METALS
JOINING
MANUAL

Differences among the many welding processes are based principally on how each process closes the distance that separates atoms. Traditionally, this has been done by a casting operation, with filler metal poured into the joint. Fusion welding still looms large today, but in addition to the conventional electric arc, plasma arcs, ultrasonic waves, high-energy beams, explosives, and frictional heat are used in welding. Moreover, solid-state diffusion welding and/or brazing has come on the scene. In this process, by some combination of deformation and diffusion at the interface, metal lattice structures can be joined without melting or without melting a filler metal and making subsequent use of diffusion.

To be practical, it does no commercial good to weld two pieces of metal together if the process of coalescence deforms one of the pieces, or puts one of the alloys in an undesirable heat-treatment condition, or otherwise detracts from the usefulness of the components. To a large extent the engineering portion of welding metallurgy activity does not concern itself with the invention of mechanisms for joining metals; rather, it concerns itself with techniques for minimizing the side effects of joining processes. For example, theoretically there is little difference between oxyacetylene welding and electron-beam welding. Both processes melt the metal at the interface, and the liquid metal overcomes or eliminates the barriers separating the surfaces. Commercially, however, the processes are quite different from each other. Electron-beam welding involves more expensive processing, but also imposes less degradation (fewer side effects) on the parts being welded.

The elements of this cost trade-off comparison are complex. The viability of such a large number of distinctly different welding processes in the marketplace attests to this complexity. To oversimplify, almost anybody can stick two pieces of metal together. However, some people make a commercial success of this activity, while others either price themselves out of competition or offer an inferior, nonfunctional, noncompetitive product.

This handbook describes a variety of joining processes which will aid the reader in selecting the process that will be a commercial success.

To some engineers, the question is, "What new materials are available for me with unique or improved properties or with promise of substantial cost savings?" Other engineers are confronted with the research and development in joining which focuses on one goal: producing defect-free joints the first time with a minimum of consumables and at the least possible cost.

Welding and brazing research is going on all over the world, some privately funded, some funded by organizations and associations—sometimes government money aids the effort. Some research is practical, involving a search for better, maybe quicker ways to join specific products. Other research is strictly "blue-sky," with no immediate applications. Add it all up and it represents the lifeblood of the joining industry.

Many of the processes described in this handbook have left the research and development laboratories and are accepted production

PREFACE

The long-heralded technological revolution in materials usage is finally about to arrive, spurred by the potential uses of composites and strong interest in secondary properties, two areas where the opportunities for progress are brightest at the moment. The radical transformation of materials usage is finally about to take place.

The increasing emphasis on structural reliability, more than anything else, is changing the nature of materials development. After years spent in devising structures of unprecedentedly high strength at unprecedentedly high temperatures, engineers are realizing that they have achieved little so long as these structures cannot be given a reasonably long operating life, or even so long as there is no certain way of predicting what the operating life of a given structure will be.

As structural reliability becomes more important, so do secondary materials properties such as stress corrosion resistance and fatigue strength. Structural designers are almost in general agreement that, in order to optimize these properties, it will now often be necessary to accept reductions in the formerly all-important primary characteristics, such as ultimate and yield strengths. What may be needed more urgently, though, is more extensive use of the latest findings of metallurgical and welding engineers. Of course, materials users are also being nudged in the direction of new techniques of fabrication and, especially, joining processes.

During the fifties and early sixties there were numerous welding and brazing processes; now there are many, many more. The reason is that engineers have been building things with a greater variety of metals than ever before, resulting in a new spectrum of welding methods. Welding results in *coalescence*, a key word meaning "to grow (solidification) or unite (solid state) into one body." Since the "one body" in this case is metallurgical, welding is the establishment of the same kinds of bond across interfaces as those that account for the sticking together of atoms to form a single metal piece. Thus, welding establishes a metallurgical bond. Welding occurs when the atoms of one body are brought sufficiently close to the nearest layer of atoms of a second body so that the forces of interatomic energy act. This statement is also true of blacksmith hammer forging, laser welding, and all degrees of sophistication in between.

CONTENTS

To Carolyn and Anne-Marie,
your encouragement, patience,
and thoughtfulness was appreciated

Library of Congress Cataloging in Publication Data

Schwartz, Mel M
Metals joining manual.

Includes bibliographical references and index.
1. Welding—Handbooks, manuals, etc. 2. Brazing—
Handbooks, manuals, etc. 3. Solder and soldering—
Handbooks, manuals, etc. I. Title.
TS227.2.S38   671.5′02′02   78-27886
ISBN 0-07-055720-9

2 3 4 5 6 7 8 9 0   HDHD   8 6 5 4 3 2 1 0

The editors for this book were Harold B. Crawford, and Joseph
Williams, the designer was Elliot Epstein, and the production
supervisor was Thomas G. Kowalczyk. It was set in Baskerville
by Intercontinental Photocomposition, Ltd.

Printed and bound by Halliday Lithograph.

METALS JOINING MANUAL

M.M.SCHWARTZ

Chief of Manufacturing Technology
Sikorsky Aircraft
Division of United Technologies

McGRAW-HILL BOOK COMPANY

*New York St. Louis San Francisco Auckland Bogotá Düsseldorf
Johannesburg London Madrid Mexico Montreal New Delhi
Panama Paris São Paulo Singapore Sydney Tokyo Toronto*

processes, while others are still being evaluated as a prototype operation or pilot plant system. Through research and development, engineers continue to make improvements, refine techniques, and prepare processes for worldwide acceptance.

There is no ultimate end to the need for research and development. Technology can be depicted as an ever-enlarging circle. The more research and development effort expended, the larger the technology in hand—and the larger the perimeter of the circle, which thus affords a wider avenue of future probing. Though there may be leaders and laggards, the search for new advances in the state of the art never terminates.

There is really no choice as to whether to *join* the "race." One can choose to lead or lag, but it is virtually impossible for a company, an industry, or a country to remain healthy and competitive without pushing the frontiers of technology or at least scrutinizing and putting to use the pioneering of others. It is a rare field of business in which a company can sustain itself over a long term with the same product in the same market.

The paths open for the future are paths of opportunity for the aggressive, capable company in the joining and joining-equipment fields, offering multiple choices of endeavor. To a degree greater than ever before, engineers are operating in an atmosphere where the stimulus and the harsh discipline of venture and risk are in force. Scientists and engineers have always felt that they are engaged in one of the most dynamic, volatile, and competitive industrial efforts on the business scene.

The years ahead promise to be at least as challenging and revolutionary as those which have passed. In all likelihood they will be more so. In the last 15 years the metals-joining industry has pioneered a new science and industry in which problems are so new and unusual that it behooves no one to dismiss any novel idea with the statement that "it can't be done." The job now is to keep everlastingly at research and experiment, to adapt our laboratory results and those of other laboratories to production as soon as practicable, to let no improvement in joining and joining equipment pass us by.

I wish to express my appreciation and acknowledge the able support of R. June Bushfield, who assumed responsibility for the preparation of the manuscript. I also wish to thank Frances T. Diver for her assistance.

M. M. Schwartz

1

ELECTRON-BEAM WELDING

Born 20 years ago in the atomic power industry and nurtured in the aircraft and aerospace industries, electron-beam welding has emerged from adolescence as a mature manufacturing technology, mainly in the automotive and related fields. Other industries, however, have been slower in recognizing the unique advantages offered by electron-beam welding. These advantages include lower welding costs, minimum energy input to the workpiece, decreased distortion, the ability to weld finished machined parts, elimination of consumables, high production rates, and quality welding of virtually every metal from aluminum to refractories—from foils to plate thicknesses.

As awareness of the process has increased, however, so have the highly sophisticated applications. Because of this, the equipment itself must, of necessity, continue to incorporate the latest developments in vacuum technology, electronic controls, optics, power supplies, and fixturing.

Electron-beam welding got its start for the simple reason that nothing else would do the job—there was no other way to join the high-melting-point refractory metals used in nuclear fuel elements. These first applications were characterized by very high quality and very low productivity. However, other advantages soon became obvious.

The electron beam is clean. In the beginning, the workpiece and the electron gun shared a common high vacuum, typically 10^{-4} torr (0.0133 Pa), which is roughly equivalent to a contamination level of 0.1 ppm. Hence, the metallurgical cleanliness of the weld is excellent. Even today, after the advent of partial-vacuum and nonvacuum electron-beam processes, hard-vacuum electron-beam welding is widely used. Experts foresee that electron-beam welding will continue to be a major growth area for the application of electron-beam technology for some time to come.

ELECTRON-BEAM WELDING—BACKGROUND

A breakthrough, in any technology, is an infrequent and long-coming phenomenon. And a breakthrough applied to a technology that is in itself newly created, conceived in Germany, and first applied in France in 1955, it is remarkable indeed. The breakthrough in the case of welding with an electron beam in soft vacuum is really only a backward step—one which takes advantage of circumstances that were passed by while the industry hurried toward the use of the electron beam for welding at atmospheric pressure.

Commercial electron-beam welding equipment, which utilizes a heat source of electrons which are accelerated by an electric field to extremely high speeds and focused to a sharp beam by electrostatic or electromagnetic fields, is used for welding a wide range of metals in thicknesses ranging from foils to extremely thick sections. The welding equipment is manufactured for welding in high vacuum of 10^{-4} to 10^{-5} torr (1.33 to 0.133 Pa), in medium or partial vacuum (PV) of 0.05 to 0.3 torr (5.7 to 39.9 Pa), and nonvacuum (NV) in air or inert-gas atmosphere. The basic welding equipment is designed to operate in one of two voltage ranges. So-called low-voltage welding units operate at 15 to 60 kV, while high-voltage welders operate at 100 to 200 kV. Either low- or high-voltage welding units can be operated in high-vacuum welding or partial-vacuum welding (PVW) applications, see Fig. 1-1, while only high-voltage welding units are capable of non-vacuum electron-beam (NVEB) welding.

Electron-beam welding (EBW) in a vacuum environment offers advantages over other types of fusion-welding equipment in the following respects: (1) the high-energy electron beam produces a deep, narrow, penetrating type of fusion weld; (2) the highly concentrated

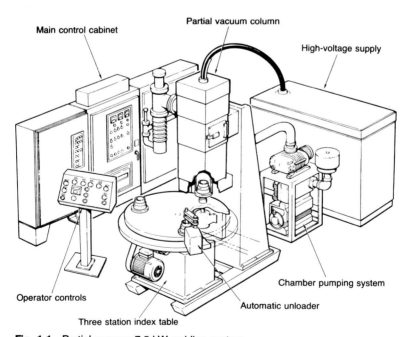

Fig. 1-1 Partial vacuum 7.5-kW welding system.

beam permits a low energy input to the material, which minimizes distortion and thermal effects on the materials; (3) weld parameters can be precisely controlled for repeatability; (4) the vacuum environment provides for weld purity from contaminating gases, so that even reactive-type metals can be welded; (5) foil gages to heavy metal sections can be welded in one pass; (6) many dissimilar metal combinations can be welded; (7) welding rates are faster than conventional fusion-welding processes; (8) electron beams can be welded with a minimum effect on material properties.

EBW disadvantages are (1) the initial high cost of the equipment; (2) the process is limited to specific types of joints; (3) metal joint gap should not exceed 0.010 in (0.25 mm) for narrow welds deeper than 0.5 in (12.7 mm), although sound welds have been obtained with joint gaps of 0.030 in (0.76 mm) by increasing weld width to 0.275 in (7 mm); (4) the weld seam can be missed if the electron beam is not precisely adjusted; (5) inspection of electron-beam welds requires accurate nondestructive tests to ensure weld quality because of the narrow weld joint; (6) careful surface preparation is necessary before welding; (7) vacuum chambers can limit the size of part to be welded; (8) weld zones in alloy steels such as 300M and D6AC are extremely hard after welding because of quenching effects from the base metal and tooling; and (9) electron-beam tooling must be constructed of nonmagnetic materials to prevent deflection of the beam from the weld seam. Nonmagnetic materials are not required if tools are degaussed.

Several of the disadvantages mentioned above are part of procedures essential for nuclear and aerospace quality which can often be relaxed in other industries to reduce electron-beam costs to competitive levels.

In item (3) of the disadvantages listed above, the gap for electron-beam joints will have to be increased as new applications occur. For example, quality EBW has been reported for oil-storage tanks as well as for structural and pressure vessel steels for pipe lines. And in regard to item (6), EBW has successfully been used to weld flame-cut plate for oil-storage tanks.

EBW in vacuum environments requires that the workpiece and its related tooling be contained in a vacuum chamber. In high-vacuum (conventional in-chamber) welding, long working distances are permissible between the electron gun and the workpiece, since no appreciable electron scattering is encountered. With partial vacuum levels, some beam spread will occur because of electron-molecule collisions. With spreading of the electron beam, weld zones become wider than in high vacuum and the gas content is somewhat decreased. For many applications, these changes are not important to the function of the workpiece. However, high or PVW processes require the use of either large or complex vacuum chambers or special small chambers, just large enough to house the workpiece. With both types of vacuum chambers, special vacuum-pumping systems are required to evaluate and maintain the necessary vacuum level during welding.

NVEB welding, wherein the workpiece is at atmospheric pressure and the electron beam is permitted to escape from the environment in which it is formed, eliminates the need for the vacuum chambers and greatly increases the production capabilities of the process. However, passing of the electron beam from a vacuum through a differentially pumped orifice system to the workpiece results in a 10% loss of power, and the electron stream becomes diffused by the gases at atmospheric pressure. A low-density protective gas such as helium has been used, but in most instances air has been satisfactorily used around the electron beam to minimize electron scattering. High accelerating voltages required for NVEB welding produce high-intensity x-rays, which must be shielded from operating personnel. The NVEB welding process does not limit the size of the workpiece, but does limit shape, since the electron-gun-to-work distance in air environment is typically 0.375 to 0.5 in (9.5 to 12.7 mm). The NVEB welding process, therefore, is limited by workpiece shape.

EBW machines are available commercially, and the type of equipment to be used for a given welding application will depend upon the basic welding requirements and the manufacturer's equipment preference. In general, low-voltage and high-voltage equipment for use in high- or partial-vacuum levels will produce similar welds in most materials.

EBW PROCESS

Low-voltage EBW machines use either a fixed electron gun mounted on the vacuum chamber or a mobile-type gun placed inside the vacuum chamber. High-voltage EBW equipment for vacuum operation uses a fixed electron gun mounted on the vacuum chamber. In special cases, a sliding-type seal can be used for moving the fixed type of electron gun. See the material on sliding seal in the section, *Equipment and Cooling.* For high-voltage NVEB welding, the electron gun is either fixed or movable, depending upon the equipment manufacturer.

In a typical low-voltage, high-vacuum welding unit the electron gun can be used in a fixed position or it can transverse the workpiece. Typical modes of electron gun and work movement are shown in Fig. 1-2. The electron gun travels on the y and z axes, while the work carriage moves on the x axis. Multiaxis movements of the gun can be accurately controlled by the weld operator or by automatic programming. High-voltage, high-vacuum welding units use a fixed electron gun assembly mounted on the chamber wall.

The location and mobility of the electron gun is an important feature to be considered for a given welding application. However, with either a fixed- or mobile-type electron gun, adequate tooling is required to move the workpiece in proper relation to the electron beam. An additional feature to be considered with the choice of a mobile interior-chamber electron gun vs. the fixed gun mounted on the chamber wall is replacement of the tungsten elements used for

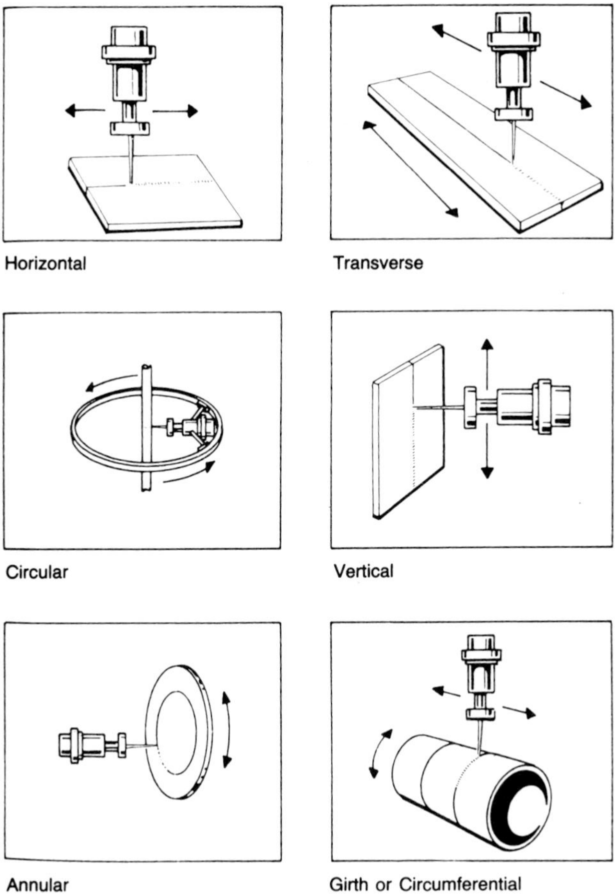

Horizontal   Transverse

Circular   Vertical

Annular   Girth or Circumferential

Fig. 1-2 Electron-beam weld positions for use with a mobile-type electron gun.

initiating the electron beam. With a mobile-type gun located in the vacuum chamber, it is necessary to break the vacuum and remove the gun for replacement of the filament. In the case of the fixed electron gun mounted on the chamber wall, separate vacuum valves and pumping systems permit changing the filament without breaking the chamber vacuum. This feature greatly shortens the time for reinitiating weld cycles when a filament failure occurs.

An additional factor that requires consideration with low- and high-voltage EBW units is the protection of personnel from x-rays generated by the electron beam striking the work surface. For low-voltage machines, under 20 kV, the x-rays generated are termed "soft" x-rays, since they are stopped by the steel walls of the vacuum chamber and leaded glass windows. The high-voltage welding units generate "hard" x-rays which must be shielded from operating personnel by means of lead sheet or other materials. If more than 20 kV is generated, periodic radiation survey of the equipment is mandatory. In some instances, it may also be necessary to view the weld operation by remote means, such as with an optical system or by means of closed-circuit television. See the section, *Safety.*

In EBW operations, the operator must adjust and manipulate the electron beam and tooling mechanism so that the beam will strike the center of the weld seam. Since the electron-beam spot size can vary from 0.005 to 0.060 in (0.13 to 1.5 mm), depending upon the type of electron gun, the focusing current (which controls the focal length of the beam), distance from gun to work, accelerating voltage, and beam current, it is possible for the beam spot to miss the joint unless the operator can accurately view the beam and weld seam, before and during the weld cycle.

Variables

The basic variables for controlling EBW are

1. Accelerating voltage
2. Beam current
3. Welding (travel) speed
4. Focusing current
5. Distance from gun to work

Increasing the accelerating voltage of beam current increases depth of penetration; the product of these two variables (called beam power) determines the amount of metal melted. Increasing welding (travel) speed without changing another process variable reduces depth of penetration almost proportionately and reduces weld width somewhat. Changing any of the other four basic control variables so as to increase beam spot size reduces depth of penetration and increases weld width if welding speed is not changed.

Beam deflection can be used to change the impact angle of the beam or to produce controlled patterns of beam oscillation for the effect of greater beam spot size or other special effects, and the beam can be pulsed to reduce effective beam power.

In NVEB welding, ordinarily all of the five basic control variables except beam current are preset and control is based on beam current. Beam current may be set at a fixed value for the application and merely turned on and off in relation to workpiece travel, or it may be programmed to vary in a predetermined pattern. Beam deflection cannot be used; beam oscillation is seldom used.

Beam Tracking

A method for precise alignment of the electron beam and the weld seam without the use of visual optics has been developed with a new electron-probe system. The electron probe, which can be fitted to any electron-beam system, uses the electron beam itself to give a direct display of its own position in relation to the seam to be welded. Electrons reflected from the work surface are detected by a pickup plate and are translated into a visible trace on a cathode-ray oscilloscope. When the beam crosses the seam, the angle of reflection of the electrons changes, altering the scope pattern and providing a topographical view of the work surface. Another recent development is a scan-record-playback system which can automatically scan a seam to be welded and record the coordinates in a computer memory. On command, the system will play back the recorded path indefinitely for production welding.

Beam Oscillation

Low-voltage and high-voltage EBW machines are designed so that the welding process can be improved by various manipulations of the electron beam. Deflection coils are used so that the beam amplitude can be varied around the center line in the x and y directions. By means of the deflection system, the beam can be made to form different waves, circles, rectangles, squares, etc. Beam deflection can greatly improve weld integrity and at the same time improve the welding process by eliminating tool manipulations. Beam oscillation is used to produce wider welds, slower cooling rates, and more uniform weld shape, without necessarily defocusing the beam. Welds somewhat wider than normal are required in joints that have relatively large root openings, or that make use of filler-metal replacements.

Lower cooling rates that result from larger welds permit more outgassing from materials containing impurities, and thus help to control porosity. Welds made in metals subject to embrittlement during or after fast cooling can benefit from beam oscillation and defocusing. One of the more useful effects of oscillated beams is the general improvement of weld shape. Oscillation with or without defocusing has been used to avoid excessive undercut and underfill. Beam oscillation is not always used, even though available. Except for penetration control, most advantages can usually be duplicated by using defocused beams. Also, the wider weld and greater heat input may be a disadvantage, as in welding thin foils. The addition of a circle generator or pulsing of the beam at various pulse widths and frequencies is a definite aid in obtaining sound welds in materials with good thermal conductivity, such as aluminum or copper, or in metals with low vapor pressures, such as magnesium. Pulsing of the beam is obtained by applying a negative signal to the grid bias cup which interrupts the beam. A pulsed beam permits dissipation of heat and metallic vapors, if required in some applications. Beam operation can be changed from continuous to intermittent on machines equipped with pulsing controls. Beam pulsation reduces the rate of heat input, but is independent of other beam conditions. Therefore, pulsation can be combined with oscillation and deflection, as well as travel speed, to influence weld behavior. At very low frequencies, such as 1 Hz, each pulse produces a separate weld, even at low travel speed. By increasing travel speed and adjusting pulse frequency and pulse length, tack welds, spot welds, or intermittent welds can be made at normal production rates.

High-Vacuum EBW

One of the major drawbacks with high-vacuum welding is the time involved in making a weld. First, the tool and the part must be put together, or if the tooling is fixed in the vacuum chamber, the part must be secured in the tool and the necessary chill blocks, runoff tabs, focusing block, and clamps must be placed in the proper locations. The weld joint or joints are then placed in proper relation to the electron gun. After the tooling and electron gun are positioned, the vacuum chamber is pumped to a vacuum of 10^{-4} to 10^{-5} torr (0.0133 to 0.00133 Pa). The operator aligns the weld seam with the joint, adjusts the electron beam to the desired focus, engages the travel mechanism, and makes the weld. The chamber is then air-released and the part or tool and part removed. For an average run in a high-vacuum EBW machine, a typical time cycle can be as follows:

1. Load part or tool in chamber with chill blocks, clamps, etc.—5 min.
2. Evacuate chamber to 10^{-4} to 10^{-5} torr—7 min.
3. Align electron beam, focus, and weld—5 min.
4. Vent chamber and unload work—5 min. Total 22 min.

The time noted above for making a typical weld can be varied considerably, depending upon the complexity of the weld, the type of tooling employed, the vacuum-pumping capacity, and the skill of the operator in aligning and completing the weld.

PVEB

In order to speed up the process, welding machines have been developed for welding in partial vacuum levels of 0.05 to 0.3 torr (5.7 to 39.9 Pa). PVEB welds are similar in quality to high-vacuum welds in most materials and the process can be greatly expedited by reduced vacuum-pumping requirements. In addition to the reduced vacuum-pumping time, equipment can also be designed with a minimum-size vacuum chamber to provide rapid pump-down times. The PVEB welding process is making the EBW process a tool for large production rates of specialized nature. Special machines of this type are producing small production parts at a rate as high as 1800 parts per hour.

PVEB welding equipment consists of two vacuum chambers and two pumping systems. One chamber houses the electron gun and the other chamber contains the workpieces. The gun housing for either low-voltage or high-voltage electron-beam systems is separately pumped into a vacuum level of 10^{-4} to 10^{-5} torr (0.0133 to 0.00133 Pa) by means of mechanical and diffusion vacuum pumps. The high-vacuum environment is required to minimize oxidation of the electron emitter. The welding chamber is also separately pumped by a mechanical pump to a vacuum of 0.01 to 0.1 torr (1.33 to 13.3 Pa). The passage connecting the gun housing to the work chamber contains an orifice to limit the leak rate and a special valve to maintain the gun housing at high vacuum. When the work chamber is pumped to the vacuum level required, the valve is opened and the electron gun activated. The vacuum level in the two chambers is not equalized, since the molecules of air or gas at 0.01 to 0.1 torr (1.33 to 13.3 Pa) have a long mean free path, so that only a few of them randomly find their way into the gun chamber, where they are removed by the diffusion pump. After welding is complete, the valve between the chambers is closed and the work chamber is air-released. Since the gun chamber is maintained in a high vacuum and the minimum-size work chamber is rapidly pumped by a mechanical pump, the complete process cycle is a matter of seconds, making the process adaptable to mass-production schedules. However, this type of equipment generally falls into the category of the special-purpose welder, as opposed to the general-purpose high-vacuum welder. Typical PVEB welding machines are shown in Fig. 1-1 and 1-3.

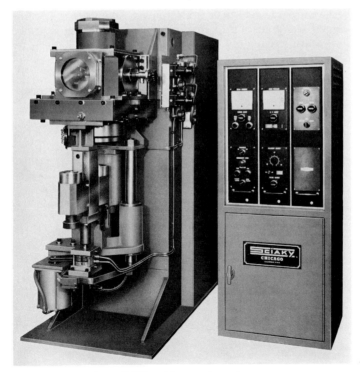

Fig. 1-3 Low-voltage PVEB welding equipment.

PVEB welding machines are recommended for true automation and high-production schedules when the vacuum chamber can be sized to fit the specific part plus necessary fixturing tools.

Protection of operating personnel from x-radiation requires the same type of precautions as noted previously for high-vacuum welding. Since PVEB welding requires considerably less time for welding than high-vacuum chamber welding, the next step is to eliminate the vacuum chamber and weld either in air or in lower density gas at atmospheric pressure [760 torr (101,080 Pa)]. The electron beam is generated in a high vacuum and is then passed through several small orifices which form distinct pumping chambers maintained at progressively lower vacuum levels until the electron beam passes to atmospheric pressure. The electron beam emerging into air will tend to degrade rapidly as the electrons collide with or graze gas molecules. To minimize this condition, helium gas, which is the lightest of the inert gases (atomic number 2), is emitted around the electron stream at the exit orifice of the beam. Since the dispersion of the electron beam is a function of gas density times the distance it travels through the gas, excessive energy loss and scatter will occur with the distance of travel. For this reason, electron beams (100 to 200 kV) are required, the working distance is not much greater than 0.75 in (19 mm), and the maximum practical metal penetration capability is limited to approximately 0.5 in (12.7 mm) in steel at a 9-kW power level. Most systems today have changed to air in lieu of helium, and the working distance has been limited to approximately 0.375 to 0.5 in (9.5 to 12.7 mm). By

Fig. 1-4 High-voltage NVEB welding equipment.[1]

Fig. 1-5 High-voltage NVEB welding equipment.[2]

welding outside the vacuum chamber, the limit to the length of the part to be welded must be controlled by the radiation shielding required to protect personnel in the area. However, the shape of the part will limit the application because of the close electron-gun-to-part requirement. Parts of odd shapes or parts containing protrusions or depressions, etc., will not be suitable for NVEB welding.

NVEB

NVEB welding equipment is made with a fixed-voltage electron gun, and a movable high-voltage welding head may be provided. The optimum welding speed will be governed by the material and gage to be welded.

NV welding, like high-vacuum or PV welding, generates x-radiation because of the high voltages employed. To protect personnel from this radiation hazard, the equipment and operator must be shielded. The protective shielding required depends upon both voltage and material being welded and is determined by federal regulations. Normally this means that most welding machines are enclosed in a shielded room. Typical NVEB welding equipment is shown in Figs. 1-4 and 1-5.

GUNS—FIXED AND MOBILE

There are many electron-beam gun designs that could be considered for either general use or for specific applications in EBW, including work-accelerated-type guns in which the workpiece is the gun anode. But, in practice, only self-accelerated-type guns are used. This is because of their superior focusing and power-handling capabilities, and the fact that they permit placing the gun (anode) and workpiece at the same electrical potential (namely, earth-ground).

Low-voltage welding guns are generally operated in the space-charge-limited condition. They can be classed into two types: (1) those in which only the accelerating voltage is varied to control power and (2) those in which the accelerating voltage and beam current are varied to control power. The former type is sometimes referred to as a "diode-type" gun because it is primarily a two-element device that is electronically similar to a diode; the latter is termed a "triode-type" gun. In either type, if the gun is operated in the space-charge-limited condition, the beam current produced at any value of accelerating voltage is proportional to the $^3/_2$ power of the accelerating voltage.

In the diode gun, when a change in beam current is desired at a given voltage, the adjustment is accomplished by mechanical change of the cathode-to-anode spacing of the gun, thereby changing the proportionally constant of the gun.

The triode-type gun is similar to the diode gun, except that the "cathode" is now provided with a variable negative voltage relative to the filament. This makes it possible to control the electron-beam current at any operating voltage; thus, both the accelerating voltage and beam current can be developed independently when welding parameters are established.

EBW guns for operation in vacuum chambers are generally of the basic types known as Pierce, modified Pierce, Steigerwald, or Westinghouse guns. The Pierce or modified Pierce guns are for low-voltage operations up to 60 kV, while the Steigerwald and Westinghouse guns are for high-voltage applications where accelerating voltages may range from 100 to 200 kV.

The Pierce triode electron-beam gun basically consists of an anode, a control electrode (cathode), and a hot filament (emitter or cathode element). The filament, which is directly heated, is manufactured from metal strip to form a square or round target (emitting) surface. Filament life will vary considerably from a few hours to approximately 20 h depending upon the beam power used. The electrons generated by the filament are accelerated by the voltage applied across the cathode-anode and are focused into a sharp beam by means of an electromagnetic focusing coil. For most welding applications, the beam is focused approximately 2 in (50.8 mm) below the bottom of the focusing coil. Control of the electron beam is handled by adjustment of the control electrode bias, accelerating voltage, and focusing current. A mobile-type electron gun is shown in Fig. 1-6.

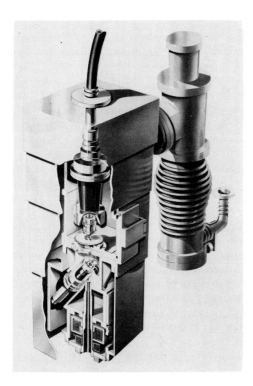

Fig.   1-6   Mobile-type high-vacuum electron-beam gun.[1]

The fixed-electron-beam-type gun mounted on the vacuum chamber requires that the movement of the part in relation to the gun be controlled entirely by the tooling of the workpiece. In practice, for general EBW operations, the advantage of a mobile gun over a fixed gun is questionable as far as weld positioning is concerned.

High-voltage electron guns are usually a Steigerwald triode system. Electrons are emitted from a thermionic emitter and are accelerated by a high potential to an anode. Interposed between the hot cathode and anode is a grid which is used to control the flow of electrons. The shape of the electrostatic field from the grid cup focuses the electron beam, which passes through an aperture in the gun anode. Once out of the gun section of the column, the electrons are focused by an electro-magnetic lens system into a beam. An optical viewing system for observing the beam impingement area is located above the magnetic lens, and a heat shield is placed at the exit end of the column to minimize heat transfer by back radiation into the column.

The high-voltage electron gun of 6 kW operating at a maximum voltage of 150 kV and 40 mA of beam current can be focused at work distances of 0.5 to 25 in (12.7 to 635 mm) below the base of the electron gun. These work distances are governed by chamber size. The electron beam can be focused to a minimum spot size of 0.005 in (0.13 mm), with 0.015 in (0.38 mm) used for most welding applications of sheet materials. With heavy-gage materials, a circle generator is used to form larger effective beam size of approximately 0.030 in (0.76 mm). The high-vacuum machines available today range from 6 to 35 kW. A research laboratory recently set out to see just how far EBW could be developed for heavy engineering applications, and an electron beam welder of 75 kW was constructed.[3] With this apparatus, welds have been made in a single pass in 7.8 in (200 mm) steel or 11.8 in (300 mm) aluminum alloy. The laboratory found that large pressure vessels may remain on the shop floor for weeks while successive weld passes are made to complete the joints by SAW and GTA welding and frequently preheat and interpass temperatures must be controlled all this time. With EBW, such work could be reduced to a few shifts.

Although the incentive to develop a high-power gun was mainly the hope of being able to weld thicknesses over 3.9 in (100 mm), there were other reasons for having ample power available. Work with lower power guns had shown the advantage of parallel-sided welds compared with narrow pointed welds in regard to porosity and other defects. Narrow pointed welds generally indicate that minimum power has been employed. The maximum thickness of steel which can be welded with 75 kW to acceptable standards of quality remains to be proved, but it will certainly be a substantial increase on the current limits for electron beam. Preliminary work on the weldability of structural steels by electron beam indicates satisfactory joint properties, and the toughness of the weld metal after stress relief is at least as good as the parent metal.[4]

The high-voltage tungsten hairpin filament can vary from 0.012 to 0.025 in (0.3 to 0.6 mm). The life of the filament will depend upon the beam power used for welding. With low beam power of 1 to 2 kW employed for welding of foil materials, the filament life can average 350 h, while at a beam power of 4 to 5 kW, the filament is reduced to 8 h. An overall average of filament life is in the range of 320 h under a vacuum of 10^{-4} torr (0.0133 Pa). The development of the gun column to permit changing the filament while the chamber is evacuated has improved productivity economics.

The high-voltage EBW gun is also used for PVW where a separate vacuum chamber is provided for the electron gun assembly and the work area. A special valve between the two chambers permits rapid welding cycles, as noted previously for low-voltage EBW equipment. The power ratings of PVW machines range from 7.5 kW to 15 kW. For high-voltage NVEB welding, the electron-gun assembly is modified with differential vacuum-pumping systems to keep the hot filament at a vacuum level of 10^{-4} torr (0.0133 Pa) and still permit the electron stream to emerge into air or inert gas atmosphere. A schematic of the electron gun assembly is shown in Fig. 1-7. The high-voltage power supply is increased from 150 kV to 175 kV to obtain an adequate energy density of the electron beam outside the vacuum column. The electron-gun assembly is fixed and the workpiece is moved past the gun.

Other high-voltage NVEB welding equipment also makes use of an electron gun assembly that contains several distinct pumping sections so that the beam generated in a vacuum of 10^{-4} torr (0.0133 Pa) can freely pass into atmospheric pressure. The electron source is derived from a tungsten rod of 0.060 in (1.5 mm) diameter that is heated to thermionic emission temperatures by electron bombardment from an auxiliary filament which encircles the rod. This tungsten rod, because of its mass, extends the operating life of the electron gun many times over the conventional hairpin filament used for other high-voltage machines.

The tungsten provides excellent beam stability with no manual realignment requirements. The entire cathode assembly, including the rod emitter, bombarding filament, inner grid cup, and heat shield, is replaceable as a plug-in unit. During operation, the electron emitter (cathode) is maintained at a high negative voltage. The emitted

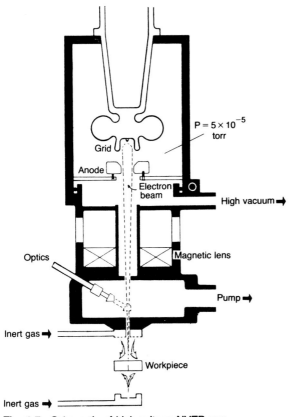

Fig. 1-7 Schematic of high-voltage NVEB gun.

electrons are electrostatically collimated by a shaping grid and accelerated by a remotely adjustable anode held at positive ground potential. The system operates at a maximum potential of 150 kV and a maximum continuous beam current of 60 mA.

The electron-gun chamber and the first dynamic pumping stage beneath the gun chamber are individually evacuated by two diffusion pumps that are rigidly mounted to the gun chamber. All mechanical pumps are mounted on a common base and are connected to the mobile welding head by means of flexible vacuum ducting. At the output orifice of the beam-transfer section, an overpressure stage is provided to minimize the welding vapors and other contaminants from entering the gun. At the exit orifice of the gun, helium gas is used to provide a minimum of interference between the beam and the gas in the transfer system. The gun assembly is moved on a fixed carriage during welding at speeds up to 280 in/min (118.4 mm/s). A schematic sketch of the electron gun assembly is shown in Fig. 1-8, and a photograph of the unit appears in Fig. 1-9.

In the last 5 years, ribbon filaments have been used almost exclusively, especially in the EBW of auto components. The ribbon filament was found to be a better source for large beam currents than the wire hairpin filament. Substitution of the ribbon filament resulted in improved beam controllability because the electron gun produces a stationary image, or apparent source of electrons, independent of the beam current or accelerating voltage. The ribbon filament has 2 to 3 times the lifetime of the hairpin filament.

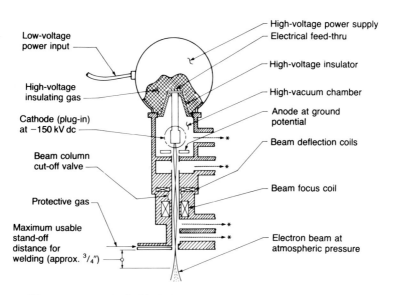

*To vacuum pumps by flexible ducts.

Fig. 1-8 Schematic of high-voltage NVEB gun.[5] (0.75 in = 19 mm)

Fig. 1-9 Mobile high-voltage NVEB welder.[6]

WELD ENVIRONMENT

In EBW, electrons are generated by heating a tungsten element or emitter to very high temperatures. Free electrons, generated by thermionic emission, are accelerated to extremely high velocities by an electrical field and are collimated into a defined beam. The tungsten emitter, if it is heated in air, will have a very short life because of oxidation, and the electrons that it generates will quickly become diffused and the emitter will lose its effectiveness as an electron source. For this reason, a vacuum environment is required for forming and controlling the electron beam. A vacuum environment of 10^{-4} torr (0.0133 Pa) or lower is used to protect the electron emitter which is heated to approximately 3632°F (2000°C).

Since the electron emitter requires a region of low pressure, most general-purpose EB welders are manufactured to utilize a high vacuum of 10^{-4} to 10^{-5} torr (0.0133 to 0.00133 Pa). In this environment, it is possible to obtain the highest-quality deep-penetrating type of welds with a minimum of contamination from pickup of impurities. The amount of impurities present in a vacuum atmosphere is many times less than that in inert gases, such as argon and helium. However, once the electron gun is activated in a high vacuum and the welding process is started, the electron beam does not continue to exist in a high vacuum, because of metallic and gaseous vapors that are discharged from the molten weld-metal pool. These vapors increase the pressure locally at the point of beam impingement.

Large high-vacuum chambers for EBW generally require a chamber size large enough to enclose the workpiece, including the tooling motions necessary for moving either the workpiece or the electron gun in relation to the weld seam. To ensure a rapid pumpdown time, large mechanical and diffusion pumps are required. The high-vacuum electron-beam welder, therefore, is used for batch-type work where production rates are relatively low and/or the part size is such that it can conveniently fit into the vacuum chamber.

To overcome the shortcomings of the high-vacuum welding process, various innovations of the process such as PV or NV EBW are used. These processes are aimed at high-production-rate welding, where the materials, design, quality, and quantities are such that high-vacuum EBW is not required. A diagram showing the differences of the three different pressure modes of operation appears in Fig. 1-10.

PVW machines utilize two chambers. In these machines, the electron beam is directed through a small orifice positioned between the anode and the workpiece, reducing the time needed by hard-vacuum equipment to pump down the work chamber. The emitting and workpiece chambers are evacuated by separate pumps to 0.0001 torr (0.0133 Pa) and 0.1 torr (13.33 Pa), respectively. Because the work chamber is evacuated more rapidly in PV electron-beam welders, production rates are increased. But, because the pressure is higher in the work chamber, the electron beam can be projected only 2.4 in (60 mm), and penetration in steel is reduced to about 4 in (102 mm).

Welding of materials such as titanium and refractory metals at increased vacuum pressures may result in contaminated welds, since these materials will absorb oxygen and nitrogen as interstitial impurities. Other materials such as iron-base alloys which are normally welded in inert-gas atmospheres are not embrittled by gas impurity levels of oxygen, nitrogen, water vapor, oil, etc., as high as 500 ppm. The impurities in PV levels are oxygen and nitrogen of ambient composition. A vacuum of 0.380 torr (50.5 Pa) corresponds to a gas impurity level of 500 ppm. In addition to the impurities that surround a metal during welding, gases are evolved from the molten weld metal. With the inert-gas-shielded arc method, the gases tend to remain in the

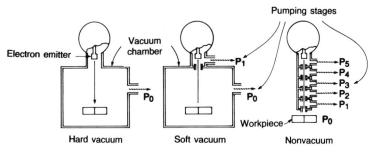

Fig. 1-10   The three different pressure modes of operation of electron-beam welders.[5]

vicinity of the molten metal because of the blanketing effect of the shielding gas, and are largely reabsorbed back into the molten weld metal. Welding in a vacuum results in the gases being dispersed and removed by the vacuum pumps.

Welding in a vacuum, whether it is a high vacuum of 0.0001 torr (0.0133 Pa) or a PV of 0.05 to 0.3 torr (5.7 to 39.9 Pa), is a definite advantage for producing impurity-free welds. However, many welding applications exist where the characteristics of the electron beam could be used to advantage by welding in a NV atmosphere. The size of workpiece, if positioned outside of the vacuum enclosure, would not be limited by the size of the vacuum chambers.

NVEB machines maintain the electron source at 0.0001 torr (0.0133 Pa), but the workpiece is at atmospheric pressure [760 torr (0.1013 MPa)]. The electron beam passes through several orifices dividing successive and distinct pumping chambers in the beam-transfer column. Each chamber is maintained at progressively lower vacuum until the electrons reach atmospheric pressure at the column output.

Because the column is continually maintained during operations and because it is not necessary to evacuate the work chamber, pumpdown time is eliminated and production rates are very high. However, beam penetration is limited and the workpiece must be positioned within 1.25 in (32 mm) of the output nozzle, and maximum penetration in steel is about 1.5 in (38.4 mm).

Welds made at atmospheric pressure will be affected more by electron scatter, so that the resultant weld will be wider than those produced under high vacuum or PV. The welds, however, will show the characteristic deep, narrow weld of EBW. Chemical purity of NV welds is controlled by the inert-gas shielding around the weld area. Because of the impurity level of the inert-gas cover, NV welds have been largely limited to materials that are weldable by inert-gas-shielded arc processes. Most NV welds today are produced in air, for economic reasons. The machines range from 12 kW to 36 kW. The choice of weld environment for a given weld application will depend upon the material purity and properties, part configuration and size, type of joint, number of parts required, and the economics of the process.

PVEB WELDING

Although general-purpose machines can be employed advantageously for short production runs, the principal development is in special-purpose machines tooled for particular parts. Figure 1-11 illustrates some typical PV tooling concepts. Note that in each case the work chamber and tooling are an integral assembly, specially designed for and limited to a single weld design.

A large number of PVW machines have been produced. For example, a machine with a single welding station and dual loading stations can have production capability in the range from 50 to 150

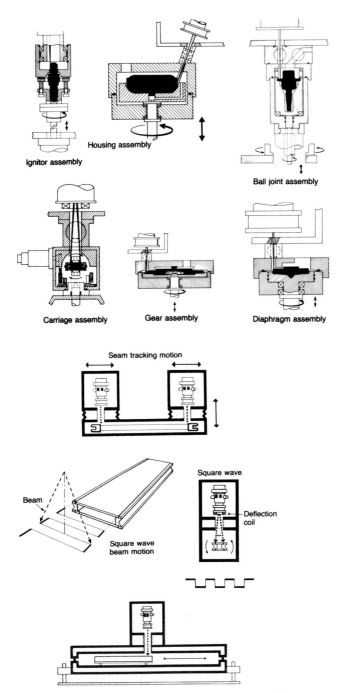

Fig. 1-11 Some typical tooling concepts in special-purpose machines tooled for particular parts.[5]

parts per hour. A dual-gun, dual-welding-station machine, on the other hand, could increase the production capability up to and perhaps above 240 parts per hour. It should be stated that the production rates in the final analysis are dependent on the design of the parts.

The PV mode of welding has found wide acceptance in the automotive industry. A particularly interesting recent introduction has been the combination of parts handling by means of a dial-feed table and PVW. Utilizing a labyrinth sliding seal technique to provide a guard vacuum before and after the separately pumped welding chamber, this concept allows the full realization of the well-known high production capability of the dial-feed table, which can range from 500 to 1500 parts per hour.

Electron-beam welders can be converted with kits which enable them to operate at 0.03 to 0.2 torr (4 to 27 Pa) partial pressures or at the 0.0001 torr (0.0133 Pa) level required for high-vacuum welding. Pump-down to partial pressures takes less than half the time to achieve than the high-vacuum level. The PV retrofit kit is offered to users of standard welders. An adapter and pumping apparatus form the nucleus of the system. The adapter section, installed below the electron-beam gun, provides a high vacuum to maintain the shape of the beam before it enters the work chamber. A variable leak system controls the degree of vacuum in the work chamber by introducing air or shielding gases into the chamber.

NVEB WELDING

Two basic technical problems had to be solved in order to produce a practical NVEB welding system. First, a technique had to be developed which permitted the electron beam to escape from the vacuum environment in which it was formed into a region of gas at atmospheric pressure without significant loss of power. Second, the electron-beam characteristics have to provide a reasonable working distance external to the gun structure before the scattering of electrons reduces the power density of the beam to a level too low for welding.

Unfortunately, some opinion seems to prevail that the distance between the electron gun and the weld, the so-called standoff distance, may not exceed 0.375 to 0.5 in (9.5 to 12.7 mm), in other words, that one has to position the gun very close to the workpiece. This is obviously inconvenient; moreover, the shape of the workpiece often prevents close access of the electron gun. But, in fact, such small standoff distances are required only if indeed a weld cross section is needed which is much deeper than wide. Where a weld of more conventional appearance is sufficient, a much greater standoff distance can be used. The process still retains many of its advantages over other welding processes, the large standoff being an additional advantage.

The electron gun can use a small jet of air or helium emanating from the same orifice as the electron beam. Welds can be made at standoff distances of 1 in (25.4 mm) and more with helium. It is thus possible to weld, for instance, the inside corner of a right-angle tee joint or to join two 3-in-diameter (76 mm) parallel tubes along their outside walls.

Standoff distance in NVEB welding is limited because the power density of the electron beam is gradually diminished by scattering. It is about 1.2 in (30.5 mm) with 36-kW beam power and air shielding. This increases to approximately 2 in (50.8 mm) with helium shielding. Weld penetration or depth, for a given welding speed, decreases as standoff distance increases.

For example, a 9-kW welder used with helium shielding can weld steel at approximately 1100 in/min (458 mm/s) but penetration will be less than 0.05 in (1.3 mm). On the other hand, penetrations of 0.1 in (2.5 mm) are possible when weld speeds are reduced to 300 in/min (125 mm/s).

Power of the electron-beam welder greatly influences weld penetration and speed. Power levels to 36 kW are now commercially available and higher power levels have been shown in experimental welders. Some companies report that their 50-kW machine can penetrate 2 in (50.4 mm) of steel and weld at speeds up to 10 in/min (4.2 mm/s).

For example, a 12-kW welder working at 40 in/min (16.9 mm/s) will

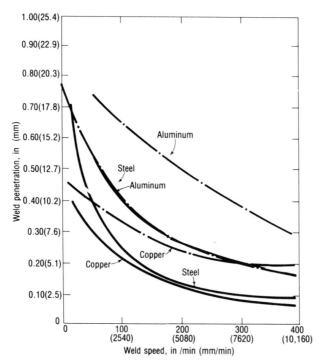

Fig. 1-12 Weld penetration vs. weld speed at 24 kW, 150 kV with 0.375-in (9.5-mm) standoff and air effluent is shown in black. The difference with helium effluent is shown in gray.

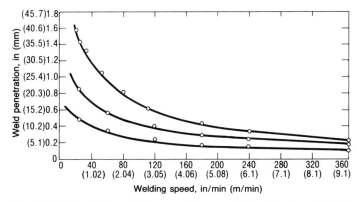

Fig. 1-13 Penetration depth vs. welding speed for three power levels. Material is 1010 carbon steel welded with a helium shield at 0.375-in (9.5-mm) standoff and 150 kV.

penetrate 0.4 in (10 mm) of 1010 carbon steel with helium shielding at 0.375 in (9.5 mm) standoff. Increasing the power to 39 kW and maintaining all other conditions the same, permits penetration of 1.2 in (30.5 mm). Increasing the welding speed at a given standoff distance, beam voltage, and beam power level decreases weld penetration. Thus, taking the same 1010 carbon steel and 0.375 in (9.5 mm) standoff distance, but increasing the welding speed to 200 in/min (85 mm/s) results in slightly less than 0.2 in (5 mm) penetration at 12 kW. Increasing power to 36 kW barely doubles the penetration. See Fig. 1-12 for additional data on weld penetration.

Three shielding or effluent gases are considered for NVEB welding, and the use of a shielding gas notably improves weld penetration. Figure 1-13 illustrates the improvement when helium is used in welding of copper, aluminum, and steel. The relative capacities of helium, air, and argon to scatter the electrons of the beam by collision of the electrons with gas molecules are indicated by their molecular weights and relative densities. The relative densities are helium, 0.14; air, 1.00; and argon, 1.38. From this it is obvious why argon is not a practical effluent gas in NVEB welding.

On the average, when helium is used for shielding, penetration is about twice that compared to NVEB welding in air, and argon is even less effective than air for shielding.

EQUIPMENT AND TOOLING

As specialized new applications come about, the PV and NVEB welding machines must be modified to accomodate production requirements. Several examples follow.

1. The PVEB facility in Fig. 1-14 currently produces 250 welds per hour. The capability of such a machine can be extended to 600 pressure vessels per hour [1200 girth welds, 33.5-in-diameter

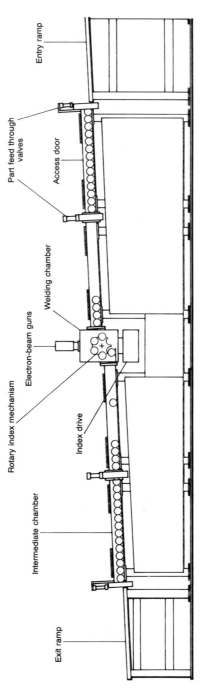

Fig. 1-14 PVEB welding facility producing pressure vessels.

(89-mm)]. This is accomplished by adding a second power supply and a unique method of preevacuating a group of parts in an intermediate chamber thus eliminating the pump-down time from the machine cycle time. The equipment is inclined for simple rolling transfer of parts through the machine.

2. The highly automated NVEB welding equipment seen in Fig. 1-15 is a three-axis CNC (computer numerical-controlled) system for welding edge seams of emission-control devices. It has combined welder and part motion. The machine rotates the part around its center line *A*, moves the horizontally mounted

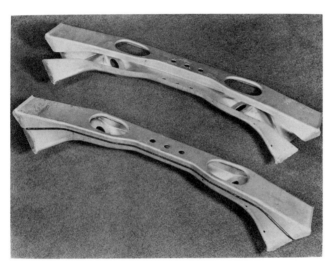

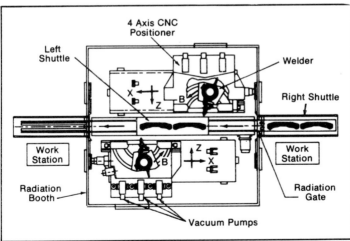

Fig. 1-15 Computer numerical controlled (CNC) setup (bottom) for NVEB welding auto frame crossmembers (top).[7]

electron-beam head in and out *B*, and rotates the head about its beam *C*. Only *A* and *B* need precise control. The CNC synchronizes all motions so that the electron beam impinges on the work at a 90° angle (1.6 rad) and moves at a constant speed relative to the work. While the welding head moves rapidly to stay perpendicular to the work, the weld puddle is steady and produces consistently high-quality welds. One CNC can control several welders at once.

3. The feasibility of joining aluminum armored vehicles by means of the EBW process is being evaluated by the U.S. government. Advantages of the process include a unique capability in the fabrication of thick aluminum armor and it offers a single-pass welding capability. Facilities which would be required to fabricate vehicles are shown in Fig. 1-16. The EBW results in improved ballistic properties at or near the weld.

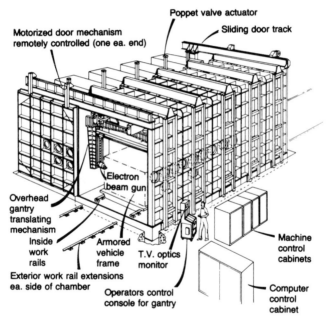

Fig. 1-16 Facility to electron beam weld future military vehicles. The overall interior chamber dimensions are:

Length	384 in	(9750 mm)
Width	158 in	(4010 mm)
Height	178 in	(4520 mm)

4. High-production welding of rimmed-steel passenger-frame parts with both PVEB and NVEB systems is both feasible and practical. After the successful laboratory welding of rimmed steel parts with the PVEB process, a production prototype was built to obtain operating data and experience. This system was based on

the principles shown in Fig. 1-17, with the workpieces held
stationary and the electron beam traveling along the weld joint
by electromagnetic deflection. From this initial prototype which
produced 4000 units in one year, a two-head system was
developed and has been used under production conditions,
welding over $9^1/_2$ million units in 7 years. As production

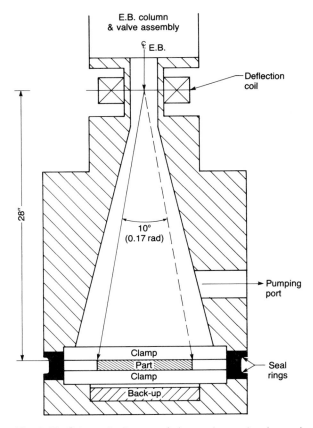

Fig. 1-17 Schematic diagram of electron-beam chamber and
deflection system used for PV production welding.

requirements for sidebar and inner rail blanks increased, work
was started to utilize the NVEB welding process because of its
potential for higher welding speeds and shorter cycle times.
Since the parts to be welded are at atmospheric pressure, no
pumping time is required. Two production NVEB systems have
been built, see Fig. 1-18, and these two NV systems have
together produced over 7 million welded blanks to date.

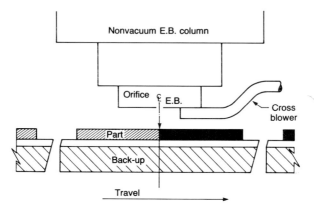

Fig. 1-18 Schematic diagram of electron-beam column and travel system used for NV production welding.[8]

5. A recent government-sponsored program designed and tested a system for producing high-pressure hydraulic tubing which is spirally welded on a continuous basis. A continuous system for producing high-pressure titanium alloy tubing by wrapping strip and EBW was designed and is shown in Fig. 1-19. The design evolved from the various approaches using inside mandrels to the final concept of forming and welding in a cavity. A cost estimate which included all elements required to produce finished tubing revealed that about 25 percent cost reduction can be achieved over present methods of producing high-pressure titanium alloy tubing.[9]

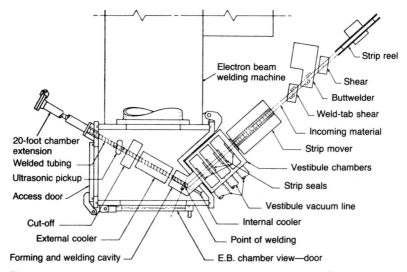

Fig. 1-19 Layout of system for continuous EBW system for tubing.[9]

6. Finally the development work on sliding-seal electron-beam (SSEB) welding equipment recently has been evaluated as a production method for EBW for diverse applications. Applications evaluated included cylinders, 120-in-long (3048-mm) plates, channel and tee shapes, and others, see Fig. 1-20. The SSEB welding facility is shown in Fig. 1-21.

Application	Rating		
	1	2	3
Center wing box			X
Wing covers & planks	X		
Tension beams			X
Landing gears		X	X
Nacelle or fuselage bulkheads	X		
Longerons or stringers	X		
Cylinders (rocket motor cases)		X	
Rotor hubs	X		

Rating 1 – Best application on basis of present work
Rating 2 – Requires development. SSEB is potential
  process
Rating 3 – Can only be efficiently welded in EB
  chambers			

Fig. 1-20 Potential titanium primary structure application areas for SSEB welding.[10]

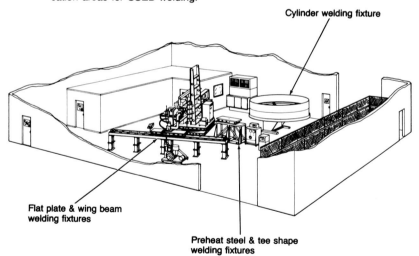

Cylinder welding fixture

Flat plate & wing beam welding fixtures

Preheat steel & tee shape welding fixtures

Fig. 1-21 SSEB welding facility.[10]

Another type of SSEB welder has been developed in France. The portable welding head consists of an electron gun mounted on a carriage; this carriage travels on a base plate which in turn rests on the joint to be welded. In order to obtain the required vacuum, the welding chamber is fitted with seals placed between the carriage and suction plate assembly and the parts to be welded. The joint to be welded is sited beneath the lower part of the welding chamber; its underside and ends are blanked by means of a continuously arc-welded bead and a special adhesive tape.

Welding in the horizontal position is accomplished simply by lowering the electron-beam welder onto the sheets. When welding in the vertical position, the welding head can be held by a lifting system (crane), and the vacuum applies it to the welding joint. A close-up of the portable welding gun is seen in Fig. 1-22.

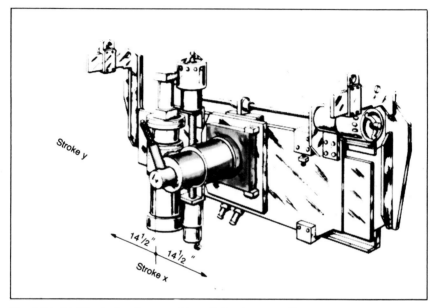

Fig. 1-22 Mobile electron-beam welder with local vacuum.[11]

Tooling

Tooling and fixturing rank second only to design in importance to EBW. Proper weld-joint design and good tooling control the success or failure of any welding process. The EBW process employs weld joints with contacting edges which have been machined to a relatively close tolerance. This is particularly true of butt-type joint configurations. Although the distortion which occurs is far less than that encountered with most other fusion-welding processes, it is still a factor that must be compensated for. It is indeed foolhardy to expend the required capital for a highly sophisticated fusion welding system, and expect it to perform miracles in metal joining, if tooling requirements and consideration have not been included in the initial planning stages when an EBW system is procured.

The tooling required by the electron-beam process is similar to, but does not have to be as strong as, tooling for automatic gas tungsten-arc (GTA) and gas metal-arc (GMA) fusion-welding processes. Since joint configurations are identical, except for minor innovations, the tool required to maintain joint alignment with minimum residual restraint is applicable to all automatic fusion-welding processes.

Prerequisites for successful tooling are as follows:

- Provide a sturdy base to hold tooling mechanisms to prevent deflections due to pressure, weight, and temperature variations during welding.
- Provide work tables and rotary fixtures for moving the work in relation to the electron beam. Smooth, accurate motion control is required at specified travel speeds. For vacuum welding, all travel motions must be easily controlled from outside the vacuum chamber by the operator.
- Design tooling to either move the part or the electron gun in proper relation with the weld seam. A contour follower or a seam tracking device on the workpiece or tooling is desirable.
- Provide backup protection under the weld bead, usually of the same material being welded. This will prevent damage to the part and/or tooling by the existing electron beam.
- Use nonmagnetic materials for tooling to prevent beam deflection. All magnetic materials to be welded should be demagnetized prior to welding.
- Provide starting and runoff tabs, preferably of the same material being welded. Angle blocks are desired to prevent undercutting at the weld edge or at weld start and stop areas.
- Provide a tungsten or copper block for preadjusting and focusing the electron beam. The surface of the block should be placed at the level where fine focusing is desired.
- Protect critical parts of tooling mechanism with tungsten or copper materials to prevent electron-beam damage.
- Provide preheat or postheat capability when required for materials being welded. In many cases, preheat and postheat operations can be controlled by using a defocused electron beam.
- Maintain tooling at ground potential.
- Provide copper chill blocks or bars along the weld seam where applicable, to minimize heat transfer and material warpage.[2]

Of particular interest to EBW fabricators is the concept of loading more than one part in an EBW chamber at one time. Figure 1-23 is a multispindle rotary fixture used to produce vacuum tubes. When tooling permits multiple-part welding in one chamber pump-down cycle, the process then actually produces higher-quality welded configurations at possibly less cost than those produced by other fusion-welding processes.

The ingenuity of the tool designer has become more important in EBW than in any other welding process. All work is done remotely and in a vacuum; the weld details must be held in practically intimate

Fig. 1-23 Multispindle welding fixture.[12]

contact; the motors for movement of the parts must be capable of operation in a vacuum; and all types of assist tools, subfixtures, and work-handling systems must be accurate and function with practically zero error tolerances.

Shown in Fig. 1-24 is a special-purpose, multiple-tooling fixture designed for EBW of 30 pressure vessel assemblies in one loading. The fixture is mounted on a rotary table in the vacuum chamber. It is electronically sequenced for precise, repeatable indexing of the parts under the electron-beam gun. After positioning, each part is held stationary as one annular plug weld is made by circular beam deflection.

Also shown in the side view of Fig. 1-24 is a fixture which has each part positioned, and is individually rotated by a mechanism which engages at the weld station to produce the required girth welds.

As requirements for EBW arise, imaginative fixturing must evolve. Applications of this type of unique fixturing include EBW of refractory metal honeycomb sandwich materials, corrugated sine wave assembly in Fig. 1-25. A successful production program employed the use of EBW to assemble a large-scale, highly stressed sheet-metal enclosure.[14] The enclosure was constructed of 6Al-4V titanium alloy, and the construction employed the use of closely spaced internal ring stiffeners which were joined to the enclosure skin with approximately 3500 in (87,500 mm) of EBW. The assembly and positioning of the stiffener segments and cylindrical skin were accomplished on a single fixture, shown in Fig. 1-26. The fixture located the zee segments vertically from the base of the skin and, in the ready-to-weld condition, mechanically

(a)

(b)

Fig. 1-24 Multiple tooling fixtures for EBW of automobile air bag bottles. (a) Top view and (b) side view.[13]

pushed the stiffener flange against the skin, with almost continuous bearing, through retractable spring-loaded shoes. Tooling can be simple as well as complex. Consider, for example, the welding of pressure vessels. Titanium spheres, 14 in (355.6 mm) in diameter, have been electron-beam-welded with the tools shown in Fig. 1-27. The

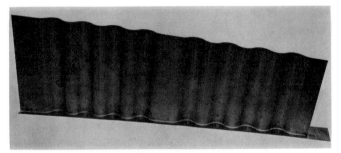

Fig. 1-25 Underside of cobalt-base welded component.

Fig. 1-26 EBW fixture for cylinder to produce skin-to-zees weldment.[14]

Fig. 1-27 Simplified tools for welding spherical motor cases.[2]

small plug in the center of Fig. 1-27 is tack-welded lightly to the sphere, which in turn is threaded for attachment to the rotary fixture within the electron-beam chamber. The ring with the slots throughout is tightened to hold the two halves of the sphere butted together. As the sphere is rotated within the chamber, a light pass of the beam (nonpenetrating) touches each open slot in the ring and fuses the two halves, like tack welding in fusion welding. On completion, the ring is removed and then a full-penetration weld is applied to the sphere, and there is neither distortion nor need for tooling.

An ingenious and practical arrangement for multiple-tier welding was used to electron-beam weld more than 12,000 terminal interconnections per pump-down, in an automated mass-production application for ferrite-core memory arrays for electronic computers. A typical stack of frames assembled in an EBW fixture is shown in Fig. 1-28. Before the core frames are stacked, the upper and lower terminals on each frame are spread apart to ensure positive contact with the mating terminals of adjacent frames, as shown in details A and B in Fig. 1-28. The frames are then stacked in an aluminum holding fixture, to which is attached a comblike aligning tool. When the assembly is completed, the holding fixture cover is bolted in place and the aligning tool removed. By this means, the 25,872 accurately formed and trimmed

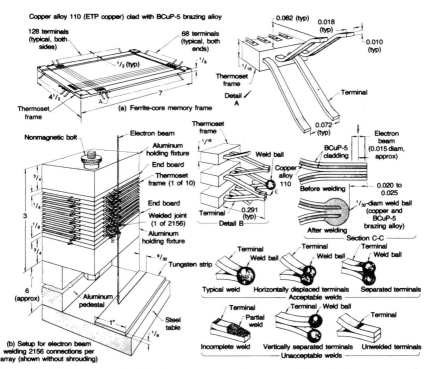

Fig. 1-28 EBW of terminals of ferrite-core memory frames used in electronic computers.[15] (0.01 in = 0.25 mm)

terminals in a batch of six arrays were aligned vertically to make 12,936 welded joints.

Whereas a few years ago most time was spent by electron-beam manufacturers in improving beam generation and control, today the emphasis has shifted to work-handling systems, tooling, and special beam control devices to turn welders into true production tools.

One type of machine sketched in Fig. 1-29 consists of a basic unit to which special tooling can be attached. Here the tooling includes the small work chamber sized to fit the specific part involved. Three typical tooling configurations are shown, two for making relatively large circular welds by workpiece rotation and the third for making small, circular welds by beam deflection. This tooling can be quickly and easily changed. With this machine, the operating parameters are set and locked at a control station. The operator merely loads the part into the machine and pushes a button, closes a door, or perhaps moves

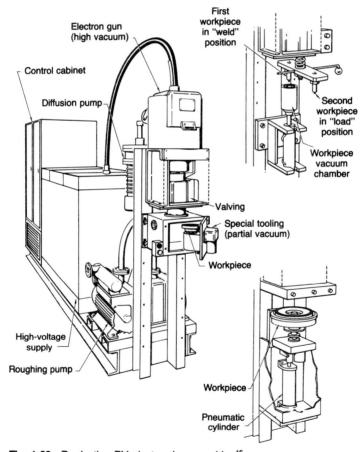

Fig. 1-29 Production PV electron-beam welder.[16]

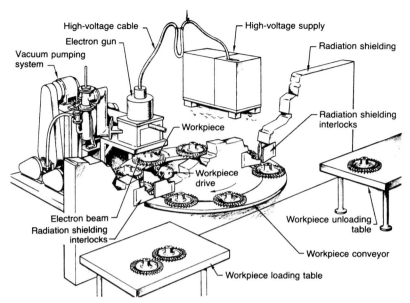

Fig. 1-30   Production system for NVEB welding wheels.

the fixture into position. The rest of the cycle is fully automatic. The tooling needed for NVEB machines presents different problems. A turbine wheel assembly welding system is shown in Fig. 1-30. The wheels, installed on individual rotary spindle assemblies, are mounted on a rotary conveyor system. The rotary conveyor system positions the composite wheel under the electron beam, where the wheel is rotated on the rotary spindle. Loading and unloading the rotor are accomplished from a separate control room that is radiation isolated by appropriate wall structures and interlocks.

JOINT DESIGN

In any welded joint, stresses are introduced into the welded assembly through unequal expansion and contraction of the metal because of large temperature variations between the molten weld metal, the heat-affected zone, and the parent metal. The molten weld metal contracts as it cools, and this contraction is resisted by the adjacent cool base metal. As a result, the weld metal is stretched and a series of opposing stresses are built up in the joint. This stress condition is accentuated by the difference in the weld width between the top and bottom of the weld, which provides different amounts of molten weld metal as well as a reservoir of temperature gradients. Arc welds in heavy-gage materials are not satisfactory in this respect, due to unequal shrinkage stresses of the V-shaped weld zone. This condition is greatly improved by producing narrow welds with parallel sides of the cast weld structure and by reducing heat input to the joint. The shrinkage force is further reduced when welds are placed on the neutral axis of the assembly and no filler metal is added. Of all the fusion-welding processes, electron-beam welds will generate the minimum amount of built-in stresses in a welded joint because of their deep, narrow weld characteristics.

In considering weld joint designs for EBW, it must be noted that the electron-beam spot size may vary from 0.005 to 0.50 in (0.13 to 1.5 mm), depending upon the type of equipment and the degree of focusing used. Because of this small focal spot size, it is mandatory that special precautions be taken to see that the joint design and fit-up are satisfactory for EBW. The edges of the joint to be welded must fit tightly together, since the electron beam will heat only the metal surfaces that it strikes. Therefore, the smaller the beam, the closer is the required tolerance for the joint.

If the weld joint should be larger than the normal beam-focal-spot size, the beam is correspondingly increased in size, or the beam is moved over a rotational pattern. This same procedure will apply where a mismatch occurs in the weld joint fit-up as a result of metal or machining tolerances.[2,17] The best weld-joint types for EBW are the butt, burn-through, tee, and lap. Fillet-type welds are difficult to make and are not usually employed.

Butt Joints

If the simplest and most common weld joint, a butt weld of two plate sections, is taken as an example illustrating the basic difference in joint preparation, for a conventional arc weld, a vee preparation would be

Preparation	Weld	Notes
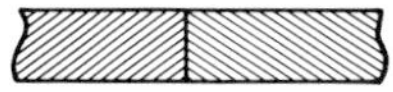		Plain butt.
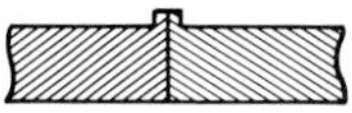		Butt joint with lip preparation to provide filler.
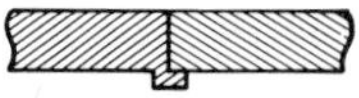		Spigot preparation
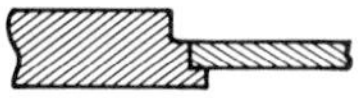		Joining a thick to thin section.

Fig. 1-31 Butt weld preparations.[17]

used and the weld built up by successive passes using filler material. For EBW, however, the mating edges of the plate sections are machined off square so as to present a solid metal interface to the beam, which fuses the joint in a single pass. Therefore, it can be seen that while the electron-beam weld joint preparation is the simpler, a somewhat higher standard of machining is called for to ensure that the mating surfaces are in close abutment. For a plain butt joint on a 0.5-in (12.7-mm) plate, a maximum gap of 0.005 in (0.13 mm) could be allowed, but this would be reduced for thinner sections. Figure 1-31 shows some variations on plain butt joints, on both similar and dissimilar section thicknesses. The lip and spigoted preparations shown are devices used to counteract undercutting and drop-through of weld metal. There are numerous other variations of these commonly used slant-groove welds.[15]

Lap Joints

This type of joint is used mainly in joining thin-gage metals or a thin to a thick section with a spike weld. Typical joints are shown in Fig. 1-32, and an instrument flexure is a good example of simulating spot welds with the electron beam.[17] In this application, link pieces are welded to stainless steel limbs of the flexure, which is used in a liquid-flow measurement system. The fatigue life of the component was doubled by changing from spot welding to EBW as a result of the elimination of oxidation in the weld zone.

Angle, Tee, Channel, Box, and H Sections

Having established that relatively distortion-free welds can be made on machined components, we can consider the EBW process as a method for fabricating various shapes in which the resulting section is built up

Preparation	Weld	Notes
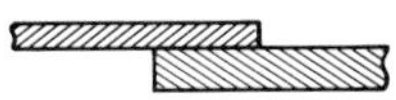		Lap joint showing stake and fillet welds
		Lap joint on thin gauges
		Alternative joint preparation for thin gauges

Fig. 1-32 Lap-joint preparations.[17]

from a number of easily machined parts. Figure 1-33 illustrates some basic joint preparations used for butt welding angle and tee sections, and these can be applied to channel, box, and H sections.

A good example of precision fabrication by EBW is an aluminum alloy frame assembly.[17] The four flat plates are fully machined prior to assembly into a welding fixture which doubles as an acceptance jig to ensure that the piece parts are within dimensional tolerance when assembled for welding.

Flange and Shaft Joints

Flanges and gears can be joined to shafts and tubes by means of either planetary or circumferential joints, as illustrated in Fig. 1-34. The planetary weld preparation normally requires an interference fit between the mating parts, usually of the order of 0.001 in per inch (0.001 mm per millimeter) diameter for shafts up to about 10-in (254-mm) diameter. Failure to make allowance for weld shrinkage in this type of joint can result in the material being left in a stressed condition and subject to cracking during welding, in subsequent heat treatment, or in service. The alternative plain or spigoted butt preparation does not present the same problem because the component parts are now more free to contract during welding.

Many variations of the basic joint and weld types described above and illustrated in Figs. 1-31 to 1-35 are used to meet the needs of individual applications. The weld preparations used for joining thin-gage bellows and diaphragms are illustrated in Fig. 1-35. The extremely low heat input from an electron-beam weld also makes it possible to hermetically seal chemical substances in containers and to encapsulate potted electronic components.

An example demonstrating the complete practicality of EBW is shown in Fig. 1-36. The wing center section, a single-cell box beam of 6Al-4V titanium, consists of four basic weld assemblies fabricated from

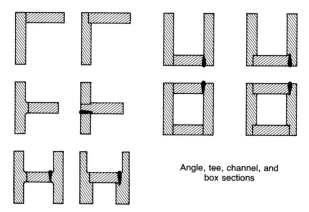

Angle, tee, channel, and box sections

Fig. 1-33 Angle- and tee-joint preparations.[17]

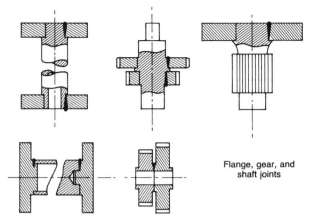

Flange, gear, and
shaft joints

Fig. 1-34 Flange- and shaft-joint preparations.[17]

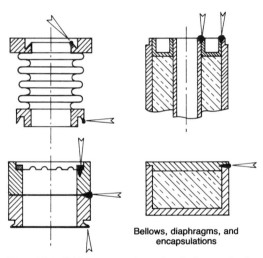

Bellows, diaphragms, and
encapsulations

Fig. 1-35 Weld preparations for bellows, diaphragms, and encapsulations.[17]

33 machined parts. It transmits wing outer panel loads (applied to wing pivots) into fuselage nacelles and center body. This beam was the first aircraft structure to include welds in tension.

Each wing box needs seventy welds in 25 setups. Fifty-seven welds are square butts and thirteen are scarfed joints. Welds join metal thicknesses from 0.5 to 2 in (12.7 to 50.8 mm). The longest weld is 65 in (1651 mm).

In most applications, the fit-up of parts for EBW must be more precise than for inert-gas-shielded metal-arc processes. A metal-to-metal fit of mating parts with zero gap size is desired, but is not practical. Gap sizes should preferably be no greater than 0.005 in

(0.13 mm). Shown in Table 1-1 are the results of a series of tests which denote the effect of gap on the strength of joint. No filler metal addition was used in these tests. As the gap size was reduced, the thickness of the weld was reduced and the heat-affected zone in the steel was minimized, thus the strength of the joint increased. Where gaps in a joint exceed the size of the electron beam, gaps or voids will occur in the weld. The degree of tolerance will vary with the materials being welded. For example, aluminum alloys can tolerate a larger gap size than can be used for steels.

As with any welding process, joint design for EBW must receive careful attention. Since the process is used to produce extremely narrow welds, it must be remembered that the beam is also very narrow. It is, therefore, mandatory that the preparation and fixturing of the workpiece are accurate. The most useful characteristic of the electron beam is its power of penetration. Because of the aforementioned electron beam stiffness, the beam produces a weld zone that assumes the joint efficiency when the part is loaded in tension, because only a small amount of weld metal is involved for each increment of loading.

Studies of other welding processes show that most failures do not originate in the weld, but rather in the zone immediately adjacent to the weld, usually referred to as the heat-affected zone. Because of its extremely small focal spot, EBW can dramatically reduce the heat-

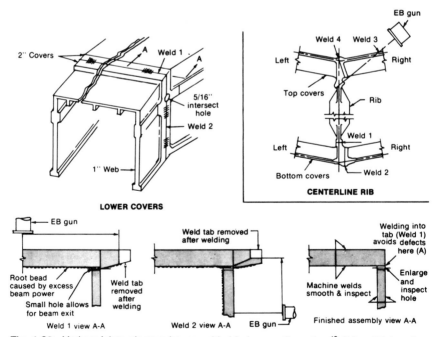

Fig. 1-36 Various joints electron-beam-welded in box configuration.[18] (1 in = 25.4 mm)

TABLE 1-1
Effect of Gap on Strength
of Electron-Beam Welds
17-7PH Annealed, 0.020-in-thick (0.50 mm);
Parent Metal Strength 125.0 ksi (862 MPa)

Gap		Strength	
in	mm	ksi	MPa
0.001	0.03	123.3	850
0.002	0.05	115.8	798
0.003	0.08	116.1	801
0.004	0.10	111.0	765
0.005	0.13	103.2	712
0.006	0.15	81.9	565

affected zone in weldments. The size of the spot can be varied, however, by simply changing the focusing current.

To make full use of the electron-beam process, we should keep in mind that welds of greater width can be obtained for joints that are to be loaded in tension. Deep, narrow welds are often more applicable to true butt joints or joints loaded in shear because the volume of cast material is reduced. However, the shear strength of metal is lower than its tensile strength, and the possibility of joining members in tension rather than in shear should be considered.

In welded joints, stresses are introduced during welding by the unequal expansion and contraction of the molten weld zone, the heat-affected zone, and the unaffected base metal. Therefore, the EBW process, which appreciably reduces the heat input to the materials, also minimizes the origin of such stresses. Characteristically, the electron beam produces welds that are rectangular as compared with the triangular shape of conventional arc welds. The configuration of the welds minimizes or, in many instances, eliminates angular distortion of the welded parts. With distortion held to reasonable limits, the parts may often be welded in the finish-machined condition.

It would be highly desirable to make a tee joint the same way that an electron-beam butt joint is made. When two very thin materials are being joined, this is sometimes possible, but for heavy materials, the optimum joint could be made only by forging or machining the horizontal plate to provide a land for the vertical member to butt against and be welded. This solution, however, is not as practical as simply producing a deep-penetration weld through the horizontal member into the neutral axis of the vertical member.

The two welds in Fig. 1-37 (tee and burn-through) are optimum for joint efficiency. Since they are 90° displaced, an angular weld position that approximates either condition also approximates the ideal weld. Although this position is the same as for a conventional arc-fillet weld, the advantage of the electron-beam weld is that by deep penetration the weld will have little or no fillet and will be lighter than a larger fillet

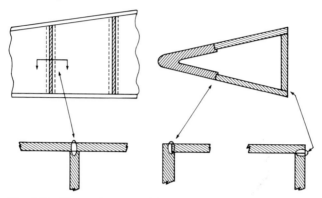

Fig. 1-37 Electron-beam weld joints in vane assembly.

weld having little penetration. This joint is illustrated by the 5254 aluminum welds in Fig. 1-38.

The joint stresses discussed previously have been primarily transverse. The amount of material melted is less and the shrinkage in the longitudinal plane is less. Also, the beam may be used to prestress the joint. This is accomplished by defocusing the beam so that it does not melt the joint, but rather heats the area near the joint, expanding the metal in a longitudinal direction. After welding, the cooling weld metal and the heat margins contract more uniformly.

In lap joints, unfavorable stress conditions can also be relieved. To arc-weld a lap joint, when both sides of the material are accessible, a double fillet is used. This same joint can be duplicated with an electron-beam weld with only one surface accessible by producing a double-fillet effect with a penetration weld at each free edge.

The strength of a joint should be determined by its design. The addition of filler metal, unless a reduction in thickness is involved, adds nothing useful to the strength of the joint, but increases its weight. In many applications, EBW eliminates the need for filler metals, unless a situation occurs when a filler metal is used to create more favorable metallurgy in the weld. An example, Inconel 713C, a vacuum-cast

Fig. 1-38 Electron-beam welds in simulated tube-to-head seam of navol tank-weld penetration.[2]

nickel alloy, when welded to itself, develops a condition that results in microcracking. However, the insertion of a strip of Udimet 500, a nickel-base superalloy, of proper thickness into the joint produces an apparently crack-free weld. Usually, elimination of filler metal reduces the effective shrinkage forces acting on the joint as does the placing of the welds as near as possible to the neutral axis of the assembly. The closer the weld is to the neutral axis, the less is the leverage exerted to pull the section out of alignment.

ECONOMICS OF EBW

Although the initial cost and capital investment of electron-beam welders are high, their commercial value has proven their worth many times. Electron-beam experience and equipment are expensive (basic equipment costs upward of $200,000). Most managements are reluctant to make that kind of investment until they have positive assurance that it will prove advantageous and profitable. The major factors in EBW which influence the cost, besides initial equipment investment, are effect of pump-down time on unit labor cost and high cost of precise joint preparation and precision tooling.

The initial cost of EBW equipment varies considerably, depending on chamber size, type and capacity of vacuum-pumping equipment, beam-power requirements, and degree of complexity and automation of control equipment. The absence of a welding chamber in NVEB systems is offset, at least in part, by the cost of a shielded work enclosure and high-speed work-handling equipment. High equipment utilization, preferably in long runs on similar parts, is needed to avoid high amortization charges in unit welding costs.

A second major factor is the effect of pump-down time on labor cost per weld. This effect can be reduced in some applications by using work chambers of minimum size for the assembly being welded, increasing pumping capacity, welding in PV instead of high vacuum, using dual work chambers or special vacuum rotary-feed systems with sliding seals, and by other mechanical expedients. Pump-down time is eliminated in NVEB welding.

A third major cost factor is precise joint preparation and the precision tooling needed for accurate tracking of the joint by the narrow electron beam.

Factors that favor the use of EBW where arc welding is also suitable include high welding speed, deep penetration in a single pass, and the ability to make most welds without using filler metal or shielding gas. In many applications, the localized heat input and extremely rapid thermal cycling of EBW eliminate, or reduce, the cost of related operations such as machining and heat treatment.

Auto parts manufacturers, taking all the above factors into consideration, are using NVEB welding for its speed, low cost, and reliability. One manufacturer builds two basic catalytic converters, and twelve 36-kW NVEB welders are used to weld 25,000 converters daily.

The converters are made from titanium-stabilized Type 409 stainless steel. The electron-beam weld is used to make continuous seam welds around the periphery of the converter. Construction of the converters is such that the weld must penetrate four layers of 0.050 in (1.3 mm), or a total of 0.200 in (5 mm). One converter is welded in 13.4 s at a weld speed of 300 in/min (127.3 mm/s).

NVEB welding is also adaptable to relatively small production runs. One automobile company had to join 1140 steel yokes to 1020 steel tubing drive shafts. Joining the yokes to the tubing required the use of Hastelloy W (nominally Ni-24.5Mo-5.5Fe-5Cr) filler metal to avoid cracking the dissimilar steels, and the welding was completed in one pass. Automobile-part producers are not the only ones to have taken to NVEB welding. For example, steel companies and metal fabricators are using the process to produce welded tubing. Welders are integrated readily with tube mills, welding tubing on a production basis at speeds up to 121.9 in/min (51 mm/s).

SAFETY

As with many processes, electron beams present an occupational hazard that must be dealt with to assure the safety of the user. This hazard involves exposure of personnel both to the accelerated electrons or to secondary radiation in the form of x-rays or neutrons, with x-rays by far the more common problem. Basically, an electron-beam facility may be thought of as a giant x-ray tube with the electron gun acting as the filament and the workpiece as the target. Instead of producing x-rays for useful purposes as with the x-ray tube, the primary goal of the electron-beam facility is the use of the electron beam itself, and x-rays became a byproduct.

Currently, electron beams involved in the metallurgical and related fields usually have required accelerating potentials of 60 to 100 kV. At these potentials, the wall thicknesses of chambers necessary for high-vacuum welding generally provide adequate x-ray shielding for 60 kV. However, lead shielding is generally added to the chamber's interior for voltage above 60 kV. Viewing windows are always a possible source of x-ray leakage in steel casing units. A thickness of lead glass is added to provide the necessary shielding in this area. It is recommended that the following suggestions be observed. "Recommended Safe Practices for Electron Beam Welding," AWS A6.4, and "Safety in Welding and Cutting," USAS Z49.1 (1a test edition), should also be consulted.

1. In compliance with existing regulations and good general practice concerning equipment capable of producing x-rays, a radiation survey should be made at installation of the equipment and annually commencing 1 year from completion of the machine installation.
2. Any time that a major disassembly or rework of the equipment is performed, it is mandatory that a radiation survey be made. This

is applicable to any work performed (or changes made) on equipment, when lead shielding is either disturbed or modified, regardless of location; for example, whenever the column shroud is moved or the column is relocated to its alternate position, a survey is required.

These requirements apply not only to existing high-vacuum EBW machines, but to NVEB and PVEB welders as well. The above requirements apply equally to shielding surrounding any tooling package associated with the basic welder. Special handling and facilities are required when welding toxic materials, such as beryllium.

REPAIR

EBW is accumulating an impressive history of cost savings through repair of castings, forgings, and fabrications. For example, a rocket engine manufacturer reported a savings of $100,000 by the repair of an assembly that had failed because of high operating temperature. A brazed Hastelloy C section was successfully electron beam repair welded without removal of the braze filler metal.

Some salvaging repairs have included the following:

1. Oversize holes that can be saved by welding a plug insert and remachining. Three similar aircraft housings (6Al-4V titanium) which contained a good deal of costly and complex machining were involved. Unfortunately, one of the bored holes, approximately 0.2 in (5 mm) in diameter, was oversize. A close-fitting titanium plug of the same alloy was inserted in the hole and electron-beam-welded with satisfactory results.

2. Some cracks can be repaired by scanning over the joint with a small piece of filler wire. An example of this was a magnesium turbine nose section that experienced fatigue cracking during operation of the engine. Sound repair of these welds was accomplished by EBW. Here the ability of the electron beam to make a very narrow weld 12 in (305 mm) below the surface of the part was a necessity. Furthermore, it was vitally necessary to locate precisely the position of the weld before turning on the beam, otherwise, extensive damage of the part would have resulted. Simpler, less costly items, such as tooling and fixturing, also can be repaired using EBW. An example is a fabricated aluminum drilling fixture which is quickly and easily repair welded without distortion. Here the fixture was fabricated by normal arc-welding techniques. However, on completion it was found that one of the welds had cracked. At that time the locating holes had been positioned to close tolerances, and repair by normal welding would have resulted in extensive distortion. EBW solved the problem.

3. Lugs which have been forgotten from a drawing during the design stages of a program can be welded onto finished parts

without danger of distortion. Precisely machined AMS 5616 control-spider housings had been manufactured on a limited production basis before complete development testing revealed the need for improved structural rigidity. Unfortunately, the area requiring stiffening was immediately adjacent to a hole finish-machined to very close tolerances. However, with EBW it was possible to add a stiffening member without affecting significantly the dimensions of the hole. During development testing it was found necessary to add two bosses to a large, complex Type 431 stainless steel casting. Because of casting problems, schedule considerations, and costs involved, it was extremely important that a means be found to add these bosses to existing semifinished and finish-machined parts. Efforts to add the bosses by arc welding resulted in cracking and excessive distortion. Fortunately, EBW solved the problem.

4. The repair of damaged or worn jet-engine fan blades by EBW has become a standard maintenance and overhaul practice. It is anticipated that airline companies can save an estimated 75% of the cost of new blades by having worn or damaged blades repaired by EBW. Previously, this was not considered feasible because of the high stress on the welded joints during engine operation. The costly blades, made of titanium, were normally

Fig. 1-39 Partially machined titanium alloy forging.[19]

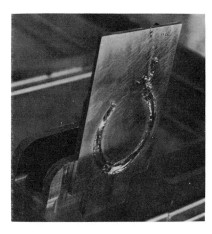

Fig. 1-40 Electron-beam weld over patched area.[19]

replaced. The leading edge of the blade is first machined, then a replacement strip is welded to it after various interim cleaning and other protective measures have been taken. Inspection by fluorescent and x-ray methods signifies the final acceptance of the repaired blade.

5. Imaginative use of electron-beam equipment for repair of seven aluminum electronic components recently resulted in a savings of approximately $10,000. The $1500 investment-cast aluminum structure had been rejected because of unacceptable flexure in the cast nuts. The choices were to scrap all seven parts and make a new mold, then recast and remachine the new parts, or to repair the castings. Two gussets machined from Type 1100 aluminum were electron-beam-welded to each of three nuts without distortion. This was done at a cost of approximately $75 for material and labor for each of the seven parts.

6. Figure 1-39 shows one of two partially machined titanium alloy forgings 84 in (2135 mm) long, each of which had a discrepancy as a result of a computer control malfunction. EBW was the only permissible method of weld repair, because of the crack sensitivity of the particular titanium alloy. Because of the length of the forging, it was necessary to position the part in the electron beam chamber at a 27° (0.47 rad) angle and machine the discrepant area to the same angle to maintain perpendicularity between the weld joint and electron beam gun. The weld joint, instead of being circular, is elliptical which immediately increased the cost of machining test specimens, fixturing, etc. Integral fixturing included copper heat sinks, titanium runoff weld tab, and titanium backup plate to stop further beam penetration. Actual welding was accomplished in two pumpdowns, the first to align and adjust the electron beam to trace the elliptical path of the weld joint. The chamber was then opened to secure a 0.100-in (2.5-mm) titanium "scab" plate over the

weld joint to prevent weld undercutting. After the second pump-down, a single elliptical weld pass of 3-s duration was made, Fig. 1-40, using less than one revolution to minimize overall heat input into the part. The "scab" welding technique was used because it prevented weld undercutting and eliminated the additional heat input of a second "cosmetic" weld pass to remove undercutting if the "scab" had not been used. The elimination of undercutting and minimum heat input was particularly important since the thickness of the part was finish-machined prior to weld repair. The cost savings on these two parts was $40,000.

Listed above are only a few of the hundreds of case histories on repair and salvage welding by EBW.

MATERIALS

The initial use of EBW was for joining metals whose mechanical or chemical properties were seriously impaired by even a minute amount of atmospheric contaminants (principally oxygen and nitrogen). These were refractory or highly active materials such as molybdenum, tantalum, tungsten, beryllium, columbium, and zirconium.

Today, as Table 1-2 indicates, the EBW process is applied not only to the refractory metals, but to a wide range of other materials. Significantly, the major emphasis has now passed from the refractory metals to those that might be best described as the structural metals, particularly in view of their extensive use in various types of structures. These applications take advantage of the higher weld-joint efficiencies and reduced distortion and shrinkage, compared with other types of fusion welds, that result from the electron-beam weld's narrower weld and heat-affected zone.

Aluminum and Its Alloys

As seen in Table 1-2, practically all the aluminums have been welded. However, certain aluminum alloys, particularly the 7000 series, are very difficult to join. Moreover, even with the readily weldable alloys, such as 6061, EBW is sometimes unsatisfactory for particular applications because of unacceptable distortion, excessive heat input, or related problems. In tests of the tensile strength of this alloy, welded in the solution-treated condition and aged to the T6 condition after welding, approximately 85% of expected base-metal strength was obtained.

Visual and radiographic inspection of most aluminum welds indicates no incidence of cracking or porosity. The high purity of the vacuum welding environment undoubtedly contributed to this favorable condition.[20]

In EBW of heavier thicknesses, such as 1.5 in (38.4 mm) of 7075 aluminum, several precautions must be taken. A slower welding speed

TABLE 1-2
Materials Joined by EBW[5]

Steels

300 series stainless

400 series stainless

Maraging

17-4PH

17-7PH

15-5PH

PH15-7Mo

14-8Mo

AM350 and 355

Carbon steels [including but not limited to 1010, 1025, 1035, 1065, 1095 and Uddeholm (UHB-15)]

Low-alloy steels (including but not limited to 4130, 4140, 4340, 52100, 8640)

Tool steels (including but not limited to H11, M2, and W2)

HY-80

HY-130

HY-150

D6AC

300M

Rocoloy

Simonds No. 73

Vascomax

Ferrous Alloys

300 series to 400 series stainless steel

300 series to austenitic precipitation-hardenable stainless

300 series martensitic precipitation-hardenable stainless

300 series stainless to mild steel

300 series stainless steel to beryllium copper

400 series to austenitic precipitation-hardenable stainless

400 series to martensitic precipitation-hardenable stainless

400 series stainless to mild-steel austenitic precipitation-hardenable to martensitic precipitation-hardenable stainless

4130 to 17-22 (V)

4130 to 4140

4130 to Transcor T

6150 to M2 tool steel

Kovar to steel

Heat-Resistant Alloys

Hastelloy B

Hastelloy C

Hastelloy N

Hastelloy W

Hastelloy X

Haynes Stellite 21

Haynes Stellite 25

Haynes Stellite 31

Haynes Stellite 36

S-816

Inconel 600

Inconel 625

Inconel 700

Inconel 713C

Inconel X-750

Inconel 718

Inconel 722

L-605

GMR-235

19-9DL

A-286

16-25-6

N-155

René 41

Udimet 500

Udimet 700

Waspaloy

TABLE 1-2 (*Continued*)

Titanium and Titanium Alloys

Commercially pure

Beta III

Beta C

5Al-2.5Sn

6Al-2Sn-4Mo-6V

6Al-4V

13V-11Cr-3Al

7Al-4Mo

3Al-1Mo-1V

8Al-1Mo-1V

6Al-6V-2Sn

6Al-2Sn-4Mo-2V

Rare and Precious Metals

Gallium

Gold and alloys

Gold to germanium

Gold to nickel plate

Gold to silicon

Iridium

Iridium to nickel

Palladium

Palladium to 347 stainless steel

Platinum and alloys

Platinum to nickel

Platinum to platinum-rhodium

Silver and alloys

Heat-Resistant Alloys

A-286 to Inconel alloy 713

A-286 to Inco 100

A-286 to Udimet 500

A-286 to Waspaloy

Elgiloy to beryllium copper

Hastelloy X to Inconel alloy 713

Haynes Stellite No. 6 to steel

Haynes Stellite No. 21 to steel

Haynes Stellite No. 21 to Nitralloy

Haynes Stellite No. 31 to AISI 8640

Incoloy alloy 901 to Inconel alloy 713

Inconel alloy 713 to mild steel

Inconel alloy 713 to Udimet 500

Inconel alloy 713 to Waspaloy

Inconel alloy X-750 to Mallory 1000

Inconel alloy X-750 to mild steel

Inconel alloy X-750 to molybdenum

Inconel alloy X-50 to Simonds No. 73

Inconel alloy X-750 to tungsten

Inconel alloy X-750 to Waspaloy

N-155 to 17-4PH

N-155 to 347 stainless steel

Udimet 500 to low-alloy steel

Udimet 500 to Inco 713

Waspaloy to low-alloy steel

Waspaloy to Inco 100

Refractory Metals and Alloys

Beryllium

Columbium and alloys

Columbium to tantalum

Molybdenum and alloys

Molybdenum to platinum

Molybdenum to titanium

Molybdenum to tungsten

Molybdenum to Kovar

Molybdenum to tantalum

Rhenium

Tantalum and alloys

Tungsten and alloys

Tungsten to beryllium copper

Tungsten to copper

Tungsten to stainless steel

Tungsten to steel

TABLE 1-2 *(Continued)*

Tungsten to titanium
Vanadium
Vanadium to 347 stainless steel
Vanadium to AISI 4340
Vanadium to titanium
Zirconium and alloys

Aluminum Alloys

1100
2014
2017
2021
2024
2219
3003
5005
5052
5083
5086
5254
5456
6061
7039
7075
7079
7178
Cast 355
Cast 356
Cast 357
Cast AMS 4291
Cast RED-X-20

Magnesium alloys

AZ31B
AZ80A
AZ91A and C
ZK60A

Cast AMS 4442 (EX33A)
HK31A
ZRE-1

Copper and Copper Alloys

OFHC
Electrolytic tough pitch
Beryllium copper
Aluminum bronze
Cupronickel
Constantan

Nonmetals

Alumina
Beryllia
Vycor
Magnesia
Thoria
Pyrex

Miscellaneous Metals and Alloys

Kovar
Invar
Rodar
Kamawire
Mumetal
Nickel
Vicalloy
Cadmium
Uranium
Mallory 1000
Ni-Span "C"
Nickel silver
Monel (nickel-copper)
Havar
Elinvar

TABLE 1-2 *(Continued)*

Miscellaneous Materials	Copper to Kovar
Alumel to Chromel	Copper to mild steel
Alumel to 347 stainless steel	Copper to nickel plate
Aluminum to beryllium	Copper to silver
Aluminum to copper (hermetic seal only)	Copper to silver alloys
Aluminum to stainless steel (hermetic seal only)	Cupronickel to SAE 1010 steel
	Dumet to nickel
Aluminum bronze to mild steel	Elkonite to Simonds No. 73
Aluminum bronze to stainless steel	Kovar to nickel plate
Austenitic stainless steel to tungsten carbide	Mallory 1000 to Simonds No. 73
Beryllium to copper	Nickel to copper plate
Beryllium to 52100 steel	Nickel to nichrome plate
Beryllium to uranium	Nickel to silicon
Brass to 94Pb-4.5Sn foil	Nickel to steel
Chromel to 347 stainless steel	Nickel silver to SAE 1010 steel
Constantan to copper	Nickel silver to silver

will allow more time for gas or vapors to escape from the molten puddle. The speed is usually of the order of 8 to 10 in/min (3.3 to 4.2 mm/s), and to reduce the level of oxides, the abutting edges and adjacent surfaces of the weld joint are brushed immediately before welding.

The results of welding 7075 aluminum in the T651 condition indicate that porosity-free welds can be produced with the EBW process. The transverse tensile strength of the weldment is low in comparison to parent-metal tensile strength. It is apparent from tensile test results that low transverse joint strength results when thick sections of 7075 aluminum are joined by the electron-beam weld process. Low transverse joint strength must be allowed for in the design of components requiring the joining of thick sections.

Recent work performed in Japan[21] shows that from the viewpoint of mechanical properties, electron-beam-welded 7075 exhibits tensile strength comparable to the yield strength of base metal, but the fracture mode seems to be rather brittle with small elongation. The fracture toughness of the weld, however, is superior to that of the base metal, so it seems that from the standpoint of fracture toughness, electron-beam-welded 7075 is useful if a proper welding procedure is applied, and a sound weld will result.

As indicated in Table 1-2, EBW of the 5000 series of aluminum alloys has been successfully accomplished. Welds have been made in

5-in-thick (12.7 mm) 5083 aluminum alloy. The weld was accomplished with a single pass, and when one considers the number of passes and the time required to produce such a weld using conventional techniques, this is quite remarkable. The application of a 5000-series aluminum alloy was recently demonstrated in the fabrication of a 5254 aluminum alloy torpedo component, as well as 5000-series aluminum pressure hulls for submersible vehicles.

The aluminum alloy 2219 has shown that significantly higher strength and joint efficiency can be developed in plate gages welded by the electron-beam process than by either GTA or GMA; that is, tensile strength efficiency is 70 to 80% for electron-beam welds and 50 to 65% for GTA and GMA.[22]

One of the most interesting phenomena with EBW of Type 2219 aluminum is that higher yield strengths are obtained with heavier gages than with the thinner material.

The following results were found in a recent investigation which evaluated EBW 2219 aluminum alloy for pressure vessel applications.

- Fit-up gaps up to 0.01 in (0.25 mm) can be tolerated prior to welding. However, a maximum specification limit of 0.005 in (0.13 mm) is recommended.
- The most uniform weld geometry is obtained from low-travel-speed, low-voltage, high-amperage, out-of-focus, and overpowered settings.
- Repair can be accomplished by rewelding, which is the most successful method to employ and produces about 10% reduction in mechanical properties.
- Mechanical property data indicate that narrow welds are superior to wide welds; however, reinforcements produced from wide welds are desired for most pressure-vessel applications.

Aluminum alloy 2021 has a combination of properties that make it an excellent choice for applications requiring exposure to cryogenic temperatures, elevated temperatures, or conditions that present potential stress-corrosion hazards. Recent work has shown that the alloy has been successfully electron-beam-welded for use in liquid-propellant storage tanks. In the heat-treated and aged condition, it is one of the strongest readily weldable aluminum alloys. The 2021 aluminum alloy is not as weldable as 2219. The alloy is very sensitive to the rate of heat input and is susceptible to porosity and cracking where adequate heat sink or chill bars are not provided. Finally in the successful EBW of 2021 alloy, a high volume of filler metal, 2319, was required to minimize cadmium and tin in the weld. Repair welding could not be satisfactorily accomplished by electron-beam or GTA welding when other filler metal additions were used. Vaporization of the cadmium appeared to be the problem.

The feasibility of fabricating 7039-T4 and -T61 aluminum alloy armor-plate hull structures by EBW has been investigated. Joint efficiencies as high as 100% were achieved in the T4 material and about

75 to 90% in the T61, without filler metal or preheat. The welds were apparently free from heat-affected-zone cracking, and preweld machining and cleaning minimized porosity. Welds in the T61 material also appeared free from stress-corrosion cracking. The best welds were obtained with the beam focused beyond the joint.

The heat-treatable alloys of series 2xxx, 6xxx, and 7xxx are crack-sensitive to varying degrees when welded. The condition of the zone immediately adjacent to the weld is critical in determining weldability. The 6xxx alloys are only slightly affected by the heat cycles of EBW. Alloys 2219, 7039, and 7005 appear to be the least affected of the alloys of their respective series. The techniques used to prevent cracking in EBW of heat-treatable aluminum alloys are

1. Special care in preweld cleaning to avoid porosity and oxide inclusions in the weld metal.
2. Prestressing joints in compression by using interference fits when possible.
3. Use of a ductile filler metal, usually in the form of a thin strip preplaced in the joint, which will yield under shrinkage stresses and fill joint openings.
4. Selection of beam power, beam spot size, and welding speed to create as narrow a weld as practical during short welding heat cycles, to avoid excessive grain-boundary melting.
5. Use of postweld heat treatment to restore the strength and ductility of the weld and heat-affected zones.
6. Other techniques such as designing or locating joints to be free of externally imposed restraints, reinforcing of joint areas, and, when possible, welding in the solution-treated condition, with postweld aging.

A U.S. government–sponsored program was conducted to evaluate EBW of 5086-H116 aluminum alloy. Some of the conclusions of the program are as follows:

1. The fatigue performance of 5086-H116 aluminum electron-beam welds in air is superior to 5086-H116 GMA welds in air. The fatigue performance of the electron-beam welds compares favorably to base-metal performance. This can be attributed to the absence of porosity and other weld defects.
2. The fatigue performance of electron-beam welds compared with GMA welds shows from 80 to 100% increase in the stress level attained at 10^8 cycles.
3. The strength and toughness properties of the 5086-H116 electron-beam-weld properties compare favorably with base-metal properties. The excellent properties of the electron-beam welds again can be attributed to the absence of porosity and other weld defects.

Beryllium and Its Alloys

Beryllium, with its low density, high modulus of elasticity, and high specific heat, is being used to an increasing extent in numerous applications. Use of beryllium for structural applications, however, has been impeded partly by the lack of satisfactory welding techniques for the production of sound and reliable joints. Conventional fusion-welding techniques have been hindered by contamination, cracking hot-shortness, and related problems, which have all led to low room-temperature strength and poor ductility. Some success has been realized with brazing and braze-welding techniques; brazed joints, however, have limited applications because of the difference in the melting point of the braze metal and the beryllium.

Although difficulties are encountered in welding and brazing beryllium by conventional techniques, EBW has produced high-strength welds. Unlike most other metals, fine grain size and random grain orientations in beryllium electron-beam welds are not dependent on fast welding speeds. Instead, best results to date have been achieved with relatively low welding speeds—15 in/min (6 mm/s). Controlled cooling, which is required to produce the optimum weld-zone micro-structures, is accomplished by moderating the power density and decreasing the welding speed. Of course, the ideal weld zone would be small in overall size while exhibiting a fine-grained, random micro-structure. The results illustrated in Fig. 1-41 indicate that this weld structure is attainable by using moderately high voltages in combination with lower beam currents while maintaining the slow welding speeds.

Results obtained from tensile testing beryllium welds at room temperature and 1000°F (538°C) show that the room-temperature ultimate strength of the electron-beam welds is consistently about 65%

Fig. 1-41   Weld cross section in 0.040-in (1-mm) beryllium.[2]

of the base-metal strength. Thus, even with the 35% drop in ultimate strength, the electron-beam welds have strengths among the highest reported. At 1000°F (538°C), even though in a series of tests all the welded specimens failed in the welds, the base-metal and weld ultimate and yield strengths are essentially the same. Similar trends have been reported for GTA welding.

Ductility appears to be the property that has suffered most from the welding process. Studies of the relationship between composition and quality of beryllium sheet and properties of electron-beam welds have determined that the quality of welds in beryllium is linked directly to the oxide content of beryllium.

During EBW, beryllium is vaporized, displacing liquid metal and causing weld undercutting to occur. Beryllium oxide is transported to the weld surface during welding and forms a surface film that retards liquid-metal flow. If the surface oxide film is sufficiently thick, the solidified weld will be undercut. When most other metals are electron-beam-welded, undercutting is not a serious problem.

The maximum permissible beryllium oxide content for single-pass, full-penetration butt welds decreases with increasing sheet thickness. For 0.020-in-thick (0.50 mm) sheet, 1.6% beryllium oxide is acceptable, while less than 0.7% must be present in order to produce sound EBW in 0.25-in-thick (6.4 mm) sheets. The amount of beryllium oxide below which sound welds can be made in 0.25-in-thick (6.4 mm) sheet is not exactly known.[23]

Recently completed work has shown:

1. Weld undercutting and porosity can be reduced for a given beryllium oxide content and sheet thickness by (a) welding at low travel speeds, (b) reducing the power density of the electron beam, and (c) lowering the energy input per welding pass by using multiple-pass welding procedures.

2. Weld cracking can be eliminated in sheets 0.062 in (1.6 mm) thick or greater by preheating. The necessary preheating temperature increases with sheet thickness and the amount of external restraint placed on the butted specimen.

3. Crack-free welds can be made in 0.020-in-thick (0.50 mm) sheet without preheat even under conditions of high restraint.

4. Because of fusion-zone grain growth, the bend ductility of electron-beam-welded beryllium is less than that of the base metal. Bend ductility of welded beryllium increases with decreasing beryllium oxide content.

5. The ultimate tensile strength, 0.2% offset yield strength, and elongation in 1 in (25.4 mm) are lower for electron-beam-welded beryllium than for the base metal. The ultimate strengths and elongation of traverse-welded specimens are less than for longitudinal-welded specimens. Yield strengths of longitudinal- and transverse-welded specimens are nearly equal.

6. EBW of beryllium, using aluminum filler-wire additions, can be

utilized to make high-quality welds having excellent strength properties (60 to 75% strength efficiencies at room temperature). No preheat is needed. Welding with filler metal additions is most applicable to thick plate and beryllium that has a high beryllium oxide content. In beryllium plate with a high oxide content (over 4%), filler metal must flow out of the weld root to prevent beryllium oxide agglomeration. Increasing the joint gap reduces the formation of this type of defect by lowering the amount of beryllium oxide and beryllium introduced into the fusion zone.

7. In electron-beam welds made without filler metal additions, intergranular microcracking is associated with the presence of aluminum, silicon, and titanium in the grain boundaries.

In another investigation relative to the use of filler metal additions in beryllium welds, it was found that electron-beam braze welds with strengths comparable to that of the base metal can be made in vacuum-cast, hot-rolled beryllium, using a preplaced shim of aluminum alloys 1100, 6061, 5052, or 5083.

Copper and Its Alloys

Copper does not exhibit the excellent weldability of many common materials. The primary defects associated with the welding of copper are gas porosity and cracks in welds. These defects have been controlled by use of a deoxidized filler metal, usually a phosphorus- or tin-bearing copper. Unfortunately, the continuity of mechanical properties, thermal and electrical conductivities, and corrosion resistance is not maintained across a weld of dissimilar filler and base metals. Also, in thin sections where no filler metal is employed, this means of eliminating the formation of weld metal defects is not available.

Molten metal may be expelled from the weld joint during EBW of nondeoxidized coppers (especially alloy 110), causing spatter and uneven weld surfaces, but this can usually be remedied by a cosmetic pass. The vacuum environment avoids possible hydrogen embrittlement; nevertheless, root voids and porosity still can occur.

Of the various copper alloys, oxygen-free copper is often of particular interest because of its good conductivity and its low rate of work hardening. A recent program evaluated the weldability and investigated various possible methods of minimizing weld defects in oxygen-free and boron-deoxidized copper. The study was directed toward situations where filler metal would not be employed, such as in welding of thin sections. The results showed that with EBW, sound welds in boron deoxidized copper can be made with one pass. However, for oxygen-free copper, at least four passes are required to produce welds which approach sound quality.

The presence of low-melting elements ordinarily makes the welding of free-machining copper alloys impractical, and the volatility of zinc prevents the welding of the brasses and other zinc-containing copper alloys. Other copper alloys can be electron-beam-welded without any unusual problems, except for alloy 175 (high-conductivity beryllium copper), for which the welding conditions must be controlled within a very narrow range to produce sound welds, and special safety precautions must be taken because of the toxicity of beryllium.

EBW of the beryllium-copper alloy 172 has been accomplished and a comparison of test results, although limited, shows the increase in strength exhibited over the conventional shielded gas processes.

Columbium and Its Alloys

Numerous companies have evaluated the EBW characteristics of first- and second-generation columbium alloys. The results have shown that all the alloys are weldable, but primarily in the first-generation alloys (FS82, D31, F48), EBW has provided a significant improvement in ductility over GTA welding. The improvement in ductility of the electron-beam welds in columbium alloys is attributed to a weld purity which is unattainable with GTA welding.

Electron-beam welds in the second-generation columbium alloys (Cb752, FS85, C129Y, D43, B66) have shown excellent ductility, improved weld transition temperatures, and joint efficiency. Joint ductilities at 70 and 2200°F (21.1 and 1204°C) in D43 are equivalent to those for the base metal, and joint efficiencies at these temperatures are within the range of 91 to 102%. Because of the marked reductions in ductility of Cb752 after welding and coating, a detailed evaluation was made of electron-beam-welded columbium-alloy panels for the thermal protection system of the space shuttle, the aerobraking system of the space shuttle, and the aerobraking system of the space tug. The results showed that:

1. EBW has no significant effect on elevated temperature tensile strength of sheet Cb752.
2. EBW has a marked reducing effect on bend and tensile ductility.
3. Postweld anneal does not improve tensile elongation.
4. R512E coating further reduced ductility of welded Cb752 material.[24,25,26]

In Figure 1-42 good weld ductility was required in joining a missile cone to a missile liner, because of differential thermal stresses in service and the need to prevent distortion.

Magnesium and Its Alloys

In spite of the high vapor pressure at its melting point, the EBW process has been applied successfully to magnesium and its alloys. Most applications have been for the fabrication of small precision components and for the salvaging of mismachined parts. The limited extent has been on commercial wrought and cast magnesium alloys that contain less than 1% zinc.

Special techniques and close control of operating variables are needed in order to prevent voids and porosity at the root of the weld, because of the high vapor pressure of magnesium, which has the lowest boiling point [2025°F (1107°C)] of any commonly welded metal. This difficulty is aggravated by the presence of zinc, which has a still lower boiling point [1663°F (906°C]. It is ordinarily impractical to electron-beam-weld magnesium alloys that contain more than 1% zinc.

Circular oscillation of the beam or the use of a slightly defocused beam is helpful in obtaining sound welds. The most satisfactory technique involves (1) the use of integral or tightly fitted backing of the same alloy and (2) close control of welding conditions to values that trial welds have shown will either minimize porosity and voids or localize them in an area where they can be machined away later or where they can be tolerated. Alloys that have been electron-beam-welded with good results include casting alloy AZ91C-T6 and wrought alloy AZ80A-T5.

In most instances, more conventional joining methods could not be employed because of the accompanying excessive weld distortion.

Molybdenum and Its Alloys

The main technical objections to the more extensive use of molybdenum have been its general brittleness, low ductility, and low impact strength. All of these problems are aggravated by joining operations. Since the detrimental effects of high-temperature heating are primarily dependent on the purity of the molybdenum, successful fusion welds can be obtained only on metal of the maximum purity with the fastest possible welding techniques, the highest cooling rates, and shielding gases of high purity. For these reasons EBW, with its low total energy input, providing fast heating and cooling, and its vacuum atmosphere, providing a high-purity surrounding atmosphere, has been investigated for application to molybdenum and its alloys, which have been primarily Mo-0.5% titanium and TZM. Figure 1-43 illustrates a welded

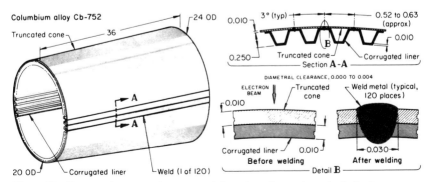

Fig. 1-42 Truncated cone and corrugated liner (members of a missile body component) that were joined by electron-beam melt-through welding.[15] (3° = 0.5 rad)

TZM container and lid for a nuclear fuel; the figure indicates that the material exhibits excellent electron-beam weldability. Weldments so produced in Mo-0.5Ti alloy also exhibit relatively good mechanical properties.

Joint efficiencies as determined by room-temperature tensile tests of electron-beam welds of 0.040 in (1 mm) of TZM have been found to be 71.1%, whereas GTA welds have exhibited 62.6%. Tensile test data show the ultimate and yield strengths of the Mo-0.5Ti electron-beam welds are substantially higher than for the GTA dry-box welds at 1600°F (871°C) and above. The strength of the electron-beam weld is approximately 20% higher than for the GTA welds. This improvement in strength is attributed to the much finer grain size of the electron-beam welds as compared with the coarse structure of the GTA welds.

Recent work in the Soviet Union concluded that electron-beam welds in molybdenum are more ductile if made faster. Samples 0.018 to 0.039 in (0.45 to 1 mm) thick, welded at about 40 in/min (16.9 mm/s) rather than 6 in/min (3 mm/s) (16,000 V at 90 mA), could be bent 40° (0.69 rad) at room temperature without cracking, while those welded at the slower speed could not be bent.

Heat-Resistant alloys—Iron, Nickel, Cobalt Base

In the family of iron-base heat-resisting alloys, A-286 has been successfully electron-beam-welded, and tensile and bend data show that optimum strength properties have been obtained in the electron-beam weldments which are welded in the solution-treated condition and postweld aged. Hot cracking may result if welding is done in the aged condition. The ultimate and yield strengths are 88 and 98%, respectively, of the base-metal strength. These strength levels compare favorably with those obtained from GTA welds using the same heat treatments and Hastelloy W filler wire. The ultimate-strength and yield-strength joint efficiencies in the GTA welds are 85 and 98%, respectively. Bend tests have indicated somewhat better bend ductility for the electron-beam welds compared with GTA welds.

Fig. 1-43 A container for nuclear fuel which shows the tube electron-beam-welded to the cap and subsequently to the cylinder.[2]

The most readily electron-beam-welded alloy of this group is 19-9DL, which has excellent weldability and on which the best results are obtained when preheating is used. Alloy N-155 has good weldability, and alloy 16-25-6 is rated fair.

Solid-solution nickel-base alloys, Hastelloy N, Hastelloy X, and Inconel 625 are readily electron-beam-welded. The recent use of Hastelloy C for fuel capsules in several SNAP power generators indicates the relative versatility of the process to handle all types of metals. See Table 1-2. (SNAP is an acronym for Systems for Nuclear Auxiliary Power.)

Precipitation-hardenable nickel-base alloys that are rated good in weldability by the electron-beam-process include Inconel 700, alloy 718, Inconel X-750 and René 41. Inconel X-750 should be welded in the annealed condition and René 41 should be welded in the solution-treated condition.

René 41 is a precipitation-hardening nickel-base austenitic alloy with good high-temperature properties which, combined with its relatively good formability and its availability as a sheet material, make it attractive as a structural material. Satisfactory fusion welds have been produced in René 41 by the electron-beam process. A unique solution to the problem of designing and fabricating a René 41 component for an aircraft gas-turbine engine was achieved by electron-beam tier welding. As indicated in Fig. 1-44, the component consisted of a cylinder with an external flange on one end, an internal flange on the other, and a tubular annulus between. The components were assembled by welding the through-shape ends of two subcomponent cylinders by a single two-tier circumferential weld.[15]

The components were made of René 41, for service at elevated temperature. The chief welding objectives were to obtain sound welds and to avoid distortion of the part, and especially the alignment of the 288 holes located in the annulus. Both welds were satisfactory as to soundness and shape. Undercutting was not a problem. The René 41 material was not a problem. The René 41 material was capable of withstanding considerable excess beam power, which was especially important in making the upper tier weld.

Successful welds have been made with one pass in 1-in (25.4-mm) René 41 plate. Welds made in solution-annealed plate and then postweld-solution-annealed and aged have exhibited tensile and stress rupture properties approximately equal to those of parent metal.

Two-pass welds in 1.5- and 1.75-in (38.4- and 44.5-mm) René 41 have been found to be free of surface cracks; however, a slight amount of fine porosity has been observed. There is a tendency for cold shuts to occur at the tip of the fusion zone of the second weld pass. This tendency does not seem to be significant. The cold shuts in René 41 appear to occur at random and not continuously, therefore in EBW thicknesses of 1.5-in (38.4-mm) or greater, care should be taken because of the tendency for cold shuts to occur and the increased tendency toward strain age cracking.

Other nickel-base alloys in this group that have fair weldability include casting alloys 713C and GMR-235 and wrought Udimet 700 and Waspaloy.

Another nickel-base alloy, Inconel 718, exhibits excellent EBW characteristics and can be welded in either the annealed or the aged condition. Although one-pass welds in Inconel 718 are possible, a higher-quality weld can be obtained with the pass from each side when welding 1.25-in (32-mm) thickness.

The relative ease of EBW cobalt-base alloys is illustrated in Fig. 1-25

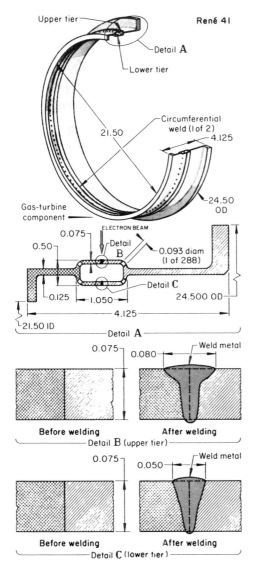

Fig. 1-44 Section through a cylindrical component of an aircraft gas turbine, showing tiered welds made simultaneously by EBW.[15] (0.01 in = 0.25 mm)

which shows the cap and inner web of a 72-in (1829-mm) spar member. The weld is a penetration weld through the cap, with an excellent fillet on the corrugation web. HS-21 has good weldability in unrestrained joints (generally poor in restrained joints). Cast alloy HS-31 has fair-to-good weldability and alloy S-816 has fair weldability.

Steels—Stainless, Precipitation-Hardened, Low-Alloy, Ultrahigh-Strength, Maraging

Most steels that have been fusion-welded by one arc process or another can be electron-beam-welded. However steels having sulfur or selenium contents in excess of 0.03% do not lend themselves to EBW. The low boiling points of sulfur and selenium cause excess porosity. Since the varieties of steels and gages are so numerous, only a few examples of the more prominent families of steels are illustrated.

Stainless

The various 300 or 400 series stainless steels have been electron-beam-welded quite easily, Table 1-2. Bend tests conducted on as-welded specimens showed these welds to be very ductile. Type 302 0.062-in (1.6-mm) specimens were bent 155° (2.7 rad) over a $1t$ radius mandrel and the welds were found to be sound. As is to be expected with annealed austenitic material, hardness of the weld zone was the same as that of the base material. Therefore, electron-beam techniques can be used to produce deep, narrow, sound welds in annealed Type 302 as well as any 300-series austenitic stainless steel. Weldment strength is equivalent to that of the base metal and no corrosion sensitization of the material occurs.

The high cooling rates typical of EBW help to inhibit carbide precipitation, because of the short time during which the steel is in the sensitizing temperature range.

Although the martensitic stainless steels (400 series) can be electron-beam-welded in almost any heat-treated condition, welding will produce a hardened, martensitic heat-affected zone. Hardness and susceptibility to cracking increase with increasing carbon content and cooling rate. Figure 1-45 describes an application in which PVEB welding replaced GMA welding.

Precipitation-hardened

In EBW of the precipitation-hardened (PH) steel alloys, no unusual problems have been encountered. As expected, fractures occurred in the weldment at strengths slightly above those for annealed material. Data obtained for Type 17-7PH welded in condition A (annealed) and subsequently solution-treated and aged have shown that base-metal strength was obtained in the weldment. The tensile strength obtained with material welded in the solution-treated condition and aged to the TH1050 condition after welding has been recorded, and weldment strengths were only slightly below the base metal properties. Foil thicknesses weld just as readily as thicker materials.

In thicknesses up to 1 in (25.4 mm) of PH15-7Mo steel, crack-free electron-beam welds have been produced with excellent tensile properties. A new steel, PH14-8Mo, which has slowly found its way into products such as pressure tanks, supersonic aircraft, and the Apollo moon vehicle, has exhibited weld tensile strengths of 205 ksi (1413 MPa) and yields of 203 ksi (1400 MPa). In EBW of PH steels the weld metal becomes austenitic during welding and remains austenitic during cooling. In the more martensitic types, such as 17-4PH and

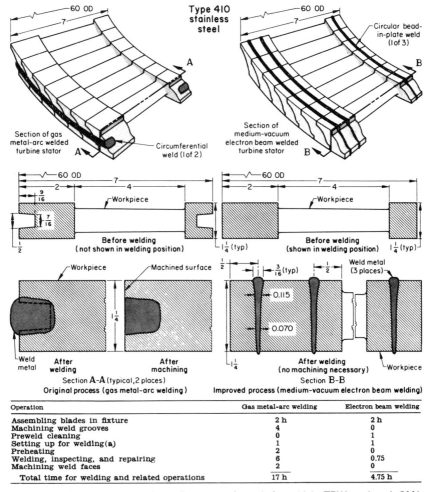

Operation	Gas metal-arc welding	Electron beam welding
Assembling blades in fixture	2 h	2 h
Machining weld grooves	4	0
Preweld cleaning	0	1
Setting up for welding(a)	1	1
Preheating	2	0
Welding, inspecting, and repairing	6	0.75
Machining weld faces	2	0
Total time for welding and related operations	17 h	4.75 h

Fig. 1-45 Sections of a turbine diaphragm (stator) for which EBW replaced GMA welding for joining the blades. Process change eliminated preheating and two machining operations, and reduced welding time.[15] (0.01 in = 0.25 mm)

15-5PH, the low carbon content precludes formation of hard martensite. Some of the precipitation-hardening stainless steels have poor weldability because of their high phosphorus content. Steels 17-10P and HNM are not usually electron-beam-welded.

Low-alloy, ultrahigh-strength

AISI 4340 and 4130, widely used deep-hardening low-alloy structural steels, respond very well to EBW. No significant problems have been encountered in producing sound, crack-free welds without preheating or postheating in low-restraint weld joints. These welds display excellent mechanical properties. Furthermore, as with austenitic stainless steel, deep narrow welds can be produced.

Tensile and fatigue tests conducted on 4340, 0.25-in (6.4-mm) thick, welded both before and after heat treatment (R_c 26–32) shows weldment strength equal to that of the base material. Similar weldments heat treated to R_c 47 exhibit the same base-metal strength.

Tensile tests have been conducted on welds made in heat-treated 4340. The results were quite remarkable in that, once again, base-metal strength was maintained in the weld zone. Results of the fatigue testing of 4340 weldments also have been outstanding. The endurance properties of weldments produced in annealed material and heat-treated to R_c 26–32 after welding approach those of the smooth base material, and they are significantly better than the endurance properties of the base material containing a standard notch. Similar data for material heat-treated to R_c 40–44 after welding have shown that fatigue strength of the weldments approaches that of the smooth base material.

The reason for the retention of strength in steels welded in the heat-treated condition can be deduced. Test results have shown that the small fusion zone and high welding speed associated with the voltage and density of the electron-beam weld have limited the overtempered or heat-affected zone to a very thin sandwich layer of softer, weaker material. This thin layer is supported by adjacent stronger material, producing triaxial stressing that prevents reduction in area. Thus the true, rather than apparent, tensile strength is realized. With normal arc welding, a significantly wider and softer overtempered region is produced; thus tensile strength is reduced.

Electron beams have been applied to gear materials. Tensile and fatigue properties of the carburizing-grade SAE 9310 (AMS 6265), the nitriding-grade Nitralloy 135 (AMS 6470), and SAE 4340 (AMS 6415) have been evaluated for comparison. The materials were heat-treated and conditioned as applicable to the fabrication of actual gears.

The results of tensile and fatigue tests indicate that electron-beam-welded joints develop properties quite adequate for fabricated gears. The welded specimens failed consistently in the heat-affected zone for AMS 6470 and AMS 6415 materials.

Fatigue tests of AMS 6265 show that the endurance limit of the welded specimens with the respective unwelded base-metal specimens have a joint efficiency in fatigue which is above 85% for all three

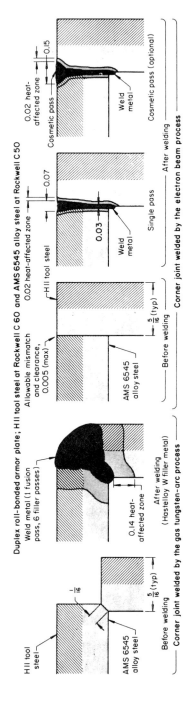

Fig. 1-46 Cross sections through corner joints and welds made in duplex roll-bonded armor plate, showing approximate differences in sizes of the welds and the heat-affected zones resulting from EBW and GTA welding.[15] (0.01 in = 0.25 mm)

materials. In addition, the service performance of the electron-beam-welded joints has been verified for several specific gear assemblies by actual gearbox and engine tests.

The H11 hot-work die steel currently in use in pressure vessels and containers exhibits welding characteristics similar to those of the SAE 4340 steel discussed previously. The chief advantage of EBW over other welding processes in joining tool steels is its ability to produce joints at high speed without annealing or other heat-treating operations.

Small dies of D2 tool steel have been electron-beam-welded in production. A larger operation is the production of bimetal band saws. Specially designed PV machines are used to produce band saw blades by welding 0.062-in-wide (1.6 mm) M2 high-speed-steel cutting-edge strips to Type 6150 steel bands. In an unusual application seen in Fig. 1-46, 0.312-in-thick (7.9 mm) duplex armor plate made of equal thicknesses of H11 tool steel and high-strength alloy steel AMS 6545 was welded without preheating or postheating.

Low-carbon steel

Commercial interest is growing in EBW of low-carbon steels. With the lower heat input and extremely rapid heating and cooling of the electron beam, the resultant grain size in both the weld and the heat-affected zone is significantly smaller than in arc welds. There are three general classes, killed, semikilled, and rimmed. All forging steels and all steel containing more than 0.25% carbon are killed. Steels containing from 0.15 to 0.25% carbon generally are semikilled. Many steels with less than 0.15% carbon are rimmed, and these make up the bulk of steel used. Killed means that the steel has been deoxidized by additions of ferrosilicon, aluminum, and other strong deoxidizers. Ferrosilicon and sometimes aluminum are added to semikilled steels. Rimming is used when the surface of the steel is important. The steel is partially deoxidized with manganese. When the molten metal begins to solidify into an ingot, gas evolves. The result is an ingot with a skin of very clean metal and a porous core containing a great deal of entrapped gas. During subsequent hot rolling, these pores are rolled shut to produce a sound product.[27]

Because it contains no deoxidizers and is thus prone to weld porosity, rimmed steel is the most difficult of the three types of low-carbon steel to electron-beam-weld. When welding with processes like EBW which do not use filler rods, deoxidizing agents must be added in the weld area. For example, in GTA welding, surfaces can be coated with aluminum-bearing paint. The technique used most often with EBW is to sandwich an aluminum shim in the joint to provide deoxidizing action. Usually, 0.010-in-thick (0.25-mm) shims are used. Naturally, the weld region is high in aluminum content, but the improved weld may more than compensate for any change in weld-zone chemical composition.

Although sound welds are easier to make with semikilled steels then with rimmed steels, some dissolved oxygen remains to cause porosity.

Thus, the addition of a thin shim of aluminum prior to EBW helps produce better welds by deoxidizing the weld material.

Killed steels usually are free of porosity caused by carbon monoxide encountered in rimmed and semikilled steels. The porosity caused by other impurities usually is scattered and of little consequence for commercial applications.

With rimmed steels, joint design is a key factor influencing the soundness of the weld. In general, successful welds are made when the weld involves surfaces that are deoxidized and a clean rim surface of the steel is present.

In case-hardened steels, the case is the source of welding problems. For example, a carburized surface may contain up to 1.5% carbon and is generally of a eutectic composition. Thus, we have a thin, brittle surface film which melts and freezes at a temperature different from that of the base material. In addition, the surface material is martensitic and shrinks more than the base material when cooling. Also, the surface has a high gas content.

As with rimmed steels, proper joint design is the key to successful EBW of case-hardened steels. Unlike rimmed steels, case-hardened steels weld best when a minimum of carburized surface material is included in the joint interface. Weldability is better with thin-case materials than with thick ones. Thus, carbonitrided materials cause less welding difficulty than deep-carburized ones.[4,28]

Maraging

In a recent comparison of the mechanical properties of electron-beam welds in maraging steel with the properties of GMA and GTA welds, the electron-beam welds were capable of developing slightly higher tensile properties than GTA or GMA welds. Two-pass welds are not recommended in maraging steel because of the possible occurrence of cold shuts, cracking, or porosity. It is recommended that sufficient beam energy be used to allow the joint to be made in one pass.

A recently completed investigation of EBW of D6AC 0.5-in-thick (12.7 mm) plate provided significant information relative to the use of this steel. The key features resulting from the program which produced quality welds were:

- No preheat was required.
- Welding was completed in a single pass.
- The use of beam oscillator, midpoint focusing, and a filler strip eliminated microcracking.
- The mechanical properties of the electron beam welds in the 220 to 240 ksi (1517 to 1655 MPa) and 260 to 280 ksi (1793 to 1931 MPa) heat-treat conditions were comparable to those of corresponding gas-tungsten arc welds.
- Fracture toughness test results were reduced and the lower fracture toughness values were attributed to microsegregation in the fusion zone.[29]

Tantalum and Its Alloys

Tantalum and tantalum alloys, Ta-10W, Ta111, Ta222, and Ta333, are readily weldable by the electron-beam process. Since the alloys are relatively new, intensive welding development programs have only recently been initiated. Because of its high melting point of 5425°F (2998°C) and good thermal conductivity, thicknesses of 0.060 in (1.5 mm) or more must be rapidly heated to high temperatures for welding. Copper chill bars are used to avoid distortion and weld sagging and to shorten the time the assembly has to remain in the vacuum chamber, thus limiting grain growth.

Weldability of tantalum alloys containing other refractory elements is somewhat lower than that of unalloyed tantalum. Because of high vapor pressure, alloys containing vanadium are better welded by the GTA welding process.

The electron-beam-welded tensile strength of Ta111 is the same as Cb752 columbium alloy up to 1500°F (816°C).

Titanium and Its Alloys

The EBW of titanium and its alloys has been accomplished with relative ease. Since titanium, a very reactive metal, must be welded with protective inert gases to produce satisfactory weld joints, the vacuum of the electron-beam chamber is a natural environment to insure clean, void-free welds.

Pure titanium (A-70)/5Al-2.5Sn/6Al-4V

Welded tensile data and the tensile properties of these three alloys are presented in Ref. 30. It is feasible to join different titanium alloys together as well as different thicknesses. The Ti-6Al-4V alloy, which has been the most frequently used alloy in the past, can be electron-beam-welded in either the annealed or the solution-treated-and-aged condition. For weldments that will be used at elevated temperatures, a preferred process sequence is anneal, weld, solution-treat, and age. For other service conditions, a process sequence of solution-treat, age, and weld gives almost the same strength properties and only slightly lower fracture toughness.

Sound welds have been produced in one pass in 1.0- and 1.75-in (25.4- and 44.5-mm) Ti-6Al-4V using the EBW process. The solution-treated and aged parent metal exhibited ultimate and yield strengths of 159 and 149 ksi (1096 and 1027 MPa) respectively. Comparable transverse weldment strengths and longitudinal weld-metal strengths from 1-in-thick (25.4 mm) weldments have exhibited 148 and 139 ksi (1020 and 968 MPa) average ultimate and yield strengths, respectively.

A comparison of electron-beam welds made in 1-in (25.4-mm) annealed 6Al-4V titanium material with GMA welds made in 1-in (25.4-mm) annealed material indicates that EBW offers porosity-free welds with tensile and fracture toughness properties comparable to those of the parent metal. Tensile and impact toughness properties comparable to parent metal have also been obtained by the GMA welding process. However, EBW offers a weld that can be made in one pass without filler material and without extensive joint preparation other than grinding.

B120VCA (13V-11Cr-3Al)/7Al-2Cb-1Ta/6Al-6V-2Sn/8Al-Mo-1V

The 13V-11Cr-3Al all-beta-titanium alloy as well as the three other titanium alloys have been welded by the high-voltage and low-voltage electron-beam processes and by the GTA vacuum-purged dry box technique in an argon atmosphere.[22]

Ti-6Al-6V-2Sn has proved the most difficult of the titanium alloys to weld. Although the welds look good visually, a center bead solidification line appears in the microstructure. Low ductility and fatigue properties dictate limited use of this alloy for EBW, particularly in thin gages.[31]

Recent work on heavier gages around 0.5 in (12.7 mm) thick is encouraging. Some work indicates weld-line microporosity causes reduced fatigue properties in this alloy.

By eliminating such porosity, it is possible to produce improved properties. Special cleaning precautions seem to help, as does multipass welding.

Beta C (6Cr-3.4Al-8V-3.7Zr-4Mo)/8V-8Mo-2Fe-3Al/ 6Al-2Sn-4Zr-6Mo/6Al-2Zn-4Zr-2Mo

While these advanced titanium alloys are weldable by electron beam, they require considerably more attention to the choice of heat-treatment cycles and sequence to produce the optimum property balance between weldment and base metal for a particular application. On the other hand, the alloys are not particularly more sensitive to weld preparation and process parameters than contemporary titanium alloys.

The Ti-6-2-4-6 and Ti-6-2-4-2 alpha-beta alloys are basically similar with respect to weldability and weldment property response. It is easier to consistently achieve good properties in Ti-6-2-4-6 welds compared with the Ti-6-2-4-2 alloy. Both of the beta alloys, Beta C and Ti-8-8-2-3, are weldable and achieved high tensile joint efficiencies. However, the 0.5-in (12.7-mm) Ti-8-8-2-3 material was clearly superior to 0.5-in (12.7-mm) Beta C alloy with respect to overall weldability, weldment properties, and base-metal machinability. Results obtained on 0.1-in (2.5-mm) thick Beta C sheet generally were better than on 0.5- and 1.0-in (12.7- and 25.4-mm) Beta C plate partly because of base-metal microstructural effects.[32]

Beta III (11Mo-6Zr-5Sn)

This is new heat-treatable titanium alloy in which aging produces ultimate tensile strengths as high as 200 ksi (1379 MPa) with good corrosion resistance, toughness, and ductility. Beta III has been successfully welded by the EBW process. The tensile properties of the base metal [196 ksi (1351 MPa)] and the electron-beam weldment [175 ksi (1207 MPa)] are comparable. The best results were obtained by welding Beta III in the solution-treated condition followed by the aging treatment. In this condition the strength of the weldment is slightly lower than the base metal, but the ductility is better.[33]

Tungsten and Its Alloys

Tungsten is the most difficult of the refractory metals to weld because of its high melting point [6170°F (3410°C)], sensitivity to thermal shock, and the room-temperature brittleness of the welds and of the heat-affected zone. Good and fair welding results have been reported for W-25Re and W-25Re-30Mo alloys, respectively. Best results are obtained when assemblies are fixtured with the joint under compression during welding. Fixtures are often released after welding, to permit the weld to cool without restraint; if the weld is restrained during cooling, cracking is likely to occur. Preheating in the range of 1300 to 1400°F (704 to 760°C) and postweld stress relieving at 1800 to 1900°F (982 to 1038°C) help to reduce stresses. Somewhat wider welds and lower welding speeds than are used for other refractory metals are desirable. Beam oscillation and pulsing are also helpful.

Zirconium and Its Alloys

Another very reactive metal is zirconium. It is rarely used as a pure metal, but is used as an alloy, Zircaloy. Zircaloy-2, which is a zirconium-base alloy containing small amounts of tin, iron, and chromium, is well known in nuclear applications. Zircaloy-2 is highly reactive at fabrication temperatures and can dissolve both oxygen and nitrogen with deleterious effects on its mechanical, physical, and corrosion properties. Particular precautions must be taken in welding this alloy to prevent its reaction with the atmosphere. The fusion of Zircaloy-2, with its 3272° (1800°C) melting point, by the GTA process requires the use of relatively high power input with a wide fusion zone in relation to the depth of penetration. In contrast, EBW provides an inherent operating vacuum of 10^{-4} torr (0.0133 Pa), which is an ideally pure atmosphere for joining Zircaloy-2 and has produced welds whose properties are equivalent to or better than the base metal.

The tensile strength of welded Zircaloy-2 has been investigated in both the longitudinal and the transverse directions. The specimens of welded material in general showed slightly higher ultimate and yield strengths, and correspondingly lower ductility (reduction in area and elongation) than did the hot-rolled plate material. These differences are the result of the quenched fusion structure, which is higher in strength than the surrounding material or base plate.

Impact test specimens made from solid Zircaloy-2 plate in which 100% penetration welds were made showed that the electron-beam-welded Zircaloy-2 had higher impact strength than GTA-welded material. EBW can be applied to Zircaloy joints up to 3 in (76 mm) thick without forming extensive porosity or fissuring. Properly developed weld joints formed by this process are characterized by mechanical and corrosion properties approximating those of the parent metal. Weld shrinkage and distortion of electron-beam-welded Zircaloy is lower than that resulting from arc welding.

Nonmetallics—Ceramics

Ceramic materials are being used extensively by the electronics industry in the construction of power electron tubes, microwave windows, and similar components. The advantages of ceramics in these applications include high dielectric strength and superior elevated-temperature properties. These advantages have not been fully realized, however, because of difficulties in joining separate ceramic sections into structurally sound, vacuumtight components. Current metallized and brazed joints present problems of matching thermal expansion. Furthermore, brazed joints exhibit lowered arc-over thresholds and reduced useful service temperatures. In addition, the joints are subject to electrode capacitance effects that limit electrical performance.

EBW is one of the few methods available for direct fusion welding of ceramics. Actual welding of ceramics is attractive, for it can minimize many of the difficulties associated with brazing. Gas or plasma torches can fuse certain ceramics; however, these methods lack the precise controllability and cleanliness possible with electron-beam techniques. Because of these advantages, EBW procedures have been developed for the joining of ceramic materials, including alumina, quartz, and magnesia, to themselves and to metals.

A need for preheating and controlled cooling are two immediate and apparent prerequisites. Without preheating, welds invariably show evidence of cracking. Therefore, two preheating techniques have been used, electron-beam heating and resistance heating. Resistance preheating techniques have been more successful because of more precise control. The heating element is a tungsten filament wound on a zirconia coil form. Multiple heat shields of tantalum and molybdenum surround and cover the unit except for a small opening at the top to allow optical viewing and welding. Weld specimens are supported on a tungsten platform inside the coil form. Temperatures as high as 3300°F (1815°C) have been obtained and field effects on the electron beam have been reduced.

Welding speed is quite critical and best results are achieved at higher travel rates. Lower speeds [15 in/mm (6 mm/s)] produce a glass structure. Although no cracks are evident in the weld zone, flexural testing has indicated that glassy welds are relatively weak. The tendency toward formation of glassy welds increases in the less-pure aluminas. By increasing welding speed to 30 in/min (12.6 mm/s), glass formation has been limited. The advantage of higher welding speed appears to result from the decreased time that the weld zone is above the 1800°F (982°C) preheat temperature. This limits the time available for segregation of the glassy constituents and for grain growth.

Flexural bend testing of welded ceramics has indicated that relatively good joint strengths can be obtained. Under simple beam bending, the base ceramic achieved a surface stress of approximately 50 ksi (345 MPa). Electron-beam-welded joints withstood as much as 20 ksi (138 MPa).

Limited tests have been conducted on the joining of alumina to metals. Techniques similar to those used in pure alumina welding have produced crack-free joints between 96% alumina and tungsten, molybdenum, and columbium. Undoubtedly, the successful joints resulted in part from the relatively closely matched coefficients of thermal expansion. See Fig. 1-47.

Various joint characteristics are primarily dependent on the beam location. Glassy-phase joints result from impingement of the beam directly on the ceramic member. Locating the beam to fuse the metallic member adjacent to the ceramic has produced interdiffusion of the two materials and yielded stronger joints.

Molybdenum feed-throughs electron-beam-welded into alumina electron tube supports have been accomplished by circular oscillation of the beam about the base of 0.040-in-diameter (1 mm) pins. Joints of this type have been tested and were helium-leak tight.

Dissimilar Metals

In the fabrication of welded assemblies with the electron beam, it is not essential that welded members be of identical material. In many applications of electron-beam technology, dissimilar materials are joined as effectively as identical materials. In some instances, problems arise as a result of differences in melting temperatures and mutual solubility, but generally these can be overcome through proper tooling or by the manner in which the electron gun is handled. For example,

Fig. 1-47 Alumina welded to molybdenum.[34]

aluminum and stainless steel are a difficult combination because their melting temperatures are 1200 and 2600°F (649 and 1427°C) respectively. Beams of sufficient density to melt stainless steel will reduce aluminum to a plasma, thus making any direct joining of the two impossible. This problem is resolved by concentrating the beam on the stainless steel to act as a high-temperature soldering iron that melts the aluminum. The resulting joint is a brazed type of low efficiency, but it proves effective for many purposes.

Problems arising from mutual insolubility of two materials can also be solved by the manner in which the beam is positioned. One example is copper and titanium which have limited solubility with each other and form mechanical mixtures if melted together. Strict control of melting of these two materials by the electron beam is necessary because a high percentage of titanium in the mixture causes the joint to become excessively brittle and subject to transverse cracking. This was exhibited in the EBW of the alloy Ti-3Al-1.5Mn to Cu-0.8Cr alloy. With preferential melting of the copper, the joints had relatively low strength [7 to 14 ksi (48 to 96 MPa)] and low ductility. There was a diffusion layer at the titanium interface that was very hard and brittle.[35] If the percentage of copper is high, however, a good weld can be produced. Additional difficulties that must be resolved arise from the fact that heat applied at the juncture of the two metals will be dissipated unevenly, since copper has a higher thermal conductivity than titanium. As in the preceding example of stainless steel and aluminum, this problem can be overcome by directing beam impingement on the copper at an angle to the joint. This compensates for differences in rate of heat dissipation while providing a high percentage of copper in the joint. Virtually all such problems in the welding of dissimilar materials can be overcome by varying the angle of beam impingement.

Table 1-2 lists numerous combinations of dissimilar metal joints. Successful welds over small areas have been obtained between titanium 6Al-4V and René 41 alloy by use of a pair of intermediate materials joined by EBW.

Development of this bond arose out of a design required for VTOL aircraft, where there was a need for combining, into one structure, high strength-to-density-ratio titanium fan blades and temperature-resistant nickel-base superalloy turbine blades. Initial attempts to weld titanium to René 41 directly were unsuccessful, as was the search for a single intermediate material compatible with both. Vanadium and Type 410 stainless steel constitute suitable intermediate materials.

A series of weldments used in a typical butt weld are shown in Fig. 1-48. Joints of this type consistently show ultimate test strength values of 40 ksi (276 MPa). Most failures occurred within 1 h at the vanadium-to-Type 410 weld at about 1000°F (538°C).

During the same program, procedures were developed to electron-beam-weld the titanium alloy to other nickel-base alloys; the base metal thicknesses ranged from 0.032 to 0.080 in (0.82 to 2.2 mm). Satisfactory joints were produced by (1) welding the titanium alloy to a columbium insert, (2) welding the nickel-base alloy to a copper-alloy insert, and (3) welding the inserts together.

A recent requirement in Japan for joining mild steel pipe to copper pipe was reported. The results showed that in the EBW of mild steel to oxygen-free copper, a 0.01- to 0.02-in (0.25- to 0.50-mm) shim aluminum addition was effective in obtaining sound dissimilar-metal joints (same tensile strength with copper-base metal, low hardness of weld zone, stable microstructure), but the high hardness of the weld zone could not be avoided in the case of 0.04-in (1-mm) aluminum shim addition. Nickel and monel inserts were also effective in producing sound dissimilar-metal joints. However, bending properties of the dissimilar metal joint were not improved by the addition of aluminum and nickel or monel insert, and this problem remains to be solved.

Current usable applications include various refractory metals, iron- and nickel-base superalloys, platinum and phosphor bronze to copper, and beryllium copper to steel.[36]

EBW has been used to join molybdenum and columbium alloys to stainless steel.[37] Flat butt and lap joints were electron-beam-welded; the amount of heat applied to the high-melting metal was regulated by moving the molten pool away from the joint or by reducing the beam current. Under the proper conditions, the molten stainless steel wet the refractory metal well and produced a well-contoured joint. Titanium

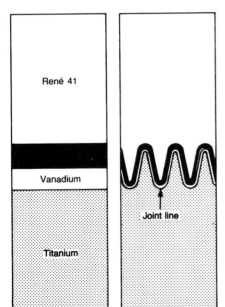

Fig. 1-48 Conventional butt joint (left) using intermediate material (vanadium and 410 stainless steel) and proposed high-shear butt joint (right).[36]

and columbium alloys D43, B66, and Cb752 have been electron-beam-welded successfully.[38] During this program, several titanium alloys were successfully joined to columbium as shown in Table 1-3. Other combinations of tungsten to molybdenum, molybdenum to columbium, and aluminum to stainless steel have been reported.[5,36,39,40,41] Table 1.4 shows 33 two-member combinations that were joined by EBW and lists the results.[42]

TABLE 1-3
Joining Columbium to Titanium Alloys[38]

	Tensile strength			
	RT (20°C)		570°F (299°C)	
Ti alloy	ksi	MPa	ksi	MPa
Ti-3Al-1.5Mn	73	503	62	427
Ti-4Al-3Mo-1V	76	524	63	434
Ti-3Al-8Mo-11Cr	75	517	61	421

RT: Room temperature.

MECHANICAL PROPERTIES—TEST RESULTS

Several of the important metals are listed below, and consideration is given to varied mechanical properties.

Aluminum Alloys

A recent study was performed to investigate the mechanical and fatigue properties of mobile-electron-beam weldments in 5456-H321 aluminum.[43] The major objectives of this study were:

1. To assess the mobile electron-beam-weld process for application to aluminum structures.
2. To establish design data for aluminum structures.
3. To develop and document mechanical and fatigue properties of mobile-electron-beam weldments.

In summary, mobile-electron-beam–welded panels $0.312 \times 20 \times 100$ in and $0.75 \times 20 \times 100$ in $(7.9 \times 508 \times 2540$ mm and $19 \times 508 \times 2540$ mm) were evaluated to determine weld-joint properties. Data were developed for tensile and fatigue specimens. Results for bend and tensile tests were within the minimum acceptable values of the applicable specification. See Table 1-5. Fatigue data were developed for both thicknesses of welded and base plate stock at stress levels equal to two-thirds the yield strength of the weld; results were comparable to published data.[44]

TABLE 1-4
Summary of Results[42]

Combination	Visual examination results	Metallo-graphic results	Transverse tensile strength	Bend ductility	Overall weld quality
Ag/Al	Good	Good	Good	Good	Good
Ag/Cu-20Ni	Fair	Good			Good
Ag/Fe-13Cr-8Ni	Fair	Good	Fair	Poor	Good
Ag/Ni-15Cr-7Fe	Good	Good			Good
Ag/Ti	Fair	Good	Good	Fair	Good
Ag/V	Fair	Good	Good	Fair	Good
Al/Cu	Poor	Poor			Poor
Al/Cu-20Ni	Poor	Poor			Poor
Al/Fe-18Cr-8Ni	Poor	Poor			Poor
Al/Ni	Fair	Good	Good	Good	Good
Al/Ni-15Cr-7Fe	Poor	Poor			Poor
Cu/Fe-18Cr-8Ni	Fair	Fair	Good	Good	Good
Cu/Ni	Fair	Fair	Fair	Good	Fair
Cu/Ni-15Cr-7Fe	Good	Good	Good	Good	Good
Cu/V	Good	Good	Good	Good	Good
Cu/V-10Ti	Good	Fair			Fair
Cu-20Ni/Fe-18Cr-8Ni	Good	Fair	Good	Good	Good
Cu-20Ni/Ni-15Cr-7Fe	Good	Good	Good	Good	Good
Cu-20Ni/V	Fair	Poor	Poor	Poor	Poor
Cu-20Ni/V-10Ti	Poor	Poor			Poor
Fe-18Cr-8Ni/Ni	Good	Good	Good	Good	Good
Fe-18Cr-8Ni/Ni-15Cr-7Fe	Good	Good	Good	Good	Good
Fe-18Cr-8Ni/V	Fair	Fair	Good	Good	Fair
Cb/Ti	Good	Good	Good	Good	Good
Cb/V	Good	Good	Good	Good	Good
Cb/V-10Ti	Good	Good			Good
Cb/Zr-2Sn	Good	Poor	Fair	Poor	Poor
Ni/Ni-15Cr-7Fe	Good	Good	Good		Good
Ni/Ti	Fair	Poor			Poor
Ni-15Cr-7Fe/V	Good	Poor			Poor
Ni-15Cr-7Fe/V-10Ti	Good	Poor			Poor
Ti/V	Fair	Poor	Poor	Good	Poor
Ti/Zr-2Sn	Fair	Good	Good	Fair	Good

Superalloys (Nickel-Base)

The potential advantages of EBW have been evaluated for the fabrication of bimetal wheels. A-286 is generally used as a disk alloy, 713C is used as a blade alloy, and depending on the application, U-500 may be used for either the disk or the blades. Spin testing of electron-beam-welded wheels produced failures at approximately 3 times service requirements.

Mechanical property tests indicated that electron beam welds of A-286 to 713C and of U-500 to 713C (all in cast form) retain excellent

TABLE 1-5
Tensile Test Results

Alloy Condition	Spec. no.	Thickness in	Thickness mm	Yield ksi	Yield MPa	Ultimate ksi	Ultimate MPa	% Elongation G.L. 2 in (50.4 mm)	% Reduction of area	Remarks
EB weld	C	0.312	7.9	35.7	248	49.8	345	7.4	18.5	Failed through weld
EB weld	E	0.312	7.9	36.5	255	48.6	338	7.0	17.0	Failed through weld
EB weld	C	0.75	19.0	29.5	207	49.2	338	14.1	26.9	Failed through weld
EB weld	E	0.75	19.0	29.4	200	47.9	331	13.1	27.3	Failed through weld
Base metal	J	0.312	7.9	37.4	255	56.3	386	18.1	25.3	
Base metal	K	0.312	7.9	37.1	255	55.7	386	18.1	24.9	
Base metal	I	0.75	19.0	33.3	228	50.4	345	22.1	31.7	
Base metal	M	0.75	19.0	33.4	228	50.7	352	22.6	32.9	
Minimum Requirements										
Base metal				33.0	228	46.0	317	12.0		Per QQ-A-250/20
EB weld				19.0	131	42.0	290			Per QQ-A-250/9

tensile and stress rupture strengths. All the test results exceeded current fusion-welded specification minimums by significant margins.[5]

Table 1-6 shows fatigue data on three commonly used nickel-base alloys tested at room temperature 68°F (20°C), 1300°F (704°C), and 1600°F (871°C).

Titanium Alloys

Figure 1-49 shows transverse yield strength results of recently completed work by an aerospace company obtained on 0.5-in (13.7-mm) thick Beta C and Ti-8-8-2-3 electron-beam welds.[32]

Fracture Toughness

In recent years extreme concern has been given by designers, metallurgists, and welding engineers to the fracture toughness of materials. Shown in Fig. 1-50 are test results for several aluminum-, steel-, and nickel-base alloys and a titanium alloy that reflects the fracture toughness of the base metal and electron-beam-welded test specimens.

APPLICATIONS

Characteristics of electron-beam welds as shown in numerous previously cited figures suggest even more exciting applications for the process. The uses, needs, and applications range from nuclear, aircraft, missiles, space, electronics, and undersea to commercial cars, saw blades, etc. EBW has also proven to be an excellent salvage tool for expensive machine components and production items. With all these applications, and they are continually increasing, EBW is not a panacea for all the welding industry. Just as there are applications for high- and low-voltage machines, so the same is true for electron beam and all the other welding processes. Table 1-7 denotes the widespread areas of electron-beam applications.

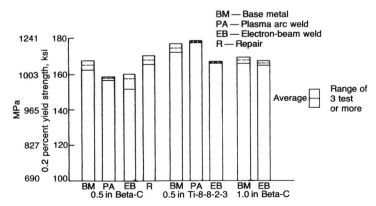

Fig. 1-49 Transverse tensile yield strength of welds compares favorably to that of base metal. (0.5 in = 12.7 mm)

TABLE 1-6
Room- and Elevated-Temperature Fatigue Strength of Several Heat-Resistant Alloys

	Test temperature		Fatigue strength, ksi (MPa) (cycles to failure)					
	°F	°C	10^5 ksi	MPa	10^6 ksi	MPa	10^7 ksi	MPa
Inco 625								
Base metal	68 (Room)	20	112	772	80	552	78	538
	1300	704	86	593	73	503	68	469
EB welded	68	20	104	717	86	593	82	565
	1300	704	76	524	66	455	62	427
René 41, ST								
Base metal	68	20	108	745	87	600	82	565
	1600	871	60	414	36	248	24	165
EB welded	68	20	108	745	87	600	82	565
	1600	871	70	483	41	283	24	165
Inco 718								
Base metal	68	20	140	965	98	676	96	662
	1300	704	141	972	113	779	102	703
EB welded	68	20	138	952	94	648	88	607
	1300	704	128	883	108	745	96	634

TABLE 1-7
Electron-Beam Applications

Fuel elements and fuel tubes	Honeycomb
Ion-propulsion systems	Band saw blades
Collimators	Jet engine fuel-control levers
Bimetal tubing (columbium-stainless steel) for liquid metals	Rocket engine injectors
Solar-heat generators	Pressure spheres
Turbine rotors	Inner and outer fan exit casings (turbofan engines)
Turbine wheels	Aircraft engine compressor cases and shafts
Finned superheater tubing for reactors	Aircraft engine turbine casing
Thermocouple and capsule encapsulation	Aircraft fuel-drive system
Hollow bearings (AISI 52100 Steel)	Jet engine heat exchangers
Roller Bearings	Turboprop engine gearshafts
Fan blades (titanium)	Manifold segments for helicopter engines
Airfoil vanes	Jet engine nozzle components
Cluster gears	Typewriter carriages
Composite gears	Aircraft landing gears
Helical pinion gears	Aircraft landing mats
Valves	Automotive planetary carriers
Belts	Automotive transmission bands
Hydrofoil drive shafts	Gimbal joints for fuel and oxidizer engine lines
Alternator and relay rotors	Helicopter rotors
Drive shaft shroud	Stator cores
Stampings in transmission subassemblies	Honeycomb panels for wing structure
Relays	Distributor cams and plates
Diaphragms	Steering column tubes
Bellows	Ball joints
Computer leaf springs	Wing beams, covers, carry-through fittings
Transmission and torque converters (trucks and earthmovers)	Bushings
Piston actuators	Gyroscopes
Pressure sensing and aneroid capsules	Bimetal pipe for Dacron
Miniature relays	18 components for lunar-module descent engine (rings, bellows, tubes, hub, throttle)
Filters	Infrared dewars
Transducers	Automotive flywheels
Pyrotechnic igniters	Automotive slip yokes
Liquid battery seals	Automotive transmission bowls
Propellant valves	Chain links for coal rippers
Thermionic generator emitters	

Alloys	Test Temperature °F	°C	Hours at temperature	Base metal K_c(ksi $\sqrt{in}$)	$K_c\left(MN\,\dfrac{1}{\sqrt{m^3}}\right)$	EB welded K_c(ksi $\sqrt{in}$)	$K_c\left(MN\,\dfrac{1}{\sqrt{m^3}}\right)$
Fracture Toughness of Three Light Alloys (Average of three)							
2219	78	26		30.3	33.3	26.9	29.5
T62	400	204	1/2	24.5	26.9	22.3	24.4
	400	204	1000	22.0	24.1		
2014	78	26		39.4	43.2	29.7	32.6
T6	300	149	1/2	35.9	39.4	28.8	31.6
	300	149	1000	33.0	36.2		
Ti-6Al-4V	78	26		89.0	97.7	82.9	91.0
Ann.	750	399	1/2	61.3	67.3	62.1	68.1
	750	399	1000	63.1	69.2	62.3	68.4
Fracture Toughness of Two PH Stainless Steels (Average of two)							
AM 350	78	26		120.5	132.3	93.8	102.9
SCT 850	800	427	1/2	78.9	86.6	66	72.4
	78	26		120.9	133.7	110.6	121.4
PH15-7Mo	700	371	1/2	84.3	92.5	76.8	84.3
TH1050	700	371	1000	86.8	95.3		
Fracture Toughness of Three Ni Alloys (Average of three)							
IN 625	78	26		66.0	72.4	63.9	70.1
Ann	1300	704	1/2	52.5	57.6	46.8	51.3
	1300	704	1000	69.8	76.3	51.7	56.7
René 41 ST	78	26		67.9	74.5	66.3	72.7
	1400	760	1/2			72.3	78.3
	1600	871	1/2	38.6	41.3	44.5	48.8
INCO 718	78	26		139.9	153.6	100.7	110.5
STA	1300	704	1/2	93.4	102.5	79.8	87.6

Fig. 1-50 Fracture toughness.

Nuclear

EBW has been applied to the fabrication of fuel elements for pressurized water reactors. The distinct advantages of the electron-beam weld are the following:

- Vacuum environment prevents contamination of the weld joint.
- Vacuum environment ensures that the weld metal possesses good corrosion resistance and mechanical properties.
- High concentration of weld heat. The extreme concentration of thermal energy is an important advantage of EBW of plate-type fuel elements.
- High concentration of heat reduces shrinkage and thermal distortion. For example, in fuel-element welding, total transverse

shrinkage per weld seam is only 0.001 to 0.0015 in (0.03 to 0.04 mm) for electron-beam welds, compared to 0.010 and 0.012 in (0.25 and 0.30 mm) for GTA welds.

The EBW of the fuel capsules for the SNAP-21 and SNAP-23 power generation systems shows the feasibility of using this process for satisfactorily sealing isotopic fuel capsules. These systems are used to produce electrical power in areas of limited access such as undersea and other remote terrestrial regions.[45]

In the next generation of nuclear reactors, such as the molten salt breeder reactor or the controlled thermonuclear reactor, and in radioisotope thermoelectric generators, molybdenum will be used because of its excellent corrosion resistance, especially to liquid metals. Complex welded structures of molybdenum, shown in Fig. 1-51, are being electron-beam-welded and tested to evaluate the material and its use in these future nuclear applications.[46]

Ion-propulsion systems, with their need for refractory metals, have made use of the electron-beam process. Contact ionizers with a molybdenum jacket have been welded to a heavy-walled tungsten cylinder.

EBW is ideally suited for fabrication of ion-propulsion systems that includes joining of similar and dissimilar refractory materials. Complex, high-restraint configurations have been successfully welded without cracks or leaks; distortion was held to 0.002 in (0.05 mm), although some cases required as much as 100 in (2540 mm) of welding for fabrication. Engine life tests of ion-propulsion systems have demonstrated that the weld and porous tungsten in the weld vicinity are capable of withstanding numerous thermal cycles and long usage without any evidence of failure or degradation.

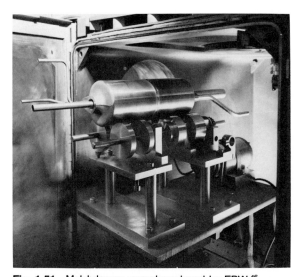

Fig. 1-51   Molybdenum vessel produced by EBW.[46]

Undersea

Experimental shells with electron-beam welded inner ribs of HY-80 steel, Fig. 1-52, are being evaluated in tests as a submarine hull structure for underwater uses.

Fig. 1-52 Full-penetration electron-beam welds in HY-80 steel cylinder.[2]

Motors, Wheels, Gears, and Engines

EBW of critical aircraft engine parts such as highly loaded power train and accessory gears have provided the engineer with a new design concept to reduce cost, decrease weight, increase reliability, and solve complicated design problems.

Current design stress levels for double helical aircraft gears require that the gear teeth be hardened after cutting. The desirability of maintaining the smallest possible gap between helices for minimum size and weight precludes finish grinding of the gear teeth after hardening because of the large gap required for grinding wheel clearance. The designer is limited in a choice of the gear material to a nitriding steel to control hardening distortion. When the gear must have integral bearing raceways, experience with nitrided steel as a bearing raceway material is limited compared with the more conventional through-hardened or carburized bearing steels.

With the EBW process, the design of a double helical gear may be improved in one of two ways:

- The double helical gear teeth can be manufactured in two pieces from carburizing steel, cut, case-carburized, hardened and ground separately, and electron-beam-welded at the center.
- The gear teeth can be from nitriding steel, cut, shaved, and nitrided, and the bearing raceways made from carburizing steel and electron-beam-welded to the gear tooth section.

EB   Welds

Fig.   1-53 Accessory   cluster   gear   electron-beam-welded   at   webs.   (Arrows   point   to   electron   beam   welds.)[47]

In the first choice, the necessity of a large gap for grinding wheel clearance is eliminated, and in the second choice, the desirable properties of two different steels are utilized on an integrated piece. On large double helical gears 20 to 22 in (508 to 559 mm) in diameter, feasibility EBW tests have indicated the potential for joining the two finished ring gear details in one operation and subsequently welding this subassembly to the web detail. See Fig. 1-53.

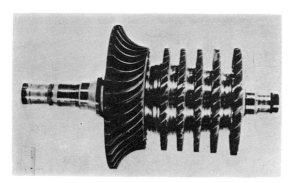

Fig.   1-54 Bladed   electron-beam-welded   titanium   rotor.[48]

Fig. 1-55 17-7PH steel electron-beam-welded for helium gas storage.

Two new applications for EBW are a compressor rotor and power shaft which are components of a rotating gas-turbine engine. The bladed rotor, 6Al-4V titanium, is shown in Fig. 1-54.

Silicon-iron laminates are stacked together to make up the stator core assembly for electrical actuator motors. Conventional welding techniques for holding the laminates together at a high rate per minute

Fig. 1-56 Preparing for EBW of landing gear.[50]

were unsuccessful. The uneven and inconsistent weld penetration and width resulted in nonuniform magnetic paths. The electron-beam process allowed the penetration to be controlled to within 0.001 to 0.002 in (0.03 to 0.05 mm) and resulted in small uniform welds that did not adversely affect the magnetic properties of the core.

Aircraft, Missiles, Reentry Vehicles and Boosters

Development programs for EBW encompassing a variety of diverse shapes, including tees, crosses, channels, angles, and combinations thereof for the SST (supersonic transport) airplane, were evaluated, and the results are to be utilized in designs and manufacturing within the next 5 years.

Titanium forgings have been joined by EBW to form a rotor hub 120 in (3048 mm) in diameter for a new helicopter. The Ti-6Al-4V alloy parts, 2.25 in (57.2 mm) thick and electron-beam-welded in one-pass welds, were 10 in (254 mm) long and were joined in four areas of the hub. The hub and blades of the helicopter were formed in four pieces, and then were joined by EBW because hub and blades could not be forged in one piece. Another portion of the hub, called the movable hub, was also electron-beam-welded.[49]

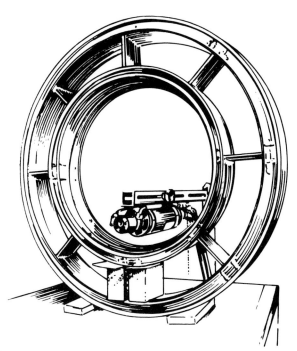

Fig. 1-57   Main engine mount of the TFE-731 turbofan jet engine.[51]

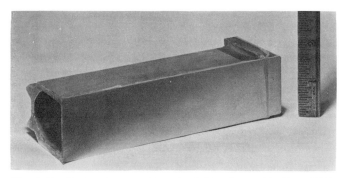

Fig. 1-58 Electron-beam welds extruded landing mat to Type 6061-T6 aluminum end connector.[50]

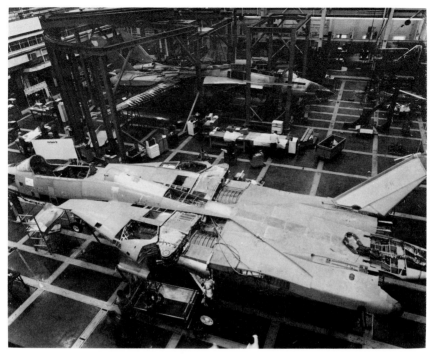

Fig. 1-59 The electron-beam-welded wing box assembly in new advanced fighter airplane.[18,52]

Pressure vessels are a constant companion in any space rocket, booster, reentry vehicle, or orbiting laboratory. EBW of pressure vessels fabricated of H11 hot-work steel, 6061 aluminum, 6Al-4V titanium, and the PH steels, see Fig. 1-55, has been extremely successful.

EBW is being adapted to more aircraft and aircraft engine assemblies as engineers realize the potentialities of the process. Shown in Figs. 1-56 to 1-58 are aircraft landing gears,[43] main engine mounts of jet engines, aircraft landing mats, engine pylon structures, and wing slat tracks.[50,51]

The use of EBW has been applied to the wing box assembly, Fig. 1-59, on an advanced fighter airplane. The section is a single-cell box beam consisting of four basic weld assemblies fabricated from 33 detailed machined parts. The box transmits wing outer panel loads, applied at each pivot, into the fuselage nacelles and center body. Electron-beam welds in 25 setups are required to fabricate a wing box. Fifty-seven welds are square butt joints and thirteen are angled or scarf joints. The longest of the 70 welds runs 65 in (1650 mm), and the overall total is about 1800 in (4570 mm).[52]

EBW has been a cost-effective process in joining titanium engine cases into finished components for modern aircraft.

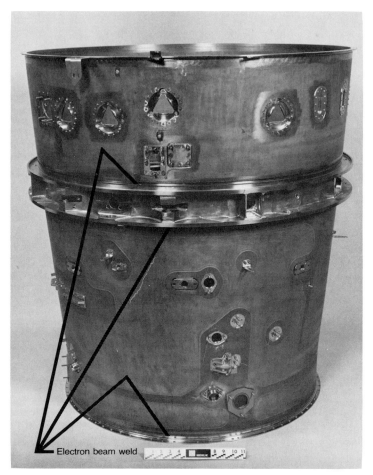

Electron beam weld

Fig. 1-60 Aft case, Type 6Al-4V titanium engine mount ring, electron-beam-welded.

In Fig. 1-60 and 1-61 are two sandwich engine cases joined into a production assembly by EBW. Over 500 assemblies like those in Fig. 1-60, have been produced without failure and over 300,000 hours of flight operation have produced no problems.

EBW is being extensively used to join Inconel 718 components together on the engines for the space shuttle. The various components being joined are seen in Fig. 1-61. Previous engines have been assembled by bolting the parts together, but welding saves weight because heavy flanges that must be used for bolting are eliminated. EBW is being used rather than other methods because it permits tight tolerances and minimizes heat distortion and heat-affected zone.[53]

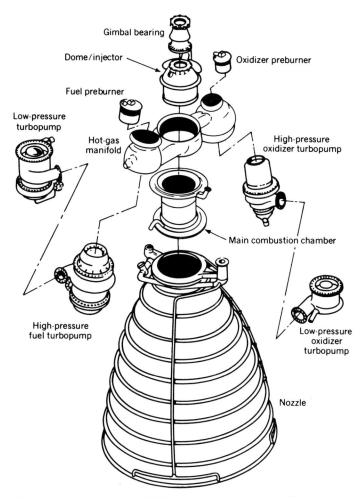

Gimbal bearing

Dome/injector

Oxidizer preburner

Fuel preburner

Low-pressure
turbopump

Hot-gas
manifold

High-pressure
oxidizer turbopump

Main combustion chamber

High-pressure
fuel turbopump

Low-pressure
oxidizer
turbopump

Nozzle

Fig. 1-61   Components for EBW for space shuttle engine.[53]

Electronics

Waveguide antennas for aircraft and the scimitar antenna for the
Apollo command module have required the use of electron beams.
Figure 1-22 illustrates the tooling used in the application of EBW for
electron tubes, and Ref. 7 is an excellent source for further information on this subject.

Electron beams are useful in hermetically sealing transistors, welding
transistor junctions, and replacing soldered connections. In this application, EBW provides a mechanically and electrically sound joint
containing no residual corrosive flux and does not affect the spring
characteristics.

Increasing reliability requirements demand that electronic circuits and other electrical devices, such as microswitches, be hermetically sealed without the danger of corrosive impurities remaining within the capsule. EBW accomplished in a vacuum provides an ideal process for such encapsulation. A high-temperature switch, used in a high performance aircraft, requires an all-welded assembly because flux residues associated with soldering cause deterioration of internal components and subsequent changes to the dielectric properties of the switch itself. In this instance, the 17-7PH cover assembly was electron-beam-welded to a cold-rolled-steel base in a vacuum and the unit subsequently backfilled with an inert gas. The welds were 0.012 in (0.30 mm) wide and were located within 0.030 in (0.76 mm) of glass hermetic seals that were not damaged during welding. Hundreds of these switches have been successfully processed.

Miscellaneous

1. Electrical connections for an entire computer-memory array have been joined by an electron beam in a single pass. In a continuous pass, precise welds connect terminals of ferrite-core planes with those immediately above and beneath in a memory array. Conventionally, each terminal is welded separately. A ferrite-core plane contains thousands of tiny magnetic doughnuts wired together. A number of these planes are interconnected in stacks to make a column of electrical terminals in the stack pass through the beam of electrons. The beam strikes each terminal and all four sides of the memory array are handled the same way, see Fig. 1-26.

2. A hammer unit that has two leaf springs is being joined to a hammer socket and hammer assembly for the computing industry. Heat buildup is at a minimum and efficiency of the beam is well over 70%, and with the beam focused to a spot only 0.001 in (0.03 mm) in diameter, the hammer and its socket are not distorted and the temper for the spring material is not affected by EBW.

3. EBW has been used successfully in welding a thin foil seal over an explosive charge in the top cap of a liquid-ammonia battery. Hermetically sealing the heat-sensitive battery compartment by EBW provides a smaller battery than would be possible if sealing were done by other, more conventional welding processes.

4. Bimetal bandsaw blades fabricated by EBW cut faster and last longer than their more costly single-metal counterparts. Traditionally, heavy-duty band saw blades are machined from strips of hardened high-speed tool steel. Because of the rigidity of the tool steel, bending stresses in the blade are concentrated at the root of the saw teeth as the band wraps around drive wheels of the saw machine. It is in this area that blade failures usually originate. In addition, the tool steel bands cannot be drawn as

taut as would be desired for high cutting speeds because of the material's rigidity. These problems have been eased by using composite blades consisting of a narrow strip of a high-speed tool steel, M2, which is electron-beam-welded to a wide strip of low-alloy carbon steel, AISI 6150. The strip of tool steel is just wide enough so that the roots of the saw teeth are machined into the low-alloy carbon steel. Thus stresses caused by bending of the blade and impact loading of the teeth are applied to the more flexible and less expensive 6150 alloy that handles flexing and tension and distributes the stresses more evenly. Again, high energy concentrating in a narrow weld zone leaves most of the steel unaffected metallurgically. This is now being done by PVEB machines.

5. EBW has been applied to a diaphragm section made of 0.001-in-thick (0.03 mm) titanium, which is part of a hydraulic-fluid flow-control system in a missile; a similar type is used in the Apollo spacecraft. On command, either pressure or an explosive charge ruptures the diaphragm to permit fluid flow in the line.

6. Electron beams have been used to weld components of infrared detector dewars, Fig. 1-62; thermionic heating devices, Fig. 1-63; and the 13-layered columbium bellows in Fig. 1-64.

7. Electron beams have recently been used as a heating and vaporizing source to improve the wetability of beryllium by braze filler metals. Titanium was chosen as a surface activator to promote wetting. Vacuum evaporation of titanium onto the surfaces to be brazed was chosen as the most desirable method for applying the activator. Silver filler metals produced relatively good joints with this method because the titanium layer and the short heating cycle prevented extensive reaction between the braze and the base metal. However, exceedingly good joints were also achieved using 1100 aluminum as the braze filler metal. In addition, titanium has been successfully used to wet graphite and tungsten carbide. Wetting and flowing of the brazing filler metal on titanium-coated base material occur by liquid metal penetrating, displacing, and tunneling under the vapor-deposited film.[54]

Fig. 1-62   Electron-beam-welded infrared-detector dewars.[2]

.020″ tantalum to .316″ solid tungsten

.005″ to .010″ tantalum

.002″ fansteel #82* to .005″ tantalum

.002″ to .002″ fansteel #82*

.002″ fansteel #82* to .005″ tantalum

.020″ tantalum to .020″ columbium

.060″ to 1.00″ solid columbium (machined after welding)

.040″ to .040″ columbium

*Fansteel composition
.33% tantulm
.60% columbium
.07% zirconium

Fig. 1-63 Electron-beam-welded thermionic heating device.[2]

8. EBW equipment and techniques have been used to a limited extent for brazing. The high vacuum used in the work chamber permits adequate flow of brazing filler metal on properly cleaned joints without a reducing atmosphere or a flux. There is no problem of flux entrapment, and no need to clean the work after brazing. The high vacuum and the absence of flux provide a brazing environment that avoids the problems associated with prepared atmospheres when certain stainless steels are brazed, as well as the more reactive metals such as titanium. Electron-beam brazing is done in the same way as EBW, except that the beam is defocused to provide a larger beam spot and to reduce the power density or the heating effect on the work. Brazing temperatures are reached quickly and heat can be localized to minimize grain growth, softening of cold-worked metal, and, in austenitic stainless steels, sensitizing of the material by carbide precipitation. Electron-beam brazing is a convenient method for brazing small assemblies such as instrument packages, combining the versatility and close controllability of electron-beam heating with the advantages of vacuum brazing. Packaged devices can be encapsulated with an internal vacuum without damaging the basic package. Tube-to-header joints in small heat-transfer

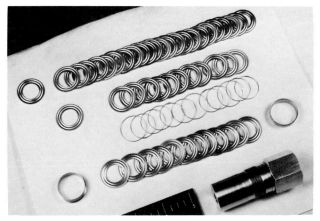

Fig. 1-64   Details and electron-beam-welded columbium bellows and holding fixture for thermionic generator.[2]

equipment made of heat-resisting alloys and refractory metals are sometimes electron-beam brazed. A recent application was for a Zircaloy-2 in-pile tube-burst specimen. There was a requirement for a long stainless steel capillary pressurization tube to be brazed into the specimen. Furnace brazing was not possible because the heat treatment of the test section would be affected. Induction brazing did not appear to be practical because of the complex shape of the specimen. The capillary tube was brazed into a molybdenum adapter with copper, and the adapter was brazed into the Zircaloy-2 specimen with 48Ti-48Zr-4Be. Both brazes were made simultaneously by impinging the defocused beam from a conventional low-voltage electron gun on the molybdenum adapter. In the application described above, visual control of the brazing cycle was used. In another tube-to-header

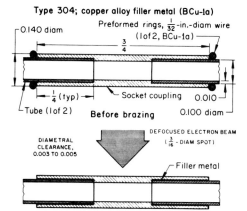

Fig. 1-65   Joint between two capillary tubes of an instrument package electron-beam-brazed in high vacuum with low-power defocused beam.[15]   (0.01 in = 0.25 mm.)

application, the joint is electron-beam-welded on the top side of the header, and brazing filler metal preplaced on the reverse side of the header at the joint is caused to melt and flow by the heat of the beam. Small-diameter, thin-wall stainless steel tubes are readily joined by electron-beam brazing as seen in Fig. 1.65.

9. One of the more recent EBW applications is the making of rock drill bits. These are used in the oil and gas drilling industry, and instead of one large forging, the drill bits are made more cheaply in three parts joined by vertical welds.

PVEB Welding

Current applications include gears, saw blades, flywheels, slip yokes, and pipe fittings. The 14-in-outside-diameter (356 mm) ring gears and counterweights as well as flywheel stampings have been electron-beam-welded in automobiles since 1968.

Double-helical aircraft engine gears assembled from two pieces are a natural application for PVEB welding. It also is quite practical to weld single gears onto relatively long shafts. Band-saw blade manufacturing has been revolutionized with the advent of EBW. These applications

Fig. 1-66 Automotive transmission turbine lockup ring.[1]

Fig. 1-67 Torque converter.[1]

have been accomplished in a high-vacuum environment, but have been now satisfactorily welded under PV.

Figure 1-66 illustrates the PV welding setup for turbine lockup rings. Low heat input and high welding speeds produce up to 375 transmission components per hour. Another significant point is that the electron-beam weld does not disturb the prior brazing of the internal parts. Thus, practical high-production rates can be realized.

A torque converter assembly is seen in Fig. 1-67. EBW meets the critical hermetic seal requirements for this component at outputs of 250 parts per hour utilizing filler wire.

NVEB Welding

NVEB welding is a much newer technique. Specific applications are developing every month and its production potential is promising. One outstanding production application for NVEB welding is in the manufacture of thin-walled tubing and steel pipe where control of weld bead geometry is important. The electron-beam tube mill has produced excellent quality tube of Types 304 and 304L stainless steel and Inconel at speeds from 480 to 960 in/min (203 to 406 mm/s). With higher-strength materials, the tube size and speed would be proportionately lower. Tubing of 0.021 in (0.54 mm) Types 304 and 304L stainless steel at 960 in/min (460 mm/s) and 0.030-in (0.76-mm) wall at 1200 to 1440 in/min (508 to 610 mm/s) has been produced.

After the work leaves the forming stands, it enters the enclosed welding station where it passes through a seam guide and squeeze rolls. The electron beam is generated in an orifice in the bottom of the gun. The beam strikes the moving tube beneath, and welding takes place in an atmosphere.

As the tubing leaves the welder, it is cooled by a water spray and enters a three-pass sizing mill which reduces it to final dimensions.

After straightening, the tubing passes onto a runout table for cutoff via a flying shear and is automatically discharged.

The future adaptation of the system extends these promising possibilities:

- Butt welding of corrugated tubes
- Sheet to sheet (different gages and material)
- Formed section to formed section
- Lap welding of strips
- Tube or shape to sheet
- Tube to tube
- Fin to shape
- Discontinuous welding of mesh or screen
- Rod to rod
- Dual wall shape
- Spiral tube welding

The electron-beam tube welder makes it possible to fabricate stainless tube, for example, which can compete economically with glass and plastic tubing used in the chemical and petroleum industries.

In desalination plants, where long-range plans call for up to 700 million miles of corrosion-resistant tube, electron-beam-welded tube is expected to find a new market.

EBW of gas-line pipe sections in the field promises to lower costs and produce better welds than presently used arc-welding methods. A feasibility and design study, recently conducted on joining steel pipe 30 in (762 mm) in diameter with 0.375-in (9.5-mm) walls, shows that electron-beam pipe welds can be produced automatically. A single electron-beam weld can be produced along the circumference of the pipes in 2 min. Present pipeline construction techniques require two teams of workers to make several welds in each joint.[55,56,57]

Two recent production jobs which went on-line in the automotive industry were collapsible steering columns and steering-gear ball joints. The machine welding and steering columns seam-welds 0.070-in-thick (1.7 mm) steel sheet to form 18-in-long (457 mm) parts. A carousel

Fig. 1-68 Electron-beam-welded steering column.[1]

conveyor feeds the parts under the machine's electron beam which produces seam welds at the rate of 500 in/min (212 mm/s). It produces 11 parts per minute, Fig. 1-68, and over 60 million have been produced. Figure 1-69 shows the automated electron-beam conveyor system for welding the die-cast aluminum manifold assemblies at a rate of 120 parts per hour.

Fig. 1-69 Die-cast aluminum manifolds set up for EBW.[1]

Refrigerator compressor shell halves are electron-beam-welded at 300 in/min (127.2 mm/s) without filler wire. This would be unusual for other EBW methods, since the shell halves do not always match perfectly. Here, wide penetration of NVEB is ideal. The beam melts the lip of the lower shell into the upper half, making a 0.187-in (4.7-mm) fillet. Automatic welders make 600 welds per hour.

A similar part, also leaktight, is the torque converter of automatic transmissions. Materials are low-carbon rimmed steel. The halves are rotary-fillet-welded with considerable mechanical runout of up to 0.025 in (0.6 mm). Because of this, and to overcome the natural porosity of rimmed steel, the maker uses welding wire, adding 1 in (25.4 mm) for every inch (25.4 mm) of weld. Weld speed is 300 in/min (127.2 mm/s). NVEB welds rimmed steel more reliably than PV because atmospheric pressure helps control the molten pool.

NVEB may one day weld the seam of roll-formed auto wheels. The hope is to replace spot welds, thereby raising quality, strength, and safety. A four-gun machine will make four welds simultaneously, each about 6 in (152 mm) long. Again, as wheels are made of rimmed steel, a 1:1 ratio of wire will be used. The machine will turn out 1000 wheels an hour. Also being investigated are welded oil-filled shock absorbers. Tests show that the coating of oil on the parts does not hurt the weld. Welding time is 2 s.

Local EB

The two local-vacuum EBW machines, mobile-type and SSEB, have future potential capabilities. As described previously in Fig. 1-21, the

Fig. 1-70 Five 108-in-long (2743 mm) SSEB-welded wing beams.[10]

SSEB equipment has successfully electron-beam-welded production 6Al-4V titanium aircraft wing beams (Fig. 1-70).

The welder shown in Fig. 1-23 has been used for numerous feasibility applications prior to any full-scale production usage. Shown in Fig. 1-71 is the schematic for tube-to-tube-sheet welding, and Figure 1-72 shows some of the completed electron-beam welds.[52] The machine shown in Fig. 1-71 has been designed in order to significantly increase the production rate of tube-to-tube-sheet welding with respect to the GTA process. In 40 h, the mobile-type machine has welded 12,250 tubes vs. 1500 tubes for the GTA process.[11]

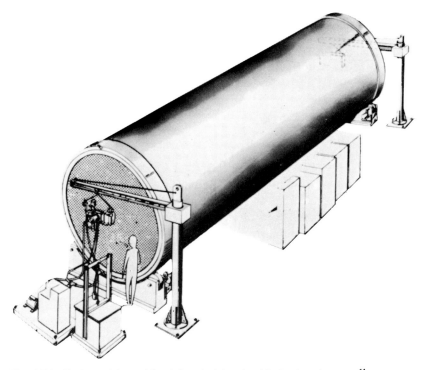

Fig. 1-71 Equipment for welding tubes to tube sheet in heat exchangers.[11]

Fig. 1-72   Finished tube welds.[11]

Welding in Space

EBW is reaching for new heights—this time in outer space. An electron-beam welder was operated aboard Skylab I. According to the developer, the astronauts were able to weld for 10 min in a space-evacuated chamber. The EBW experiments were to study the effect of weightlessness on molten metal. The welder was designed for maximum compactness.

In space, of course, it is easy to obtain the necessary vacuum in the work chamber; it is simply vented to space. The resulting vacuum is far better than any obtainable on earth, leaving no contaminants to affect the quality of the weld.[58] Similar experiments were conducted in EBW and cutting by the Soviet Union on stainless steel, aluminum alloy, and titanium in the Soyuz experiments. Visual observation of the welding and cutting processes in the conditions of weightlessness and overloading detected no differences, as compared with similar operations under conventional conditions on earth.[59] The completed tests proved that it is possible to obtain sound welded joints of various metals and alloys with EBW under the conditions of short-time weightlessness. Electron-beam cutting also was found to perform with little change compared with routine conditions on earth.

Future

The history of EBW is typical of new processes. There were few applications at first, while today 50 fully automatic electron-beam welders are working two and three shifts every day. This equipment is proving it can produce commercial parts in a production-shop atmosphere. Still, this is only the beginning. The number of parts now being designed or redesigned to use electron-beam welding will result in a significant increase in its use in the coming years. An example of this growth is the auto industry. In 1962 this slow start had grown to about three assemblies per car. In 1971, this figure rose to 30 per car. The forecast is for 40 electron-beam-welded assemblies in every car in 1978.

For the future, a PV machine is foreseen that follows the joint by deflecting the beam magnetically instead of moving the part or the gun. Multigun electron-beam welding is a promising idea, mostly because a number of guns bearing on one part increase output, and welding speed increases productivity. If the work is 0.10-in-thick (2.5 mm) low-carbon steel, each gun could be welding 120 in/min

(51 min/s). This would equal 1000 in (25,400 mm) of welding every minute.

The beams will follow any path, straight or curved, and will change direction almost instantaneously. Eight beams, then, could cover a part of almost any shape. This, plus welding speed, means that multigun welding is a very likely part of future production lines.

Electron beams are being used to drill close-tolerance holes and grooves in diamond, alumina ceramics, and difficult-to-machine metals. The potential application of electron-beam drilling of diamond is for wire drawing dies. By mechanical methods, it takes 24 h to pierce the initial hole in a 20-point stone. The electron beam does the job in minutes.

High-alumina ceramics can be machined accurately with electron beams.[60]

But perhaps the most significant application to ceramics is production of metallized ceramic wafers. The vacuum required for electron-beam generation is also the environment required for vacuum deposition of metals. In fact, drilled substrates with metallized through-connections were formed simultaneously with hole drilling.

Electron beams melt through many kinds of rocks like a hot knife through wax. When fully developed, the device could be used for tunnels, trenches for pipes, quarries, and mines. It even cuts through iron rods in reinforced concrete. It works as well under water as above. Indications are that the electron-beam rock cutter will be economically competitive with other methods. Because the electron beam does not produce a mechanical "kick," it does not require elaborate bracketing and support. An experimental unit consists of a power supply and electron gun. Recently a government contract was let to field-test an electron-beam rock-excavation machine. Demonstrations have shown that the beam makes use of high-energy electrons to melt deep but narrow cuts in rocks. The beam is passed through a series of small partially evacuated chambers, each separated by a 0.10- or 0.05 in-diameter (2.5 or 1.3 mm) aperture. In the process, the beam is focused electromagnetically and delivered to the surface where it is needed.

Recently developed in the laboratories of Osaka University was a 100-kW-output EBW machine which can weld steel plates up to 8-in-thick (203 mm) in one pass. Particularly suitable for jobs on atomic reactors, boilers for thermal-electric generators, and various types of high-pressure vessels, the machine operates on two accelerating voltages—100 kV and 200 kV.

The 100-kW machine requires high vacuum for welding, but researchers are now working on a similar system that can be operated under normal atmospheric pressure.

Other metalworking areas include:

- Superrefinement of metals and their alloys on a volume basis.
- Continuous high-speed annealing.
- Rapid, economical production of ultrapure metal foils.
- Fusion treatment and hardening.

Finally, will outer space ever become a practical manufacturing site? Experts think so. Their confidence was put to its first test in a series of experiments conducted aboard Skylab I.

In the weightlessness and vacuum of space it may be possible to process materials in ways that would be impossible or prohibitively difficult on earth. Metals could be melted and solidified without absorbing contaminants from their containers. Casting metals is tricky on earth because of thermal convection. Additional nonuniformity results when heavier elements in a molten alloy settle toward the bottom of the mold.

Materials engineers do not always know why molten metals act as they do. But they know metals would be much stronger and more ductile if they could be crystallized more perfectly.

If the crystal structure of steel were perfect, steel could be made several times stronger than it is today. Obviously, no one expects to manufacture huge steel beams in space, but a better understanding of how crystals form could result in improved production techniques on earth.

If only an understanding of the effects of gravity on the solidification process were found, then a great contribution to science would have been made.

A perfectly grown silicon crystal could be sliced into chips capable of supporting as many as 750,000 electronic devices on an area less than 1 in (25.4 mm) across. It may also be possible to produce a block of pure metal in space, then draw it into wire on earth. These fine wires could increase the reliability of critical devices such as heart pacemakers. It may also be able to produce perfect ball bearings.

The Skylab I experiments include melting small samples of nickel, both pure and alloyed with tin, silver, and copper, which are attached to circular disks called "strings." An electron beam will be concentrated on the samples one at a time, causing them to melt and float free of the disks. The molten metal should form perfect spheres and solidify with uniform grain structure.

The end is not in sight relative to electron beams and especially EBW.

REFERENCES

1. Samuelson, F., Leybold-Heraeus Inc., private communication, March 1978.
2. Schwartz, M. M., "Modern Metal Joining Techniques," Wiley-Interscience, New York, 1969, pp. 1–142.
3. Sanderson, A., "A 75 KW Electron Beam Installation for Thick Section Welding," *Proc. Conf. on Advances in Welding Processes*, The Welding Institute, 1974.
4. Russell, J. D., Rodgers, A. J., and Stearn, R. J., "A Study of the Application of Electron Beam Welding to Structural Steels," *Met. Constr.*, **6**(10), 307–312, October 1974.
5. Schwartz, M. M., "Electron Beam Welding," *WRC Bull.* 196, July 1974.
6. Lanyi, R., Westinghouse Corp., private communication, March 1978.
7. "CNC Steers Nonvacuum EB Welder," *Am. Mach.*, **118**(13), 43–44, June 24, 1974.

8. Hinrichs, J. F., Ramsey, P. W., Ciaffoni, R. L., and Mustaleski, T. M., "Production Electron Beam Welding of Automotive Frame Components," *Weld. J.*, **53**(8), 488–493, August 1974.
9. McGregor, W. P., and Bailey, B. G., "Manufacturing Methods for Spiral Welded Titanium Tubing," Solar Div. of International Harvester, Contr. F33615-72-C-1331, AFML-TR-74-59, April 1974.
10. Ellison, H. P., and Witt, R. H., "Sliding-Seal Electron Beam Welding," Grumman Aerospace Corp., Contr. F33615-73-C-5030, AFML-TR-76-3, January 1976.
11. "Local Vacuum E.B. Welders (L.V.E.B.W.),"Sciaky Technical Booklets, October 5, 1975.
12. Kohn, M. L., Schollhamer, F. R., and Meier, J. W., "Electron Beam Techniques for Fabrication and Assembly of Parts for Electron Tubes," Final Report 21067, Contr. DA-36-039-AMC-03625 (E), July 1, 1963 to March 31, 1966, pp. 63–81B.
13. Brolmmelsiak, R., Union Carbide Corp., private communication, March 1978.
14. Whirlein, J., and Bosna, A., "EBW of a Sheet Metal Enclosure," 5th Nat. SAMPE Tech. Conf., Doc. 73SD 2157, Oct. 9, 1973.
15. "Metals Handbook," vol. 6, "Welding and Brazing," 8th ed. 1971, pp. 519–564.
16. Meier, J. W., "Electron Beam Welding at Various Pressures," *2d Internat. Conf. Electron and Ion Beam Science and Technology*, New York, April 1966.
17. Becket, F. J., "Designing for Electron Beam Welding," *Weld. Met. Fabr.*, pp. 210–216, June 1973.
18. "The Superstrong Wing Box of Tomcat," *Weld. Des. Fabr.*, pp. 33–36, May 1974.
19. Provancher, D. A., "Repair by Electron Beam Welding," *IIW Electron Beam Colloq.*, Dusseldorf, September 1973.
20. Sanderson, A., Taylor, A. N., and Stearn, R. V., "Electron-Beam Weldability of Three Aluminum Alloys," *Met. Constr. Br. Weld. J.*, **4**(7), October 1972.
21. Arata, Y., Ohsumi, M., and Hayakawa, Y., "Electron Beam Welding of High Strength Aluminum Alloy (Report 1)," IIW Doc. IV-196-76, *Trans. JWRI*, **5**(1), 1976.
22. Brennecke, M. W., "Electron Beam Welded Heavy Gage Aluminum Alloy 2219," *Weld. J.*, **44**(1), 27s–39s, January 1965.
23. Hicken, G. K., "Effects of Beryllium Oxide on the Base Weldability of Beryllium," *Weld. J.*, **49**(2), 364s–370s, February 1970.
24. Tavassoli, A. A., "Bend Ductility of Columbium Alloys WC 3015 and Cb752," *Weld. J.*, **50**(10), 451s–455s, October 1971.
25. Tavassoli, A. A., "Mechanical Properties of Weld, Base Metal and Coated Columbium FS85," *Weld. J.*, **52**(7), 323s–328s, July 1973.
26. Tavassoli, A. A., "Mechanical Properties of Weld, Base Metal and Coated Columbium Alloy Cb 752," *Weld. J.*, **52**(4), 168s–172s, April 1973.
27. Sciaky Brothers, "Turbine Engine Fabrication Repair and Overhaul Using Electron Beam Weld Techniques," Sciaky Engineering Rep. Bull. 363, Feb. 1971.
28. Hokanson, H. A., and Meier, J. W., "Electron Beam Welding of Aircraft Materials and Components," *Weld. J.*, **41**(11), 999–1008, November 1962.
29. McHenry, H. I., Collins, J. C., and Key, R. E., "Electron Beam Welding of D6AC Steel," *Weld. J.*, **45**(9), 419s–425s, September 1966.
30. Witt, R. H., "Electron Beam Welding Titanium," *Weld. Eng.*, pp. 66–76, May 1970.
31. Schwenk, W., Kaehler, W. A., Jr., and Kennedy, J. R., "Weldability of Titanium Alloy Sheets 6Al-6V-2Sn and 8Al-1Mo-1V," *Weld. J.*, **46**(2), 64s–73s, February 1967.
32. Duvall, P. S., and Nessler, C. G., "Manufacturing Technology for Joining Titanium Alloys," Contr. F33615-72-C-1624, AFML-TR-75-93, Feb. 28, 1975.
33. "Welding of 1″ Thick Ti-6Al-4V and Beta III by EBW," AFML-TR-73-197, Lockheed Missiles & Space Co., Palo Alto, CA.
34. Slaughter, G., Oak Ridge National Laboratory, private communication, February 1978.
35. Strizhevshaya, L. G., and Starova, L. L., "Fusion Welding of Certain Dissimilar Metals," *Weld. Prod. (USSR)*, **13**(1), 8–13, January 1966.
36. Schwartz, M., "The Fabrication of Dissimilar Metal Joints Containing Reactive and Refractory Metals," WRC Interpretive Rep. 210, October 1975.
37. D'Yachenko, V. V., Sivov, E. N., and Morozov, B. P., "Welding Molybdenum and Niobium to Stainless Steel," *Weld. Prod. (USSR)*, **13**(1), 2–7, January 1966.

38. Welty, J. W., Valdez, P. J., Smeltzer, D. E., Jr., and Davis, C. P., "Joining of Refractory Metals," Technical Documentary Rep. ASD-TDR-63-799, pt. 2, November 1964, AFML, Contr. AF 33(657)-9442.
39. Gatsek, K. F., "Joining Aluminum to Stainless Steel," *Weld. Des. Fabr.*, **38**(9), 61–62, September 1965.
40. Schwartz, M. M., "Electron Beam Welding of Refractory Metals," SAE 1962, *Aero-Space Mfg. Forum*, Los Angeles, October 1962.
41. "Electron Beam Welding Data Manual," Hamilton Standard, Division of United Aircraft Corp., April 1964.
42. Metzger, G., and Lison, R., "EBW of Dissimilar Metals," *Weld. J.*, **55**(8), 230s–240s, August 1976.
43. Nagler, H., "Evaluation of Mobile Electron Beam Weldments in AL5456-H321 Plate," Mfg. Res. Rept., Rohr Industries, April 23, 1975.
44. Hardy, R. R., Jr., "High Cycle Fatigue Behavior of 5086-H116 Aluminum Alloy Electron Beam Welds," *Weld. J.*, **56**(1), 8s–12s, January 1977.
45. Gunkel, R. W., Donnelly, R. G., and Slaughter, G. M., "Electron Beam Welding of Strontium-Fueled Capsules," *Weld. J.*, **48**(12), 950–955, December 1969.
46. Moorhead, A. J., and Slaughter, G. M., "Welding Studies on Arc-Cast Molybdenum," *Weld. J.*, **53**(5), 185s–191s, May 1974.
47. Bratkovich, N. F., Roth, R. E., and Purdy, R. E., "Electron Beam Welding Applications and Design Considerations for Aircraft Turbine Engine Gears," *Weld. J.*, **44**(8), 631–640, August 1965.
48. Silverstein, S. M., Strautman, V., and Freeman, W. R., "Application of Electron Beam Welding to Rotating Gas Turbine Components," *9th SAMPE Symp.*, Paper 1–3, November 1965.
49. McGregor, W. P., "Electron Beam Welding of the First AH-56A (Cheyenne) Helicopter Rotor Hubs," *Weld. J.*, **49**(11), 876–881, November 1969.
50. "Electron Beam Welding Developments," Sciaky Engrg. Rep., Bull. 353, October 1968, pp. 2–15.
51. "Ceramic X-Ray Tube's Small Focal Spot Size is Key to Short Film-Focal Distance," *Weld. Des. Fabr.*, pp. 62–67, October 1975.
52. "EB Welding Teams Up with NDT Techniques," *Weld. J.*, **54**(2), 97–100, February 1975.
53. "Engines for the Space Shuttle," *Am. Mach.*, pp. 36–39, Feb. 1, 1975.
54. Westland, E. F., and Lohmann, H. G., "Vapor Plating Aluminum on Beryllium for Welding," *Weld. J.*, **46**(3), 207–210, March 1967.
55. Williams, V. A., "Electron Beam Welding Goes Mass Production," *Production*, pp. 126–129, November 1967.
56. Vaccari, J. A., "Special Report: Four Processes," *Mater. Eng.*, pp. 40–43, April 1970.
57. Williams, V., "Electron Beam Welding Closes the Gap," *Production*, pp. 80–82, June 1973.
58. McKeown, D., "Space Welding in the Skylab," *Weld. Engr.*, pp. 18–20, December 1974.
59. Paton, B. E., "Welding in Space," *Weld. Eng.*, pp. 25–29, January 1972.
60. "Electron-beams Do More than Weld," *Automation*, p. 12, December 1975.
61. Arata, Y., Shima, K., Terai, K., and Nagai, Y., "The Forecasting of Welding Processes in the Future by the Delphi Method," *Weld. Res. Abroad*, pp. 31–32, August–September 1973.
62. Arata, Y., Terai, K., Nagai, H., Futami, I., Shimizu, S., and Satoh, K., "Insert-Type EB Welding Technology (Report 2)," IIW Doc. IV-146-74, *Trans. Jpn. Weld. Soc.*, **4**(2), 93–100, 1973.
63. Arata, Y., and Tomie, M., "100-KW Class EB Welding Technology (Report 1)," *Trans. of JWRI*, **2**(1), 17–20, 1973.
64. Sanderson, A., Taylor, A. N., and Stern, R. M., "Electron-beam Weldability of Three Aluminum Alloys," *Met. Constr. Br. Weld. J.*, **4**(7), July 1972.
65. Lawrence, G. S., "Some Improvements in Beam Quality for High Voltage Electron Beam Welders," *Electron and Ion Beam Science and Technology 5th Internat. Conf.*, 1972.

66. "An Investigation of Technological Parameters of Welding," IIW Doc. IV-160-74, Study Group of EB Welding, Shengyang Metal Research Institute, People's Republic of China, 1974.

67. Brooks, J. A., and Krenzer, R. W., "Progress Toward a More Weldable A-286," *Weld. J.*, **53**(6), 242s–245s, June 1974.

68. Mara, G. L., Funk, E. R., McMaster, R. C., and Pence, P. E., "Penetration Mechanisms of EB Welding and the Spiking Phenomenon," *Weld. J.*, **53**(6), 246s–251s, June 1974.

69. Gooch, T. G., "Stress Corrosion Cracking of Welded Joints in High Strength Steels," *Weld. J.*, **53**(7), 287s–306s, July 1974.

70. Andersson, T., and Lundqvist, B., "Properties and Structure of Welded Joints in Ti-3Al-2.5V Hydraulic Tubing," *Weld. J.*, **53**(7), 314s–320s, July 1974.

71. O'Brien, T. P., Pence, P. E., Funk, E. R., and McMaster, R. C., "Suppression of Spiking in Partial Penetration EB Welding with Feedback Control," *Weld. J.*, **53**(8), 332s–338s, August 1974.

72. Staudt, J. W., Corle, R. R., and Schleissman, J. A., "Scribeline Technique Detects Incomplete Fusion in EB Welds," *Weld. J.*, **52**(9), 580–586, September 1973.

73. Fink, J. H., "Analysis of Atmospheric EB Welding," *Weld. J.*, **54**(5), 137s–153s, May 1975.

74. Brooks, J. A., "Weldability of High Ni, High Mn Austenitic Stainless Steel," *Weld. J.*, **54**(6), 189s–195s, June 1975.

75. Sayegh, G., and Dumonte, P., "EB Welding of Heavy Sections and Large Components," *4th Internat. EB Processing Seminar*, Apr. 22–26, 1976, Long Island, NY.

76. Paton, B. E., Lebedev, V. K., Nazarenko, O. K., and Lokshin, V. E., "Equipment and Technology of EB Welding of Thick Metals," *4th Internat. EB Processing Seminar*, Apr. 22–26, 1976, Long Island, NY.

77. Bosna, A., and Krishnaswamy, H., "EB Welding of a Large Titanium Alloy Shroud Structure," *4th Internat. EB Processing Seminar*, Apr. 22–26, 1976, Long Island, NY.

78. Turner, A. J., "Industrial Applications of the EB Welding Process," *4th Internat. EB Processing Seminar*, Apr. 22–26, 1976, Long Island, NY.

79. Seifert, K., Jueptner, W., and Draugelates, V., "EB Welding of Fine-Grained Structural Steel in Partial Vacuum," *4th Internat. EB Processing Seminar*, Apr. 22–26 1976, Long Island, NY.

80. Lowrie, R., "Welding E-Brite 26-1 to Other Alloys," *Weld. J.*, **52**(11), 500s–506s, November 1973.

81. Tews, P., Pence, P., Sanders, J., Funk, E. R., and McMaster, R. C., "EB Welding Spike Suppression Using Feedback Control," *Weld. J.*, **55**(2), 52s–55s, February 1976.

82. Papin, M., and Bordes-Pages, H., "Soudage et fusion par fais-ceaux d'electrons," *1st Internat. Colloq. on EB Welding*, June 1970.

83. Niebuhr, F. W., and Fritz, D., "Extreme Tiefschweissungen in der Praxis," DVS-Bericht 21, Strahltechnik v.

84. Böcher, D., "Electronenstrahlschweissen," *Ind.-Anz.*, 59, 1972, Leybold-Heraeus.

85. Albrecht, C., and Lamatsch, H., "Electronenstrahlschweissen von Kupferstabililisierten Supraleitern für einen Blas enkammergrossmagneten," *Schweissen and Schneiden*, Johrgang 24 (1972), Heft 10.

86. Terai, K., Toyooka, T., Nagai, Y., Murakami, T., and Kurose, T., "EB Welding of Mild Steel to Oxygen Free Copper," IIW Doc. IV-90-72, July 1972, pp. 1–28.

87. Arata, Y., Terai, K., Nagai, H., Shimizu, S., and Aota, T., "Superalloys for Nuclear Plants (Report 1)," *Trans. JWRI*, **5**(2), 119–126, December 1976.

88. Paton, B. E., et al., "Special Features of EB Welding and Cutting Apparatus and Processes for use in Space," *Autom. Weld. (USSR)*, **24**(3), March 1971.

89. Terai, K., Toyooka, T., and Nagai, Y., "Effects of Process Parameter on the Penetration Depth in High Voltage EB Welding," *Trans. Jpn. Weld. Soc.*, **3**(1), April 1972.

90. Kanzler, P. J., "Another Application of EB Welding," Navmiro, *Manuf. Tech. Bull.*, **52**, 2–3, March 1974.

91. Huber, R. A., and Turner, P. W., "EB Welding at the Oak Ridge Y-12 Plant," *Weld. J.*, **48**(10), 787–798, October 1969.
92. Privoznik, L. J., Smith, R. S., and Heverly, J. S., "EB Welding of Thick Sections of 12% Cr Turbine Grade Steel," *Weld. J.*, **50**(8), 567–572, August, 1971.
93. Konkol, P. J., Smith, P. M., Willebrand, C. F., and Lonnor, L. P., "Parameter Study of EB Welding," *Weld. J.*, **50**(11), 765–776, November 1971.
94. Robelotto, S. M., and Morse, R., "Small Component EB Welding," *Weld. Eng.*, pp. 37–39, February 1972.
95. Murphy, J. L., and Turner, P. W., "Wire Feeder and Positioner for Narrow Groove EB Welding," *Weld. J.*, **55**(3), 181–190, March 1976.
96. Hegland, D. E., "Electron Beams Come Down to Earth," *Automation*, pp. 64–70, March 1976.
97. Bryant, W. A., and Gold, R. E., "Weldability of Three Forms of Chemically Vapor Deposited Tungsten," *Weld. J.*, **54**(11), 405s–408s, November 1975.
98. "Practical Considerations for Electron Beam Welding," Hamilton-Standard, pp. 1–16, 1970.
99. Fraikor, F. J., Hicken, G. K., and Grotsky, V. K., "Precipitation in EB Welded Beryllium-Ingot Sheet," *Weld. J.*, **52**(5), 204s–211s, May 1973.
100. Adler, P. N., Kennedy, J., and Satkiewicz, "Localized Hydrogen in Titanium Welds," *Weld. J.*, **52**(4), 180s–186s, April 1973.
101. Lucas, M. J., Jr., and Jackson, E. C., "The Welded Heat-Affected Zone in Nickel Base Alloy 718," *Weld. J.*, **49**(2), 46s–54s, February 1970.
102. Campau, J., and Unger, R., "EB Joins Roller Bearing Industry," *Weld. Eng.*, pp. 50–51, October 1970.
103. Burns, T. E., "Production of Aneroid Capsules," *Weld. Met. Fabr.*, pp. 336–338, September 1973.
104. Dietrich, W., and Kluger, H. D., "Rationelle Fertigungsmethoden durch Electronen-strahl-Schweissen," Leybold-Heraeus GmbH., 1972.
105. "Some New Thinking on Plate Fabrication," *Iron Age*, pp. 63–66, Sept. 13, 1976.
106. Lobb, A. E., Lindh, D. V., Wahlin, B. M., and Lovell, D. T., "Titanium Alloy Welding," Rept. FAA-SS-72-09, SST Technology Follow-On Program—Phase I, Final Report, D6-60209, July 1972.
107. "Here are the Facts about EB," *Weld. Des. Fabr.*, pp. 62–63, October 1971.
108. Weidner, C. W., and Shuler, L. E., "Effect of Process Variables on Partial Penetration Electron Beam Welding," *Weld. J.*, **52**(3), 114s–119s, March 1973.
109. Schumacher, B. W., "Atmospheric EBW with Large Stand-Off Distance," *Weld. J.*, **52**(5), 312–314, May 1973.
110. Groves, M. T., and Gerken, J. M., "Evaluation of Electron Beam Welds in Thick Materials," Tech. Rept. AFML-TR-66-22, pp. 1–324, February 1966.
111. Goodman, I., "Applications of Electron Beam Welding in Aeronautics, Electronics, and Machine Design," *IIW Electron Beam Colloq.*, Dusseldorf, September 1973.
112. Meleka, A. H., White, H., and Johnson, T. K., "The Application of Electron Beam Welding in Aero Engine Manufacturing," *IIW Electron Beam Colloq.*, Dusseldorf, September 1973.
113. Hagan, D., "Electron Beam Applications in Ford of Europe," *IIW Electron Beam Colloq.*, Dusseldorf, September 1973.
114. Becket, F. J., and Russell, J. D., "Electron Beam Welding Applications in General Engineering," *IIW Electron Beam Colloq.*, Dusseldorf, September 1973.
115. Welin, A. H., "Introduction of Electron Beam Welding Method in Production of Aircraft Engines at Volvo Flygmotor AB," *IIW Electron Beam Colloq.*, Dusseldorf, September 1973.
116. Ohsumi, M., Higuchi, K., and Hayakawa, Y., "Present Status of Applying Electron Beam Welding to High Strength Aluminum and Magnesium Alloy Parts," *IIW Electron Beam Colloq.*, Dusseldorf, September 1973.
117. Szucs, T., and Naderi, H., "The Position of Electron Beam Welding and the Objects of its Development in Hungary," *IIW Electron Beam Colloq.*, Dusseldorf, September 1973.

118. Leonhardt, W., and Siepman, W., "Evidence from Electron Beam Welding In Engine Manufacturing," *IIW Electron Beam Colloq.*, Dusseldorf, September 1973.

119. Binder, H., Luxemburger, R., Fritz, D., and Dietrich, W., "Solution of Actual Manufacturing Problems by Electron Beam Welding," *IIW Electron Beam Colloq.*, Dusseldorf, September 1973.

120. Gauthier, J., "Industrial Applications of Electron Beam Welding Process to Mechanical Parts," *IIW Electron Beam Colloq.*, Dusseldorf, September 1973.

121. de Burbure, S., de Boeck, P., and Groeseneker, P., "Electron Beam Welding at C.E.N.I.S.C.K.," *IIW Electron Beam Colloq.*, Dusseldorf, September 1973.

122. Scott, D. G., Estes, C. L., Huber, R. A., and Turner, P. W., "Successful Joining of Beryllium," *Weld. J.*, **51**(1), 15–24, January 1972.

123. Miller, J. A., "Manufacture of an Electron Beam Welded Turbine Engine Compressor Rotor," *Weld. J.*, **56**(5), 24–29, May 1977.

124. Roblin, M. J., and Robelotto, S. M., "Electron Beam Welding is Economical," *Weld. Des. Fabr.*, pp. 90–94, May 1977.

2

LASER WELDING

Almost 20 years have passed since the first lasing action was announced in 1959; however, lasers have appeared in very few factories although a great many have been installed in research laboratories. Because it was so revolutionary, scientists were quick to envisage the broadest range of potential applications. In those days, everybody felt that if there were not a laser in every home in the seventies, there at least would be one in every industrial facility.

Now rapid technological developments have combined to bring lasers into daily use. This desirable state of affairs resulted from the extension, not only of laser technology, but also of a number of related systems components. Higher power, new wavelengths, tunability, improved ruggedness, reliability, reproducibility, and stability were among these developments.

The highly collimated light beam of high wavelength purity generated by the laser permits this metalworking tool to become multifaceted. It can be used to measure and align; to weld, drill, or cut; to heat-treat and alloy. It is a tool that never gets dull, is easily manipulated for automated processes, and could eventually be piped throughout the shop from one central laser source.

THEORY AND PRINCIPLES OF PROCESS

Just what is this very special light beam generated by a laser? How is it generated? If one thinks of a battery as a generator of electrons (bunches of electrical energy), one can think of a laser as a generator of photons (bunches of light energy). The current of electrons from the battery can be used to heat the filament in a bulb, as in a flashlight. The combination of battery and bulb then becomes another photon generator. The difference between these two photon generators—laser and flashlight—is that the photons from the flashlight's filament are randomly emitted in all directions. Even when they are directed by a flashlight reflector they form a rapidly diverging beam of light in a broad range of wavelengths (colors) over the visible spectrum. In contrast, the photons from a laser are emitted quite precisely in a well-collimated (parallel) beam, all at about the same wavelength. This is called a coherent beam. Absolute coherence is impossible, but the extent of coherence depends on the narrowness of the wavelength region (sharpness of color) and the parallelism of the individual photon paths. One of the properties which make the laser so valuable and account for the ever-lengthening list of laser applications is coherence. This term describes the particular relationships between frequency, phase, amplitude, and direction. The different portions of the beam tend to reinforce each other where they coincide in the same phase, and tend to cancel each other where they coincide in opposite phase. The coherence gives the laser a unique property of being mono-chromatic.

To send several messages simultaneously by flashlight, several flash-lights, each with a different colored filter, can be used as multiple communication channels over the same path. However, with more than 10 colors, it would be hard for each receiver to discriminate among the messages and pick the one intended for it. With a laser, thousands of distinct information channels (1 Å in bandwidth*) can be transmitted over the same spectral region.

When high power is required to weld a material, that power must be focused in the smallest possible region so as not to waste energy. If power is required at a specific wavelength band, e.g., 1 Å wide, the monochromaticity (singleness of color) of the laser permits the concen-tration of several hundred thousand watts per square centimeter in 1-Å bandwidths.

Laser is an acronym for *l*ight *a*mplification by *s*timulated *e*mission of radiation. To understand what is meant by *light amplification*, it helps to reach an understanding of *amplification* in terms of sound. There are many kinds of amplifiers, all of which make large signals out of small signals so that they can be *heard* in the presence of *noise*.

The audio amplifier in an auto operates with transistors or vacuum tubes, which have an essential characteristic called *gain*. This means that a large current of electrons will flow through the tube if the "grid" or trigger voltage is slightly offset. Small fluctuations in the grid voltage will produce similar, but larger, fluctuations in the *amplified* current flow through the tube. The difficulty we sometimes have in sharply "tuning in" one radio station on the dial, without hearing an adjacent station simultaneously, illustrates the importance of amplification in narrow frequency bands. Efforts to find sharply tuned low-noise amplifiers led in 1954 to the *maser*, an acronym of *m*icrowave *a*mplifi-cation by *s*timulated *e*mission of *r*adiation. The principles of the maser have been extended to apply to the *amplification of light signals* of much smaller wavelengths.

The neon sign, or fluorescent light, as a light source is similar to a laser but without *gain*, which is an essential characteristic of a laser. The neon sign is a gas-filled, transparent tube which emits light from narrow-wavelength regions, has sharp colors, and is at the red end of the optical spectrum. A transformer excites the gas electrically with a

*1 Å = 10^{-10} m.

discharge of electrons. The electrons boost the gas atoms to high energy levels. Having been boosted, the gas atoms relax, while emitting their excess energy in the form of *photons*, packets of light energy. The activity in this gas is a disorderly conglomeration of spontaneous emission, absorption, and some *stimulated emission*. Again, the neon tube does not have *gain*, which is necessary for light amplification.

Gain can be provided in a gas by selectively exciting atoms to upper energy levels of certain transitions, from the lower energy levels of which rapid relaxation to the ground state (the lowest energy level) will occur naturally. These atoms can be continually reexcited to the upper level; with rapid depletion from the lower level, there are always more atoms at the upper level. This condition, in which the gas is out of equilibrium, is called *population inversion*. Population inversion permits *gain* in the medium.

When this condition of population inversion is produced through the external excitation of the lasing medium, it is commonly called "pumping" and may be achieved optically or electronically.

When photons of spontaneous emission (between the upper and lower energy levels) hit molecules in the upper level, each collision *stimulates* the *emission* of another photon, which in turn stimulates the emission of more photons from collisions with other excited molecules at the upper energy level. Every successive photon is stimulated to emit in precisely the same direction, and at exactly the same frequency as the last. This cascade of identical photons becomes a *coherent beam* of *l*ight *a*mplified by *s*timulated *e*mission of *r*adiation, *laser*!

This cascade of identical photons becomes the output, the coherent beam of light energy amplified by stimulated emission. In order to build up this cascade of photons, the stimulated-emission process is generated inside a resonant cavity, which acts like an amplifier by ensuring that the radiation will make many passes through the active laser medium, thereby affording maximum propagation of stimulated emissions.

So, essentially, a laser consists of a reservoir of active atoms, which can be excited to an upper energy level, a pumping source to excite the available active atoms, and a resonant cavity to provide feedback for the laser oscillations. It is an electrooptical device that converts electrical energy into electromagnetic energy.

KEY VARIABLES

Three things are essential to achieve laser action—suitable materials, appropriate energy (pump) sources, and a design to promote stimulated emission.

Laser Material

The prime requisite of a laser material is its ability to undergo stimulated emission. The material must also have the following properties:

- It must luminesce when excited by optical, electrical, radio-frequency, or other type of energy.
- The emission transition must have a long spontaneous emission decay time so that a population inversion can be achieved.
- The absorption properties of the material must be such that a large fraction of the exciting energy is absorbed and is effective in producing a population excess in the upper level of the emission transition.
- The spectral width of the emission transition must be relatively small so that sufficient gain per pass can be obtained to overcome the losses through the partially reflecting end surfaces.
- The optical quality of the crystal must be sufficiently good so that scattering caused by imperfections, strains, or inhomogeneities does not result in excessive loss of the emitted radiation.

A number of solids and several gases meet these requirements. See Table 2-1.

A typical lasing medium is a single-crystal rod of yttrium-aluminum-garnet (called yag) containing ions of neodymium. Neodymium-doped yag (Nd:yag) has replaced most other material (including the original ruby laser) for high-energy crystal-laser applications because it allows high pulse rates, has a relatively good efficiency, and can be operated with simple cooling systems.

Argon, helium, krypton, neon, oxygen, and xenon have turned out to be active laser substances. Now, carbon dioxide (CO_2), hydrogen, and nitrogen (N_2) have also been made to lase. Oxygen is used in mixtures of argon or neon. Neon produces laser action either as a single gas or as a constituent of helium-neon mixtures. The other

TABLE 2-1
Lasers for Welding[1]

Laser	Operation	Pulse length, ms	Pulse energy, J	Peak power, W	Max weld thickness*		Speed of welding	
					in	mm	in/min	mm/s
Ruby	Pulsed	3–10	20–50	1–5 k	0.005 to 0.020	0.13 to 0.50	3.0	1.2
Nd:glass	Pulsed	3–10	20–50	1–5 k	0.005 to 0.020	0.13 to 0.50	1.5	0.63
Nd:yag	Pulsed	3–10	10–100	1–10 k	0.005 to 0.025	0.13 to 0.60	5.0	2.1
CO_2	Pulsed	5–20	0.1–10	1–5 k	0.005	0.13	3.0	1.2
Nd:yag	CW			1000	0.150	3.81	30.0	12.7
CO_2	CW			1000	0.025	0.60	30.0	12.7
Gas dynamic	CW			20 k	0.750	19.0	50.0	21.2

*Maximum thickness given here is for Type 304 stainless steel.

gases—argon, krypton, and xenon—produce laser action when used in their pure form.

A typical CO_2 laser actually uses a mixture of three gases: carbon dioxide, helium (He), and nitrogen for high-power operation. The CO_2 supplies the molecular action required for photon generation, the N_2 acts to sustain and reinforce the molecular action, and the He provides intracavity cooling. In flowing-gas systems, this mixture is constantly pumped through the resonator cavity to sustain the lasing action, seen in Fig. 2-1.

There are advantages to the various types of lasers. The gaseous type is superior in frequency stability and monochromaticity, but has low efficiency (less than 0.1%). The solid state is more efficient (up to 10% for a perfect ruby), but most will not transmit continuous-wave. An exception is the continuous-wave, Nd:yag machine recently introduced. This 1000-W machine utilizes krypton-arc-lamp excitation, and at this power level the unit is capable of welding 0.12-in (3-mm) thick stainless steel at 10 in/min (4.2 mm/s) and thinner gage material at proportionately higher welding speeds.[3]

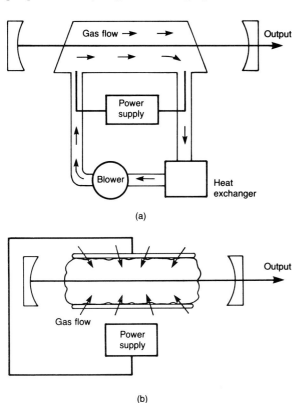

(a)

(b)

Fig. 2-1 Flowing-gas laser systems.[2] (a) Axial flow; (b) cross flow.

Pump Energy

Another key factor is getting the pump energy into the laser material. Given the laser material and the energy source, this factor largely determines the strength and duration of the output beam. Solid-state lasers are pumped optically by a flash lamp mounted in a reflecting cavity, which also contains the laser rod. Flash lamps have been usually filled with xenon or krypton gas. Gas lasers are generally pumped by

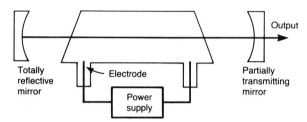

Fig. 2-2 Schematic of sealed-tube laser system.[2]

an electric discharge in the gas tube. Typically this form of electrical discharge is applied by electrodes, Fig. 2-2. In one production shop a special electron-beam-arrangement is used.

LASER PROPERTIES

There are several important distinguishing features of laser light. Monochromaticity and coherence have been discussed earlier.

Divergence

Lasers produce very nearly parallel beams of light, and it is this directionality that makes it possible to collect laser light and deliver it to a localized area with high efficiency. Because the beams are almost parallel, the laser energy is not greatly dissipated as the beam travels over long distances. Divergence is a measure of the increase in beam diameter with distance from the laser's exit aperture. The divergence is so slight that it is measured in milliradians (mrad); because of this particular property, the laser beam can be focused by a lens into extremely small spots.

Intensity

The output of a well-collimated light source, such as the laser beam, can be focused to a very small spot. This is a result of low divergence, and the smaller the spot size, the higher the energy concentration. In fact, lasers are presently capable of producing light that is more than 7 magnitudes brighter than the light from the sun. However, such levels are available only in very short pulses.

Lasers are operated in either a continuous-wave (CW) or pulsed mode. Solid-state lasers, such as Nd:yag, are usually operated in the pulsed mode because of flash lamp limitations, but continuous operation is also available, as mentioned earlier.

Q-switching is a means of achieving high peak powers by temporarily storing some of the energy in the laser cavity and then releasing it in a short burst. This is commonly achieved by preventing reflection from one of the end mirrors to build up the population inversion, and then suddenly changing this condition to permit reflection. The sudden feedback condition then produces a high-power pulse with a rapid time rise.

Gas lasers are usually operated in a continuous-wave mode and are capable of developing higher continuous average power than are solid-state lasers.

Mode Structure

One other property of laser beams worth mentioning is mode structure, which is the configuration of the electromagnetic field generated by the laser, and which affects the intensity distribution of the beam. TEM (transverse excitation mode) is the ability of a laser to oscillate in the laser cavity along one or more paths parallel to the axis of the cavity, and subscript numbers are used to describe the distribution pattern in a plane perpendicular to the beam.

TEM_{00} indicates the fundamental mode, in which lasing occurs only along the cavity axis. Most lasers generate multimode beams, and although the total power of such a beam may equal that of a TEM_{00} beam, the power density at its focal point may be as much as 2 orders of magnitude less. And a TEM_{00} laser beam can be focused to the smallest theoretical spot.

WELDING

In order to place laser-beam welding (LBW) in its proper frame of reference with respect to arc welding and EBW, we must compare thermal events which occur in these processes. During the formation of an arc weld, liquid is moved from an area directly under the arc toward the rear of the pool, and this movement is rapid. Metal also moves from the rear of the pool toward the arc. In an electron-beam weld, a similar situation develops. The principal difference is the depth of penetration. The concentrated energy spot produces deep penetration and the liquid moves up the side of the crater and toward the surface. In EBW, the liquid is moved around the hot beam and close to the rear of the weld pool. This movement can be so rapid that the liquid may be lifted from the crater. Craters have been observed where the liquid metal rose above the surface and formed a solidified spout.

LBW is similar to the events observed in arc and electron-beam welds where liquid is moved very rapidly away from the area of energy

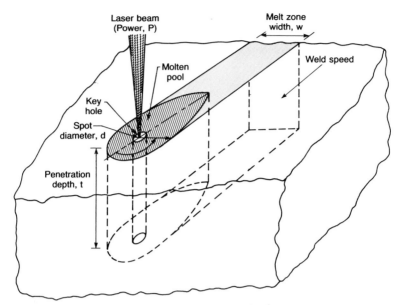

Fig. 2-3 Deep-penetration laser weld characteristics.[4]

impingement. These events occur because of violent convective movement in the weld pool.

The deep-penetration welding mode established by a focused laser beam is represented schematically in Fig. 2-3.[4] With reference to the figure, the laser radiation penetrates into the material, since energy is delivered to the surface too rapidly to be removed by thermal conduction. A deep-penetration cavity containing metal vapor is formed. Relative motion between the focused beam and the workpiece maintains the deep-penetration cavity in dynamic equilibrium with the molten zone around it. The cavity is translated through the material, with melting at the leading edge of the resultant molten weld pool and solidification at the trailing edge. The molten weld zone formed is also illustrated by the photograph in Fig. 2-3, which shows a top view of the weld zone formed in stainless steel at a laser power of 6 kW and a welding speed of 25 in/min (10.6 mm/s). The keyhole near the leading edge of the melt zone appears as the brightest region, since it exhibits the characteristics of a black body. The trailing edge of the tear-shaped zone defines the representative solidification lines of the top surface weld bead.

One can readily see an analogy between the three welding processes. In the low-energy-density arc-weld process, liquid is moved toward the rear of the pool at a relatively slow rate and acts as a coolant to remove heat from beneath the arc source. In the electron beam, the motion is more violent. Similar conditions exist with a laser where concentrated energy in a single overpowering pulse causes the liquid metal to move away from the point of energy impingement.

The optimum laser output required for welding depends on the absorptivity, thermal conduction, density, heat capacity, melting point, and surface conditions of the metals to be joined, as well as on the duration of the laser pulse. For example, metals with high thermal conductivity, such as copper and silver, require greater energy than do less-conductive metals, such as iron and nickel. Greater output energy is also required for highly reflective surfaces than for dull or rough surfaces.

EQUIPMENT AND TOOLING

In general, most solid-state laser systems available for welding are of the pulsed-output type. The elements of this system are seen in Fig. 2-4. The pulsed laser delivers bursts of energy at rates up to 200 per second. Each pulse lasts a few microseconds or milliseconds. The machine makes high-quality spot welds as deep as 0.080 in (2.2 mm). Shallower seam welds can be made at rates over 2 in (50.8 mm) per second. In LBW, spot size and power intensity are chosen so that, when reflection factors are considered (they may vary from approximately 70% for most metals to as high as 98% for metals such as silver and gold), typical absorbed power concentrations are on the order of 6.5×10^5 W/in² $(1 \times 10^5$ W/cm²) or less. Actual energies and pulse lengths necessary are determined empirically for each material, according to penetration and spot size desired.

The welding ability of a pulsed laser is determined by both its energy-per-pulse capacity and its average-power-output capability. In

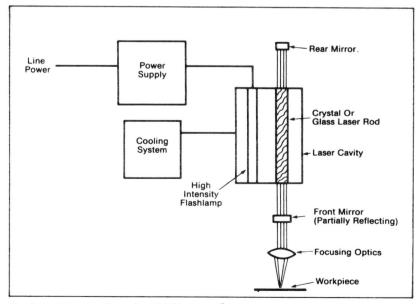

Fig. 2-4 Elements of a pulsed LBW system.[5]

general, a high energy-per-pulse capacity is necessary for the production of welds of a substantial size (penetration and nugget diameter). Desired product throughput (spot welds per second or seam weld rate) affects the average power capability required.

There are several CO_2-type lasers commercially available. One is a convectively cooled closed-cycle CO_2 laser which is capable of a maximum power output of 2 kW. Since this is a convectively cooled system it should be readily amenable to adaptation, and higher power level units are being designed.

Other suppliers have multikilowatt, CW CO_2 laser systems available. An example in Fig. 2-5 is a 6-kW unit equipped with extensive tooling and computer control for an automotive-underbody welding application.[6,7] In the unit, excitation is provided by a direct-current, high-voltage discharge and zinc selenide output optics are utilized.

A 10-kW CO_2 laser system (HPL-10) is shown schematically in Fig. 2-6, and an advanced 15-kW system is shown in Fig. 2-7. The compact system utilizes electron-beam discharge stabilization to provide high power output. One of the difficulties with gas tube lasers is that the available output power for a given tube length is limited by two factors: the ability to cool the gas and to stabilize the gas discharge. However, these two factors have been overcome.

In the HPL-10, the working gas is pumped at high speed normal to

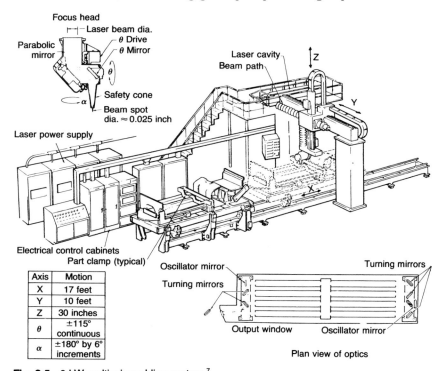

Axis	Motion
X	17 feet
Y	10 feet
Z	30 inches
θ	±115° continuous
α	±180° by 6° increments

Fig. 2-5 6-kW multiaxis welding system.[7]

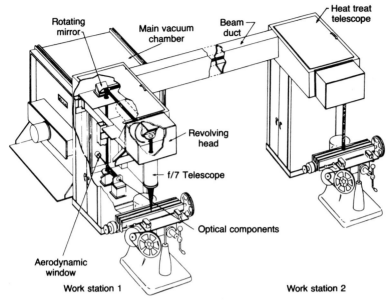

Fig. 2-6 Schematic of 10-kW CO_2 laser system.

the direction of the emitted laser beam. The heated gas is thus removed from the laser cavity by cross flow and is then passed through a heat exchanger before it is returned. The system operates like a closed-cycle wind tunnel, and the thermal restraints on power output are greatly reduced.

The discharge is stabilized by preionization of the gas using a board-area electron beam. The preionization technique makes for geometric freedom of the laser cavity because the volume per unit length is no longer limited by the maximum diameter of the cavity. The cross-flow/electron-beam preionization combination allows the laser to reach power levels over 15 kW, see Fig. 2-7.

At the very high power levels of this system there are no reliable window materials available to allow transmission of the laser beam from the low-pressure laser cavity to the atmosphere. For this reason the HPL-10 uses an "aerodynamic window"—a hole in the laser chamber wall with an annular set of exhaust vanes designed to balance the pressure differential between the chamber and the atmosphere while preventing any exchange of air and gas. This hole allows photons to pass freely, but discourages the leakage of air in or of the gas working medium out, Fig. 2-6.

Once the beam is outside the lasing chamber, it passes through a beam director, which focuses it into the workpiece through appropriate optics. In fact, at this point any number of work stations can be coupled to the laser beam through the use of appropriate mirrors to deflect the original beam and aim it to another station. Such time-sharing techni-

Fig. 2-7 Newly developed 15-kW HPL system.[8]

ques can greatly increase the utilization of the laser system by allowing several time-synchronized operations, such as those on a production line, to use the same laser source. If a part requires two different processes, such as welding and heat treatment, one work station could be set up for welding and the other could perform the heat treatment.

In addition to the currently available commercial systems described here, convectively cooled, multikilowatt laser systems are being developed by several companies.[9,10] It is obvious that potential users of high-power, industrial laser equipment may soon have a broad range of units from which to select the most appropriate for their application.

JOINT DESIGN

Most weld-joint geometries used in conventional fusion-welding processes are suitable for LBW. It must be remembered, however, that the laser beam is focused to a spot of only a few thousandths of an inch, and fit-up tolerances and alignment requirements are also on that order of magnitude. The most frequently used laser weld geometries are the butt, lap, and flange types.

Butt joint, full-penetration type: It is not necessary to bevel the edges of material to be laser-welded, and sheared edges are acceptable if they are square and straight. Fit-up tolerance should be closer than 15% of material thickness, as shown in Fig. 2-8a, to avoid laser beam wandering. Misalignment and out-of-flatness of the parts should be less than 25% of the thickness of the material. Transverse alignment should be within 0.005 in (0.13 mm). Compressive clamping of the material is recommended; buckling is not a problem unless the material to be welded is thinner than 0.010 in (0.25 mm).

Lap joint, burn-through, or seam-type weld: Air gaps between the pieces to be welded severely limit the penetration and/or rate of the weld. Compressive clamping as shown in Fig. 2-8*b* should be used to maintain separation less than 25% of the material thickness. Welding a 0.002-in (0.05-mm) foil would require a separation of 0.0005 in (0.01 mm) or less which clearly presents a challenge to the tool designer. When materials of different thicknesses are welded, the thinner material should be welded to the thicker.

Flange joint: Most comments about butt joints also are directly applicable to flange joints. Straight, square edges, good fit-up, compressive clamping and precise transverse alignment are all necessary. This geometry is a good choice for welding materials with high shrinkage rates, such as aluminum.

Typical results from the aforementioned joint designs are presented in Table 2-2. A recently completed study[11] utilizing a 5-kW CW CO_2 laser evaluated the aforementioned joints and others, Fig. 2-9, proved the successful joining of cold-rolled steel for automotive applications.

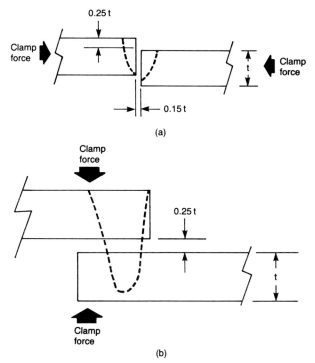

Fig. 2-8 Clamping and tolerances for (*a*) butt joint and (*b*) lap joint. Dimensions are in units of material thickness *t*.

TABLE 2-2
CW CO$_2$ LBW, Typical Results

Material	Thickness		Rate		Weld		Remarks
	in	mm	in/min	mm/s	in	mm	
Butt Welds							
321 stainless steel	0.005	0.13	90	38.1	0.018	0.45	Full penetration
321 stainless steel	0.010	0.25	35	14.8	0.028	0.71	Full penetration
321 stainless steel	0.0165	0.42	11	4.7	0.030	0.76	Partial penetration
17-7 stainless steel	0.005	0.13	110	46.5	0.018	0.45	Full penetration
302 stainless steel	0.005	0.13	50	21.2	0.020	0.50	Full penetration
302 stainless steel	0.008	0.20	30	12.7	0.020	0.50	Full penetration
302 stainless steel	0.010	0.25	10	4.2	0.040	1.00	Full penetration
Inconel 600	0.004	0.10	150	63.5	0.010	0.25	Full penetration
Inconel 600	0.010	0.25	40	16.9	0.018	0.45	Full penetration
Nickel 200	0.005	0.13	35	14.8	0.018	0.45	Full penetration
Monel 400	0.010	0.25	15	6.0	0.025	0.60	Full penetration
Commercial pure titanium	0.005	0.13	140	59.2	0.015	0.38	Full penetration
Commercial pure titanium	0.010	0.25	50	21.2	0.022	0.55	Full penetration
Lap Fillet Welds							
Tin-plated steel	0.012	0.30	20	8.5	0.030	0.76	Full penetration
302 stainless steel	0.016	0.40	175	74.0	0.030	0.76	Partial penetration
302 stainless steel	0.030	0.76	30	12.7	0.025	0.60	Partial penetration
302 stainless steel	0.010	0.25	15	6.0	0.025	0.60	Full penetration
Corner Weld							
321 stainless steel	0.010	0.25	20	8.5			
Edge Welds							
321 stainless steel	0.005	0.13	85	36.0			Weld type 1
321 stainless steel	0.010	0.25	25	10.6			Weld type 1
321 stainless steel	0.0165	0.42	15	6.0			Weld type 2
17-7PH stainless steel	0.005	0.13	45	19.0			Weld type 1
Inconel 600	0.004	0.10	160	67.7			Weld type 1
Inconel 600	0.010	0.25	35	14.8			Weld type 1
Inconel 600	0.0165	0.42	25	10.6			Weld type 2
Nickel 200	0.005	0.13	18	7.6			Weld type 1
Monel 400	0.010	0.25	25	10.6			Weld type 1
Ti-6Al-4V alloy	0.020	0.50	27	11.4			Weld type 2

TABLE 2-3
Comparison of EBW and LBW Processes

Characteristic	Laser	Electron beam
Heat generation	Low	Moderate
Weld quality	Excellent	Excellent
Weld speed	Moderate	High
Initial costs	Moderate	High
Operating/maintenance costs	Low	Moderate
Tooling costs	Low	High
Controllability	Very good	Good
Ease of automation	Excellent	Good
Range of dissimilar materials	Very wide	Wide

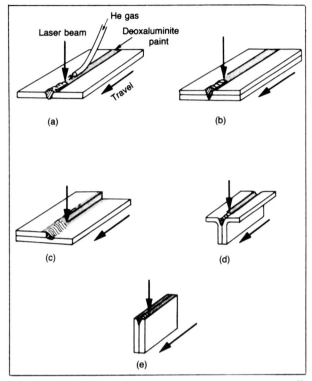

Fig. 2-9 Five types of weld joints for automotive applications.[11]
(a) Full-penetration bead on plate; (b) seam weld on lap joint; (c)
fillet weld on lap joint; (d) flare vee-groove weld in coach joint; (e)
square-groove weld in edge joint.

ADVANTAGES, DISADVANTAGES, AND ECONOMICS

Perhaps the best way to locate the niche of laser metalworking is via
comparison with the better-known welding methods. LBW most closely
resembles EBW since both processes use a stream of energy to fuse
metals to be joined. In EBW electrons supply the energy, whereas
lasers utilize light. For a comparison of the two processes see Table 2-3.
With resistance spot welding, the best welds require a close adherence
to proper part-design practices. The main disadvantages are its limited
material range and the influence of current flow through the part on
previous spot welds or on the material itself. For other comparisons see
Table 2-4. When low currents (below 10 A) are required to make a
weld, the gas-tungsten arc is unstable and is very sensitive to joint
mismatches or electrode standoff. The main advantage of gas-tungsten
arc is the price of equipment. For other comparisons see Table 2-5. A
comparison of LBW and plasma-arc welding (PAW) techniques would
be difficult, since they are used in different areas, the former for
small-part welding and the latter for large parts.

There are inherent advantages associated with LBW:

- No direct contact with the weld area is required, permitting welding through a glass window or some desired atmosphere, since the heat source is a light beam.
- Welds all metals: welds involving even dissimilar metals are possible since high power density can fuse metals of widely varying physical properties.
- Precise, well-defined welds: microwelding applications are possible because of the extremely small spot, on the order of 0.005 in (0.13 mm), which can be obtained.
- Small heat-affected zones: the extent of heat-affected zones is small, permitting welds to be made close to heat-sensitive parts.
- Ability to weld at right angles or in areas impossible to reach by conventional processes, since the laser beam can be reflected by a mirror.
- Lack of effect of magnetic fields on the laser beam.

LBW has its limitations, since the CW multikilowatt systems, at present, are bulky and expensive. Thus, they are only practical for applications which are not weldable by the conventional processes. The accuracy of parts to be welded and fixtures to hold these parts must be closely controlled since another problem of LBW is part fit-up.

SAFETY

Light can create atomic radiation from an impinged surface. However, to be measured or be significant, tremendous amounts of light energy are necessary. The wavelength of the impinging light also plays an important role in the amount and the character of the radiation.

The vapor plume provides intense ultraviolet, white-light, and infrared radiation, especially at higher welding power. LBW presently does not pose any atomic radiation problems; however, the higher

TABLE 2-4
Comparison of Resistance Spot Welding and LBW Processes

Characteristic	Laser	Resistance
Heat generation	Low	Moderate to high
Weld quality	Excellent	Good
Weld speed	Moderate	Moderate
Initial costs	Moderate	Low
Operating/maintenance costs	Low	Low
Tooling costs	Low	High
Controllability	Very good	Low
Ease of automation	Excellent	Fair
Range of Dissimilar materials	Very wide	Narrow

TABLE 2-5
Comparison of GTA Welding and LBW Processes

Characteristic	Laser	Gas-tungsten arc
Heat generation	Low	Very high
Weld quality	Excellent	Excellent
Weld speed	Moderate	High
Initial costs	Moderate	Low
Operating/maintenance costs	Low	Low
Tooling costs	Low	Moderate
Controllability	Very good	Fair
Ease of automation	Excellent	Fair
Range of dissimilar materials	Very wide	Narrow

energies of the future will have to be carefully analyzed; both as to atomic ultraviolet and infrared secondary radiation.

The most important safety hazard from lasers is damage to the eye retina, which can occur at very low output levels. The laser outputs are in the wavelength where the eye itself will tend to focus the light to the most critical eye area—the retina. Any laser, regardless of size, is a potential eye hazard. This does not mean the equipment is dangerous if properly utilized. The hazard is from improper use. There are no complete guidelines established for laser eye safety. Some suggested and recommended procedures are as follows: (1) The equipment should be designed with all safety considerations. This includes fail-safe viewing apparatus so that the laser cannot operate while not welding, and fail-safe prevention of operation by possible unauthorized personnel. (2) Not only the operator, but also personnel in the general area, should be educated about the hazards of direct and indirect laser light. (3) Partitions and opaque surfaces should be provided to protect people in the general area, or any unsuspecting visitors. (4) Warning signals or lights should be provided to alert unsuspecting visitors, passers-by, etc. (5) Continuous and regular inspection of mechanical safety alarms, solenoid relays, etc. (6) High-voltage safety systems such as limit switches, dumping relays, and audio pulsing alarms should be inspected regularly. (7) Stringent rules should be observed regarding misuse of the laser optics and the equipment in general. (8) Operational rules should require that more than one person be responsible for laser safety. Safety maintenance depends not only on a knowledge of the physics of objects, but an ability to guess what the equipment or people might do.

OSHA has incorporated the ANSI Z-136.1 1973 standard ("Safe Use of Lasers") into broader OSHA regulations. All installations of laser equipment must conform to OSHA requirements, and enclosures or housings must be completely safe for use in an open manufacturing area.

Electrical hazards associated with laser devices are comparable to those encountered with electron-beam welders and RF equipment, and require similar safety measures.

MATERIALS

A large variety of alloys (steel, heat-resistant, titanium, aluminum) have been welded with the pulsed or CW laser. It is evident that most LBW effort has been expended and the greatest capability has been accomplished with the ferrous alloys, followed by titanium and aluminum alloys, respectively. Until the first reported demonstration of deep-penetration LBW,[4] most welds were performed by pulsed lasers.[12] Table 2-6[7,12] describes various plate thicknesses of different materials which have been laser-welded.

TABLE 2-6
Materials Welded by High-Power Lasers[7,13]

Material	Thickness		Laser power, kW
	in	*mm*	
Ship steel, grades A, B, C	1.125 butt	28.6	12.8
	1.0 butt	25.4	12.0
	0.75 butt	19.0	12.0
	0.625 butt	15.9	12.0
	0.50 butt	12.7	12.0
	0.375 butt	9.5	10.8
	0.375 to 0.5 tee	9.5 to 12.7	11.9
Low-alloy carbon steel	0.375 to 0.5 tee	9.5 to 12.7	7.5
AISI 4130	0.60 butt	15.2	14
Low-alloy high-strength steel 300M	0.75 butt	19.0	14
Arctic pipeline steel X-80	0.52 butt	13.2	12
D6AC steel	0.25 butt	6.4	15
	0.50 butt	12.7	15
HY-130 steel	0.25 butt	6.4	5.5
HY-180 steel (HP9-4-20)	0.062 butt	1.6	5.5
	0.062	1.6	10.5
	0.64	16.3	5.5
Titanium alloy 6AL4V	0.60 butt	15.2	13.5
	0.125, 0.25	3.2, 6.4	5.5
Nickel-base alloy—Inco 718	0.57 butt	14.5	14
Stainless steel-AISI 321	0.57 butt	14.5	14
Aluminum alloy:			
2219	0.50 butt	12.7	13
2219	0.25 butt	6.4	5
2219	0.25 butt	6.4	16
5456	0.125 butt	3.2	5.5
5456	0.187 butt	4.7	5.5

Power: 5 kW

Speed: 60 ipm (2.54 cm sec)

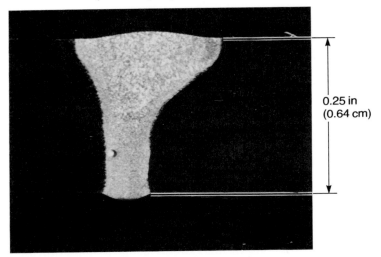

0.25 in
(0.64 cm)

Fig. 2-10 Laser weld in Type 2219 aluminum alloy.[7]

Aluminum and Its Alloys

In LBW studies[14] using the high-power CO_2 laser, aluminum alloys have proven to be most difficult to weld due to the high initial surface reflectivity for CO_2 laser radiation. The main difficulty in the formation of laser welds in aluminum alloys has been the generation of porosity, which is also the area of greatest difficulty in arc welding. Some success, however, has been achieved in LBW of 2219 alloy, Fig. 2-10, and 5456 alloy, Fig. 2-11. Both of these materials have been welded in thicknesses up to 0.375 in (9.5 mm) with acceptable bead geometry and microstructure. It has not yet been possible to completely eliminate porosity. Tensile tests on these welds resulted in failure by diagonal shear through the welds at an average strength of 49.7 ksi (342 MPa) vs. a parent-metal ultimate tensile strength (UTS) of 50 ksi (345 MPa). Results of laser butt-weld bend tests over a 1-in (25.4-mm) radius, seen

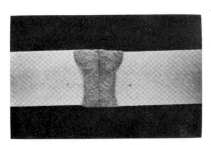

Fig. 2-11 Laser weld and bend test specimen of Type 5456 aluminum alloy.[7]

Fig. 2-12 Laser butt weld bend test.[13]

in Fig. 2-12, were acceptable.[12] Bend-test results of laser fillet welds, tee-to-plate, are shown in Fig. 2-13.[12] The web tee extrusion of Al alloy 5456, 0.125 in (3.2 mm), was welded to Al alloy 5456, 0.187 in (4.7 mm), sheet metal. In addition, Fig. 2-13 shows the different resultant bend configurations of fillet welds using a web with and without an upset web, as well as the bend configurations of a GMAW 0.125-in (3.2-mm) fillet, welded tee to plate, of identical materials for comparison purposes. All specimens were bent under identical bending conditions. The results of the tests indicate the following:

Fig. 2-13 Fillet weld bend test.[13]

- The laser fillet weld joint without the upset web produced a very minimal fillet reinforcement and after bending produced the sharpest bend radius; however, the laser weld did not fracture.

Steels

Although full-penetration 0.25-in (6.4-mm) stainless steel welds were first formed in 1969,[15] little, if any, formal characterization work on these earliest welds was conducted. Tests and examination of a deep-penetration laser weld in 0.125-in-thick (3.2 mm) Type 304 stainless steel was found to be acceptable under x-ray evaluation.[4] This weld specimen failed in the base metal when tensile tested. It was also noted at this time that the laser welds examined showed less tendency for underbead spiking than electron-beam welds. At the same time, the capability for LBW of rimmed steel sheet was evaluated, and it was noted that although the welds possessed some gas porosity, the characteristics of these welds appeared to be suitable for automotive sheet-metal joining applications. Results in HY-alloy steels were evaluated and reported in 1972.[16] These initial welds in HY-130 exhibited embrittlement and low fracture toughness as compared with base metal; however, it was also noted that welds having tensile and Charpy-impact strengths equivalent to or greater than base metal had been formed in several low-carbon and low-alloy steels. It was anticipated that problems in the HY steels could probably be solved by improved gas shielding, with possible use of preheating, postheating, or filler metal addition.

More recently, detailed analysis of the mechanical properties of laser welds in several ferrous-base alloys has been made. Fracture toughness test results of laser-beam-welded modified 4340 alloy have been excellent. Figure 2-14 depicts the typical weld joints that have been

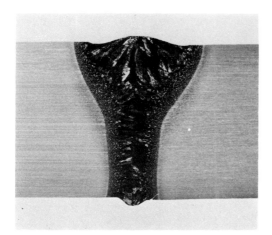

Fig. 2-14 Weld cross section of modified Type 4340 alloy 0.5-in (12.7-mm) laser weld.[17]

attained.[17] These include tanker construction steels,[18] HY-130 alloy,[19] and X-80 Arctic pipeline steel.[20] In the study of the applicability of LBW to merchant ship construction, grades A, B, and C ship steel were welded in thicknesses ranging from 0.375 in (9.5 mm) to 0.5 in (12.7 mm) for grade A; 0.5 in (1.27 mm) to 0.75 in (19.0 mm) for Grade B; and 1.0 in (25.4 mm) to 1.125 in (28.6 mm) for grade C. See Table 2-7. These steels are all in the 0.23% maximum carbon, 0.60–1.03% Mn class, and increase in deoxidation from grades A through C. Welding was accomplished with a CW, convectively cooled, high-power CO_2 laser at power levels from 5.5 to 12.8 kW. At these power levels, it was necessary to weld the 0.75-in- and 1.0-in-thick (19.0 and 25.4 mm) materials in two passes, one from each side.

Material properties of the welds are summarized in Table 2-8.[7] All welds made within the thickness capability of the equipment passed x-ray inspection, but porosity appeared at the roots of deeper welds which were somewhat marginal in penetration. The generation of root porosity was deemed to be speed/power related. Root porosity in dual-pass welds was thought to be related to evolution of gas without sufficient time for removal from the melt and was reduced by appropriate selection of welding parameters.

Tensile properties of welds in grades A, B, and C steel were shown to be excellent, with fractures occurring in the base plate rather than the welds. Adequate weld ductility was demonstrated with side bend tests. Charpy impact tests were also conducted as a qualitative demonstration of weld soundness in this material, which is not impact qualified. In conclusion,[18] high-power laser systems offer significant potential for shipyard applications. Autogenous, deep-penetration laser welds exhibited mechanical properties which compared favorably with conventional arc welds using filler metal. Since the weld energy per unit

TABLE 2-7
Demonstration Butt Welds[13]

Thickness		Laser power, kW	Weld speed		Comment
in	mm		in/min	mm/s	
0.375	9.5	10.8	50	21.2	Single pass
0.375	9.5	10.8	45	19.0	Single pass
0.5	12.7	12.0	27	11.4	Single pass
0.5	12.7	12.0	30	12.7	Single pass
0.625	15.9	12.0	24	10.2	Single pass
0.75	19.1	12.0	45	19.0	Dual pass
1.0	25.4	12.0	30	12.7	Dual pass
1.0	25.4	12.0	30	12.7	Dual pass
1.125	28.6	12.8	27	11.4	Dual pass
0.375–0.5	9.5–12.7	11.0	90	38.1	Tee joint
0.375–0.5	9.5–12.7	7.5	65	27.5	Tee joint
1.0	25.4	12.0	27	11.4	Dual pass*
1.0	25.4	12.0	25	10.6	Dual pass*

*0.001-in (0.03-mm) aluminum foil preplaced at weld interface.

TABLE 2-8
Weld Properties of Tanker Construction Steels[7]

Number and grade	Thickness		X-ray	Tensile	Side bend	Charpy impact energy at 0°F (−15°C)			
						Weld		Haz	
	in	mm				ft-lb	J	ft-lb	J
1-A	0.375	9.5	OK	Failure in base plate	OK	14.3	19.4	12.7	17.2
2-A	0.375	9.5	OK	Failure in base plate	OK	8.0	10.8	10.3	14.0
3-A	0.5	12.7	OK	Failure in base plate	OK	9.7	13.1	7.3	9.9
4-A	0.5	12.7	OK	Failure in base plate	OK	11.7	15.8	11.7	15.8
5-B	0.625	15.9	OK	Failure in base plate	OK	36.0	48.8	14.0	19.0
6-B	0.75	19.0	OK	Failure in base plate	OK	10.7	14.5	5.0	6.8
7-C	1.0	25.4	Aligned root porosity	Failure in base plate	OK	12.7	17.2	11.7	15.8
8-C	1.0	25.4	Aligned root porosity	Failure in base plate	OK	26.7	36.2	15.3	20.8
9-C	1.125	28.6	Large scale porosity	No mechanical tests					
12-C	1.0	25.4	OK	Failure in base plate	OK	8.8	11.9	5.3	7.1
13-C	1.0	25.4	OK	Failure in base plate	OK	8.0	10.8	11.5	15.6

length is relatively low, narrow fusion and heat-affected zones were obtained and thermal distortion was reduced to a minimum.

LBW of longitudinal or spiral seams for line pipe offers the possibility of making square butt welds without filler and with decreased edge preparation requirements. A high-strength, low-alloy material, X-80 Arctic pipeline steel,[13,20] was successfully laser-welded by both single- and dual-pass techniques in 0.52-in (13.2-mm) thickness. Dual-pass welds exhibited smaller grain structure than single-pass welds and the upper shelf energy for dual-pass welds was also in excess of 264 ft-lb (358 J) and the transition temperature was below −60°F (−51°C), Table 2-9. The results of this investigation showed that X-80 alloy can be laser-welded to provide direct-fusion, square-butt welds with mechanical properties exceeding those of the base metal. Prospects for the potential application of high-power LBW to the production of high-quality, large-diameter pipe appear highly promising for this material.

Weld parameter results shown in Table 2-10 and subsequent testing, Table 2-11 indicate that direct laser butt-welding of HY-130 and HY-180 steels in thicknesses suitable for high-speed surface vessel fabrication is a highly feasible process. Further LBW tests are required for these high-yield-strength steels with principal attention directed toward the process of weld metal refinement during the welding process. Emphasis should be placed on establishment of conditions for attainment of maximum zone refinement and anticipated maximum improvement in weld-zone strength and ductility.

Another steel, D6AC, has been laser-welded, and good-quality welds were achieved in 0.25- and 0.5-in (6.5- and 12.7-mm) thicknesses with a CW laser at 15 kW. For the D6AC steel, a limited amount of preheating at 450°F (232°C) is needed to prevent cracking. The resultant welds appear to be free of porosity. The 0.25-in (6.4-mm) welds were

TABLE 2-9
Impact Test Results for Dual-Pass Laser Welds[13]

Specimen number	Test temperature		Notch configuration and direction*		Charpy energy		Comment
	°F	°C			ft-lb	J	
1	−100	−73.3	Side	i	12.5	16.9	Visible pores in fracture
2	−24	−31.1	Side	o	245.0	332.2	One pore in fracture
3	70	21.1	Side	i	185.0	250.8	Grouped porosity at one corner
4	−18	−27.8	Side	o	160.0	216.9	Small pores only
5	−62	−52.2	Side	i	>264.0	358.0	Fine root porosity
6	−60	−51.1	Side	o	>264.0	358.0	Fine root porosity
7	−105	−76.1	Side	o	16.0	21.7	Considerable porosity in plate
8	−21	−29.4	Side	i	44.0	59.7	Considerable porosity in plate
9	−18	−27.8	Side	i	163.0	221.0	Considerable porosity in plate
10	−103	−75.0	Side	o	38.5	52.2	Considerable porosity in plate
11	−100	−73.3	Side	i	96.0	130.2	Fine root porosity
12	−24	−31.1	Side	o	39.0	52.9	Fine root porosity
13	−100	−73.3	Side	o	34.5	46.8	Planar defect and pores
14	70	21.1	Side	i	239.5	324.7	Considerable porosity
15	−80	−62.2	Side	o	22.0	29.8	Considerable porosity
16	−100	−73.3	Side	i	23.5	31.9	Large flaw
17	−40	−40.0	Side	o	178.0	241.3	
18	−20	−28.9	Side	i	226.0	306.4	
19	−20	−28.9	Side	o	>246.0	358.0	
20	75	23.9	Side	i	247.0	334.9	Small pore
21	−100	−73.3	Side	o	198.0	268.4	
22	−80	−62.2	Side	i	7.5	10.2	
23	−38	−38.9	Side	o	>264.0	358.0	
24	−80	−62.2	Side	i	6.0	8.1	
25	−80	−62.2	Side	o	68.0	92.2	

*i—in welding direction; o—opposite welding direction.

TABLE 2-10
LBW Test Parameters[13]

Material	Thickness in	Thickness mm	Weld type	Laser power, kW	Weld speed in/min	Weld speed mm/s	Number of pieces
HY-130 steel	0.25	6.4	Butt	5.5	50	21.2	3
HY-180 steel	0.062	1.6	Butt	5.5	160	67.7	2
HY-180 steel	0.062	1.6	Lap	5.5	140	59.2	1

TABLE 2-11
Results of Impact Tests on HY-130 Laser Welds[13]

Welding speed in/min	Welding speed mm/s	Temperature °F	Temperature °C	Weld impact strength ft-lb	Weld impact strength J	Base-metal impact strength ft-lb	Base-metal impact strength J
45	19.0	30	−1.1	39.0	52.9	26.4	35.8
45	19.0	75	24	39.0	52.9	27.0	36.6
35	14.8	75	24	28.3	38.4	24.0	32.5
20	8.5	75	24	27.0	36.6	25.0	33.9

extremely consistent and reproducible, and preliminary tensile tests in both 0.25- and 0.5-in (6.4- and 12.7-mm) weld specimens resulted in fracture within the base metal, indicating a high-quality weld.[21]

The mechanical and metallurgical properties of welds in low-carbon and high-strength, low-alloy(HSLA)-grade steels used in actual industrial applications has been found most satisfactory.

Properties equivalent to base metal in HSLA steel welds were found,[22] whereas the higher heat input necessary for arc welding often results in a decrease in strength below base metal values in these alloys. One application has been a heater motor yoke assembly for automotive use.

Heat-Resistant Alloys

LBW investigations and feasibility studies have been conducted successfully on many nickel- and iron-base alloys using pulsed and continuous-wave CO_2 lasers.

Laser weld assemblies in 0.25-in-thick (6.4 mm) Inco 718 alloy were fabricated using a continuous-wave CO_2 laser at power levels ranging from 8 to 14 kW. Mechanical properties for the 0.25-in-thick (6.4 mm) weld assemblies are shown in Table 2-12.

Alloys AMS5525 and 5544 (A-286 and Waspaloy), which are materials primarily used for parts requiring high strengths up to 1300 and 1500°F (704 and 816°C) and oxidation resistance up to 1500 and 1750°F (816 and 954°C), have been successfully laser-welded in specimens up to 0.031 in (0.8 mm) with a CW CO_2 laser.[23] Pulsed LBW of René 41 shows that the mechanical performance of welds, Table

TABLE 2-12
Inco 718 Nickel-Base Alloy Tensile Results[13]
Specimen Thickness 0.25 in (6.4 mm)

Description	Identification	Elongation (%)		Ultimate strength			
				Tensile		Yield	
		1 in (25.4 mm)	2 in (25.4 mm)	ksi	MPa	ksi	MPa
Transverse	TTB-1N		16.4	201.1	1387	175.7	1211
base metal	TTB-2N		16.4	201.0	1386	177.6	1225
Longitudinal	LTB-1N		17.0	204.1	1407	177.9	1227
base metal	LTB-2N		20.0	204.3	1409	178.6	1231
Longitudinal	ALT-1N		5.2	200.2	1380	174.6	1204
welded	ALT-2N		10.5	200.0	1379	173.2	1194
	ALT-3N		6.0	198.5	1369	170.2	1174
Transverse	ATT-1N	5.7	3.9	198.8	1371	179.3	1236
welded	ATT-2N	3.1	2.2	194.9	1358	180.9	1247
	ATT-3N	5.0	3.2	197.3	1360	180.4	1244

TABLE 2-13
Tensile Properties of Weld Joints in 0.005 in (0.13 mm) René 41[12]

Condition	Test temperature		Ultimate tensile strength		Yield strength		Elongation in 2 in (50.8 mm), %
	°F	°C	ksi[a]	MPa	ksi[a]	MPa	
Base metal	RT[e]	20	124.8(L)	860	80.7(L)	556	b
			110.3(T)	761	71.8(T)	495	13.5(T)
Welded	RT[e]	20	124.3	859	80.1	552	16.0
Base metal	1000[d]	538	103.4	713	72.2	498	14.2
Welded	1000[d]	538	96.9	668	74.7	515	8.5
Base metal	1400[d]	760	108.5	748	91.5	631	5.0
Welded	1400[d]	760	99.7	687	86.0	593	2.5
Base metal	1800[d]	982	42.6	294	39.0	269	9.8
Welded	1800[d]	982	42.4	292	37.5	259	3.3

[a]L—longitudinal; T—transverse.
[b]Specimens broke outside the 2 in (50.8 mm) gage length.
[c]All values are average of three samples.
[d]At elevated temperatures, welds failed in heat-affected zone.
[e]At room temperature (RT), welds failed in base metal.

2-13, compares quite favorably with the respective base-metal properties. The weld-joint efficiencies ranged from 90 to 100% with only small reductions in ductility. Test specimens failed usually in the base metal or heat-affected zone. The small decreases in ductility are attributed to the as-cast weld structures plus possible interstitial contamination during welding. During the same investigation, the columbium alloy D36 was evaluated, and results similar to those achieved with René 41 were obtained, Table 2-14.

TABLE 2-14
Tensile Properties of Weld Joints in 0.005 in (0.13 mm) Cb D36[12]

Condition	Test temperature °F	°C	Ultimate tensile strength ksi[a]	MPa	Yield strength ksi[a]	MPa	Elongation in 2 in (50.8 mm), %
Base metal	RT[e]	20	73.4(L)	506	64.6(L)	445	15.2
			72.0(T)	496	64.6(T)	445	17.7
Welded	RT[e]	20	76.8	530	69.6	480	10.3
Base metal	1600	871	52.5	362	37.1	256	18.9
Welded	1600[d]	871	50.8	350	40.3	278	7.9
Base metal	1900[d]	1038	37.9	261	34.5	238	35.0
Welded	1900[d]	1038	36.0	248	34.4	237	4.7
Base metal	2200[d]	1204	23.6	163	20.8	143	[b]
Welded	2200[d]	1204	24.0	165	24.0	165	16.5

[a]L—longitudinal; T—transverse.
[b]Specimens broke outside the 2 in (50.8 mm) gage length.
[c]All values are average of three samples.
[d]At elevated temperatures, welds failed in heat-affected zone.
[e]At room temperature (RT), welds failed in base metal.

The most extensive research on LBW of high-temperature alloys has been conducted in Great Britain,[24] where a fast-axial-flow CO_2 laser with an output of up to 2.0 kW has been used to weld nickel-base alloys such as PK33, N75, and C263 and a ferrous-base alloy, Jethete M152, in thicknesses of 0.039 and 0.079 in (1.0 and 2.0 mm). In 0.039-in (1-mm) material, the depth-to-width ratio is nearly unity as the result of parameter selection to promote a slower cooling rate in the weld zone to prevent cracking. In 14 of the 18 tensile specimens of Jethete 152 that were tested, failure occurred in the base metal, away from the weld zone. The Nimonic 75 specimens, however, failed preferentially at the edge of the fusion zone at about 90% of parent-metal strength. Ductility in these specimens was 12 to 13% as compared with 33 to 35% in the parent material. Tensile-test data for the laser-welded ferrous- and nickel-base alloys are summarized in Table 2-15.

For welding nickel- and ferrous-base heat-resistant alloys, it was found that an energy density threshold existed below which the reflectivity of the workpiece was high and prevented useful welding. This has also been found to be true for other metals and alloys. For heat-resistant alloys, it was possible to exceed this threshold only with a low-order-mode laser. Above this threshold, reflectivity was low and the laser energy could be used for welding efficiently. It was concluded that a 2-kW, low-order-mode CO_2 laser could weld a significant amount of material used in aircraft engine fabrication. The nickel- and iron-base alloys appeared to demonstrate good response to LBW and exhibited acceptable mechanical properties in the thickness range shown in Table 2-15.

TABLE 2-15
Tensile Properties of Laser Welds in Nickel-Base and Iron-Base High-Temperature Alloys[7,24]

Alloy and weld or parent material	Nominal thickness		Average UTS		Elongation in 1.98 in (50 mm), %	Fracture location
	in	mm	ksi	MPa		
PK33-W	0.039	1.0	142	982	20.0	Weld
PK33-P	0.039	1.0	147	1014	23.0	—
PK33-W	0.079	2.0	155	1067	26.0	Parent
PK33-P	0.079	2.0	151	1041	27.0	—
C263-W	0.039	1.0	145	1000	31.0	Parent
C263-P	0.039	1.0	141	973	30.0	—
C263-W	0.079	2.0	141	973	23.0	Weld
C263-P	0.079	2.0	143	986	35.0	—
N75-W	0.039	1.0	104	714	13.0	Weld
N75-P	0.039	1.0	117	807	34.0	—
N75-W	0.079	2.0	106	729	18.0	Weld
N75-P	0.079	2.0	117	807	32.0	—
JM152-W	0.039	1.0	129	887	15.0	Parent
JM152-P	0.039	1.0	133	917	16.0	—
JM152-W	0.079	2.0	126	869	11.0	Parent
JM152-P	0.079	2.0	126	869	16.0	—

Titanium and Its Alloys

A comparison study[25] of electron-beam, laser, and plasma-arc welds in Ti-6Al-4V alloy in thicknesses of 0.040, 0.060, 0.080, and 0.250 in (1, 1.5, 2.2, and 6.4 mm) has been conducted. Radiographically sound welds were produced by all three techniques, and all welds exhibited tensile strengths equivalent to or exceeding base-metal values following a stress relief of 2 h at 1000°F (538°C).

Two other investigations are pertinent. One investigation determined the fatigue properties of laser butt welds in 0.230-in (5.8-mm) and 0.14-in (3.6-mm) Ti-6Al-4V sheet.[24] The fatigue properties of the welds showed that, under proper welding conditions, laser welds can be made in Ti-6Al-4V which exhibit base-metal fatigue characteristics. The technique of LBW was concluded to be promising for welding of thin to medium sections of Ti-6Al-4V.

The other investigation[17] determined the laser-weld properties of Ti-6Al-4V in thicknesses from 0.25 to 0.5 in (6.4 to 12.7 mm). Results of tensile tests shown in Table 2-16 were comparable to the properties of the base metal for both the 0.25- and 0.5-in (6.4- to 12.7-mm) thicknesses.

Dissimilar Metals

LBW is sometimes used to weld dissimilar metals when other methods prove unsatisfactory. Combinations shown in Table 2-17 have been successfully welded with a pulsed laser.

TABLE 2-16
Ti-6Al-4V Titanium Alloy Tensile Results[27]

| | | Elongation, % | | Ultimate strength | | | |
| | | | | Tensile | | Yield | |
Description	Identification	1 in (25.4 mm)	2 in (50.8 mm)	ksi	MPa	ksi	MPa
Transverse	TTB-1T	23.6	13.1	160.3	1105	144.6	997
base metal	TTB-2T	21.0	13.3	162.0	1117	148.7	1025
Longitudinal	LTB-1T	24.0	13.2	151.5	1045	144.3	995
base metal	LTB-2T	22.1	13.3	152.3	1050	145.2	1001
Transverse	ATT-1T	4.5	1.5	156.8	1081	154.0	1062
welded	ATT-2T	5.0	1.3	156.3	1078	156.0	1076
	ATT-3T	4.7	0.8	155.8	1074	155.0	1067
Longitudinal	ALT-1T	11.7	7.6	158.0	1089	149.0	1027
welded	ALT-2T		8.3	159.6	1100	148.0	1020
	ALT-3T		6.5	159.8	1102	142.0	979
Transverse	TTB-5T	22.1	13.3	152.0	1048	146.0	1007
base metal	TTB-6T	22.5	15.0	153.0	1055	150.0	1034
Longitudinal	LTB-5T	22.5	14.6	154.0	1062	148.0	1020
base metal	LTB-6T	21.8	13.5	153.0	1055	149.0	1027
Transverse	ATT-7T	25.0	13.3	157.2	1084	148.0	1020
base metal	ATT-8T	11.0	8.2	157.5	1086	146.0	1007
	ATT-9T	24.5	13.7	156.0	1076	147.0	1014
Longitudinal	ALT-7T	16.1	9.5	159.0	1096	148.0	1020
welded	ALT-8T	20.8	12.0	157.0	1083	147.0	1014
	ALT-9T	19.8	12.0	159.0	1096	148.0	1020

TABLE 2-17
LBW of Some Dissimilar Metals[29]

| | Thickness | | | Thickness | |
Metal	in	mm	Metal	in	mm
Nickel wire	0.020	0.50	Tantalum wire	0.025	0.60
	0.020	0.50	Copper	0.015	0.38
	0.020	0.50	Tungsten wire	0.003–0.005	0.08–0.13
	0.005	0.13	Silicon carbide		
Copper wire	0.002–0.003	0.05–0.08	fibers	20 μ	20 × 10⁻³
	0.002–0.003	0.05–0.08	Brass	0.019	0.48
	0.002–0.019	0.05–0.48	Mild steel	0.002–0.003	0.05–0.08
	0.015	0.38	Stainless steel	0.031	0.80
Stainless			Tantalum wire	0.015	0.38
steel wire	0.030	0.76	Tantalum wire	0.025	0.60
Nichrome	0.0025	0.06	Silver-plated		
wire	0.020	0.50	brass	0.040	1.01
René 41	0.005–0.025	0.13–0.60	Monel rod	0.140	3.60
	0.025	0.60	Cb-D 36	0.125	3.20
Phosphor			Hastelloy X	0.025	0.60
bronze wire	0.005	0.13	Palladium	0.005	0.13
Titanium			Gold	0.016	0.40
wire	0.031	0.80	Copper-nickel		
Kovar			Stainless steel		
Columbium			Tungsten		

APPLICATIONS

The unique capabilities of the laser have led to a number of important laser processing applications, Table 2-18. Historically, some of the first

TABLE 2-18
Applications

Welding system	Type of part	Material
Pulsed mode	Pacemaker components and cases	
	Mechanical instrumentation components (flexure assemblies, load-cell covers)	
	Lithium battery sealing	
	Microwave components	Tungsten and molybdenum
	Lamp-terminal feed-throughs	
	Gyroscope bearing assemblies	
	Thermal and magnetic sensor probes	
	High-reliability thermocouples	
	High-speed printer belts	
	Special ordnance parts, such as exploding bolts	
	Strain gages	Ni Span C to 430 stainless steel
	Watch components	Powdered tungsten to 304 stainless steel
	Watch main spring and collet assembly	Free machining brass and spring steel
	Bellows	Beryllium copper to copper
	Capacitor can	Aluminum
	Drive belt	Stainless steel
	Motor brush mounts	Beryllium copper
	Relay can	Nickel-plated steel
	Mercury sensor switch	Inco 123 nickel powder
	Fluorescent lamp	Copper to brass
	Cigar lighters	nichrome to alloy steel
	Collars for klystron tubes	Tantalum to molybdenum
	Fuel pin bundle to tube sheet	304 to 316 stainless steel
	Bridgework for tooth dentures	Chrome-cobalt and palladium-gold
	Thermistors	AISI 1151 steel to 321 stainless steel
Continuous wave	Acid storage battery	Lead
	Lined vessels and pipes	Carbon steel to stainless steel, nickel alloy, titanium, tantalum
	Valves for emission control systems	Steel

Fig. 2-15 Computer-controlled laser.[5]

applications of LBW involved spot welding of very small wires, Fig. 2-15. Currently, most industrial applications involve average pulsed or CW power levels up to approximately 1 kW. A second category of applications, involving laser power levels from 1.5 to 10 kW, is under advanced development and several production applications are imminent. Finally, research is being conducted on a number of potentially important applications at power levels above 10 kW.[8] It is anticipated that this work will contribute significantly to the development of future industrial processes.

Low-Power Applications (<1 kW)

An example of current industrial LBW applications which utilize the precision and control that LBW affords to weld very small parts is the welding of wire leads on small contact wires for wire-wound relays.[30] Three typical pulsed LBW applications are

- *Wire-to-terminal welding.* A variety of materials can be chosen for the terminals, including steels, nickel, Kovar, beryllium copper, and phosphor bronzes. Brass can be used, but not with the flexibility of the others because of the problem of zinc outgassing. The best alloys for terminals have been found to be copper-nickel alloys. Computer-controlled LBW systems are presently performing automated wire-to-terminal welding on relay plates for electronic switching circuits, Fig. 2-15. Another terminal-welding application unique to the laser involves salvaging a defective image-display tube worth several thousand dollars. Because the glass wall of the tube is transparent to the laser light, it is possible to focus through the walls of the tube and create a weld in the vacuum environment of the tube, Fig. 2-16.

- *Seam welding.* Tantalum capacitors have been hermetically sealed in which the capacitor consists of a pressed-powder tantalum slug submerged in a sulfuric-acid electrolyte contained within a pure-tantalum case, which must be welded shut. Further, a glass-to-metal seal insulates the central wire feed-through from the cell body. With LBW, the total heat input is normally very low and can be controlled to weld with very little heat buildup. Some samples have been welded in 30 s with virtually no heat sinking and without damage to either the glass seal or the contents.
- *Mixed spot and seam welding.* A typical jet-engine component welded with a pulsed laser is Waspaloy baffle, Fig. 2-17. The welding consists of a seam weld along the top edge and a series of spot welds to anchor the "comb" to the baffle. Because of the flexibility of the pulsed-laser system, both the seam weld and spot welds are performed on the same equipment with identical energy levels for the two welds.

In addition to the above applications, which are representative of a wide range of present-day industrial LBW applications utilizing pulsed lasers, there are automated LBW transfer lines for manufacturing metal-enclosed gas-protected contacts for telephone switch gear. The first operation joins two armatures to a spring to form a twin contact. Next the contact is bonded to the switch cover, and a separate welding

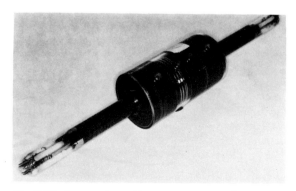

Fig. 2-16 Laser-salvaged image display tube.[5]

Fig. 2-17 Laser-welded Waspalloy jet engine baffle.[5]

station, operating under a protective gas atmosphere, seals the device.

For many years, aerospace manufacturers have been interested in establishing a method for the welding of adhesive-bonded honeycomb panel joints that causes little or no loss of strength of the adhesive bond in the area of the weld. The honeycomb panels shown in Fig. 2-18 were fabricated of Ti-6Al-4V face sheets bonded to a high-temperature polyimide core with polyimide adhesive. The localized heat input of the laser proved ideal for this application. Though the adhesive had to be removed from directly underneath the weld root to avoid contamination and cracking of the weld metal, there was no thermal degradation of the adhesive or core. Not only can large panels be butt-welded to each other, but damaged panels can be repaired by LBW repair plugs in the damaged area.

The design of larger and more powerful jet engines places greater demands on the materials used in their fabrication. Designers often utilize nickel-base heat-resistant alloys because of their high strength at high temperatures. Unfortunately, these alloys are susceptible to microcrack formation in weld heat-affected zones (HAZ), especially in dissimilar combinations. Thus, great difficulty was encountered in the electron-beam joining of Hastelloy X tips to Udimet 700 hollow turbine blades. However, the lack of an HAZ in many laser welds in these

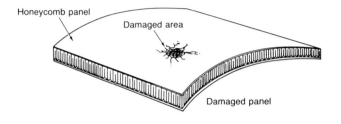

Honeycomb panel

Damaged area

Damaged panel

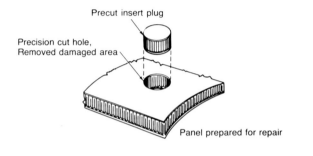

Precut insert plug

Precision cut hole,
Removed damaged area

Panel prepared for repair

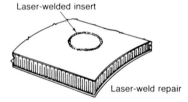

Laser-welded insert

Laser-weld repair

Fig. 2-18 Honeycomb panel repair technique.

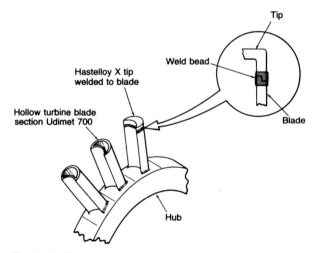

Tip

Weld bead

Hastelloy X tip
welded to blade

Hollow turbine blade
section Udimet 700

Blade

Hub

Fig. 2-19 Required weld joint in jet-engine turbine blade.[31]

materials suggested that microcracking could be avoided by using this process. Figure 2-19 shows a turbine blade fabricated by laser-beam welding of a Hastelloy X tip to a René 41 base section. Metallographic examination revealed the welds to be crack-free.

Medium-Power Applications (1.5 to 10 kW)

Several LBW applications have recently evolved in this power range. Because the laser provides a basis for cost-effective, high-volume production, strong interest has centered around applications in the automotive industry.[29]

The LBW setup for the underbody welding system is shown in Fig. 2-20. The flexibility of the computer-controlled system allows welding parameters for a number of different underbody designs to be stored in the central computer memory and selected as required. Further, since weld parameters may be programmed readily for other designs, the cost of retooling the system to accept new shapes is dependent only on requirements for new clamping structures. The underbody welding offers striking proof of the ability of the laser to produce high-speed welds in large, complex parts.

Current and future applications for LBW are for close-tolerance assemblies in which precision parts can be fixtured closely together for welding. The high power densities used require good part fit-up to obtain quality welds. Conceptually, LBW could be used for many body assembly operations. However, this is not practical today because metal stampings of component parts are too inaccurate to provide proper fit-up requirements. This situation may change gradually in the future.

Fig. 2-20 Laser-beam body-pan seam weld system.[33]

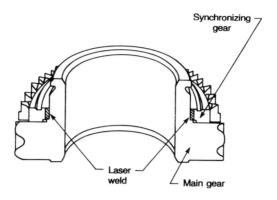

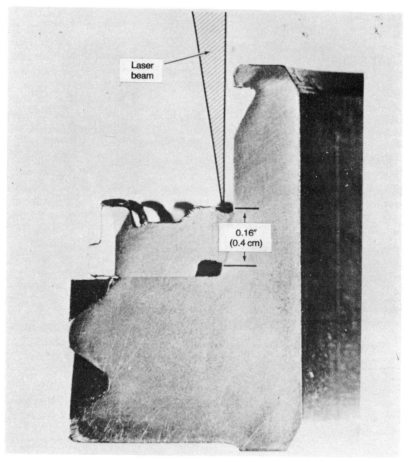

Fig. 2-21 Transmission gear cluster.[34]

Another example of a production LBW application in the medium-power category is a lead-welding process.[30] This application for lead batteries requires a precisely controlled, partial-penetration weld which is readily facilitated by the close control of energy input provided by the laser process. The high welding speed and minimal specific weld energy also promote rapid cooling so that metal does not slump out of the weld zone during processing. A unique capability for high-speed welding of lead is demonstrated by this application. Other sample applications in the medium-power range include welding of transmission gear clusters, Fig. 2-21, and box beams for the automotive industry.

High-Power Welding Applications (>10 kW)

As available laser power increases, more attention is being directed toward heavy industrial welding, where the laser can provide economic advantage over conventional techniques. Relatively little detailed information on heavy section welding has appeared in the literature, although applications have been considered in the areas of thick-wall pipeline welding,[20] shipbuilding,[18] drill bit manufacturing, nuclear plant fabrication, and farm machinery manufacturing. Heavy section welding has been demonstrated in thicknesses up to 1 in (25.4 mm) by welding from both sides.

Basic laser advantages in heavy section welding stem from the lack of filler-metal requirement (which can dominate the welding cost for certain closely controlled, high-strength, low-alloy steel types such as used in gas-line construction), from high welding speed, and from reduced thermal distortion. Further, for quality-critical applications such as the welding of gas lines for use in Arctic environments, unique weld characteristics have been demonstrated with LBW.[20]

Filler-metal addition to welds in 300 series stainless steel has been performed, and these experiments demonstrated that no special difficulties exist in filler-metal addition. It should, therefore, be possible to add filler metal when desirable to change fusion-zone composition to prevent undercut. It has been shown that the weld bead is narrower when filler is added. This is a result in part of the fact that energy is expended in melting the filler which would otherwise be available for melting of the base metal. It was further observed that the welds with filler-metal addition exhibit good melt-back of filler into the base metal.

As commercially available laser power continues to increase and new welding techniques are developed, it is anticipated that many new applications in the area of heavy section welding will be developed with substantial fabrication cost savings to industry. Recently narrow welds in 2-in-thick (50.8 mm) HY-80 steel were formed with a penetration weld by a 77-kW gas dynamic laser system. Other tests on Type 304 stainless steel and HY-80 steel at laser powers up to 100 kW have also been achieved.

REFERENCES

1. Acharekar, M. A., "Lasers," *Weld. Eng.*, pp. 9–11, December 1974.
2. Schaffer, G., "Lasers in Metalworking," AM Special Rep. 679, pp. 42–56, July 1, 1975.
3. Staff Report, "State of the Art in Continuous Nd-YAG Laser Welding," *Met. Prog.*, November 1970.
4. Brown, C. O., and Banas, C. M., "Deep-Penetration Laser Welding," *AWS Annual Mtg.*, San Francisco, April 1971.
5. Bolin, S. R., "Bright Spot for Pulsed Lasers," *Weld. Des. Fabr.*, pp. 74–77, August 1976.
6. Ball, W. C., and Banas, C. M., "Welding With a High-Power CO_2 Laser," SAE 740863, Nat. Aero. Engrg. and Mfg. Mtg., pp. 1–9, October 1–3, 1974.
7. Breinan, E. M., Banas, C. M., and Greenfield, M. A., "Laser Welding—The Present State-of-the-Art," IIW Annual Mtg., Tel-Aviv, Doc. IV-181-75, pp. 1–53, July 6–12, 1975.
8. Bellaforte, D., Avco Everett Research Lab., private communication, March 1978.
9. "British Welding Institute Works with 2 kW, CO_2 System," *Lasersphere*, 3(1), 3, Jan. 15, 1973.
10. "New 10 kW Laser to be Available Shortly," news release, Culham Laboratories, Oxford, England, 1973.
11. Baardsen, E. L., Schmatz, D. J., and Bisaro, R. E., "High Speed Welding of Sheet Steel with a CO_2 Laser," *Weld. J.*, **52**(4), 227–229, April 1973.
12. Schwartz, M. M., "Laser Welding and Cutting," WRC Bull. 167, Nov. 1971.
13. Nagler, H., "Feasibility, Applicability, and Cost Effectiveness of LBW of Navy Ships, Structural Components and Assemblies," Contr. N00600-76-C-1370, vols. 1 and 2, Dec. 22, 1976.
14. Breinan, E. M., and Banas, C. M., "High Power Laser Welding of Aluminum Alloys," unpublished report, United Technologies Research Center, E. Hartford, Conn., 1974.
15. Banas, C. M., "The Role of the Laser in Materials Processing," Canadian Welding and Materials Technol. Conf., Toronto, Sept. 29–Oct. 1, 1969.
16. Banas, C. M., "Laser Welding Developments," *Proc. CEGB Internat. Conf. on Welding Research Related to Power Plant*, Southampton, England, Sept. 17–21, 1972.
17. Seaman, F. D., and Hella, R. A., "Establishment of a Continuous Wave Laser Welding Process," IR-809-3 (1 through 10), AFML Contr. F33615-73-C-5004, October 1976.
18. Banas, C. M., and Peters, G. T., "Study of the Feasibility of Laser Welding in Merchant Ship Construction," Contr. 2-36214, U.S. Dept. of Commerce, Final Report to Bethlehem Steel Corp. August 1974.
19. Breinan, E. M., and Banas, C. M., "Fusion Zone Purification During Welding with High Power CO_2 Lasers," Second Internat. Symp. Japan Welding Society, Osaka, Aug. 25–29, 1975.
20. Breinan, E. M., and Banas, C. M., "Preliminary Evaluation of Laser Welding of X-80 Arctic Pipeline Steel," *WRC Bull.* 201, December 1971.
21. Banas, C. M., "Electron Beam, Laser Beam and Plasma Arc Welding Studies," Contr. NAS 1-12565, NASA, March 1974.
22. Yessik, M., and Schmatz, D. J., "Laser Processing in the Automotive Industry," SME Paper MR74-962, 1974.
23. Alwang, W. G., Cavanaugh, L. A., and Sammartino, E., "Continuous Butt Welding Using a Carbon Dioxide Laser," *Weld. J.*, **48**(3), 110s–115s, March 1969.
24. Adams, M. J., "CO_2 Laser Welding of Aero-Engine Materials," Rep. 3335/3/73, British Welding Institute, Cambridge, England, 1973.
25. Banas, C. M., Royster, D. M., Rotz, D., and Anderson, D., "Comparison of Electron Beam, Laser Beam and Plasma-Arc Welding of Ti-6Al-4V," 56th Ann. Mtg. American Welding Society, Cleveland, Apr. 21–25, 1975.
26. Breinan, E. M., and Banas, C. M., "Fatigue of Laser-Welded Ti-6Al-4V Alloy," *ASM/WRC Conference on Joining of Titanium for Aerospace Applications*, Beverly Hills, CA, Feb. 5–6, 1975.
27. Locke, E., Hoag, E., and Hella, R., "Deep Penetration Welding with High Power CO_2 Lasers," *Weld. J.*, **51**(5), 245s–249s, May 1972.
28. Seretsky, J., and Ryba, E. R., "Laser Welding of Dissimilar Metals: Titanium to Nickel," *Weld. J.*, **55**(7), 208s–211s, July 1976.

29. Mauchel, G. A., "The Laser Arrives ... Finally," *Ind. Res.*, pp. 49–51, August 1973.
30. Gaglinano, F. P., "Interaction of Laser Radiation with Metals to Produce Welds," SME Paper MR74-954, 1974.
31. Kloepper, D., "Laser-Beam Welding Process Development," AFML-TR-70-216, Contr. F33(615)-69-C-1837, September 1970.
32. Ball, W. C., and Banas, C. M., "Welding with a High-Power, CO_2 Laser," SAE Paper 740863, October 1974.
33. Chang, Uck, Ford Mfg. Devel. Center, private communication, March 1978.
34. Seaman, F. D., and Locke, E. V., "Metal-Working Capability of a High Power Laser," SAE Paper 740864, 1974.
35. Arata, Y., and Miyamoto, I., "Some Fundamental Properties of High Power Laser Beam as a Heat Source" (Reports 1, 2, and 3), *Trans.-Jpn. Weld. Soc.*, 3(1), March 1972.
36. Swift-Hook, D. T., and Gick, A. E. F., "Penetration Welding with Lasers," *Weld. J.*, 52(11), 492s–499s, November 1973.
37. Bastien, J., "Application of the Laser to Welding and Machining," *Soudage Tech. Connexes*, 25(11/12), 437–448, November–December 1971.
38. Burwell, W. G., "Review of CW High-Power Laser Technology," UAR-M132, *3d RPI Workship on Laser Interaction and Related Plasma Phenomena*, Rensselaer Polytech. Inst., Troy, NY, August 1973.
39. Benson, L., Nussenbaum, J., and Mulvaney, D., "Laser Welding Simplified," *Amer. Mach.*, pp. 81–85, April 20, 1970.
40. Conti, R. J., "Carbon Dioxide Laser Welding," *Weld. J.*, 48(10), pp. 800–806, October 1969.
41. Arata, Y., Miyamoto, I., and Kubota, M., "Some Fundamental Properties of High Power CW Laser Beam as a Heat Source," Dept. of Weld. Engr., Osaka University, IIW Doc. IV-4-69, pp. 1–14, March 1969.
42 Gerry, E. T., "Industrial Applications of Gasdynamic Lasers," *Amer. Physical Soc. Mtg.*, Washington, DC, April 1970.
43. Estes, C. L., and Turner, P. W., "Laser Welding of a Simulated Nuclear Reactor Fuel Assembly," *Weld. J.*, 53(2), 66s–73s, February 1974.
44. Moorhead, A. J., "Laser Welding and Drilling Applications," *Weld. J.*, 50(2), 97–106, February 1971.

3

PLASMA-ARC, NEEDLE ARC–MICROPLASMA, AND PLASMA-GMA WELDING

PLASMA-ARC WELDING

Plasma, an ionized gas that was little more than a laboratory curiosity a decade ago, is becoming an important industrial tool. Sometimes called "the fourth state of matter," a plasma resembles a gas in many respects, but with an important difference: the particles (atoms or molecules) of a gas do not carry electrical charges. Unless energy is supplied continuously to maintain the plasma, it will degenerate quickly into an ordinary gas. If a plasma has been heated to a condition where it is at least partially ionized it is, therefore, capable of conducting electric current. When an arc is established through the gaseous column separating two electrodes, some of the gas molecules are ionized. The ionized zone, or plasma stream, consists of positively charged ions from the arc gas, an essentially equal number of electrons, and neutral atoms or molecules. A plasma exists to some extent during any arc occurrence. The term "plasma" as applied to arc processes has become associated with constricted-arc techniques. The arc constriction is brought about by forcing the arc through a reducing nozzle as it passes from the electrode to the workpiece.

The plasma-arc process, developed about 25 years ago, has a high degree of arc stability. Most of the early plasma-arc work was mechanized at currents up to 500 A. In recent years, small manually operated systems have been developed for use at currents as low as 0.1 A.[1,2]

THEORY AND PRINCIPLES

The plasma-arc welding (PAW) process is a specialized form of conventional gas tungsten-arc welding (GTAW). In PAW the use of a constricting orifice results in a stable, high-energy, concentrated arc. The constriction of the arc produces a high concentration of energy in the arc column center which takes the form of a stable and unidirectional jet. When an arc is squeezed, its cross section gets much smaller, and the voltage gradient, current density, and heat-transfer intensity increase. Surrounding the arc column adjacent to the nozzle wall is an annular layer of cooler gas having a very steep radial temperature gradient. This relatively cool nonconductive thin layer forms a tube of electrical and thermal insulation which stabilizes the arc and protects the nozzle. For a given current, the gas flow rate must be high enough to sweep out the radial flow of heat to the nozzle. At too low a gas flow or too excessive a current, the protective gas layer is disturbed and punctured—then the nozzle may be damaged by melting or by a phenomenon known as double arcing.

Nozzles

The nozzle is the important part of a plasma gun. It narrows the arc (nozzle bore must be smaller than arc diameter), and keeps the plasma traveling parallel along the length of the nozzle. The smaller the nozzle bore, the higher the temperature. The longer and narrower the nozzle constriction, the more uniform the path of the plasma, the higher the temperature, and the more concentrated the energy. Two types of nozzles are used; a simple one-orifice nozzle and a nozzle having two more orifices perpendicular to the weld axis. The latter one is the more widely used, since it allows for narrower welds and higher speeds than the simple nozzle. See Fig. 3-1.

Transferred and Nontransferred Arc

The gas-tungsten arc is well known and further comments on it are not necessary, except to note that the arc shape is conical and that it expands rapidly as it leaves the electrode. Two arc systems may be used to generate a welding plasma arc, transferred arc or nontransferred arc. The systems are shown schematically in Fig. 3-2. PAW is a dc process and is most often used with the tungsten electrode negative (straight polarity) and the work positive, as a transferred arc. Figure 3-2 also shows how the nontransferred arc operates. Note that a stream

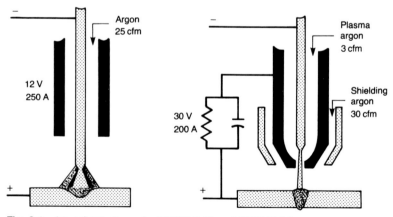

Fig. 3-1 Arc column shape for GTAW (left) and PAW (right).

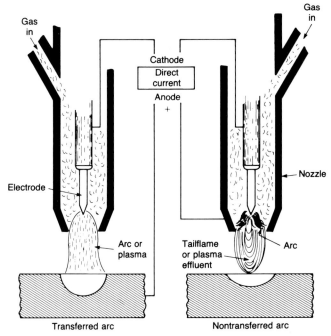

Fig. 3-2 Schematic diagram of a PAW system.

of hot plasma emerges from the plasma arc torch nozzle when either the transferred or the nontransferred arc modes are used.

Transferred arcs are usually preferred for welding because of the greater energy transfer. They do require that the work be electrically conductive. Nontransferred arcs are most often used to weld nonconductive materials as well as for cutting and spraying. A transferred arc sometimes is used as a pilot arc. The latter is used to initiate a transferred arc, and is turned off after the arc has been started. The transferred arc consists of a central core of extremely high temperature surrounded by a sheath of relatively cool gas. The electrical circuit from the electrode is completed through the workpiece. In the nontransferred arc, there is no electrical flow between the electrode or nozzle of the workpiece.

Key Variables

The choice of shielding gas and the orifice gas for PAW is important, but the gases available are the same as those used for GTAW. The shielding and orifice gases are almost always the same; hence, arc effluent variations are avoided. Argon, argon-helium, and argon-hydrogen, the most common gases for PAW, give the best results. The orifice gas ionizes in the arc, and the shielding gas goes through an outer cup to cover the work and surround the arc. The plasma will be wild and uncontrollable if the flow of orifice gas is high enough to also shield the weld. The separate shielding gas provides suitable weld coverage, permitting a low orifice gas flow to give a workable jet.

Argon is suitable for welding all metals, but is not always the best choice. Hydrogen additions to argon make a hotter arc, allow better heat transfer, and permit higher welding speeds. Hydrogen additions cannot be used when reactive metals such as titanium or zirconium are welded. Argon-helium mixtures are used on the reactive metals. Pure helium causes high heat loads on the torch components so it is used only where relatively low heat inputs are needed.

Using a straight helium orifice gas or mixtures over 75% helium with argon overheats the nozzle, and current-carrying capacity in the torch is low. For hotter flames than possible with straight argon, mixtures under 75% helium should be used. In PAW of stainless steels and nickel alloys, a shielding gas of argon-hydrogen mix (to 15% hydrogen) has been found to be the best choice, while argon has been found to be the best choice in joining carbon and high-strength steels.

Weld Modes

The plasma process can be operated in two different welding modes. The first is "puddle-type" or "melt-in" welding. During melt-in welding, the arc impinges on the work and melts it to some depth, but does not penetrate through the work. A low flow of plasma gas is used which will not deform the weld puddle. In general, materials and joints that can be welded with the direct-current, straight-polarity GTA process can also be handled by the puddle-type process, e.g., square butt, fillet, lap, edge, blind tee, and prepared butt joints. The second mode is referred to as keyhole welding. The term keyholing has been applied to a technique whereby the operating parameters are adjusted to produce a plasma jet forceful enough to penetrate completely through the workpiece but not strong enough to expel the molten metal from the joint. This technique produces a small hole which is carried along the weld seam. The metal which has been melted during this cutting action is drawn together immediately behind this hole by surface tension forces to produce the weld bead, without the addition of filler metal.

The advantage of the keyhole mode is the assurance of full penetration. The keyhole can be observed during welding and is an indication of complete and uniform penetration. Filler metals can be added with PAW by the techniques that are conventional for GTAW.

Variations of Current Process

PAW, which started years ago, found its applications in two specific areas, differing from each other by their electrical energy level. At low energy, there is microplasma welding, which operates at current from 0.2 to about 10 A and is applied to light-gage assemblies. Microplasma

TABLE 3-1
Synopsis of the Actual Development of Plasma
from Low- to High-Current Welding (Single Run)

	Microplasma	Intermediate plasma	Conventional plasma
Current, A	0.2–10	10–100	100–300
Operating technique		Melt-in and keyhole	Keyhole
Thickness, in (mm)	0.0008–0.032 (0.02–0.8)	0.020–0.17 (0.5–4.3)	0.10–0.28 (2.5–7.1)

is used either manually or mechanically with the melt-in (or weld-puddle) technique. At high energy, there is conventional PAW operating in the range of 100 to 300 A with the keyhole technique and applied to heavy thicknesses with automatic equipment.

Until recently, PAW has been used only in these two areas, and has been considered as complementary to conventional GTAW process. But some recent developments promise an extension of the scope of PAW in the range of 10 to 100 A, previously regarded as the main field of GTAW and corresponding approximately to thicknesses from 0.020 to 0.2 in (0.5 to 5 mm). The intermediate current for PAW has several advantages over the standard GTAW process and is essentially employed as a manual operation with the melt-in technique.

Table 3-1 indicates approximately, for each range of current plasma arc, the corresponding thicknesses for stainless steel welding.

NEW VARIATIONS TO PLASMA-ARC PROCESS

Pulsed-current methods have been applied to the PAW process. When used with PAW, pulsed current produces a continuously welded seam consisting of overlapping arc spot welds as illustrated in Fig. 3-3.

Pulsed-current operation has a very significant effect on penetration with the plasma process. The use of pulsed current PAW can be extended into the keyhole mode of operation with enhancement of depth-to-width ratio over nonkeyhole full-penetration welds.

A new application is plasma arc plus hot wire. The intense heat of the plasma arc makes it ideal for use in hot-wire welding. When the plasma arc is combined with the arcless deposition technique, it is particularly suited for surfacing. The hot wire provides virtually limitless molten metal addition which wets, and spreads over, the plasma-melted surface. Deposition rates of up to 60 lb/h (7.56 × 10^{-3} kg/s) are not unusual. A wide range of dilution control is possible by changes of the plasma-arc operating condition without a change in the hot-wire operation. Dilution of less than 2% has been achieved.

The high deposition rates possible with plasma arc make it impractical to feed a single wire at the required speed. Therefore, two hot wires or more are used. The ability to use two wires instead of one gives an

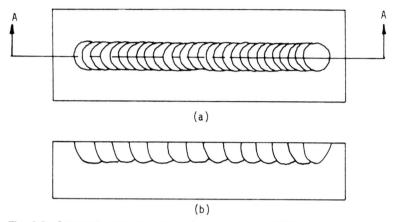

Fig. 3-3 Schematic representations of pulsed-current PAW showing series of overlapping fusions. (a) Top view; (b) section A-A.

added feature to the system. This added feature has virtually eliminated arc blow.

Manual plasma arc, also referred to as needle arc and microarc, is a plasma arc that conforms to all the principles of plasma-arc behavior. It is used in transferred and nontransferred arc modes. This process will be covered later in the chapter.

A very recent development, plasma-GMA, is a process that combines features of the plasma-arc and the inert gas metal arc processes. This process will also be covered in more detail later in the chapter.

EQUIPMENT AND TOOLING

The mechanized PAW equipment consists of a power supply, torch, nozzle and accessory generator, travel devices, and gas supply. The equipment today has both ac and dc capability. The ac mode is generally useful for welding aluminum and magnesium; it tends to lift the oxide and leaves a cleaner weld with fewer inclusions. The dc mode is more useful in welding stainless steel, steel, copper, silicon bronze, and other materials.

Torches are available for straight- or reverse-polarity operation, and

Fig. 3-4 Typical commercial PAW torch.[1]

a torch is shown in Fig. 3-4. Water-cooled power cables are connected at the top of the torch to supply power and cooling water to the electrode. Fittings are provided on the lower torch body for the plasma gas hose, the shielding gas hose, and cooling water for the nozzle.

There are two types of electrodes used in the plasma-arc torch. The tungsten electrode is used for straight-polarity operation and is available in several diameters, depending on the current to be used. A water-cooled copper electrode is used for reverse-polarity operation. The tungsten electrode is usually used for stainless steels and most other metals. The copper electrode is used for aluminum, zirconium, and other reactive metals. One of the advantages of the copper electrode is that it permits the process to operate on reverse polarity. The cleaning action of reverse polarity scours the weld zone free of harmful oxides.

A second advantage involves the welding of metals such as titanium and zirconium. Certain codes prohibit the use of GTAW on these metals because of the risk of tungsten inclusions in the weld. Obviously, a copper electrode eliminates this problem.

The equipment available today is compact, reliable, and easy to maintain. The welding operator must be concerned with only two factors in order to weld with the plasma arc: first, the choice of current rating and hence nozzle or orifice size suitable for a given material thickness; and second, the plasma gas flow rate. The shielding-gas flow rate, in general, is fixed by virtue of the torch cup size and the need for gas coverage. The choice of plasma gas–argon, argon-hydrogen, or argon-helium mixtures—is governed by the current used and material thickness welded.

In most instances fixturing for PAW is similar to that used for GTAW, as seen in Fig. 3-5. The upper plates are adjustable for varying gap width beneath the joint. The plates must be thick enough to produce adequate underbead coverage to accommodate the keyholing plasma, Fig. 3-6. The lower sections of the fixture are movable to permit flat and tee-type welds. For keyholing conditions, the piercing arc is an important factor in tooling design for PAW. The underbead

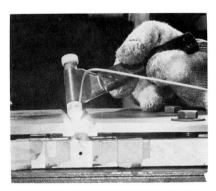

Fig. 3-5 PAW in horizontal position.[3]

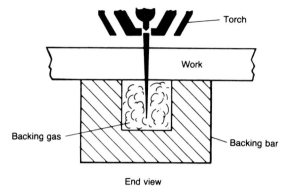

End view

Fig. 3-6 Keyholing sketch.[1]

gas chamber must be approximately 0.75 in (19 mm) × 1.5 in wide (38.1 mm) to prevent weld contamination and to prevent excessive heating of the tooling. It is not necessary, therefore, to employ expensive close-fitting backing bars with their attendant problems of varying chill and mechanical tolerances. This simple backing bar supports the weldment, contains underbead shielding gas, and provides venting for the plasma jet.

JOINT DESIGN

In general, plasma-arc welds can be used with many of the common joint types, including tee, plug, slot, fillet, and longitudinal or circumferential butt welds. A good clean-sheared or saw-cut edge has been found to be adequate joint preparation for most butt-joint applications. The edge preparation must be sufficient to allow a tight, even fit-up. Any substantial gap in the joint will result in a weld less than full cross section. A lack of joint registry may lead to undercutting along one side of the joint.

The face and root side of the joint should be free of all oxide, dirt,

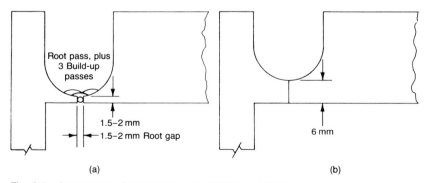

(a)

(b)

Fig. 3-7 Comparison of joint sections by GTAW and PAW.

oil, and other contaminants, since clean starting material is essential to producing a consistent high-quality weld.

From the simple butt-type joints which were the initial joint designs for PAW, the capability has been extended to include a variety of the more complex joints than are common in structural welding. Such joints now include tapered welds, welds from two sides, multipass from one side, and tee joints by burn-down and by burn-through techniques. This has been accomplished for titanium, but the development is essentially and more easily applicable to stainless steels. Figure 3-7 depicts the U joint currently being plasma-arc-welded, a process that is replacing the GTAW process in fabricating table rollers for steel mills.

ADVANTAGES, DISADVANTAGES, AND ECONOMICS

PAW can be used almost every place that GTAW is used. The advantages noted below are nearly always available. PAW is an extension of GTAW; however, because of the nature of the constricted arc, PAW has several advantages over the standard GTAW process:

- Improved arc direction and stiffness leads to improved control of heat input to the work without arc wander or jump.
- Greater welding standoff distances (equivalent to using longer arc length) allow greater tolerance for arc-length variation by the operator, less sensitivity of puddle size to arc-length changes.
- Less sensitivity to mismatch or poor joint fit-up.
- Controlled penetration by use of a keyhole welding technique.

Keyholing is limited to a finite range of material thicknesses. However, experience has shown that this range may be expanded by proper control of the factors involved. Below a minimum material thickness, the hole generated by the plasma column is of sufficiently greater size than the amount of metal melted so that it is not filled. Above a maximum thickness, the plasma column cannot penetrate and pass through the workpiece. The minimum and maximum thicknesses are believed to be determined by the following interrelated factors:

- Size and design of orifice
- Type and amount of orifice gas
- Electrical power input
- Thermal characteristics of the workpiece
- Geometry of the joint, including fit-up

Generally, a single type and size of orifice may be used for a range of material thicknesses by varying the orifice gas flow rate and power input. Keyholing in titanium has been reported for thicknesses from 0.020 to 0.5 in (0.5 to 12.7 mm), but not with a single orifice.

Keyholing is not the only advantage of PAW. It also may be used as a conventional heat source similar to GTAW. In this case the plasma column does not penetrate the workpiece, but impinges on it, and can be used, for example, to make multipass or fillet welds. The major advantage of using plasma arc in this manner is its relative insensitivity to arc length, or length of the plasma column. The heat input to the workpiece remains relatively constant as the arc length is changed, whereas it changes radically in the GTA process. Operator training is easier, and the completed weld is more uniform. A second benefit is almost total freedom from tungsten inclusions in the weld, since the tungsten cannot come in contact with this molten filler metal or weld pool.

The most striking feature of a plasma arc weld made in the keyhole mode is the smooth and consistent root penetration. The root, or back side of the weld bead, tends to be convex with a sharply defined underbead. The import of this may be lost on the designer or materials engineer, but is readily appreciated by those responsible for producing weldments.

A second characteristic is the relatively narrow and parallel-sided fusion zone. This reduces distortion when compared with other arc processes. Depth- (of penetration) to-width (of fusion zone) ratios approaching unity are possible, and are exceeded in commercial processes only by EBW. An axiom of welding states that distortion is inversely proportional to the depth-to-width ratio, all other factors being equal. Distortion is also reduced in comparison with GTAW, because only one pass is required for plasma arc, whereas several may be needed to complete a GTA weld.

Other advantages are

- Higher speeds. Because the plasma arc is a more concentrated, higher-energy heat source it does produce higher welding speeds than GTA, especially on metals with a thickness above 0.125 in (3.2 mm). In addition, plasma is capable of welding stainless steel up to 0.5 in (12.7 mm) thick in a single pass, whereas GTA is normally limited to 0.125 in (3.2 mm).
- Reduced joint preparation. With keyhole PAW it is possible to weld metals up to 0.5 in (12.7 mm) thick with a simple square edge preparation, although at the upper limits a small top-edge vee preparation is sometimes an advantage.

The tungsten electrode in a plasma torch is more effectively cooled and is, therefore, less susceptible to melting.

Whether or not PAW will be more expensive than another welding process will be determined only by careful evaluation of the application and the welding processes.

Equipment. PAW equipment is 2 to 5 times more expensive than GTAW equipment of the same capacity, but is far less costly than EBW equipment of the same capacity.

Maintenance. Cost is greater for PAW than for other arc-welding processes. Frequent replacement of orifices is the principal contributor to the high maintenance cost of PAW equipment.

Productivity. Capability of PAW is high, and its potentiality for high production must be evaluated before it can be determined whether or

TABLE 3-2
Comparison of PAW vs. GTAW for 120-in-Diameter (3 m) Rocket Motor Case

Operations	Cycle time		Personnel	Worker-hours and consumable materials	
	GTA	Plasma arc		GTA	Plasma arc
Preheat, h	2.0	2.0	Electrician	17.5	9.0
Fit-up inspection, h	1.0	1.0	Inspector	1.0	1.0
Weld procedure			Welding engineer	12.0	3.5
inspection, h	1.0	1.0	Welders (2)	24.0	7.0
Weld, h	7.0	1.5	Fitters (2)	22.0	5.0
Interpass cleanup, h	4.0	1.0			
Postheat, h	2.5	2.5	Total worker-hours	76.5	25.5
			Total filler metal, lb (kg)	34 (15)	14 (6)
Total cycle time, h	17.5	9.0	Total inert gas, ft³/h (L/min)	560 (264)	325 (153)

not the high cost of equipment would be justified. In applications where PAW is up to 4 times as fast as alternative processes, equipment costs are rapidly amortized if production quantities are high.

Several examples below show the time and cost savings resulting from the use of PAW in preference to an alternative process.

Three metals used for aerospace components were welded by plasma-arc and gas tungsten-arc processes to compare times required for making welds. Samples welded were 0.25-in-thick (6.4 mm) Type 410 stainless, 0.25-in-thick (6.4 mm) maraging steel (18% Ni), and 0.085-in-thick (2.4 mm) 6Al-4V titanium alloy. PAW took one-fifth to one-tenth as long to complete 100 in (2.5 m) of weld as GTAW, partly because fewer passes were required and partly because travel speed was greater. An example of estimated costs for PAW vs. GTAW in producing 120-in-diameter (3 m) D6AC steel rocket motor cases is shown in Table 3-2. Note that PAW requires about one-half the total cycle time, one-third as many worker-hours, and considerably less filler metal and inert gas to do the job.[4]

Finally, the housings for power relays shown in Fig. 3-8,[2] which are used in aircraft and missiles, were plasma-arc-welded after consideration of soldering, brazing, GTAW, and EBW. Soldering and brazing were eliminated because welding was more convenient, less expensive, and produced better joints. EBW was ruled out because of the high cost of equipment, the welder skill required, and the effect of the vacuum on various electrical components. The PAW equipment and its operation required less welder skill than GTAW. All housings required a hermetic seal, and the plasma-arc operation also satisfied this requirement.

Some limitations have been recorded, however, for PAW.

The plasma-arc torch often is quite large, thus close corner work may be difficult.

A disadvantage of keyhole welding is a tendency to undercut. Undercutting is characterized by a concavity at the edges of the weld, below the original material surface. Undercut tends to become worse as either material thickness or welding speed is increased. There are several methods for reducing or entirely eliminating undercut. For example, a slight decrease in welding speed may be effective in marginal cases. Where undercut is more severe, a wash or cosmetic pass may be used. In this case, a second, nonpenetrating weld pass is made to smooth the weld bead contour. Filler wire may or may not be added, as the situation requires.

A second pass, of course, increases welding costs and requires totally different welding conditions. Another procedure which has been

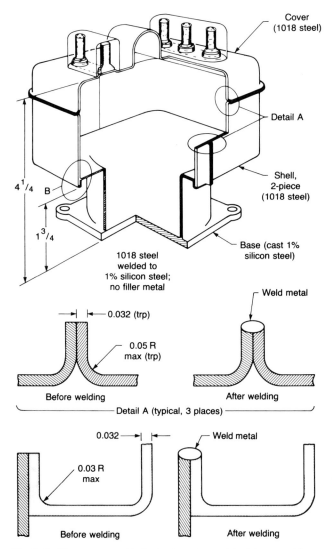

Fig. 3-8 Plasma-arc-welded relay housing and the joints used.[2]

TABLE 3-3
Comparison of PAW with Other Welding Methods

	PAW	GTAW	GMAW	EBW
Equipment cost	Moderate	Low	High	Very high
Welding cost (less equipment)	Low	High	Moderate	Low
Ease of application	Good	Excellent	Fair	Difficult
Ease of welding	Excellent	Good	Difficult	Good
Joint quality	Excellent	Good	Good-fair	Excellent
Wire required	Sometimes	Often	Always	No
Joint (vee) required	No	Often	Always	No
Automatic or manual	Both	Both	Automatic	Automatic
Distortion	Low	High	High	Very low

shown to be of value[5] is to add filler wire while making the keyhole weld. The wire is added ahead of the arc. A relatively small amount of wire addition will eliminate undercut.

Before one chooses one process over another, subjective comparison and consideration should be made. In Table 3-3 is an example of what one should do before making a selection. The obvious conclusions that one may make from this table is that no one welding method is "best" for all the engineering factors which should be evaluated in any given application. Rather, the welding engineer should have a group of evaluation of factors available and use sound judgment in their development.

MATERIALS AND THEIR PROPERTIES

The PAW process has been applied to numerous materials.

Aluminum and Its Alloys

Work performed under government sponsorship[6] investigated the use of plasma arc techniques to weld aluminum alloys for space vehicle applications. The work was primarily directed to the welding of Type 2219 aluminum. The transferred mode was used because of its efficiency in transferring energy to the workpieces. DC reverse polarity produced the most satisfactory welding results with a gas mixture rich in argon as the plasma gas. Under these operating conditions, the workpieces were cleaned cathodically while welding was in progress. Satisfactory welds were made in 0.25-in-thick (6.4 mm) aluminum plate with a tightly butted square-butt joint preparation. Full penetration was assured by keyholing. Ultimate tensile strength of about 37 ksi (255 MPa) was obtained in as-welded Type 2219-T87 plate.

Nickel and Its Alloys

Successful high-quality plasma arc welds have been produced in thicknesses up to approximately 0.3 in (7.6 mm) in alloy 200, essentially pure nickel, alloy 400, nickel-copper, alloy 600, nickel-chrome, and alloy 800, nickel-iron-chrome.[7]

TABLE 3-4
Room-Temperature Tensile Properties

Alloy	Type test	Tensile strength	
		ksi	MPa
200	Transverse weld	60	414
200	Base metal	61	419
600	Transverse weld	83	572
600	Base metal	90	621
800	Transverse weld	74	510
800	Base metal	75	518

It was found that "keyholing" could be used for material above approximately 0.090 in (2.3 mm). Materials less than 0.090 in (2.3 mm) gage can be welded with the plasma arc process; however, the "puddle" technique is used.

Welds essentially free of porosity can be produced with the proper welding conditions in all of the alloys. Very little difficulty has been experienced with the nickel-chromium and nickel-iron-chromium alloys. Somewhat more care is needed to assure a porosity-free weld in the nickel and nickel-copper alloys. Porosity can be a problem in the start and crater areas. This problem can be resolved by using a run-on and runoff tab or the appropriate gas- and amperage-sloping device. Table 3-4 shows a comparison of the base-metal and transverse-weld room-temperature tensile properties. Nearly 100% joint efficiency can be expected when fully annealed base material is welded. When cold-worked base metal is welded, the weld and heat-affected zone will be in the annealed condition and joint efficiencies of less than 100% are to be expected. The ductility of plasma arc welds has been shown to be generally good.

Other nickel-base alloys, including Inconel 718, Incoloy 800, Inconel X, Hastelloy X, and René 41, have been successfully welded.

Steels

A wide range of steels have been plasma-arc-welded, such as low-alloy, carbon, maraging, 304, 321, 410, 310 stainless, D6AC, 4130, 17-4PH, HY-180, and HP9 Ni-4Co-0.20C steels. Thicknesses have ranged from 0.125 in (3.2 mm) to 1 in (25.4 mm). In some fracture toughness tests[8] of Inconel 718, plasma welds tested higher than GTA welds. The fracture toughness figures for 17-4PH show over 100% joint efficiency for the plasma welds.

Copper and Copper Alloys

Several copper alloys such as 95Cu-5Sn, 70Cu-30Zn, and 70Cu-30Ni and pure copper have been welded in thicknesses up to 0.125 in (3.2 mm).

Titanium and Its Alloys

Plasma-arc welds have been used in a wide variety of titanium applications, both for development and in production. While it has been overshadowed in the aerospace field by the more glamorous electron-beam process, it has also been used there. However, it is very likely that many applications that have been electron-beam-welded are more suitable to plasma arc and can be done much more economically by the latter process. Alloys welded include Type 6Al-4V titanium alloy[9] in a variety of joints that are common in structural welding and in taper joints (see Fig. 3-9 and the section *Joint Design*). PAW was done for material exceeding 0.10 in (2.5 mm) where keyholing was practical.[9]

Several new titanium alloys have been plasma-arc-welded under government sponsorship[10] to evaluate mechanical properties for 0.10- and 0.5-in-thick (2.5 and 12.7 mm) Ti-6-2-4-6 and Ti-6-2-4-2 alloys. Satisfactory properties were generally obtained with the plasma-arc process.

Fig. 3-9 PAW: a vertical taper weld of 6Al-4V titanium.[9]

Fig. 3-10 PAW: a seam-welded titanium tee section.[11]

Welding techniques and parameters were developed for PAW of 0.1- and 0.5-in-thick (2.5 and 12.7 mm) Beta C (Ti-3Al-8V-6Cr-4Mo-4Zr) and 0.5-in-thick (12.7 mm) Ti-8Mo-8V-2Fe-3Al (Ti-8-8-2-3). The best combinations of yield strength and ductility, as well as fatigue endurance strength, were obtained in plasma-arc-welded 0.5-in-thick (12.7-mm) Ti-8-8-2-3. Plasma arc welded Ti-8-8-2-3 exhibited 169 ksi (1163 MPa) average yield strength with 3.5% elongation and 60 ksi (414 MPa) fatigue endurance strength. To further demonstrate the merits of the process, a Ti-8-8-2-3 subscale airframe component (wing pivot actuator-to-cover splice joint) was plasma-arc-welded, and further testing of the component yielded fatigue endurance strengths of 60 ksi (414 MPa).

A second program has extended the plasma-arc process capability to include titanium butt joints 1.0 in (25.4 mm) thick and arc seam-welded tee sections with cap members up to 0.25 in (6.4 mm) thick as seen in Fig. 3-10.

Other alloys plasma-arc-welded include A-286, alloy 25, and Zircaloy.

APPLICATIONS

All materials that are considered fusion weldable by other processes can be plasma-arc-welded. Mechanical tests of a wide variety of metals and alloys indicate no significant differences in properties between welds produced by other processes and plasma arc welds. The advantages derive primarily from the ease of control, increased speed, and insensitivity to arc-length change. The data in Table 3-5 demonstrate these gains. The ease of control, especially, makes the process very useful for thin-material welding and for repair operations where it is desirable to minimize effects of repair on other areas.

There are many applications where PAW has been used successfully in production. This new process has been used to make both longitudinal and girth welds in stainless steel and titanium tubing. It is especially useful for large-diameter applications where the wall thicknesses are great enough to permit the use of the keyhole mode. On such sizes and materials, it is faster to weld with a plasma arc than with GTA. Reject and repair rates are also lower.

The first extensive use of PAW occurred in the tubing industry, where its ability to produce seam welds without mechanical-backing fixturing could be used to advantage. For example, the longitudinal seam on stainless steel tubing whose diameter exceeds 1 in (25.4 mm) can be plasma-arc-welded at speeds up to 150% greater than those achieved with the GTA process; these are single-pass welds in tubing with wall thicknesses of 0.090 to about 0.25 in (2.3 to 6.4 mm). The continuously formed stainless steel pressure tubing is made from strip rolled into tube form and butt-welded, generally without filler metal.

A schematic view of plasma-arc tube welding is shown in Fig. 3-11. Weld bead shape and reinforcement are controlled by adjusting four variables: the welding current, the location of the arc relative to the center line of the pressure rolls on the tube mill, the force exerted by the pressure rolls, and the backing gas pressure inside the tube.

PAW has also been used to make circumferential joints in stainless steel pipe and in pipe of some other materials, in the horizontal and vertical pipe positions. This type of weld would normally be made by multiple-pass GTAW using a backing ring and filler metal on a prepared joint. The use of PAW permits keyhole welding of pipe with square-groove butt joints in one pass. Welding of circumferential joints in tanks or vessels is an extension of the technique used to weld circumferential pipe joints. The vessel must be positioned and rotated so that the joint is in the horizontal position. PAW on a vessel, involving the joining of girth seams on a D6AC steel missile case 10 ft (3 m) in diameter, was evaluated and proven of equal quality to a GTA-welded case.

PAW is very adaptable in making seal welds in thin-wall items such as electronic equipment, cans, bellows, and copper shading poles on electric motors. PAW with its reliability in starting, even with variations in torch-to-work distance, and consistent concentration of heat makes this application ideal. Consistent fusion of all copper wires is critical, and plasma ensures that the arc will not wander or jump to the nearest point of ground. Plasma has replaced GTA on motor stator lamination stacks because of its reliable arc-starting characteristic and consistent repeatability, which has reduced the number of rejected pieces. Other

TABLE 3-5
PAW vs. GTAW for Three Aerospace Metals[2]

| Condition | 410 Stainless Steel | | Maraging steel: 18% Ni | | Alloy Ti-6Al-4V | |
	Plasma arc	Gas-tungsten arc	Plasma arc	Gas-tungsten arc	Plasma arc	Gas-tungsten arc
Thickness of metal, in (mm)	0.25 (6.4)	0.25 (6.4)	0.25 (6.4)	0.25 (6.4)	0.095 (2.4)	0.095 (2.4)
Number of passes	1	2	1	3	2*	5†
Current, A	240	170 to 200	240 to 250	180 to 200	90 to 175	120 to 175
Travel speed, in/min (mm/s)	12 (5)	4 (2)	12 to 13 (5 to 5.5)	4 (2)	15 (6)	6 (3)
Time per 100 in (25 m) of weld, min	8.3	50	7.4	75	13.4	83.5

*One keyhole welding pass and one filler metal pass on the outside of a rocket motor case.
†One root pass without filler metal and two passes with filler metal on the outside of a rocket motor case. The root pass was back-gouged and two filler passes were made on the inside.

applications include the welding of copper thermostat elements for capillary tubes and in platinum glass-making equipment. Platinum dies for making glass fibers are built up and repaired without tungsten contamination, since the filler material cannot touch the tungsten, which is held inside of the torch in PAW.

Some recently developed applications include vacuum tubes and thermocouple joining. Filling an evacuated chamber with argon and then plasma-arc welding the work inside the chamber sounds more than slightly exotic for ordinary production work. But this is being done to join special high-quality sheathed thermocouples. A vertical plasma jet is programmed so the arc joins six thermocouples in sequence, then the plasma arc is programmed to seal the metal sheath closures on all six assemblies, also in sequence. The equipment does about 50 thermocouples per hour, as compared with about half that rate for manual welding.

The equipment welds junctions of nickel-chrome and nickel-aluminum, or iron and constantan, and seals sheaths of stainless steel or Inconel. The resulting thermocouples are used where the need for accurate temperature measurement may be accompanied by corrosion problems.

Vacuum power tubes for radio transmitters require welding cupro-nickel to monel, a joint that demands excellent shielding. Anything less lets in impurities, causing a porous weld and a vacuum tube that does not hold a vacuum. Currently PAW has replaced GTAW since the extremely hot gas shield of PAW has been found to decrease the number of porous welded tubes.

Included among jet engine components are thin metal compressor vanes, collector cones, combustion cases, and bearing housings. Appli-

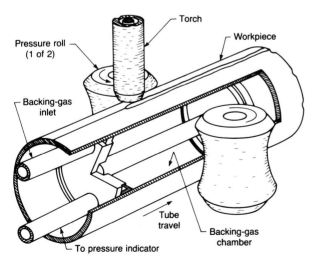

Fig. 3-11   Setup for welding longitudinal seams in stainless steel tubes, employing internal backing with inert gas.[2]

cations have even extended to helicopter control links, and a production PAW process has been established for joining 6Al-4V titanium alloy using a straight butt joint, 0.45 in (11.4 mm) thick.

Hydrofoil boats have been partly constructed by blind (from one side) PAW. Each boat requires about 800 lineal ft (2.6 km) of plasma weld on 0.187- to 0.5-in-thick (4.7 to 12.7 mm) 15-5PH stainless steel struts for the hydrofoil. After welding the equivalent of a boat-and-a-half of joints, it was found that the plasma system gave a 12:1 production advantage in hours over GTAW, and less than $1/4$% of the welds failed to meet the critical nondestructive testing requirements after welding.

PAW has made major contributions in the area of jet engine repair. Tip shroud seals on aircraft engines are now weld-repaired by low-current plasma-arc equipment. Procedures have been perfected for the repair of several other engine parts such as the buildup of worn Type 410 stainless steel spacer abutments, air seals, vanes, vane case assemblies, exhaust cones, and titanium compressor fan blades.

An example of a dramatic use for PAW was the development of its use for supersonic-aircraft stiffened panels. The PAW machine that can weld 65 ft (20 m) long 6Al-4V titanium assemblies in one continuous operation is shown in Fig. 3-12. The unit was capable of attaching L-shaped stiffeners to machined wing skin sections up to 30 ft (9 m) long. The machine was capable of welding one panel while another was being loaded, and used the same head for both panels.

Another novel commercial application is the PAW of sponge compacts of titanium and zirconium to form primary melt electrodes for consumable electrode furnaces. In considering the case of reactor-

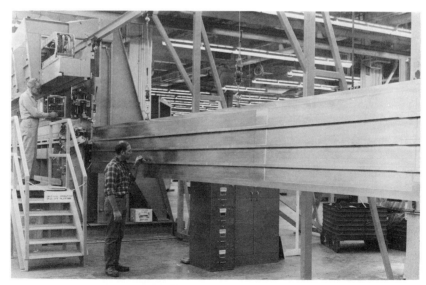

Fig. 3-12 Largest PAW machine.[12]

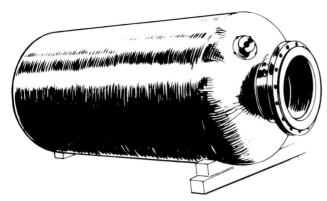

Fig. 3-13 Cylindrical vessel made of 0.2-in-thick (5 mm) titanium plates by PAW.[14]

grade zirconium, it must be borne in mind that government specifications prohibit use of GTAW for joining compacts because of the possibility of tungsten inclusions in the base metal. GMAW has been used, but is expensive because of the cost of zirconium welding wire and occasional burn-backs of the guide tubes, which result in excessive copper deposits.

Recently PAW has been used to produce office and hospital furniture, heat-exchanger tubes, and cryogenic vessels. In Japan PAW is being developed for mild-steel pipeline welding for on-site application.[13] PAW is also being used to fabricate 0.2-in-thick (5 mm) pure titanium cylindrical vessels for industrial use, as shown in Fig. 3-13. Feasibility of PAW underwater work has been shown in Japan.[15] In this process, viscous liquid is used in place of shielding gas to protect the part being welded from the surrounding water and to stabilize the plasma arc.

Welding experiments using mild steel as the base metal have proven the successful welding of 0.25-in-thick (6.4 mm) material, and it has been ascertained that this process can be put to practical use.

Results of this work are summarized as follows:

1. Water glass is used as a typical viscous liquid.
2. Water glass shielding for the part being welded has a marked effect on stabilization of the underwater plasma arc.
3. Water glass shielding has the effect of heat-insulating the part being welded and lowers the solidification rate of molten metal. Because of this feature, the weld metal does not include blowholes and the maximum hardness of the heat-affected zone adjacent to the bond is lowered considerably.
4. The weld produced by this process has excellent mechanical properties, and especially its ductility and notch toughness can be improved remarkably, compared with those of the weld produced without shielding.

PAW is also being applied in production shops to stainless steel (Types 304, 304L, and 316) for specialized boilers in the food and chemical industry in France.[16]

Fabricators of commercial products such as automobiles are well aware of the progress made in the development of plasma-arc equipment, particularly that for low-current operation. Several production applications are being evaluated. As more flexible controls and gas-flow-sloping devices become available to simplify the keyhole mode of welding, the use of the process will expand. PAW equipment is presently more expensive than GTA equipment, but this disadvantage should be offset by the advantage of increased production speeds.

REFERENCES

1. "Welding Handbook," 6th ed., sec. 3b, American Welding Society, Miami, 1971.
2. "Metals Handbook," 8th ed., vol. 6, American Society of Metals, 1971, pp. 142–147.
3. Union Carbide Corp., private communication, May 1978.
4. Privoznik, L. J., and Miller, H. R., "Evaluation of Plasma Arc Welding for 120 in (305 mm) Diameter Rocket Motor Case," *Weld. J.*, **45**(8), 717–725, September 1966.
5. Mitchell, D. R., "Evaluation of Plasma Arc Welds," final rep., Proj. CW-11-1, Titanium Metals Corporation of America, West Caldwell, N.J., 1967.
6. Pattee, H. E., Meister, R. P., and Monroe, R. E., "Cathodic Cleaning and Plasma Arc Welding of Aluminum," *Weld. J.*, **47**(5), 226s–233s, May 1968.
7. Lingenfelter, A. C., "Plasma Arc Welding Nickel Alloys," *Weld. Eng.*, **49**(1), January 1970.
8. Langford, G. J., "Plasma Arc Welding Various Metals," GDC-ERR-AN-1172, Mfg. R&D, General Dynamics, Convair Div., December 1967.
9. Langford, G. J., "Plasma Arc Welding of Structural Titanium Joints," *Weld. J.*, **47**(2), 102–113, February 1968.
10. Nessler, C. G., and Duvall, D. S., "Manufacturing Technology for Joining Titanium Alloys," IR-838-2-VI, AFML Contr. F33615-72-C-1624, August 1974.
11. Brubaker, D., Muser, C., and Sidbeck, P., "Manufacturing Methods for Plasma Arc Welding," Contr. F33615-74-C-5036, AFML-TR-76-152, January 1974–September 1976.
12. Turner, A., The Boeing Co., private communication, April 1978.
13. Narita, K., Takagi, K., Kimura, T., and Mitsui, A., "Plasma Arc Welding of Pipelines: A Study to Optimize Welding Conditions for Horizontal Fixed Joints of Mild Steel Pipes," *Int. J. Pressure Vess. Piping*, **3**(4), October 1975, and *Weld Res. Abroad*, **23**(2), 9–41, February 1977.
14. Katsura, H., Katsube, J., and Hirayama, S., "Some Experiments on Plasma Arc Welding of Titanium Plates," IIW Doc. IV-87-72, pp. 1–9, May 1972.
15. Hasui, A., Kinugawa, J., and Suga, Y., "Development of Underwater Plasma Welding (The Second Report)," *Trans. JWRI*, **1**(2), 56–68, October 1972.
16. Schultz, J. P., "Principal Industrial Applications of Plasma Welding in France," IIW Doc. IVB-2-73, pp. 1–6, 1973.
17. Sipkes, M. P., "State of The Art of Plasma Welding Investigations at TNO-Netherlands," IIW Doc. IV-121-B, pp. 1–11, 1973.
18. Tsuchiya, K., Kishimoto, K., Matsunaga, T., and Nakano, E., "Plasma Arc Welding Procedures for Thick Steel Plate," IIW Doc. IV-117-73, pp. 1–34, September 1973.
19. Hasui, A., and Inomata, H., "Development of Underwater Plasma Welding," National Research Institute for Metals, IIW Doc. IV-52-70, pp. 24–35, 1971.
20. Arata, Y., and Inoue, K., "Automatic Control of Plasma Arc Welding," Dept. of Welding Engineering, Osaka Univ., IIW Doc. IV-54-71, pp. 1–25, March 1971.
21. Miller, H. R., and Filipski, S. P., Automated Plasma Arc Welding for Aerospace and Cryogenic Fabrications," *Weld. J.*, **45**(6), 493–500, June 1966.

22. "Plasma Arc Welding for Gas Turbine Engine Fabrication," Allison Div., General Motors, Contr. F33615-69-C1893, AFML-TR-70-131, July 1969–October 1970.
23. Kennedy, C. R., "Plasma Welding," *Aust. Weld. J.*, **20**(3), 26–28, May/June 1976.
24. Marquardt, E., "Plasma Welding Studies," *ZIS Mitt.*, (2), 228–237, February 1967.
25. Demars, P., "Plasma Welding," *Soud. Tech. Connexes*, **22**(5/6), 181–202, May/June 1968.
26. Evrard, M., and Blanchet, B., "Study of the Arc Plasma From the Point of View of Welding," *Soud. Tech. Connexes*, **24**(7/8), 281–298, July/August 1970.
27. Marquardt, E., "Performance Limits in Plasma Welding," pp. 41–49; Borner, Wietal, "Plasma Welding of High Alloy Cr-Ni Steel with Currentless Filler Material," pp. 50–58; Sabisch, G., "Plasma Welding of Mild Steel Sheet," pp. 59–66; *ZIS Mitt.*, **13**(1), January 1971.
28. Lundin, C. D., and Ruprecht, W. J., "The Effect of Shielding Gas Additions on the Penetration Characteristics of Plasma Arc Welds," *Weld. J.*, **56**(1), 1s–7s, January 1977.
29. Metcalfe, J. C., and Quigley, M. B. C., "Keyhole Stability in Plasma Arc Welding," *Weld. J.*, **54**(11), 401s–404s, November 1977.
30. Metcalfe, J. C., and Quigley, M. B. C., "Heat Transfer in Plasma Arc Welding," *Weld. J.*, **54**(3), 99s–103s, March 1975.
31. Steffens, H. D., and Kayser, H., "Automatic Control for Plasma Arc Welding," *Weld. J.*, **51**(6), 408–418, June 1972.
32. Tomsic, M. J., and Jackson, C. E., "Energy Distribution in Keyhole Mode Plasma Arc Weld," *Weld. J.*, **53**(3), 109s–115s, March 1974.
33. Drews, P., and Böhme, D., "Investigations Concerning The Technology of Plasma Arc Welding of Structural Steels," IIW Doc. IV-175-75, Institute für Schweisstechnische Fertigungsverfahren der Rhein—Westf. Technischen Hochschule, Aachen, Germany (Fed. Rep.), April 1975.
34. Brubaker, D., and Perkins, W., "Plasma Arc Welding," IR-849-4B (III), AFML Contr. F33615-76-C-5231, February 1977.

NEEDLE ARC–MICROPLASMA WELDING

Manual plasma-arc welding was developed to obtain a very stable, controllable arc at low currents for welding thin metal. This process combines a continuously operating pilot arc within the torch and arc constriction to provide an arc which is stable at currents as low as 0.1 A. Because of the long needlelike arc, the process has been called needle arc welding in the United States. It has been called microplasma in Europe because of the low currents employed.

CHARACTERISTICS OF PROCESS

Figure 3-14 shows a schematic diagram of the plasma needle arc welding system. The basic elements of the torch are the electrode and the orifice from which the plasma and transferred arc emerge on their way to the weldment. A small flow of argon is supplied through the orifice to form the arc plasma. Shielding of the arc and the weld is obtained from a second gas flow through the gas lens and cup assembly. Shielding gas can be argon, helium, or mixtures of argon with either hydrogen or helium.

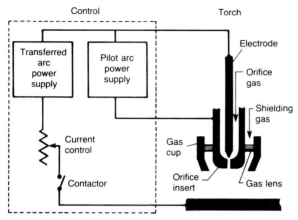

Fig. 3-14 Schematic diagram for low-current PAW.

The initial plasma is formed by an internal low-current pilot arc between the electrode and the orifice insert. This internal arc heats the orifice gas to very high temperatures so that it becomes ionized, i.e., a plasma. The plasma forms a conductive path between the electrode and the weldment to permit instant ignition of a welding arc, which in this case is called a transferred arc. The pilot arc and transferred arc have separate dc power supplies.

After the pilot arc has been established, the transferred arc can be started by closing the contactor in the lead to the workpiece. This provides a smooth reliable start which eliminates the "tracks" or etch marks sometimes left on the work by high-frequency starting and the tendency toward "blasting through" caused by current surges associated with touch starting.

When compared with a gas-tungsten arc, the low-current plasma arc or jet has improved directional properties, improved arc stability, and greatly reduced sensitivity to variations in torch-to-work spacing. In addition, contamination of the weld by tungsten is avoided because the tungsten electrode is positioned behind a water-cooled copper orifice. These factors make manual welding much easier, especially for new welding trainees, even when filler metal is added. Also, there is no chance of contaminating the electrode either by accidentally dipping it into the weld puddle or by touching it with the filler metal. Thus, arc stability can be maintained and there is little chance for tungsten contamination in the weld.

At very low currents, the needle arc process employs the melt-through type of welding associated with gas tungsten-arc welding. At the higher currents used for welding heavier metals, the keyhole mode of penetration can be achieved with the plasma torch by increasing the orifice gas flow.[35] Low-current plasma torches can be used either manually or mechanized.

OPERATING CHARACTERISTICS

At very low currents, the plasma needle arc process was found to have special merit for the fusion welding of thin metal.[36] In Fig. 3-15 is a 0.010-in (0.25-mm) stainless steel relay case being repaired with a 3-A arc. Manual welding of this thickness and less represents a great departure from previous practice with the gas tungsten-arc process which would have required more torch movement. With either process, however, the weld is the same, a smooth fusion weld.

The operating lengths of plasma needle arcs are longer than gas-tungsten arcs. For example, needle arc lengths are normally 0.25 in (6.4 mm) whereas gas-tungsten arcs are about half that or 0.125 in (3.2 mm) at currents above 30 A dc straight polarity. These differences in arc lengths are not particularly important for skilled welders. However, as currents are reduced for the welding of light-gage metals, gas-tungsten arcs tend to become unstable and wander over the surface of the weldment. To overcome this, smaller electrodes are used at very short arc lengths. These critical operating parameters require the highest manual skills for welding foils and very thin metals. The other alternative is to mechanize the welding operation in order to achieve reasonable production and quality. Thus it is in this low-current foil-welding area that the characteristics of the needle arc become most significant because of its ability to provide long, stable arcs and with wide operating tolerances.

If a comparison were made in the changes in arc lengths and tolerances for both the gas tungsten and needle arc processes operating in the 10-A welding range one would find the needle arc 10 times longer and the arc tolerance more than 10 times greater. Thus the needle arc process makes it possible—in fact quite easy—to weld foils manually.

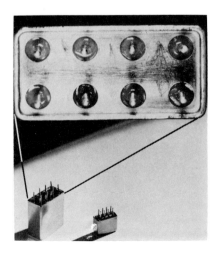

Fig. 3-15 Needle arc in use repairing a weld in relay case.[1]

Foil and very thin sheet thicknesses of common metals have been welded using a system of 15 A compacity. Typical welding conditions are shown in Table 3-6. Note that for stainless and high-alloy steels, there is a preference for the use of shielding gas mixtures composed of argon and about 1% hydrogen. This hydrogen addition helps to promote good puddle fluidity and wetting action on the stainless steel welds. As the limits of current and thickness for the system are approached, use is made of the added heating capacity of the high hydrogen mixtures. For other metals such as titanium or copper, however, where hydrogen cannot be tolerated, helium or a helium-argon mixture is used.

TABLE 3-6
Manual Needle Arc Welding Butt Joints in Foils and Thin Sheet

Thickness		Welding current, A, dc straight polarity	Speed		Shielding gas†
in	mm		in/min	mm/s	
Stainless Steel					
0.001‡	0.03	0.3	5	2.1	Argon-1% H_2
0.003‡	0.08	1.6	6	3.0	Argon-1% H_2
0.005‡	0.13	2.4	5	2.1	Argon-1% H_2
0.010	0.25	6	8	3.3	Argon-1% H_2
0.020	0.5	15	10	4.2	Argon*
0.020	0.5	17	24	10.2	Argon-5% H_2
0.030	0.76	10	3	1.2	Argon*
0.030	0.76	10	5	2.1	Argon-1% H_2
0.030	0.76	17	10	4.2	Argon-5% H_2
0.050	1.3	13	4	2.0	Argon-5% H_2
0.062	1.6	17	3	1.2	Argon-10% H_2
Titanium					
0.003‡	0.08	3	6	3.0	Argon*
0.008	0.20	5	6	3.0	Argon*
0.015	0.38	8	5	2.1	Argon*
0.022	0.55	12	9	3.8	Helium-25% A
Inconel 718					
0.012	0.30	6	15	6.0	Argon-1% H_2
0.016	0.40	3.5	6	3.0	Argon-1% H_2
Hastelloy X					
0.005‡	0.13	4.8	10	4.2	Argon-1% H_2
0.010	0.25	5.8	8	3.3	Argon-1% H_2
0.020	0.5	10	10	4.2	Argon-1% H_2
Copper					
0.003‡	0.08	10	6	3.0	Helium-25% A

*Argon flow rate: 0.5 ft³/h (0.24 L/min) through a 0.030-in-diameter (0.76 mm) orifice.
†Shielding gas flow: 20 ft³/h (9.44 L/min).
‡Flanged butt joint.

Higher-current systems with current capacities of up to 100 A have been developed.[36] In extending the current range up to 100 A for the needle arc process, which will allow welding up to 0.18 in (4.5 mm), several advantages are gained:

- Greater versatility
- Very good point visibility
- No electrode pollution from the filler metal on the weld puddle
- No tungsten inclusion because of short-circuiting
- Very good arc rigidity
- Larger permissible variations of arc length

As arc currents are increased, the orifice diameters and the argon flows must be increased. With this increase in arc currents, and as a result of the capacity of the system, the keyhole welding mode can be used in which, with a relatively high flow rate of orifice gas, the plasma jet actually pierces the weldment. The presence of a keyhole during welding is visual proof that full penetration is being obtained in the weld. Manual keyhole welding in 0.125-in-thick (3.2 mm) stainless steel made at 70 A yields welds which are about half the width of those produced by normal melting, where heat from the arc soaks in until full penetration is reached.

FIXTURING AND JOINT DESIGN

Although a plasma needle arc is easier to manage than a gas-tungsten arc as a heat source, the melting behavior is the same for the two processes. Therefore, joint-fixturing requirements are much the same for either process. When thin metals are welded, it is essential that both joint edges be in continuous contact and that both edges melt simultaneously to fuse together into a single weld puddle. Separation between the joint edges before or during welding will allow the edges to melt separately and remain separate. Butt and edge joints have the following requirements:

- *Butt joints.* Illustrations showing tolerances for joint fit-up and fixturing are shown in Fig. 3-16 for butt joints in metal thicknesses below 0.030 in (0.76 mm). No filler metal is used. Gas backing is recommended to assure good puddle fluidity and wetting attachment on both sides of the joint. As can be seen, the backing groove dimensions are narrower for square-butt than for flanged-butt joints.
- *Edge joints.* Figure 3-17 shows the fit-up and fixturing tolerances for edge joints. Tolerances are much greater than those for butt joints. Because of this, the edge joint is the easiest and most reliable joint for welding. Successful welding of foil thickness assemblies is much surer when some form of edge joint can be used.

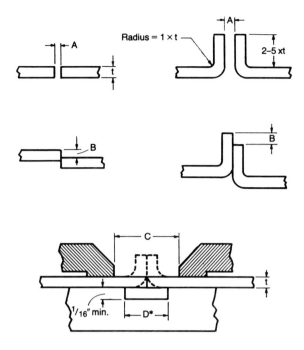

Butt joint type	Gap "A" max.	Mismatch "B" max.	Clamp spacing "C"		Backup groove "D"	
			Min.	Max.	Min.	Max.
Square	0.2 t	0.4 t	10 t – 20 t		4 t – 16 t	
Flanged†	0.6 t	1 t	15 t – 30 t		10 t – 24 t	

*Gas backing, either argon or helium, is required
†Flanging of butt joints is recommended for thickness below 0.010 in.

Fig. 3-16 Joint design and fixturing tolerances for butt joints in metal thicknesses up to 0.030 in (0.76 mm).

An example of a fixture used for needle arc-microplasma welding of nickel-base alloys, René 41 and Inconel 718, is shown in Fig. 3-18. The clamps and backing plate are made of copper to give maximum heat conduction away from the weld zone and so reduce heat input and distortion of the workpiece. The 0.22-in-thick (5.6 mm) copper clamps were supported by a stainless steel bar section. The backing bar contains a channel which supplies argon backing gas to the underside of the workpiece. The plasma torch is placed as near to the work as possible to reduce arc length.

Strict attention to surface cleaning becomes increasingly important as metal thicknesses approach those of foils. The parts to be welded should be cleaned shortly before welding and standard cleaning procedures should be followed.

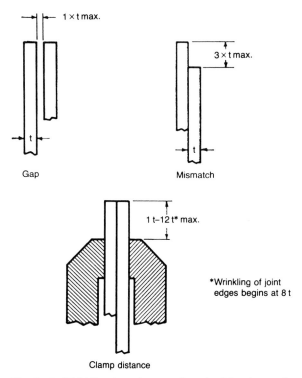

Gap

Mismatch

*Wrinkling of joint
edges begins at 8 t

Clamp distance

Fig. 3-17 Weld fixturing tolerances for edge joints in metal
thicknesses up to 0.030 in (0.76 mm).

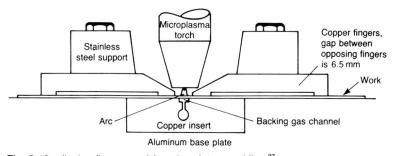

Fig. 3-18 Jigging fixture used for microplasma welding.[37]

SHIELDING

Inert-gas shielding of the top and bottom of the weld puddle is
especially important on thin metals. Good shielding preserves puddle
fluidity and assures good wetting and attachment of the melt from both
joint edges into a common pool. For butt welds, backing shielding can
be provided through a relief groove in the weld jig as shown in Figs.

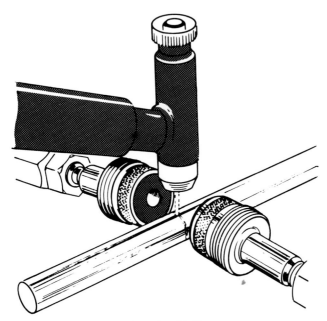

Fig. 3-19 Auxiliary shielding of welds.[38]

3-16 and 3-18.[37] For small parts, gas lenses (i.e., devices which project coherent streams of shielding gas) can be used instead of a chamber. Two lenses directly opposed to each other—with the weldment between—can provide a quick and easy method for overall shielding. Figure 3-19 illustrates the use of lenses for shielding a butt weld joint in thin-wall titanium tubing.

MATERIALS

The plasma needle arc welding system produces fusion welds in thin metals with exceptional ease and reliability. It does this by providing a

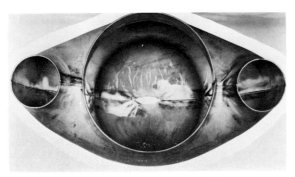

Fig. 3-20 Stainless steel jet engine casing.[38]

stable, low-current plasma arc which can be adjusted to provide just the right heat input for delicate weldments. The process is easy to operate, because it is not overly sensitive to arc-length changes; hence, relatively long arc lengths can be used. Also, the long needlelike arc formed through a small orifice can be aimed reliably and precisely. The plasma needle arc process has been applied to stainless steels, titanium and its alloys, refractory metal alloys, copper, Kovar, and several nickel-base alloys. In some recent work[37] butt welds having satisfactory mechanical properties and good fatigue properties were made in 0.010-in-thick (0.25 mm) Nimonic PK33 and 0.015-in-thick (0.38 mm) René 41 by the microplasma process.

A variety of low-current welding applications have been plasma-arc-welded. Examples include a computer drive belt made of a 0.003-in-thick (0.08 mm) by 0.625-in-wide (15.9 mm) band of stainless steel.[38] The flange acts as a preplaced filler metal and greatly increases the tolerance for variations in joint fit-up.

Needle arc welding is used for fabricating complex structures employed on small jet engines. One such example is the welding of an outer combustion case made of 0.025-in-thick (0.6 mm) Type 347 stainless steel, shown in Fig. 3-20. The process is useful as a repair tool. Fig. 3-21 shows the rebuilding of worn edges on simulated turbine blades, and the welds were made with a cobalt-base alloy filler metal. Worn seal rings have also been successfully repair-welded. Other types of repair welds include hard-surfaced seats of truck valves, ducting, and other thin-wall structures.[39,40]

Other applications include welded capsules made from stainless steel hypodermic tubing for encapsulating radioactive materials, float gauges of stainless steel for liquid-level indicators, stainless steel bellows, and hermetically sealed relay cases seen in Fig. 3-15. An example of the

Fig. 3-21 PAW used for turbine blade repair.[38]

Fig. 3-22 Manual needle arc welding of filter screens to the end connections.[1]

outstanding directional stability of the needle arc is shown in Fig. 3-22, which illustrates the welding of a stainless steel filter assembly. This item was designed for furnace brazing using preformed braze filler metal to join the ultrafine-mesh wire cloth to the heavy end fittings. The finished part can be made faster by welding than by brazing, and welding has improved service temperature and corrosion resistance.

Industry has adopted the process for a variety of foil weldments, jet engine parts, electronic and instrumentation assemblies, and as a repair tool. Now that a proven method is available, welding engineers can confidently fabricate complex assemblies of thin metals.

REFERENCES

35. O'Brien, R. L., "Arc Plasmas for Joining, Cutting and Surfacing," WRC Bull. 131, July 1968.

36. Wagenleitner, A. H., "Micro-plasma Welding," *Schweisstechnik*, **22**(3), 25–29, March 1968.

37. Adams, M. J., "Plasma, Electron Beam and Laser Welding of Thin Nickel-base Alloys," *Met. Constr. Br. Weld. J.*, August 1974, and *Weld. Res. Abroad*, **21**(2), 37–43, February 1975.

38. Gorman, E. F., "New Developments and Applications in Manual Plasma Arc Welding," *Weld. J.*, **48**(7), 547–556, July 1969.

39. "Plasma Arc Welding; More Reliability for Less Money," Staff Report, *Met. Prog.*, pp. 106, 109–110, July 1968.

40. MacAbee, P. J., Dyar, J. R., and Bratkovich, N. F., "Plasma Arc Welding of Thin Materials," Tech. Rep. AFML-TR-67-177, June 1967.

41. "Plasma Arc Welder Will Aid Duct Life," *McClellan Spacemaker*, McClellan AFB, Sacramento, **9**(25), 2, June 21, 1968.

42. Feustel, E., "Microplasma Welding," *Lastechniek*, **34**(8), 188–193, August 1968.

43. Braken, M. J. G., "Microplasma Welding Tests With Temperature Measurement," *Lastechniek*, **37**(3), 43–46, March 1971.

44. Granier, M., Demars, P., "Laser and Plasma Arc Welding and Cutting," *Weld. Res. Abroad*, **28**(1), 35–41, January 1972, and *Aust. Weld. J.*, **15**(7), September 1971.

45. Braken, M. J. G., "Welding of Thin Materials," *Lastechniek*, **36**(11), 243–247, November 1970.

PLASMA-GMA WELDING

Plasma-GMA welding is a form of welding in thermally ionized gas in which a consumable electrode is fed towards the workpiece through a copper nozzle which also guides a plasma stream.[46,47] The potential of the process and its resultant properties offer a substantial improvement over GMAW. The cost of the equipment is, of course, higher because of the more complex construction, but there is gain in quality and in welding speed which can lead to improved economics. The appearance, shape, and soundness of the welds can be considerably improved and the applicable ranges of process parameters such as wire extension, current, arc length, deposition rate, and traverse speed are much enlarged by the presence of plasma around the filler wire.

PROCESS DESCRIPTION

The process can be described as GMAW with a stream of plasma around the lower part of the filler wire. Figure 3-23 is a schematic representation of a torch and the connections of the power sources. The plasma is generated in a stream of argon gas by an arc discharge between the workpiece and a nonconsumable electrode in the torch. A water-cooled copper nozzle is used to guide the plasma arc around the filler wire. In order to avoid pickup of air, shielding gas—which can be carbon dioxide, argon, helium, nitrogen, hydrogen, or mixtures of these gases, depending on the kind of metal to be welded—is applied around the arc system. The composition of the shielding gas further influences the welding properties. For mild steel or stainless steel, the shielding gas consists of argon with a few percent CO_2, and for aluminum and copper, the shielding gas consists of a mixture of argon and helium.

Plasma-GMAW can be carried out with both electrodes (the nonconsumable electrode and the filler metal) using direct current, straight polarity as well as reverse polarity. For straight polarity, the nonconsumable electrode consists of a pointed thoriated tungsten rod. Under balanced conditions, plasma-GMAW with straight polarity is a stable process, especially when the plasma gas contains a small amount of

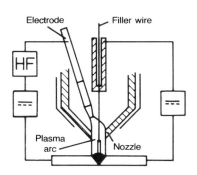

Fig. 3-23 Schematic diagram of plasma-GMA system with a tungsten or copper electrode.[48]

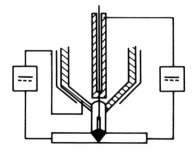

Fig. 3-24 Schematic diagram of plasma-GMA system with the nozzle as the nonconsumable electrode.[48]

oxygen. However, most of the work to date and applications have been done with direct current, reverse polarity. For welding with reverse polarity, the nonconsumable electrode may be a thick tungsten rod or a thick copper rod. The copper electrode is preferred because of its longer life at high plasma currents. The electrode is directly water cooled. During the welding procedure, the plasma arc is ignited with the help of a high-frequency discharge. This arc forms an electrically conductive path in the nozzle and from the nozzle to the workpiece. Then the gas metal-arc circuit is closed and filler metal is fed along the axis of the plasma stream. The very moment the filler metal touches the plasma, current flows through it to the workpiece. Thus no short-circuiting between filler metal and workpiece is necessary to start the filler metal current. Spatter, therefore, is totally absent during the igniting procedure. This is in contrast to conventional GMAW where ignition is always accompanied by some degree of spatter.

Other electrode arrangements and different power source connections can be used to provide the plasma around the filler wire.[49] One of those which has been found very satisfactory in industrial practice is shown in Fig. 3-24. In this form the water-cooled copper nozzle of the torch acts as the plasma electrode. This alternative manner of plasma-GMAW is so-called nozzle plasma-GMAW. Here the nonconsumable tungsten or copper electrode has been left out and the nozzle is connected to the plasma power supply. The welding procedure is now as follows. First the arc between filler metal and workpiece is ignited by short circuiting the two, as is usual with GMAW. Then the plasma arc between nozzle and workpiece ignites spontaneously.

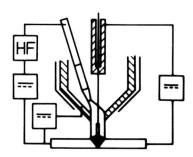

Fig. 3-25 Schematic diagram of plasma-GMA system with an extra plasma current supplied via the nozzle.[48]

A disadvantage of nozzle plasma-GMAW is that starting is accompanied by some spatter. Directly after the ignition, however, this process is just as spatter-free as normal plasma-GMAW. A great advantage of nozzle plasma-GMAW is that the equipment is less complicated. The high-voltage, high-frequency generator can be left out, like the extra copper electrode in the torch. Because the nozzle has a relatively large volume of copper, high plasma currents can be used.

A third mode of plasma-GMAW is shown in Fig. 3-25. Here again the plasma arc is generated from an internal copper or tungsten electrode. Hence the same sequence of operations must be followed as was mentioned in the discussion of Fig. 3-23. Now, however, it is possible to add extra current to the plasma arc via the nozzle. A third power supply, therefore, can be used. This method will be especially useful for welding materials with a high thermal conductivity.

DEPOSITION CHARACTERISTICS

The circumstance that the flow of current from the wire makes use of an already existing current path governs the welding properties. Rather coarse droplets may be formed at low current, but their transfer to the workpiece is not disturbed by erratic arc forces as happens with low-current GMAW, so the low-current coarse-droplet mode can actually be used. The magnitude of the current from the wire depends on the potential difference between the wire and the surrounding plasma, and when it increases the droplets become smaller.

Because the filler wire is in contact with the electrically conductive plasma over a considerable length, the location at which the wire current enters the plasma is not necessarily confined to the tip of the wire. Depending on the potential difference between wire and ambient plasma, current transfer may be spread over a large area. With thin wire having large electrical resistance this effect may be substantial and can lead to a lowering of the melting rate.[47] In most cases, however, with thicker wire having lower resistivity, the presence of plasma will considerably increase the melting rate. An increase in melting rate has also been found with a 0.05-in-diameter (1.3 mm) wire, which is a very suitable size for a number of applications where increased deposition rate and improved weld shape play a role.

Very large melting rates can be obtained at long wire extensions at which control over material transfer would be lost with GMAW, but is retained with plasma-GMAW. This is specifically in the range of rotational transfer. There are two types of metal transfer with plasma-GMAW: axial and rotational transfer.[50] The plasma-GMAW system with "metal" has a tendency to spatter much less compared with GMA, probably because the current is more gradually transferred from the wire to the plasma, and because the plasma current, which is parallel to the solid part of the wire, has a tendency to reduce the width of the rotation.

Although most applications investigated up until now make use of modest wire extensions and nonrotational, jetting transfer, the rotational mode is a very practicable condition for plasma-GMAW. The liquid metal transfers as a rain of fine drops to the workpiece without spatter.

WELD PENETRATION AND SHAPE

In comparison with conventional GMAW where the current through the filler metal is the only source of energy input to the workpiece, with plasma-GMAW there is the additional source of the plasma current. The influence of this extra heat source on the penetration of the weld metal into the workpiece is shown in Fig. 3-26. With these experiments

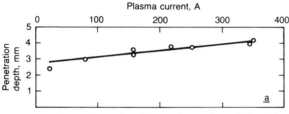

Fig. 3-26 Penetration of weld metal showing width of the weld.[48] (0.04 in = mm)

the current through the electrode and the feed speed have been kept constant, as has the travel speed of the workpiece. Thus the only variable has been the plasma current.

It appears that the plasma current has only a slight effect on the penetration depth of weld metal. A rise of 300 A in the plasma current results in an increase of only 0.04 in (1 mm) penetration depth. This holds, of course, for that particular plate thickness. For thinner plates, the plasma current has a somewhat greater effect on the penetration. High plasma currents result in a small contact angle, hence high plasma currents promote good "wetting-in." The influence of plasma on the bead shape appears, therefore, to be confined mainly to the surface in case of thicker plate. In thin plate, however, the increase in penetration is an important effect which makes higher traverse speeds possible.

APPLICATIONS

Plasma-GMAW has found its first applications in that field of welding where GMAW fails in one or more respects, for instance, deposition rate, welding speed, heat input into the workpiece (this can be lower with plasma-GMA because of the high welding speed), weld porosity, spatter during the ignition and spatter during welding, flexibility of welding parameters, manageability of the process, the possibility of preheating the workpiece with the solitary plasma before adding the filler, and the possibility of using rotating transfer.

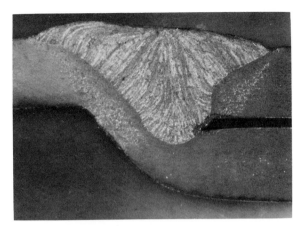

Fig. 3-27 Plasma-GMA-welded cross section of a lap joint on a pressure vessel.[48]

Also, the plasma-GMAW process has several advantages over submerged arc welding. In addition to the features mentioned above, plasma-GMAW is a clean process when compared with submerged arc welding. In this comparison the extremely low energy input per unit of weld length, because of the high deposition rate in the case of great extension of a relatively thin electrode, must be mentioned again. This can be of advantage for welding and filling vee-groove butt joints in alloyed steel plate.

One of the most promising applications of plasma-GMAW is welding thin plate, namely stainless steel and mild steel from 0.04 to 0.24 in (1 to 6 mm) thickness. The extra heat source of the plasma sheath offers the possibility of welding very fast. This type of welding will be used for longitudinal welding of stainless steel tubes.

Figure 3-27 is a cross section of lap weld in a pressure vessel. The mild steel plate was 0.09 in (2.3 mm) thick. A third application is shown in Fig. 3-28. In this car wheel, the disk was welded in the rim. The welding speed was twice the speed obtained with GMAW. The absence of spatter is very important in this case.

Another promising field of application for plasma-GMAW is joining

Fig. 3-28 Plasma-GMA-welded disk in the rim of a car wheel.[48]

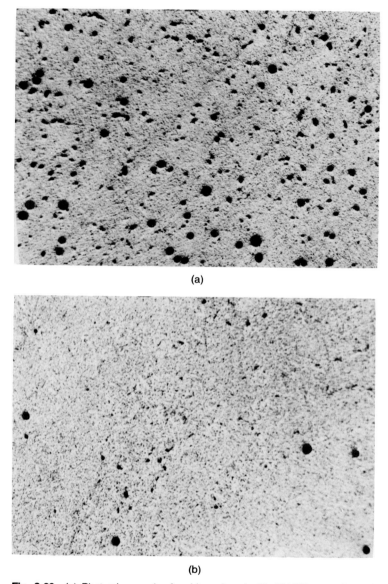

(a)

(b)

Fig. 3-29 (a) Photomicrograph of weld produced with GMAW on uncleaned aluminum. (b) Photomicrograph of weld produced with plasma-GMAW on uncleaned aluminum.[48]

aluminum. Good results have been obtained with thin plate as well as with thick. In this case it is not only the high welding speed which makes the system preferable, but also the high quality of the weld metal. One of the disadvantages of GMAW of aluminum is that the welds produced by this process are often porous. Most of this porosity

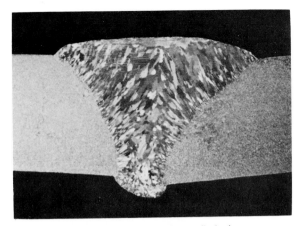

Fig. 3-30   Cross section of a 90° (1.6 rad) single vee-groove weld in 0.40-in-thick (10 mm) copper.[48]

is caused by the trapping of hydrogen during cooling and solidification of the melt. Hydrogen may come from the plate material as well as from the filler metal (hydrated oxide films).

Figure 3-29*a* shows a cross section of a bead-on-plate weld of aluminum with ordinary GMAW. The weld was made on an uncleaned plate. Figure 3-29*b* is a similar weld, but now made with the plasma-GMAW process. The difference in porosity is striking. The lower porosity in the case of plasma-GMAW is most likely caused by the cleaning action of the plasma sheath. During welding one can see the cathode spots of the plasma arc moving on the workpiece relatively far in front of the molten weld pool and leaving behind a bright surface.

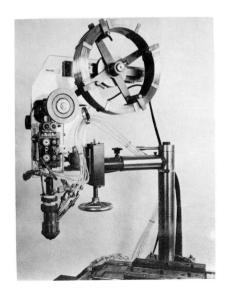

Fig. 3-31 Plasma-GMAW gun and wire-feed system.[51]

For welding metals with a high thermal conductivity, the plasma-GMAW process has the great advantage of having an additional heat source, namely the plasma sheath. High plasma currents up to 500 A allow the welding of relatively thick copper plate without preheating. An example is shown in Fig. 3-30. This depicts a cross section of a weld in 0.4-in-thick (10 mm) copper. The weld was made in two passes.

Although plasma-GMAW is a mode of GMAW, it can compete with some applications of submerged arc welding. The process is distinguished by a high degree of flexibility at low as well as at high filler-metal currents. With one diameter of the filler metal a wide range of currents can be used. See equipment setup in Fig. 3-31. Both ignition and welding are spatter-free.

One of the greatest advantages of the additional plasma sheath is the possibility of using large electrode extensions with their attendant high deposition rates. The process is 3 years old and has excellent potential and economic advantages in production shops.

REFERENCES

46. Essers, W. G., Liefkens, A. C., and Tichelaar, G. W., Paper 40, *Proc. Conf. on Advances in Welding Processes*, Harrogate 1969, The Welding Institute, 1970.
47. Essers, W. G., Jelmorini, G., and Tichelaar, G. W., *Met. Constr. Brit. Weld. J.*, **4**(12), 439, 1972.
48. Essers, W. G., "Plasma with GMA Welding," *Weld. J.*, **55**(5), 394–400, May 1976.
49. Essers, W. G., Tichelaar, G. W., van den Heuvel, G. J. P. M., and Jelmorini, G., "Welding in Thermally Ionized Gas," Paper 15, *3d Internat. Conf. Advances in Welding Processes*, Harrogate, 1974.
50. Ton, H., "Physical Properties of the Plasma-MIG Welding Arc," *J. Phys. D; Appl. Phys.*, **8**, 922–933, 1975.
51. Tichelaar, G. W., Phillips Laboratories, private communication, December 1977.
52. Essers, W. G., Jelmorini, G., and Tichelaar, G. W., "Electrode Phenomena with Plasma-MIG Welding," *Proc. 2d Internat. Conf. on Gas Discharges*, London, 1972, pp. 135–137.
53. Taver, E. J., and Shorshorov, M. Kh., *Svar. Proizvod.*, **1971**(10), 26–28; English translation in *Weld. Prod. (USSR)*, **18**(10), 43, 1971.
54. Smars, E., Paper 9, *Internat. Conf. on Exploiting Welding in Production Technology*, London, 1975.
55. Vennekens, Ir. R., "Plasma-MIG Welding and Surfacing," IIW Doc. IV-192-76.

4

HIGH-FREQUENCY WELDING

High-frequency welding may be divided into two categories: (1) high-frequency resistance welding, in which the high-frequency current is introduced into the work by direct electrical contact; and (2) high-frequency induction welding, in which the high-frequency current is induced in the work by an inductor coil, without electrical contact. (High-frequency induction welding is sometimes called induction resistance welding.)

The high-frequency resistance welding process is an important but not widely known commercial process. Many thousands of tons of steel pipe alone are produced by the process every year. The process offers unique characteristics, such as high welding speed, which produce substantial economic advantages for its users.

Although high-frequency induction heating has been used commercially for many years, attempts to apply this type of electrical energy directly to the weldment resisted all attempts, until a breakthrough in 1950. This advance in the state of the art resulted from meticulous reevaluation of traditional concepts of the behavior of electrical energy, and unorthodox but practical solution of "impossible" problems of high-frequency power generation, transmission, and control.

High-frequency currents (10,000 to 500,000 Hz) have been used for several years to make welds in a variety of materials and shapes. In some cases, the high-frequency current is used to melt metal which then forms the weld. However, in most high-frequency welds, the welding current is used to heat the faying surfaces of the parts being welded so that a good solid-state weld can be produced. If molten metal is produced, it does not remain in the joint and does not contribute directly to the coalescence which is the weld.

THEORY AND KEY VARIABLES

To understand high-frequency resistance welding, an understanding of solid-state welding is useful. Solid-state welding processes can be divided into two types—diffusion welding and deformation welding. High-frequency welding is a deformation process.

All solid-state welding processes have one problem in common—overcoming the barrier presented by metal surfaces to producing welds by atomic forces acting across the weld interface. The major problem in solid-state welding is to put clean metal surfaces into contact so that the interatomic forces can act.

In general, high-frequency resistance welding employs a number of surface-conditioning operations to aid in producing welds. Faying surfaces are heated to high temperatures, usually above the melting point, and relatively large amounts of plastic deformation are used to remove contaminated metal from the faying surfaces and bring these surfaces into intimate contact.[1]

The high-frequency current is used to heat the faying surfaces to an appropriate temperature. High-frequency current is used because its behavior when flowing in a conductor offers the unique advantages of high welding speeds, welding without joint pickling or shot blasting, and welding of heavy wall thicknesses.

Deformation Welding

Making useful solid-state welds means that the surface roughness and barrier layers must be overcome during the welding process. Clean metal surfaces must be brought together if a weld is achieved. Heating to high temperatures coupled with deformation is one way of overcoming these surface problems.

Deformation welding includes any process where gross plastic flow is used to overcome the surface conditions that prevent welding on contact. Surface conditioning may be accomplished by plastic flow alone. Increasing the surface area of the faying surface breaks up the oxide skin into islands. Between these islands uncontaminated metal is brought into intimate contact and welding occurs. The interface area may be heated to make it easier to deform plastically.

High-Frequency Resistance-Welding Characteristics

The high-frequency resistance-welding process has a number of characteristics that are considered important in preparing high-strength joints in a large number of materials and configurations. One characteristic of the process is that welds with very narrow heat-affected zones can be produced. The welding current tends to flow only near the surface of the materials because of the skin effect, which is a result of the use of high-frequency welding current. The heat for welding, therefore, is developed in a small volume of metal along the edges to be joined. A narrow weld zone is desirable because it is capable of producing a stronger weld than the wider zone produced by other welding processes. The metal that becomes molten during welding is squeezed out of the joint during the upsetting or forging portion of the cycle.

High frequency current flow is controlled by two factors.[2] The high frequency makes the current flow in a thin layer on the surface of the conductor. The current also flows in the path of lowest impedance.

This path may not be the shortest path available to the current from a geometric point of view. These phenomena are called the "skin effect" and the "proximity effect."

Skin effect

Current distribution within the materials and near the edges to be welded is extremely important to successful high-frequency resistance welding. To produce narrow welds and weld-heat-affected zones, the depth of heat penetration must be limited. The depth of heating obtained with high frequency is limited by two effects: (1) the skin effect, and (2) the proximity effect. Skin effect is the term applied to the crowding of alternating electrical current toward the surface of a conductor.

Proximity effect

The proximity effect is that effect which causes current in a conductor to be attracted to a nearby return conductor. High-frequency current flowing in metallic conductors tends to flow on the surface of the material at relatively shallow depths. For example, at 450 kHz the depth of penetration of the current in steel at a temperature of 2000°F (1093°C) is about 0.030 in (0.76 mm); at 10 kHz the depth in steel at a temperature of 2000°F (1093°C) is about 0.2 in (5 mm). High-frequency current introduced into the work by means of contacts or by induction may have its path in the work controlled by variations in the inductance of the circuit and the nearness of its own return circuit, which is called the proximity effect.

When high-frequency current is used, the proximity effect makes it possible to confine heating to predetermined paths. A schematic example is shown in Fig. 4-1. In this example an auxiliary conductor is connected in series with the part to be heated.

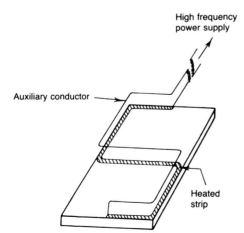

High frequency
power supply

Auxiliary conductor

Fig. 4-1 Sketch of use of proximity effect to restrict heating path of high-frequency current.[3]

Heated
strip

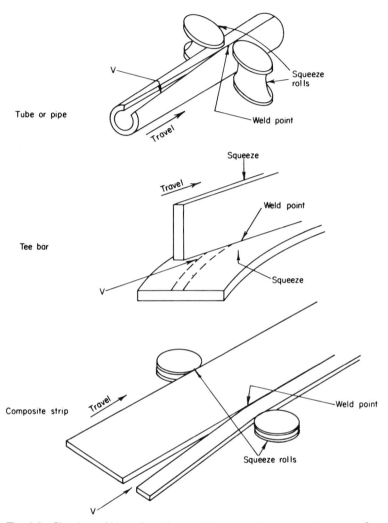

Fig. 4-2 Sketches of V configuration used to make three types of products.[3]

Process Principles

Both the skin effect and the proximity effect are used to make the heating current flow along the faying surfaces of the weld joint in high-frequency welding. To make most welds, the edges of the parts to be joined are brought together in the form of a vee. Three different configurations of vees for producing different products are shown in Fig. 4-2. The shape of the vee is important in producing satisfactory welds.

If the angle is less than 5°, the apex (weld point) does not stay at a fixed point, and weld variations occur. Also, arcing may occur upstream from the weld point. If angles larger than 7° are used, control over the part edges may be lost and the edges may wrinkle or stretch.

High-frequency current is introduced upstream of the apex, either through small sliding contacts at each edge of the joint, or through specially designed coils. High-frequency current flows along one seam edge to the apex of the vee at the squeeze rolls, then back upstream along the opposite edge. Current at such high frequencies flows along the metal surface to a depth of only a few thousandths of an inch. Each edge of the joint acts as the proximity conductor for the other, heating is concentrated at the surface of one edge, and in its mirror image in the opposing edge. Very high heating efficiencies and unusually close control of heating are possible because of the "proximity" and "skin" effects.[4]

High-Frequency Resistance Welding

High-frequency resistance welding (HFRW), in which the current is introduced by means of direct contact, may be utilized for a large number of configurations and types of welding. In turn, it may be divided into continuous HFRW in which two or more pieces of metal are continuously welded together at a high rate, and into finite-length or individual-piece HFRW, in which the whole area to be welded is heated at once and a weld produced. Induction welding (IW) of any kind can be used only in cases where there is a closed-loop path, or a complete circuit for the flow of current wholly in the work; this may, in turn, be divided into fixed-position static butt and lip-type welding,

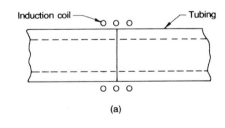

(a)

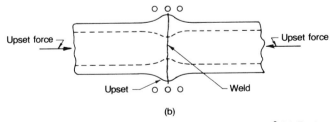

(b)

Fig. 4-3 Upset-butt-welding tubing by induction heating.[3] (a) During heating; (b) after upset.

generally of a circular nature (such as for pipe ends), and into continuous high-speed welding (such as for side seams of tubing.)[5]

Welds are also made by using high-frequency current to heat the ends of bars, tubes, pipes, or other shapes. The heated ends are then upset together and a weld obtained. This technique is often called IW although the proper name is upset-butt welding by induction heating. In this kind of welding no vee is used. The method is shown in Fig. 4-3. Some longitudinal welds in tubing have been made in a similar way. A long bar-shaped inductor is positioned over the closed longitudinal seam and as the pipe seam passes under the inductor, it is heated to welding temperature. A set of squeeze rolls makes the weld.

Electrical resistance heating has been employed for many years using frequencies as low as 25 Hz for purposes such as (1) melting, (2) heating heavy masses of metal for annealing, (3) preheating and postheating, and (4) forging. Subsequently, with the requirement for heating less massive structures (and in order to gain the advantages of the skin effect produced by high frequencies) high-frequency motor-generator sets and high-frequency vacuum-tube units were employed (usually with the current being induced into the work by means of an inductor). The high-frequency heating current was employed for operations such as heat treating, brazing, and soldering. This equipment has been adapted to many of the welding applications that were formerly reserved for low-frequency resistance and arc welding methods.[5]

Current

The current for high-frequency welding of either type may be produced by high-frequency motor-generators, solid-state inverters, or for higher frequencies, by vacuum-tube oscillators. Frequencies used are in two ranges; the lower is from 3 to 10 kHz, and the upper is from 300 to 500 kHz.

Welding current can be introduced to the parts being welded by induction or through contacts which ride on the part.

Welding with an induction coil

When the current is introduced by induction, the parts are usually of regular shape. This technique has been applied primarily to tubular products.

A work coil of some type is placed around the tube and used to induce current in the tube. A typical setup is shown in Fig. 4-4. With the coil shown in this figure, the current will be spread out around the circumference of the pipe, but will be concentrated along the vee. The work coil is always cooled, usually by internal water cooling.

Inducing the welding current in the work with a coil has certain advantages. It makes it possible to:

- Produce tubing with unmarked, highly polished surfaces.
- Produce tubing from coated metals.
- Produce tubing from patterned strip.
- Eliminate die or contact marks from the surface of thin-walled tubing.
- Weld materials where friction and interaction between contacts and skelp is a problem.
- Use a wide range of frequencies for welding, from 10,000 to 450,000 Hz.

The major disadvantages of IW are first that the process requires somewhat higher powers for equivalent material thicknesses and speeds than the contact process. Some resistive losses occur over the circumference of the tube. These are higher than circumferential resistive losses in the contact technique. A second disadvantage is the limited shapes of products that can be welded. There is no evidence that shapes other than tubes have been welded by the induction process.

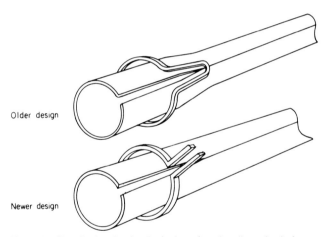

Older design

Newer design

Fig. 4-4 Sketch showing basic design of work coil used to induce current in the part being welded.[1]

Welding with contacts

When contacts are used to introduce the welding current the edges of the material being welded are also brought together to form a vee as shown in Fig. 4-5. Contacts ride on the surface of the materials being welded and current is transferred directly from the contacts to the part. Since even in a tube the path down one side of the vee and back the other side is the lowest-impedance path (because of the skin and proximity effects), almost all of the current flows around the vee. Because high currents have to be handled through the contacts, they are water-cooled internally.

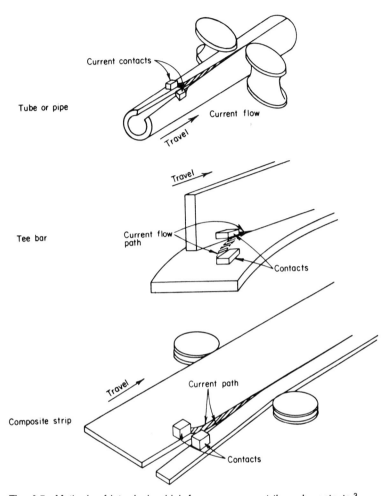

Fig. 4-5 Methods of introducing high-frequency current through contacts.[3]

High frequencies are used with contacts, of the order of 450,000 Hz. There are a number of reasons for using such high frequencies. First the skin and proximity effects are increased since they are proportional to frequency. The skin depth decreases as frequency increases and the proximity effect increases as frequency increases. Another reason for using such high frequency is that it reduces contact problems. It has been found that introducing current of 1000 to 2000 A through rubbing contacts is much easier at 450,000 Hz than at 60 or even 10,000 Hz. All metals have an oxide layer on their surfaces. Commercial metal surfaces may be covered with oxide skins or scale of appreciable thickness. At low frequencies the contact must either break through this skin and make contact with the metal or produce considerable heating through contact resistance. With high frequencies, the voltage is high and there is continuous arcing or puncturing of surface films under the contact. Most of the current is carried by the arc. Some portion of the current may also be transferred by capacitance through the oxide film on the work. In any event, the contact does not need to break through the oxide coating. Only enough pressure is needed to assure that continuous contact with the surface is maintained. This feature makes it possible to weld thin materials without bending or collapsing them. Contact wear is not a problem. Production life for a pair of contacts of 40,000 to 50,000 ft (12.2 to 15.2 km) of weld on hot-rolled steel has been reported.

As with the high-frequency induction welding (HFIW) process, the contact process has advantages and disadvantages. A major advantage is the ability to weld a given tube shape with less power. Power losses with the induction process are larger because the circumferential flow of current is greater than when contacts are used. The circumferential flow may be reduced by placing a ferrite rod in the proper position on the axis of the tube for tube making, and increasing the impedance of the circumferential current path. Of course, the same thing can be done when contacts are used, and often is, especially for small tubing.

Process Control

The control of HFRW is highly dependent on the configuration of the vee and other parameters.

When induction welding, the vee shape must be controlled. In addition, the inductor should be designed so that it transmits energy to the load with minimum loss. The inductor should be properly spaced from the work. The inductor is generally fairly wide as it encircles the tube. This spreads out the current in the circular path around the tube. At the vee the current concentrates along the edges to be welded. For power levels up to 100 kW a hairpin or nose is used on the coil as shown in Fig. 4-4. This hairpin helps to concentrate the current in the edges of the vee. A parameter which is also important is the placement of the coil with respect to the apex of the vee. Excessive power losses occur if this placement is not correct.

For contact HFRW, the vee can be defined more exactly as shown in Fig. 4-6. The vee is defined by:

- The width of the vee (or edge separation) w at the downstream, inside tip of the contact shoes.
- The contact-to-squeeze-roll center line distance $d_{c\text{-}sr}$ measured from the downstream, inside tip of the contact shoes to the center line of the squeeze rolls.

Temperature distribution within the materials and near the edges to be welded is extremely important to successful HFRW. To produce narrow welds and heat-affected zones, the depth of heating by the current must be limited. This can be done by proper relationships between the vee shape, the power input, and the speed of welding.

Maximum usage of the proximity effect is limited in HFRW because the strip separation must be sufficient to prevent arcing across the vee. Arcing across the vee is undesirable because it causes nonuniform heating of the strip and may pit the edges. The tendency for arcing to occur and the strip separation required to prevent arcing varies with the welding conditions and materials being welded.

Variation in the separation and length of the vee during welding will cause corresponding variations in the amount of power drawn from the generator and in the heat developed at the strip edges. Variation in the width of the vee during welding changes the distribution of current at the edges of the strips and causes changes in the depth of heating and the final surface temperature of the edges. To produce consistent welds, the width of the vee and the contact-to-vee-apex distance must not fluctuate.

There is no question about the need for accurate control of the relative positions of the edges when two edges are welded together. The ideal relationship is, of course, to have the two edges parallel and matched in the vertical direction. Mismatch will cause uneven heating of the faying surfaces. Serious angular mismatch may cause overmelting of the edges and arcing near the apex of the vee. Poor welds will result. In general, it is probably best to be sure that the faying surfaces are parallel and at the same level. However, in welding thick skelp into pipe, deliberate angular mismatch has been used. In this case the inside edges of the faying surfaces are melted off and as the edges approach the apex of the vee, they approach parallelism.

Materials would be expected to vary in the allowable ranges of energy inputs which will result in high-strength welds. Some materials

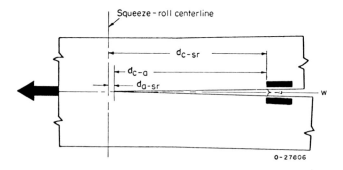

w = Width of the vee or strip separation at the contacts

d_{c-a} = Contact to apex distance

d_{c-sr} = Contact to squeeze-roll centerline distance

d_{a-sr} = Apex to squeeze-roll centerline distance

Fig. 4-6 Definition and nomenclature of the V for contact high-frequency welding.[3]

should possess sufficient tolerance to variations in energy input that a broad range of energy input will result in high-strength welds. Other materials may have critical energy-input requirements.

A second parameter related to weld characteristic is the power density, or heat-source intensity. As has already been mentioned, the heat-generation region in HFRW is confined by the skin and proximity effects to a thin band along the edge of the moving strip between the electrodes and the squeeze point, and approaches closely a strip heat source. The power density is the idealized energy release per unit area of a strip heat source moving along the strip edge at welding speed. Therefore, the width of the heat-affected zone in a high-frequency resistance weld should be linearly related to power density.

BASIC PROCESS TYPES

There are two basic process types; one is for high-speed welding of pipe, structural I beams, and other products from continuous metal strip, and the other is for welding drums, frames, and other finite-length products. Both depend on high-frequency current introduced directly to the workpiece through small electrical contacts. A current of 400 kHz is used for the "continuous" welding process, and 10 kHz current is used for the "finite-length" welding processes. In addition, specialized coils for heating and welding processes, based on 400-kHz induction heating, have also been developed for longitudinal pipe and tube welding.

Continuous High-Frequency Resistance Welding

Continuous HFRW is generally performed by introducing current into work at about 400 kHz by means of small sliding contacts. The parts to be joined are brought together in a vee of about 5 to 7°. The two edges to be welded are resistance-heated by the high-frequency current at a shallow depth, thus creating a high effective resistance. Speed and power level are adjusted so that the two facing edges are brought together at welding temperature, and then squeezed with forging pressure to produce the weld. Metal and impurities are squeezed out into two external upsets, which may be cut off, leaving smooth surfaces. Figure 4-7 shows configurations for butt welding the seam in a continuously moving tube while Fig. 4-8 shows the actual operation.

The benefits gained in using this process are:

- Higher joint-heating efficiencies, with resultant lower energy costs than in conventional processes.
- No special surface or joint preparation, since contact resistance factors are minimal; hot-rolled steel need not be cleaned prior to welding.
- A very narrow weld zone is produced because of extremely rapid heating and cooling caused by proximity and skin effects.
- Forge pressures force contaminants out into upset weld bead.

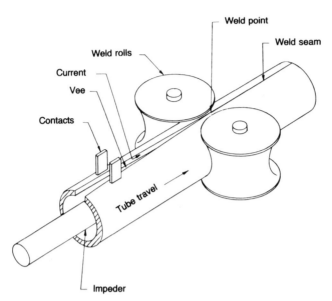

Fig. 4-7 Continuously butt welding a tube seam by HFRW.

Fig. 4-8 Close-up of 16-in-diameter (1216 mm) pipe mill with HFRW.[6]

Continuous HFRW—Current Penetration

This type of continuous HFRW utilizes 10 kHz for a variation of low-frequency seam welding. By use of the depth of current penetration possible with HFRW, the process is capable of joining from two to four layers of uncoated steel or stainless steel strip and sheet up to a total

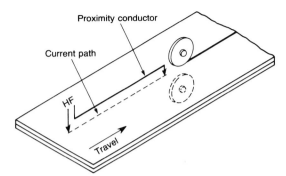

Fig. 4-9 Setup for continuous CP lap welding.

thickness of 0.25 in (6.4 mm). Current is introduced to the weldment through two contacts sliding against one of the moving surfaces, and is directed by a return conductor suspended above and parallel to the seam. A "hot line" is produced in the weldment directly beneath the return condutor, with penetration of up to 0.23 in (5.8 mm) in steel, when 10 kHz current is utilized. Squeeze rolls immediately downstream of the trailing high-frequency contact forge the heated metal into a continuous seam weld, at rates up to 150 ft/min (45 m/min), as seen in Fig. 4-9. Heating of the path to plastic welding temperatures takes place in all layers in milliseconds, with the "hot line" ranging from 0.5 to 6 in (12.7 to 152 mm) long, depending upon the distance between high-frequency contacts. This continuous current-penetration (CP) welding process can produce benefits such as:

- High-quality joint free of discontinuities
- Electrical contact made only from one face of the weldment
- Welds can be linear or nonlinear

Finite-Length Current-Penetration HFRW

Techniques have been devised for bringing the ends of two strips together, and passing a high-frequency current through the joint area. The high-frequency current is confined to the joint area by means of proper positioning of a return, or proximity conductor, over the weld. By selection of the proper frequency, the current will penetrate deeply enough to heat the joint all the way through. When the joint is at welding temperature, pressure is applied and upset automatically takes place. Joints with small upsets are made in this fashion at very high rates of speed.

The finite-length CP bar butt-welding process has been compared to flash welding; however, it provides the following additional advantages:

- No fumes, or spatter of molten metal
- Uniformly high-quality welds
- Low metal consumption equivalent to approximately the thickness of the base metal

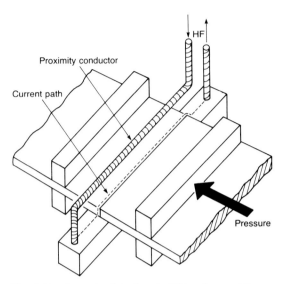

Fig. 4-10 Setup for finite-length CP bar butt welding.

The process is especially suited for joining finite-length flat, cylindrical, and other shapes, as seen in Fig. 4-10. Butt welds 3 to 36 in (76 to 900 mm) long can be made in steel 0.025 to 0.187 in (0.6 to 4.7 mm) thick. Slit or sheared steels and stainless steels, as well as aluminized, galvanized, and terne-plated steels, are readily joined. Multiple welds can be powered from a single power source. A 7.5-in (191-mm) joint in 0.118-in (3-mm) mild steel can be welded in 1.1 s. Dissimilar steels and sizes are readily joined. Workpieces are fed manually or automatically to the weld station, where they are positioned and clamped in a fixture.

Butted bars resting on a copper bar are brought together under pressure. Over the work and in line with the weld joint, a proximity conductor carried 10-kHz current to the copper bar. The current flows along the top of the copper bar and up to the upper edge of the joint. The current then flows along the joint, and the skin effect keeps the flow at the joint close to the surface. When the current reaches the end of the joint, it returns to the top surface of the copper bar and then goes out.

Resistance heats the joint within a second, and forging pressure completes the weld.

The finite-length CP bar lap or lip-welding process has been compared to resistance seam welding and has the following additional advantages:

- Continuous high-quality joints produced in one "shot," without work or weld head movements.
- Less lip width required than for normal resistance seam welding.

The process is capable of joining two or more thicknesses of uncoated steels and certain stainless steels in a projecting lip as shown

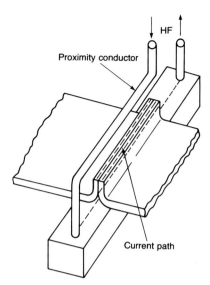

HF

Proximity conductor

Current path

Fig. 4-11 Setup for finite-length CP bar lip welding.

in Fig. 4-11. Welds can be straight or curved, from 3 to 36 in (76 to 900 mm) in length, in a total lip thickness up to 0.3 in (7.6 mm). A 24-in (0.6-m) lip weld in four thicknesses of 0.050-in (1.3-mm) Type 409 stainless steel can be made in approximately 2 s. Production equipment can be automatically or manually loaded. Current travels along the outer edge of the lip to a depth of 0.23 in (5.8 mm) in steel. In the lip-welding process, the upper edge of butting flanges on plates or sheets is prepared for joining in the same way as bar butt welds. A squeezing device or set of hammers, Fig. 4-12, forge-welds the heated top edge of the lips. An ideal joint fit is full contact over the entire length of the lip; nevertheless, gaps of 0.005 in (0.13 mm) are permissible on unclamped edges. Poor fits are easily pressed together as in Fig. 4-13. Hammers above the squeezer shown in Fig. 4-13*b* do the forge welding. This system requires deeper lips than the scheme of Fig. 4-13*a*, which uses nonconductive ceramics of high density such as aluminum oxide or silicon nitride on a combination clamping and

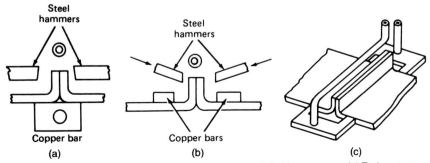

Steel
hammers

Steel
hammers

Copper bar

Copper bars

(a)   (b)   (c)

Fig. 4-12 (a) Squeezing device. (b) Copper bars in parallel with squeezers. (c) End contacts.

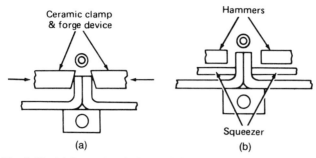

Fig. 4-13 (a) Squeezing device made from ceramics. (b) Hammers used in forge welding.

forging squeezer. After the lips are pressed together, and the high-frequency current heats the lip edges, added pressure forges the weld. The ceramic material must resist high pressures, high heat, and thermal shock. Figures 4–14a and b illustrate the various thickness combinations possible for lip welding, while Fig. 4-14c shows shapes other than straight lips that are weldable. The current penetration process is also adaptable to welding lips on round or oval objects. Production rates up to 900 parts per hour are attainable.

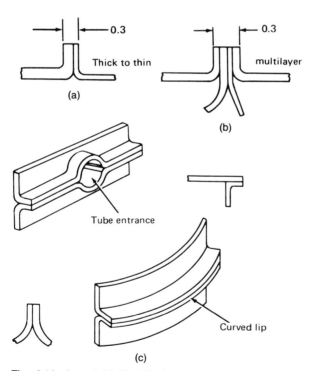

Fig. 4-14 (a and b) Combination thicknesses used for lip welding. (c) Weldable straight-lip shapes.

Continuous IW

Continuous IW can be used only in cases where there is a short-circuit path (or closed loop) wholly in the work, so that the induced current may circulate in the weld area. Typical is butt welding of tubing. In induction butt welding of tubing, the tube's edges are brought together in a 5 to 7° vee just downstream of the weld point. At the open end of the vee, an inductor encircles the tube. High-frequency current in the inductor induces a circulating current around the back of the tube and in the vee produced by the convergence of the edges of the tube. The current heats the edges; by control of the speed and power level, the edges are brought together at the proper welding temperature. Squeeze rolls press the edges together, producing a weld while liquid metal and impurities are squeezed out into an upset. This upset is then cut off, leaving a smooth surface. This technique of tube welding is advantageous for coated metals. Figure 4-15 is a representation of the induction butt welding of continuous tubing.

   IW of individual pieces is also performed when there is a closed-circuit path permitting the circulation of induced high-frequency current in the piece. Typical of these applications are the butt welding of pipe, or tube ends, in which the two ends are pressed against one another with a force sufficient to produce a weld when welding heat is reached.

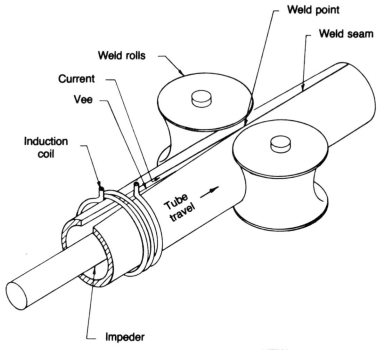

Fig. 4-15 Continuously butt welding a tube seam by HFIW.

EQUIPMENT AND TOOLING

Power Sources

Power generators for high-frequency continuous welding (either by high-frequency resistance or induction) above 10 kHz are usually restricted to vacuum-tube oscillators. Mercury-tube rectifiers are used to convert the plant input voltage into the high-voltage direct current utilized by the oscillator circuit. Solid-state rectifiers are now in use as a substitute for tube rectifiers. The output portion of the circuit is an induction coil (or inductor) surrounding the metal to be heated. The inductor can also be placed adjacent to the metal, when it is not practical to surround the parts being welded.

High-frequency RF generators range from 1 to over 60 kW output to handle the wide range of materials and production requirements called for in welding. For frequencies in the range of 3 to 10 kHz, used for some continuous HFRW applications and for some individual parts or pieces, high-frequency welding power is generally produced by motor-generators or by solid-state inverters. Shown in Fig. 4-16 is a fixture for continuous HFRW.[6]

The motor-generators used for this purpose usually consist of a high-frequency alternating-current single-phase alternator driven by an induction motor.

Fig. 4-16 Continuous high-frequency welding of H beams using two 160-kW power sources.[6]

The inverters usually consist of a solid-state rectifier that converts three-phase alternating current to direct current. The direct current, in turn, is converted by a controlled solid-state device to high-frequency alternating current with frequencies up to 10 kHz.

Matching Devices

Vacuum-tube oscillators inherently have high output impedances and should be fed into a high-impedance load. Since the inductors and the contacts used for HFRW are both low-impedance loads, some impedance-matching device is necessary in order to transfer energy efficiently from the generator to the work. This device is basically a transformer connected directly to the generator output. The transformer, or impedance-matching device, is generally of simple construction. It consists of a primary winding composed of multiple turns of water-cooled copper tubing surrounded by a secondary of one or several turns of water-cooled copper tubing.

In motor-generator and solid-state low-frequency power sources, the output of the device is normally fed through high-current cables to the primary of a transformer that is somewhat like a 60-Hz transformer utilizing a laminated iron core. Capacitors are connected in parallel with the primary of the transformer in order to improve the power factor of the high-inductance load so that the generator or inverter is operated as close to unity power factor as possible. The output of the transformer is at low voltage and high current; it feeds an induction coil or contact system through very short and closely spaced leads.

Contacts

Contacts are means through which high-frequency current is conducted into the workpiece for HFRW. The material used for high-frequency contacts, either fixed or sliding, is usually of the copper-silver group of alloys. The contacts are required to carry rather large currents, so that it is necessary in most instances to provide water cooling for the contacts and mounts. The force of the contacts on the material being welded is generally low. It is usually in the order of 5 to 50 lb (2.3 to 22.7 kg) on continuous welding, and 5 to 100 lb (2.3 to 45.4 kg) on static welding operations. The forces required are dependent upon the thickness and condition of parts being joined, as well as on the current density.

The contacts have a relatively long life on continuous welding of nonferrous materials. They last as much as several hundred thousand feet of tubing before having to be replaced. Life on ferrous metals which are clean or have tight scale is around 50,000 to 100,000 ft (15.2 to 30.5 km) of tubing, or more. On static welding operations, the contacts will last for many thousands of operations before requiring dressing or replacement.

Contacts are silver brazed to heavy copper mounts so that replacements can be made by replacing the mount and contact tip assembly. Repairs can be made easily by rebrazing new contact tips on the mount.

Induction Coils (Inductors)

The induction coil is the means through which the high-frequency alternating current flows to set up the alternating magnetic field required for the high-frequency induction heating of a workpiece. They are generally formed from copper tubing, copper bar, or copper sheet, and are water-cooled internally. The life of induction coils is usually dependent on whether physical damage occurs. The coil can be of the single- or multiple-turn variety, with the geometry conforming to the workpiece or to the area to be heated.

Impeders

In tube or pipe welding with either high-frequency resistance or high-frequency induction, there is a wasted current flowing around the inside surface of the tube. This current is in parallel with the welding current and is of no value. Therefore, in many tube-welding installations, a magnetic core called an impeder is placed inside the tube in the weld area. This core increases the inductive reactance of the current path inside the tube and reduces the inside current significantly. This, in turn, makes more power available for heat in the weld zone with a corresponding increase in welding speed for a given power input. See Fig. 4-7.

Control Devices

HFRW is by nature a mass-production system. Only a few hundredths to a few thousandths of a second is required to bring the metal from room temperature to welding temperature. Thus, it is important that the power source be automatically and continuously regulated. The most commonly used regulators are

- Motor-generator with high inertia to provide a constant output voltage, installed for one or a group of machines, but specifically devoted to feeding and controlling the high-frequency equipment.
- Electromechanical regulators, such as an induction regulator, installed on the individual equipment or on a group of machines.
- Electronic and saturable-core reactor regulators. These are employed mostly on high-frequency equipment in the lower capacity ranges, but are now available for the larger-capacity units. (Electronic and saturable-core reactor type regulators have faster response than induction regulators, but cannot isolate the high-frequency equipment from short-duration power line peaks in the way a motor-generator does.)[7]

Generator Power Controls

It is general practice to utilize a high-frequency generator of greater capacity than called for by the application; thus it is desirable to have a control for raising and lowering the level of high-frequency power to meet the individual demands of the welding operations. There are numerous types of high-frequency power controls; all basically perform the function of lowering or raising the current flowing in the contacts or the inductor coil.

Thyratron or phase-shift control, using a simple phase shifting of the voltage applied to the grid of the thyratron, is effective in raising and lowering the high-frequency level. Saturable-reactor control placed in the circuit before or after the main plate transformer provides a smooth power control. By the addition of a magnetic amplifier and instrumentation, automatic controlling can be accomplished. Variable-impedance control is accomplished by connecting a variable impedance in series with the secondary winding of the welding transformer and the inductor or contacts. This is the most direct method of raising or lowering the high-frequency power level.

Another recent innovation in control is the use of a system utilizing a controllable vacuum-tube device as a variable resistor placed in series with the dc output of the power supply to the oscillator.

In continuous HFRW operations, it is considered essential that the welding power be continuous and ripple-free, particularly for high-speed light nonferrous metal welding. For heavy ferrous metal welding, this is of much less importance. In high-frequency motor-generator power sources, power control is performed manually or automatically by varying the dc field on the high-frequency generator.

ECONOMICS

HFRW is making an impact on the auto, truck, and wheel producing industry as well as tube and pipe manufacturers.[8]

Tube and pipe produced by 400-kHz welding processes use almost 60% less electric power than the same tubing produced by low-frequency welding process. This saving can be translated into increased production capacity, without increasing the consumption of electrical power.

Tests made in a plant operating both 360-Hz rotary electrode and 400-kHz induction tube welders show that in producing 1.0-in-OD by 0.034-in-wall (25.7 by 0.86 mm) steel tubing at 113 ft/min (34 m/min), the rotary electrode welder costs $2.51 per hour to operate. The 400-kHz welder, operating under the same electrical conditions to produce the same tubing, costs only $0.93 per hour to operate. (This is based on a rate of $0.02 per kWh). On a three-shift production basis, the yearly saving is $7800. The plant can increase its production capacity from 113 ft/min (34 m/min) to 334 ft/min (102 m/min)—triple the rate possible with the ERW (rotary electrode) welder—while consuming the same amount of power. Also, low power requirements avoid the need for large transformer substations and allow production during periods of short power supply or brownouts.

Power savings increase with increase in tubing wall thickness. For example, 3.0-in-OD by 0.190-in-wall (76 by 4.8 mm) tubing welded at 47 ft/min (14 m/min) with a high-frequency welder, instead of rotary electrode welding, would result in a power bill savings approximately $8700. Further, power savings increase again as larger high-frequency welders are used. In producing a 3.0-in-OD by 0.160-in-wall (76 × 4 mm) tube at 169 ft/min (51 m/min), power savings from using the high-frequency welder would be $21,900 annually.

By using high-frequency CP bar butt welding the cost of welding automobile wheel rims, see Fig. 4-17, has been cut to one-third the cost by manual flash-butt methods. The equipment and fixtures, see Fig. 4-18, recently developed for the wheel production lines is capable of welding up to 1000 rims per hour, or about twice the rate possible with flash welding. Joint heating with 10-kHz currents normally produces less than one-half the weld upset or material burn-off resulting from flash welding. This saves about 0.25 in (6.4 mm) of blank length per trim.

Line input power of about 150 kW is required, only one-third of that used for a 600 kVA flash welder which produces only half as many rims. Initial tests show higher weld quality and elimination of pinhole leaks that often result during flash welding.

Operational benefits include elimination of sparks and spatter during welding. Programmable heating power and weld forging pressure facilitate simple automation; no operator is needed.

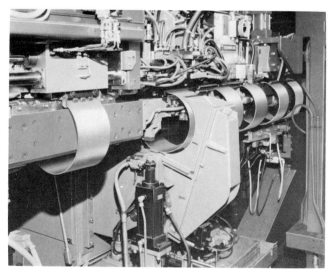

Fig. 4-17 Cut rim blanks in successive stages of fabrication.[6]

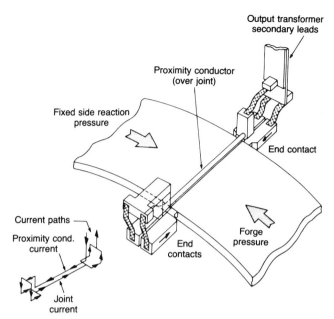

Fig. 4-18 Butt penetration welding fixture. Sketch at lower left shows current flow pattern.

In auto plant installations, eliminating two workers from each existing rim welding line can yield savings of $30,000 annually per shift. Savings in a steel strip can average 1% per rim or about $6 per hour of production. Other CP welding is currently being performed on auto frame blanks.

The fabrication of I and H beams used primarily in lightweight truss applications in commercial and residential building construction, and increasingly in truck and trailer construction, are produced by HFRW. The economics of the process are evident in the uptime or operating efficiencies which are 85 to 90%. Strip-to-beam conversion rates are said to be at 95%-plus level, and labor and operating costs are significantly lower. In a mill operating in Japan, single-size beam production runs have been conducted with a mill uptime rate in excess of 90%. Because of this, beam and scrap losses are less than 5%. Virtually automatic operation of the mill has also reduced cost of labor.

Mill downtime for size changes is at a minimum because of quick-change, modular design of the fixtures for feeding, processing, aligning, and welding strips into beams. Quick-change systems are built into the mill to aid in rapid retooling.

MATERIALS

A wide variety of materials have been welded by HFRW. Table 4-1 lists materials which have been successfully welded by the process.

Recent development work evaluated the feasibility of using the HFRW process to produce 20-ft (6-m) lengths of 5456-H111 alloy, 3 in (76 mm) high, T-extrusion-welded to 4-in (102-mm) weld strip of 0.187-in-thick (4.7 mm) 5456-H116 sheet. This type of structure is to be used in several new high-speed aluminum ships, and the welding setup is seen in Fig. 4-19.

Aluminum and copper have low resistivity and high thermal conductivity, but with HFRW these properties are not a disadvantage. A large variety of aluminum tubing made of various alloys in Table 4-1 is being successfully welded in diameters from 0.5 to 16 in (12.7 to 406 mm), with walls up to 0.25 in (6.4 mm) thick. Copper, having a conductivity as high as 101%, is successfully welded without change in grain size at or near the weld. Figure 4-20 shows the microstructure of a weld in copper.

Brass, normally difficult to weld because of its natural tendency to lose zinc when hot, can be joined with high frequency without a shielding atmosphere. The high resistivity of brass makes it weldable at very high speed.

TABLE 4-1
Materials Successfully Welded by HFRW Process[5]

Carbon Steels	Aluminum
API Grade B	1100
API Grades X42 through X60	1002
Boiler tube	2014
A7	2017
A36	2219
Galvanized	5051
SAE 1010 to 1020	5052
	5056
Alloy Steels	5083
	5456
Cr-Mo high-temperature steels	6061
4340	7179
4130	
Tool steel	*Zirconium*
430 stainless	
301 stainless	Commercially pure
310 stainless	Zircaloy
17-7PH	
18% maraging	*Titanium*
	Commercially pure
Copper	6-4
	8-1-1
OFHC	
Bronze	*Nickel*
63-37 brass	
70-30 brass	René 41
Cupronickel	Inconel
Beryllium-copper	
Monel	

Fig. 4-19 Welded T stiffened panel.[9]

Steel is very well suited to HFRW. Scaled hot-rolled steel can be welded without difficulty; hot-rolled, pickled, and cold-rolled steels are also easily welded. Stainless steels in the 300 and 400 series are also welded by the high-frequency process.[11]

Zirconium and zircaloy have been welded successfully with a protective argon atmosphere. Many other materials such as bronze, silicon bronze, German silver, and Inconel are welded successfully with both the continuous HFRW and HFIW processes.

Titanium structural shapes for high-speed aircraft currently are fabricated by extrusion or by machining from thick plate or bar. Extruded shapes may have poor transverse properties and require overall finishing to remove contaminated surfaces and achieve the required dimensions. Fabrication by machining is expensive and wasteful of material. HFRW has been demonstrated to be a promising method for economic high-speed fabrication of titanium structural shapes that have good mechanical properties. Several government-sponsored programs showed the feasibility of producing titanium tee shapes from 0.030- to 0.060-in-thick (0.76 to 1.5 mm) in Ti-6Al-4V and Ti-8Al-1Mo-1V alloy strips. A recently completed program showed the successful fabrication of I shapes from titanium strip.

The I sections were fabricated from Ti-6Al-4V strip. The straight I

Fig. 4-20 Photomicrograph of HFRW in electrolytic copper, 150×.[10]

sections were made using 2-in-wide (50.8 mm) strip 0.080 in (2.2 mm) thick for the web. The material for the tapered I sections was the same except that the width of the web strip tapered in 8 ft (2.4 m). These sections simulate actual components used in fabricating aircraft structures.

In the process, the titanium is shielded from the air during heating and subsequent cooling. Since the strips are hot from the contact-shoe location to the weld point, argon-filled chambers are used to protect the heated metal. In subsequent testing and evaluation of the shapes produced, in the static mode of loading, the welded sections were equal to or superior to extruded titanium sections or the unwelded base material. Butt sections were tested by loading transversely across the weld; the tee sections were loaded both transversely and longitudinally. Tee sections also were tested in compression. See Table 4-2.

Various types of fatigue loadings were applied, and the relative superiority of welded or extruded tee sections depended on the mode of loading. Two transverse loading directions were used, parallel and perpendicular to the weld bond line, and in both cases the welded tees were equal in fatigue strength to extruded tee sections. The welded tee sections loaded longitudinally demonstrated slightly reduced fatigue strength compared with the extruded tee sections. Fillet fatigue tests indicated that the fillet radius could be reduced to $0.5T$ without degrading the flexing fatigue strength.

Currently several HSLA (high strength, low alloy) steels, although they cannot be rolled into structural shapes, will shortly be used to make I beams by HFRW. The practicability of fabricating beams of HSLA steels by HFRW was shown recently in tests on Armco Formable 80 and J&L Van 80 alloys with a minimum yield strength of 80 ksi (552 MPa), and Republic X-W-45 with a minimum yield strength of 45 ksi (310 MPa). No postweld heat treatment is required on most

HSLA steels with low carbon and manganese. The main use for the I beams will be as lightweight, high-strength frame sections in truck trailers.

HFRW has also been used to weld dissimilar metals together. Following are examples of dissimilar metal weldments which have been produced:

- Double-walled tubing made from two types of steel to obtain unusual sonic properties.
- Carbon steel to OFHC copper for high-strength, high-conductivity bar.
- OFHC copper to aluminum alloy to produce high-strength lightweight conductor.
- Tool steel to carbon steel for band-saw blades.
- Beryllium copper to brass for electrical contacts.
- Type 430 stainless steel to galvanized carbon steel for automotive trim.
- Structural shapes of alloy and carbon steel for architectural use or strength improvement.
- Clad steel to carbon-steel sheet.

TABLE 4-2
Static Tensile Properties of Welded and Extruded Sections

Material	Form[a]	Condition[b]	Fillet, r/t	Nominal thickness		Tensile strength	
				in	mm	ksi	MPa
Transverse-Rib Test							
Ti-6Al-4V	W	SR	0.34	0.085	2.2	146	1007
	E	MA	1.0	0.085	2.2	145	1000
	W	STA	0.34	0.085	2.2	157	1083
	E	STA	1.0	0.085	2.2	154	1062
7075 Aluminum	E	T6	1.0	0.140	3.6	74	510
Longitudinal-Rib Test							
Ti-6Al-4V	W	SR	0.34	0.085	2.2	138	952
	W	STA	0.34	0.085	2.2	151	1041
Stem-Transverse Test							
Ti-6Al-4V	W	SR	0.34	0.085	2.2	121	834
	E	MA	1.0	0.085	2.2	140	965
	W	STA	0.34	0.085	2.2	115	793
	E	STA	1.0	0.085	2.2	147	1014
7075 Aluminum	E	T6	1.0	0.140	3.6	73	503
Compression-Crippling Test							
Ti-6Al-4V	W	SR	0.34	0.085	2.2	126	869
	E	MA	1.0	0.085	2.2	138	952
	W	STA	0.34	0.085	2.2	125	862
	E	STA	1.0	0.085	2.2	143	986

[a]W = Welded, E = extrusion.
[b]SR = stress relieved; MA = mill annealed; STA = solution treated and aged.

JOINT DESIGN

Three basic types of joints can be made using the HFRW process—butt, lap (flat lap or scarf lap), and tee. Sketches of these joints are shown in Fig. 4-21. With these basic joint configurations, a wide variety of products can be produced. A variety of products that have or could be produced by HFRW are shown in Fig. 4-22. These products will be discussed in more detail under *Applications.*

It should be noted that, in general, IW is used exclusively with the butt-joint configuration and for tube shapes. However, when a circular inductor is used, this method of welding might also be used with the scarf configuration to make tubing or pipe.

In certain cases in IW, a circular joint may be made by melting the two edges of the lip together with an induced current. Surface tension

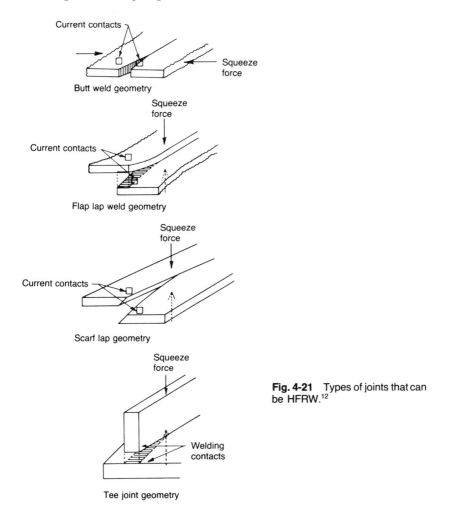

Current contacts

Squeeze force

Butt weld geometry

Squeeze force

Current contacts

Flap lap weld geometry

Squeeze force

Current contacts

Scarf lap geometry

Squeeze force

Fig. 4-21 Types of joints that can be HFRW.[12]

Welding contacts

Tee joint geometry

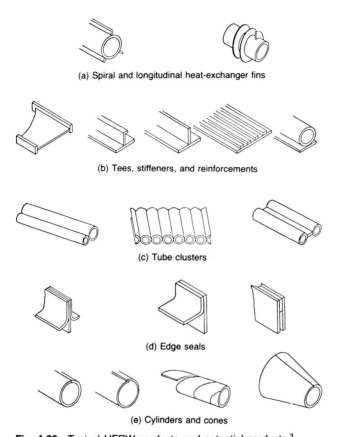

(a) Spiral and longitudinal heat-exchanger fins

(b) Tees, stiffeners, and reinforcements

(c) Tube clusters

(d) Edge seals

(e) Cylinders and cones

Fig. 4-22   Typical HFRW products and potential products.[3]

of the liquid metal causes the two edges to flow smoothly together. Figure 4-23 shows typical cross sections of three of these joints.

Another very recent form of IW of individual pieces is performed by induction heating a joint, such as a lap joint, between two pipes. After the parts are at welding temperature, a very large extra pulse of current in the inductor produces magnetic forces in the work that press and forge the hot parts together to make the weld.

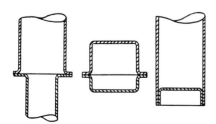

Fig. 4-23   Typical joint types for induction welding.

TABLE 4-3
HFRW Used on End Products

Metal furniture	Auto side rail and frame cross-member
Propeller shaft	tubing
Auto tailpipe	Lamp posts
Steel structures	Filters
Bimetallic strip	Well casings
Cable sheathing	Mufflers
Can (tin plate and aluminum)	Band saw blades
Copper tubing	Auto decorative trim
Irrigation tubing and pipe	Furnace water-wall tubing
Auto drive shaft tubing	Heater tubes
Automotive radiator	Nuclear reactor finned tubing (Zr)
Auto and truck axle and housing tubing	Bearing races
Appliance tubing	Mirror support system for space telescope
Bicycle tubing	(Ti-6Al-4V)
Catalytic converter enclosures	Wheel rims
Water tanks	Gas transmission line piping
Signpost frames	Vacuum cleaner tubing
Display racks	

APPLICATIONS

The number of applications for HFRW is growing at a rapid rate. Industry acceptance of the process is now general throughout the world, particularly for continuous welding operations. Equipment manufacturers have been working steadily on the process, and with new developments in technology, users of high-frequency equipment have begun to seek out other applications; see Table 4-3.

The process is one of high efficiency. Well-designed installations use as much as 60% of the energy drawn from the power line; this appears as useful heat in the work. Practically all high-frequency welding machines use a balanced three-phase power system.

Since the time required in HFRW is short and the heat localized, there is minimum oxidation, discoloration, heat-affected zone, and distortion of the parts. Containers, which cover materials that would normally be damaged by excessive heat, can be high-frequency welded. Included in the latter is the continuous welding of electrical cable sheaths, with the cable inside the sheath while it is being welded.

Tube and Pipe

Both IW and HFRW are used for manufacturing tube and pipe. These processes have produced a significant percentage of the world's output of pipe and tube. They are usable for the manufacture of nonferrous and ferrous tubing, as well as heavy-wall pipe.

Welds can be made in tubular shapes either as longitudinal welds (parallel to the axis of the tube) or as "spiral" welds (weld is a helix around tube). In general, for high-speed production of pipe and tube, longitudinal welds are made. With spiral techniques, large-diameter pipe can be made from skelp which is too narrow to make the same diameter by longitudinal welding.

Tubular forms for making tubing and pipe may be made in many ways. However, to make the maximum use of the high-frequency processes, they are usually made in a rolling form mill. Figure 4-24 shows a modern high-speed mill for making steel pipe up to 24 in (0.6 m) in diameter. The same techniques have also been used for small-diameter tubing.

A major advantage of the HFRW process is its capability to weld very thin tube forms. Wall thickness of at least 0.030 in (0.76 mm) and perhaps thinner can be butt-welded by either the induction or contact process. If very thin walls are to be welded, the contact process can be used to make lap welds. Three different techniques of making cans from 0.005- to 0.015-in-thick (0.13 to 0.38 mm) metal have been investigated. These involve:

- Continuously forming a longitudinal mash lap joint, then cutting the tube to a can length.
- Continuously spiral forming and mash lap welding, then cutting the tube to can length.
- Longitudinally mash lap welding individual can blanks by first heating the full length of the joint and then mash lap welding the whole length simultaneously.

Fig. 4-24 Modern high-speed manufacturing mill.[10]

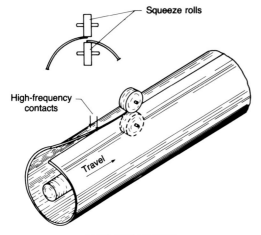

Longitudinal mash lap

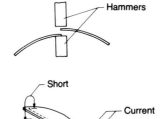

Spiral mash lap

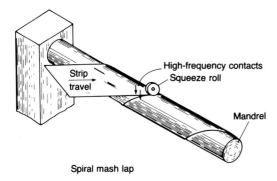

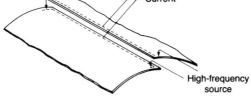

One-blow mash lap

Fig. 4-25   Three techniques for welding thin-wall cans.[11]

Fig. 4-26 Spiral-welding-produced wire-mesh tubing.[6]

Figure 4-25 shows sketches which describe how the techniques work. These same techniques can be applied to any thin-walled tubular shape.

Spiral welding has many uses other than for cans. A wide variety of pipe diameters can be produced by spiral welding using the contact process. Figure 4-26 shows a piece of wire mesh tubing produced by this technique.

It is possible to make tube forms that are not circular by HFRW. An important example is the production of rectangular tubing to be used in automobile frames. This tubing can be made by forming two channels and welding them together. However, a better way is to form the rectangular section with a single seam and then weld the seam closed in much the same way as round tubing is welded. Figure 4-27 shows an automobile frame made from welded rectangular tubing.

HFRW is also used for cable sheathing. Sheathing is used to keep moisture out of and oil or other impregnating liquid in power and communication cables.[13] The sheath must resist mechanical stresses in a

Fig. 4-27 HFRW-produced auto frame from rectangular tubing.[6]

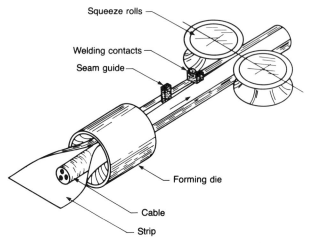

Fig. 4-28 Die-forming technique for cable sheathing.[3]

wide variety of environments. An ideal sheath is strong, light, and corrosion resistant. Aluminum and steel sheathing can be applied by HFRW. One way of accomplishing this is shown schematically in Fig. 4-28.

Structural Shapes

In the past, structural shapes generally have been made in steel by hot rolling. The major advance in HFRW has been its adaptation to

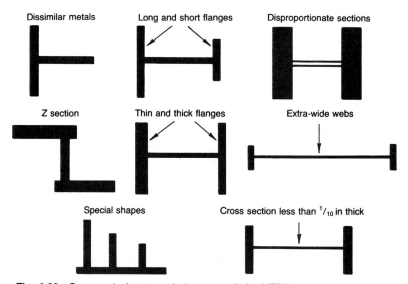

Fig. 4-29 Some typical structural shapes made by HFRW.

structural shapes. It has been found that the process can be used to produce economically shapes that are not otherwise feasible. Shapes made up from dissimilar metals, shapes whose sections have significantly different web and flange thicknesses, those with asymmetrical sections, and those with thin components are possible. Some examples are shown in Fig. 4-29.

Tee welds hypothetically can be made in any metal. They are easiest to make in a metal such as titanium which dissolves its own oxide at elevated temperatures. They are hardest to make in a metal such as

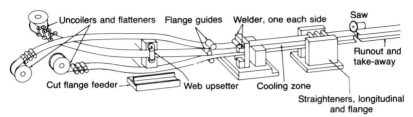

Fig. 4-30   Production operation to weld structural beams.

aluminum which has a tenacious oxide which is not dissolved by the parent metal at elevated temperatures. Carbon and low-alloy steels fall somewhere between titanium and aluminum in ease of tee welding. In welding steel, enough metal is squeezed out of the tee that it is not necessary to descale the faying surfaces before welding. This is true even for hot-rolled steels.

Structural shapes that are considered practical for welding are tees, angles, I's, H's, channels, and special shapes. The standard shapes can be easily produced with uneven flanges or legs, different thicknesses of flanges or legs, extra wide webs, stems or legs, and very thin webs, stems or legs. Special shapes that cannot be rolled can be made. In addition, shapes can be made of dissimilar metals. Tees with a stainless steel flange and carbon-steel stem can be made. H or I sections with high-strength alloy steel flanges and carbon-steel webs are easily produced. Galvanized and aluminum steels can be welded.[14]

An advantage of producing structurals by HFRW is that the process is adaptable to large-scale production. If the parts being made can be produced from hot-rolled strip, the mill sketched in Fig. 4-30 can produce beams continuously and at high speeds.

Finned Tubing

Finned tubing is useful in heat exchangers of all types because of the extended surface which the fin provides.[15]

Within the last 15 years a number of mills have started to produce finned tubing and pipe by HFRW. See Fig. 4-31. Tubing with either spiral or longitudinal fins is produced. Most of this material is carbon-steel tubing with carbon-steel fins for use in steam-generation service.[16]

Fig. 4-31 High-frequency spiral finning of pipe. Inset shows close-up of weld area.[6]

Other spiral tubing joined by HFRW includes aluminum fins to aluminized steel and copper-nickel tubing. The composite finned tubes are being considered for heat-exchanger applications in power generating, heating, cooling, and desalination equipment. See Fig. 4-32.

Fig. 4-32 Welded aluminum-finned steel tubing.

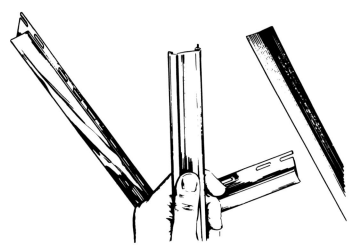

Fig. 4-33 Dual-metal trim for automotive use.

Metal Molding

Dual-metal automotive trim and moldings, seen in Fig. 4-33, are being produced commercially by HFRW. The process also is used to produce decorative moldings for office and kitchen furniture, appliances, and architectural shapes. One company has even made dual-metal saw blades by combining high-speed steel for the cutting edge with a flexible steel backing. The "stainless" molding consists of a thin outer strip of stainless steel and a thicker backing strip of less-expensive carbon steel. The costly metal may comprise one-fourth or less of the total thickness, thereby substantially reducing material costs.

Dual-metal strips also can be made for electrical contacts, terminals, and similar components by welding narrow strips of tungsten-copper or silver alloys to less-costly backing material.

Where are tomorrow's products? In the aerospace industry, structural shapes besides tee sections are required in modern aircraft. Development programs are necessary to explore other shapes, such as L's, Z's, or H's, which could be fabricated successfully by HFRW. The ultimate objective, of course, would be to fabricate stiffened panels by this process. Although many procedure and tooling problems must be solved, panel fabrication should be feasible. In all of this military and commercial applications, the savings in fabricating costs would be appreciable. As needs arise HFRW will find its niche.

REFERENCES

1. Osborn, H. B., Jr., "High Frequency Welding of Pipe and Tubing," *Weld. J.*, **42**(7), 571–577, July 1963.
2. Wollaston, K. H., "High Frequency Welding of Titanium tube," *J. Inst. Met.*, **90**, 33–37, December 1961.

3. Martin, D. C., "High Frequency Resistance Welding," WRC Bull. 160, April 1971.

4. Heald, S. T., "Radio Frequency Resistance Welding of Carbon Steel Pipe and Tubing," *5th Mechanical Metal Working Conference, AIME Metallurgical Society Conference, Metallurgical Working of Steel*, 21 (1963).

5. Kirdo, I. V., and Skachko, Yu. N., "The Radio Frequency Welding of Brass Tubes," *Avtom. Svarka* (Automatic Welding), **11**, 44–50, 1963 (BWRA translation available).

6. Thermatool Corp. private communication, June 1978.

7. "High Frequency Resistance Welding," *Weld. Met. Fabr.*, August 1968, pp. 285–292.

8. Rudd, W. C., "High Frequency Resistance Welding," *Metal Prog.*, October 1965, pp. 239–240, 244.

9. Reichelt, W., Alcoa, private communication, March 1978.

10. Kearns, W., editor, "Welding Handbook," private communication, April 1978.

11. Rudd, W. D., "High Frequency Resistance Welding of Cans," *Weld. J.*, **4**(42), 279–284, April 1963.

12. Wolcott, C. G., "High Frequency Welded Structural Shapes," *Weld. J.*, **11**(44), 921–926, November 1965.

13. Tudbury, C. A., "Cable Sheathing by Electronics in Sweden," *IEEE Internat. Conv. Rec.*, 1963.

14. Rudd, W. C., "High Frequency Resistance Weldings of Structural Shapes," *IEEE Electrical Heating Conf.*, September 1965.

15. Oppenheimer, E. D., "Helically and Longitudinally Finned Tubing by High Frequency Resistance Welding," American Society of Tool and Manufacturing Engineers, Technical Paper AD67-197, 1967.

16. "High Frequency Welded Thinwall Tubing for Radiators," *Automot. Ind.*, Dec. 1, 1973, pp. 34–36.

17. DeSaw, F. A., Mishler, H. W., and Monroe, R. E., "Development of a Manufacturing Method for the Production of Aircraft Structural Components of Titanium by High Frequency Resistance Welding," Rep. AFML-TR-71-222, Battelle Memorial Institute, Columbus, OH, Contr. F33615-70-C-1416, August 1971.

18. "High Frequency Welder Spits Out I-Beams for Mobile Homes," *Weld. Des. Fabr.*, **45**(7), 42–43, July 1972.

19. Rudd, W. C., "Lip Welding with High Frequency Currents," *Weld. Des. Fabr.*, January 1973, pp. 54–55.

20. Rudd, W. C., "Current Penetration Seam Welding—A New High Speed Process," *Weld. J.*, **46**(9), 762–766, September 1967.

21. Rudd, W. C., "Bar Butt Current Penetration Welding," *Weld. J.*, **49**(10), 788–794, October 1970.

22. Brosilow, R., "How to Make a Wheel Rim—In Four Seconds," *Weld. Des. Fabr.*, February 1976, pp. 57–59.

5

EXPLOSIVE WELDING

In recent years, many "new" processes have been introduced, some of which have been used only briefly, some of which have turned out to be extensions of older, established processes, and a few of which have developed into really new and substantially useful tools. While explosive welding (EXW) is not in any usual sense a mature technique, it seems apparent that it is an important new metal-joining technique because of its ability to handle unique joining problems and large areas, and because it is potentially economically competitive with other joining processes.

If we compare the development of EXW with that of explosive forming, to which it is less related than one might first suppose, we see that EXW faced a distinctly different attitude and climate than did explosive forming. The concept of using the force from an explosive charge instead of a large press to form metal into a die is easily grasped and therefore credible, while the idea that two metals can be made to join by simply "banging" them together at ambient temperature is less credible. Because of these differing attitudes, explosive forming was immediately and enthusiastically accepted, while EXW until very recently met mainly skepticism and a corresponding paucity of interest and support.

Although it has been less than a decade under development, EXW is in general use by the technological community.

The controlled application of the enormous power generated by detonating explosives gives rise to phenomena not intuitively expected by those accustomed to more traditional velocities and pressures. EXW offers the opportunity to clean metal surfaces of contaminants such as oxide and nitride films, oil, adsorbed gases, etc. and to immediately press these thoroughly clean surfaces together at pressures of several million pounds per square inch (newtons per square meter). Further, the relatively small amount of energy involved with the process gives rise to minimum melt accumulation at the metal/metal interface. These are ideal conditions for effective welding.

Combinations of metals such as aluminum to steel and titanium to steel, which form brittle intermetallics when exposed to the elevated temperatures of conventional welding methods, are readily joined by

EXW. The only metals that cannot be welded by the process are those too brittle to withstand the impact of the explosive impulse. As a rule of thumb, those metals with 5% or greater tensile elongation in a 2-in (50.8-mm) gage length or a Charpy V-notch impact value of 10 ft-lb (13.5 J), or greater, are acceptable. (EXW is like slapping your hand down hard on water when swimming. If your hand is at a slight angle with the water, the impact will cause a jet of water to emerge from your fingertips.)

THEORY AND KEY VARIABLES

The phenomena that occur during or are related to EXW, as well as the EXW process itself, have been the subject of considerable study by investigators throughout the world. The welding mechanism is an oblique plate collision process that results in a jetting effect at the collision point. The jetting effect is thought to be responsible for the effacement of surface films between the colliding plates, which are held in intimate contact by the explosive pressures such that interatomic and intermolecular forces between the plates produce a weld. To fully appreciate and understand the nature of the EXW process, it is necessary to understand the requirements for metallurgical welding and the nature of the detonation of solid high explosives.

Metallurgical Welding

To achieve a metallurgical bond between two similar or dissimilar pieces of metal, the atomic structure of metal A must be brought sufficiently close to the atomic structure of metal B that the cohesive atomic forces of each array of atoms can effectively act on the other. This normally requires an intimacy of contact on the order of an interatomic spacing. Because metal and metal-alloy surfaces in a normal atmospheric environment are always covered with films of oxides, nitrides, and adsorbed gases, the surfaces of mating metal plates, even under very high direct pressure, will not metallurgically bond because sufficient intimacy of contact cannot be established. The removal or effacement of surface films and the establishment of the necessary intimacy of contact, then, must be achieved in any metallurgical bonding process. Fusion welding, brazing, and soldering are examples of joining processes that effectively disrupt surface films by dissolution or melting and establish the necessary intimacy of contact by wetting of the molten phase. On the other hand, HFRW, friction welding, and ultrasonic welding disrupt surface films by severe localized deformation of the mating surfaces while the surfaces are maintained in intimate contact by high pressure. The EXW process meets the requirements for metallurgical bonding by the elimination of surface-film material from the joint interface and the concurrent development of a very intimate interfacial contact, each as the result of the high-pressure collision.

Explosive Detonation

To one being introduced to EXW for the first time, it is often not clear how the cladding plate is made to strike the backer plate at an angle, especially when the plates are set up for welding in a parallel manner. This is usually the result of an intuitive misconception that an explosion is an instantaneous occurrence. Although an explosion appears and sounds like an instantaneous phenomenon, it actually is a progressive reaction.

Detonation can propagate at a rate as high as 28,000 ft/s (8538 m/s), generating approximately one liter (1×10^{-3} m^3), of gaseous products for every gram of explosive detonated. The pressure in the vicinity of the detonation from the sudden generation of gas may be as high as 4000 psi (27×10^3 MPa).

In EXW it is this high pressure, developed in a narrow zone in the layer of explosive, that forces the cladding plate across a predetermined interfacial separation to collide with the backup plate. The zone of high pressure developed by the explosive acts progressively on the surface of the cladding plate as it moves over the surface. The cladding plate, in turn, is accelerated in the region where the explosive has detonated and remains essentially undisturbed where the explosive has not yet detonated.

Actually the picture presented above of the events that occur during an explosion and the response of the metal cladding plate to the detonation pressure is grossly oversimplified. The subject is extremely complex and in some cases not well understood. Many papers and books have been written on the subject of explosive detonation and the reaction of solid materials to explosive forces. To fully appreciate the complexity of the phenomenon, one should consult some of the many books and papers that have been written on the subject, for example, Refs. 1 through 4.

Mechanisms and Principles

The mechanism of EXW involves high-pressure mechanics and fluid flow. Simply stated, bonding is accomplished when the high-pressure developed by a chemical explosive is used to impinge metal surfaces at a critical velocity and in a critical angled configuration. When the collision velocity and angle are controlled within certain limits, the surfaces at the point of collision become fluid and are expelled from the apex of the collision angle. This flow process and expulsion of the surface layers is known as jetting. The severe deformation and extension of the colliding surfaces by hydrodynamic flow and the resulting jet act to break up the bond-inhibiting surface films, leaving behind film-free surfaces pressed into intimate contact. Unless an excess of energy remains in the system (resulting from reflected shock waves, residual stresses, and/or interfacial melting), the mating surfaces will remain metallurgically bonded.

Shock

Shock puts metal in a strange state. As a metal is compressed severely by a shock wave, its temperature, internal energy, and entropy increase. Particles of the metal even attain a unidirectional velocity.

After the shock wave passes and the metal is again exposed to a normal environment, it returns to its original volume. Of course, if a shock wave causes permanent deformation—as in EXW—there will be a change in shape.

Principles

The process is basically simple. Typical setups are shown in Figs. 5-1 and 5-2. The prime metal is oriented to the backer metal with an air gap separating them. The explosive, in plastic, liquid or granular form, is placed uniformly over the prime metal. The base of the backer rests on an anvil appropriate to the thickness of the backer and to the

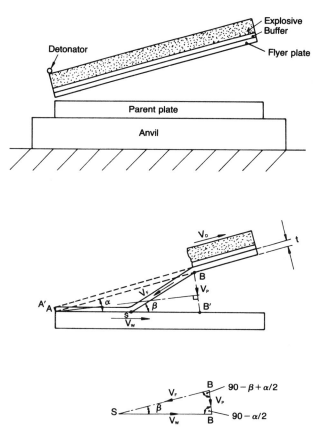

Fig. 5-1 Inclined arrangement for EXW.[5]

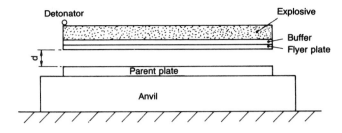

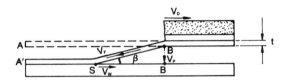

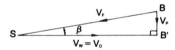

Fig. 5-2 Parallel arrangement for EXW.[5]

allowable distortion of the final product. For thick backers a bed of sand is an entirely satisfactory anvil; thinner backers require stronger anvils such as a slab of steel or possibly concrete. The air gap is maintained by supports tack-welded to the prime and to the backer, or by metallic inserts between the prime and backer at the very edges. If the prime is of such a thickness or dimension that it tends to sag in the middle, internal support in the form of thin metal ribbons stood on edge are positioned between the prime and the backer.

Many operators choose to place a moderating layer (e.g., polyethylene, water, or rubber) between the explosive and the prime metal. This serves to protect the surface of the prime from the effects of the explosive. The explosive is then initiated so that the detonation wave front progresses across the surface of the prime in a straightforward and uncomplicated manner.

An acceptable weld results after the following conditions are satisfied:[5]

1. V_W/V_{SP} and V_F/V_{SF} should be less than 1.2, where V_W is the velocity of point of impact (Figs. 5-1 and 5-2), V_{SP} is the sonic velocity in the parent plate, V_F is the velocity of the flyer plate relative to the point of impact (Figs. 5-1 and 5-2), and V_{SF} is the sonic velocity in the flyer plate.

2. The impact angle β (see Figs. 5-1 and 5-2) should exceed a limiting value below which welding does not take place.
3. A minimum value of impact velocity must be exceeded to get welding.
4. Above this minimum of impact velocity the conditions for an acceptable weld is dependent upon the impact energy, not impact pressure. The weldability of a given material combination is governed by the stronger of the two materials, regardless of which material constitutes the flyer or the parent plate. The minimum impact energy for an acceptable weld is proportional to the ratio of strain energy to dynamic yield of the material.
5. There appears to be a maximum impact energy above which the weld is weakened by excessive melting, which may be related to the heat required to raise the temperature of the lowest-melting-point material to its melting point.
6. For optimum use of explosive, the standoff distance should be between $^1/_2$ and 1 times the flyer plate thickness.
7. High detonation velocity explosives should not be used because of damage to the flyer plate resulting from the high pulse pressure.
8. The effect of using air or steel as an anvil plate does not significantly change the weld quality.

Very recent experiments have shown the limitations of these proposals. For instance, a melted interlayer is not necessarily weakening unless harmful intermetallics are formed, or the thickness of the melted layer formed is sufficiently great as to allow the reflected tension wave to separate the two surfaces before solidification occurs. It also appears that, although in similar-density materials melting is concentrated in the vortices as long as the energy is not excessive, in dissimilar density metals there is a very thin melt zone at the interface even at low impact energies. This confirms that though some welding parameters can be defined, the process is so complex that it is still not possible to predict and control all the significant parameters with certainty.

Two important variables in the welding process are: (1) the collision velocity and (2) the collision angle. Other important factors are the physical and mechanical properties of the metals being welded and their dimensions.

Collision velocity

The nature of the explosive used determines the detonation velocity, which in combination with the preset angle between the plates establishes the collision velocity. If the plates are preset parallel (Fig. 5-2) to one another, the collision velocity is equal to the detonation velocity. Experiments have established that there is a collision velocity below which no welding occurs. For jetting and welding to occur, the collision velocity has to be in the vicinity of the sonic velocity of the plates. Table 5-1 presents the bulk sonic velocity of several metals.

TABLE 5-1
Bulk Sonic Velocity of Some Common Metals[6]

	Sonic velocity	
Metals	ft/min	m/s
Al	1.1	5.6×10^{-3}
Cu	0.8	4.1×10^{-3}
Mg	0.9	4.6×10^{-3}
Mo	1.0	5.1×10^{-3}
Ni	0.9	4.6×10^{-3}
Stainless steel (Type 302)	0.9	4.6×10^{-3}
Ti	0.9	4.6×10^{-3}
Zr	0.7	3.6×10^{-3}
Zn	0.6	3.0×10^{-3}
Steel	0.9	4.6×10^{-3}

Collision angle

There is also a minimum collision angle below which no jetting occurs regardless of the collision velocity. In the parallel plate cladding arrangement shown in Fig. 5-2, this angle is established by the distance between the two plates called "standoff." In the case of angle cladding (Fig. 5-1), the preset angle plus the standoff will establish the collision angle. The amount of explosive, metal thickness, and material properties of the prime plate have direct influence on the collision angle.

Jetting

In order to obtain a metallurgical bond in EXW, jetting has to occur. In order for jetting to occur, two metal plates are made to collide at a high velocity and in an angular fashion.

The word "jetting" is most often used to describe the division of a fluid stream into component streams as it strikes an impenetrable surface, as illustrated in Fig. 5-3. During the angular collision of two metals at a velocity of between 1000 and 3000 ft/s (305.8 and 914 m/s), high pressure is generated at the collision point. But when the collision occurs at a specific angle and velocity, the compressed metal in the vicinity of the collision point, which behaves as a fluid, flows toward the apex of the collision angle, relieving the unequal distribution of

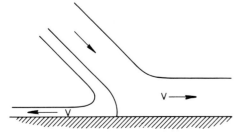

Fig. 5-3 Illustration of division of fluid stream striking an impenetrable surface.

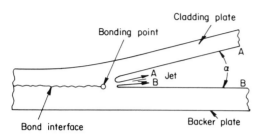

Fig. 5-4 Plate-collision process and subsequent setting.

pressure that tends to occur. An illustration of the angled collision is shown in Fig. 5-4. The high pressure and resulting fluid behavior of the metal extend only a short distance from the collision point; therefore, only the surfaces in the vicinity of the collision point take part in the hydrodynamic flow. When the surfaces of metal A and metal B divide from their parent masses and flow in the same direction, jetting has occurred. The division of the metal surfaces accomplishes two important functions. First, the bond-inhibiting films which are attached to the surfaces are broken up and expelled from the point of collision. Second, the division of the surface exposes virgin metal in the vicinity of the collision point of the adjacent metal plates. These virgin surfaces are brought into intimate contact by virtue of the collision and the extreme shearing action of the dividing streams of metal. The intimacy of contact is of atomic dimensions and the forces of atomic attraction that hold metal A and metal B in the solid state interact, forming a union of metals A and B by their cohesive atomic forces; therefore, a metallurgical bond results.

Bonded Interfaces

Probably the most noted effect and certainly the one that evokes the most curiosity is the rippled or wavy appearance of the explosive weld interface. However, the metallurgical bond between the two metals has essentially three configurations: (1) straight, direct metal-to-metal bond, (2) wavy, or (3) straight butt with a continuous layer between the plates. These three configurations are shown in Fig. 5-5. They result from variations in collision velocity and collision angle.

A straight metal-to-metal bond configuration is obtained when the collision velocity is below the critical velocity required for the formation of waves. The jet escapes completely, and the plates are bonded in a straight line. This type of bond is satisfactory; however, in practice it is not easy to achieve, since slowing the collision velocity below the critical value can result in nonbonds.

At the correct collision velocity and collision angle, the wavy type of bond configuration is formed. A greater degree of freedom is available in choosing the angle and velocity for the wavy bond than exists for the straight bond. This wavy type of bond is stronger than the other type bonds and is more reproducible. The rippled interface is the result of fluctuations in the dividing fluid stream or jet at the collision point. The fluctuations in jet flow are thought to be caused by the buildup of a hump of material ahead of the collision point, as the collision point races across the surface, which interferes with the flow-division process. The jet flow meets resistance from the hump of material as the hump increases in size, eventually interrupting the jet flow momentarily. The cladding plate then flows over the hump, relieving the resistance to the jet flow, and the process is free to repeat itself.

The straight bond with a continuous layer occurs when the clad is made at higher collision velocities than those employed for the wavy bond configuration. The continuous layer is essentially an alloy composed of the two plate materials. It is thought to be caused by the instantaneous heat generated by the severe plastic deformations encountered at the interface. Where the two metals form solid solutions, such as copper and nickel, the presence of such a layer may not be detrimental to the bond strength. However, when the two metals form brittle intermetallics, such as steel and tantalum, the layer represents a weakness. In general, a continuous layer bond is not considered an optimum bonding condition.

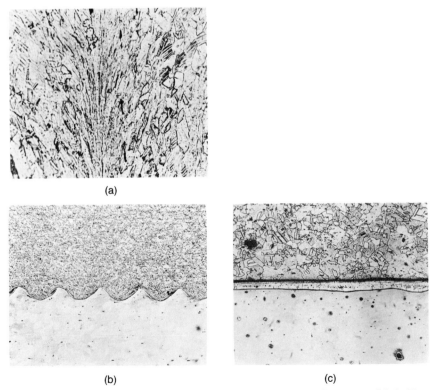

(a)

(b)   (c)

Fig. 5-5 (a) Copper weld; (b) copper-nickel with a wavy interface; (c) copper-nickel with a continuous-layer bond zone.[6]

Bond Nature and Interfacial Heating

Microscopic study of the typical wavy bond zone in Fig. 5-6 reveals that a heavy plastic flow occurs at the crest of the waves. Electron-probe analysis indicates that the melt pockets in front and in back of the waves are composed of mixtures of the two plates.

In metal systems that form solid solutions, these melt pockets are ductile. In systems that form a series of intermetallics, these melt pockets are brittle and may show flaws; however, extensive mechanical tests have shown that these flaws are very localized and are not harmful to the mechanical properties of the bonded plates.

The strength and quality of an explosive weld often depends on the amount of interfacial melting that occurs, from which two major detrimental effects can result: brittle intermetallic compounds and shrinkage voids. Metal combinations that form brittle intermetallic compounds from diffusion or fusion interaction will exhibit poor explosive-weld strengths if extensive interfacial melting occurs; see Fig. 5-7. The solidified melt will be made up of the two metals being joined and therefore will exist as the brittle-compound phase. If the brittle compound is distributed as discrete pockets and not as a continuous layer, the strength of the weld may not be significantly impaired.

For metal combinations that are metallurgically compatible, a small amount of interfacial melting will not degrade the strength of the joint. But if a large amount of melting has occurred, the solidified melt is likely to contain shrinkage voids. These shrinkage voids can act as sites for crack initiation and, if numerous, they will simply decrease the effective weld area. In addition, the cast metal structure associated with the solidified melt will generally have inferior mechanical properties.

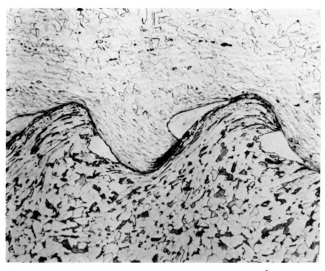

Fig. 5-6 Interface between carbon and low-alloy steel.[6]

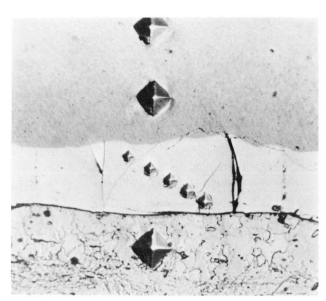

Fig. 5-7 Interface of tantalum and iron.[6]

The amount of interfacial melting is controlled by the EXW parameters, which normally are chosen so that a continuous layer of melt is eliminated and the pockets of melt associated with the wavy interface are kept to a minimum.

Process Variables

From a mechanistic point of view, the important factors involved in EXW are the kinetic energy and the collision angle of the cladding

TABLE 5-2
Material and Process Parameters of EXW

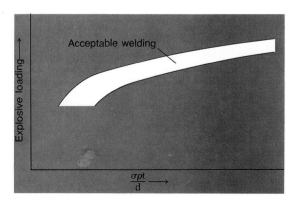

plate at the moment of collision. But, for engineering applications, these factors are meaningless unless a suitable expression can be found to relate them to process parameters and material properties. The role of the material and process parameters of EXW is expressed by the relationship of the explosive loading, or the weight of explosive per unit area of cladding plate, to the cladding plate's strength σ, density ρ, and thickness t, and the gap d between cladding plate and base plate. Shown in Table 5-2 is in generalized form for explosives of low detonation velocity, a relationship which has been empirically determined for a wide variety of metal alloys, so that it is now possible to predict, with fair accuracy, the optimum conditions for explosively welding almost any alloy to itself or to another alloy.

Practices

Although a relatively small number of firms and institutions are working with EXW, their practices with regard to types of explosives used, handling of noise and air blasts associated with detonating explosives, EXW procedures, and evaluation of weld quality vary greatly from one to the other.

Explosives

The energy for the process is provided by the detonation of a high explosive. The detonation velocity of the explosive is important because it must fall within the limits necessary to produce the required impact velocity between the two metals being welded. Investigators[7] have established that the maximum detonation velocity of the explosive should not normally exceed 120% of the highest sonic velocity within the materials being welded to produce jetting and prevent shock damage to these materials. When explosives having higher detonation velocities are used, special equipment and procedures are necessary.

The explosives that have been utilized for welding vary both in

TABLE 5-3
Explosives Used for EXW

High velocity, 15–25,000 ft/s (4572–7620 m/s)	TNT, RDX, PETN, composition B, composition C4, Detasheet, Primacord
Low–medium velocity, 5–15,000 ft/s (1524–4572 m/s)	Ammonium nitrate, ammonium perchlorate, amatol, nitroguonidine, dynamites, diluted PETN

detonation velocity and physical form. Some of the explosives used by category of detonation velocity are shown in Table 5-3. In addition to the explosives shown in Table 5-3, special explosives may be made or blended for specific EXW purposes. The physical forms of explosives utilized for welding include plastic flexible sheet, cord, pressed shapes, cast shapes, and powder or granulated explosives.

The low- and medium-detonation-velocity explosives listed in Table 5-3 fall within the detonation-velocity limits generally required for EXW and are used extensively where large areas of materials are being welded. These explosives require little or no buffering and are generally used in direct contact with the cladding metal. In addition, they are usually considerably cheaper; the cost may be as little as 1/50 that of the high-detonation-velocity plastic explosives.

Low- and medium-detonation-velocity explosives are also used for specialized EXW such as lap, seam, and spot welding. This will be discussed later in the chapter.

As pointed out above, explosives having detonation velocities greater than 120% of the sonic velocity within the materials being welded are used in the more specialized applications of the EXW processes. When they are used for welding larger surface areas such as flat plates, more elaborate techniques [including (1) buffer materials or air gaps between the explosive and the prime or cladder metal, (2) angled interface clearances, or (3) minimal parallel-plate interface clearances] are required to prevent material shock damage.

Noise and Air Blast

The problems of noise and air blast associated with detonating explosives have been discouraging to many who have considered the application of explosive metalworking processes. The principal restrictions to the size of composites that can be explosively welded are the noise, air blast, and ground vibrations generated by the detonating explosive.

The approach most commonly used has been to locate the EXW facility in a remote area in order to avoid the consequences of these effects. With increasing population density, remote areas are becoming more difficult to find; therefore, techniques must be employed to lessen the effects of the explosion which, under the certain conditions, may extend for many miles. These techniques involve various forms of barricading, and burying the explosive and the components to be bonded under sand and water. Also, a very important factor in outdoor EXW operations is the weather, especially in the northern, midwestern, and eastern states where a large portion of the nation's manufacturing is concentrated.

One attractive solution to the problems of noise and air blast, as well as environmental problems, for EXW operations involving smaller explosives charges has been the use of low-grade-vacuum chambers. Figure 5-8 shows a vacuum chamber presently being used for EXW.

Fig. 5-8 EXW vacuum chamber.

PARAMETERS

Basically, two geometries and their modifications are utilized for EXW. These are (1) constant interface clearance or standoff and (2) angular interface clearance, both of which are shown schematically in Fig. 5-9. When low- and medium-detonation-velocity explosives are being used, a constant finite clearance is normally employed, without any buffering material between the explosive and the cladding plate. With the use of high-detonation-velocity explosives and a constant interface clearance, buffering materials such as Plexiglas, rubber, etc., and in some instances, air gaps, are employed between the explosive and the cladder plate.

A variation of constant clearance bonding in which buffering is used is shown in Fig. 5-10. This technique, called explosive lock cladding, differs from most other constant clearance techniques in that separation is maintained by knurling or threading the base-metal weld surface to depths from 0.001 to 0.100 in (0.03 to 2.5 mm).

Angled interface clearance is used with high-detonation-velocity explosives. The technique produces good small-area seam, lap, tee, and flat coupon welds.

EXW in air generally produces a satisfactory joint, but some investigators use a vacuum because they feel that air in the interface is detrimental.[8] Whether or not useful for improving welds, a vacuum environment helps eliminate noise and air blast. Some EXW[9] is performed underwater; however, the interface is nearly always in air or vacuum.

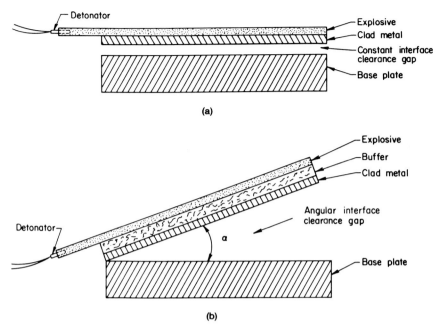

Fig. 5-9 Explosive-metal geometries utilized to accomplish EXW.

The most important parameters in EXW[8] are thought to be the type and mass or charge loading of explosive, mass and mechanical properties of the cladding metal, and the distance through which the cladding metal is accelerated before it collides with the base metal. Determining the optimum combination of these parameters for welding any particular combination of metals has been done empirically by many of the people in the field, often requiring a large number of experiments. Investigators[9] have recently developed an empirical relationship of the important material and process parameters to cladding-plate velocity and quality of welding for a wide variety of metals and alloy combina-

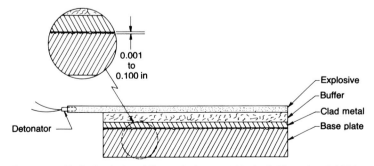

Fig. 5-10 Explosive lock welding technique—0.001 in (0.03 mm) to 0.100 in (2.5 mm).

tions, thus making it possible to predict more accurately the optimum EXW parameters for most metal and alloy combinations.

Depending on the configuration, types of materials, and material thicknesses, postbonding treatment of explosively welded composites will vary from no required treatment to machining, flattening, reshaping, and stress-relief annealing. In many instances, clad flat plates have a curvature which exceeds allowable tolerances after the welding operation; therefore, the plates must be flattened. Explosively welded composites may normally be stress-relief-annealed to remove the cold work introduced during the welding operation. Caution must be exercised in heat treating metallurgically incompatible metal composites so that the heat treating temperature does not result in diffusion across the weld interface to form undesirable compounds.

WELD QUALITY

A large number of tests, both nondestructive and destructive, are used to evaluate the weld quality or integrity and the effect of the process on the parent metals in explosively welded composites.

Nondestructive Evaluation

Ultrasonic inspection

Ultrasonic inspection is the most commonly used nondestructive technique for determining weld quality in explosively welded products. Ultrasonic inspection will not confirm the strength of the welded interface, but it will clearly locate the nonwelded and partially welded areas usually found around the periphery of explosion-welded composites. It has been used to evaluate the welds in a wide variety of composite configurations from flat plate to spot welds.[10] Care must be exercised in ultrasonic inspection to compensate for discrepancies in the test results caused by specimen curvature, surface finish, and material distortion.

Radiography

Radiography has been investigated as a nondestructive technique for determining weld continuity by numerous investigators.[10,11] Reports indicate that it can be used as a reliable technique for determining weld quality.

Destructive Evaluation

Peel

Peel or chisel testing is a rough, quick technique widely used by most people in the EXW field to determine weld soundness. The test involves peeling the cladding metal back against itself or driving a chisel into the weld interface. Generally, if the weld is of sufficient quality, failure will occur in one of the parent metals, however, if the weld is of less than optimum quality, failure will occur along the weld interface. The ability of the interface to resist the separating force of the chisel provides an excellent qualitative measure of bond ductility and strength. Nonuniform weld quality will often result in a combination of failure in the base and cladding metal and along the weld interface in advance of the chisel point.

Bend

The bend test is used to evaluate both weld integrity and ductility of the composite. In accordance with applicable ASTM and ASME boiler and pressure vessel code specifications, bend specimens cut from explosion-welded plate have consistently withstood 180° (3.14 rad) bending without separation of the weld. Testing is usually done with the prime metal in tension and compression. Figure 5-11 shows bend test samples from explosion-welded plate.

The general experience has been that the majority of the explosively welded composites with good-quality welds will successfully withstand a full 180° (3.14-rad) bend in the as-welded condition with the cladding metal both in tension and in compression. Titanium-[12] and zirconium-alloy claddings require a stress-relief anneal before they can withstand such a bend with the cladding in tension. In the as-welded condition, these metals will exhibit localized fissuring at the weld zone during bending. Although Stellite 6B can be successfully explosively welded to other metals, it cannot be bent through a 180° (3.14-rad) bend in tension without fracturing. It can, however, be bent in compression without failure.

Fig. 5-11 Explosive-welded bend test specimens.[6]

Tensile

The tensile test is utilized to determine the influence of the metallurgical EXW in the composite and to determine the effects of the EXW process on the parent metals. The specimen used for this test is usually a standard tensile specimen of the integral composite, and yield strength, ultimate strength, reduction of area, and elongation are determined.

A special "ram" tensile test has been developed by some researchers to evaluate the weld-zone tensile strength of explosion-welded composites. As shown in Fig. 5-12, the specimen is designed to subject the welded interface to a pure tensile load.

The specimen typically has a very short tensile gage length and is intended to cause failure at the welded interface. The ultimate tensile strength and relative ductility of the explosion-welded interface can be obtained by this technique. Perhaps the most important thing learned from the test is related to the mode of fracture of the specimen.

Shear

The shear test is used to determine weld strength and involves subjecting the weld zone of the explosively welded composite to a shear

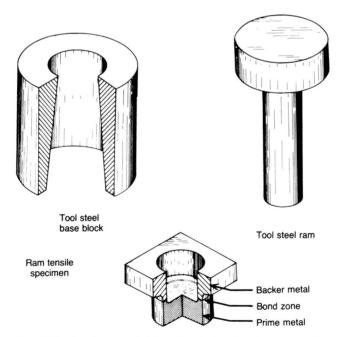

Tool steel base block

Tool steel ram

Ram tensile specimen

Backer metal

Bond zone

Prime metal

Fig. 5-12 Specimen and fixture for testing bond zone tensile strengths.[6]

TABLE 5-4
Typical Shear Strengths for Commercially
Available Explosive-Welded Plates[6]

	Typical shear strength	
Cladding metal on carbon-steel backers	ksi	MPa
Stainless steels	66.7	460
Nickel and nickel alloys	60.5	417
Hastelloy alloys	56.7	391
Zirconium	49.0	338
Titanium	39.5	212
Cupronickel	36.4	251
Copper	22.0	152
Aluminum (1100-H14)	13.9	96

load. In general, failure in shear testing of a high-quality explosive weld will occur in the weaker of the two materials rather than at the weld. This test is normally conducted in accordance with the standard ASTM test, Specification A264-64. The ASTM and ASME specifications require a minimum weld shear strength of 20 ksi (138 MPa) for nickel- and stainless-steel-clad plate. Typical shear strengths for commercially available explosion-welded plates are shown in Table 5-4.

Fatigue

Fatigue tests have been employed to determine both weld quality and the effects of the EXW process on the parent metals of the composite. The fatigue properties of the parent metals are not adversely affected by the EXW process and fatigue fractures are not initiated in the plane of the weld zone.

Thermal Fatigue

Thermal fatiguing involves heating specimens from explosively welded composites to elevated temperatures followed by quenching to near room temperature in short time cycles. After thermal cycling, the specimens are usually bent and/or shear-tested to determine the effect of the cycling on the ductility and weld strength of the composite.

Researchers[15] have reported that plates of Type 304 stainless-steel-clad steel and 55A titanium-clad steel withstood 2000 cycles of heating to 1000°F (538°C) followed by quenching in cold water, while tantalum-clad steel plates withstood 2500 cycles at 650°F (344°C) with no decrease in weld strength. Although the shear strength is often lowered slightly by thermal cycling, the reduction is a result of partial stress-relief of one or both of the parent metals. Shear fracture still occurs in the weaker parent metal.

Hardness

Hardness testing is utilized to determine the effects of the EXW process on hardening of the metals in the welded compact. The test involves conducting a microhardness profile study on a cross section of the explosively welded composite. In general, it has been found that the greatest hardness increases occur adjacent to the weld zone or interface. The amount of hardening depends upon the metal or alloy being welded—those metals or alloys that are more susceptible to work hardening, such as Type 304 stainless steel, will develop considerably higher hardness during the welding operation than metals such as aluminum.

Postbonding heat treatment will reduce or remove the work hardening introduced by the welding operation. Low-carbon steels, aluminum alloys, copper alloys, and titanium composites can be stress-relief-annealed at relatively low temperatures, while stainless steels, nickel-base alloys, etc. require higher annealing temperatures.

Corrosion

Corrosion testing involves subjecting the explosively welded composite to the standard corrosion test which will best describe its performance in the corrosive atmosphere in which the composite is intended for use, and then monitoring the composite in its actual field application. Companies[16] report that they have experienced no impairment of corrosion resistance attributable to explosive cladding. Explosively clad Type 304L stainless steel has successfully passed boiling nitric acid and boiling ferric sulfate–sulfuric acid tests for intergranular corrosion. Further, the corrosion resistance of explosively welded titanium, as tested in boiling 65% nitric acid "hot wall" lab tests, has not been altered. An explosively welded titanium sample behaved normally in a 2-year exposure to nitric acid vapor in a plant batch reactor that operated at 400°F (204°C) and 2 ksi (14 MPa).

Miscellaneous

Electrical and thermal conductivity studies have demonstrated that the welded interface does not impede the free flow of electricity or heat. Impact and torsion tests have also verified the quality of explosion welded metals.

EQUIPMENT AND TOOLING

An important consideration in producing explosive-welded joints in metals is getting rid of the shock wave after the weld has been formed. The compressive wave caused by the high-speed collision propagates through the metal until it reaches an interface. All or part of the wave is reflected, and it is converted from a compressive to a tensile wave. If

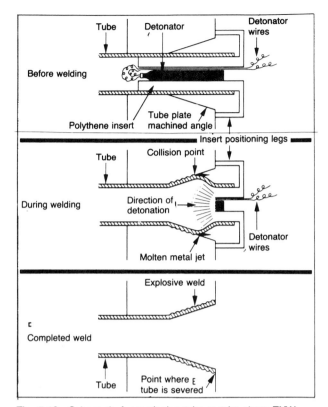

Fig. 5-13 Schematic for explosive tube-to-tube-sheet EXW.

the magnitude of the reflected tensile wave exceeds the strength of the weld it can rip the weld apart. Metal-to-air interfaces reflect nearly all wave energy. Thus, proper selection of support tooling and its geometry is important for successful EXW.

The equipment and tooling required for EXW varies with the application, joint configuration, and materials being joined.

The geometries used for tube-to-tube-sheet and plug welding are based on the angular geometrical setup seen in Fig. 5-13.

Plug welding, being a maintenance operation, is usually carried out on site. More often than not, the tube sheet is in a relatively inaccessible position, and in many instances the operator is working in conditions of close confinement with a hot, steamy, undesirable atmosphere. Figure 5-14 is a schematic showing an application of the tooling developed to demonstrate the location of an explosively loaded plug assembly inside a tube and welding the plug to the tube, all from a remote location.

One of the primary advantages of the EXW process is the ability to clad dissimilar metals to each other. Dissimilar metals can be explosively clad since the explosion weld does not have a molten zone at the

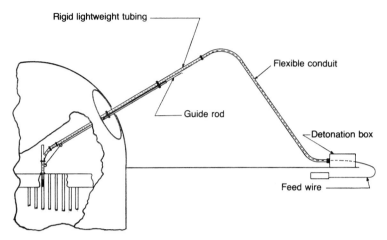

Rigid lightweight tubing

Flexible conduit

Guide rod

Detonation box

Feed wire

Fig. 5-14 Schematic of tooling for EXW plugs from remote location.

interface. Lead and steel are among dissimilar metals which may be explosively clad to each other. Normally, lead and steel are immiscible. This means that before they can be welded by means other than EXW, the steel surface has to be tinned. Tinning of the steel followed by casting molten lead on the surface presents health problems. Successful EXW of lead to steel has utilized compacted sand as a satisfactory anvil system. Tooling for EXW is shown in Fig. 5.15.

Fig. 5-15 Tooling for EXW.[17]

ECONOMICS (ADVANTAGES AND LIMITATIONS)

The mechanism of welding combined with the nature of the weld makes EXW a unique and versatile welding technique. Many of its advantages result from the fact it is a cold-welding process. Some of the advantages of EXW are

- A high-strength metallurgical weld can be formed not only between similar metals, but also between those dissimilar metal joint systems that are incompatible when fusion or diffusion joining methods are used. Over 260 combinations of similar and dissimilar metals have been welded by this process, including dispersion-strengthened alloys.
- Welding can be achieved between alloys without significantly disturbing the effects of cold work, dispersions, or precipitates that are necessary to strengthen various alloys.
- The explosive energy is self-contained, cheap, safe to handle, and for special applications can be portable.
- Welding can be achieved quickly in applications involving weld areas from less than 1 in^2 (6.5×10^2 mm^2) to over 100 ft^2 (9.3 m^2).
- The facility required for welding is simple, and only a small equipment investment is needed.
- Joint surfaces do not require extensive cleaning other than removal of heavy oxides and scale followed by degreasing.
- The low cost of using explosives for fabrication is most attractive—usually 50 cents to $1 per pound.

Disadvantages and limitations of the process are

- The metals being welded must possess sufficient ductility and impact resistance to withstand the forces of the detonating explosive and the ensuing collision of the components. Although gray cast iron has been successfully clad with 304 stainless steel without damage, most materials of low impact resistance will not practically survive EXW.
- Because of the complexity of the welding mechanisms and the need to maintain controlled collision conditions, EXW is generally confined to welding simple geometries such as flat plates, cylinders, and cones.
- The thickness of the base or stationary component in EXW is essentially unlimited; however, the cladding-plate (component accelerated by the explosive) thickness is limited. Cladding-plate thicknesses ranging from 0.001 to 2 in (0.03 to 0.8 mm) have been explosively welded.
- The noise and air blast associated with the detonation has been a discouraging factor in utilization of the EXW process. The use of remote locations or burying of the explosive under sand or dirt to suppress the noise and air blast add to the cost of the process. One practical solution to this problem developed by a research institute has been the construction of a blast containment structure specifically for explosive metalworking operation.[18]

JOINT DESIGN

The versatility of the EXW process has been demonstrated in the many geometric configurations that have been welded by the process. The geometries that have been explosively welded include flat plate and sheet, cylindrical configurations, configurations employing linear welds such as lap joints, tee joints, panels, spot welds, and other more complex configurations such as honeycomb structures. The area of weld ranges from small areas in spot welds to extremely large areas in clad plates.

Flat Plate and Sheet

To date, the widest application of EXW has been in the area of cladding and welding of flat plate and sheet, which involves the simplest and most straightforward of EXW procedures. The major commercial application of the EXW process is the sheet and plate composite. The total thicknesses of sheet and plate that have been welded range from a few mils to over a foot with cladding metal thickness ranging from 0.001 in (0.03 mm) to more than 1.5 in (38.1 mm). The sizes of sheet and plate explosively welded range from small coupons to areas as large as 10×24 ft (3×8 m).

Figure 5-16 illustrates a large explosively clad composite. This particular composite is 15×24 ft (4.5×8 m), consisting of 0.187-in-thick (4.7 mm) Type 304L stainless steel clad to 3-in-thick (76.5 mm) plain carbon steel. The versatility of the process enables engineers to produce the aforementioned clad composite in Fig. 5-16 as well as thin foils of 0.005-in-thick (0.13 mm) tantalum clad to Inconel. To prevent damage to thin metal sheets or foils during EXW, a buffer material or metal is usually required between the explosive and the metal being welded. Thin composites are normally deformed to a greater extent than thicker composites during the EXW operation.

An extension of flat plate or sheet welding is the welding of multiple-layer composites, Fig. 5-17. This type of structure may be built up by explosively welding a single layer of metal at a time on the

Fig. 5-16 Type 304L stainless steel explosively welded to plain carbon steel.[17]

Fig. 5-17 Multiple-layer composite.[17]

composite in a series of successive steps, or may also be fabricated in a single step through one EXW operation. Multiple-layer composites having more than 100 sheets or foils have been welded in a single welding operation.[19]

Explosively welded sheet and plate in general are not utilized in the as-bound condition, but are fabricated into a usable configuration, as will be discussed later under applications.

Clad Tube

Tubular cladding is a simple extension of the flat sheet cladding or welding technique. All that is normally required in addition to the equipment needed for welding flat sheet is a supporting die or mandrel to prevent fragmentation or collapse of the tube during the welding operations, depending on whether the cladding is internal or external. The internal cladding of the tube normally requires the use of an external supporting die, while the external cladding of a tube requires an internal supporting mandrel.

Explosive tube cladding has been reported by several organizations.[11,20,21] A section of a Zircaloy-4 tube internally clad with aluminum is shown in Fig. 5-18.

Fig. 5-18 Zircaloy-4 tube internally clad with aluminum.[22]

Tubular Transition Joints

EXW offers a unique method for effecting a high-strength metallurgical bond between two dissimilar or metallurgically incompatible metal tubes. Transition joints are made by overlapping the tubes to be joined, either by tapering the mating ends or using a telescoping arrangement. As with tubular cladding, transition joints require die or mandrel support during the welding operation. Welding may be accomplished by positioning the explosive in the interior or on the exterior of the tubular joint. Small-diameter joints are usually welded with the explosive on the exterior, while large-diameter joints are often welded with an internally positioned explosive charge.

The sizes of tubular transition joints that have been welded range from less than 0.5 in to 8 in (12.7 to 204 mm) in diameter. The material combinations welded include Inconel and Zircaloy, stainless steel and Zircaloy, stainless steel and 6061-T6 aluminum, stainless steel and SAP aluminum, 6061-T6 aluminum and titanium, and 1100 aluminum and magnesium.[9] Tubular transition joints are known to have been explosively welded by various investigators.[19,23]

Seam and Lap Welds

Seam and lap welds are additional modifications of the EXW process which have been utilized for joining similar and dissimilar combinations of sheet metal.

Four types of joints have been developed, and materials have been selected for their strength in the most useful conditions of maximum hardness and temper. Lap joints of dissimilar and similar thicknesses as well as sandwich butt and scarf joints have been tested. The method provides a totally confined linear seam weld and has been used to make narrow, continuous, airtight joints in various aluminum alloys, titanium, copper, brass, and stainless steel.

The totally confined explosive-seam-welding concept uses a flattened steel tube, as shown in Fig. 5-19. Totally confined seam welding

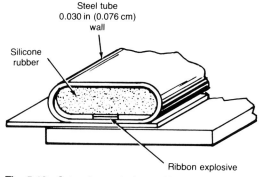

Fig. 5-19 Setup for explosive weld.

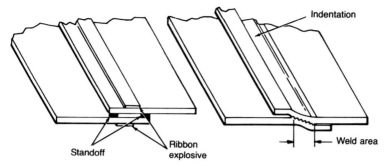

Fig. 5-20 Setup for producing scarf joint and finished scarf joint.

eliminates the noise, flame, smoke, lead sheating, and masking tape that are associated with the normal explosive seam welding. The confinement permits EXW in areas sensitive to contamination or in close proximity to personnel, and is being considered for use in the Space Shuttle docking system. The confinement tubes would be placed inside and outside the concentric cylinders to be welded and, on simultaneous firing of the two explosive ribbons, would form an airtight, continuous joint.

A scarf joint, as shown in Fig. 5-20, permits splicing of sheet stock in thicknesses to 0.090 in (2.3 mm) without addition of material, and produces joints that show strength up to that of the parent metal. This type of joint is particularly suited for longitudinal tankage and large-diameter pipe joints requiring high strength.

Rib-Reinforced Structures

The EXW process has been successfully employed to fabricate a number of rib-reinforced structural elements ranging from tee joints to complex panel structures. EXW permits a freer choice of materials, thermal-mechanical state, and configuration for supported panel structures. It is also potentially more economical than some of the competing processes. Since no external heat is applied, alloys often can be explosively welded in the desired mechanical- or thermal-treated condition, and will require no postbonding thermal treatment to develop the desired properties.

Rib-reinforced structures are fabricated by two techniques, which are basically the same as those used for (1) seam welding and (2) flat-plate cladding. In both approaches the base plate or stationary component is replaced with a composite consisting of the desired rib configuration supported by extractable tooling. Welding is then accomplished either by explosively seam welding the cladder plate or skin to each rib, or explosively welding the cladder plate or skin in flat-plate-cladding fashion to the ribs and tooling. After welding, the expendable tooling is removed, leaving the cladding plate or skin welded to the remaining ribs. It may be seen that rib-reinforced structures require

Fig. 5-21 Explosively fabricated titanium panel.[22]

the most elaborate and complex setup and support tooling of any of the geometric configurations that are explosively welded; however, the technique is still economically competitive with many other techniques for fabricating reinforced structures. A section of a more complex rib-reinforced titanium panel structure having double-face skins is shown in Fig. 5-21.

Spot Welds

Explosive spot welding has many advantages for joining a variety of metals and dissimilar combinations of metals that have been unweldable by conventional spot-welding techniques. For this reason, a considerable amount of effort has been put forth in recent years into developing this unique welding process. In addition to its capacity to join otherwise unweldable metal combinations, explosive spot welding is of interest because the small explosive charges that are required for welding can be packaged and utilized in a hand-held tool. This tool, seen in Fig. 5-22, weighs approximately 10 lb (4.5 kg). This tool, which has a self-contained electrical power supply with safety interlocks, has been used to spot-weld thirty-five different metal combinations. This tool and other types of hand-held tools with explosive cartridges are completely self-contained, mobile spot-welding systems that can be used in remote environments where it is impossible or impractical to transport more conventional electrical energy systems.

Joints have been made by explosive spot welding in 2024-0, 2024-

Fig. 5-22 Explosively spot-welded lap joint of 6061-T6 aluminum alloy.[24]

T3, 6061-T6, and 7075-T6 aluminum, Types 304, 347, and 17-7PH stainless steel, and titanium alloys 6Al-4V and 8Al-1Mo-1V. In addition, dissimilar-metal combinations which have been joined by explosive spot welding include aluminum to titanium and stainless steel, and stainless steel to titanium, cobalt-base alloys, and nickel-base alloys. A spot-welded lap joint between two plates of 6061-T6 aluminum alloy is shown in Fig. 5-22.

Other Configurations

Other configurations which have been explosively welded include a honeycomb grid fabricated by a novel approach. The structure was made by simultaneously explosively compacting and welding a bundle of copper-plated aluminum wires inside a copper tube. After welding, the aluminum cores were chemically dissolved out of the structure, leaving the copper in a hexagonal honeycomb structure. This and similar structures have been made from a variety of materials.

EXW has been employed to weld complex curved surfaces. In welding more complex shapes, the primary difficulties are in design and fabrication of the necessary support tooling and in setting up and maintaining the necessary uniform interface standoff and explosive loading. An example of an explosively welded complex curved surface is a hemispherical configuration produced from Type 2219 aluminum explosively welded to AISI 301 stainless steel.

Another series of unique explosively welded configurations involves wire-reinforced structures. The fabrication of these structures requires the same techniques used for flat plate or sheet welding, with a wire grid or screen structure located in the interface. After EXW, the wire structure is imbedded in the interface with the matrix metal welded around it. Both flat and hemispherical structures have been made; the latter were formed either simultaneously with welding or by explosive forming after welding. In addition to Type 304 stainless steel wire and strip, titanium 6Al-4V strip has also been explosively welded in a 6061 aluminum matrix.

MATERIALS

Since no external heating is employed in the EXW process and the time of the welding operation is extremely short, dissimilar combinations of metals which have widely different melting points, hardnesses, and thermal expansion characteristics may be joined. Dissimilar metals may be joined without diffusion and without the subsequent formation of brittle intermetallic phases at the weld interface which occurs with more conventional heat- and fusion-dependent joining processes.

In general, it may be said that any metal or alloy possessing sufficient ductility and impact resistance such that it will not fracture as a result of the dynamic forces involved may be explosively welded. Cladding metals with elongation as low as 5% have been explosively welded.

TABLE 5-5
Explosive Welded Metal Combinations

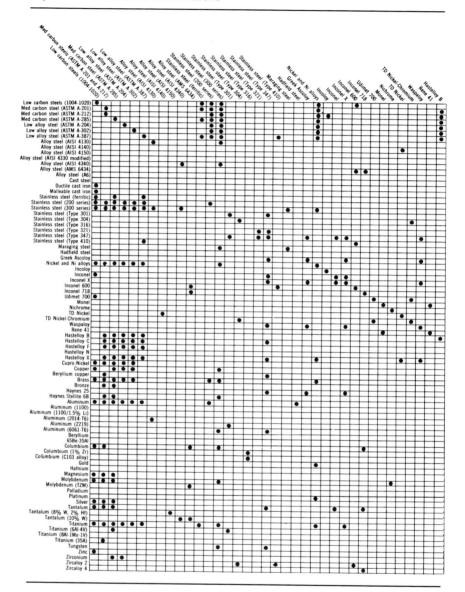

TABLE 5-5
(Continued)

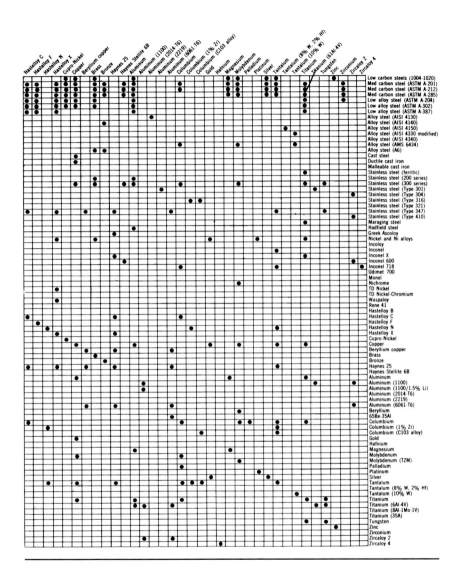

Many metal combinations have been explosively welded by various firms and institutions. The majority of these metals have been welded in the wrought condition, although some metals have been explosively welded in the cast condition. Table 5-5 lists metals that have been explosively welded to themselves and dissimilar metal combinations that have been explosively welded. Many of the combinations listed in this table have not been welded in useful configurations, but only in small coupon configurations to demonstrate that the EXW process can be used to join these metals, Fig. 5-23.

Besides the combinations shown in Table 5-5, an example of a unique materials combination which has recently been welded is Hastelloy X to malleable cast iron. This materials combination is particularly interesting in that the cast iron was able to withstand the impact of EXW. This materials combination would be useful in erosive

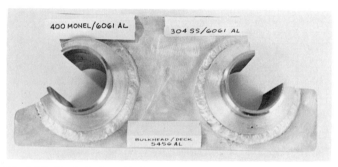

Fig. 5-23 Explosively welded monel and stainless steel to aluminum for ship applications.[25]

or high-temperature applications (for example, the pistons in large marine diesel engines) for protecting the cast iron. Another series of interesting combinations involved Invar—a Fe-36Ni alloy—as the common component with brass, stainless steel, aluminum, and high-expansion Mn-base alloy containing 72% Mn, 16% Cu, and 12% Ni. Figures 5-24 and 5-25 illustrate the microstructure of the welded joint for some of the metals joined.

In regard to mechanical properties, at a confidence level of greater than 99.5%, the bond strength of titanium-clad steel can be expected to exceed 20 ksi (138 MPa). Titanium clads are in the stress-relieved condition to assure maximum available ductility. No ASTM/ASME standard of shear strength has been established to date for titanium-clad plate. However, minimum ductility, yield strength, and tensile strength requirements prescribed for austenitic stainless steel integral clads have been met by explosion-welded plate products. Titanium clads also meet the requirements specified for stainless and nickel clads.

Field exposure tests and service applications to date show no impairment of the corrosion resistance of clads. Clad titanium has

Fig. 5-24 TD nichrome to TD nichrome weld produced by EXW.[22]

withstood 2 years nitric acid vapor exposure, whereas solid stainless steels used in this same application lasted 6 to 18 months. In addition, room-temperature bend ductility and bond shear strength of titanium clads were not altered by 3000-h exposure to air at 600°F (316°C).

Considerable data evaluating the weld strength of explosive welds have been generated through shear testing. Typical shear strength data are shown in Table 5-6. Available data[26,27] on the fatigue properties of explosive welds and welded materials are extremely limited.

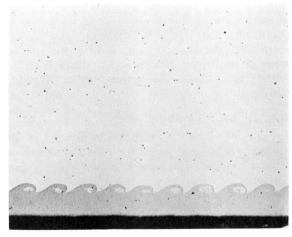

Fig. 5-25 0.005-in (0.15-mm) tantalum explosion-welded to Inconel 600.[22]

TABLE 5-6
Strength of Explosive Welds in Several Materials

Explosion-welded combination	As-clad shear strength		Reference
	ksi	MPa	
304 stainless steel to ASTM A-212-B	49.8	343	21
TMCA 35A titanium to ASTM A-212-B	39.0	269	21
Hastelloy C to ASTM A-212-B	59.0	407	21
Inconel 600 to ASTM A-212-B	63.0	434	21
1100-H14 Aluminum to ASTM A-212-B	12.4	86	21
DHP Copper to ASTM A-212-B	24.7	170	21
410 stainless steel to ASTM A-212-B	49.5	341	21
6061-T6 aluminum to same	26.0	179	22
AISI 1018 hot-rolled steel to same	42.0	290	22
TD Nickel to 304 stainless steel	88.4	610	23
Hastelloy X to Inconel 718*	114.0	786	23
304 stainless steel to same	90.0	621	23

*Solution-heat-treated and aged.

APPLICATIONS

The major incentive to the use of clad chemical-process vessels is utilization of the corrosion or erosion resistance of a thin inner layer of a more expensive metal supported by a thicker, less expensive metal. Chemical vessels with their interiors clad with titanium have found important applications as lined pressure vessels and retorts in the chemical industry because of improved heat-transfer characteristics, simplified design, and lower fabricating cost than could be obtained with loose liners. Some of these vessels are 8 ft (2.4 m) in diameter and 23 ft (7 m) high.

Tube sheet for heat-exchanger application has utilized welded composites of nickel and copper alloys on steel and produced 100% reliable joints between titanium tubes and steel tube plates as shown in Figure 5-26. Heat exchangers which have been explosively welded include sulfur dioxide coolers, ethylene glycol calandrias, nitric acid calandrias, experimental multiflash distillation plants, and turboalternator condensers.

By far the largest-tonnage application of EXW to date has been the cladding of billets which were subsequently hot- and cold-rolled to strip for production of United States subsidiary coinage. Figure 5-27 shows

Fig. 5-26   Titanium tubes explosively welded to stainless steel header assembly.[6]

rolling billets in which 0.9-in-thick (22.9 mm) 75/25 cupronickel was simultaneously clad to both sides of pure copper about 3.5 in (89 mm) thick. The billets weighed 3400 lb (1542 kg) each and were rolled to the gage thickness of 10- and 25-cent coins. Other examples of rolling billets which have been commercially produced were used to produce strip for 50-cent coinage and gilding metal clad to both sides of SAE 1008 steel strip for military bulletproof jackets. Explosively welded plate is also being examined and tested for lightweight metallic protective armor. By properly combining two or more metals with widely different physical and mechanical properties, armor with superior ballistic properties has been obtained.

Other explosively welded products utilized commercially include clad tubular products with either internal or external clads. Probably one of the most noteworthy applications of explosively welded products was the use of titanium/stainless steel transition joints in the Apollo lunar excursion module. The use of these joints in such an application attests to the confidence placed in their fabrication.

A number of applications for explosively clad tube and its modifications include work[20] directed toward lining the bores of high-strength-steel gun barrels with high-temperature-resistant alloys. It was intended that liners of these alloys would provide corrosion and erosion

Fig. 5-27   Cupronickel clad to copper for U.S. coinage.[6]

resistance needed in gun barrels, which are subjected to the effects of high-temperature propellant gases, high-velocity projectiles, and high rates of fire.

Several manufacturers of chemical process equipment have been interested in cladding the inside surfaces of tubes and pipe sections with stainless steel, titanium, tantalum, and other corrosion-resistant materials.[16] The techniques for cladding cylinder bores and pistons, a modification of both internal and external tube cladding for high-performance internal combustion engines, has also been demonstrated.

The broadening technology in the reactor, aerospace, and cryogenics industries has increasingly required the joining of pipes and tubing of dissimilar and often incompatible metals in metallurgical, strong, leaktight welds. It is for these requirements that explosively welded tubular transition joints have found application.

Transition joints for reactor applications normally involve Zircaloy to stainless steel or nickel-base alloy combinations.[28] Other combinations welded in transition joints for reactor applications include columbium-0.1 Zr to Type 316 stainless steel and Type 304 stainless steel to SAP aluminum.

It is often desirable to join two incompatible materials. Such joints are difficult to make by conventional welding practices in field applications and they generally exhibit low strength and ductility. Mechanical fastening techniques are therefore used. However, explosion-welded transition joints remove the limitations of bolting and riveting. Examples of bimetallic transition couplings include Inconel and Zircaloy,

Fig. 5-28 Explosively welded bimetallic couplings.[6]

Fig. 5-29 Explosively welded monel to titanium.[25]

stainless steel and 6061-T6 aluminum mild steel and 1100 aluminum, stainless steel and molybdenum, 6061-T6 and titanium, and 1100 and magnesium. Figures 5-28 and 5-29 illustrate typical couplings and penetration fittings.

Recent advances in the state of the art have demonstrated that structures having complex channeling can be fabricated by EXW, as shown in Fig. 5-30.

As the design of aircraft and aerospace structures becomes more sophisticated, there is an increasing requirement for the use of integrally stiffened members and panel structures in a wide variety of metal alloys including high-strength aluminum alloys, titanium-, iron-, and nickel-base alloys, and the refractory metals. In many cases, these alloys cannot be fabricated to meet existing design requirements, and in other instances, currently used fabrication processes have proved to be very costly both in processing and material costs. It is expected that explosively welded rib-reinforced structures will find increasing application in the aircraft and aerospace fields in the future.

Aluminum, copper, and steel are the most common metals used in high-current, low-voltage conductor systems. EXW is routinely employed by the primary aluminum reduction industry in anode rod fabrication. The connection is free of the aging effects characteristic of mechanical connections and requires no maintenance. The mechanical properties of the explosive weld (shear, tensile, and impact strength) exceed those of the parent Type 1100 aluminum alloy.

Although the application of explosive spot welding has been somewhat limited, its future potential is becoming increasingly evident in the amount of development work being conducted on both the process and on portable hand-held spot-welding tools. It provides rapid operation both in conventional situations and in remote or extreme environ-

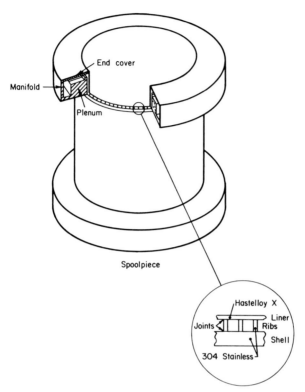

Fig. 5-30 Hastelloy X explosively welded to Type 304 stainless steel channel.

ments, excellent examples being an orbiting space laboratory or a deep-submergence undersea station. In the latter case, it has been demonstrated that EXW can be accomplished underwater without removing the water from the interface gap initially separating the plates to be bonded.[9]

The application of explosive spot welding to attaching electrical connector tabs has been developed. Normally the tabs are used to attach electrical cables to railroad rails, bus bars, etc. with bolts or other types of mechanical fasteners; however, with the use of a small prepackaged explosive charge and hand-held welding tool, cables can be attached by explosive spot welding with a considerable savings in time and money.

A unique EXW application has recently been developed[9] for joining tubes to tube sheets. This process combines the elements of the explosive tubular cladding and spot-welding techniques and can be implemented with a hand-held tool using packaged explosive charges. Inconel, aluminum, stainless steel, and titanium tubes have been welded in steel tube sheets and brass tubes welded in bronze tube sheets by this process. A section of a condenser tube sheet model with explosively welded tubes is shown in Figure 5-31.

The EXW tube-to-tube-sheet welding process has several advantages over other tube-to-tube-sheet welding processes. The explosive process can give greater flexibility in the selection of materials, since combinations that are incompatible by normal joining techniques can be welded by this technique (e.q., aluminum to steel). The tube welding can be performed accurately with a hand-held tool, and thus the process can be applied in the field.

Fig. 5-31 Titanium tubes explosively welded in a steel tube sheet.[17]

Many other applications of EXW have been examined, such as line cladding,[29] cladding the inside of large water storage tanks in Japan,[27] and cladding the bores of long tubes[12,31] and on the outside of bars and tubing, Fig. 5-32. Perhaps the most recent application of EXW has been the fabrication of wire reinforced metals.[32,33] Reasonably large plates have been produced in which volume fractions of up to 20% of fine high tensile wire and wire mesh have been incorporated into an aluminum matrix.

Other areas in which EXW can be expected to be utilized in the future are tube-to-tube-sheet welding, repair of worn or damaged areas, seam welding of sheets and plates, and fabrication of fiber-reinforced materials.

The use of explosives, whether it be for:

- Forming
- Welding
- Sizing
- Perforating
- Controlled hardening
- Compaction

has progressed quite rapidly and has been accepted by industry. In the case of EXW, during the early years of its development the process was applied mostly to simple flat and circular components, but in recent years its capability to weld more complicated shapes and fabricate complex structures has been demonstrated. One of these applications has been the EXW of aluminum to steel for deck houses for naval ships.

Fig. 5-32 4.5-in-OD (115 mm) × 0.187-in-thick (4.7 mm) steel tube with 0.062-in-thick (1.6 mm) Inconel cladding.[22]

EXW to date has seen limited commercial and industrial application because of psychological and educational factors. Future industrial usage of EXW will be found in applications where the unique advantages of the process can be utilized fully. This could include the fabrication of unique products, or the improvement of existing products so as to extend their useful life or upgrade their performance.

Better communication between industry and the scientific community and the support of industry in developing the process for specific applications should lead to a fuller utilization of the process as a commercial tool.

REFERENCES

1. Taylor, J., "Detonation in Condensed Explosives," University Press, Oxford, 1952.
2. Zeldovich, I. B., and Kompaneets, A. S., "Theory of Detonation," Academic Press, New York, 1960.
3. Cook, M. A., "The Science of High Explosives," Reinhold, New York, 1958.
4. Rinehart, J. S., and Pearson, J., "Explosives Working of Metals," Pergamon Press, New York, 1963.
5. Wylie, K. W., Williams, P. E. G., and Crossland, B., "An Experimental Investigation of Explosive Welding Parameters," *Proc. of Conf. on Use of Explosive Energy in Manufacturing Metallic Materials of New Properties and Possibilities of Application Thereof in the Chemical Industry*, Marianske Lazner, Czechoslovakia, 1970.
6. "Welding Handbook," 6th ed., American Welding Society, 1971, Chap. 51, pp. 51-3–51-28.
7. Cowan, G. R., Douglass, J. J., and Holtzman, A. H., U. S. Patent 3,137,937 June 3, 1964; assigned to E. I. Du Pont de Nemours and Co.
8. Carlson, R. J., "The Application of Explosive Energy to Material Fabrication," *High-Velocity Metalworking Seminar*, Midwest Research Institute, Kansas City, MO, Oct. 5–6, 1966.
9. Wittman, R. H., "The Explosive-Bonding Process: Applications and Related Problems," ASTME AD67-177, April 1967.
10. Doherty, A. E., et al., "Develop Manufacturing Methods to Utilize Explosives as a High Energy Source to Spot Weld Metals," Interim Engineering Prog. Rep., Aerojet-General Corp., Research Division, Downey, CA, Air Force Contr. AF33(615)-5354, January 1967.
11. Addison, H. J., and Betz, I. G., United States Army, Frankford Arsenal, Philadelphia, private communication, May 1978.
12. Holtzman, A. H., and Cowan, G. R., "Bonding of Metals with Explosives," *Weld. Res. Counc. Bull.* 104, American Welding Society, New York, April 1965.

13. DeMaris, J. L., and Pocalyko, A., "Mechanical Properties of Detaclad Explosion Bonded Clad Metal Composites," ASTME Tech. Paper AD66-113, 1966.
14. Doherty, A. E., "The Utilization of High Energy Pressures to Form, Bond and Compact Space-Age Shapes," Aerojet General Corp., Downey, CA, Rep. 1313-64(01)ER, February 1964.
15. "Guide to du Pont Detaclad Explosion Bonded Clad Metals," E. I. Du Pont de Nemours and Co., Wilmington, DE.
16. Pocalyko, A., "Explosion Clad Plate for Corrosion Service," North Central Region Conf., Nat. Assn. of Corrosion Engineers, Sept. 28-30, 1964.
17. Yoblin, J., E. F. Industries, private communication, April 1978.
18. Flint, R. S., and Linse, V. D., "Design and Operation of a Blast Containment Structure," Symp. on Behavior and Utilization of Explosives in Engineering Design, New Mexico Sec., ASME, and The University of New Mexico, College of Engineering, Albuquerque, NM, March 2-3, 1972.
19. Bayce, A. E., "Explosive Welding," Stanford Res. Inst. J., 13, January 1967.
20. Breitzig, R. W., "Explosive Welding (Cladding) of High Temperature Metals to High Strength Steels; First Phase Report," Tech. Memo. T-27/75, U.S. Naval Weapons Laboratory, Dahlgren, Va., 1965.
21. Philipchuk, V., "Explosive Welding Status—1965," ASTME Tech. Paper SP 65-100, 1965.
22. Carlson, R., Northwest Technical Industries, private communication, April 1978.
23. Wright, E. S., and Bayce, A. E., "Current Methods and Results in Explosive Welding," NATO Advanced Study Institute on High Energy Rate Working of Metals, Sandifjord/Lille-Hammer, Norway, September 1964.
24. Pattee, H., Battelle—Columbus Labs, private communication, April 1978.
25. Grollo, R., Naval Ordnance Station, private communication, March 1978.
26. De Maris, J. L., and Pocalyko, A., "Mechanical Properties of Detaclad ® Explosion Bonded Clad Metal Composites," ASTME Tech. Paper AD 66-113, 1966.
27. Banerjee, S. K., and Crossland, B., "Mechanical Properties of Explosively Graded Plates," Met. Constr. Brit. Weld. J., July 1971.
28. Carlson, R. J., "Explosive Welding," Western Metals Cong., Los Angeles, Feb. 22-26, 1965.
29. Polhemus, F. C., "Explosive Welding Development," 1st Internat. Conf. of the Centre for High Energy Forming, 1967.
30. Fukuyama, I., "Explosive Welding and Explosive Cladding," CEER, p. 15, July 1970.
31. Doherty, A. E., and Knop, L. H., "Practical Applications of Explosive Welding," Proc. 2d Internat. Conf. of the Centre for High Energy Forming, p. 7.4.2, 1969.
32. Wylie, H. H., Williams, J. D., and Crossland, B., "Fabrication of Metal/Metal Wire Composite Materials by use of Explosives," Weld. Met. Fabr., May–June 1971.
33. Wylie, H. K., Williams, J. D., Crossland, B., "Fabrication of Fibre Reinforced Aluminum," Proc. 3d Internat. Conf. of the Centre for High Energy Forming, 1971.
34. Carpenter, S. H., and Wittman, R. H., "The Theory and Application of Explosion Welding," Metallurgy Division, Center for High Energy Rate Forming, Denver Research Institute, University of Denver, Denver, 1970.
35. Smith, E. G., Jr., Laber, D., Linse, V. D., and Ryan, M. J., "Development of Explosive Welding Techniques for Fabrication of Regeneratively Cooled Thrust Chambers for Large Rocket Engine Requirements," Rep. NASA-CR-72-878, NASA—Lewis Research Center, Contr. NAS3-10306, June 15, 1971.
36. Segel, A. W. L., "Explosive Bonding of Dissimilar Metal Tubes," Rep. AECL-2209, Atomic Energy of Canada, Ltd., Chalk River, Canada.
37. Porembka, S. W., Wittman, R. H., and Carlson, R. J. "Explosively Welding Duplex Zircaloy-Aluminum Tubing," Battelle—Columbus Labs, Rep. BMI-X-412, April 1966.
38. Crossland, B., Bahrani, A. S., Williams, J. D., and Shribman, V., "Explosive Welding of Tubes to Tube-Plates," Weld. Met. Fabr., 35, 88, 1967.
39. Stone, J. M., "Applications of Explosion-Bonded Clads," Met. Constr. Brit. Weld. J., 1, 29–34, 1969.
40. Nishio, Y., Ohmae, T., Yoshida, Y., and Oka, T., "Welding of Tantalum and Newly Developed Tantalum Clad Steel," Tech. Rev. Mitsubishi Heavy Ind., 8(2), 1971; Weld. Res. Abroad, 18(1), 26–34, 1972.

41. Erokhin, V. A., et al., "Properties of Explosive Welded Titanium-Aluminum Joints," *Svar. Proizvod.*, (7), 26–27, 1972; *Weld. Prod. USSR*, 43–45.
42. Belousov, V. P., Sedykh, V. S. and Trykov, Yu. P., "Mechanical Properties of Explosive Welds Between Titanium and Steel (In the Intermediate Layers)," *Svar. Proizvod.*, (9), 19–21, 1971; *Weld. Prod. USSR*, 29–33.
43. Lieberman, E., and Kennedy, J. R., "Joining Cylinders of Ta-10W and 4340 Steel by Explosive Welding," *Weld. J.*, **46**(11), 509–515, November 1967.
44. Johnson, W. R., "Explosive Welding Plugs into Heat Exchanger Tubes," *Weld. J.*, **50**(1), 22, January 1971.
45. Lucas, W., Williams, J. D., Crossland, B., "Some Metallurgical Observations on Explosive Welding," *Proc. 2d Internat. Conf. of the Centre for High Energy Forming*, Denver, 1969.
46. Deribas, A., Matreenkov, F., Sobolenko, T., and Teslenko, T., "Investigations of Changes in the Zones of Collision by Explosive Joining of Metals," *Symp. on High Dynamic Pressures*, Paris, 1967.
47. Polhemus, F. C., "Establishment of Parameters and Limitations of Explosive Welding," Final Rep., NASA Contr. NAS8-11738, Pratt & Whitney Aircraft, FR-1528, Aug. 27, 1965.
48. Kögel, H., "Aufschweissen mit Sprengstoffen," *ZIS Mitt.*, **13**(1), 75–83, 1971.
49. Meyer, G., and Gottsmann, R., "Explosivumformung und ihre Anwendung in der Fügetechnick," *ZIS-Mitteilungen*, **13**(1), 84–90, 1971.
50. Wiesner, P., "Neue Energieguellen fur die Schweisstechnik," *ZIS Mitt.*, **11**(1), 7–23, 1969.
51. Naumann, E., "Die Anwendung von Elektromagnetischen Feldern und Schockwellen in der Schweisstechnik," *ZIS Mitt.*, **11**(1), 145–162, 1969.
52. "Erfolgreiche Anwendung der Sprengschweisstechnik," *Schweisstechnik*, **24**(11), 11, 1974.
53. Pennanech, J. L., "Explosive Welding and Cladding," Review de la Saudure—Lastijdschrift, **26**(3), 157–169, July–September 1970.
54. Frey, A. P., "Explosive Welding and Cladding," *Soud. Tech. Connexes*, **23**(1-2), 20–28, January–February 1969.
55. Horn, V., "Explosive Welding," *ZIS Mitteilungen*, **13**(1), 67–74, January 1971.
56. Douglass, J. J., "Applications of Explosion Bonding," ASTME Tech. Paper SP65-94, 1965.
57. Pearson, J., and Hayes, G. A., "Research in Explosive Welding," Studies of Various Metals Systems, ASTME Creative Manufacturing Seminars, SP63-97, 1962–1963.
58. Lieberman, I., Zernow, L., and Knop, L. H., "High Velocity (Explosive) Fabrication Applied to Refractory Metals," Advanced High Energy Rate Forming, Book III, ASTME Creative Manufacturing Seminars, SP63-69 (1962–1963).
59. Addison, H., Jr., Fogg, W. E., Betz, I. G., and Hussey, F. W., "Explosive Welding of Aluminum Alloys," *Weld. J.*, **42**(8), 359–364, 1963.
60. Irving, R. R., "LNG Tankers Take on Made in USA Labels," *Iron Age*, **218**(20), 43–48, Nov. 15, 1976.
61. Jefferson, T. B., "Welding Aluminum to Steel," *Weld. Des. Fabr.*, pp. 80–82, May 1977.

6

FRICTION WELDING

Friction welding is a well-established commercial process which is used extensively in numerous countries and industries throughout the world. Current estimates of the global situation indicate that more than 2000 friction-welding machines are installed in factories and laboratories, and these produce more than 400 million joints per year. Friction welding (FRW), although originally introduced as a mass production tool, mainly for the automobile industry, is now widely used for both quantity and batch production. Although most of the machines are employed for the manufacture of welds in ferrous materials, many installations are used in the mass production manufacture of dissimilar metal joints that are used in the electrical, chemical, nuclear, and marine industries. The energy required to achieve a friction weld is provided by the frictional heat generated at the rubbing surfaces under heavy pressure. The basic idea of friction welding is not new. A patent was granted as early as 1891 in which the concept of using frictional heat for extrusion and welding purposes was applied.[1]

The process initially promoted in Eastern Europe in the late fifties was introduced in the United States in 1960. In the midsixties a new version of friction-welding machine was exhibited which utilizes a different concept of providing energy for the welding process.[2] The process uses a flywheel attached to a rotating spindle in order to store all the energy required for welding in the form of kinetic energy before the welding is started. In other words, the power required for heat generation at the interface comes from the "inertia" of the rotating mass. Hence, the process has been specifically named inertia welding[3] or flywheel friction welding[4] as compared with the so-called conventional friction welding[5] or continuous-drive friction welding.[6]

ELEMENTS OF PROCESS

Continuous-Drive Friction Welding

The basic requirement to achieve a friction weld is to generate sufficient heat quickly to raise the temperature at the interface high enough for forging; the mating surfaces are then forged together immediately to form a metallurgical bond. Figure 6-1 illustrates the

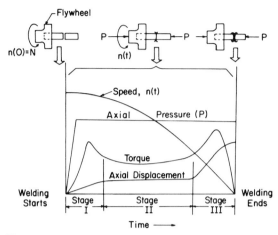

Fig. 6-1 Characteristics of typical continuous-drive FRW.[7]

principle of a typical conventional or continuous-drive friction welding (FRW) process. The rotating part is first brought up to a constant speed N. The welding cycle starts when the nonrotating part is pushed against the rotating part under a moderate pressure P_1 while the speed is kept constant. This is the heating phase, which results in rapid temperature rise at the interface. When the interface temperature reaches the forging range of the work material, the rotation is arrested promptly by applying a brake; i.e., the speed curve represented by $n(t)$ drops from N to zero in the braking period. During this period, the axial pressure is often increased (to P_2) to forge the parts together by upsetting. An appreciable amount of shortening of the workpiece* is realized in the heating phase and during the forging phase while the materials near the interface are softened and squeezed out to form a flash.

Inertia Welding

The inertia welding is slightly different as illustrated in Fig. 6-2. The rotating spindle with a replaceable flywheel (or a combination of flywheels of various sizes) attached is also brought up to a preset initial speed of N r/min. The welding cycle also starts when the nonrotating part is pushed against the rotation part, but the driving power is cut off simultaneously and results in a rapid drop of rotating speed and rotation stops completely in a very short time. Therefore, the inertia welding is basically carried out under a constant axial pressure, but at variable speed as compared with the stepped pressure and constant

---

*The shortening of the workpiece during the heating phase of continuous-drive FRW has been frequently called "burn-off," although actual "burning" either does not occur or is insignificant.

speed for a typical continuous-drive process. In essence, inertia welding tends to blend the heating and forging phases rather quickly with all stored energy being practically "dumped" at the interface all of a sudden. On the other hand, the continuous-drive process usually has a distinct heating period before forging takes place.

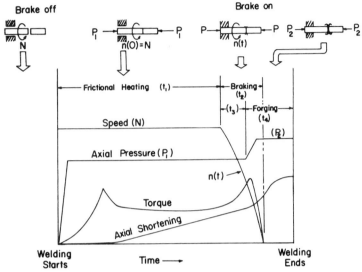

Fig. 6-2 Characteristics of typical inertia welding.[7]

Flywheel FRW

Flywheel friction welding is similar to conventional FRW and inertia welding in the basic process. The flywheel method, however, stores energy in a flywheel, and this energy can be released in specific quantities through an integral clutch system.

The primary advantage of the flywheel welder is its ability to store energy in the flywheel during the material loading cycle, and thus reduce the total floor-to-floor time per weld. This advantage is most noticeable when large weld areas are involved. The primary disadvantage is also most noticeable when large weld areas are involved. The primary disadvantage is the complexity added by the clutch, and the limitation on welding small-area parts.

PROCESS CHARACTERISTICS

Weld Parameters

For inertia welding, there are only three independent welding parameters to set up the process. As shown in Fig. 6-2, they are the initial rotating speed N, also called initial sliding velocity at the faying surface, which relates to the flywheel, spindle revolutions per minute, and the weld diameter; the moment of inertia I of the attached flywheel-spindle system; and the axial pressure P, also called axial thrust force, in pounds per square inch (megapascals) at the weld interface.

The first two parameters determine the total kinetic energy available for the welding, and the axial pressure dictates the welding cycle time. The process tends to adjust itself adaptively, so to speak, as long as the parameter settings are properly selected. The simplicity of inertia welding facilitates the optimization procedure, and probably less effort is required to find the optimum condition than with the continuous-drive process. As one would expect, different metals prefer different values for these parameters. For the purpose of illustrating the effects resulting from varying these parameters, we will consider only the case for welding steel to steel.

Literally hundreds of welds have confirmed the presence of a range of sliding velocities which will produce the best weld properties. This preferred velocity range for steel bars extends from 350 to 1000 ft/min (1.8 to 5.1 m/s) and refers to peripheral velocity at the start of the weld cycle. Velocity of course decreases as the flywheel and spindle slow, and eventually becomes zero, at which time the weld is complete. Good welds can be made outside this preferred velocity range, in a range extending down to 275 ft/min (1.4 m/s) and up to 1500 ft/min (7.6 m/s). However, welds made at these extreme velocities do not have the most desirable weld flash formation or heat-affected zone widths and shapes. At very low speeds, for example, 225 ft/min (1.1 m/s), the flash is very rough and uneven and inadequate center heating results. Excessive velocity produces inadequate peripheral heating and very little flash. If borderline velocities are used for extending the capacity range of a machine, appropriate adjustments of pressures and energies can be made to partially counteract the strong velocity effect.

Effects similar to those resulting from varying the velocity result from varying the pressure. Normally low-pressure welds resemble high-velocity welds with reference to flash formation and heat-affected zores. Increasing pressure fivefold on a 1.75-in-diameter (44.5 mm) bar produces a pinched-off heat-affected zone at the center and a considerable volume of flash as would result from the use of low velocities. The pressure-velocity equivalents have been determined and adjustments are made to compensate for this relationship when calculating parameters for a prescribed weld.

The third weld parameter is flywheel moment of inertia. Flywheels are sized not only to produce the desired amount of kinetic energy, but also to produce the desired amount of forging. Flywheel forging is a unique aspect of inertia welding. It results from the characteristic torque rise which occurs at the weld interface as the flywheel slows and comes to rest. Notice that as the speed in Fig. 6-2 decreases, the torque is rising quite rapidly. This increased torque, in combination with the axial load, produces forging. Because forging begins at some critical velocity, about 200 ft/min (1 m/s), the amount of forging is dependent on the amount of energy remaining in the flywheel. This in turn is a linear function of the flywheel moment of inertia. Large, low-speed flywheels, therefore, produce more forging than small, high-speed flywheels, even though they contain the same amount of kinetic energy.

This forging action expels any residual impurity or oxides from the joint, exposing clean material. At a critical speed, a solid-state bond is made, and additional working of the heat-affected zone continues until the flywheel stops which is usually 1 to 2 revolutions later. The rotation after bonding causes adiabatic work to be done beyond the weld interface. It is, therefore, usual to have a fine-grained, well-worked structure considerably beyond the bond interface. This prevents the formation of a sharp discontinuity or stress concentration in the joint. The maximum torque developed at the end of the weld cycle correlates with the torsional strength of the material at the indicated temperature. By the use of the flywheel and a given speed, a very specific quantity of energy is released to the part; therefore, the process is not power dependent. The controllable variables for a specific part are only speed and pressure. The flywheel mass requirements are developed from empirical equations that have a fairly broad tolerance. Therefore, in manufacturing a specific part, the operator must control only pressure and adjust the speed to attain a certain energy per square inch of bond area.

The inertia welding process is amenable to both theoretical and empirical analysis. While there are only three variables in the system (speed, flywheel mass, and pressure), each must operate within a specific range to produce sound joints, and each interacts with the others. Flywheel mass has a momentum effect that influences the depth of the heat-affected zone. Surface speed determines the quantity of energy to be released to the joint. Ram pressure on the joint determines the frictional coefficient which controls the energy release rate. The interactions between inertia welding variables are summarized in Fig. 6-3.

Continuous-drive FRW, on the other hand, has more parameters to control. These parameters, as referred to in Fig. 6-1, are the rotating speed N, friction pressure P_1, frictional heating time t_1, deceleration

	Variation from optimum	
Parameter	Too much	Too little
Flywheel mass	Bond fracture Incomplete bond	Interface overtemperature
Surface speed	Narrow heat-affected zone (HAZ) HAZ overtemperature	Incomplete bond Insufficient upset
Pressure	Bond fracture Excessive upset	Interface overtemperature Insufficient upset Wide heat-affected zone

Fig. 6-3 Inertia welding parametric interactions for cylindrical sections.

time t_2, delay time t_3, upsetting or forging time t_4, and the upsetting or forging pressure P_2. In practice, however, not all the parameters need to be controlled. For instance, the pressure can be kept constant throughout the welding cycle as in inertia welding, thus $P_2 = P_1$. Others may have the forging phase started when the rotation is completely stopped, that is, $t_3 = t_2$. If the pressure is kept constant and no internal braking force is applied, the process essentially becomes inertia welding without an explicit flywheel. This case, of course, would be only applicable to very limited conditions when the kinetic energy built up by the rotating parts of the machine (chucks, spindle, etc.) is sufficient for welding.

In general, the continuous-drive FRW machine has more parameters to be set up than in inertia-welding machine. The larger number of parameters often makes the search for the optimum condition more difficult before experience is obtained. The capability to store energy in the flywheel makes the power requirements of inertia welding inherently lower than the continuous-drive process, in which a high power motor is usually needed to maintain the constant speed during the frictional heating phase. In fact, it is mandatory to keep the friction pressure P_1 at a moderate level in the continuous-drive process in order to avoid the need for an excessive-size motor. This is evidently at the expense of a longer heating period, and thus the total welding cycle time is also longer.

It has been realized that the major variables to be considered are speed of rotation (surface speed), applied pressure during heating (friction pressure), duration of heating (burn-off), and applied pressure during forging (upsetting). These variables are to some extent interrelated and must be considered with secondary factors such as rate of buildup of force during heating and forging, stopping time, condition of the surface before welding, and geometry and thermal and physical character of the material being welded. In addition, from a detailed study of the relationships between torque, rotational speed, and applied pressure in mild steel, a general approach has been derived. If a satisfactory weld requires certain minimum values of torque, pressure, and burn-off, and in general if these minima are exceeded, the welds are sound.

It is generally agreed that satisfactory friction-welded joints can be produced using many combinations of speed of rotation and axial pressure, e.g., by rotating the component to produce relatively low peripheral speed and exerting a high pressure (the English and Soviet practice) or by rotating it at a higher speed and exerting a lower pressure (American practice).

High speed or low friction pressure give a low deformation rate, causing long weld-cycle times and overheated parts. Conversely, low speed or high pressure gives a high deformation rate and short weld time. The short cycle, desirable perhaps for high productivity, excessively hardens the weld zone, particularly of high-carbon-equivalent steels. Yet for most materials, the task of making friction welds with good mechanical properties means little more than acquiring the ability to determine and use the right combination of speed and pressure. The process burns off some metal; the amount depends on the material, dimensions, rotation speed, and axial pressure. For solid sections of commercial steel, allow for a loss amounting to 20% of the diameter of the workpiece. To find exact losses, experiments must be conducted, as seen in Fig. 6-4. Burn-off time for most steels is expressed in the relation

$$t = 3.25d^2$$

where t = burn-off displacement time,
  d = bar diameter, in (mm).
This relation does not apply to high-alloy steels, stainless steels, and to surface-treated components.

The heating time must be long enough to clean the faying surfaces by friction and to raise the weld-zone temperature to the required plasticity. When the two components are hot enough, rotation stops and forging pressure is applied. It must not be so high as to cause excessive weld upset and excessive working of the weld zone, nor must the pressure be so low as to give an incomplete weld and insufficient hot working. The trick is to select the FRW conditions which will give a fine-grained microstructure free from excessive working.

It has been realized that probably the most important parameter is the applied pressure, since it not only influences the driving torque or heat generation but also determines the maximum temperature at the interface. The effect of pressure on the torque (power) and the interface temperature is summarized in Table 6-1,[7] which shows that higher pressures produce higher torques and lower temperatures. It is also apparent that there is an approximately linear relationship between the interface temperature and the torque, which appears to be

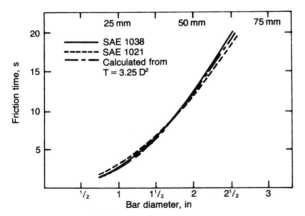

Fig. 6-4 Burn-off time vs. bar diameter for Types 1038 and 1021 steel. Calculated and experimental curves are almost identical.

TABLE 6-1
Effect of Varying Weld Parameters on Peak Temperature, Torque, and Power for 0.5-in-Diameter (12.7 mm) Mild Steel[8]

Rotation speed, r/min	Relative sliding velocity at periphery, ft/s (m/s)	Friction force, tons (kg)	Friction pressure, tons/in² (kg/mm²)	Peak recorded temperature, °F (°C)	Torque, lb·ft (kg·m)		Steady state power, hp (kW)
					Peak	Steady state	
3200	7 (2.1)	1/2 (508)	2.5 (3.9)	2426 (1330)	18 (2.48)	3.9 (0.54)	2.4 (1.8)
		1 (1016)	5.1 (8.1)	2345 (1285)	17 1/2 (2.42)	6.1 (0.84)	3.7 (2.8)
		1 1/2 (1524)	7.6 (12.0)	2336 (1280)	17 (2.34)	7.5 (1.38)	4.6 (3.5)
5000	11 (3.3)	1/2 (508)	2.5 (3.9)	2435 (1335)	17 1/2 (2.42)	2.8 (0.39)	2.7 (2.0)
		1 (1016)	5.1 (8.1)	2417 (1325)	12 1/2 (1.72)	4.0 (0.55)	3.8 (2.9)
		1 1/2 (1524)	7.6 (12.0)	2381 (1305)	15 (2.07)	4.8 (0.66)	4.6 (3.5)

independent of applied pressure and relative speed. Therefore at high pressures the material in contact at the interface will be cooler and less fluid, and the rotational force, i.e., torque, will also be greater with high pressures. It can be concluded that if this relationship between torque and temperature is linear, then the interface temperature for mild steel could not exceed about 2534°F (1390°C), since the torque would then decrease substantially to zero.

The actual value of pressure to produce satisfactory friction welds is dependent on the material being welded, and must be selected so as to cause uniform heating at the interface and to maintain the two surfaces in intimate contact to prevent penetration of the interface by the atmosphere. It is to be noted that, in general, the pressures used for upsetting in FRW are similar to those employed in flash welding.

It has been established that in order to produce satisfactory joints, certain minimum values of duration of heating must be exceeded, so as to ensure that the weld interface has reached a uniform temperature and that surface impurities present on the original interfaces are removed. In addition, sufficient heating of the parent material adjacent to the interface is needed to permit the pieces to be forged together. When this condition is reached, the weld cycle is usually terminated. Failure to reach this situation will result in irregular heating, with the occurrence of inclusions and unbonded regions of the interface because inadequate plasticity has not been reached. Heating times in excess of optimum lead to lower productivity and greater consumption of material, but not appear to produce any measurable deterioration in weld quality.

PROCESS DIFFERENCES

Despite the difference in the number of welding parameters and the rate of energy input, inertia and continuous-drive FRW exhibit similar characteristics of frictional torque at the interface. As shown in Figs. 6-1 and 6-2, both processes have a torque history with two peaks, one during the initial stage and the other near the end of the welding cycle. Because the initial stage of FRW is dominated by the dry friction and wear behavior under severe load, there are fluctuations in the rising torque curve[8] as the rubbing surfaces change from partial to complete contact. The torque reaches the first peak and drops slightly to a steadier or equilibrium level for the rest of the heating period. Control of the peak as well as the equilibrium torque is considered crucial to the quality of a friction weld in the continuous-drive process. A feedback control system has been suggested[9] in order to maintain the equilibrium torque substantially constant throughout the weld cycle before forging starts. This is accomplished by controlling automatically the axial force, which appears to have a linear relationship with torque in the operation range. Such a system offers the advantages of preventing overload of the machine and helping to maintain constant weld quality.

Inertia welding, on the other hand, depends more on the initial rotating speed and the size of flywheel to ensure that the proper amount of kinetic energy is supplied to the process. Initial speed is of particular importance; a minimum value for a given material has to be reached in order to provide sufficient power for welding. Empirical equations have been proposed to estimate the specific power required at various stages of the weld cycle.[10] On the basis of the yield strength of the material and the required power, engineers have calculated the lower critical surface speeds for a group of materials using an empirical formula. Table 6-2 shows these values for several materials in which some correlation between the specific power and the lower critical speed prevails. Lead requires the least amount of specific power of 50 hp/in^2 (5.78 kW/cm^2) and can be welded at a very low surface speed of 50 ft/min (2.5×10^{-2} m/s); tungsten, on the other hand, requires 1750 hp/in^2 (202.13 kW/cm^2) of specific power and a minimum initial surface speed of 2500 ft/min (12.7 m/s) in order to obtain a good weld.

It has been noted that an appreciable shortening of workpiece is realized in both FRW processes when the material near the interface is squeezed out to form a flash. The magnitude and shape of the flash formation, in fact, often serves as a reliable indicator for the weld quality. By the nature of the processes, there are some differences in the history of workpiece shortening between the inertia welding and the continuous-drive FRW. As shown in Fig. 6-1, there is substantial shortening (or burn-off) during the heating phase of the continuous-drive process when the mating surfaces are first settled and then brought into complete contact. The rate of shortening (or the burn-off rate) is approximately constant throughout the equilibrium-torque period. The hot metal at the interface is gradually forced out under the axial pressure P_1 to form a flash. It has been reported[6] that the burn-off rate is linearly proportional to the axial pressure and it also has been noted that the burn-off rate is generally higher at lower speed for a given

TABLE 6-2
Power Requirement and Lower Critical Speed for Inertia Welding of Tubing[11]

Material	Specific power		Lower critical initial surface speed	
	hp/in^2	kW/cm^2	ft/min	m/s
Lead	50	5.78	50	2.5×10^{-2}
Stainless steel	260	30.03	200	1.0
Aluminum	380	43.89	250	1.3
Tool steel	430	49.67	275	1.4
Low-carbon steel	470	54.29	350	1.8
Nickel	650	75.08	650	3.3
Titanium	800	92.40	750	3.8
Copper	950	109.73	1800	9.1
Molybdenum	1250	144.38	2000	10.2
Tungsten	1750	202.13	2500	12.7

axial pressure. Therefore, it has been suggested that controlling the burn-off rate by manipulating the axial pressure and the speed can be used as a measure of quality control.

Inertia welding, on the other hand, does not have appreciable shortening in Stage II as indicated in Fig. 6-2. The upset occurs essentially during the forging phase in Stage III when the torque reaches the second and higher peak. It is at this stage that the fresh subsurface materials are brought into intimate contact at atomic level to form a metallurgical bond after the contaminated original surface layers are forged out to the flash. The high torque and the forge action is attributed to the remaining angular momentum carried by the flywheel. Since the rotating speed at the forging stage is very low, the torsional forging force is dependent on the size of the flywheel. Thus, the welding of difficult-to-forge materials would normally require a larger flywheel which tends to prolong the forging period and to raise the level of the peak torque slightly. Because of the combined torsional and axial forging force occurring in inertia welding, the materials are squeezed out along a spiral path as compared with a radial flow in the continuous-drive process caused by axial force alone.

One characteristic of the inertia-welder-produced joint is the flow line pattern. Most forge-type butt welds, including friction and flash, are forged by thrust, not rotation. Flow lines are radial, as seen in Fig. 6-5. In inertia welding the joint is forged by torque and thrust. Plastic metal has axial, radial, and circular movement as it is squeezed from the joint. Flow lines spiral into the weld, as seen in Fig. 6-6.

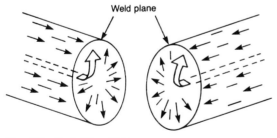

Fig. 6-5 Radial flow lines.

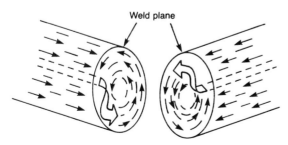

Fig. 6-6 Spiral flow lines.

TEMPERATURE DISTRIBUTION

Because of the importance of knowing the thermal behavior in the weld zone during FRW, considerable efforts have been made to investigate the temperature variation during the weld cycle.

The question of whether melting occurs at the interface has been a controversial one. Experimental results by many scientists[8,12,13] showed no evidence of melting for dissimilar metal welds, and melting is highly unlikely for similar metal welds based on their extrapolated temperature curves. Metallurgical examination of specimens and the fact that the high-level torque curve is essentially continuous without any significant disruption by liquid formation also tends to substantiate this conclusion. It is conceivable that even under relatively moderate pressure during the heating phase, the thermally softened material would have been forced out to the flash long before a liquid phase would appear.

In inertia welding, the temperature rise is much more rapid because of the higher rate of energy input and shorter welding-cycle time.

METALLURGICAL CHARACTERISTICS

In general, friction welds of identical materials consist of a thin layer of severely deformed but highly refined grain structure near the weld interface. There is a narrow region of heat-affected zone between the weld and base-metal structures. Figure 6-7 is a typical macrosection of a low-alloy steel bar weld showing the hardness, the heat-affected zone, and the metal flash. The shape of the heat-affected zone and the flash

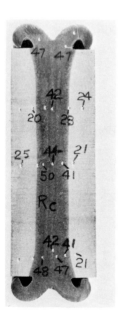

Fig. 6-7 Heat-affected zone (HAZ) and hardness in SAE 86B30 steel. Numbers represent Rockwell C hardness values in the as-welded condition.[14]

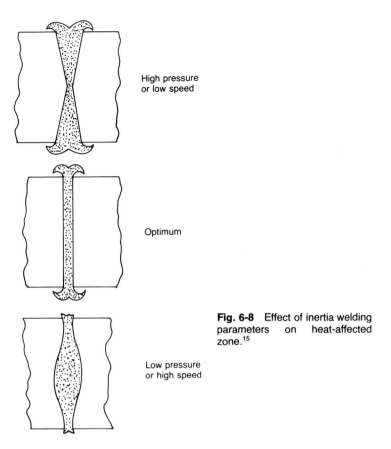

High pressure
or low speed

Optimum

Fig. 6-8 Effect of inertia welding parameters on heat-affected zone.[15]

Low pressure
or high speed

depends on materials and the welding conditions. In general, high pressure or low speed will result in a wedge-shaped heat-affected zone toward the center, as shown in Fig. 6-8. On the other hand, high speed or low pressure will produce a heat-affected zone slightly bulged at the center. The heat-affected zone produced under an optimum welding condition should be relatively uniform and narrow throughout the entire section.[15] Should the energy stored in the flywheel be excessive, it will force a large amount of material out of the interface to form a long flash. In inertia welding, the rotating speed, which dictates the kinetic energy more than any other parameter, is a very important factor affecting the welding performance. A minimum critical speed usually has to be reached for a successful weld.[16]

Because of the complex interplay between mechanical, thermal, and metallurgical factors during the welding process, microstructures at different regions are considerably different. Near the interface, fine and severely elongated grains prevail as a result of mechanical deformation. Recovery, recrystallization, and grain growth of the deformed material take place in the neighboring heat-affected zone to various degrees, depending on the thermal effect in the region. Figure 6-9 shows a part of the microstructures of a mild-steel weld exhibiting gradual change of grain structures from the interface to the base metal. The micrograph also shows the metal flow pattern at the midradius region for a weld having a wedge-shaped heat-affected zone similar to that shown in Fig. 6-7.

Microstructures are also affected by welding conditions. For the continuous-drive process, it was found[17] that higher pressure generally produces a fine interface grain structure with a narrow and double-wedge-shaped heat-affected zone. Increasing speed, on the other hand, tends to slightly offset the effect of pressure. These findings are conceivable in view of the fact that high speed will cause the thermal effect to be dominant over the mechanical effect on microstructures, which, in turn, dictate the hardness and tensile strength in the weld zone. It has also been reported[18] that forging of the overheated weld interface will weaken the metal in the heat-affected zone. A postweld normalizing heat treatment would eliminate the adverse effects of forging at the overheated weld interface.

The importance of thermal behavior in FRW could have resulted in a major difference between the inertia and continuous-drive processes in terms of hardness distribution. In inertia welding of mild steel bars, it was found that the average Knoop hardness across the interface is about 27% higher than the base metal.[19]

The fact that the weld is stronger than base metal is evidenced by the result of a typical tensile test shown in Fig. 6-10. The fracture occurred outside the weld region even after it was slightly machined down to reduce the cross-sectional area at the weld. On the other hand, similar mild steel welds by the continuous-drive process appear to have generally lower hardness at the heat-affected zone than the base metal.

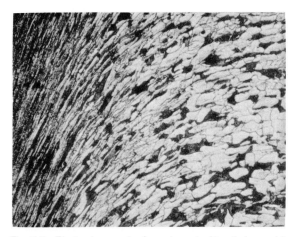

Fig. 6-9 Photomicrograph of a carbon-steel inertia bar weld (250×).[7]

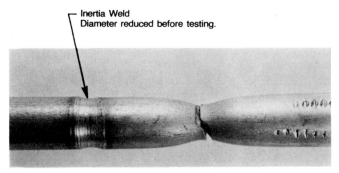

Inertia Weld
Diameter reduced before testing.

Fig. 6-10 A tensile test specimen of an inertia weld.[7]

The tensile strength at the weld was reported[6] to vary from 77 to 100% of that of the base metal, depending on welding conditions. The difference in weld strength resulting from the thermal effect may have been a contributing factor to a slightly higher fatigue strength of inertia welds than continuous-drive friction welds reported for some superalloy materials.[20]

INTERFACIAL BONDS

For FRW of identical metals under proper conditions, the metallurgical bonds are usually achieved by expelling contaminated surface layers and bringing together the nascent sublayers close to the range of atomic attraction. To a certain extent, diffusion may be expected to take place across the interface during the heating and forging phases. In fact, postweld annealing of mild steel friction welds causes the interface completely to disappear, and the equiaxial grains are restored throughout the weld as if there had not been a weld. The bonding mechanism of dissimilar metal welds, however, appears to be much more complex. Among others, factors such as physical properties, surface energy, crystalline structure, mutual solubility, and possible formation of intermetallic compound from the materials being welded may all play a role in the bonding mechanism. The complexity makes the prediction of weldability of a metal pair almost impossible without running extensive experiments. It is obvious that much more work is needed to analyze systematically the mechanisms of bonding for better understanding of the process.

Since the key to achieving a metallurgical bond in the solid state is to break up and remove the contaminated surface layers, materials with substantial difference in hardness are generally more difficult to weld. The hard material incurs practically no deformation while the soft one is already severely deformed or extruded. Examples include stainless steel in aluminum alloy and copper-to-aluminum welds in which the stainless steel and the copper show no obvious sign of deformation. In these cases, complete removal of surface layer from hard metal may

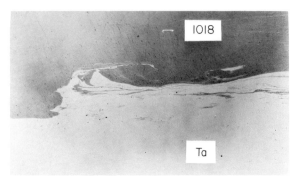

Fig. 6-11 Inertia weld of SAE 1018 steel and tantalum (250×).[7]

not be possible because of the lack of subsurface flow. Some debris of surface contaminants are expected to remain embedded at the interface.

Despite the fact that only a partial bond may have been formed at the interface of dissimilar metal welds, the mechanism of mechanical mixing and interlocking may play an important role in achieving a sound weld. It has been found[16] that a depth of about 0.002 in (0.05 mm) of mechanical mixing exists across the interface of inertia welds of tantalum to SAE 1018 steel (Fig. 6-11) and GMR 235 superalloy to SAE 1040 steel (Fig. 6-12). The degree of interfacial mixing depends on materials and the location at the interface. An inertia weld between mild steel and tungsten carbide (Fig. 6-13) indicates very little mixing. The bond is apparently formed between the steel and the cobalt binder within the cemented carbide.

Although the FRW process appears to be too fast for diffusion to take place as compared with the typical diffusion welding, microprobe analyses have indicated a smooth transition from a cobalt-enriched zone to the low-carbon steel when such an inertia weld was scanned. Other microprobe investigations[13,21] of aluminum to steel and low-

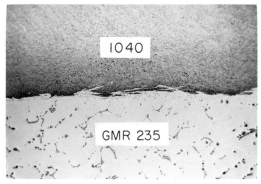

Fig. 6-12 Inertia weld of SAE 1040 steel and GMR 235 superalloy (67×).[7]

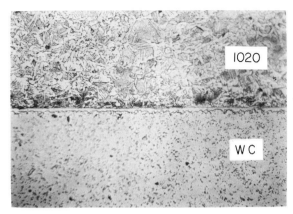

Fig. 6-13 Inertia weld of SAE 1020 and tungsten carbide (67×).[7]

carbon steel to titanium have found evidence of element mix. One elaborate probe found the existence of a thin decarburized layer on the steel side followed by an iron-in-titanium solid solution and/or iron-titanium intermetallic compound. Although formation of the alloy layers varies from place to place and the exact nature of these layers was not identified, these observations tend to indicate that some degree of diffusion has occurred at the weld zone during the process.

EQUIPMENT AND TOOLING

The conventional-type machine shown in Fig. 6-14 shows schematically that the workpieces are aligned axially to each other and one workpiece is rotated with respect to the other, which is held stationary. The surfaces of the workpieces are slid relatively under welding force. When the workpieces are heated sufficiently to accomplish a weld, a mechanical brake is applied to stop the relative rotation between the

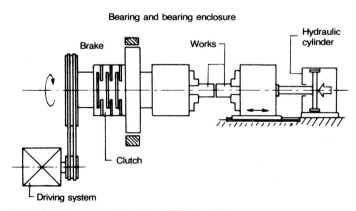

Fig. 6-14 The conventional-type FRW machine.

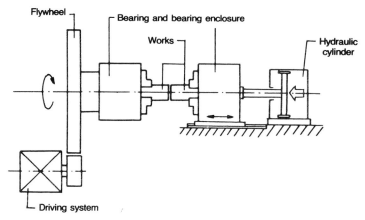

Fig. 6-15 The flywheel-type FRW machine.

workpieces. In the flywheel method seen in Fig. 6-15, one workpiece is chucked to the rotating spindle provided with a flywheel, which has stored the desired kinetic energy. This rotating workpiece is pushed against the other workpiece held stationary under a welding force. When the kinetic energy of the flywheel is converted to frictional heat at the contact area, a weld is formed.

In both methods, the flash (upset) is formed at the joint. If it is required to remove the flash (upset) from joint, a suitable process as well as the flash-removing equipment must be incorporated. If the flash at the joint can be removed simultaneously during the welding cycle, versatility, productivity, and production efficiency of the FRW process will be increased considerably.

As a result, a new lathe-type FRW machine has been introduced in Japan. It is designed to remove the flash simultaneously with its formation at the joint. Thus, by the time when welding is completed, the flash will have been removed and machines.

Since flash removing in the heating phase keeps the contact area unchanged during the entire welding cycle, a true welding pressure results at the contact area between the workpieces. Therefore, a sound weld can be obtained with a lower welding force by this method than by either the conventional or flywheel method for welding workpieces of the same size. Consequently, this advantage makes the design and manufacture of the machine much easier, as seen in Fig. 6-16.

The requirements placed on the design of FRW machines are many. One of the major requirements must be an ability to handle heavy production demands with minimum downtime, while maintaining part reliability. The major functions of the external machine are

1. Clamping and centering of the workpiece
2. Rotating and friction under pressure
3. Braking
4. Upsetting

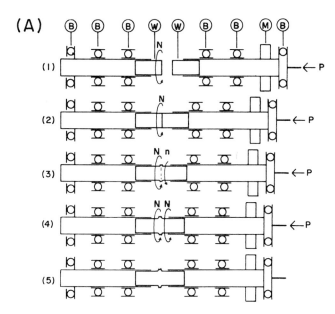

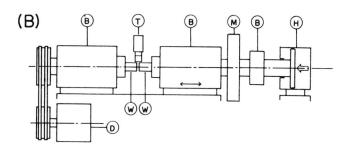

(W) Workpieces to be welded
(M) Rotating Mass
(T) Cutting Tool
(B) Bearing and Bearing Enclosure
(H) Hydraulic Cylinder
(D) Driving System

Fig. 6-16 A new FRW machine type.[22]

The overall design of the machine is determined in some measure by the part to be welded, the upsetting forces required, and the torque and vibrations originating at the weld.

An analysis of the torques to be transmitted is important for the structural layout and selection of drive motors, the transmission elements, and the clamping devices. As noted earlier, friction generates vibrations which must be dampened by the design of the machine and

Fig. 6-17 Double-ended machine used to produce truck axle housings.[23]

the choice of the process parameters. This has a direct influence on the weld and the life of the machine, and will vary based on the condition of the material and the shape of the part. Extensive investigations regarding the generation and damping of vibrations are necessary in order to obtain satisfactory results.

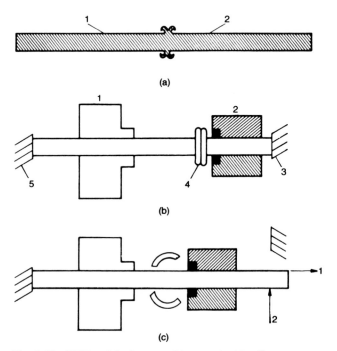

Fig. 6-18 FRW and flash removal in one chucking.[17]

Chuck requirements are critical because of the high torques and axial and radial forces transmitted. Hydraulically operated chucks generate the forces which reliably prevent the parts from slipping through. Special attention must also be given to the shaft bearings. Thus far, in all equipment built, braking has caused no problems once the rotating masses have been balanced.

The upsetting process essentially determines the size of the installation. While with flash butt welding the upsetting velocity plays a decisive role along with other factors, this is not the case with FRW. The upsetting process affects the entire concept of the machine. Figures 6-17 and 6-18 illustrate FRW machines fabricated for specific uses.

It is difficult to track the total number of FRW machines currently employed in the world for producing parts; however, as an example, FRW machines are used in approximately seventy companies in the United Kingdom, but more than 40% of all such equipment is employed in the automobile and allied industries. Details of the

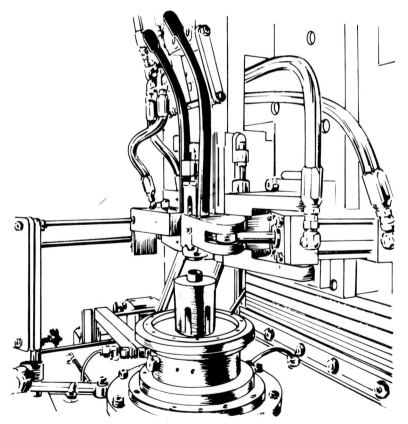

Fig. 6-19   The tailstock holds the fork, the flywheel holds the stem. Inertia welding is all over in 1 to 10 s.

number of machines and their distribution in British industry are summarized in Table 6-3. All machines but four are of the continuous-drive type; sixteen are of vertical configuration, while the remainder have a horizontal spindle axis.

Another new experimental impulse FRW machine is being developed in the U.S.S.R. which employs an impulsator in the machine drive for conventional FRW. This machine has established a sharp reduction in heating time and upset displacement, and has finally enabled engineers to obtain a high-quality joint.

Inertia and FRW machines are either horizontal or vertical. The machine must control all parameters and have devices that shut it down for overtravel, low pressure, and too little speed.

Fixtures must be able to locate the part accurately, hold it, and resist high thrust and axial forces. The rotating part of the machine should exert equal clamping pressure on the piece. Welding thrust should tend to tighten it. Usually stationary two-jaw chucks with vee or wrap-around jaws are used. The setup should be kept as simple and

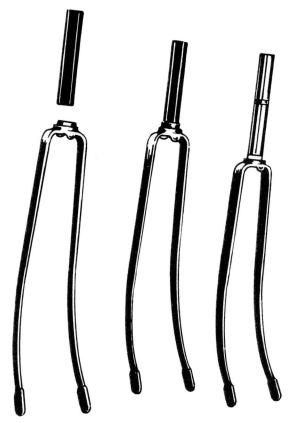

Fig. 6-20 From left: stem and forging before welding, after welding with flash, after lathe machining.

TABLE 6-3
Distribution of FRW Machines in the United Kingdom[9]

Industry or type	No. of machines	Percent of total
Automotive		
Structural parts	22	14
Engine parts	24	16
Transmission parts	14	9
Steering parts	2	1
Other	4	3
Total automotive	66	43
Hydraulic	3	2
Wire	8	5
General	13	9
Dissimilar metal	11	7
Plastics	12	8
Job shop, research and development organizations	39	26
	152	100

rugged as possible, since rotating mass affects weld parameters; too much energy can be stored in the flywheel because of an oversized fixture. Tailstock tooling can be either a two-jaw chuck or a simple clamping device as long as the tooling will not yield to the thrust and torques involved and guides the part properly. As an example of the tooling and fixturing previously described, Figs. 6-19 and 6-20 illustrate

Fig. 6-21 Rigid jigging for the FRW of truck axle housings.[23]

the welding of the forged fork and tube stem for a bicycle. There are 6000 fork-stem assemblies welded per day on one assembly line.

Another example of an axle housing, Fig. 6-21, demonstrates that careful jigging to fix parts is very important. In this example, the jigs and fixture must be made with enough rigidity to keep the precise center of parts in production because the axle has a cast steel part on one side and forged tubes on both sides.

A single model of an inertia-welding machine will span a range of weld diameters of about 3:1, with models available to weld mild-steel bars ranging from 0.125 to 0.25 in (3.2 to 6.4 mm) diameters. Thrust forces range from a few hundred to over a half-million pounds (227,000 kg). A schematic of the essential design features of an inertia welder is shown in Fig. 6-22.

All gripping devices used for holding the weld members must be reliable. Slippage of the part in relation to the chuck results either in a poor weld, or in damage to the gripping device.

Thrust supporting and chucking surfaces of the gripping devices must be rigid and located as near as possible to the weld interface to reduce deflection, thus minimizing eccentricity and nonparallelism. Grip diameter must be as large or larger than the diameter of the weld. Serrated gripping jaws are recommended for maximum clamping reliability.

Basic tooling divides into two categories—rotating and nonrotating. Each category, in turn, subdivides into manual and power-operated. Rotating tooling must be well balanced, have the smallest possible moment of inertia, have high body strength, and have a high gripping power when rotated at high speeds.

The most commonly used nonrotating gripping device is a self-centering viselike fixture with a provision for absorbing thrust.

Self-centering of the piece part allows for larger variations of tolerances of the welded pieces, while maintaining concentricity with the piece held in the collet chuck. Non-self-centering devices may be used where concentricity is of little concern.

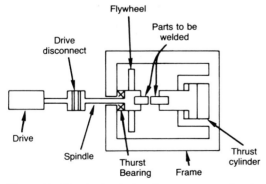

Fig. 6-22 The basic design features on an inertia welder.[14]

Fig. 6-23 Tooling for large inertia welding: (1) ways, (2) retracting cylinders, (3) rotary actuator, (4) replaceable jaws, (5) steadyrest, (6) backstop, (7) backstop latch, (8) pendant tailstock control.[14]

Wedgelike fixtures capable of withstanding torque and thrust can be used for welding long pieces. Weld parallelism and concentricity depends not only on the accuracy of the parts to be welded, but also on the length of overhang from the fixture to weld interfaces, as well as the rigidity of the tooling. As a rule, the larger the pieces welded, the greater the eccentricity, rigidity, and ruggedness of required tooling, shown in Fig. 6-23.

In short tubular welds, tooling can be piloted with considerable improvement of weld concentricity.

When large quantities of the same-shaped parts are welded, machines are built fully automated. Parts are fed into hoppers, and from the hoppers into gripping devices, then welded and ejected.

Figures 6-24 and 6-25 depict the use of a part now being produced by inertia welding in lieu of electron-beam welding. The shaft and wheel of four turbocharger models presently are welded in a vertical machine. The shaft is securely locked in the stationary upper check, while the wheel is held by a web-shaped saddle in the rotatable chuck at the base. As the spindle begins to rotate, it also rises to a predetermined position with a small clearance between parts. At a speed of 1350 r/min (141.3 rad/s), power is cut off, the spindle and attached flywheel press against the stationary shaft with a thrust of 17,000 lb (7718 kg), and the forging of the weld is complete. Inertia welding has reduced processing time at least 30%. While electron-beam welds were performed in a vacuum, inertia welding requires no special atmospheric conditions. The machine can be placed at any convenient location because welding operations produce no bright flashes, spatter, or objectionable fumes. Standard safety glasses provide adequate eye protection.

In addition to the conventional-drive, inertia, and flywheel types of FRW machines, there are several variations of machine design intended for various applications as summarized in Fig. 6-26. Figure 6-26*a* shows the principle of one design in which both parts are

Fig. 6-24 At start of weld the shaft is held stationary; rotor turns before parts are pressed together.

Fig. 6-25 Turbine wheel of heat-resistant alloy now is inertia-welded to Type 4140 steel shaft; EBW had been used.

rotating but in opposite directions. Such a machine will be suitable for those welds which may require very high relative rubbing speed. Another design, shown in Fig. 6-26b, has two stationary pieces pushing against a rotating piece between them. This machine is evidently desirable if the parts are very long or in such an awkward shape that rotation is difficult or impossible.[24] A similar situation shown in Fig. 6-26c involves two rotating pieces pushing against a stationary piece at the middle. The same principle can be applied for the reason of improving productivity. Figure 6-27 is a machine which can make two welds back to back at the same time with one rotating spindle at the center. This specific machine is fully automated for mass production of

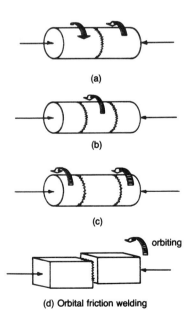

(a)

(b)

(c)

orbiting

(d) Orbital friction welding

Fig. 6-26 Variation of FRW machines.[7]

Fig. 6-27 Automated dual-head inertia welder for engine valves.[7]

exhaust valves for internal combustion engines at an average rate of 1200 parts per hour.

Figure 6-26d is another design of so-called "orbital" FRW.[25] Instead of rotating around its own axis, the moving piece rubs against the stationary piece in an orbital motion with a small offset. As soon as the interface temperature reaches the welding condition, the two pieces are realigned quickly to their desired orientation and forged together. This design is particularly suitable for welding parts with noncircular cross sections. Rectangular bars of different size have been successfully welded by this process. No friction brake is required to stop the unit and more than a single pair of components can be welded at one time. An improved version of the machine is expected to produce 2000 welded parts per hour.

Other variants of FRW machines include "microfriction welding,"[26] which is capable of joining pins of a diameter as small as 0.04 in (1 mm). Such a machine is usually small and portable. For large-size pipes, FRW machines have been proposed for pipe lines up to 36 in (900 mm) in diameter.[27]

BASIC JOINT DESIGN

The very nature of FRW is such that the joint face of at least one of the members must be essentially round. The revolving member should be somewhat concentric in shape since it must be revolved at relatively high speeds, and as long as the surface in contact is a continuous one. Figure 6-28 illustrates the basic joint designs, consisting of combinations of bars, tubes, and plates. Where bars or tubes are welded to plates, most of the flashing occurs from the more easily forged bar or

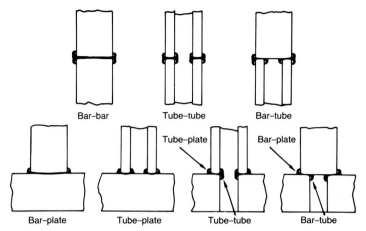

Fig. 6-28 Typical joint designs showing flash formation and HAZ.[14]

tube member. Each of the types of joints has its own distinct flash-flow pattern. The joints are between bar and bar, tube and tube, bar and plate, and tube and plate. The first two types refer to those joints where the diameters of the workpiece at the joint are the same. Thus a bar-to-bar joint with one diameter greater than the other is considered as a bar-to-plate weld. The parts are basically butt-welded at the interface, which can be either perpendicular or at an angle to the axis of rotation.

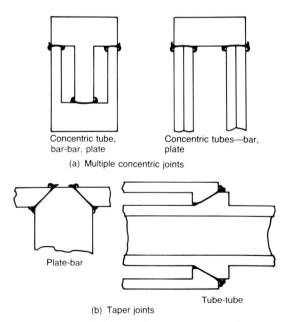

Fig. 6-29 Special joint designs showing multiple welds and welds made on a taper.[14]

Figure 6-29 illustrates "special" joint designs consisting of simultaneous welds on concentric cylinders. The requirements here are to produce both welds within suitable speed limits, and to ensure that both welds contact at appropriate times during the weld cycle to distribute energy proportionately. In addition to the square butt welds, angular or taper welds are feasible.

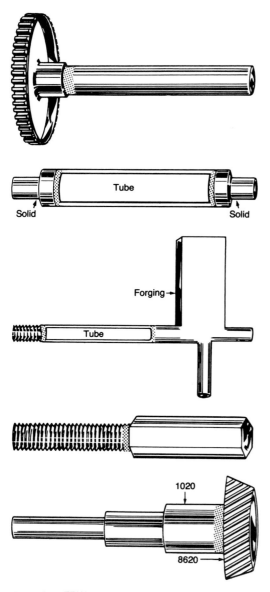

Fig. 6-30 FRW can handle all forms of metal.

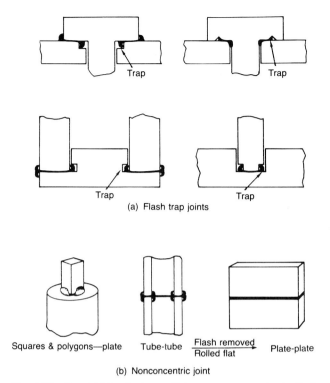

(a) Flash trap joints

Squares & polygons—plate   Tube-tube $\dfrac{\text{Flash removed}}{\text{Rolled flat}}$ Plate-plate

(b) Nonconcentric joint

Fig. 6-31 Special joint designs utilizing traps to contain the flash, and joints of noncircular geometries.[14]

Angle joints are usually designed with faces 30 to 45° (0.52 to 0.78 rad) from the center line, although angles as low as 8° (0.14 rad) have been made. Successful welds have been made in various forms of metals as shown in Fig. 6-30. For the more easily forged materials, the greater angles are preferred, to prevent pushing the one part through the hole. Some other special joint designs are shown in Fig. 6-31. The "flash trap" joints are intended for applications where the flash is not accessible for removal, and it must not be exposed for functional or aesthetic reasons. Noncircular members have been welded successfully, although the flash produced is very rough and unsymmetrical, and presents problems if it must be removed.

A requirement for noncircular joints is that the area of the mating member must be sufficiently large to completely accept the sweep of the noncircular rotating member. Plate-to-plate welds are not feasible by rotary FRW. However, such a joint can be produced, as illustrated in Fig. 6-31, by rolling a tube into a plate section.

Some welds between dissimilar materials with widely different forging temperatures or thermal diffusivity values require relative size adjustments at the interface, to produce proper balance of forging and upsetting of each member.

Joint Surface Conditions

Since the original butting surfaces of most welds are completely forged away in the process, joint surface preparation is not critical. As-forged, sheared, flame- and abrasive-cut, or sawed surfaces are usually satisfactory if adequate energy is provided to correct for out-of-squareness and the excessive flashing is not detrimental. Excessive out-of-square faces, however, may produce radial forces affecting weld concentricity. Center projections left by cutoff tools present no problems. However, pilot holes with concave surfaces should be avoided to prevent entrapping of air and oxides in the weld. Heavy forge or mill scale should be removed, since it acts as a bearing surface and sometimes cannot be flashed out of the weld interface. Carburized, nitrided, and plated surfaces should usually be avoided.

Joint Design for Forging Balance

Both welding faces must be heated to forging temperature and some of the material of each part must be moved into the flash. This requirement, generally, puts no restrictions on the relative sizes of the two interfaces. Heat losses to the cold metal are low. Heating rates as high as 100,000°F (55,000°C) per second make the weld cycles very short. Bar-to-plate and tube-to-plate welds are perfectly feasible.

Some welds between dissimilar materials of widely different forging temperatures or conductivity do require adjustments of size at the interface. For example, in a tube-to-tube weld, a nickel-base turbocharger rotor is 0.062 in (1.6 mm) smaller in OD and 0.062 in (1.6 mm) larger in ID than its mating hollow steel shaft. The additional 0.031-in (0.8-mm) overhang of the alloy steel provides enough thermal balance at the periphery of the nickel-base alloy.

Without this heat-sink effect, too much steel would be flashed away to achieve adequate forging action on the nickel alloy.

Another example is a small keyway cutter blank. A tool-steel shank was readily welded to the cutter blank as a bar-to-plate joint. When the shank was changed to alloy steel, the blank had to be modified to present a bar-to-bar joint. A situation where geometry will affect heat balance arises when a tube is welded to a thin plate with a hole of the same ID. It may be necessary to make the hole in the plate smaller to avoid excessive heat at the ID.

Joint Design for Machine Size

The material at the center of the bar-to-bar or bar-to-plate joint requires more welding energy because it must be extruded farther to form the flash. This material at the center of the bar, however, contributes very little to torsional or bending strength of the weld, being near the neutral axis. In some cases it is practical to design the joint with a center relief in one or both parts to eliminate this nonworking but hard-to-weld material. This center relief may be used to permit the part to be joined on a smaller machine than the original design, or perhaps simply to speed up the welding cycle.

A simple example is a 3-in-diameter (76 mm) solid shaft of C1020 steel to be welded to a forged gear blank. This joint requires a 4-in-capacity (102 mm) inertia-welding machine. By forging a 1.25-in-diameter (32 mm) indentation in the center of the gear, the assembly becomes suitable for a 2.5-in (64-mm) machine. The revised part is not quite as strong; for equal torque load, the maximum shear stress is about 3% more than before. If this is significant, the part can be made as strong as before by increasing the OD of the shaft by only 0.031 in (0.8 mm). Even with this additional diameter, the new design is readily welded on the smaller machine.

Similarly, a bar-to-plate weld can be redesigned to a bar-to-bar joint if desirable to bring it within capacity of a particular machine. A sprocket-to-hub joint is another example of similar design approaches. In this case, a full interface weld was not required, but inertia welding was preferred to fusion welding because it avoided heat-distortion of the flat sprocket plate. These principles can be applied in reverse, of course, if the limitation is the minimum capacity of a particular machine.

Joint Design for Flash Consideration

If the joint design would restrict flow of flash from the weld, clearance for the extruded material must be provided. Flash traps may be deliberately incorporated in the design where flash removal would be impossible or where flash removal cost can be avoided. Volume of flash is calculated by multiplying the upset length loss by area of the weld. The precombustion chamber shown in Fig. 6-32 is a production part where flash removal would have been impossible. Shoulder-weld joints must be designed to provide flash clearance. In addition, there must be

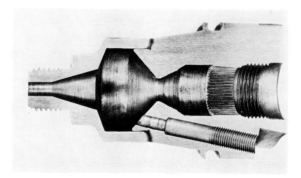

Fig. 6-32 Flash traps are designated into a part in which flash removal is impossible. The precombustion chamber shown incorporates a void to accept internal flash.[14]

clearance to avoid rubbing of the shaft in the ID. Rubbing robs part of the flywheel energy unpredictably and diminished weld repeatability.

For a tight, flash-free internal corner, a joint can be designed with just enough protrusion for an internal shoulder to make contact as the weld is completed. It is necessary to balance design and parameters so that the shoulder will brake residual energy without getting hot enough to produce its own flash.

Welding Forces

The value of welding torque and thrust and clamping forces necessary to resist the torque must be considered in design of the components to be welded and design of holding devices. Thrust values will vary with materials and areas of contact. In Table 6-4 are representative thrust loads for 1-in (25.4-mm) bars of several materials. These are "middle-of-the-road" values and may be varied to suit the needs of specific applications. For other bar sizes, unit thrust pressure varies as the square root of the diameter. For tubular welds, thrust pressure is based on wall thickness. The OD minus ID (twice wall thickness) is about equivalent to solid bar diameter in estimating unit weld pressure. Example: a 0.5-in (12.7-mm) wall tube will have about the same pressure as a 1-in (25.4-mm) bar.

TABLE 6-4
Welding Thrust—1 in (25.4 mm) Bars

Material	Pounds	Kilograms
Low-carbon steel	12,000	5,500
Medium-carbon steel	14,000	6,400
Low-alloy steel	15,000	6,800
Superalloys	50,000	22,700
Maraging steel	20,000	9,100
Stainless steel	18,000	8,200
Tool steel to carbon steel	40,000	18,200
Copper or brass	5,000	2,300
Titanium	8,000	3,700
Aluminum (1100)	6,000	2,700
Aluminum (6061)	7,000	3,200

ADVANTAGES, LIMITATIONS, AND ECONOMICS

FRW has been developed to such a stage that it will produce reliable welds with many technical as well as economic advantages over other comparable welding methods. Ideally, each new application should have complete and thorough research. However, many FRW applications have had successful production results without total metallurgical research.

FRW solves many of the problems encountered in electric butt welding and eliminates the particular disadvantage of the flash in flash welding. The following are some of the obvious advantages which FRW offers over other processes:

- FRW makes the joining of dissimilar materials possible at high production and low cost. This provides design engineers greater flexibility in designing for cost and performance.
- The solid-state bond achieved by FRW generally yields better mechanical properties and a narrower heat-affected zone than welds by fusion-welding processes.
- Great economic advantage can be realized from FRW by fabricating parts with standard bar or tubular stock instead of expensive forgings or castings.
- FRW machines can be readily automated for mass production of quality parts; hence, skilled labor is not required.
- Lower electrical power requirements. There is no single-phase, short-time peak electrical load during the welding process. With lower power demand and power consumption, the process frequently can be considered in installations where flash butt welding would be impossible. Power costs in some applications are 70 to 80% lower than other processes.
- Better use of floor space. Because FRW produces no disconcerting flashes or showers of sparks, the machines can be installed closer to other operations in manufacturing areas.
- Material savings. The smaller loss of length in FRW and the possibility of combining materials not suitable for welding by electrical methods has provided substantial material cost savings.
- Easier workpiece preparation. Clamping prior to welding is in most cases much simpler, and weld surface conditions are less critical than those required for electrical flash butt welding.
- Less adjustment to maintain dimensional tolerance. The electrical flash butt process requires highly conductive and relatively soft clamping devices that must have frequent machining and adjustment to maintain tolerances. Chuck linings of FRW machines are hardened and ground to provide better accuracy and longer service life.
- Adaptable to automatic processes. In many applications, automatic loading and unloading of the machine, as well as indexing of the parts and transfer to other operations, is possible.
- Better control of welding variables. The reliability of the weld is not influenced by the welding current or the electrical resistance at the welded joint. These critical variables in electric welding are dependent upon the part, the welding machine, the electrical power available at the time of welding. With FRW the dependent variables can be easily controlled and adjusted by production personnel.
- Elimination of weld inclusions. FRW largely eliminates the inclusion of foreign matter in the weld area. This leads to a higher weld joint quality and provides some metallurgical advantages.

Limitations

Despite all the advantages, FRW has several limitations. At least one of the objects to be joined must have a symmetrical shape to permit the high-speed rotation that is required. In flat-faced joints, considerable upset is produced because of plastic deformation in the final phases of the welding cycle, and upset removal may be necessary. Surfaces to be welded should be perpendicular to the rotating axis, angular butt-weld joints are not easily made, and good alignment of the parts is critical.

Economics

Whether parts are inertia-welded or conventionally friction-welded, engineers are improving their basic understanding of the process and are finding the economic advantages inherent in the friction-weld process. With better accuracy of alignment and scrap-loss reduction, the shutdown-control shaft seen in Fig. 6-33 is now conventionally friction welded in lieu of flash welding. The trunnions shown in Fig. 6-34 illustrate again an example of the economic benefits derived by flywheel FRW over GMAW.

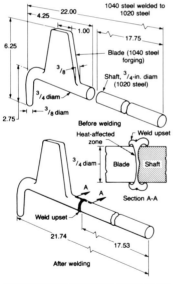

Fig. 6-33 Shutdown control shaft that was made by joining a steel forging to a steel shaft at lower cost by FRW than by flash welding.[28] (0.001 in = 0.03 mm)

Item	Welding process	
	Flash	Friction
Cost Comparison		
Production, parts per hour	240	300
Steel savings (a)	—	$5500
Scrap loss (b)	6 to 7%	1/2 to 1%
Forging scrap loss	3.5%	1.5%
Fixture maintenance (c)	$1830	$1050

(a) For each 100,000 units. (b) From misalignment, burns and other causes. (c) Cost per year.

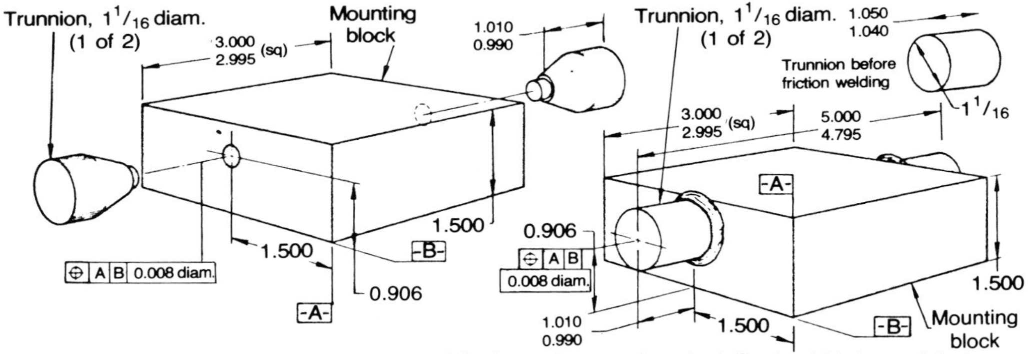

Trunnion, 1 1/16 diam.
(1 of 2)
3.000
2.995 (sq)
Mounting
block
1.010
0.990
1.500
-B-
1.500
0.906
-A-
⊕ A B 0.008 diam.
Trunnion, 1 1/16 diam.
(1 of 2)
1.050
1.040
Trunnion before
friction welding
1 1/16
3.000
2.995 (sq)
5.000
4.795
-A-
0.906
⊕ A B
0.008 diam.
1.010
0.990
1.500
-B-
1.500
Mounting
block

Original method (gas metal-arc welding) Improved method (flywheel friction welding)

Operation	Gas metal-arc welding	Flywheel friction welding
Comparison of Costs per Mount		
Machine two trunnions	\$0.90	\$0.06
Drill two holes in block	0.12	—
Assemble trunnions to block	0.10	—
Weld	0.85	0.50
Total cost per mount	\$1.97	\$0.56
Saving per mount		\$1.41

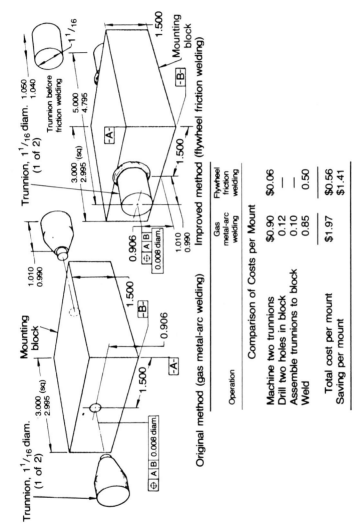

Fig. 6-34 Original and improved methods of welding trunnions to a mounting block to make a trunnion mount for air and hydraulic cylinders. Cost per mount was reduced by 71% when flywheel FRW replaced gas metal-arc welding.[28] (0.001 in = 0.03 mm)

WELD QUALITY AND PROCESS CONTROL

The quality of friction welds is primarily dictated by process control, once the weldability of a metal pair is established. The simplicity of inertia welding makes the determination of process parameters relatively easy. On the basis of theoretical analyses, supplemented by experimental data, the manufacturers of inertia-welding equipment have worked out a number of graphs and tables which can be used as a guide to determine welding parameters.[29] These parameters were successfully used to produce the fabricated compressor wheel, shown in Fig. 6-35, which represents a weldment where close tolerances must be maintained in the finished product. Blank preparation was carefully controlled and rigid tooling used to hold concentricity. The compressor wheel of Inconel 718, a nickel-base alloy, was designed to operate at a temperature of 1000°F (538°C) and inertia-welded in 2.5 s.

Such manufacturer's data would usually provide a good starting point, and many easy-to-weld metals can probably be set up successfully by first trial. For difficult-to-weld metals, the process parameters can further be refined and optimized through a systematic procedure as described in Ref. 19.

Continuous-drive FRW is probably a little harder to optimize because it has more variables to be manipulated. However, years of experience have revealed that weld quality very much depends on such factors as the rate and the total amount of workpiece shortening (or

Fig. 6-35 Inertia-welded compressor wheel of Inconel 718. The 14-in (356-mm) weld joining each 24-in-OD (0.6 m) wheel was made in 2.5 s.

burn-off) during the heating phase, and the shortening during the forging phase.[30] These indirect parameters are in turn affected by machine settings and material properties. To ensure weld quality, it has been suggested that these parameters be controlled automatically by incorporating in-process monitoring and feedback control devices on the welding machine.

Nondestructive testing techniques such as radiographic and ultrasonic inspections have been used for checking friction welds with various degrees of success.[31–33] On critical applications, quality can be further checked by loading the weld area in tension or torsion to as high as 85% of the yield strength. However, these tests usually become unnecessary as confidence is established.

MATERIALS

Considerable effort has been made to determine the weldability of metal pairs by FRW processes. In principle, almost any metal that can be forged and is not a good dry-bearing material can be welded by the friction process. Figure 6-36 is a weldability chart for commercially developed inertia welds; and a more detailed list of welds claimed to have been successfully made by inertia welding is shown in Table 6-5. A similar chart[34] and a list of welds claimed to have been successfully made by the continuous-drive process are shown in Fig. 6-37 and Table 6-6.

The ferrous-base materials, from mild steel to high-speed tool steel, can all be welded. The mild steels are relatively easy to join and have a wide range of parameters. Highly alloyed steels, such as high-speed steels, can also be efficiently joined, but with a much narrower operating band of parameters and more axial thrust force, commensurate with their higher forging flow stress. Their lack of toughness and their sensitivity to notches and thermal shock may dictate that weld flash be removed prior to thermal quench treatments to prevent crack propagation from the flash.

The macrostructure of a typical friction weld between SAE 4140 and 4340 is shown in Fig. 6-38. This friction-welded blank used in the oil-well equipment industry shows that the heat is generated very locally and uniformly at the interface as reflected by the narrow width and shape of the heat-affected zone. The metal at the interface is continuously hot-worked at high strain rates, and this results in considerable refinement of the structure over a narrow band when the heating ceases.

Titanium alloys are readily inertia-welded. Within the range of parameters investigated, properties of joints are acceptable, provided sufficient upset is achieved. Most titanium-alloy inertia weldments can be used in the as-welded condition, although somewhat better tensile elongation and fatigue lives will be achieved by postweld stress relief or reheat treatment. The titanium alloys which have been inertia-welded and exhibit consistent welds after fatigue and tensile property evalua-

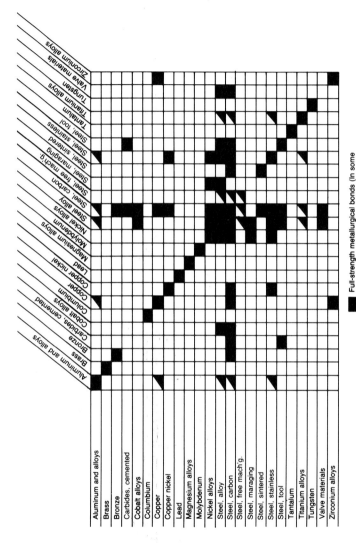

Fig. 6-36 A reference weldability chart for inertia welding.[14]

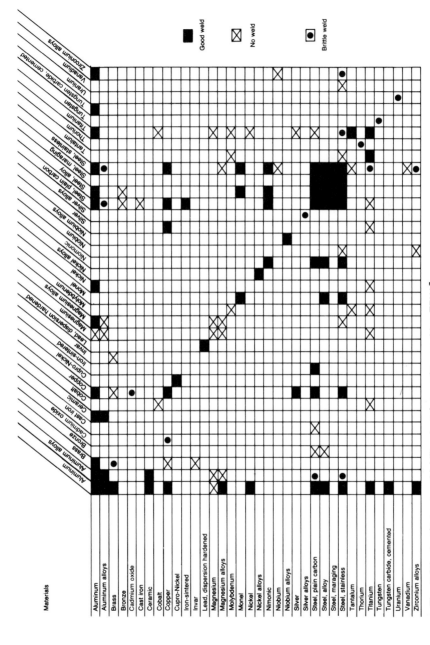

Fig. 6-37 A reference weldability chart for continuous-drive FRW.[7]

TABLE 6-5
Successful Welds by Inertia Welding Process[15]

1. *Carbon and Alloy Steels*

SAE 1008 to 1037, 1052

SAE 1010 to self, *1113, 1213,* 8620

SAE 1013 to 1010, 1018, *1117*

SAE 1017 to 1085

SAE 1018 to self, 1013, 1117, 5130, 8620, sintered 1024, 1080, ausformed 1060

SAE 1020 to self, 1037, 1052, 1095, *1141, 1144, 1215,* 4140, sintered 1080

SAE 1025 to self

SAE 1025 to *5120L*

SAE 1035 to 4130, 4140

SAE 1036 to Inconel 713C

SAE 1037 to 1008, 1020

SAE 1040 to 52100

SAE 1045 to self, *1141,* 4150, 8620

SAE 1047 to 21-4N

SAE 1049 to self

SAE 1052 to self, 1008, 1020

SAE 1060 ausformed to 1018

SAE 1070 to M-1

SAE 1080 to self

SAE 1085 to 1017

SAE 1095 to self, 1020

SAE 1117 to *self, 1013, 1018*

SAE 1137 to *self*

SAE 1141 to *self, 1144, 1018, 1020, 1045*

SAE 1144 to *self, 1141, 1020*

SAE 1213 to *1010*

SAE 1215 to *1020*

SAE 14B36 to self

SAE 3140 to Sil SB

SAE 4032 to self

SAE 4038 to self

SAE 4115 to self

SAE 4130 to self, 1035

SAE 4140 to self, 1020, 1035, T-1

SAE 4142 to self

SAE 4150 to self, 1045

SAE 4340 to self

SAE 5120L to *self, 1026*

SAE 5130 to 1018

SAE 5140 to self

SAE 52100 to self, 1040, 8620, 8630

SAE 6150 to 8650

SAE 8150 to Sil 10

SAE 8615 to self

SAE 8620 to self, 1010, 1018, 1045, 8820, 52100

SAE 8625 to self

SAE 8630 to self, 52100

SAE 8645 to Inconel X

SAE 8650 to 6150

SAE 8740 to self

SAE 8822 to 8620

SAE 9310 to self

SAE 98BV40 to self

USS T-1 to 4140

2. *Sintered Steels*

SAE 1024 to wrought 1018

SAE 1080 to self, wrought 1018, 1020

3. *Maraging Steels (18% Nickel)*

250 to self, Waspaloy

300 to self, 4340

350 to self

4. *Stainless Steels*

302 to self, 404, 410, 1020, 1045, 8620, 8630

304 to self, 1020, 1045, nickel-copper

309 to 1010

310 to 17-4PH

316 to 1018, 1020

TABLE 6-5
(Continued)

321 to self, 8630

347 to 17-4PH

404 to 8655

410 to 1045

416 to *self, 440, 1018, 1045, 1113*

440C to self

17-4PH to self, 310, 347

Ca-5 (centrif. cast) to self

Ca-20 to 1020, 1045

HK to self

5. *Tool Steels*

M-1 to 1040, 1045, 1050, 1070, 1080, 8645, 8650

M-2 to 1045

M-4 to carbides (with a minimum of 10% Co)

M-7 to 1045

M-10 to 1045

M-50 to self

S-1 to 1080

6. *Special Alloys and Nonferrous Materials*

Aluminum

1100 to self, 6061, copper

2024 to *self*

6061 to self, 6063, 1100, Cast 356 *copper*

6063 to self, Cast 856

7075 to *self*

Cast 356 to 6061, 6063

S A286 to GMR 235

S AMS6304 to Inconel 713LC, Waspaloy

S Astroloy to self

S B1910 to SAE 4340

Brass (70-30) to self

Bronze (alum) to self, SAE 1020, 1045

Carpenter 5 SS (centrif. cast) to self

Carpenter 20 SS to SAE 1020, 1045

Copper (pure) to SAE 1020, 1045, *1100, 6061*, chrome copper, Zircaloy

Copper (leaded) to 1100

Copper-beryllium 25 to self

Copper-nickel to nickel-copper

Copper-tungsten to chrome-copper

Chrome-copper to copper-tungsten, silver, tungsten, pure copper

D979 to Inconel 713LC

S GMR 235 to SAE 1040, 4130, 8620, 8630, A286

S Hastelloy to self

V Hastelloy X to SAE 1045

Inconel 100 to 718

Inconel 600 to self, 304 SS, SAE 1018

S Inconel 713C to SAE 1036, 1040, 4140, 5140, 8630, EN24, Nitralloy J

S Inconel 713 LC to 718, SAE 4140, 5140, D979, EN24, Nitralloy J

S Inconel 718 to self, 100, 713LC, 901, AMS6304, Waspaloy

V Inconel 751 to SAE 1045, 4140

S Inconel 901 to self, 718, Waspaloy

V Inconel X to SAE 8645

Lead (lead oxide dispersed) to self

S Mar M246 to SAE 5140

Molybdenum (sintered) to self

Monel 400 to self

Nickel 200 to self

Ti-Ni to self

Nickel-copper to self, copper-nickel, 304 SS, SAE 1018

Nitralloy to self

Nitralloy J to Inconel 713C, 713LC

S René 41 to self, SAE 4340

V Silchrome #1 to SAE 3140, Stellite 6

V Silchrome #10 to SAE 8150

V Silchrome SB to SAE 3140

TABLE 6-5
(Continued)

Silver tungsten to chrome copper	S Udimet 700 to self
V Stellite 6 to SAE 3140, 4140, 8645, Silchrome #1	S Udimet 710 to SAE 4140
Stellite 21 to self	V Valve material 21-4N to SAE 1045, 1047, 3140
S Stellite 31 to SAE 1036, 8630	V Valve material 21-12 to SAE 3140
S Stellite 151 to SAE 8630	V Valve material 21-55N to SAE 8650
Stellite 220 to self	Vascomax 250 (maraging steel) to Waspaloy
Tantalum to self, *302 SS*, *SAE 1018*	S Waspaloy to self, SAE 8645, AMS 6304, Inconel 901, Vascomax 250
V Thompson VMS-488 to SAE 1041	
Titanium (pure) to self	Zircaloy 2 to self
Titanium (6AL-4V) to self, pure titanium	Zircaloy 4 to self, copper
Tungsten (sintered) to self	
Tungsten carbide to *SAE 1018, 1020 M4 Tool Steel*	

NOTES:
1. All material combinations listed above have been inertia-welded and in all cases a sound metallurgical bond was formed. For italicized materials, however, the bond does not possess inherent 100% parent metal strength. In other cases appropriate postweld treatment may be required to develop full weld-zone strength in materials that have been quenched and tempered, precipitation-hardened, or work-hardened. Stress relieving may be required in hardenable materials.
2. V denotes valve materials and S denotes Superalloys.

tions include Ti-6Al-4V, Ti-6Al-2Sn-4Zr-2Mo, Ti-6Al-6V-2Sn, Ti-8Al-1V-1Mo, and Ti-6Al-2Sn-4Zr-6Mo. The major advantages of this process for titanium are its potential reproducibility and control, consistent attainment of essentially base-metal properties, and insensitivity of weld quality to process parameters and joint preparation. Inertia welding is an effective method of joining titanium alloys for applications where critical metal properties are required. See Fig. 6-39.

Stainless steels, sintered steels, and maraging steels are comparatively easy to join with good properties without much care being given to the joining parameters. The heat-treatable stainless alloys, like other highly alloyed steels, are more sensitive to processing variables, in that the heat-affected zone will require further processing to produce the desired properties.

Maraging steel (18% Ni) components should be friction-welded in the solution-annealed condition, since the heat generated during welding is sufficient to cause resolution of the strengthening precipitates, and thus additional aging is required to achieve full maraged properties.

The welding of wrought superalloys to cast superalloys is a new area for inertia welding which is useful because of the ability of the flywheel to deliver the high energy input rates needed to forge-weld these

TABLE 6-6
Successful Welds by Continuous-Drive FRW[7]

1. *Carbon and Low Alloy Steels*

SAE 1018/SAE 1018	6150/6150
SAE 1020/SAE 1020	6150/C1020
SAE 1021/SAE 1021	6150/C1040
SAE 1035/SAE 1035	4118/C1020
SAE 4147/SAE 4147	4320/4320
C1008/C1008	C1042/C1042
C1020/C1020	C1045/C1030
C1022/C1022	C1060/C1060
C1026/C1026	C1040/C1030
C1030/C1030	C1039/C1039
C1040/C1040	1330/C1035
C1040/C1020	C1055/C1055
C1040/C1038	C1010/C1010
C1040/C1010	C1020/5120
C1040/C1020	C1030/C1020
C1038/C1038	C1049/C1049
C1042/C1042	4130/4130
C1027/C1027	5115/5115
C1027/1524	1340/1340
Jalloy No. 1/Jalloy No. 1	4140/1335
Jalloy No. 1/C1020	4150/4150
Jalloy No. 1/C1040	4320/4320
5140/5140	
4140/4140	**2.** *Stainless Steels*
4140/C1020	410/410
4140/C1042	410/C1020
4340/4340	410/4140
4340/C1020	431/C1020
4340/C1040	431/321
C1050/C1050	321/C1020
C1046/C1040	316/C1020
C1046/C1050	316/C1026
C1046/5140	316/C1040
C1046/C1046	316/316
	316/C1009

TABLE 6-6
(Continued)

3. *Heat Resistant Materials*	C1016/C1016
Dreadnought 30BW/Dreadnought 30BW	4615/C1040
Carpenter 20/C1020	1019/1019
Hastelloy B/C1020	4718/4718
Hastelloy C/C1020	4781/C1020
Vacon 1ST/St330TS	Nitralloy 125 (H)
Stellite G60/C1020	8622/8622
Stellite G60/C1040	**6.** *Nonferrous*
Stellite G60/AISI316	Al/C1020
Monel/Monel	Al/C1040
Monel/C1020	Al/Cu
Incoloy/Incoloy	Al/Al
Incoloy/C1020	Ti/Ti
Ni/Ni	Ti/Al
	Cu/316
4. *Powder Products*	Cu/Cu
Iron powder/9255	CA260/CA260
Iron 2% copper/C1008	CuZn-37Mn-2Al/CuZn-37Mn-2Al
	Niobium/niobium
5. *Case Hardening and Nitriding*	**7.** *High-Speed Steel*
C1009/C1009	M-2/C1055
C1016/C1027	T-1/C1055
C1016/316	

heat-resistant materials. Table 6-7 lists some of the weldable combinations of iron-, nickel-, and cobalt-base superalloys and steels for gas turbine and turbocharger construction.

Material with high thermal-diffusivity values, or materials that tend to seize and cold-work at the faying surfaces, require high speeds to produce high heat input rates while limiting the torques. Copper and molybdenum are two examples of materials that require high speeds.

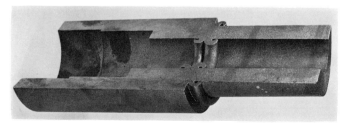

Fig. 6-38 Friction-welded blank of SAE 4140 to SAE 4340 steel.[23]

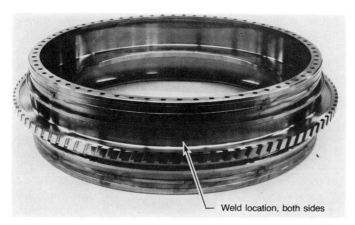

Fig. 6-39 Typical Ti-6Al-4V structure fabricated by inertia welding.[33]

Inertia welding and continuous-drive welding are by no means limited to similar-metal joining. Combinations have proved to be suitable for joining most commercial steels, including plain carbon steel/stainless steel, heat-resisting steels/wear-resisting steel, plain carbon steel/tool steel, and stainless steel/maraging steel.

TABLE 6-7
Material Combinations Welded for Turbine Applications[7]

Superalloy to Superalloy

IN713C-IN718	IN713LC-IN718	GMR235-A286
U700-U700	IN100-IN718	Waspaloy-IN718
Waspaloy-IN901	Waspaloy-Waspaloy	IN901-IN901
Stellite 220–Stellite 220	HastX-HastX	René 41–René 41
TD nickel–TD nickel	Astroloy-Astroloy	HS 21–HS 21
	IN600-IN600	

Superalloy to Steel

IN713C, LC-1036	IN713C, LC-4140	IN713C, LC-5140
IN713C, LC-Nitralloy J	IN713C-8630	IN713C, LC-EN24
IN713C-AMS6304	IN713LC-D979	HS 31–1036
GMR235-1040	HS 31–8630	GMR235-4130
GMR235-8620	GMR235-8630	Stellite 21–8630
B1900-4340	U710-4140	M246-5140
Waspaloy-Vascomax 250	Waspaloy-AMS6304	Waspaloy-8645
IN718-AMS6304	IN901-AMS6304	HastX-1045
René 41–4340	IN751-1045	IN751-1020
IN600-1018	IN600-304	

Steel to Steel

410-1045	416-416	416-1040
17-4PH–17-4PH	17-4PH–310	17-4PH–347
CARP 20–1020	CARP 20–1045	

Titanium to Titanium

Ti(6-4)-Ti(6-4)	Ti(6-4)-Ti

The use of FRW in the manufacture of tubular transition pieces, particularly in the nuclear field and for vacuum insulating vessels for the storage and handling of liquid gases, has also received a great deal of attention. The combinations which are of considerable interest to design engineers are stainless steel to pure aluminum, copper, cupronickel alloys, zirconium alloys, or titanium alloys. FRW is suitable for joining zirconium to austenitic stainless steel, since a very narrow fusion zone is produced because of the axial loading during welding. The fusion zone produced by FRW this metal combination is so narrow that the eutectic zone is almost indiscernible. However, a metallurgically sound joint between the two metals has been produced.[35]

Limitations on the weldability of materials are based on the characteristics of the process, which requires frictional heating and forging at the joint. Metals to be welded must be malleable at high temperature. Therefore, for the following materials, FRW will usually not be successful:

- Cast iron in any form—free graphite limits frictional heating. Any incipient welding that may occur with cast iron is of such a brittle nature that it has no commercial value.
- Bronzes and brasses having a high lead content (over 0.3%).
- Free-machining steels containing over 0.13% of sulfur, lead, or tellurium; e.g., SAE 1141 is weldable whereas SAE 1144 is not.
- Highly anisotropic materials, e.g., beryllium, which has almost no transverse ductility.
- Any material with a distinct weak phase present in the microstructure, e.g., graphite, manganese sulfide, free lead, tellurium, etc.

There are a number of metal combinations which have exhibited marginal weldability. Examples are aluminum alloys with copper, steels, and stainless steels, and titanium with steels. High thermal conductivity, large differences in forging temperatures, and some tendency to form brittle intermetallic compounds all can cause problems. Inertia welds of Type 6061 aluminum to pure copper and to austenitic stainless steel, and stainless steel to pure aluminum have been reported[15] to achieve nearly full strength.

Material Properties

Room-temperature and 800°F (427°C) tensile strengths of inertia-welded Waspaloy (nickel-base superalloy) was found to be comparable to electron-beam-welded joints [188 ksi (1296 MPa)], and ductility at 800°F (427°C) was 10%. At 800°F (427°C) low- and high-cycle fatigue strengths for both processes were the same, and torsional fatigue strengths of both joining processes equaled base-metal strength.

Table 6-8 shows the tensile properties of both age- and non-age-hardening alloys. These tests indicate full strength in the weld with the various post-heat treatments given. Weld strength is usually equivalent to that of the parent material. Steel to Type 6061 aluminum welds are

TABLE 6-8
Tensile Properties of Various Inertia-Welded Alloys[14]

Alloy	Condition	Test temperature °F	Test temperature °C	UTS ksi	UTS MPa	0.2% Y.S. ksi	0.2% Y.S. MPa	Elongation %	Failure location
4340	W	RT	20	220	1517	206	1420	12	Parent
321 stainless	W+SR	RT	20	87	600	34	234	65	Parent
Ti-6-6-2	W+SR	RT	20	182	1255	177	1220	12	Parent
		600	316	147	1014	120	827	16	Parent
Ti-6-2-4-2	W+SR	RT	20	145	1000	133	917	14	Parent
		900	482	110	758	83	572	18	Parent
200 grade marage	W+A	RT	20	227	1565	218	1503	12.5	Parent
Udimet 700	W+HT	RT	20	189	1303	135	931	13.5	Parent
		1400	760	144	993	125	862	15	Parent
Inconel 718	W+A	RT	20	210	1448	172	1186	13.5	Parent
	W+A	1200	649	162	1117	146	1007	8	Parent
Ti-6-4	W	RT	20	144	993	131	903	12	Parent
	W+1750°F (954°C) +1300°F (704°C)	RT	20	136	938	125	862	14	Parent
	W	600	316	104	717	84	579	16	Parent
	W+1750°F (954°C) +1300°F (704°C)	600	316	104	717	83	572	17	Parent

W = Weld.
SR = Stress relief.
HT = Heat treatment.
A = Age.
RT = Room temperature.

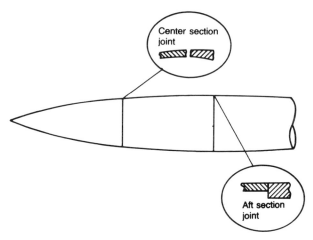

Fig. 6-40 Schematic diagram of the inertia-welded center section (tapered butt) and aft section (step butt) joints in SAE 4340 steel.

notable examples where inertia welds have produced full-strength welds in which both the static and the fatigue strength of the weld exceeds the strength of the aluminum. Steel-aluminum inertia welds have been tested in fatigue and found to have fatigue strengths at 10^7 cycles of 11 ksi (76 MPa).

A recent evaluation of the strength and ductility of SAE 4340 steel inertia welds were found to be of equal quality to that of the base metal and were evaluated in the application shown in Fig. 6-40.

Hydraulic piston rods, friction- and inertia-welded, have better fatigue strength than flux-cored arc welds shielded with carbon dioxide. The materials of the rods were Types 4130 and 4140 steel. As a result of tensile testing in which all failures occurred in the parent

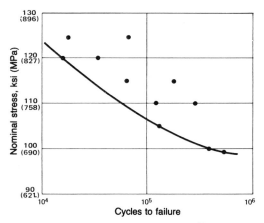

Fig. 6-41 Torsional fatigue test results.[14]

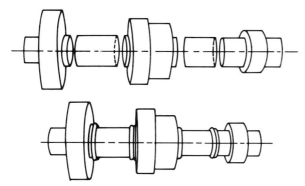

Fig. 6-42 Gearbox shafts made by FRW simple forgings or bar offcuts.

material, the joining of production solid-steel-rod pistons has been changed to FRW. Tensile strengths attained were about 83 ksi (572 MPa), yield strengths were about 54 ksi (372 MPa), and elongation in 2 in (50.8 mm) was 14.5%.

Friction welds recently performed on Udimet 700, a high-strength nickel alloy, have been shown to be equal to the parent metal in tensile and stress-rupture strength at 1400 and 1796°F (760 and 980°C). FRW does not appear to be applicable to TD-Ni or to U-700/TD-Ni weldments.

Rotating-beam tests of most common steels prove that fatigue resistance of the inertia-welded joint is equal to the parent metal. This is demonstrated in Fig. 6-41, where a 2-in (50.8 mm) shaft of SAE 1035 boron-treated steel was welded to a T1 steel flange. The torsional fatigue test results were equal to the solid Type 1035 steel with failures originating in a radius, not in the weld. As expected, some started near the flange and progressed into the weaker T1 material. Surprisingly, some failures were completely away from the weld through the solid shaft.

Finally, Fig. 6-42 shows some typical inertia welds in Types 5083 and 7039 aluminum that alloy that have been reported.[9] All Type 7039 welds failed in the base metal, so the strength of the welds was greater than that of the base metal. The average base-metal properties were:

- Ultimate tensile strength (UTS)—57.6 ksi (397 MPa)
- Yield strength—35.5 ksi (245 MPa)
- Elongation—18% in 1 in (25.4 mm)
- Reduction of area—42%

It may be stated generally that the various versions of the FRW process are frequently replacing pressure or flash welding where these welding processes have, in the past, been considered the standard method of joining. As previously stated, one important restriction with the FRW process, however, is that one of the members being joined must have essentially axial symmetry, because of the high rotational speeds involved.

APPLICATIONS

Transportation

Application of the process to the transportation industry has received a great deal of attention because FRW may simplify or cheapen the part, or make procurement of components easier. As a result of this successful work, FRW is now extensively used in the mass production of a variety of parts used in passenger car and bulk-carrying vehicles. Examples include axle cases where a forging or axle spindle is welded to a tubular banjo or beam. For this specific application alone, more than 3000 axle cases per hour are produced in England. Others are drive transmission and gearbox shafts, seen in Fig. 6-42, and S cams for air-brake-equipped trucks, tractors, and trailer vehicles. Precombustion chambers for diesel engines have been inertia-welded. This assembly forms a part of the fuel injection system, and is subject to high combustion temperatures and pressures. To date, 3 million precombustion chambers have been produced and not one field failure has been reported.

Production is over 4000 a month on the turbocharger wheel previously discussed in which the cast nickel-base GMR-235 wheel is inertia-welded to SAE 4140 steel shafts.

A spring-retainer assembly, see Fig. 6-43, for a heavy-duty tractor steering clutch originally was made from a forged, machined, and tapped baseplate into which hexagon-head bolts were inserted. When the product design was changed so that studs could be inertia-welded to a steel plate, the cost of each assembly was reduced by $0.71.

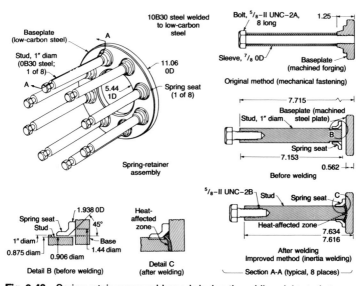

Fig. 6-43 Spring-retainer assembly made by inertia welding eight studs to a base plate at lower cost than by tapping a forged plate and inserting bolts.[28] (0.001 in = 0.03 mm)

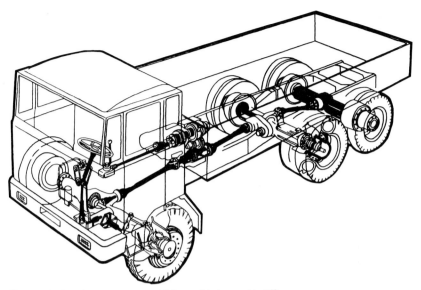

Fig. 6-44   Truck components which are friction-welded.[23]

Figure 6-44 illustrates (shaded areas) typical production components that are friction-welded in many truck manufacturing plants today. Even a marine engine manufacturer found savings of $50,000 a year when it started inertia welding bimetallic outboard-motor propeller shafts several years ago. In the last 7 years, over 2 million parts have been inertia-welded. The propeller shafts are fabricated from 9620

Fig. 6-45   Typical friction-welded components include hydraulic rams and track rollers.[23]

alloy steel and welded to Type 410 stainless. Recently a snowmobile, which is powered by a rotary combustion engine, was produced with a crankshaft specifically designed for fabrication by inertia welding as a tube-to-bar application. The metals joined are 8620 and 86B17 alloy steel.

An example of a part not welded before is a lever shift lock that has to be joined to a small plate. Now inertia welding joins the parts. A bus and truck manufacturer is producing speed-change spindles, 200 parts per week, 35,000 rods for automobile jacks per week, and 90 hand-rail support bars per hour. The earth-moving machinery industry utilizes FRW for various components as depicted in shaded areas of Fig. 6-45. The hydraulics-industry equipment makers, especially, apply the process to pipeline control equipment, particularly valves, where flanges are welded to valve body blanks. They also friction-weld cylinders, piston rods, gear pump rotors, railway buffers, and shock absorbers. In cylinder welding, the joint design contains the initial weld upset in a small cavity so that machining of the bore can be avoided. Chrome-plated piston rods are friction-welded to up ends with no damage to plating. Engineers recently converted the joining of telescoping hydraulic cylinders to inertia welding; heretofore these were joined by hand welding, submerged arc welding, and threading. The plant is producing 1500 cylinders a month which have 10,500 inertia welds. See Fig. 6-46.

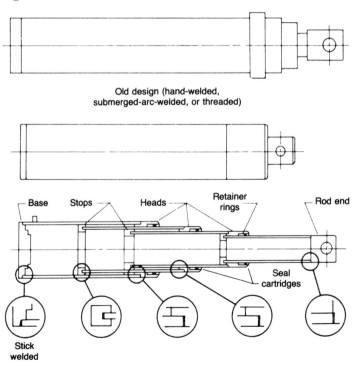

Old design (hand-welded,
submerged-arc-welded, or threaded)

Fig. 6-46 Typical inertia-welded areas.

Oil and Gas Industries

Pump shafts and control valve shafts, often requiring joints between plain carbon and corrosion-resistant-alloy steels, are made for the oil and gas industries in quantity. FRW is a natural way to fasten tools to drill pipes. Joints acceptable to the industry have been made between SAE 4140 tool joints and low- or mild-steel pipe. The hydrocarbon and mineral exploration industries have utilized friction-welded parts; one plant is producing 1000 parts per year. Inertia welding is critically

Fig. 6-47   Friction-welded heat pipes, for raised pipeline, keep soil frozen near footings.

important to the success of the Alaska pipeline. FRW of 112,000 above-ground heat-pipe supports, called stabilizers, for 390 mi (628 km) of the line, where pipe contact with the ground could upset permafrost stability and damage the environment, has proven successful. See Fig. 6-47.

Power Transmission, Nuclear Power, and Chemical Industries

The ability of FRW to join together dissimilar steel was proven in the manufacture of bimetal fasteners that are used to support insulation covers for use in nuclear plant construction. The materials involved are AISI C1009 carbon steel and AISI Type 316 stainless steel.

FRW is well suited for welding copper-aluminum transition pieces for bimetallic connections for power transmission and electrochemical plants. Where aluminum has replaced copper or transmission cables, copper-aluminum transition pieces are essential because reliable mechanical connections between aluminum parts cannot be made. Insulating oxides, corrosion, and creep at stress points lessen conductivity. Transition pieces join aluminum conductors to copper conductors.

In the chemical industry, special electrodes require the joining of titanium or steel cell elements to aluminum connecting studs, and FRW makes it possible.

Aerospace and Engine Industries

Inertia welding is just taking hold as the jet engine industry finds a niche for the process. The applications range from eight-stage compressor rotors of Inconel 718, illustrated in Fig. 6-48; Astroloy turbine disks; and

Fig. 6-48 An eight-stage compressor rotor fabricated from Inconel 718 by inertia welding.

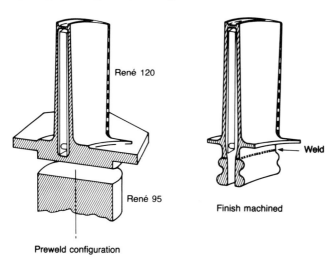

René 120

René 95

Preweld configuration

Weld

Finish machined

Fig. 6-49 Sketch of René 120 blade form inertia-welded to René 95.

Fig. 6-50   Left to right: 15-5PH bar to 15-5PH bar, 6061-T6 aluminum bar to 6061-T6 aluminum bar (two each), and 7075-T6 aluminum extruded bar.

René 95 six-stage integral rotors and René 120 turbine blades, seen in Fig. 6.49.

Hydraulic fittings of 6061-T6 for aircraft and 4130 steel drop-off wing tank fittings have been inertia-welded. More than 10,000 parts have been welded without a single reject. Besides making possible a design that is better because of simplification, FRW eliminates the need for several machining operations and reduces inspection time drastically. Figure 6-50 shows the use of inertia welding in joining a small diameter to a

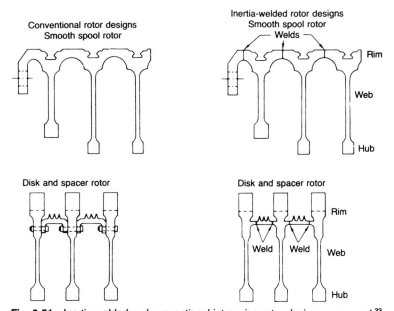

Fig. 6-51   Inertia-welded and conventional jet engine rotor designs compared.[33]

larger diameter for various fittings. All of the above welds were proof-tested to assure 100% weld strength.

A commercial aircraft engine currently contains friction-welded gearbox components and an Inconel 718 shaft fitting. FRW permitted shortening and lightening of the gear box, and replacement of a forged solid shaft fitting with a tube and stamping. In both, the gains were longer life and lower cost.

Medium-carbon steel to superalloy butt joints in turbocharger rotors are another example of the use of the process in engine rotating equipment. There appears to be little doubt that friction-welded components will be used in new-generation jet engines and in similar applications. Future welded rotor designs are compared with present designs in Fig. 6-51.

Miscellaneous

There are numerous new applications for inertia welding and FRW. These include reamers, cutters, refrigeration compressor crankshafts, rollers for copying and photo processing machines, taps, and woodworking tools.

Use of FWR in joining SAE 1045 bar-stock lift link assemblies, which have to absorb heavy shock loads, in joining coils of wire has recently been explored. The materials joined are 0.8% carbon steel and aluminum alloys.

One obvious application of FRW is the joining of high-speed steel to carbon and low-alloy steel to make twist drills.

During the last several years there have been many studies of the possible application of FRW to site operations. Prototype welds demonstrated that welding of the appropriate materials and components was possible, so special-purpose equipment was developed to exploit and process. Machines were built with particular design characteristics —light weight, compactness, remote operating features, etc.—so that welding could be performed on site or in extremes of environment. One example is the development of a small machine for attaching small dissimilar-metal connectors on the side of live cable conductors for tee joining. The unit weighs less than 11 lb (5 kg) and is capable of joining connectors of up to 0.23 in (5.8 mm) diameter.

FRW of rollers for printing presses has meant the elimination of a number of machining processes for the manufacturer of printing equipment; see Fig. 6-52.

More recently, work has shown that FRW can be applied to the fabrication of plastics and also to the joining of metallic to nonmetallic materials, e.g., aluminum and aluminum alloys to an alumina-base ceramic for the manufacture of metal/ceramic seals.

Although it has been proved empirically that a large range of materials are compatible with FRW, the exact mechanism of bond formation is not clearly understood, and further studies must continue.

A good design of joint configuration can not only improve weld

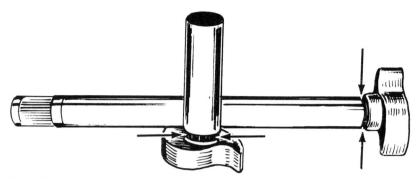

Fig. 6-52 Printing press rollers.

quality and appearance, but with a proper design, can also provide better thermal balance for materials with large differences in thermal conductivity. In some cases, by modifying a bar-to-bar weld with a center relief in one or both parts, it may be possible for the parts to be welded on a smaller machine than the original design without much sacrifice of weld strength. Undesirable flash, such as is present inside a tube-to-tube, can be eliminated by providing clearance for the extruded material. In short, ingenious design of joints would greatly broaden the applications of FRW to its full advantage.

REFERENCES

1. Crossland, B., "Friction Welding," *Contemp. Phys.*, **12**(6), 559–574, November 1971.
2. Irving, R. R., "Welders are Stirred 'Inertia'," *Iron Age*, **195**(18), 29, May 1965.
3. Oberle, T. L., Loyd, C. D., and Calton, M. R., "Caterpillar's Inertia Welding Process," *SAE Trans.*, Sec. 3, **75**, 28–35, 1967.
4. Kiwalle, J., "Flywheel Friction Welding as a Design and Production Tool." ASTME Paper AD67-198, 1967.
5. Eichhorn, F., and Schaefer, R., "Investigation of the Processes in the Welding Zone during Conventional Friction Welding of Steel," *Weld. Res. Abroad*, pp. 2–20, November 1969, translated from *Schweissen + Schneiden*, **20**(11), 1968.
6. Ellis, C. R. G., "Continuous Drive Friction Welding of Mild Steel," *Weld. J.*, **51**(4), 183s–197s, April 1972.
7. Wang, K. K., "Friction Welding," WRC 204, April 1975.
8. Squires, I. F., "Thermal and Mechanical Characteristics of Friction Welding Mild Steel," *Br. Weld. J.*, **13**(11), 652–657, November 1966.
9. Needham, J. C., and Ellis, C. R. G., "Automation and Quality Control in Friction Welding," *Weld. Inst. Res. Bull.*, 12, 333–339, Part 1, December 1971; 13, 47–51, Part 2, February 1972.
10. Johnson, P. C., Stein, B. A., and Davis, R. S., "Inertia Welding," unpublished technical report, Caterpillar Tractor Co., 1966.
11. Oberle, T. L., "Inertial Welding," SAE Paper 730103, *International Automotive Engrg. Congress*, Detroit, January 1973.
12 Weiss, H. D., and Hazlett, T. H., "The Role of Material Properties and Interface Temperatures in Friction Welding Dissimilar Metals," ASME Paper 66-MET-8, 1966.
13. Hasui, A., Fukushima, S., and Kinugawa, J., "Experimental Studies on Friction Welding Phenomena," *Trans. Nat. Res. Inst. Metals-Jpn.*, **10**(4), 53–71, 1968.
14. "Welding Handbook," 6th ed., Chap. 50, pp. 50-3–50-38, American Welding Society, Miami, 1970.

15. "Inertia Welding—Application Principles," Caterpillar Tractor Co., Peoria, Ill., 1971.
16. Sluetz, E. J., Oberle, T. L., and Brosheer, B. C., "Inertia Welding," *Am. Mach.*, Spec. Rep. 621, October 1968.
17. Ellis, C. R. G., and Nicholas, E. D., "Metallurgical Characteristics and Mechanical Properties of Cold Drawn Mild Steel Friction Welds," BWRA Bull. P/39/69, May 1969.
18. Lucas, W., "Effect of Selected Process Parameters on Joint Strength and Microstructure of Mild Steel Friction Welds," BWRA Bull. P/48/71, July 1971.
19. Wang, K. K., and Rasmussen, G., "Optimization of Inertia Welding Process by Response Surface Methodology," *Trans. ASME, J. Eng. Ind.*, **94**, Series B (4), 999–1006, November 1972.
20. Johnson, T. K., and Daines, J. W., "A Comparison of the Capabilities of Continuous Drive Friction and Inertia Welding," SME Paper AD73-221, 1973.
21. Wang, K. K., and Lin, W., "Flywheel Friction Welding Research," *Weld. J.*, **53**(6), 233s–241s, June 1974.
22. Hasui, A., Fusushima, S., and Kinogawa, J., "Some Experiments with a New-Designed Friction Welding Machine," *Bull. JSME*, **12**(51), 656–664, 1969.
23. Ellis, C., Thompson Friction Welding, Clarke Chapman Ltd., private communication, March 1978.
24. "Both Ends at Once Now Friction-Joined," *Prod. Eng.*, **38**, 104, July 1967.
25. Searle, J. C., "The Orbital Friction Welding Process for Non-circular Components," *Eng. Dig.*, **32**, 33–36, August 1971.
26. "Microfriction Welding," *BWRA Annual Report*, p. 31, 1969.
27. O'Donnell, J. P., "Friction Welding Proposed for Lines," *Oil Gas J.*, **68**, 57–50, March 2, 1970.
28. "Metals Handbook Welding and Brazing," vol. 6, 8th ed., American Society of Metals, Metals Park, Ohio, pp. 507–518, 1971.
29. "Inertia Welding Application Principles," Production Technology Inc., Peoria, Ill., 1974.
30. Ellis, C. R. G., and Needham, J. C., "Quality Control in Friction Welding, IIW Doc. III-460-72, 1972.
31. Adams, D., and Taylor, S., "Detection of Faults in Friction Welded Studs by Ultrasonics," *Weld. Met. Fabr.*, pp. 412–421, October 1969.
32. Doyle, J. R., Vozzella, P. A., Wallace, F. J., and Dunthorne, H. B., "Comparison of Inertia Bonded and Electron Beam Welded Joints in a Nickel-Base Superalloy," *Weld. J.*, **48**(11), 514s–520s, November 1969.
33. Nessler, G. C., Rutz, D. A., Eng, R. D., and Vozella, P. A., "Friction Welding of Titanium Alloys," *Weld. J.*, **50**(9), 379s–385s, September 1971.
34. Ellis, C. R. G., "Friction Welding—What It Is and How It Works," *Met. Constr. Br. Weld. J.*, **2**(5), 185–188, May 1970.
35. Hazlett, T. H., "Properties of Friction Welds Between Dissimilar Metals," *Weld. J.*, **41**(10), 448s–450s, October 1962.
36. Wadleigh, A., Interface Welding, private communication, March 1978.
37. Vill, V. I., "Investigation and Application of Friction Welding in the USSR," Comm. I Colloq., 21st IIW Annual Meeting, Warsaw, 1968.
38. Duvall, D. S., Nessler, C. G., "Manufacturing Technology for Joining Titanium Alloys," IR-838-2-VI, Contr. F33615-72-C-1624, AFML, August 1974.
39. "Flywheel Inertia Friction Welding," *Engineer*, **226**, 148–149, July 26, 1968.
40. Vill, V. L. "Friction Welding of Metals," American Welding Society, Miami, 1962.
41. Hazlett, T. H., "Properties of Friction Welded Plain Carbon and Low Alloy Steels," *Weld. J.*, **41**(2), 49s–52s, February 1962.
42. "Friction Welding in Japan," Japan Friction Welding Association, IIW Doc. III-384-69, 1969.
43. Rajala R., "High Strength Turbine Blade Dovetails," AFML-TR-74-154, August 1974.
44. Fukushima, S., "Study on Selection of Welding Conditions in Continuous Drive Friction Welding Process," *Trans. Nat. Res. Inst. Met. (Jpn.)*, **18**(4), July 1976.
45. Holko, K. H., "Friction Welding Alloy 800," *Weld. J.*, **56**(5), 140s–142s, May 1977.

7

ULTRASONIC WELDING AND SOLDERING

ULTRASONIC WELDING

The possibility of joining by ultrasonic vibration was discovered by accident in the 1940s. It happened while some experimental work was being conducted in which ultrasonic vibration was being applied to improve the grain structure during conventional electric-resistance spot welding. By accident, however, the main welding current had not been switched on, although normal pressure and ultrasonic vibration were being applied to the workpiece by the electrodes. It was then found that occasionally a weld was nevertheless produced. Soon after this discovery in Europe, a complete investigation of the whole process was undertaken, which ultimately led to the ultrasonic welding process.

THEORY

Ultrasonic welding (USW) is a solid-state joining method which uses no fluxes or filler metals. The process combines atoms at the interface of the parts to be joined through interatomic attraction. It is also a "cold" bonding process because atomic combination and diffusion occur while materials are in a semisolid or solid state. While some heating occurs, welding depends more on cleaning than on material melting. Low heat and relatively low distortion characterize the process, since welding temperatures are generally below the melting temperatures of the metals. Some recently conducted studies have shown the formation of a continuous layer of very fine grains during USW, and investigators[2-4] could relate this formation only to a short-time melting and rapid cooling of thin surface layers during the welding.

The theory is relatively simple. It was found that the close contact and friction developed with the passage of high-frequency vibratory energy through two abutting metals would cause them to adhere together without welding current.

PROCESS

The workpieces are clamped together under moderately low static force between a rigid anvil and a welding tip, and ultrasonic energy is transmitted into the top for a brief interval. Friction between the metal surfaces to be joined breaks up oxides and other contamination, exposing clean fresh metal on each surface and thus bringing the surfaces within an atomic distance of each other.

Once the surfaces are within an atomic distance, a metallic-type bond occurs, and because the ultrasonic cleaning action is continuous, there is no time to form new films to prevent atomic proximity. The resultant metallurgical bond is produced without arc or spatter, without fusion of the weld metal, without the cast structure resulting from fusion, and with negligible thickness deformation.

The significant variables during the welding operation are the applied clamping force, the power level, and weld time for spot-type welding or welding rate for continuous-seam welding. These three factors can not be determined separately for a given combination of materials, since their interaction is important in the bonding process. The particular settings for a given application depend primarily upon material properties and thickness. Clamping force may vary from a few ounces (grams) to several hundred pounds (kilograms). Electrical power input may vary from milliwatts to several thousand watts. For spot welds, the weld time is usually in the range of 0.01 to about 1.2 s. For continuous-seam welds, welding rates as high as several hundred feet per minute (meters per second) may be obtained with thin foil material. In general, it has been found that high power and short weld times produce better results than lower power and longer weld times. In addition, there is an optimum clamping force at which effective bonding of a given material combination is achieved with minimum vibratory energy.

KEY VARIABLES

Variables under the control of the welding machine operator are tip radius and surface; clamping force; power level; weld time interval for spot, ring, and line welding; and welding rate for continuous seam welding.

Tip Radius and Surface

Tip radius, while not highly critical as to specific values, is a very important general consideration that requires prime attention, since it affects weld area and thus the machine settings of clamping force, power, and pulse time or rolling rate.

For spot welding of overlapping flat-sheet materials, the radius of the active sonotrode tip should be on the order of about 50 to 100 times the thickness of the sheet in contact with the active sonotrode.* The opposing anvil is flat, not curved. Too large a tip radius results in

---

*Sonotrode is a coined name for the vibratory power-delivery element which contacts the work; it includes the tip. This term has come into general use in recent years to differentiate from the electrodes used in resistance welding.

large unwelded islands near the center of the weld spot and considerable variation in weld quality and reproducibility. A tip radius that is too small causes excessive indentation, as well as variation in quality and reproducibility.

When wires are joined to sheets, a grooved tip may be desirable; when wires are small, such as those used for connections to semiconductor devices, machine tips must be precise as to both dimensions and finish.

Clamping Force

A proper value of clamping force is important to accomplish a weld under conditions of minimum energy; i.e., for any particular welding machine; a proper clamping force permits the shortest weld interval. The ideal clamping force is sufficient to permit no sliding between the sonotrode and weldment, while not being so great as to impair welding. Within fairly broad limits, there is really no fundamental requirement of a welding contact force.

Excessive force produces needless surface deformation and increases the required welding power. Insufficient force causes tip slippage, surface damage, tip damage, excessive heating, and poor welding. If the clamping force is substantially lower than is required, damage to the transducer coupling is quite possible, although welding machines are usually equipped with safety interlocks to prevent power application under such conditions.

The proper clamping force is determined by developing a threshold curve of welding. The clamping force used for any specific application depends on the thickness and hardness of the components. Serrated or abrasive tips are effective means for reducing clamping force; such use reduces weld size while maintaining weld quality.

Power

The power setting is routinely indicated in terms of the high-frequency electrical watts delivered to the transducer. Energy (therefore power) requirements vary with the properties and thickness of the materials being welded. When dissimilar thicknesses of the same material are welded, the power input is determined by the thickness of the thinner member when it is adjacent to the sonotrode tip. Transducer coupling systems have been developed that can handle up to about 25 kW for the heavier or more difficult-to-weld materials, while fine semiconductor- or microcircuit-type welding may require only a fraction of a watt.

Welding Time or Rate

The spot-type, ring, or line welding interval during which vibratory energy is transmitted to the workpieces is usually within the range of 0.005 s for very fine wires to about 1.0 s for heavier materials. The necessity for a longer weld time indicates insufficient power. High power and short weld times usually produce results superior to those achieved with lower power and longer weld times. Not only poor surface appearance, but also internal heating phenomena and internal cracks can be expected from excessive weld times.

The same factors are significant in the rate of production of continuous-seam welds. With presently available equipment, the rate for the harder and thicker materials may be a few feet per minute (meters per second).

Power-Force Programming

Certain materials, such as the refractory metals and their alloys, are more effectively welded when power-force programming is used. This involves incremental variation in power and clamping force during the weld cycle.

Measurements of power delivery to the weldment under conditions of constant force and constant power have revealed an initial period wherein coupling between the tip and the workpiece is established and during which actual power delivery is low. This is followed by an interval of substantially higher power delivery. Coupling is more effectively established by initiating the weld cycle with low power and high clamping force. After a brief induction interval, the power is increased to form the weld.

Surface Preparation

Surface cleaning of most materials is not highly critical for USW. The welding mechanism disrupts and disperses normal oxide layers and other surface films on the mating surfaces. The more readily weldable materials, such as aluminum clad alloys, brass, and copper can be welded in the mill-finish condition and usually require only the removal of surface lubricants with a detergent. Welding of heat-treated materials exhibiting heat-treat scale is best accomplished after mechanical abrasion or descaling in chemical etching solution. Once the surface scale is removed, the elapsed storage time before welding is not important.

A good surface finish contributes to the ease with which ultrasonic welds may be made. As-rolled, as-drawn, or as-extruded finishes are usually satisfactory. Roughened surfaces resulting from oxidation, heat treating, or deep etches have occasionally been troublesome. There are a variety of chemical solutions that result in a bright finish and usually provide surfaces that are satisfactory.

It is possible to produce ultrasonic welds through surface deposits or coatings, although somewhat higher energy levels are required. For example, heavily oxidized Inconel X sheet has been successfully welded without prior removal of the oxide coatings, and sound welds have been produced in aluminum having anodized coatings up to 0.0001 in thick (less than 0.01 mm). This capability is particularly important in restricted applications in which cleaning is not possible. In the joining of electrical or electronic components, it is often required that a bond be produced through insulating enamel or plastic films. USW has been effective in this application, and films such as polyvinyl chloride or polyethylene have been penetrated. Insulations having a silicone base are more difficult to penetrate and may require removal prior to welding.

JOINT DESIGN

Almost any lap-type joint configuration within existing sheet thickness limitations is amenable to USW. The type of welding (spot-type, ring, line, or continuous-seam) used for a specific application depends on the joint design. Several aspects of joint design differ from those associated with other joining processes.

Edge distance is not critical in USW. Line welds and ring welds can be made with an overlap of but 4 to 6 times the thickness of the sheet, the only restriction being that the welding tip should not crush or gouge the sheet edge. Such welds in structural aluminum alloys 0.032 and 0.050 in thick (0.8 to 1.3 mm), for example, have shown the same strength at 0.125 in (3.2 mm) as at 0.75-in (19-mm) edge distance.

Spot Welds

USW places no restrictions on spot spacing or row spacing. Spot-type welds may be spaced at any desired interval and even overlapped. Rows of welds of any of the four types may be spaced as desired or overlapped. Consequently there is a flexibility in joint design.

Ring Welds

For some structural applications, ring welds may be preferable to spot-type welds. The ring diameter can be as large as desired (within the power capability of present equipment), providing more uniform stress distribution and substantially reducing stress concentrations. Ring welding appears to have other advantages. The parts-resonance problems occasionally encountered with spot-type welding are virtually nonexistent with ring welds. In addition, the tendency toward cracking associated with the tension and compression fields on the fore and aft edges of spot-type welds apparently does not exist in the simple shear fields around the periphery of ring welds.

WELDING SYSTEM

The source of energy in USW can be either piezoelectric or magnetostrictive. The piezoelectric effect refers to the capability of certain crystals to change size when used to conduct an electrical current.

Although the size change is extremely small, it can be amplified to several thousandths of an inch. The magnetostrictive effect is similar in that a magnetostrictive material changes size when placed in an electromagnetic field. Both effects are used extensively in ultrasonic applications.

The generation of ultrasonic energy starts with a power supply—essentially a unit that converts 60-Hz electrical energy to frequencies of either 10 or 20 kHz. This high-frequency current is received by a converter or motor containing a piezoelectric crystal, and thus the vibratory effect is established. There are various types of transducers utilized in USW equipment: the magnetostrictive type usually comprises a stack of nickel or nickel-alloy laminations, and exhibits overall efficiencies in the range of 20 to 40%. Electrostrictive transducers are associated with somewhat complicated mechanical assemblies incorporating electrostrictive ceramic washers such as lead titanate zirconate as the active energy-converting material. Such transducers have shown overall efficiencies exceeding 90% in the laboratory; in USW applications their efficiency appears to be in the range of about 55 to 80%.

The third component in this system is the horn. A horn is a resonant bar which transfers energy from the converter to the workpiece. Thus the horn equipped with a welding tip shown in Fig. 7-1 effects the high-velocity scrubbing action needed for welding. Several types of horns are used in this type of work—the step horn, exponential horn, and catenoidal horn.[5]

Titanium horns for ultrasonic tools have been recently evaluated.[6] Titanium has superior acoustical properties in comparison with stainless steel, it stands up better under the intense vibrational energy imparted than aluminum, and it is just as easy to machine as aluminum in producing horns.

Horns are evaluated on the basis of their gain, a term that expresses the ratio between output amplitude and input amplitude. The step horn exhibits higher gain than the other two, but it also has the highest stress concentration, a factor that limits its use. In contrast, exponential

Fig. 7-1 Metal welding tips are designed to suit individual applications.

horns have excellent stress curves, but low gain factors. The catenoidal horn represents a compromise between the desirable characteristics of the step and exponential horns.

Several other types of horns are available, namely the bar horn and circular horn, which are specialized tools. Of greater importance is the fact that virtually all horns are made of titanium and machined to extremely close tolerances. Size is extremely important, since it affects the resonance of the horn.

Again, it is not absolutely necessary that a horn resonate ultrasonically to effect all welds. Some welds are better made at frequencies in the audible range, specifically 10 kHz. Further, the process is best used only in certain applications. These can be summarized as applications involving highly conductive materials, highly resistive materials, metals with dissimilar resistive values, metals with large differentials in thickness, and the like. In the course of welding, the process performs its joining action without embrittlement and formation of high-resistance intermetallic compounds in dissimilar-metal welds. Further, it has no effect on temperature-sensitive metals such as beryllium-copper.

EQUIPMENT

USW equipment consists basically of a frequency converter to provide high-frequency electrical power at the design frequency of the welding system; a transducer coupling system to convert the high-frequency electrical power into elastic vibratory energy and deliver it to the weld zone; an anvil which serves as a backing support for the workpieces; a force application mechanism; a timing device to control weld interval in spot-type, ring, and line welding, or a rotating and translating mechanism for continuous-seam welding; and appropriate electrical, electronic, and hydraulic or pneumatic controls. Currently equipment operates at 20 kHz (from 200 to 1500 W) and 10 kHz (700 to 8400 W). There are basically four types of machines.

Spot-Type Machines

These machines all operate on the same principle; i.e., they deliver shear-type vibration to the sonotrode tip and subsequently into the weld interface to produce a weld spot with a single pulse of high-frequency vibration. Two different transducer coupling systems may be employed: a wedge-reed system and a lateral-drive system. The force-actuating mechanism may be hydraulic, pneumatic, or mechanical.

Wedge-reed system

In the wedge-reed system, Fig. 7-2,[7] the transducer drives the wedge in longitudinal vibration. The upper end of the reed is rigidly supported in a mass, and the wedge is attached to the reed to produce flexural vibration therein. The tip thus undergoes essentially lateral vibration in a plane parallel to that of the weldment. Clamping force is applied through the mass and reed member.

The wedge-reed system has been favored for the larger spot-type welding machines, such as the 1500-W (acoustic) machine shown in Fig. 7-3.[5]

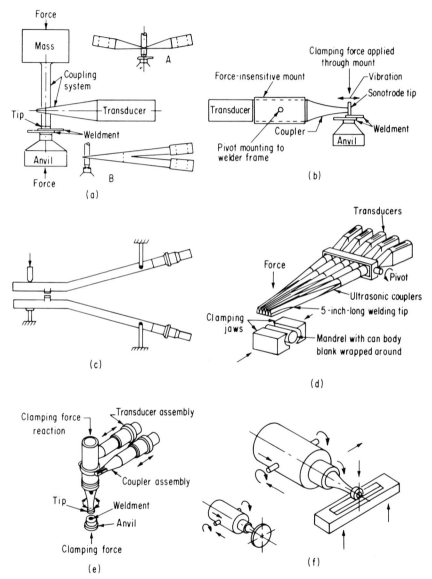

Fig. 7-2 Various ultrasonic welding machines: (a) wedge-reed spot welder, (b) lateral-drive spot welder, (c) overhung-coupler spot welder, (d) line welder, (e) ring welder, and (f) continuous-seam welder.[7]

Fig. 7-3 Commercial ultrasonic spot-welding machine equipped with a conventional tip and anvil.[5,8]

Lateral-drive system

Small USW machines usually incorporate the lateral-drive system illustrated schematically in Fig. 7-2. In this case the tip is attached to a lateral sonotrode, which vibrates longitudinally to produce tip movement parallel to the weld interface. Force is applied by a bending moment, indicated by the arrows.

Spot-type welds can be overlapped to produce an essentially continuous bonded area. This type of seam may contain as few as 50 to as many as 10 welds per inch (25.4 mm); closer weld spacing may be necessary if a leaktight joint is required.

Ring-Type Machines

Ring-welding machines utilize a torsionally driven coupling arrangement in which the axial-driving coupling members are tangent to the torsional coupler and produce a torsional vibratory displacement of the welding tip in a plane parallel to the weld interface. A schematic diagram of the essential components of a typical design is shown in Fig. 7-2.

These welding machines are available in sizes ranging from 500 to about 4500 W (acoustic) capacity. They are capable of making circular ring welds in diameters ranging from 0.125 to approximately 3 in (3.2 to 76 mm), as well as welds of oval, square, or rectangular shapes.

An uninterrupted perimeter weld can thus be produced with a single weld-power interval. These welds need not be circular; they can be square, elliptical, rectangular, or irregular in shape as long as the overall length to overall width does not exceed a ratio of about 3 : 1. Ring welds may be overlapped to produced a seam that resists eccentricity effects.

Line-welding machines

These machines usually incorporate an overhung lateral-drive transducer coupling system; the couplers extend beyond the welding tip, and force is applied to the overhung portion of the coupler. This design provides a force-insensitive mounting and eliminates high bending moments in the coupler under high clamping forces. High bending moments are characteristic of the previously described lateral-drive system, Fig. 7-2.

A cluster of multiple transducer coupling units attached to a single welding tip is ordinarily used for weld lengths greater than about 1 in (25.4 mm). An array for making 5-in (127-mm) line welds incorporates five such units with an interconnecting tip. Force is applied through hydraulic cylinders separately to each coupler, and the force is thereby equalized for each increment of weld length.

Continuous-seam welding machines

Continuous-seam welding machines usually incorporate antifriction bearings and lateral-drive transducer coupling systems, with provisions for rotation of the entire transducer-coupling-tip assembly by a motor drive. The rotating tip operates in rolling contact with the work along the desired path by either a roller-roller system, a traversing-head system, or a traversing-bed system, Fig. 7-4. Continuous-seam welds may be overlapped to produce total bonding over extended surface areas with materials such as aluminum.

Fig. 7-4 Typical traversing head of continuous-seam USW machine.[9]

ADVANTAGES AND DISADVANTAGES

Some of the advantages of USW are

- Temperatures are kept well below the melting points of the metals to prevent contamination. The temperature rise which occurs can be controlled within limits by appropriate adjustment of the welding machine settings.
- Sound junctions can be obtained between many dissimilar metals previously difficult or impossible to join.
- Intermetallic combinations are seldom formed in the weld zone of dissimilar metal junctions.
- With no current passing through the weld zone, there is no arcing or sparking to contaminate surrounding areas.
- Thin foils or fine wires can be joined to themselves or to larger and heavier components.
- A wide variety of configurations can be effectively welded.
- Helium-leaktight seam welds can be reproducibly obtained.
- The process and associated equipment can be readily incorporated in automated production lines for many applications.
- Welds highly conductive and resistive metals.
- Requires no precleaning, post-welding operations such as annealing or cleaning.
- Since no consumables are required, it eliminates gas, electrodes, fluxes, and solders that are necessary with other methods. The process also eliminates the need for venting for odors and toxic fumes.

Some of the limitations of the process in its present state of development are as follows:

- With any given material there is an upper thickness limitation for the production of sound welds with currently available equipment.
- Techniques have not yet been developed for producing butt welds with USW.

MATERIALS AND PROPERTIES

Almost every metal and alloy can be ultrasonically welded, although other welding processes may be more economical for certain of the more readily weldable materials. USW is particularly useful for materials and certain geometries that are difficult or impossible to join by other techniques, for materials which require unusually high power for satisfactory bonding, for bimetallic combinations, or for applications which cannot tolerate some of the side effects caused mainly by heat that may occur with other joining methods.

TABLE 7-1
Metals and Alloys Which Have Been Successfully Joined by
Ultrasonic Welding, or in Which Welding Feasibility
Has Been Demonstrated

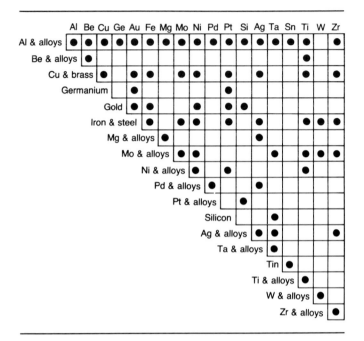

	Al	Be	Cu	Ge	Au	Fe	Mg	Mo	Ni	Pd	Pt	Si	Ag	Ta	Sn	Ti	W	Zr
Al & alloys	●	●	●	●	●	●	●	●	●	●	●	●	●	●	●	●		●
Be & alloys		●												●				
Cu & brass			●	●	●	●	●					●	●			●		●
Germanium					●							●						
Gold					●	●			●		●	●						
Iron & steel						●		●	●		●					●	●	●
Mg & alloys							●				●							
Mo & alloys								●	●					●		●	●	●
Ni & alloys									●		●			●				
Pd & alloys										●			●					
Pt & alloys											●							
Silicon												●						
Ag & alloys													●	●				●
Ta & alloys														●				
Tin															●			
Ti & alloys																●		
W & alloys																	●	
Zr & alloys																		●

Table 7-1 illustrates some of the monometallic and bimetallic combinations that are ultrasonically welded on a commercial basis. In general, the blank spaces represent those combinations in which welding has not been attempted, and do not indicate that such combinations are impossible or impractical.

As may be noted in Table 7-1, many combinations of the metals mentioned below can be joined by USW. Where not precluded by geometric considerations, the thinnest member is located adjacent to the sonotrode top. With materials of equal thickness, power requirements are lower when welding is done through the softer material.

Aluminum and Its Alloys

Among the most readily weldable materials are aluminum and its alloys, including high-strength structural alloys such as 2014, 2020, 2024, 6061, and 7075. These may be joined in any available form: cast, extruded, rolled, forged, or heat-treated. Soft aluminum claddings on the surface of these alloys facilitate bonding. In Fig. 7-5[5] is an ultrasonic weld utilized to make hermetic closures in a Type 1100-H14 aluminum tube.

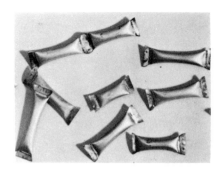

Fig. 7-5   Ultrasonic crimp weld in a type 1100-H14 aluminum tube.[5,9]

Copper and Copper Alloys

Copper and its alloys [such as brass, beryllium copper (Cu-2.25Be), cupronickel (90Cu-10Ni), and gilding metal] and other comparatively soft metals are also relatively easy to weld.

Iron and Steels

Satisfactory bonds can be produced in iron and steel of various types, including ingot iron, low-carbon steels, nonhardening steels such as the austenitic stainless steels, tool-and-die steels, precipitation-hardening steels, and others.

Precious Metals

No particular difficulties have been encountered with the precious metals such as gold, silver, and platinum, or alloys of these metals. As noted in Table 7-1, these and other metals such as aluminum have been satisfactorily bonded to semiconductors such as germanium and silicon.

Refractory Metals

The refractory metals, including molybdenum, columbium, tantalum, and tungsten and some of their alloys, have demonstrated good metallurgical susceptibility to USW, as have beryllium and rhenium. Thin sheets of these materials have been welded with the use of power-force programming. The quality of the welds appears to depend on the quality of the metal, i.e., its freedom from contamination and surface and internal defects.

Other Metals and Materials

Some other metals and materials which can be effectively joined via USW are nickel, titanium, zirconium, and some of their alloys; René 41, Hastelloy, and dispersion-strengthened materials such as sintered

TABLE 7-2
Electrical Conductors That Have Been Ultrasonically Welded to Thermal-Sprayed Surfaces

Substrate	Thermal-sprayed film	Material	Thickness range in	Thickness range mm
Glass	Aluminum	Aluminum wire	0.002–0.010	0.05–0.25
	Aluminum	Gold wire	0.003	0.08
	Nickel	Aluminum wire	0.002–0.020	0.05–0.50
	Nickel	Gold wire	0.002–0.003	0.05–0.08
	Copper	Aluminum wire	0.002–0.010	0.05–0.25
	Gold	Aluminum wire	0.002–0.010	0.05–0.25
	Gold	Gold wire	0.003	0.08
	Tantalum	Aluminum wire	0.002–0.020	0.05–0.50
	Chromel	Aluminum wire	0.002–0.010	0.05–0.25
	Chromel	Gold wire	0.003	0.08
	Nichrome	Aluminum wire	0.0025–0.020	0.06–0.50
	Gold	Aluminum wire	0.010	0.25
	Platinum	Aluminum wire	0.010	0.25
	Gold-Platinum	Aluminum wire	0.010	0.25
	Palladium	Aluminum wire	0.010	0.25
	Silver	Aluminum wire	0.010	0.25
	Copper electroplated on silver	Copper ribbon	0.028	0.07
Alumina	Molybdenum	Aluminum ribbon	0.003–0.005	0.08–0.13
	Gold-Platinum	Aluminum wire	0.010	0.25
	Molybdenum-Lithium, gold-plated	Nickel ribbon	0.002	0.05
	Copper-plated Molybdenum-	Nickel ribbon	0.002	0.05
	Manganese, Silver-plated	Nickel ribbon	0.002	0.05
Silicon	Aluminum	Aluminum wire	0.010–0.020	0.25–0.50
	Aluminum	Gold wire	0.002	0.05
Quartz	Silver	Aluminum wire	0.010	0.25
Ceramic	Silver	Aluminum wire	0.010	0.25
	Copper electroplated on molybdenum metallized with manganese	Copper foil		

aluminum powder and TD-Ni; and metal foils or wires and thermal-sprayed surfaces on glass, ceramic, or silicon. Such welds are particularly useful in the semiconductor industry, and have been applied as shown in Table 7-2.

BIMETAL JUNCTIONS

Bimetal junctions of many materials are feasible and practical, Fig. 7-6. A number of aluminum alloys and steel have been joined: (1) 0.005-in-thick (0.13 mm) Type 1100 aluminum to 0.016-in-thick (0.40 mm) stainless steel; (2) 0.04-in-thick (1 mm) Type 3003 aluminum to 0.028-in-thick (0.71 mm) AM-350 steel; and (3) 0.031-in-thick (0.8 mm) Type 6061 aluminum to 0.030-in-thick (0.76 mm) Type 301 stainless steel.

Joints were made between 0.024-in-thick (0.61 mm) Ti-5Al-2.5Sn alloy and 0.028-in-thick (0.71 mm) Type 430 stainless steel; the shear strength of these joints was about 940 lb (406 kg). Additionally, joints were produced between 0.018-in-thick (0.45 mm) A-70 titanium alloy and 0.020-in-thick (0.50 mm) Type 316 stainless steel; the joint strengths were about 200 lb (91 kg).

USW procedures have been used to join a beryllium disk to a Type 321 stainless steel ring for use with low-energy-radiation detectors.

Type 430 and low-carbon steels have been successfully joined. Examples include 0.005-in (0.13-mm) low-carbon steel to 0.008-in (0.20-mm) Type 430 stainless steel; 0.004-in (0.10-mm) zirconium to 0.005-in (0.13-mm) low-carbon steel; 0.004-in (0.10-mm) zirconium to 0.008-in (0.20-mm) Type 430 stainless steel.[10]

There is an upper limit to the thickness of any given material that can be effectively welded, because the power-handling capacity of available equipment is limited. For a readily weldable material such as unalloyed aluminum, the maximum thickness in which reproducible high-strength welds can be produced with presently available equipment is approximately 0.10 in (2.5 mm); for some of the harder metals, the present upper limit may be in the range of 0.015 to 0.072 in (0.38 to 1.8 mm). This limitation applies only to the thinnest member of the weldment when it is adjacent to the welding tip; the other member may be of greater thickness. There appears to be no lower limit to weldable thickness.

In instances when a junction is difficult to achieve at available power levels, good-quality joints have been made by inserting a foil interleaf of another material between the workpieces. For example, a 0.0005-in (0.01-mm) foil of nickel or platinum has been used between components of molybdenum. In another instance, 0.001-in (0.03-mm) beryllium foil has been welded to 0.015-in (0.38-mm) AISI Type 310 stainless steel using an interleaf of 0.001-in (0.03-mm) 1100-H14 aluminum foil. The weldable thickness range of 2014-T6 aluminum alloy has been extended by using a foil interleaf of 1100-0 aluminum.

Aluminum and some alloys to:	Copper, germanium, gold, kovar, molybdenum, nickel, platinum, silicon, steel, zirconium, magnesium, beryllium, iron, stainless steel, chromel wire, constantan wire
Copper to:	Gold, kovar, nickel, platinum, steel, zirconium
Gold to:	Germanium, kovar, nickel, platinum, silicon
Steel to:	Molybdenum, zirconium
Nickel to:	Kovar, molybdenum
Zirconium to:	Molybdenum

Fig. 7-6 Bimetallic junctions.

Design criteria, including allowable stresses, have not yet been developed to establish USW as a standard joining method for structural applications such as are found in aircraft, missile, and space vehicles. By analogy with the older types of welding, much concentrated effort will be required to accumulate and statistically analyze test data before reliable design criteria can be released. Meanwhile, designers must rely on existing experimental data, supplemented, when necessary, with their own evaluations. In such cases, actual or simulated service test of the assembly will denote final acceptance. Usually in the thinner gages of aluminum and its alloys, and often in the intermediate gages, failure under tensile load occurs by fracture of the base metal or by tear-out of the weld button rather than by shear failure of the weld itself.[9]

Line welds or seam welds show approximately the same strength as the base metal, at least with thin gages. For example, spot seam welds in structural aluminum alloys have shown strengths equivalent to 85 to 95% of the ultimate tensile strength of the material under both shear and hydrostatic tests. Five-inch line welds in 0.010-in (0.25-mm) 5052-H16 aluminum alloy average 85 to 92% of the base metal strength. Continuous-seam welds in thin-gage 1100 aluminum have shown 88 to 100% joint efficiency.

APPLICATIONS

The versatility of USW in joining many materials and material combinations in a variety of joint geometries and the unique characteristics of the welds thus obtained, have led to its acceptance as a production technique for numerous applications. In some instances it permits the welding of components that cannot be satisfactorily joined by other techniques. In other instances, joining is accomplished more effectively, more reliably, or more economically than by other methods.

Spot welding may be used to produce a conventional structural bond or for applications in which mere attachment of the component is the primary requirement. Spot seam or continuous seam welding is effective where a continuous bond is required, either for strength purposes or for hermetic sealing of components, as in packaging. Ring welding can also be used for hermetic sealing, as in capping small tubular members or for other applications in which an annular weld is desired. Area welding can be used where bonding over an extended area is required, as in the cladding of one material to another.

Here are some of the specific areas in which USW has been successfully applied:

1. Structural applications in automobiles, nuclear reactors, aircraft, missiles, and rockets.
2. Electrical applications, such as the attachment of leads to transformer coils; of contact buttons to sheet, plate, or ribbon; and of stranded aluminum wire to copper terminals.

3. Electronic applications, particularly for joining miniaturized components that are difficult to join by other methods. These applications include attachment of leads to semiconductor materials, assembly of bridge wire or electrically matched components, bonding of components for electronic tubes, welding of leads to high-temperature printed-circuit boards, and hermetic sealing of electronic components requiring special atmospheres or freedom from contamination.
4. Packaging applications, particularly the hermetic sealing of metal foil packages of various sizes and shapes, e.g., sealing of aluminum cans and squeeze tubes and the packaging of foods, drugs, and the like.

Electronics

One production process is the attachment of fine aluminum or gold lead wires to transistors, diodes, and other semiconductor devices. Wires ranging in size from 0.0005 to 0.020 in (0.01 to 0.50 mm) can be joined to plain or thermal-sprayed surfaces of silicon or germanium. Good-conductivity bonds with high reliability are thus obtained, with yields being in the range of 95 to 100% (see Fig. 7-7). USW permits the substitution of aluminum for gold wires for attachment as leads to aluminized surfaces on silicon, thus eliminating the brittle gold-aluminum intermetallics normally produced in such junctions.

Similarly, wires and ribbons can be welded to thin-film or micro-miniaturized circuits. Leads of aluminum, copper, gold, and nickel have been bonded to a variety of thermal-sprayed films on ceramic or glass substrates, as was shown in Table 7-2. Reliable joints with low ohmic resistance are thus produced without contamination of the thin film or the conductor element and without thermal distortion of the components.

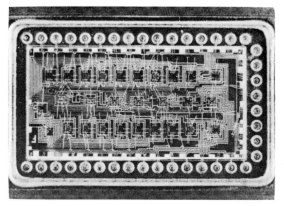

Fig. 7-7 Hybrid thin-film circuit containing 28 integrated circuits and 800 ultrasonic welds.

The encapsulation of microcircuits and other electronic components has been effectively accomplished by ultrasonic ring welding. Containers such as transistor or diode cans can be hermetically sealed without contamination of the high-purity internal components. The capability of producing a complete annular weld with a single weld pulse of 1 s or less offers a substantial time and cost saving. Ring welding is used to bond a vanadium disk in telephone headsets as well to seal aluminum and tantalum capacitors and bond and hermetically seal photoamplifier tubes.

USW can be used to produce joints in electron-tube assemblies. In addition, its capability for joining dissimilar metals permits the use of tube component materials such as titanium and rhenium which provide superior operating characteristics.

Electrical Connections

USW is effective for producing current-carrying junctions involving various combinations of aluminum, copper, silver, and other metals.

One such application involves the attachment of fine wire filaments to larger terminal posts in the fabrication of various igniter devices which rely on high-resistance bridge-wire elements to initiate explosive or other chemical reactions. Filament wires of 0.001 in diameter (0.03 mm) of such materials as nickel-chromium and tungsten-platinum have been joined to terminal posts of copper, iron, phosphor bronze, and other materials.

Thermocouple junctions involving a wide variety of dissimilar metal combinations have been produced by this means. Iron-constantan, chromel-constantan, chromel-alumel, and the more recently developed high-temperature tungsten-rhenium couples have been joined to aluminum, steel, copper, and other base metals.

Copper foil leads can be attached to aluminum transformer coil windings, even when the coil is coated with certain insulating plastic films, without damage to the foil and without introducing impurities to shorten the life of the joint.

Electrical wires of the same or dissimilar metals have been joined through certain insulation coatings, and stranded aluminum wire has been joined to copper terminals, Fig. 7-8.

Fig. 7-8 Aluminum wire welded to copper strip for auto air-conditioner clutch.[11]

Fig. 7-9 Ultrasonically welded armature coil.[11]

Both copper and aluminum wire armature windings are ultrasonically welded to copper commutators. In some instances, the windings are anodized aluminum wire; welds to the commutator are made directly through the coating without removal of the anodizing. Ultrasonic welds are also used to attach "formed" (anodized) aluminum ribbon leads to external connector terminals of tubular electrolytic capacitors.

Ground connections and jumpers for aircraft and missile application can be ultrasonically welded, so that the necessity for bolted connections through drilled holes is eliminated.

Pollution-control devices required on automobiles increase running temperatures of high-performance engines and strain starters; too much heat melts the solder and ruins the armature. An automotive company welds copper armature coils to copper-commutator starter assemblies, producing a strong joint and high temperatures; high-speed rotation and constant starting will not weaken it (Fig. 7-9). Shown in Fig. 7-10 is a half-hard copper clip yoke welded to a copper bus connector. The problem posed by conventional welding is that of annealing the clip. Annealing, in turn, leads to loss of the spring

Fig. 7-10 Fuse holder consisting of half-hard copper clip welded ultrasonically to a copper bus connector.[11]

characteristics needed to hold a fuse in place. With USW, no annealing is encountered, and the bond is stronger, since it is distributed over a larger area than possible with a spot welder.

Encapsulation and Packaging

The characteristics of the USW process have instigated a wide variety of packaging applications which range from soft foil packets to pressurized cans. These junctions are produced via ring, seam, or line welding. Applications to cans include side seams on aluminum can bodies whereby the USW unit joins lapped edges without plastic flow of the metal. Ring welding is used to seal the patch on the pot tabs on the majority of aluminum beverage containers. Weld time is less than one second, and production rates on the aluminum cans are 900 or more welds per hour.

The process is uniquely useful for encapsulating contents which are sensitive to the usual conditions, such as heat, of other joining methods, or which cannot be exposed to ambient air. These contents range from primary explosives through slow-burning propellants and pyrotechnics, high-energy fuels and high-energy oxidizers, living tissue cultures, and the like.

In USW of ordnance items, no ignition of sensitive materials is known to have ever occurred, even when such material dust was present in the weld locale.

Since USW can readily be accomplished in a protective atmosphere (or in vacuum), it permits sterile packaging of hospital supplies, precision instrument parts, ball bearings, or other materials which must be protected from dust or contamination. This capability also permits encapsulation of chemicals (such as phosphorus, lithium aluminum hydride, and ammonium perchlorate) which would react in air. After welding, the hermeticity of the seal provides permanent contents protection, and permanent containment of volatile materials such as inhibited red fuming nitric acid, alcohol, and bromine trifluoride.

Structures

A nuclear power generator for space vehicles incorporates expandable bellows assemblies between an outer shell of 6061-T6 aluminum alloy and an inner shell of AISI 321 stainless steel, Fig. 7-11.[10] Fabrication of the bellows requires strong, leaktight bonds between the aluminum and the stainless steel, each 0.031 in thick (0.8 mm), and this was achieved with ultrasonic overlapping spot welds, Fig. 7-12.[10]

Lightweight aluminum honeycomb core for structures and insulations is being commercially manufactured with USW.

USW is being evaluated as a method to join airframe structures. The first application will be doors on a helicopter. This application will

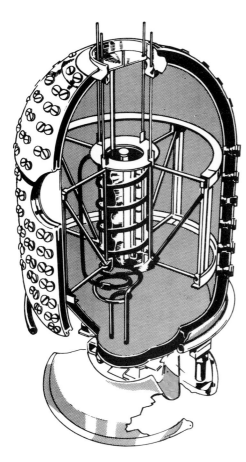

Fig. 7-11 Cutaway view of ultrasonic welded generator for direct conversion of nuclear energy to electrical energy for space applications.[12]

produce a reduction of 75% or more in the worker-hours previously required for adhesive bonding, and will eliminate fasteners and the labor to install them. The technique later will be extended to primary airframe structures.

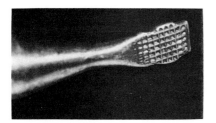

Fig. 7-12 Ultrasonic weld provides hermetic seal.

Miscellaneous

Applications in other areas have also been successful. For example, continuous-seam welding has been used to assemble components of corrugated heat exchangers. Strainer screens have been welded without clogging the holes. The ends of evacuation tubes have been simultaneously crimped and welded to provide a hermetic seal, Fig. 7-12. Multilayer welding is feasible; for example, as many as 20 layers of 0.001-in (0.03-mm) aluminum foil have been joined simultaneously with both single-pulse and continuous-seam welds. A multilayer welded field coil is shown in Fig. 7-13.

Fig. 7-13 Field coil assembled by USW which includes aluminum ribbon to itself, to copper ribbon, to consolidated stranded copper wire, and to copper terminals.[8]

Aluminum temperature-sensing devices have been welded in 0.15 s. Tooling of the machine is such that finished parts are automatically ejected into a chute and thus removed from the machine. Production is 6000 parts per day per machine, Fig. 7-14.

The aforementioned applications are representative of those in which USW has been effectively used. New applications are constantly being explored, and the areas of usefulness of the process extended. One extension is into the field of plastics.

USW of metals differs from the USW of thermoplastics in that the mechanical energy of vibration dissipated as frictional heat between the faces of the plastic parts is enough to raise the temperature of the plastic above its melting point at the interface. Coalescence of melted material is, therefore, an important part of ultrasonic plastic welding. Efficient USW of plastic depends on (1) material, (2) joint design, (3) the shape of the part, (4) the distance of the joint from the sonotrode tip, (5) sonotrode shape, (6) part support, and (7) energy delivered to the part.[7,13–15]

Other new areas of development and future exploitation include development of the thermoacoustic upset-butt welding process, which differs from USW in the following ways:

1. The type of joint welded—lap for USW vs. butt for thermo-acoustic.
2. The mode of vibration utilized—transverse vs. longitudinal.
3. The type of energy utilized—kinetic vs. potential.
4. The role played by heating in the welding mechanism—passive vs. active.[16,17]

Fig. 7-14   USW of aluminum sensing devices. Operator activates unit with two hand buttons and weld is made in 0.15 s.[11]

The homemaker of the future may do the family "sewing" ultrasonically with a titanium horn instead of needle and thread as cloth with increasing plastic-fiber content becomes more widely used.

An ultrasonic welder, the first hand-held portable unit for joining wire under field conditions, is shown in Fig. 7-15. It welds through polymer insulation, plastic coatings, and varnish, eliminating the need for wire stripping and crimped connections. The welder handles single strand wire and makes mono- and bimetallic welds in copper, aluminum and brass alloy. The welder is intended to provide easy field service and to make permanent repair welds on wire in radio and radar installation and on vehicles.

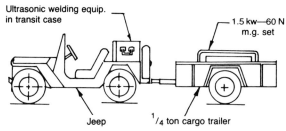

Fig. 7-15   Design for portable ultrasonic welder for field operation.

The future usefulness of the process lies in increasing the range of welding thicknesses and the variety of weldable metals, particularly in dissimilar combinations.

REFERENCES

1. Joshi, K. C., "The Formation of Ultrasonic Bonds Betweem Metals," *Weld. J.*, **50**(12), 840–848, December 1971.
2. Kreye, H., "Melting Phenomena in Solid State Welding Processes," *Weld. J.*, **56**(5), 154s–158s, May 1977.
3. Kuznetsev, V. A., and Dubasov, A. M., "An Approximate Method of Calculating the Thermal Processes which Take Place During the Ultrasonic Welding of Metals," *Weld. Prod. (USSR)*, May 1969, and *Weld. Res. Abroad*, **26**(7), 86–90, August–September 1970.
4. Hazlett, T. H., and Ambekar, S. M., "Additional Studies on Interface Temperatures and Bonding Mechanisms of Ultrasonic Welds," *Weld. J.*, **49**(5), 196s–200s, May 1970.
5. Estes, C. L., and Turner, P. W., "Ultrasonic Closure Welding of Small Aluminum Tubes," *Weld. J.*, **52**(8), 359s–369s, August 1973.
6. *Focus on Titanium*, newsletter, Timet Division, Titanium Metals Corporation of America, **2**(3), December 1975.
7. Dallas, D., "Tool and Manufacturing Engineers Handbook," 3d ed., McGraw-Hill, New York, pp. 28-120–28-132, 1976.
8. Wohlraven, T., Sonobond Corp., private communication, April 1978.
9. "Welding Handbook," 6th ed., American Welding Society, Miami, Chap. 59, 1971.
10. Gencsoy, H. T., Adams, J. A., and Shin, S., "On Some Fundamental Problems in Ultrasonic Welding of Dissimilar Metals," *Weld. J.*, **46**(4), 145s–153s, April 1967.
11. Denslow, C., Branson Ultrasonics Corp., private communication, April 1978.
12. Koziarski, J., "Ultrasonic Welding: Engineering, Manufacturing and Quality Control Problems," *Weld. J.*, **40**(4), 349–358, April 1961.
13. Menges, H., and Potente, H., "Studies on the Weldability of Thermoplastic Materials by Ultrasound," *Weld. Res. Abroad*, **27**(8), 47–55, October 1971, and *Weld. World*, **9**(1/2), 1971.
14. "Ultrasonic and Electromagnetic Bonding of Thermoplastics," *Manuf. Eng.*, pp. 46–47, April 1976.
15. Shin, S., and Gencsoy, H. T., "Ultrasonic Welding of Metals to Nonmetallic Materials," *Weld. J.*, **47**(9), 398s–403s, September 1968.
16. Yeh, C. J., Libby, C. C., and McCauley, R. B., "Ultrasonic Longitudinal Mode Welding of Aluminum Wire," *Weld. J.*, **53**(6), 252s–260s, June 1974.
17. Fischer, G. N., and McMaster, R. C., "Development of the Thermo-Acoustic Upset-Butt Welding Process," *Weld. J.*, **56**(2), 38s–50s, February 1977.
18. Kholopov, Y. K., "Determining The Principal Parameters of Ultrasonic Welding Conditions," *Aut. Weld.*, (4), 1974, and *Weld. Res. Abroad*, **21**(10), 33–34, December 1975.
19. Wunderlich, D., "Advanced Welding Techniques and the High Nickel Alloys," *Revue Soudoure*, (3), 1970, and *Weld. Res. Abroad*, **27**(4), 28–36, April 1971.
20. "Ultrasonics Gets Bigger Jobs in Machining and Welding," *Iron Age*, Sept. 13, 1976.
21. Dorn, L., "Welding and Soldering in Microelectronics," pp. 1–19, IIW Doc. IV-189-75.
22. "Rub Metals Together; Get Sound, Cool Weld," *Mod. Met.*, pp. 93–96, October 1977.

ULTRASONIC SOLDERING

Uses of ultrasonic energy are increasing. This form of energy— mechanical vibrations at 20 kHz and above—has long been used in nondestructive testing, in cleaning parts, in cutting brittle materials, and to assist a variety of metal-cutting and metal-forming operations. Plastics are being welded and staked ultrasonically, with considerable savings in assembly time and expense. Synthetic fabrics are being sewn ultrasonically in the garment industry. A new application for ultrasonic energy is an ultrasonically assisted soldering process that solders metals without flux.

Why the stimulus now for this process? A flux soldering procedure has been available for a number of years to meet the joining requirements of aluminum air conditioners, heat exchangers, and other applications. The use of flux requires flux-cleaning equipment, coil-drying and dehydration equipment, and wastewater treatment facilities. Potential problems from incomplete flux removal and new environmental legislation have necessitated the development of a fluxless joining system. This new process promises to have an impact on metal-joining operations and the utilization of materials.

PRINCIPLES

Soldering

Soldering is a group of joining processes wherein coalescence is produced by heating parts to a suitable temperature and by using a filler metal having a liquidus not exceeding 800°F (427°C) and below the solidus of the base metals. The solder is usually distributed between the properly fitted surfaces of the joint by capillary attraction.

The bond between solder and base metal is more than adhesion or physical attachment, although this does contribute to the strength. When a molten solder leaves a continuous, permanent film on the metal surface, it is said to wet the surface. Wetting is frequently incorrectly referred to as *tinning*, which actually means precoating with solder, whether or not it contains tin. Without wetting there can be no soldering action. In order for wetting to occur, there must be a stronger attraction between certain atoms of the solder and the metal than between the atoms of the solder itself. Intermetallic reactions usually take place at the interface between the metal and the solder. This wetting action is partly chemical in nature.

Ultrasonics

The term "ultrasonic" does not refer to a mode of heating for soldering, but rather it refers to an additional device used to facilitate soldering without any significant changes in the temperature of the assembly.

The principles of ultrasonics started with the early developments of ultrasonic welding prior to 1939.[23] Ultrasonic fluxless soldering appears to have been first conceived in Germany in 1936. The first such soldering iron was patented there in 1939. Since then numerous devices have been reinvented with the main purpose of eliminating flux in conventional soldering operations.

The initial successful application of ultrasonic soldering methods to an aluminum bell and tube joint in 1966 was realized when 95Zn-5Al solder was used to presolder parts, and the solder reflowed at assembly. Only marginal success was obtained in prior years using Cd/Zn alloys deemed best suited for aluminum at the time. By 1969 sufficient interest was generated to develop a soldering system in which a tube-and-fin aluminum air-conditioning coil assembly could be made using the presolder-reflow method. By 1971, the reflow process proved to be acceptable and the single-dip method of producing coil assemblies was promising and deemed feasible as a production process.

Removal of the Oxide Film Using Ultrasonic Energy

An oxide film can be removed from a metal (such as aluminum) surface using ultrasonic energy. An electronic power oscillator is used to generate electrical impulses (currents) of frequencies from 15 to 50 kHz. These electrical impulses are converted to mechanical motion by two basic types of transducers—the magnetostrictive (iron/nickel) and the piezoelectric (lead/zirconate/titanate). Desirable characteristics of transducers are reliability, frequency stability, power output stability, tolerance to environment and ease of maintenance. Both means of changing electrical to mechanical energy can be and are being used and will be discussed later in this chapter.

In the simplest terms, a solid-state electronic power supply generates high-frequency current, which is conducted to the transducer. The transducer changes electrical energy to mechanical energy, which is transmitted through a tuned solid-metal part called a "horn" and propagated into the molten solder. The resultant vibrations will produce numerous holes or voids within the liquid. This phenomenon is known as cavitation. If a piece of aluminum is immersed in the liquid solder, the collapse of the voids will create an abrasive effect known as cavitation erosion on the surface of the metal. This erosive action removes the oxide film from aluminum and permits the molten solder to wet the aluminum.

In practice, the ultrasonic vibrations are transmitted from the transducer to the work in the following manner. A "horn" (metal rod that connects the transducer to the soldering tip) of suitable length is attached to the transducer so that maximum disturbance will result at the free end. The free end of the horn forms the soldering tip and is immersed in a small pool of molten solder that contacts the surface to be soldered. As the horn is moved across the surface of the aluminum, the ultrasonic vibrations break up the oxide on the surface, exposing the underlying metal to the action of the molten solder. If the end of the horn is used as the bottom of a soldering pot, the ultrasonic vibrations will be transmitted through the bath of molten solder, and the surface of an object immersed in the bath will be subjected to cavitation erosion. A large amount of power is required to initiate cavitation action over large areas; for this reason, commercial ultrasonic soldering baths are quite small. One commercial soldering pot is $8 \times 36 \times 4$ in ($203 \times 900 \times 102$ mm).

The forces generated by ultrasonic soldering devices also tend to promote liquid metal penetration, and the cavitation action can erode the soldering tip or sidewalls of the container unless care is exercised. Equipment has been developed for measuring the ultrasonic effect in an ultrasonic solder bath with reproducible results.[24]

The measurements show that the ultrasonic effect depends very strongly on the length of the transmitting ultrasonic horn, the chemical composition of the solder, and the distance between the transmitting and receiving horns. Further, the effect is independent of the temperature of the solder bath. The maximum effect occurs at a horn length fixed at 5.5 in (139 mm). If the length of the horn is increased or decreased, the output effect decreases. The fraction of ultrasound transmitted to the solder bath depends upon the chemical composition of the solder. Thus, the measured ultrasound effect is dependent on the solder composition.

The ultrasonic effect measured in the solder decreases rapidly as distance between the transmitting and receiving horns increases.

During operation of the ultrasonic equipment, the ends of the horns erode and the output decreases. By measuring the effect in the solder bath it is now possible to reject the horns before they produce unacceptable joints, and therefore to have better process control.

Ultrasonic soldering has produced proven 100% uniformity of coating. If a copper strip is dipped in the solder for several seconds without application of ultrasonic power, there will be little or no visible solder coating on the piece. On the other hand, if a strip is dipped and ultrasonic power is applied, a few seconds of immersion produces a bright, uniform-thickness coating of solder on the copper.

Now if these two strips are examined under the microscope, this is what one sees:

- On the piece that did not receive any ultrasonic energy, there are some extremely small beads of solder, not visible to the naked eye. Most of the surface is still coated with the usual oxides and soil.
- On the piece that did receive ultrasonic energy, the solder coating is thick, flat, and mirror-finished, and coverage is 100%. There are no pinholes and no areas where oxides or smuts remain.

EARLY DEVELOPMENTS

The initial development work was performed with a flat-type soldering head and small, hand-operated units; see Fig. 7-16. The flat-type heads varied in size from 0.375×1.5 in (9.5×38.1 mm) to 0.5×6 in (12.7×152 mm). These were used for tinning large areas quickly or for tinning grooved parts, long, narrow parts, small parts, or small areas on large parts. See Figs. 7-17 and 7-18.

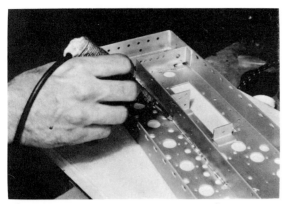

Fig. 7-16 Small hand operated solder gun.[8]

Fig. 7-17 Special tips are used on solder gun for tinning inside of opening in aluminum forging.[8]

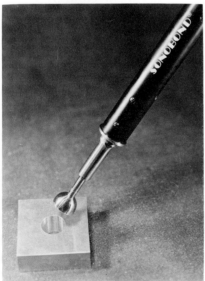

Fig. 7-18 Special soldering tip for tinning inside holes.[8]

Fig. 7-19   Ultrasonic soldering unit with integral tip heater and interchangeable tips.[8]

Ultrasonic soldering equipment was obtained in small hand-model sizes, the standard floor model, or the large flat-type units. The size and type of unit was carefully selected to suit the production job; see Fig. 7-19. Development work continued, and the resultant industrial production process currently in use is based on the application of ultrasonic vibration energy to a heated vessel containing a molten solder filler metal.

KEY VARIABLES OF PROCESS

There are several variables in ultrasonic soldering which must be considered. Whether the part being soldered is an electronic component, heat exchanger, air conditioner, or refrigeration unit, the evaluation of joint quality is critical.

The evaluation of soldering variables requires a quantitative measure of the solderability or soldered quality of a part. The functional and safety requirements of the part can be used to establish testing procedures. Pressure tightness may be the primary functional requirement of the joint, and leak-testing procedures are available as quantitative measures. However, almost all joints pass these tests and a large number of samples are required to obtain statistically significant results.

Soldering conditions for the ultrasonic soldering process have been developed and include some of the variables such as part temperature, solder composition, and solder temperature, which are similar to values established for the flux soldering process. However, the mechanism in flux soldering differs from the mechanism of oxide removal in ultrasonic soldering, which has been previously discussed. Other variables, such as joint clearance, and the introduction of a new variable, submersion depth, require examination.

Joint Clearance

An aluminum air-conditioner coil is used as an example. When the tubular members of this coil are immersed in the solder, the areas to be joined should not be too close to the surface of the molten solder, which is the area of lowest cavitation intensity. The joint must be immersed deep enough to reach an area where sufficient cavitation intensity exists to achieve adequate wetting of the joint.

Joint strength and solder filler-metal corrosion considerations require a lap joint, as shown in Fig. 7-20. Joint clearances are small, so capillary forces must be considered. During conventional flame soldering, wetting is accomplished by the use of a flux, and the molten filler metal is distributed between the surfaces of the joint by capillary attraction. In the ultrasonic soldering process, wetting does not occur during immersion when the molten solder comes in contact with the aluminum surfaces unless ultrasonic energy is present. Consequently,

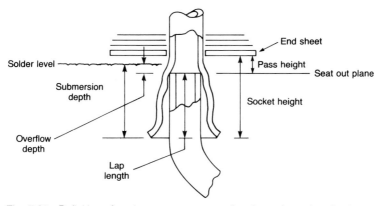

Fig. 7-20 Definition of socket parameters as related to submersion depth.

with no ultrasonic cavitation, a capillary depression exists in the joint. The magnitude of the depression depends on surface tension and joint clearance. Wetting in the joint occurs only when molten solder is present in the joint and in intimate physical contact with the aluminum surface, and sufficient cavitation exists in the joint area to remove the aluminum oxide.[25]

Submersion Depth

Joint requirements of the aforementioned coil result in a new soldering variable, submersion depth. It is the depth the open end of the socket is submersed beneath the surface of the molten solder during soldering, see Fig. 7-20. The joint length of a coil is a function of many soldering and equipment parameters. Submersion depth is the most important factor in the operation of a production soldering line. The general relationship between submersion depth and joint length is shown in Fig. 7-21. The submersion depth must be greater than D_1 to produce wetting on the inside of the socket.

Joint length increases with submersion depth. There is an upper limit to joint lengths, the lap length, that causes a departure from linearity. At depth D_o the resultant average joint length will be Q_o. The

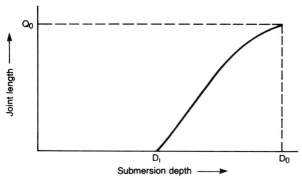

Fig. 7-21 The general relationship between submersion depth and joint length for ultrasonic soldering of coils.

maximum length attainable is the lap length. Since determination of joint length is based on the minimum wetted length on each socket of a coil, the average joint length Q_o is always less than the lap length. Submersion depth is a dimension. Therefore, dimensional control is one of the key elements in process control of production ultrasonic soldering. Any dimension that affects submersion depth affects joint quality.

Other Variables

There are four variables that have significant effects on the joint-quality-vs.-submersion-depth curve. They are the ultrasonic solder pot, socket design, preheat, and soldering time.

Each ultrasonic solder pot will have its own characteristic curve. The magnitude and distribution of the ultrasonic energy within the bath of molten solder has an effect on D_1 and the slope of the curve. However, different solder pot models may have different energy distributions because of differences in the size and shape of the pot, type of transducer, and transducer location.

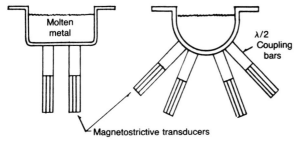

Fig. 7-22 Cross sectional view of rectangular and semicircular type solder pots showing the relative areas available for the half wave coupling bars which are welded to the pot and brazed to the transducers.

There are two types of ultrasonic soldering pot shown in Fig. 7-22. The semicircular type has the advantage of more "bottom" area, i.e., more space on which to put the transducers and heaters to maximize the ultrasonic energy driving the pot.[25] In both types of pot, ultrasonic energy must be injected without permitting the 800°F (427°C) molten metal temperature to affect the transducer performance. Because of the available surface area, the semicircular pot produces a higher power level. Sometimes, the higher power level may be essential, as, for example, in soldering of complex heat-exchanger coil structures where the acoustic nature of the product is not ideal.

The particulars of the joint design, such as lap length, have an effect on all of the submersion-depth curves. The molten bath of solder is a secondary preheat source. The significance of the primary flame preheat on the submersion-depth curve depends on the size of coil being soldered.

Soldering time affects the slope of the curve and the depth limit, D_o. Typical soldering times for a production soldering process range from 3 to 6 s. Shorter times flatten the curve, decrease the slope, and shift D_o to the right. Very short times do not provide adequate oxide removal and wetting. The limit, D_o, decreases as the soldering time increases.

PROCESS CONTROL

There are currently two basic processes that have been developed for aluminum heat-exchanger coils, see Figs. 7-23 and 7-24. Several steps in each process are similar, including cleaning, assembly, and soldering.[25,27]

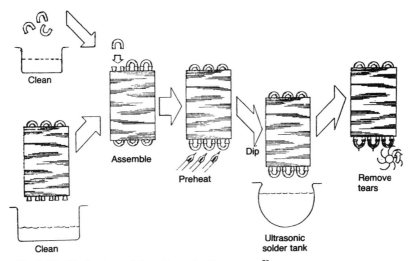

Fig. 7-23 Basic steps of the ultrasonic dip process.[26]

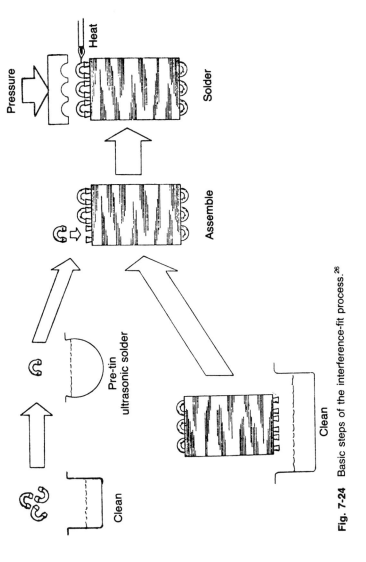

Fig. 7-24 Basic steps of the interference-fit process.[26]

Fitting the Joint

Clearances between the parts being joined should be such that the solder can be drawn into the space by capillarity, but not so large that the solder cannot fill the gap. A clearance of 0.005 in (0.13 mm) is suitable for most work except when solder precoated metals are used, in which case a clearance of 0.001 in (0.03 mm) or less is advisable.

Precleaning

Normally a clean, oxide-free surface is imperative to ensure uniform quality and a sound soldered joint. If all grease, oil, dirt, and oxides have been carefully removed from the base metal by cleaning before conventional soldering, there is a much better chance of obtaining a sound joint because only then can uniform capillary attraction be obtained. With ultrasonic soldering, only solvent vapor degreasing is used in precleaning to achieve the same results.

Ultrasonic energy is applied to the solder bath for the purpose of removing all oxides from the work surface and thus producing a chemically clean surface and allowing thorough wetting of that surface by the chosen solder. Ultrasonic horns pass through seals in the solder-bath walls and terminate close to the work surface—within about 0.062 in (1.6 mm).

Preheating

The preheat temperature is controlled by the length of time the coil or other part being soldered is in the preheat station. It is recommended that the preheat temperature be equal to or greater than the solder temperature. On a production basis, a preheat temperature below the solder temperature results in additional loading on the solder-pot heater system.

Soldering

When the system is activated, a cavitation process occurs, and minute bubbles or globules of solder implode against the work surface and scrub off the soil or oxides, leaving bare metal. In fact, if the work is allowed to remain too long in the active area, it will be eaten away and eventually disappear into solution.

While the work is immersed in the solder bath, it is impossible for new oxides to form on the clean surface. The work is completely sealed from air at this point, and the treated area is wetted with solder. When the part is withdrawn from the solder bath and examined with a microscope, it will be seen that the solder is nonporous, that 100% of the surface is covered, and that the smooth, shiny layer of solder is of uniform thickness. There are two very important secondary advantages of ultrasonic soldering. First, in most instances, the work need not be pickled or acid-treated to remove soil and oxides. This is an expensive step, and often the fumes are hazardous to workers and destructive to property and equipment. Second, both fluxing prior to tinning and postcleaning of parts are eliminated. The shelf or service life of components or products is not impaired by chemical attack from residual flux.

The process shown in Fig. 7-24 permits joining with only one component tinned. This development, along with the use of a tapered joint, has reduced processing time to less than 50% of that previously required for two-component tinned joints and has substantially improved joint reliability and fatigue life.

After degreasing of the tubing coil and return bends, the return bend ends are solder coated and placed in the bare aluminum hairpin bells. A pressing platen can be placed on the return bends prior to heating or can be attached to a press. When the platen is attached to a press, the assembled coil is fed down a conveyor and registers with the platen. The platen engages the return bends as they are being heated.

Heat is applied only to the joint area, and the return bends are pressed into the hairpin bells at soldering temperature 800°F (427°C). The elevated temperature causes some crazing of the oxide surface of the bare component and relative movement at the joint interface causes physical disruption of this oxide and allows joining to take place. To assure complete disruption of the surface, the taper joint provides compression as well as shear forces. This condition is also responsible for the increased joint reliability of the taper joint compared with a straight interference joint.

Since only the joint area is heated in most cases, for less than 1 min, there is little or no anneal of the fin component. Another benefit of the

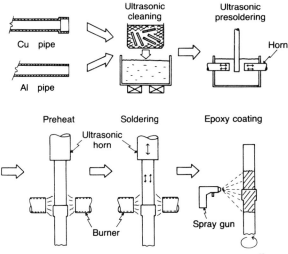

Fig. 7-25 Basic steps of ultrasonic soldering process.[28]

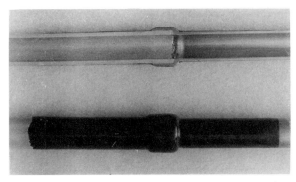

Fig. 7-26 Ultrasonically soldered aluminum-copper pipe joints.[28]

short heat cycle and cold coil is that, once heat is removed from the joint area, the coil will immediately drop the joint temperature, allowing immediate handling of the coil.

Since the processes described in Figs. 7-23 and 7-24 have gone into production, investigators have examined the application of ultrasonic soldering to copper-aluminum pipe joints, which are prefabricated parts that are widely used for connecting the aluminum evaporators to the remaining copper piping of refrigerators, dehumidifiers, and similar equipment. The process has been adapted to semiautomatic production for the joining of copper-aluminum pipe joints, Fig. 7-25.[28] In the last step of this production process, the pipe is coated with an epoxy resin for corrosion protection, Fig. 7-26.

EQUIPMENT

Two methods of ultrasonic soldering have previously been discussed. The first, Fig. 7-27, illustrates the use of an ultrasonic soldering iron.

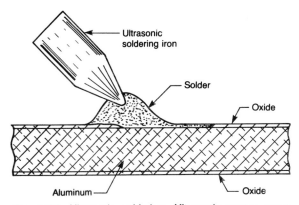

Fig. 7-27 Ultrasonic soldering. Ultrasonic waves cause cavitation, breaking up the oxide and floating it to the top of the solder puddle.

In soldering aluminum ultrasonically, the area to be "tinned" is heated to soldering temperature, a suitable quantity of solder is melted on the surface to form a molten puddle, and the end of the transducer is swept over this surface. Two such "tinned" areas are then placed together and heated until the solder coat melts and forms a bond. A frequency of 20 kHz is often used, since it is not noticed by most humans but causes active cavitation. The ultrasonic technique works satisfactorily on anodized, alodized, or irridized aluminum surfaces. The primary advantages of this process are:

- No flux is required.
- Joint quality is equal to that of joints prepared by any other process using the same solder and parent metal.

The primary disadvantages are:

- Volume of work must justify high initial investment in equipment.
- Small capacity of the units.
- Direct soldering of lap or crimp joints is not practical.

Solders usually recommended for joining aluminum by ultrasonic soldering iron techniques are the low-melting solders, and include those having the following composition:

96% Sn–4% Zn	85% Sn–15% Cd	35% Sn–65% Cd
97% Sn–3% Cu	85% Sn–15% Zn	80% Sn–20% Zn

The second method is ultrasonic dip soldering in a molten-solder pot. The equipment usually consists of a heating device, a transducer, a transmission rod, and a high-frequency generator. A range of ultrasonic solder-pot sizes[25,26] are available in both piezoelectric and magnetostrictive transducer designs. Further selection is available in either a standard pot of rectangular construction or a special pot of circular construction, Fig. 7-24. Electrical power supplied to the transducers ranges from less than 1 kW to several kilowatts. Additional electrical power on the order of 10 kW is required for the pot heating system. Electrical power to the transducers for circular pots is on the order of 10 kW, with an additional rating of 20 kW provided for the heating system. Ultrasonic pots are generally fabricated of 300 series stainless steel alloy.

Magnetostrictive transducers are basically a coil of wire wrapped around a plastic bobbin which is slipped over an iron-nickel laminated core, Fig. 7-28. When an alternating voltage is applied to the coil, the iron-nickel laminated core expands and contracts at the same rate as the alternating potential.[26]

The materials of the core change dimensions (the Joule effect) when introduced into a magnetic field. By oscillation of the magnetic field, a mechanical motion can be generated at ultrasonic frequencies. Magnetostrictive devices for soldering usually operate in the range between 18 and 26 kHz. The lower the frequency, the larger the effect of

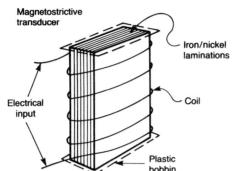

Magnetostrictive
transducer

Iron/nickel
laminations

Electrical
input

Coil

Plastic
bobbin

Fig. 7-28 Basic components of a magnetostrictive transducer.

cavitation on the surface to be soldered. Magnetostrictive devices are usually very temperature-sensitive. As the nickel alloys used reach 180 to 200°F (82 to 93°C), they lose their magnetostrictive efficiency.

Piezoelectric devices consist of 0.25-in-thick (6.4 mm) disks of a ceramic material, lead zirconate titanate. When an alternating voltage is applied across the disks, they expand and contract at the same frequency as the electrical circuit. Basic components of a typical piezoelectric transducer are shown in Fig. 7-29. Their maximum temperature capabilities are 500°F (260°C). Piezoelectric devices for soldering usually range between 20 and 60 kHz. They are more temperature-stable than magnetostrictive devices. The efficiency of piezoelectric transducers is much higher than that of magnetostrictive devices.

Efficiencies of well over 95% have been produced consistently with the piezoelectric devices, while 30 to 60% efficiencies have been generated by the magnetostrictive transducer. This has resulted in a lower price for magnetostrictive generators and the rest of the equipment for a given cavitation.

There are certain frequencies, dictated by the physical size and shape of the transducer, at which the unit has mechanical resonance. These frequencies result in a higher degree of efficiency, and are therefore utilized for soldering. Inasmuch as these frequencies are

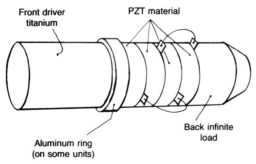

Front driver
titanium

PZT material

Aluminum ring
(on some units)

Back infinite
load

Fig. 7-29 Basic components of a piezoelectric transducer.

usually dependent on the load put on the transducer during the specific operation, the generator is provided with a "tuning" facility. Many devices are "tuned by ear." However, automatic frequency control, also incorporated in industrial units, is usually achieved by the use of an additional piezoelectric crystal which translates dimensional changes into currents with a high degree of accuracy. This feedback is used for automatic tuning.

Because of the thermal sensitivity of most transducer materials, which must remain below soldering temperatures, it is necessary to keep the transducer away from the immediate soldering area and to cool it by either air circulation or water jackets. This is achieved with the aid of a transmission coupling.

The transmission coupling is attached to that end of the transducer which is subjected to the largest vibratory energy. This is transferred through the coupling to the molten solder. The length of the coupling rod is a direct function of mechanical resonance. Stainless steel is an excellent material for transmission couplings because it has relatively poor heat-transfer properties and minimal damping characteristics.

The last important component of an ultrasonic soldering unit is the generator. These are the power units which drive the transducers and supply the heat for the soldering operation. The heat is usually supplied through resistance coils or other conventional methods. The heat is often generated in a component external to the soldering tool. This is one of the inherent problems in the ultrasonic soldering setup; the heat supplies are usually small in order to prevent overheating of the transducers. However, additional heating units can be used if more heat is needed.

Desirable characteristics of a power supply are reliability, frequency stability, and power-output stability. Three types of power supplies are the vacuum-tube, transistor, and silicon-controlled-rectifier (SCR) types.

The oldest type, which is still in use, is the vacuum-tube power supply. Two advantages of vacuum-tube power supplies are that they are relatively simple and usually have few components. However, frequency drift and power deterioration require constant monitoring.

The second type, the transistorized power supply, has been in general use throughout the ultrasonic industry for many years. It is relatively easily controlled by design, is not subject to gradual deterioration of output power, and is easily controlled by feedback circuits to automatically maintain a given output frequency. One disadvantage is the inherent low output power per transistor, necessitating many transistors to provide the high power output required for ultrasonic solder tanks.

The third type, the SCR supply, has been manufactured for some years and has proven to be extremely reliable under severe production environments. The SCR power supply provides the ability to automatically compensate for loading variables, and is extremely desirable for production applications.

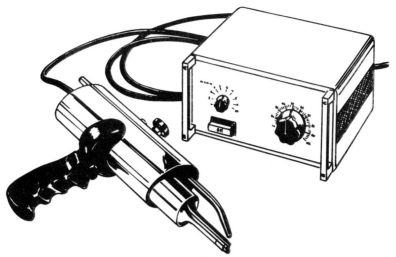

Fig. 7-30 Ultrasonic flame soldering tool.[29]

A new ultrasonic flame-soldering tool, Fig. 7-30, is now available commercially and is finding many uses in industry. This soldering tool combines an ultrasonic contact probe and an acetylene air torch into a compact, convenient soldering unit. It can be used for soldering new or previously soldered joints in aluminum or other nonferrous metals without the use of flux. The soldering tool provides two devices in one package to easily perform related operations necessary for ultrasonic soldering. The first is the heat source needed to heat the workpiece to the soldering temperature and the second is an ultrasonic horn, designed to fit the configuration of the part, which transfers ultrasonic energy into the joint, effecting a metallurgical bond without flux.

SOLDER COMPOSITIONS

While there are countless solder alloy compositions, the most widely used alloy system is the Pb-Sn combination. The addition of up to 6% antimony in place of some of the tin in Pb-Sn solders improves the mechanical properties of the solder, especially at elevated temperatures. These solders have about the same flow characteristics and wettability as straight Pb-Sn solders containing about 5% more tin.

Certain solders, Sn-Ag and Pb-Ag-Sn, have good tensile and shear strengths relative to the other solders, as well as high creep strength. The addition of 1 to 1.5% tin enhances corrosion resistance, wetting, and flow in the Pb-Ag solders.[30]

Some indium solders, notably the 54Sn-26Pb-20In filler metal, are useful in soldering aluminum. The Zn-Cd, Zn-Al, and Sn-Zn solders are used in ultrasonically soldering aluminum, Table 7-3.

Solders for aluminum can be broadly classified under three headings: zinc base, tin base, and those of a more complex and highly

TABLE 7-3
Solders for Aluminum[29]

Composition	Liquidus temperature		Corrosion resistance	Wetting ability with ultrasonics
	°F	°C		
100Zn	787	420	Very good	Excellent
10Cd-90Zn	750	399	Fair	Good
95Zn-5Al	720	382	Very good	Excellent
30Sn-70Zn	708	376	Good	Good
60Sn-40Zn	645	341	Good	Very good
40Cd-60Zn	635	335	Fair	Very good
70Sn-30Zn	592	311	Fair	Fair
34Sn-63Pb-3Zn	492	255	Poor	Poor
40Sn-60Pb	455	235	Poor	Poor
91Sn-9Zn	390	199	Fair	Fair

alloyed nature. In the binary alloys of tin and zinc, suggested compositions range from 90 to 30% tin and from 70 to 10% zinc. Another binary system, the zinc-cadmium series has been proposed; however, the ternary system Sn-Zn-Cd provides the basis for future solder filler metal developments for aluminum. This system forms a ternary eutectic melting at 320°F (160°C) with a composition of 73Sn-24Cd-3Zn.

Many alloy additions have been made to the various solders. No precise conclusions can be reached; however, the general effect of the addition of each material can be summarized as follows.

Aluminum	Increases strength of joint; however, seems to embrittle tin-lead solders.
Copper	Increases strength and hardness, lowers corrosion resistance.
Manganese, bismuth, and antimony	Increase hardness.
Phosphorus	Acts as a deoxidant for tin and improves fluidity, but may retain phosphorus or phosphates which would lower strength.
Iron	Reduces fluidity and corrosion resistance.
Silver	Increases corrosion resistance.
Cerium	With tin-rich tin-zinc solders, increases corrosion resistance and fluidity.
Cadmium	Gives high corrosion resistance to zinc-base solders.

WETTING

Recent development work has disclosed that other means of ultrasonic tinning are being investigated and evaluated.[31] One tinning method is performed with alumina dies immersed in molten solder. The aluminum tube is preheated and rubbed against the alumina die in the liquid solder, physically disrupting the oxide surface to allow tinning of the aluminum surface. Abrasion tinning may also be accomplished by preheating the aluminum above the solder melting temperature and abrading the surface with stick solder.

Another method being examined is electroplating. Aluminum and copper tubes electroplated with pure zinc have been joined in a manner similar to tubes ultrasonically pretinned with 95Zn-5Al solder. Metallographic evaluation of these joints show that metallurgical bonds resulted, similar to those from ultrasonically coated parts. Work is continuing in this area to develop the full potential of electroplating for solder-coating components for subsequent fluxless soldering.

CHARACTERISTICS OF JOINTS

The average strengths of soldered aluminum joints range from 2.5 to 5 psi (17 to 35 kPa), normally calculated for the overlap of lap joints. The strength of a joint is affected by the composition of the solder and parent metal, the thickness of the solder layer, the susceptibility of the joint to corrosion, and the design. Since the thinner the layer of solder, the stronger the joint will be, joints should be made with as little solder as possible, compatible with complete joint filling and adequate fillet size.

Some recent fatigue testing of ultrasonic one-side-tinned and two-side-tinned joints 0.375 in (9.5 mm) in diameter produced 1.6 million cycles and a failure for two-side-tinned joints. One-side-tinned joints went without a failure to 2 million cycles.

DESIGN CONSIDERATIONS

Solder strengths will seldom, if ever, approach the strength of the metal being joined. Therefore, joint designs require that advantage be taken of the structural properties of the base metal assembly. Good joint designs take advantage of interlocking seams, rivets, edge reinforcing straps, etc.

In general, soldered joints should be of the lap, scarf, or sleeve type; straight butt joints should be avoided. The lap and sleeve types provide increased strength because of the larger area of joint; however, it is customary to reinforce the joint with a small fillet of solder applied around it.

Joint clearances recommended are between 0.0025 and 0.0035 in (0.06 and 0.09 mm) to permit best capillary flow and highest joint strength.

METALS JOINED BY ULTRASONIC SOLDERING

Aluminum alloys 1100, 1235, 3003, 1200, 3102, and 7002-clad are commonly used tube alloys and are readily joined to themselves, Fig. 7-31, as well as to copper and steel by ultrasonic soldering in a bath of

Fig. 7-31 Return bends and sockets of an all-aluminum air conditioner coil before and after ultrasonic soldering. Insert shows cross section of soldered joint. Coil is inverted for soldering.[32]

molten Zn-5Al solder at 800°F (427°C). An interesting point is that recently the addition of small amounts of beryllium (less than 0.5%) to the molten bath has been found to prevent too rapid oxidation of the solder and to promote better flow by creating a capillary action which draws solder into the tubing areas to be joined.

Tin, brass, copper, beryllium-copper, nickel, nickel-iron, and columbium-zirconium materials, as well as molybdenum, titanium, carbon, Kovar, gold, silver, and even some ceramics (alumina), have been successfully ultrasonically soldered either in production, in prototype operations, or in development laboratories, Fig. 7-32. Recently additional applications such as wetting of silicon and germanium have been found. It is possible to solder nearly any metal without flux using ultrasonics. However, the economics of the problem have to be studied and evaluated before a commitment to ultrasonics is made.

Copper can be tinned by ultrasonics successfully with 85Sn-15Zn or 73Sn-23Zn-4Al solders. High-zinc solders such as 95Zn-5Al and 60Zn-40Cd are also very compatible with copper. Magnesium can also be ultrasonically tinned with a cadmium-tin-zinc solder which produces a strong joint.

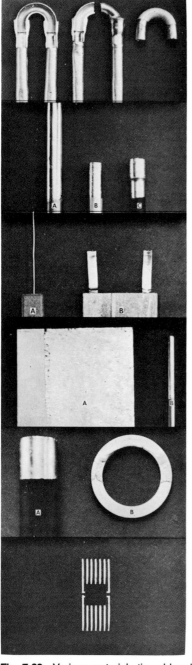

Hairpin-return bend joint (aluminum) soldered with 95-5 zinc-aluminum solder.

a. 0.375-in (9.5-mm) copper tubing tinned with 60-40 tin-lead solder.
b. Aluminum tubing tinned with 95-5 zinc-aluminum solder.
c. 0.312-in (7.9-mm) copper-coated steel tube tinned with 95-5 zinc-aluminum solder.

a. Copper resistor lead tinned with 60-40 tin-lead solder.
b. Nickel ribbon leads from capacitor tinned with 60-40 tin-lead solder.

a. 2-in (50.8-mm) aluminum strip tinned with 95-5 zinc-aluminum solder.
b. Ti-6Al-4V 0.125-in (3.2-mm) rod tinned with 60-40 tin-lead solder.

a. Carbon rod 0.75 in (19 mm) diameter tinned with 95-5 zinc-aluminum solder.
b. Aluminum ring tinned with 95-5 zinc-aluminum solder.

Gold-plated Kovar integrated circuit leads tinned with 60-40 lead-tin solder.

Fig. 7-32 Various materials tinned by ultrasonics.

Fig. 7-33 Dissimilar metals joined by ultrasonic soldering. Copper appliques soldered to aluminum bus bars.[8]

Ultrasonic soldering has been used for some dissimilar metal joints such as copper- and/or silver-to-aluminum electrical bus bars shown in Fig. 7-33. Another dissimilar joint consisting of a 75Cb-25Zr wire ultrasonically coated with indium and subsequently cold-welded to copper is shown in Fig. 7-34. This joint has been used in the manufacturing of devices for the field of superconductivity.

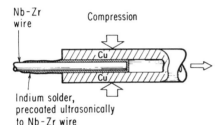

Fig. 7-34 Ultrasonic coating and cold welding.

A recent breakthrough in ultrasonic soldering of titanium and titanium alloys has been reported in the literature. With special solder alloys, titanium metals may now be joined to themselves or to other difficult-to-solder materials, with resultant tensile strengths of 25 ksi (172 MPa).

APPLICATIONS

Your next automobile may have an ultrasonically soldered gasoline tank. Soon you may have an aluminum radiator or an aluminum air conditioner, because a metallurgical bond of molten solder and aluminum can be achieved ultrasonically in a few seconds and without flux. Obviously, large savings will be made by substituting aluminum for copper, now that ultrasonic soldering is a practical joining process for industrial use. In fact, the applications of ultrasonics in soldering are growing, ranging from tinning tiny iron-nickel leads on small electronic components (Figs. 7-35 and 7-36), joining steel gas tanks, copper-aluminum connections in motor windings, aluminum radiators, air conditioners, and refrigerator liners and coils (Fig. 7-37).

Ultrasonic soldering has been applied in the tinning of aluminum sheet, extrusions, wire, cables, sand castings, and even die castings. Many leads on electronic parts are gold-plated to prevent tarnishing; however, when these leads are soldered, the resulting gold-lead-tin alloy may develop cracks that will impair electrical characteristics. The cavitation effect from ultrasonic soldering scrubs off the gold and puts it into solution in the solder, and the latter is free to wet the conductor material directly.

Below are some applications that either are in production or have been processed in feasibility studies prior to production implementation, all without flux.

- Appliances
    - Aluminum wire—pretin wire ends.
    - Motors—pretin aluminum wire ends.
    - Controls—tin-beryllium-copper capillaries.
    - Refrigeration—pretin aluminum tubing.
- Automotive
    - Aluminum wire—pretin wire ends.
    - Alternators and starter motors—aluminum wire in place of copper for end connections.
    - Steel containers—seal components without flux, Fig. 7-38.
- Aircraft
    - Aluminum wire—pretin wire ends.
    - Motors—aluminum wire in place of copper.
    - Pressure vessels—seal without flux.
- Electronics
    - Integrated circuits—remove gold plate.
    - Component leads—no flux.
    - Capacitors—tin aluminum foil.
    - Connectors—tin exotic materials.
    - Aluminum wire—pretin wire ends.
    - Coils and transformers—aluminum in place of copper.

Manufacturers are using ultrasonic soldering in joining aluminum and galvanized steel with 95Zn-5Al solder. Double-glazed windows have a space of dead air between two sheets of glass to insulate against the cold. Any seepage of air into the dead space carries moisture which condenses on the glass, ruins the clarity, and emphasizes the need for a perfectly airtight seal. To ensure hermetic seals, one company employs an automatic system for ultrasonic soldering of window-spacer corner joints.

A low-melting-temperature indium-tin filler metal enables an electrical manufacturer to solder leads to ferrite memory cores without risk of heat cracking. The solder softens at 240°F (116°C) and flows at 260°F (127°C). The firm says it will adhere to metal, glass, mica, quartz, thermosetting plastics, and some glazed ceramics; because of its low vapor pressure, it can be used in vacuum apparatus. Reports indicate that the joint can withstand 0.4-lb (200-g) pull tests.

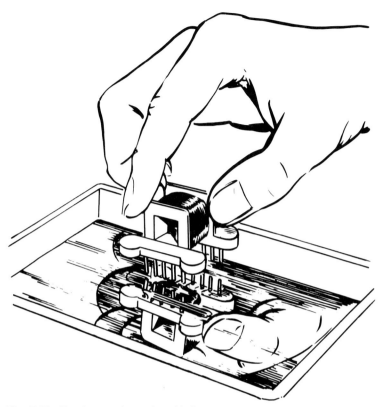

Fig. 7-35 Bench-type ultrasonic soldering system.

Integrated circuits have been joined to thick film substrates by ultrasonic soldering. High-strength, low-resistance joints are obtainable under a wide variety of processing conditions, but because of large deviations in shear strength, the process is not yet practical for production. The variations appear to be caused by variations in pedestal properties. A possible solution is to make pedestals ductile so that deformation of high pedestals will allow contact to lower pedestals. Also, successful commercial use of ultrasonics will hinge on improving substrate uniformity and testing of chip bonds for resistance to thermal shock, formation of intermetallics, and aging effects. Related work on hybrid circuits shows that very high stresses caused by thermal mismatches can occur in bonding of titanate ceramics to aluminum oxide substrates. Fractures and possible circuit failures can be compensated for by using a soft solder capable of providing a good compromise of metallurgical and thermal characteristics.

Ultrasonic energy in conjunction with brazing has been used. A large number of stainless steel instrumentation tubes, 0.004 in (0.09 mm) in diameter, were brazed into a stainless steel seal plug in the wall of a pressure vessel. The brazed assembly had to withstand a

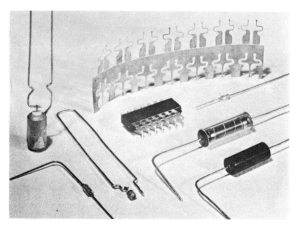

Fig. 7-36 Ultrasonically soldered electronic components.

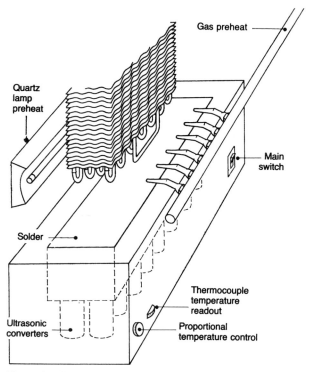

Fig. 7-37 Elements of ultrasonic soldering system. Heat exchanger coil is preheated by gas or electric heater, then immersed in ultrasonically agitated solder bath.

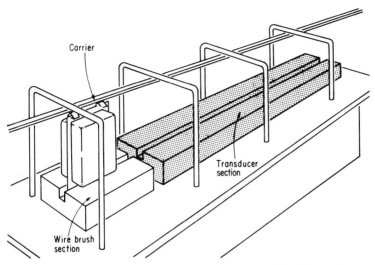

Fig. 7.38 Gas tanks for automobiles may soon be soldered in equipment designed along these lines.

pressure of 0.6 ksi (4 MPa) of hydrogen, and the brazing could not be done with flux since residual flux could not be removed from this assembly after brazing.

The solution was ultrasonic vibration of the assembly with an ultrasonic transducer during the brazing operation. This ensured that the brazing material would flow down the length of each stainless tube in contact with the seal plug.

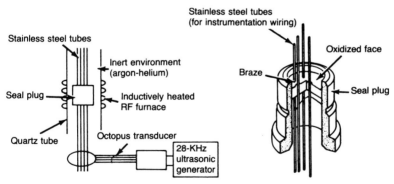

Fig. 7-39 Seal plug assembly.

The brazing filler metal for this application was Ag-1 with 0.5% lithium. The transducer was attached to the stainless steel tube assembly shown in Fig. 7-39. The brazing temperature was 1375°F (746°C). This technique can be used in applications requiring brazing of complex miniature assemblies.

FUTURE POTENTIAL

Ultrasonic tinning and soldering is not a new process, but the recent efforts of several raw material suppliers, ultrasonic equipment manufacturers, and users are making it important in the electronics, electrical equipment, automotive, and refrigeration industries. Perhaps some impetus in this direction was furnished by development of an experimental ultrasonic mass-soldering machine to solder printed-circuit boards. This machine can achieve solderability of 95% as compared with an initial solderability of 15%.

A concept for automation for soldering return bends in tubing for the air-conditioning industry is shown in Fig. 7-40.

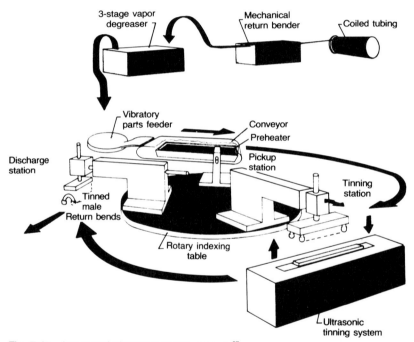

Fig. 7-40 Automated ultrasonic tinning system.[27]

Automation of the various steps of the ultrasonic soldering system, as well as improvements and developments of new equipment, are being actively pursued.

The ultrasonic flame-soldering tool, Figure 7-30, was conceived and designed primarily as a companion to the ultrasonic dip-soldering pots as a means of repairing and/or connecting dip-soldered aluminum refrigeration coils. However, the tool is not limited to these functions. In its standard configuration, or with slight modifications to the ultrasonic tip, the tool is well suited for a number of other proven and potential applications. Among them are the following:

- Repair of aluminum heat exchangers with other than fin tube configurations.
- Ultrasonic soldering of transition joints.
- Soldering of small areas on aluminum plates or castings.
- Aluminum lap-joint soldering.
- Patching of aluminum plate.
- Ultrasonic staking.

The largest areas of future activity will be the auto and home air-conditioning and refrigeration industries. It has been estimated that in 1977, 85% of all automobiles will be equipped with air conditioning.[27] As a result of the introduction of more ultrasonic soldering units into production plants, savings will become sizable. As an example, a company which recently introduced an automated high-speed ultrasonic soldering line has indicated that its savings will be anywhere from $300,000 to $1.5 million annually, depending on the volume.

One coil manufacturer currently flux-soldering aluminum estimates that it will save $2 million annually by switching to ultrasonic soldering. An added savings found by this manufacturer is that it will not be necessary to install scrubbers to handle flux fumes and waste-treatment systems to purify waste discharges.

Since ultrasonic soldering offers reductions in material costs, facility investments, and labor, the process will be adopted by many industries and has a growing future potential.

REFERENCES

23. Crawford, A. E., "Ultrasonic Engineering," Academic Press, New York, 1955.
24. Lystrup, A., "Measurement of the Ultrasonic Effect in an Ultrasonic Solder Bath," *Weld. Res. Suppl.*, **55**(10), 309s–313s, October 1976.
25. Hunicke, R. L., "Ultrasonic Soldering Pots for Fluxless Production Soldering," *Weld. J.*, **55**(3), 191–194, March 1976.
26. Denslow, C. A., "Ultrasonic Soldering Equipment for Aluminum Heat Exchangers," *Weld. J.*, **55**(2), 101–107, February 1976.
27. Jenkins, W. B., "Fluxless Soldering of Aluminum Heat Exchangers," *Weld. J.*, **55**(1), 28–35, January 1976.
28. Oelschlagel, D., Abe, H., Yamaji, K., and Yonezawa, Y. "Ultrasonic Soldering Method for Copper-Aluminum Pipe Joints," *Weld. J.*, **56**(4), 20–27, April 1977.
29. Fuchs, F. J., "Solve Soldering Problems with Ultrasonics," *Assem. Eng.*, July 1972.
30. "Soldering Aluminum," *Weld. J.*, **51**(12), 851–856, December 1972; **52**(1), 35–37, January 1973.
31. Antonevich, J. N., "Fundamentals of Ultrasonic Soldering," *Weld. Res. Suppl.*, **55**(7), 200s–207s, July 1976.
32. Alcoa Research Labs, private communication, May 1978.
33. Lystrup, A., "Ultrasonic Soldering Horn Lifetime," *Weld. J.*, **55**(2), 109, February 1976.

8

WELDBOND

The weldbonding process is essentially spot-resistance welding of parts that subsequently have their overlapping areas adhesive-bonded. The Soviet Union initially perfected this technology, which is known there as "glue welding." The approach was a "flow-in" method, whereby parts were welded together first, then the adhesive was flowed into the joint. A low-viscosity adhesive was used which penetrated the overlap joint by capillary action and was subsequently cured. The acceptance of weldbond structures has been general throughout Europe and the

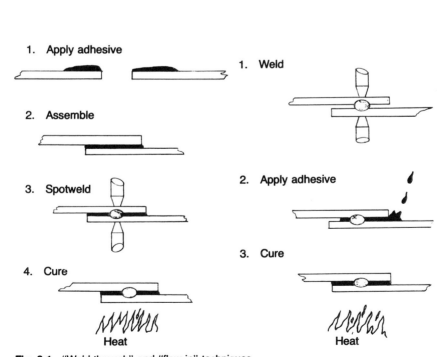

Fig. 8-1 "Weld-through" and "flow-in" techniques.

Soviet Union. The process combines two seemingly diverse disciplines, resistance spotwelding and adhesive bonding, into one process.

The technique used in the United States is the "weld-through" method, Fig. 8-1, whereby the adhesive is applied to the parts to be joined, spot-welded, and subsequently cured.

Compared with ordinary spot welding, strength of a weldbonded joint is increased fourfold in lap shear and tenfold in fatigue life. Compared with fusion welding, it offers lower cost. And compared with riveting, greater strength and fatigue resistance—and at times, lower costs (in the case of thin skins)—are the major benefits.

While the weldbonding process has been evaluated for various military aircraft and space vehicle components, it has not been used in production. However, the trucking industry has implemented weldbonding on a production basis.

THEORY AND KEY PARAMETERS

Actual joining of parts using a combination of resistance spot welds and adhesive is relatively straightforward. The adhesive is applied to most parts by laying a small bead of adhesive on the part surface and spreading it with a nylon spatula. The parts are then brought together and temporarily clamped. The parts are placed between the electrodes of a conventional-type spot welder and welded together. The weld setup used to join the parts is only slightly modified from a conventional setup. After welding, the structure is heated, usually in an oven, until the adhesive is cured. Time and temperature are dependent on the type of adhesive used and the type of metal bonded.

In establishing a reliable manufacturing weldbond process, the adhesive properties are significant. These fall into the following categories: physical and handling properties of the material, actual bonding characteristics, and the weldbond characteristics of the adhesive.

PHYSICAL CHARACTERISTICS

The desirable physical characteristics of a weldbond adhesive system consist of (1) good flow during processing, (2) 100% solids with practically no release of volatiles during cure, and (3) sufficient working life for adhesive application and welding time. For cost reasons, low-pressure-curing adhesives generally are used, even though higher cure pressures will enhance the properties of some adhesives.

Capillary Adhesives

For capillary weldbonding, there is no pressure acting on the bondline to assist adhesive flow. The ability of the adhesive to flow in and fill the faying surface is entirely dependent on gravity flow and capillary action of the adhesive. These adhesives must be extremely fluid (low viscosity) either at the time of application or during the heat cure and must not contain any filler which settles out. These highly fluid adhesives may tend to flow out of joints which are contoured or positioned away from a horizontal plane. Also, if the spacing between joints is greater than about 0.015 in (0.38 mm), complete filling may not occur because the adhesive has a tendency to flow out of the joint and leave a void area.

Adhesives are available in fluid form which when applied at the edge of a welded joint will penetrate into the joint by capillary action. Highly viscous adhesives, whose flow would be inhibited at ambient temperatures, may be heated after application to permit flow.

Spreading a liquid over a solid will occur if the maximum reversible work of adhesion, W_{adh}, of the liquid (subscript L) to the solid (subscript S) is greater than the work of cohesion, W_{coh}, of the liquid, or

$$W_{adh} - W_{coh} > 0 \tag{1}$$

The maximum reversible work of adhesion is

$$W_{adh} = F_{S^o} + F_{LV^o} - F_{SL} \tag{2}$$

where F_{S^o} is the surface free energy of the solid in vacuum, F_{LV^o} is the surface free energy of the liquid in contact with saturated vapor of the liquid, and F_{SL} is the equilibrium surface free energy of the solid-liquid interface. The work of cohesion of the liquid is

$$W_{coh} + 2F_{LV^o} \tag{3}$$

From Eqs. (2) and (3), Eq. (1) may be represented as

$$F_{S^o} - F_{LV^o} - F_{SL} > 0 \tag{4}$$

or

$$F_{S^o} > F_{LV^o} + F_{SL} \tag{5}$$

That is, for spreading of a liquid on a solid to occur, the surface free energy of the solid must exceed the sum of the surface free energies of the liquid (in contact with its saturated vapor) and the solid-liquid interface. Hence, for a given solid, the lower the surface free energies of the liquid and solid-liquid interface, the more readily will spreading of the liquid occur. Spreading of a given liquid over a given solid surface will continue until an equilibrium condition is reached. Viscous effects can retard the rate of attainment of equilibrium.

If a continuous liquid film is to be maintained in a joint between two plane surfaces, not only must the liquid (adhesive) spread over each surface, but the surface free energy of the liquid must be sufficiently great to maintain a meniscus and continuous volume of liquid between the surfaces. For a vertical joint, the liquid will rise between the plane solid surfaces until the surface energy is balanced by the gravitational forces. This capillary rise, or the height of the center of a curved interface above the reference plane of an infinite plane interface, is expressed by

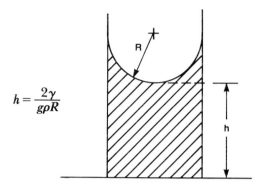

$$h = \frac{2\gamma}{g\rho R}$$

for an axially symmetrical curved meniscus, where γ is the surface tension, or surface energy, g is the gravitational constant, R is the radius of curvature at the center of the meniscus, and ρ is the density of the liquid. Thus, it may be seen that the higher the surface tension or the smaller the radius of curvature of the meniscus (resulting from narrower gaps and greater wettability of the surface), the greater will be the penetration of the liquid into the joint. For too large a space between adherends (large radius of curvature), the capillary rise will be insignificant, and only individual surface spreading may occur, leaving a gap in the adhesive bond.

The liquid adhesives may be applied along the edges of a joint after welding by ejection from a sealant gun or an orifice from a metering and mixing machine. Although injection into the joint under pressure would enable the use of a thixotropic adhesive which would have less tendency to flow out of the joint, the thinness of the gap between the welded adherends would preclude insertion of a pressure nozzle into the glue line. Spreading of the liquid adhesive on the adherend surface outside the joint may be prevented by coating the surface of the metal with a substance of low surface energy.

Weld-Through Adhesive

For weld-through weldbonding, the only pressure available to assist the adhesive in flowing is that provided when the sheet is pinched together at the spot-weld area. The pitch of the spot welds and thickness of the adherend have an influence on the intensity of the pressure exerted on the trapped adhesive. With a low-viscosity liquid adhesive, this relatively low cure pressure ordinarily is not a problem. Also, for high-flow solid or film adhesives which liquefy readily on the application of heat, no serious effect on bond strength and adhesive characteristics is anticipated. However, many of the higher-temperature-resistant adhesives require high curing pressures, either because of their low flow characteristics or the type of volatile outgassing reactions which occur during the adhesive cure. Inadequate cure pressure can result in a porous glue line, poor adhesion, and consequently greater susceptibility to environmental degradation. Adhesives which exhibit a detrimental effect from the lower cure pressures involved in weldbonding display initially inferior properties. Adhesive bond strength after environmental aging is also affected if the adhesive is not satisfactorily cured.

ADHESIVE APPLICATION

The physical form of the material is significant in determining the method of adhesive application and adaptability to mechanized or automated adhesive-processing technology. Adhesives considered for weldbonding are in liquid, paste, film, or solid form. The use of a primer improves bonding of certain adhesives and maintains a bondable surface for a prolonged period of time, if required.

The application of a paste adhesive to the joint area before welding will normally be a manual operation. The use of a skrim carrier can provide fairly even adhesive thicknesses. While adhesive could be applied by doctor blade to flat parts, this would not be practicable for highly contoured details. A hot-melt roller coat could be used for applying solid adhesives in an even coating thickness on moderately contoured parts.

The use of a standard air-spray technique to apply adhesive primer is practical and fairly efficient for either flat or contoured detail parts. Hot airless spray can be utilized to reduce the amount of solvent included in the adhesive system and permit thicker coating per pass of the gun. Solvent can be eliminated entirely by the use of 100% solid powder coatings. Electrostatic powder spray guns or fluidized beds charge the particles, which are then attracted and adhere to any slightly conductive surface. The powder is subsequently fused by heating.

BONDING CHARACTERISTICS

Aside from the inherent temperature-resistance and load-carrying (cohesive strength) characteristics of the adhesive itself, the primary factor which influences the strength and environmental durability of the adhesive bond is surface preparation. The surface preparation selected must be compatible with both welding and adhesive bonding. In the past, metal expulsion problems arose when the selected surface preparation was modified for adhesive bonding. To eliminate this condition, a compromise combination of various etchants was developed.[1] The results of this compromise of surface treatments between surface durability and weldability has shown that Class A welds, either on single-phase ac or three-phase frequency-converter-type spot-welding machines, can be produced with a phosphoric acid/sodium dichromate anodization on both bare 2024-T3 and bare 7075-T6 aluminum alloys. The anodizing solution has a bath life suitable for production use, and the treated surface maintains its weldability and durability for a minimum of 3 weeks. This period of time is sufficient for most production operations. There are no special handling or protection requirements related to this surface treatment other than those normally used in adhesive bonding.[2] Unfortunately, only a paste adhesive exhibited these excellent results. The weldability through film adhesives was rather poor, resulting in both expulsion and inconsistent welds.

The surface treatment for weldbonding must permit optimum development of adhesive strength and durability. Investigative studies have shown that while normal humidity, salt-spray, water-boil, and elevated-temperature strength testing may not reveal great differences between some surface preparations, aging under high humidity and moderately elevated temperatures while the specimen is subjected to mechanical stress can often distinguish differences fairly rapidly.[3]

METAL ADHERENDS

The first materials evaluated for lightweight, inexpensive aerospace structures were aluminum alloys. Subsequently, titanium alloys, boron-aluminum composites, and recently, stainless steel for transit vehicles have been considered.

Three factors most significantly affect the quality of the weld nugget. They are (1) the metal alloy, (2) electrical surface conductivity, and (3) uniformity of surface conductivity.

Processing factors also must be observed, since the surface characteristics of a chemically prepared metal surface are greatly influenced by:

- *Surface treatment uniformity.* Manually performed cleaning has a greater fluctuation in surface variability than automated cleaning techniques.
- *Humidity control.* High humidities affect metal surfaces, adhesives, primers, and even the surface-wetting characteristics of the adhesive upon application.
- *Temperature control.* Adhesive advancement, viscosity, and wetting characteristics are influenced by temperature. Unless temperature is controlled, a large scatter in load-carrying strength will result.
- *Particle count control.* Airborne contaminates such as smog, oil, dust, acid fumes, salts, abrasive fines, release agents, and solvents all influence the surface resistivity of the metal.

- *Solvent wipe.* "Recleaning" the surface just prior to welding with a solvent wipe can cause more harm than help. The surface can be further contaminated rather than cleaned by unclean solvent, contaminates on cloth, cloth ingredients dissolving in solvent, or a general smearing of surface contaminates.
- *Adhesive control.* Mixing of filled adhesives, storage control, and in-process controls used for the adhesive influence the ability of the adhesive to move from under the electrode pressurized area. Any appreciable adhesive residue will result in a high dielectric resistance to current flow and metal expulsion.
- *Aluminum alloys.* The chemical composition of the aluminum alloy affects the welding and bonding characteristics. High copper content tends to produce a "smut" condition on the surface of the cleaned surface and results in a high surface resistivity which promotes metal expulsion. High zinc content has a tendency to degrade the bonding strength of the adhesive systems. Comparatively, 2024 alloy would be more prone to metal expulsion than 7075, but its adhesive bonding characteristics should be better. Clad aluminum is more susceptible to bond-line corrosion than bare.

EQUIPMENT

The equipment and facilities required for weldbonding are relatively inexpensive. They include spot welders (Fig. 8-2) and, in some cases, seam welders for the welding portion of joining (Fig. 8-3), ovens for curing the adhesive, cleaning facilities for metals, and a clean area for assembly.

Fig. 8-2 Spot welding corrugated panel.[4,5]

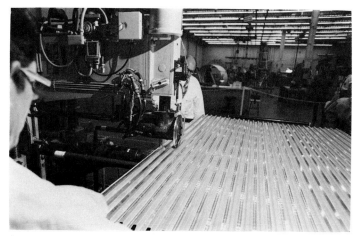

Fig. 8-3 Seam welder used in weldbond process.[4,5]

DESIGN

In designing for the weldbonding process, engineers must be aware that weldbonding will influence the load path within the joint, hence the strain patterns in a weldbonded joint are different than the strain patterns of a joint consisting of either adhesive bonding or spot welding. It is known from the many analyses performed on bonded overlap joints that stress concentrations occur at the ends of the joints. The amount of stress peaking is a function of the adherend thickness and material, and also the adhesive thickness and shear modulus. The overlap length also influences the peak end stresses, but its effects are minor except for very short overlaps.

The strain patterns for a spot-welded overlap joint would be similar to those of a mechanically fastened joint, since the load is transferred at discrete points. Generally, a row of spot welds or fasteners in line with the load do not transfer a load uniformly. Strain in the adherends causes the end spot weld to transfer a greater proportion of the load than the central spot welds. A row of spot welds perpendicular to the load line, on the other hand, will be loaded equally.

Consideration of the stress concentrations occurring at the spot weld must be included in the joint analysis. The local peaking is caused by the load redistribution caused by local bearing. Adjacent spot welds also interact to produce load peaks which in turn affect joint load-carrying capability.

The combination of the two different types of load-transferring mechanisms, an area for bonding and discrete points for the spot welding, set up complex stress patterns. A supposition at this point is that in a weldbonded joint the majority of the load is transferred by the spot weld. The adhesive acts as a cushion which reduces the peak stresses at the weld nugget. This supposition is not too unreasonable, since previous studies of weldbond joints indicate an improved fatigue strength due to the adhesive influence. The adhesive, by reducing stress concentration, allows the joint to perform better in a cyclic load environment. Since the adhesive reduces the stress concentration, there is an increased load-carrying capability.

Some test data depicting overlap vs. static tensile strength is shown in Fig. 8-4. In this figure, a 1.5-in (38.4-mm) overlap was required before the joint strength exceeded the metal strength. The adhesive bond strength for a 1.0-in (25.4-mm) overlap exceeded the weldbond strength. No significant difference was found between weld-through and flow-in techniques of adhesive application. No significant difference was found in the static load-carrying strength of a 1.0-in (25.4-mm) overlap center spot weld vs. a double-edge spot-weldbonded specimen. Finally, the static load strength of a 1.5-in (38.4-mm) weldbond specimen was 390% stronger than the spot weld.

Another series of tests, Fig. 8-5, was performed to evaluate the center spot weld using the same adhesive and adherend as in Fig. 8-4. The results showed that the edge tack-spot-weld specimens were

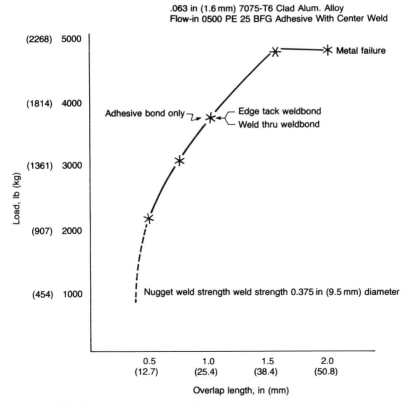

Fig. 8-4 Weldbond overlap vs. strength.

stronger (29% of ultimate) and more rigid than the center spot weld (18% ultimate) specimens. It must also be noted that both specimens failed at 0.0004-in (0.01-mm) elongation. The static tensile strength of edge tack-weldbond specimens (78% ultimate) exceeded the center weldbond (71% ultimate) specimens.

Finally, a series of tests on weld nugget size showed that edge spot-weld specimens were stronger than center spot-welded specimens whether they were adhesive bonded or not; for center spot-welded specimens (with or without adhesive), the larger the nugget weld, the greater its static tensile load strength; however, for edge spot-welded specimens (with or without adhesive), the increasing size of the weld nugget did not seem to influence its static tensile load strength.

Figure 8-6 shows a weldbond design recently incorporated into a

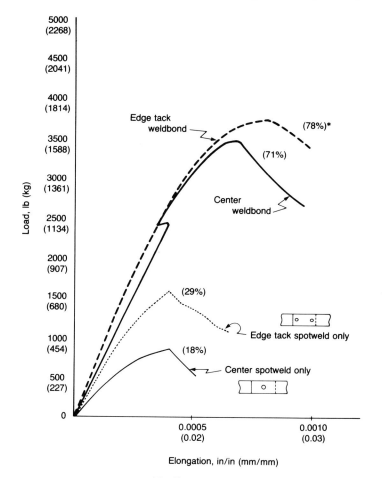

*% ultimate metal adhered strength

Fig. 8-5 Aluminum weldbond—edge tack vs. center weld.

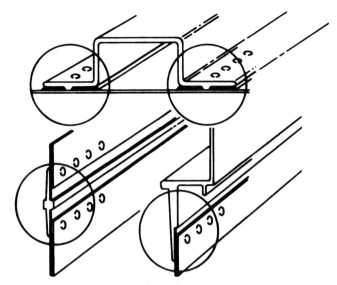

Fig. 8-6 Weldbond design in truck body.

truck body. The front and sidewall hat-shaped posts are spot-welded to the upper and lower rails and center dividers. Then the posts are bonded to the prepainted aluminum exterior skin with a structural adhesive.

ECONOMICS OF PROCESS

The weldbond process has the following distinct advantages over spot welding:

- Applicable to aircraft design
- Higher static strength
- Improved fatigue strength (mechanical and sonic)
- Eliminates sealing operations
- Improved corrosion resistance

In comparison with mechanical fasteners, weldbonding offers these benefits:

- Reduced manufacturing costs and adaptability to mechanization and automated concepts
- Higher static strength, Fig. 8-7
- Improved fatigue strength (mechanical and sonic), Fig. 8-8
- Eliminates holes (stress risers)
- No misalignment or fastener fit problems
- Improved corrosion resistance (no dissimilar metals)
- Eliminates sealing operation
- Eliminates shop noises from rivet or drill motors
- Allows for designs with thinner sheet-metal gages

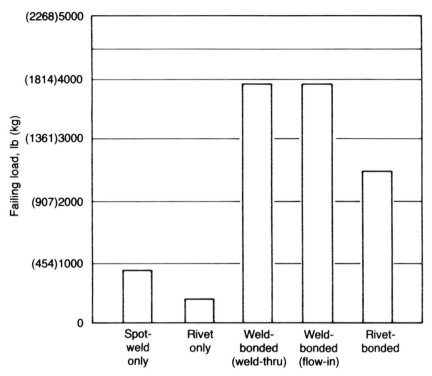

Fig. 8-7 Axial load fatigue strength of weldbond compared to rivets.

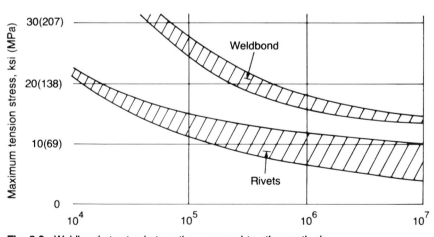

Fig. 8-8 Weldbond structural strengths compared to other methods.

In relation to adhesive bonding, weldbonding's advantages are as follows:

- Eliminates expensive facilities (autoclaves, platen press)
- Simplified tooling
- Reduced shop labor
- Fewer processing operations
- Adaptable to large structures (not limited to press or autoclave size)

MATERIALS AND THEIR PROPERTIES

Aluminum Alloys

The recently introduced all-weldbonded truck cab for the heavy-duty truck industry utilizes aluminum body sheet alloys 2036-T4 and X5085-H111 as primary cab metal; 5182 and 5052 alloy were also used, as well as body sheet steel. All these materials were weldbonded with various adhesives, including vinyl plastisols and one- and two-part modified epoxies. The aluminum weldbond joints were subjected to an exhaustive series of tests and their durability in various environments was usually equal to any of the adhesive-bonded joints and distinctly superior to the vinyl plastisol adhesive-bond joints. The fatigue strength of the weldbonded 0.040-in (1.0-mm) aluminum joints exceeded 0.032-in (0.80-mm) steel weldbond joints made with polysulfide and high-peel-strength epoxies.

Other aluminum alloys which have been tested include 2219-T87, 2219-T37, and 7075-T6 in various thicknesses. When examining the cross section of a typical lap shear specimen, one will normally see the excellent condition of the weld nugget, with proper penetration and no contamination.[2,6] The adhesive film is continuous, varying in thickness from zero around the edge of the spot welds to about 0.007 in (0.18 mm) at the ends (midpoint between spot welds in the case of actual joints). The strength of such joints is typically on the order of 3 ksi (21 MPa). These results are based on tests performed on 1-in-wide (25.4 mm) specimens having a 1-in (25.4-mm) epoxy-bonded overlap with a single spot weld in the center. By comparison, without adhesive, such joints can withstand a force of only about 850 lb (385 kg), or two-thirds less. In fatigue tests the life of the weldbond joint was found to be 13 times that of the conventional spot weld. Table 8-1 depicts basic data that has been gathered from a large number of room-temperature tests. The scatter in the data is exaggerated, since data have been taken from a wide range of tests run under various conditions; the scatter in more recent tests seldom exceeds ±5%.

An evaluation was conducted that compared rivet bonding and weldbonding as joining techniques using 2024-T3 aluminum alloy for a durable, fatigue-resistant, and cost-effective structure for a 350°F (177°C) service temperature. Table 8-2 illustrates the superiority of the weldbond joints in fatigue in an axial-tension series of tests.

TABLE 8-1
Summary of Lap Shear Tests of Aluminum Alloy Weldbond Joints[4]

Overlap L (in)	Overlap L (mm)	Number of specimens	Material	Sheet thickness t (in)	Sheet thickness t (mm)	L/t	Ultimate Load Min (ksi)	Min (MPa)	Max (ksi)	Max (MPa)	Avg. (ksi)	Avg. (MPa)	Failure mode
0.50	12.7	10	2219-T37	0.035	0.89	14.3	1.8	12	1.9	13	1.9	13	B
		2	2219-T87	0.072	1.8	7.0	2.0	14	2.0	14	2.0	14	B
0.65	16.5	2	2219-T87	0.072	1.8	9.0	2.7	18	2.9	20	2.8	19	B
0.84	21.3	2	2219-T87	0.072	1.8	11.7	3.0	21	3.5	24	3.3	23	B
1.00	25.4	40	2219-T37	0.035	0.89	28.5	2.0	14	2.2	15	2.1	15	30%B, 70%PM
		25	2219-T87	0.035	0.89	28.5	2.4	16	2.5	17	2.5	17	BM
		16	7075-T6	0.058	1.5	17.2	3.0	21	3.8	26	3.5	24	B
		49	7075-T6	0.062	1.6	16.2	2.7	18	4.4	30	3.6	25	B
		42	2219-T87	0.070	1.7	14.3	3.1	21	4.5	31	3.9	27	B
1.10	27.9	2	2219-T87	0.072	1.8	15.3	3.8	26	3.8	26	3.8	26	B
1.30	33.0	6	7075-T6	0.060	1.5	21.6	4.1	28	4.5	31	4.3	30	PM
		12	2219-T87	0.073	1.8	17.8	4.2	29	4.5	31	4.4	30	B
2.00	50.8	26	2219-T87	0.072	1.8	27.8	4.4	30	4.9	34	4.6	32	15%B, 85%PM

All tests conducted at ambient temperature (20°C).
Adhesive: EC 2214.
B = Bond.
PM = Parent Material.

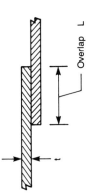
Overlap L

TABLE 8-2
Axial Tension Fatigue Results

Specimen configuration	Conditioning	Average cycles to failure
Bonded/riveted	Control	117,500
	7 days at 350° (177°C) plus 7 days humidity	61,800
Weldbonded	Control	111,600
	7 days at 350° (177°C) plus 7 days humidity	187,200
	7 days at 350° (177°C) plus 30 days salt spray	174,000

Titanium Alloys

At present, the principal method of joining aircraft structures is mechanical fastening; the relatively high cost of titanium and stainless steel fasteners is a significant factor which contributes to the magnitude of the mechanical fastening costs. Moreover, future aircraft will require the use of titanium to achieve higher performance and payloads at elevated temperatures. Accordingly, weldbonding in lieu of mechanical fasteners is a potentially cost-effective, structurally efficient joining procedure.

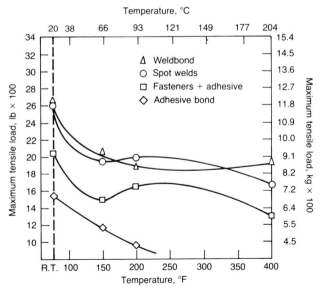

Fig. 8-9 Comparisons of joining methods for Ti-6Al-4V alloy from tensile test data.

TABLE 8-3
Titanium Weldbond Adhesives[6]

Adhesive system	Wet strength	Nugget cross section	Weldbonding properties, overlap tensile shear strength						Welding properties
			Room temperature ksi	20°C MPa	300°F ksi	(149°C) MPa	400°F ksi	(204°C) MPa	
EA 929, filled	S	S	3.3	23	3.6	25	3.6	25	Satisfactory at 180°F (82°C)
EA 929, unfilled	S	S	3.3	23	3.3	23	3.2	22	Satisfactory at 180°F (82°C)
Plastilock 729-3	S	S	3.5	24	3.5	24	3.6	25	Satisfactory
Plastilock 729-1	S	S	3.5	24	3.5	24	3.4	23	Satisfactory at 180°F (82°C)
FM 400	S	S	3.2	22	3.5	24	3.5	24	Satisfactory at 180°F (82°C)
EA 958									
ADX 516									
ADX 41.2	S	S	3.4	23	3.4	23	3.5	24	Satisfactory
ADX 41.4	S	S	3.3	23	3.3	23	3.2	22	Satisfactory
Kerimid 501									
Nolimid A380									

NOTES:

1. Adherends: Ti-6-4 Annealed, 0.050 in (1.3 mm).

2. Wet strength—uncured strength of spot-weld joint; S—meets MIL-W-6868 minimum requirements.

3. Nugget cross section—uncured specimen; S—meets MIL-W-6858 minimum requirements.

4. Overlap tensile shear values are average of five tests.

TABLE 8-3 *(Continued)*

	Adhesive properties, overlap tensile shear strength											
Adhesive system	Room temperature ksi	(20°C) MPa	300°F ksi	(149°C) MPa	350°F ksi	(177°C) aged MPa	400°F ksi	(204°C) MPa	400°F ksi	(204°C) aged MPa	450°F ksi	(2°C) aged MPa
EA 929, filled	2.7	18	3.2	22	2.5	17	1.9	13				
EA 929, unfilled	2.4	16	2.4	16	2.1	15	1.5	10				
Plastilock 729-3	4.5	31	3.1	21	2.3	16	.9	6				
Plastilock 729-1	4.1	28	4.1	28	3.4	23	1.9	13				
FM 400	2.1	15	1.8	12	2.4	16	2.2	15				
EA 958	1.6	11	1.6	11	1.4	10						
ADX 516	2.9	20	.7	4	.8	5						
ADX 41.2	2.6	18	2.6	18	1.3	9	.8	5				
ADX 41.4	3.4	23	3.2	22	2.3	16	1.4	10				
Kerimid 501												
Nolimid A380	2.8	19					2.5	17	2.2	15	2.1	15

NOTES:
1. Adherends: TI-6-4 Annealed, 0.050 in (1.3 mm).
2. Wet strength—uncured strength of spot-weld joint; S—meets MIL-W-6868 minimum requirements.
3. Nugget cross section—uncured specimen; S—meets MIL-W-6858 minimum requirements.
4. Overlap tensile shear values are average of five tests.

8-17

A comparison of tensile data for several processes is seen in Fig. 8-9. Investigators have recently examined the feasibility of titanium weld-bonding, and have produced the results shown in Table 8-3.

Composites and Dissimilar Metals

Since weldbonding of aluminum has been applied to several structures in production aircraft, its application to the joining of aluminum-boron composites seems logical. The rough surface finish of the composite was found to increase the surface area of bonding, thereby increasing the joint strength. Several test specimens showed that the joint strengths were so high that failure took place in the parent material. Therefore, the strengths shown in Fig. 8-10 represent conservative values for this type of joint. The strength was at least 4 times higher than obtained in a spot-welded Al-B joint. The orientation was 0° for these test specimens. For other tension-shear test specimens with a ±45° (0.78 rad) orientation, the weldbonded joints were 1.7 times stronger than the spot-welded joints.

Feasibility studies have been initiated to determine the economic potential of joining aluminum to steel, Table 8-4.

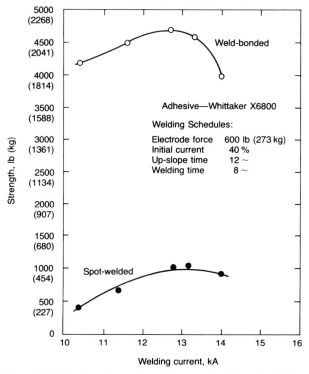

Fig. 8-10 Tension-shear strength as a function of welding current for spot-welded and weldbonded Al-B composite sheet, 0° orientation.

TABLE 8-4
Weldbond Results of Dissimilar Joints

Adherends	Adhesive system		Overlap		Tensile shear strength	
	Primer	Adhesive	in	mm	ksi	MPa
0.063-in (1.6-mm) 2024-T3 to 0.063-in (1.6-mm) 17-7PH	None	FM-24	1.0	25.4	2.2	15
0.063-in (1.6-mm) 2024-T3 to 0.063-in (1.6-mm) 17-7PH	None	BFG0050 PE 95	1.0	25.4	2.5	17
0.032-in (0.08-mm) 302 ann. to 0.032-in (0.08-mm) 302 ann.	None	EC 2214	1.0	25.4	1.8	12
0.032-in (0.08-mm) 302 ann. to 0.032-in (0.08-mm) 302 ann.	None	ADX 347	1.0	25.4	1.9	13
0.032-in (0.08-mm) 302 ann. to 0.032-in (0.08-mm) 302 ann.	None	EC 3419	1.0	25.4	1.7	11
0.032-in (0.08-mm) 302 ann. to 0.032-in (0.08-mm) 302 ann.	None	ADX 373	1.0	25.4	1.9	13
0.032-in (0.08-mm) 302 ann. to 0.032-in (0.08-mm) 302 ann.	None	Resinweld 7043	1.0	25.4	1.5	10
0.032-in (0.08-mm) 301 ann. to 0.032-in (0.08-mm) 302 ann.	None	ADX-370.1	0.5	12.7	5.2	36
0.032-in (0.08-mm) 301 ann. to 0.032-in (0.08-mm) 302 ann.	BR-127	ADX-370.1	0.5	12.7	4.8	33

APPLICATIONS

The degree of acceptance of weldbond applications has been increasing as the process has been understood and its mechanical properties developed. In the Soviet Union there are six types of transports, a helicopter, and railcars which are utilizing weldbonding. Similarly, the United States has applied weldbonding to 5% of the frame structure of a production-type helicopter, fuselage barrels for a transport (Fig. 8-11), and major load-bearing sections of the fuselage for a new close-air-support fighter. Over 1430 flight hours have been accumulated on the transport with no problems indicated.

Fig. 8-11 Dotted area is weldbonded panel.

Shelters for housing missiles and their radar tracking equipment have employed weldbonding, and the process was chosen to avoid possible radio-frequency leakage caused by rivets. Weldbonding has replaced a conventional riveted structure on a missile casing, Fig. 8-12.

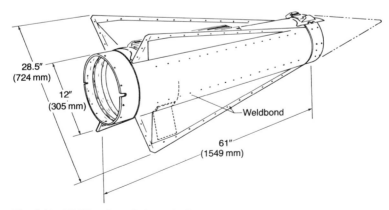

Fig. 8-12 Weldbond applied to missile skin.

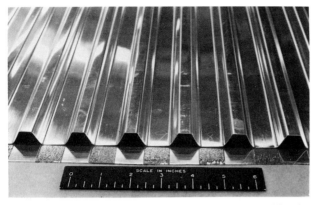

Fig. 8-13 Typical corrugation assembly prior to seam welding for weldbonded rocket shroud.[4,5]

A recent Viking spacecraft probe had weldbonded aluminum shrouds consisting of a clamshell assembly with corrugated sheet weldbonded to a smooth inner skin, Fig. 8-13.

Finally, one promising application of the weldbond process is propellant tanks. The assembly procedure allows certain manufacturing tolerances to be relaxed (i.e., gore width and length) while still maintaining tight dimensional control on critical parameters such as overall length, diameter, and volume. Moreover in the weldbonded tank one can, without weight penalty, use as-rolled sheet to form cylindrical and spherical gores. This avoids expensive chemical or

Fig. 8-14 Stainless steel weldbonded rail car structure.

mechanical milling operations necessary to increase the thickness in weld-land regions for fusion welding. Thus the weldbond process offers the potential of significant cost reduction in tank fabrication when compared with fusion welding. Tanks 10 ft (3 m) in diameter and 16 ft (5.5 m) long have been fabricated.[4]

The ground transportation industry has seen the potential of weldbond as demonstrated in Figure 8-14, which shows a stainless steel simulated railway car body and the new all-weldbonded aluminum heavy-duty truck cab mentioned previously.

A more universal acceptance and future uses of the process will come when a foolproof, nondestructive technique to inspect the quality of a weldbond adhesive joint is developed. The reason for complications is the need to inspect the quality of both the weld nugget and the adhesive bond. Radiographic and ultrasonic techniques have been used effectively in both spot-welding and adhesive-bond inspection to detect inclusions, voids, porosity, bond delamination, metal exposed nugget configuration, and diameter. However, destructive techniques must be relied upon to determine shear strength, weld penetration, and sheet separation. Currently, destructive testing remains the device necessary to determine these latter characteristics.

REFERENCES

1. Wu, K. C., "Resistance Spot Welding of High Contact-Resistance Surfaces for Weldbonding," *Weld. J.*, **54**(12), 436s–443s, December 1975.
2. Wu, K. C., and Bowen, B. B., "Advanced Aluminum Weldbond Manufacturing Methods," Contr. F33615-75-C-5083, AFML-TR-76-131, June 1975–March 1976.
3. "Manufacturing Methods for Resistance Spot Welding-Adhesive Bond Joining of Titanium," Rohr Industries, Internal Doc. 871-73-056, October 1973.
4. Sullivan, F., and Forsberg, K., "Application of Weldbond to Aerospace Structures," LMSC 6-C5-70-1, Rev. 1, January 1971.
5. Lockheed Missiles & Space Co., Missile Systems Division, Sunnyvale, CA, private communication, February 1978.
6. Mahon, J., Vizzi, C., and Sisco, W., "Manufacturing Methods for Resistance Spotweld-Adhesive Bond Joining of Titanium," Contr. 33615-74-C-5073, LTN Proj. 408-4, November 1975.
7. Fields, D., "Resistance Spot Weld—Adhesive Bonding Process," Contr. F33615-69-C-1867, AFML-TR-70-227, November 1970.
8. Fields, D., "Manufacturing Methods Development of Spot-Weld-Adhesive Bonded Joining for Titanium," Contr. F33615-71-C-1099, AFML-TR-71-93, June 1971.
9. Krohn, H., and Tscherneg, H., "Spot Welding and Spot Weld-Bonding of Al Alloys in Three and Single-Phase Welding Machines," *ZIS Mitt.*, **21**(10), 1452–60, October 1970.
10. Oldenburg, B., "Technological and Design Prerequisites for the Application of Spot Weld-Bonding with a ZIS 542 Adhesive," *ZIS Mitt.*, **21**(10), 1461–64, October 1970.
11. Szabo, R. L., "Feedback-Controlled Spotwelding," Contr. F33615-75-C-5229, AFML-TR-76-35, April 1976.

9

VACUUM BRAZING

Brazing has embarked on a vastly successful new era. Sparking this progress in recent years has been the continuing development of more and improved braze filler metals, availability of new forms and shapes of the braze filler metals, the introduction of machines that have brought brazing processes to the fore in high-production situations, and increased use of vacuum in brazing.

As new base metals and alloys were developed and used during the last twenty-five years, new brazing compositions were developed to join them. Aluminum is brazed with low-melting-point aluminum filler metals. Copper-nickel-titanium has been found effective for joining titanium and some of its alloys. Numerous brazing filler metals with excellent hot strength and increased resistance to oxidation have been developed for various superalloys so important to jet flight and the exploration of space. The development of new brazing techniques such as vacuum brazing has kept pace with filler-metal development. The brazing of ceramics to metals, for example, is now an accepted technique.

The use of vacuum in metal processing has grown steadily since the first announcement in 1948 of vacuum-melted metals and alloys. Vacuum brazing, a logical evolution in vacuum metallurgy arising from vacuum sintering and vacuum melting, is currently being used extensively in various industries and shows promise of becoming an increasingly important production process.

Vacuum brazing is the most modern brazing process and is at present, far from being completely understood. It was first used, possibly accidentally, for assembling evacuated electronic valves. Added impetus was given to the development of the process by the demand for a flux-free method of brazing for those heat-resisting alloys that cannot be processed in controlled atmospheres. By brazing under high vacuum, in an atmosphere free of oxidizing gases, a superior product, with greater strength, ductility and uniformity, may be obtained more economically than by brazing methods previously used.

THEORY

Vacuum brazing has been found to be successful in the production of joints of unequaled quality in the fluxless brazing of many similar and dissimilar base-metal combinations. The process also imparts a standard of cleanliness to the work that could not be achieved by any other method. This second aspect is so important in some instances that components that could be brazed by easier methods are being vacuum-brazed. Engineers theorized that the excellent properties found in vacuum-brazed joints were the result of metallic oxides present being dissociated when heated under low gas pressures. This is apparently unlikely, for a vacuum is simply an effective means of screening the work from oxidizing gases and other impurities.

The combination of vacuum and brazing requires examination.

Vacuum

The first vacuum pump was developed by von Guericke in about 1650. This device was the first machine by which air could be progressively removed from a chamber. In the famous Magdeburg experiment, two hemispheres were joined and exhausted by this pump. Two teams of horses pulled on the hemispheres but were unable to separate them. Other experimenters, notably Torricelli, produced vacuums; however, Guericke's pump remained the basic type of pump mechanism until the end of the nineteenth century. Other improvements were produced by Boyle, Hooke, and Hawksbee.

In 1905 Gaede, one of the most outstanding vacuum inventors, introduced his rotary mercury pump, and subsequently introduced an improved rotary mechanical pump which is the basis of most modern rotary mechanical pumps. Finally, in 1915, Gaede introduced the vapor-stream or diffusion pump. This type of pump is efficient and relatively inexpensive, and is in widespread use today.

"Vacuum" means the absence of gas, i.e., the condition of having fewer gas molecules present than exist at atmospheric pressure. Vacuum is created when molecules of gas are removed from a chamber until as few as possible remain. Present methods of eliminating gas from a chamber involve pumping. When pumping is applied to a system at atmospheric pressure, gas flows from the direction of the volume being evacuated to the pump. The gas expands into a chamber defined by a fixed stator and a rotary element. The gas expands into the chamber and is compressed by vanes until it is finally ejected at the outlet through a valve. The entire mechanism is usually submerged in a bath of special low-vapor-pressure vacuum oil to prevent air from leaking back into the chamber.

A point is reached, however, where pressure here is so low that the random molecular motion is no longer directed. There is no longer enough gas to constitute a flow. Thereafter pressure can be reduced further only by catching a molecule wandering into this area and dragging it out. A mechanical pump cannot do this, but the diffusion pump can. The diffusion pump operates on the principle that when a liquid such as oil, or mercury is boiled, the vapor rises. Heat drives the vapor up the chimney where it hits jets that force it against the walls of the chamber. The walls are kept cool by a coil arrangement so that this working fluid condenses, flows back into the boiler, is reheated, and refluxes all over again. Any molecules of gas in the chamber to be evacuated which wander into the oil stream are captured and directed toward the base of the pump. Here the pressure is built up to a point at which a mechanical pump can remove the gas. From the above explanation, one can see that the diffusion pump acts as a compressor.

Brazing

Brazing is defined as a group of welding processes in which coalescence is produced by heating to suitable temperatures above 800°F (427°C) and by using a ferrous and/or nonferrous filler metal that must have a liquidus temperature above 800°F (427°C), but below that of the base metals. The filler metal is distributed between the closely fitted surfaces of the joint by capillary attraction.

This definition brings out four distinct parts:

1. The coalescence, joining, or uniting of an assembly of two or more parts into one structure is achieved by heating the assembly or the region of the parts to be joined to a temperature of 800°F (427°C) or above.
2. Assembled parts and filler metal alloy are heated to a temperature high enough to melt that alloy but not the parts.
3. The molten filler metal spreads into the joint.
4. The parts are cooled to freeze the filler metal and anchor the part together.

A comprehensive theory of the wetting or spreading of liquids on solid surfaces has been presented by Hawkins.[1] The complete detailed derivation of the quantitative relationships is not repeated here; however, it can be concluded that wetting is the ability of the molten brazing filler metal to adhere to the surface of a metal in the solid state and, when cooled below its solidus temperature, to make a strong bond to that metal. Wetting is a function not only of the brazing filler metal but of the nature of the metal or metals to be joined. There is considerable evidence that in order to wet well, a molten metal must be capable of dissolving, or alloying with, some of the metal on which it flows.

MECHANISMS AND KEY VARIABLES

A careful and intelligent appraisal of the following variables will produce satisfactory brazed joints.

- Flow
- Base-metal characteristics
- Filler-metal characteristics
- Surface preparation
- Joint design
- Temperature
- Time
- Rate of heating

Flow

Wetting is only one important facet of the brazing process. If the molten filler metal does not flow into the joint, the use of the filler metal is greatly restricted. Flow is facilitated by capillary attraction, which in turn results from surface energy effects.[2,3]

It is apparent that a high liquid surface tension, a low contact angle, and low viscosity are desirable. Thus a low contact angle, which implies wetting, is a necessary but not sufficient condition for flow. Viscosity is also important. Filler metals with narrow freezing ranges that are close to the eutectic composition generally have lower viscosity than those with wide freezing ranges.

Flow is the property of a brazing filler metal that determines the distance it will travel away from its original position because of the action of capillary forces. To flow well, a filler metal must not suffer an appreciable increase in its liquidus temperature even though its composition is altered by the addition of the metal it has dissolved. This is important because the brazing operation is carried out at temperatures just above the liquidus.

Compositions and the surface energies of liquids and solids are assumed to remain constant. However, in real systems interactions occur:[4] (1) alloy formation between liquid and base metal, (2) diffusion of base metal into filler metal, (3) diffusion of filler metal into grains of base metal, (4) penetration of filler metal along grain boundaries, and (5) formation of intermetallic compounds.

These interactions can alter surface energies and viscosities, thus leading to changes in wetting and flow. The rate at which these interactions take place depends on the temperature, the time at temperature, and the materials involved. Generally, the extent and type of interaction, for simple systems, can be predicted from the appropriate phase diagrams and from diffusion data. However, if either the filler or base metal, or both, are alloys, these predictions become very difficult and experimental data are required.

In practice, interactions are usually minimized by (1) selecting the proper filler metal, (2) keeping the brazing temperature as low as possible, but high enough to get flow, and (3) keeping the time at temperature short and cooling down as quickly as possible without cracking or distortion.

Base-Metal Characteristics

The base metal has a prime effect on joint strength. A high-strength base metal produces joints of greater strength than those made with softer base metals (other factors being equal). When hardenable metals are brazed, the joint strengths become less predictable. This is because there are more complex metallurgical reactions involved between hardenable base metals and the brazing filler metals. These reactions can cause changes in the base metal hardenability and can create residual stresses.

Some of the metallurgical phenomena that influence the behavior of brazed joints, and in some instances necessitate special procedures, include these base-metal effects: (1) alloying, (2) carbide precipitation, (3) oxide stability, (4) stress cracking, and (5) hydrogen, sulfur, and phosphorus embrittlement. The extent of interaction varies greatly depending on compositions (base metal and filler metal) and thermal cycles. There is always some interaction, except when mutual insolubility permits practically no metallurgical interaction.

Filler Metal Characteristics

The second material involved in joint structures is the brazing filler metal. The term "brazing filler metal" is essentially synonymous with the commonly employed "brazing alloy." Its selection is important, but not for the reasons many engineers think. A specific filler metal cannot be chosen to produce a specific joint strength, which is unfortunate, but true. Actually, strong joints can be brazed with almost any good commercial brazing filler metal if brazing methods and joint design are done correctly.

Several characteristics that braze filler metals must possess are:

- Proper fluidity at brazing temperatures to assure flow by capillary action and provide full alloy distribution.
- Stability to avoid premature release of low-melting-point elements in the filler metal.
- Ability to wet the base-metal joint surfaces.
- The alloying elements of the braze filler metal must have low volatilization characteristics at brazing temperatures.
- It is desirable that it alloy or combine with the parent metal to form an alloy with a higher melting temperature.
- Washing or erosion between the brazing filler metal and the parent metal must be controllable within the limits required for the brazing operation.
- Depending on the requirements, the ability to produce or avoid base-metal–filler-metal interactions.

One of the most broadly misunderstood facts relating to brazing filler metals is that brazed-joint strength is in no way related directly to the melting method used. This fact is hard to accept because it seems to contradict a long-established metallurgical truth with regard to the manufacture of steels or other constructional metals. The effect of melting practice on brazing filler metals, however, is not the same as that of melting practice on steels. If constructional metals are produced by vacuum melting, for example, there is a definite relationship between the vacuum-melting practice and the final strength of the ingot, bar, or rolled sheet. That is not true with a brazing filler metal, since joint strength is dependent on such factors as joint design, brazing temperature, amount of filler metal applied, location and method of application, heating rate, and many other considerations that make up what is termed "brazing technique."

The degree to which braze filler metal penetrates and alloys with the base metal during brazing is referred to as diffusion. In applications requiring strong joints for high-temperature, high-stress service conditions (such as turbine rotor assemblies and jet engine components), it is generally good practice to specify a filler metal that has high diffusion and solution properties with the base metal. When the assembly is constructed of extremely thin base metals (as in honeycomb structures and some heat exchangers), good practice generally calls for a filler metal with a low diffusion characteristic relative to the base metal being used. Diffusion is a normal part of the metallurgical process that can contribute to good brazed joints in brazing, for example, of high-temperature metals with nickel-base filler metals.

Surface Preparation

In vacuum-furnace brazing the wetting action of braze filler metals is a little different from water spreading on glass because we are dealing with metals at elevated temperatures, and in most situations the attraction between the brazing filler metal and the parent metal is sufficiently great to cause alloying between the two. The condition of the surface of the parent metal, however, greatly influences the behavior of the brazing filler metal from the standpoint of wetting and the tendency to creep or to ball up. These tendencies depend on the relative surface tension—whether there is sufficient attraction by the surface of the parent metal to draw the brazing filler metal out in a thin film, or whether the surface tension of the brazing filler metal is sufficient to draw it up into balls or lumps on the surface of the parent metal when compared with a lack of attraction by the surface to draw it out in a film.

A clean, oxide-free surface is imperative to ensure uniform quality and sound brazed joints. A sound joint may be obtained more readily if all grease, oil, dirt, and oxides have been carefully removed from the base and filler metals before brazing, because only then can uniform capillary attraction be obtained. It is recommended that brazing be done as soon as possible after the material has been cleaned. The length of time the cleaning remains effective depends on the metals involved, atmospheric conditions, storage, handling, etc. Cleaning is commonly divided into two major categories: chemical and mechanical. Chemical cleaning is the most effective means of removing all traces of oil or grease. Trichlorethylene and trisodium phosphate are the usual cleaning agents employed. Various types of oxides and scale that cannot be eliminated by these cleaners are removed by other chemical means.

In a new technique, aluminum is cleaned of its oxide film and is sealed immediately with a polymeric material, making it suitable for vacuum brazing. The time between cleaning and brazing is no longer a critical factor. First, the surface of the aluminum is degreased with any common degreaser, such as naptha, a liquid chlorinated hydrocarbon. After degreasing, the aluminum oxide is removed by chemical cleaning with an alkali wash of sodium hydroxide and sodium bicarbonate. A water rinse at 140 to 160°F (168 to 174°C) and an acid washing follows. After the acid treatment, the aluminum is rinsed in distilled water. It is then immersed in an organic solvent miscible with water, such as acetone, to remove all water from the surfaces. Immediately after this step, the clean surfaces to be joined are coated with a sealer.

The sealer used may be any polymeric material which prevents substantial permeation of oxygen to the coated surface and which can be volatilized from the surface during the joining process, leaving essentially no residue. One of the better sealers comprises polystyrene in toluene and acetone. Sealed aluminum surfaces can be stored for several days without any appreciable surface oxidation.

The selection of the chemical cleaning agent depends on the nature of the contaminant, the base metal, the surface condition, and the joint design. Regardless of the cleaning agent or the method used, it is important that all residue or surface film be removed from the cleaned parts by adequate rinsing to prevent the formation of other equally undesirable films on the faying surfaces. Objectionable surface conditions may be removed by mechanical means such as grinding, filing, wire brushing, or any form of machining, provided that joint clearances are not disturbed. In grinding of surfaces of parts to be brazed, care also should be taken to see that the coolant is clean and free from impurities so that the finished surfaces do not have these impurities ground into them.

When faying surfaces of parts to be brazed are prepared by blasting techniques, several factors should be understood and considered. The purpose of blasting parts to be brazed is to remove any oxide film and to roughen the mating surfaces so that capillary attraction of the brazing filler metal is increased. The blasting material must be clean and must not leave a deposit on the surfaces to be joined that restricts filler metal flow or impairs brazing. It should be a fragmented material rather than spherical so that the blasted parts are lightly roughened rather than peened. The operation should be done so that delicate parts are not distorted or otherwise harmed. Vapor blasting and similar wet blasting methods require care because of possible surface contamination.

Solid and liquid brazing fluxes are normally not used in a vacuum.[5] In a few cases, gaseous fluxes have been used with some success; boron trifluoride is an example. Its disadvantage is that it is a noxious air pollutant. The effect of a flux would be to aid in cleaning the braze surface and to prevent further contamination under imperfect vacuum conditions. Another method of reducing contamination in vacuum is by "gettering." Lithium, magnesium, sodium, potassium, calcium, titanium, and barium can be vaporized in the chamber to reduce the volume of oxides and nitrides present in the vacuum atmosphere. These materials may condense on the chamber walls. Their disadvantage is that most of them will either react with the workload or form a coating on the wall when exposed to atmospheric moisture. For most materials best results are obtained by exercising due care with regard to cleanliness of materials to be vacuum-brazed and then using nothing but a high vacuum. Aluminum is one exception.

Successful brazing in vacuum depends on the presence of a promoter, either a metal or reactive gas. The key action of metal promoters in vacuum brazing is to reduce chemically the aluminum oxide films to permit alloy wetting. In addition, they must also scavenge remaining oxygen and moisture in the vacuum, but these are not the key mechanisms. Many metals can fulfill the function of a braze promoter, but magnesium is the best. Magnesium contained in the brazing filler metal does double duty. As it vaporizes, it tends to disrupt the aluminum oxide at the aluminum boundary layer, and later as a vapor in the vacuum chamber, it reacts with oxygen and oxides (mainly water) to reduce or eliminate formation of additional aluminum oxide surface films that could inhibit good wetting and capillary flow. Table 9-1 shows the metal activators and their actions in vacuum brazing.

Certain halide vapors promote brazing through a double decomposition reaction with the aluminum films. Bromides and iodides of phosphorus and boron have been most successful.

TABLE 9-1
Possible Actions of Activating Metal in Vacuum Brazing[6]

Activating metal	Removes oxygen	Removes water vapor	Vaporizes	Reacts with aluminum oxide	Promotes vacuum brazing
Rare earths, beryllium, scandium, yttrium	Yes	Yes	No	Yes	Yes
Magnesium, calcium, strontium, lithium	Yes	Yes	Yes	Yes	Yes
Barium, sodium, zinc	Yes	Yes	Yes	No	No
Antimony, bismuth	Yes	No	Yes	No	No

Joint Design

A brazed joint is not a homogeneous body. Rather it is a heterogeneous assembly that is composed of different materials with differing physical and chemical properties. In the simplest case, it consists of the base metal parts to be joined and the added filler metal. Diffusion processes, however, can change the composition and therefore the chemical and physical properties of the boundary zone formed at the interface between base metal and filler metal. Thus, in addition to the two different materials present in the simplest example given, further dissimilar materials must be considered.

Why should small clearances be used? The smaller the clearance, the easier it is for capillarity to distribute the brazing filler metal throughout the joint area. There will be less likelihood of voids or shrinkage cavities as the filler metal solidifies. small clearances and correspondingly thin brazing filler-metal films make sound joints and sound joints are strong joints. The soundest joints are those in which 100% of the joint area is wetted and filled by the brazing filler metal. They are at least as high in tensile strength as the brazing filler metal itself and often higher. If brazing clearances ranging from 0.001 to 0.003 in (0.03 to 0.08 mm) are designed, they are designed for the best capillary action and strongest joint.

Joint clearance is probably the most significant factor in vacuum-brazing operations. Naturally, it receives special consideration in design of a joint for room temperature before brazing, into which the brazing filler metal will be flowed. Actually joint clearance is not the same at all phases of brazing operations. It is one value before brazing, another value at brazing temperature, and still another value after brazing, especially if there has been diffusion of the filler metal into the base metal. To avoid confusion it has become general practice to specify clearance in the joint design as being a certain value at room temperature before brazing.

Optimum clearance ranges have been worked out for each type of brazing filler metal that will be suitable in brazing of all similar-metal combinations with which that filler metal can be used. Generally, clearances in the lower portion of the ranges should be used in order to obtain maximum joint strength.

Recommended joint clearances are based on joints having members of similar metals and equal mass. When dissimilar metals and/or metals of widely differing masses are joined by brazing, special problems arise which necessitate more specialized selection among the various filler metals, and the joint clearance suitable for the job at hand must be carefully determined.

Although there are many kinds of brazed joints, the problem is not as complicated as it may seem because butt and lap joints are the two fundamental types. All others, such as the scarf joint, are modifications of them. It is identical with the butt joint at one extreme of the scarf angle and approaches the lap joint at the other extreme of the scarf angle. See Fig. 9-1.

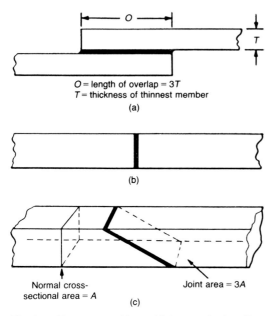

O = length of overlap = $3T$
T = thickness of thinnest member

(a)

(b)

Normal cross-
sectional area = A

Joint area = $3A$

(c)

Fig. 9-1 Basic types of brazed joints are (a) lap, (b) butt, and (c) scarf.

In general, lap joints are preferred for brazing. These joints depend for their strength on penetration between close, conforming surfaces, rather than on external fillets; the joints are usually intended to be stressed in shear.

In designing for brazing, butt joints are generally avoided. If the use of a butt joint is unavoidable, the entire assembly must be designed to ensure that there will be no deflection or bending stresses at the brazed joint. Concentration of bending stresses at the joint will cause the brazed filler metal to tear, especially if the base metal has a higher modulus of elasticity than the filler metal.

When a brazed assembly is subjected to bending stresses or fatigue, an abrupt change in section thickness in the joint area will promote failure at the joint, just as in a welded joint. This type of failure is caused by the relative flexibility of the thin section and rigidity of the heavy section. Failure can be avoided by tapering the heavy section in the joint area, thereby providing the two components with approximately equal stiffness at the point where failure would otherwise occur. This reduction in section also facilitates brazing, because it provides more uniform heating, uniform clearance, and uniform filler-metal flow.

Selection of the type of joint to use is influenced by the configuration of the parts, as well as by stress requirements and other service requirements such as electrical conductivity, pressure tightness, and appearance. Also influential in selecting joint type are fabrication techniques, production quantities, method of feeding filler metal, etc. Lap joints are generally preferred for brazing operations, particularly when it is important that the joints be at least as strong as the weaker member. The lap joint length should equal 3 times the thickness of the thinner member joined for maximum strength.

Time and Temperature

The temperature of the braze filler metal naturally has an important effect on the wetting action because the wetting and alloying action improves as the temperature increases. Of course, the temperature must be above the melting point of the braze filler metal and below the melting point of the parent metal. Within this range, a temperature is generally selected that will give the best satisfaction from an overall standpoint.

Usually the lowest brazing temperatures are preferred to (1) economize on heat energy required, (2) minimize heat effects on base metal (annealing, grain growth, warpage, etc.), (3) minimize base-metal–filler-metal interactions, and (4) increase the life of fixtures, jigs, or other tools.

Higher brazing temperatures may be desirable in order to (1) use a higher-melting but more economical brazing filler metal, (2) combine annealing, stress relief, or heat treatment of base metal with brazing, (3) permit subsequent processing at elevated temperatures, (4) promote base-metal interactions in order to modify the brazing filler metal (this technique is usually used to increase the remelt temperature of the joint), (5) effectively remove surface contaminants and oxides with vacuum brazing, and (6) avoid stress cracking.

The time at brazing temperature also affects the wetting action, particularly with respect to the distance of creep of the braze filler metal. If there is a tendency to creep, the distance generally increases with time. The alloying action between braze filler metal and parent metal is, of course, a function of both temperature and time. In general, for production work, both temperature and time are kept at a minimum consistent with good quality.

In conclusion, the braze filler metal and process for brazing must be selected with a true understanding of both the physical metallurgy of the base material and the interactions of the base material with the braze filler metals.

EQUIPMENT AND TOOLING

Equipment

Modern machines ensure accurate and repetitive brazing results through a system of automatic controls regulating temperature, time, and, when applicable, atmosphere. These three factors, incidentally, are the basis for selecting a proper brazing furnace.

Vacuum furnaces for brazing can be described as one of three types:

1. *Hot-retort, or single-pumped retort furnace.* This consists of a sealed retort, usually of fairly thick material. The work load is placed into the retort and the retort is sealed, evacuated, and heated externally. Most brazing work requires that the vacuum pumping be continued throughout the heat cycle to remove the gases that are continuously given off by the work load. The furnaces used are either gas-fired or electrically heated. The hot retort vacuum furnace is limited in size and maximum operating temperature by the ability of the retort material to withstand the collapsing force of atmospheric pressure. Another disadvantage is that some units are designed to be heated and cooled while evacuated and therefore require substantial time for heating and cooling of the heavy-wall retort. The maintained-high-temperature equipment is usually inefficient from a space viewpoint because only a small segment of the hot zone provides the even radiation source needed to maintain low thermal differentials within the workpiece. Vacuum brazing furnaces of this type have been built for operation at temperatures as high as 2100°F (1149°C), but most hot-wall vacuum retorts are limited to 1600°F (871°C) or lower. Leakage into hot-wall retorts is sometimes a problem, particularly if the materials to be brazed require a maximum pressure of 10^{-3} torr (0.13 Pa) or lower. Argon, nitrogen, or other gas is often introduced into the retort to accelerate cooling.

2. *Double-pumped, or double-wall hot-retort vacuum furnace.* A typical furnace of this type consists of an inner retort containing the work load. The inner retort is contained within an outer wall, or vacuum chamber. Also within the outer wall is the thermal insulation and electrical heating elements. A "rough" vacuum, typically 1.0 to 0.1 torr (0.13 to 0.013 kPa), is maintained within the outer wall, and a much finer vacuum, typically 10^{-2} torr (1.3 Pa) or lower, is maintained within the inner retort. Most brazing work requires that the vacuum pumping of the inner retort be continued throughout the heat cycle to remove the gases that are continuously given off by the work load.

   The double-pumped vacuum furnace is not limited in size or maximum operating temperature, since the hot inner retort is not subjected to the forces of atmospheric pressure. The outer wall is usually maintained at around room temperature, and thus may also be of any size.

   This type of furnace has a particular advantage in that the elements and thermal insulation are not subjected to the high vacuum. Heating elements are typically of nickel, nickel-chromium, graphite, stainless steel, silicon carbide, or other commonly used furnace-element materials. Thermal insulation material is usually silica or alumina brick, castable ceramic, or wool materials.

3. *Cold-wall vacuum furnace.* A typical cold-wall vacuum furnace consists of a single vacuum chamber, with the thermal insulation and electrical heating elements located inside of the chamber. The vacuum chamber is usually water-cooled. The maximum operating temperature of cold-wall furnaces is determined by the materials used for the thermal insulation (or heat shield) and the heating elements. The thermal insulation and heating elements are subjected to the high vacuum as well as the operating temperature of the furnace. Heating elements for cold-wall vacuum furnaces are usually made of molybdenum, tungsten, graphite, tantalum, or other high-temperature, low-vapor-pressure materials. Thermal insulation or heat shields are typically made of multiple layers of molybdenum, tantalum, nickel, or stainless steel, or they consist of high-purity alumina brick, graphite, or alumina wool sheathed in stainless steel. The maximum operating temperature and vacuum obtainable for cold-wall vacuum furnaces depends on the materials used for the heating elements and the thermal insulation of heat shields. Temperatures up to 4000°F (2204°C) and vacuum down to 10^{-6} torr (0.13 mPa) is obtainable. See Fig. 9-2.

All three of the above types of furnaces are constructed in either a side-loading (horizontal), bottom-loading (elevator or bell-type), or top-loading (pit-type) configuration. Work zones are usually rectangular for side-loading furnaces, although bottom or top loaders usually have a circular work zone.

Vacuum pumps for brazing furnaces may be of the oil-sealed mechanical type for pressures ranging from 10 to 0.1 torr (133 to 0.013 kPa). Brazing of base materials containing chromium, silicon, or

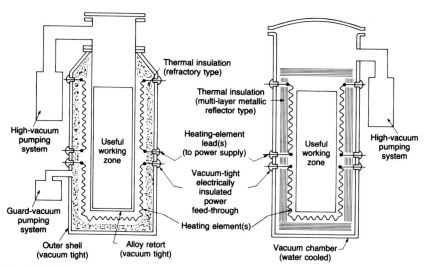

Fig. 9-2 Schematic of hot-retort (left) and cold-wall furnace (right).

other metals forming oxides of intermediate stability usually require pressures of 10^{-2} to 10^{-3} torr (1.3 to 0.13 Pa), which is best obtained by a high-speed dry mechanical-type pump of the Roots or turbomechanical type. Vacuum pumps of this type are not capable of exhausting directly to atmosphere, and require a "roughing" or "backing" pump usually of the oil-sealed mechanical type. This kind of pump compresses the gas which flows into it from the vacuum system and exhausts the compressed gas to the atmosphere. In general, it employs one or more rotors, usually with a radial sliding vane or vanes. As the rotor turns inside the pump housing, gas is taken in at one point on the circumference, swept along by the rotor and vane, and expelled at a point which is a considerable angular distance from the intake. As the rotor continues to revolve, it reaches the intake again and the cycle is repeated.

Brazing of base materials containing more than a few percent of aluminum, titanium, zirconium, or other elements that form very stable oxides: require vacuum of 10^{-3} torr (0.13 Pa) or lower. Vacuum furnaces for this type of brazing usually employ a diffusion pump which typically obtains pressures of 10^{-2} to 10^{-6} torr (0.001 to 0.13 mPa). The diffusion pump is usually backed by a mechanical pump or by dry-type Roots pump and mechanical pump.

The vapor stream from the diffusion pump operates in such a way as to concentrate the individual gas molecules at one location in a vacuum system. The oil vapor passes through jets imparting a portion of its velocity to the individual gas molecules, giving them a new velocity direction that forces them towards the bottom of the pump. This action causes a high molecular concentration at the bottom of the pump, where the pressure increase allows for removal of the gas by a mechanical pump. In order for the vapor stream to form, a roughing pressure generally below 1 torr (13.3 kPa) must be achieved in the vacuum system. This vacuum, of course, is well within the range of most mechanical pumps. The walls of the diffusion pump are usually cooled by water, so that the vapor striking the wall will condense and return to the boiler.

Another method of brazing using vacuum is by induction heating. Induction heating is used extensively on parts that are self-jigging or that can be fixtured in such a manner that effective heating will not be interfered with or reduced by the fixture. Induction heating is also used where very rapid heating is required. It is used primarily when it is necessary to heat parts economically or when a large number of parts can be adapted to special machines.

Most of the heat generated by this method is relatively near the surface. The interior is heated by thermal conduction from the hot surface. As a rule, the higher the frequency, the shallower the heating. It is necessary to make certain that there is no significant radiation from the generator or the work coils to avoid interference with reception on any of the allotted broadcast frequencies. Proper generator design and equipment installation will ensure against the violation of FCC regulations.

The parts to be brazed are sometimes held in a refractory chamber (quartz or tempered glass) that contains a vacuum atmosphere. The coil is placed around either the work or the refractory to heat the parts. Another technique which combines vacuum and induction heating utilizes induction generator leads, brought through the vacuum chamber walls, surrounding a graphite cylinder, called a *susceptor*, which is heated by the induction field. The theoretical temperature limit attainable is the sublimation temperature of graphite.

Tooling

When assemblies are put through the furnace to be vacuum-brazed, the relationship of the parts must be maintained, of course, from start to finish. There are a number of ways this can be done. When an assembly is complicated, it might be necessary to resort to a combination of several different methods.

The method of holding the assemblies together, the design of the joints, and the means of applying the braze filler metal are all very closely related. It is possible to design the parts so that they may be assembled and brazed without the use of fixtures. In other instances, it may be necessary to provide clamps and supports to ensure that the parts are held in correct alignment.

One of the most important things to remember in furnace brazing is the force of gravity. Assemblies have a tendency to fall apart after they become heated and the joints become loosened because of expansion. Also, the braze filler metal naturally tends to flow downward more than in any other direction. It creeps horizontally or upward on the surfaces of the metal, but it flows downward quite freely and collects at low spots if applied in excess quantity. Therefore, in designing an assembly for vacuum-furnace brazing, one must keep in mind how the assembly will be held together within the furnace and how it will be set up in the furnace both to direct the flow of the braze filler metal into the joints to the best advantage and to give minimum distortion or movement of the parts. These points are generally easy to determine by cut-and-try methods, and when a proper procedure is found, the braze filler metal can be made to flow into all joints, leaving neat fillets and clean surrounding surfaces; the job can usually be done without distortion.

Some of the various methods of holding assemblies together within the furnace follow.

Laying parts together

Perhaps the simplest method of joining two parts is simply to lay one on top of the other with braze filler metal either in between the members or wrapped around one of the members near the joint. In this case the weight of the upper member would be required to assure good metal-to-metal contact or a weight could be added to assure it. The scheme sometimes lacks the advantage of having a definite means of indexing or keeping the parts from moving in relationship to one another.

Pressing parts together

The most common method of assembling parts for vacuum-furnace brazing is simply to press them together. In general, regardless of the degree of tightness, some scheme is usually employed in order to prevent slippage of the parts when they become heated in the furnace, particularly if the joint has a vertical axis.

Snug fit desirable

In pressing parts together, the usual tolerances from machining the parts naturally give variations in the amount of press fit which cannot be avoided. An effort should be made, however, to have a snug fit at all times, if possible. When brazing with lower-melting braze filler metals, particularly on nonferrous assemblies, it is desirable to have a clearance of 0.001 to 0.003 in (0.03 to 0.08 mm) within the joint to permit the best flow of the braze filler metal.

Spot welding and tack welding parts together

Spot welding is frequently employed for holding definite relationships between the parts assembled for vacuum-furnace brazing. It is fast, inexpensive, and generally a neat operation.

Auxiliary fixtures

All of the foregoing methods of holding assemblies together are used for vacuum-furnace brazing, the choice of any method depending on the characteristics of each individual product. In some instances, however, it is found impracticable to use any of the suggested methods, and it is then necessary to resort to auxiliary fixtures to locate properly the members with respect to one another while they are being furnace-brazed. These fixtures sometimes take the form of graphite blocks or heat-resisting-superalloy and/or refractory-alloy supports or clamps.

Auxiliary fixtures have several disadvantages. They present additional mass that must be heated, they are subject to warpage that might make them unusable for repeated operations, and they present an extra item of maintenance expense. However, two examples where auxiliary fixtures have been used to advantage are as follows:

- *Blocks.* This type of tooling, consisting of weighted blocks, has been successfully utilized to produce brazed refractory and diffusion-welded reactive-metal components. The tools are usually of the same material as the parts being brazed, thus minimizing any thermal expansion problems.
- *Pellets.* This new tooling concept has resulted in an economical and reusable approach to produce a fluid-pressure effect on parts being brazed. Using this approach has resulted in removing the distortion problems in elevated temperature brazing and/or DFW. Thus a control over the mass of the fixturing, weight of the fixturing, and continuous use of the fixturing without any thermal warpage has been attained. An example of this type of tooling is shown in Fig. 9-3.

Therefore, in selecting fixtures for assembling parts for vacuum brazing, the following factors should be considered:

- The mass of the fixture should be kept to the minimum that will adequately accomplish its purpose. The fixture should be designed to provide minimum interference with even heating of the parts by removing heat by conduction from the brazing area. It is also important that the fixture not hamper the flow of the braze filler metal.
- Vacuum is a determining factor in the selection of the material to be used in the fixture. These materials must withstand the

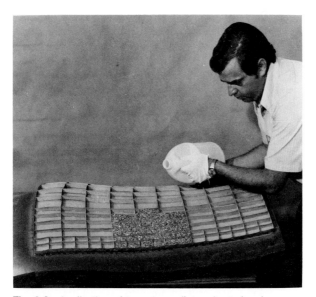

Fig. 9-3 Application of tungsten pellets prior to brazing.

temperatures involved without being appreciably weakened, distorted, or vaporized.

- Consideration should be given to the expansion and contraction of the fixture in relation to the parts being brazed to assure a combination that will maintain the proper joint clearance and alignment at the brazing temperature. Therefore, the coefficient of expansion of the fixture material as well as of the parts should be considered. Taking advantage of the coefficient of expansion of stainless steel vs. several nickel-base superalloys, a new technique for vacuum brazing honeycomb sandwich panels has been developed that makes $360°$ (2π rad) joints on cylinders, cones, and compound contours in cylindrical configurations. These components were formerly brazed in $120°$ ($2\pi/3$ rad) segments. The new process has been used on parts up to 52 in (1321 mm) in diameter with acceptable fillet size and no excessive braze filler-metal flow. See Fig. 9-4.
- Titanium has been brazed successfully with aluminum by a novel tooling method. The general technique is to mount and clamp the parts on a mandrel, with the aluminum filler metal in position, and then rotate the mandrel slowly inside a furnace held at about 1250°F (677°C). Rotation prevents the alloy from flowing out of the joints by gravity. Speed is approximately 1 r/min (1.05×10^{-1} rad/s).
- The fixture should be made of material that will not readily alloy at elevated temperatures with the material of the assembled parts. The fixture should be so designed that it will not contact the braze filler metal.

There are certain other requirements for brazing fixtures that are peculiar to the vacuum-brazing process. In vacuum-brazing fixtures, materials should be selected that will not expel gas or otherwise contaminate the inner furnace environment. Whereas graphite and various steels and superalloy heat-resisting materials are satisfactory as tooling materials up to 2000°F (1093°C) brazing temperatures, the tooling material for use at 3000°F (1649°C) is limited. Refractory metals and/or their alloys, ceramics, graphite, newly developed carbides or borides, and refractory-coated graphite are the only materials available for fixturing in the 3000°F (1649°C) and above furnace temperature range.

Of the tooling materials discussed for use in vacuum atmosphere at 3000°F (1649°C) and above, ceramics such as alumina, zirconia, and beryllia have exhibited reaction with refractory metals, contamination, and problems of thermal expansion and contraction. Graphite is another unsatisfactory material. It has excellent dimensional stability; however, it embrittles the refractory metals that are usually the heating element material of the furnace. The newly developed carbides and borides (ZrB, ZrC, TiC) are still in limited use. This leaves only the refractory metals and/or their alloys.

Fig. 9-4   Inconel 625 brazed honeycomb sandwich on steel fixture.

STOP-OFF AND PARTING AGENTS

Frequently, it is necessary to prevent the braze filler metal from wetting portions of assemblies, fixtures, and metallic supports. It is customary to turn to refractory oxides: levigated alumina, calcium and magnesium oxide, magnesium hydroxide, and titanium dioxide. They are used as extremely fine powders suspended in alcohol, lacquer, acryloid cement, water, or acetone. Two types of stop-off mixtures are available. One is fast drying and behaves much like a commercial lacquer. The second is a nonwicking type, composed of oxides in a gelled vehicle, that does not settle out on standing; this type dries slowly. Slurries usually are brushed on with a paintbrush or paint roller. The use of an artist's brush is ideal for precision applications of fine areas of stop-off, although the operation is time-consuming and requires considerable skill.

In practice, flow may not stop when the joint is filled, and braze filler metal may flow onto areas where it is not wanted. For example:

- In brazing a threaded stud into a part, the braze filler metal is likely to follow the threads and render them out of tolerance.

- Support points on fixtures used in furnace brazing may become wetted by the braze filler metal, producing an unwanted braze and perhaps resulting in loss of the fixture and assembly, because it may be impossible to separate them without damage.
- Some parts, such as turbine and compressor brazements, are designed to close tolerances and excess braze filler metal may be dimensionally objectionable.
- Tubular assemblies, particularly small capillary tubes [0.062-in (1.6-mm) ID or less], can easily become partly or completely blocked with braze filler metal.
- Excess braze filler metal may be unacceptable because of appearance.
- In production brazing, where it may be necessary to use more braze filler metal than called for to allow for variations in fit-up between parts, some joints will have excess braze filler metal which will flow away from the joint area.

Although these coatings can prevent wetting by braze filler metals on portions of assemblies that contact the coated surfaces, they will not necessarily form barriers for creep of braze filler metals on the assemblies. Braze filler metals often creep beneath the coatings. This problem becomes more acute when brazing in vacuum. Because many stop-off materials are oxides, the vacuum does remove the oxide, leaving a slight residue that is ineffective as a stop-off material. When zirconium oxide (ZrO_2) is mixed with a suitable nitrocellulose lacquer, it produces an effective parting agent for brazing in vacuum above 1600°F (871°C). Since ZrO_2 is only a parting agent and not a stop-off, usually thin separator sheets are used between the braze tools and the assembly to be brazed.

In certain types of work it is necessary to confine the flow of braze filler metal to definite areas. It may sometimes be accomplished by controlling the amount of braze filler metal used and its placement in the assembly.

ADVANTAGES, DISADVANTAGES, AND ECONOMICS

The brazing process itself has distinct advantages over other joining methods. When metals can be joined without melting them, the problems caused by high heat are eliminated or reduced to a minimum. Parts do not tend to warp or burn because the application of heat is general. The entire joint area is evenly heated to the flow point of the braze filler metal. In welding, the heat is intense and localized, applied directly to the weld filler metal and the joint. Furthermore, almost any metal can be formed in a single assembly by simply selecting a braze filler metal that melts at a temperature lower than that of the metals to be joined.

The ability to join dissimilar metals permits the use of the metals best suited for their functions in the assembly. Some further advantages of the vacuum-brazing process are increased strength of brazed joints, increased wetting and flow of braze filler metal, bright surfaces that dispense with expensive postcleaning operations, removal of unwanted gases, minimum interference with basic properties of material and improved corrosion resistance. Many metals are easy prey for harmful gases, such as oxygen and nitrogen, which is found in the cleanest of furnace brazing atmospheres. Oxides and nitrides form on the parts being brazed and these films prevent a good braze. Vacuum eliminates these films.

Furthermore, vacuum brazing is especially suited for brazing very large, continuous areas where (1) solid or liquid fluxes cannot be removed adequately from the interfaces during brazing, and (2) gaseous atmospheres are not completely efficient because of their inability to purge occluded gases evolved at close-fitting brazing interfaces.

Vacuum is most suitable for brazing refractory and reactive base metals. The characteristics of these metals are such that even very small quantities of atmospheric gases may result in embrittlement and sometimes disintegration at brazing temperatures.

Any difficulties experienced with contamination of brazing interfaces because of base-metal expulsion of gases are negligible in vacuum brazing. Occluded gases are removed from the interfaces immediately upon evolution from the metals.

Whether or not a clean surface is achieved depends upon the type and level of oxide or nitride formation on the surface of the alloy. If low-vapor-pressure oxides are present, brazing temperatures may not be high enough or vacuum high enough to remove or dissociate them. Under these conditions, either a higher vacuum and/or a mechanism to break the surface film are required. Superalloys containing titanium and aluminum are examples. Vacuum brazing of aluminum alloys depends on the presence of magnesium in the braze filler metal, base material being joined, or vapors to diminish the influence of persistent aluminum oxide surface layers.

Vacuum brazing is economical because it is adaptable. If there are a few parts to be joined or if there are hundreds of thousands of parts to join, it is economical to use vacuum brazing, with modern mass-production methods. This adaptability is the reason vacuum brazing is becoming one of the most widely used of metal-joining processes.

Why is vacuum brazing so adaptable? Because it is simple. To braze metal parts these three elements are needed: a braze filler metal to fill the joint, vacuum to prevent oxidation, and a way of getting heat to the parts.

In summary, the following advantages can be attained by designing for vacuum brazing:

- Economical fabrication of complex and multicomponent assemblies
- Simple means for achieving extensive joint area or joint length

- Excellent stress distribution and heat transfer
- Ability to join cast materials to wrought metals
- Ability to join certain nonmetals to metals
- Ability to join dissimilar metals and dissimilar metal thicknesses
- Ability to fabricate large assemblies in stress-free condition
- Ability to preserve metallurgical characteristics of metals being joined
- Capability for precision production tolerance
- Reproducibility and close process control

MATERIALS

The advancements in the field of brazing during the past ten years are impressive. The need to fabricate complex assemblies for service at elevated temperatures along with the need to develop braze filler metals that are compatible with the base metals being used has changed the nature of the brazing process itself. The introduction of vacuum into the brazing process used with many metals, nonmetals, and alloys previously brazed with other protective atmospheres and heating methods has been a part of this change. In fact, it is generally recognized today that brazing has become a sophisticated process.

Because of ever-changing requirements in components and generation of new data and properties, the following sections on materials and applications will cover many of the numerous new metals and alloys as well as the standard ones. Many of the metals can be joined by more than one braze filler metal, depending on the end use (temperature and function), and where applicable this will be noted.

Aluminum and Its Alloys

The advancements in aluminum brazing have been:

- Alloying additions to base metals, brazing sheet cladding, or filler metals which aid wetting, Table 9-2.
- Development of vacuum brazing procedures.

The use of aluminum heat exchangers in automotive applications has been increasing significantly the last few years. Alloying additions and vacuum brazing often are used together although vacuum brazing can also be accomplished without the use of the improved alloys. The cleaning and preparation are critical to all fluxless aluminum brazing operations and especially to the unaided vacuum procedures.

Within the last ten years, vacuum brazing of aluminum alloys has left the laboratory and entered into production plants. One braze filler metal used has been 88% aluminum and 12% silicon (BAlSi-8); however, new aluminum brazing sheets with magnesium alloyed into the aluminum-silicon claddings BAlSi-6, BAlSi-7, and BAlSi-8 have been developed as well as other new braze filler metals.[7]

TABLE 9-2
Best Braze Filler Metal and Parent Metal Combination in Long-Cycle Brazing[7]

Base metal	Braze filler metal	Core alloy	Temperature °F	Temperature °C
Alum. alloy 3003	No. 11 braze sheet (Al-7.5Si) cladding	3003	1150–1160	621–626
Alum. alloy 6061	No. 23 braze sheet (Al-10Si) cladding	6951	1070–1100	577–593
Alum. alloy 3003	No. 21 braze sheet (Al-7.5Si) cladding	6951	1100–1130	593–610
Alum. alloy 6061	No. 21 braze sheet (Al-7.5Si) cladding	6951	1075–1100	579–593
Alum. alloy 3003	X7 braze sheet (Al-9.7Si-1.5Mg) cladding	3003	1080–1120	582–604

These new braze filler metals being developed for vacuum brazing consist of three basic types. One is an aluminum-silicon system, with indium, germanium, or yttrium additions. Another is a binary aluminum-yttrium alloy, with minor additions of germanium or indium. The third is a silver-aluminum combination, with germanium or indium.

All three perform well in vacuum brazing at temperatures below 1112°F (600°C). They all flow on aluminum alloy 6061 in vacuum without the use of flux. The Al-Si-In filler metals exhibit flow temperatures in the range of 1075 to 1095°F (580 to 590°C), and the Al-Si-Y filler metals exhibit flow temperatures in the range 1095 to 1140°F (590 to 616°C). Filler metals in the Al-Si-Ge system are particularly promising and exhibit flow temperatures of 1020 to 1095°F (549 to 590°C). Of particular interest in this system are the 55Al-5Si-40Ge, 45Al-5Si-50Ge, and 35Al-5Si-60Ge filler metals, all of which flow at 1020°F (549°C); these flow temperatures are approximately 50°F (10°C) below those of commercial filler metals. A silver-aluminum-germanium filler metal shows promise in joining 2024 and 7075 aluminum, since it will melt at about 932°F (500°C).[8]

The following aluminum alloys have been vacuum brazed successfully in development laboratories and in production of automotive and aircraft heat exchangers:

1. 6061
2. 1100
3. 3003
4. 2219
5. 7005
6. 6071
7. 6062
8. 6066
9. 6070
10. 356 casting

Brazing has varied from 1070 to 1160°F (577 to 627°C) in furnaces operating in 10^{-5} torr (1.33 mPa) range.

Heat exchangers[9] have been brazed and hydrostatically and pneumatically tested with no leaks found. After artifical aging, tensile strengths of greater than 40 ksi (275 MPa) have been obtained in the cross-sectional areas of the brazed end product.

A complete aluminum radiator can be brazed in one step, whereas copper and bronze radiators conventionally go through separate operations in joining the tube and fin assembly. One auto manufacturer has introduced aluminum radiators as standard equipment on some high-production-model cars.

The new aluminum alloy 7005 is very attractive for vacuum brazing because of the very high strengths possible in joint configurations that normally entrap fluxes. Full and strong fillets were obtained with the 88% aluminum–12% silicon braze filler metal.

For most brazeable aluminum alloys, an overlap distance twice the thickness of the thinnest member is recommended to make the joint as strong as the base metal. This is not true for 7005, however, because of its high base-metal strength after brazing sheets of 0.125-in (3.2-mm) 7005 alloy brazed at lap distances of 0.25 and 0.5 in (6.4 and 12.7 mm) failed through the joints at 35 and 45 ksi (241 and 310 MPa) tensile strength, respectively. Brazed 7005 alloy structures should be designed, when possible, so that direct tension loads are not applied to the joints. One precaution should be observed, that of holding 7005 assemblies at brazing temperature only long enough to ensure complete flow of the braze filler metal because the silicon alloy filler metal penetrates very rapidly.

Beryllium

Beryllium is not considered to be easily brazed since beryllium's chemical activity requires that care be taken to prevent contamination and oxidation of joints. Brazeability is affected by the process as well as the filler metals used. Problems in brazing beryllium increase with increasing temperatures; those not familiar with beryllium should choose a braze filler metal with the lowest brazing temperature and suitable mechanical properties.

Several commercially available braze filler metals, as well as several newly developed braze filler metals, have been used to braze beryllium in vacuum. Vacuum-furnace brazing has been used to join relatively simple shapes. Aluminum, silver, silver-aluminum (28% Al) eutectic, and silver-copper eutectic (28% Cu) have been found to be some of the most suitable braze filler metals for joining beryllium to itself. Vacuum brazing of beryllium with aluminum results in high-tensile-strength joints. The process involves preplacing the aluminum and applying less than 1 psi (6895 Pa) pressure to the joint during brazing. Pure aluminum (Type 1100) and aluminum–12% silicon filler metal are within a few thousand pounds per square inch (pascals) of the beryllium base-metal yield strengths [33 and 40 ksi (228 and 276 MPa)]. Brazing temperature is 1330°F (720°C). Variability in the joint strengths, however, would limit design stress to about 20 ksi (138 MPa).[10] In addition, various investigators have concluded that titanium–6% beryllium, titanium-copper-indium, silver–15 wt% lead–20 wt% copper, silver–5 wt% lead, and copper–18 wt% lead can also be successfully used to vacuum-braze beryllium joints.

Beryllium components should be degreased and pickled in 10% hydrofluoric or nitric-hydrofluoric acid mixtures prior to brazing. Ultrasonic rinsing with deionized water is a further requirement. A precoating of the joint faying surfaces by special vacuum-metallizing techniques or electroplating prior to brazing has been found very effective for subsequent wetting by various braze filler metals. Silver, titanium, copper, aluminum, or BAlSi-4 precoats provide reliability for the difficult-to-wet beryllium material.

The utilization of vacuum evaporation and deposition of titanium vapor was found to be very effective in promoting wetting on beryllium. The titanium evaporation treatment drastically changes the surface of the beryllium and promotes extensive spreading and wetting when pure aluminum filler metal is used. The ultimate strength obtained at room temperature for joints butt-brazed with commercially pure aluminum compares very favorably with that for the beryllium base metal.

Brazing of beryllium is generally carried out on lap joints because they are easiest to make. In beryllium, however, these joints are undesirable because of the inherent notch present in this type of joint. Therefore, joints that contain no notches are required to achieve maximum usefulness of brazed joints for beryllium. Step joints, scarf joints, or butt joints have also been used when possible.

Copper and Its Alloys

A vacuum is a suitable atmosphere for brazing copper and copper alloys when the alloys contain minimal or no amounts of elements (lead, zinc, etc.) having high vapor pressures at brazing temperature. The braze filler metal should also be restricted to those containing few or no elements of high vapor pressure, such as zinc, phosphorus, and cadmium.

Magnesium and Its Alloys

In the past ten years, a very limited amount of work has been performed and reported on the vacuum brazing of magnesium or its alloys. Wettability programs have evaluated a magnesium–zinc–rare-earth alloy (ZE 10) and magnesium-lithium alloy (LA 141A) using AZ 125 as the braze filler metal. The wettability tests included bare base metal as well as silver-plated specimens. The silver-plated specimens exhibited wetting at brazing temperatures of 1080 to 1100°F (582 to 593°C). Considerable work is still necessary before magnesium can be considered brazeable by vacuum techniques.

Steels—Low Alloy, Stainless

Practically every braze filler metal that has been manufactured or recently developed for use above 1600°F (871°C) will wet steel in vacuum. Since the list of steels and alloys is too long, a few examples are briefly discussed. No major problems to date have been encountered in using the high-temperature silver-, gold-, palladium-, copper-, and nickel-chrome-base filler-metal systems in vacuum brazing steels. Depending on the application and temperature environment, one of these braze filler-metal systems has been adequate and suitable for the job requirements.

Experimental containers of 4130 low-alloy steel were brazed with the AMS 4777 braze filler metal (7Cr-3Fe-4.5Si-3B-Rem Ni) at 1925°F (1051°C). The containers showed excellent braze filler-metal flow and filleting, Fig. 9-5, and subsequent testing produced helium-leaktight joints.[11]

Figure 9-6 shows the results of vacuum brazing low-carbon-steel experimental land mines.[11] The same braze filler metal used for the 4130 alloy containers was applied. The interesting points of this development program were:

- Mine assembly contained eight brazed joints
- All joints brazed simultaneously
- Assembled unit held by resistance tack welds and vacuum brazed without benefit of tooling

Vacuum brazing studies have been conducted on a relatively new austenitic stainless steel, 21Cr-6Ni-9Mn-0.3N. The corrosion resistance of this alloy equals or exceeds that of Type 304 stainless steel in most

Fig. 9-5 Type 4130 steel containers vacuum-brazed and heat treated by gas quenching.[11]

Fig. 9-6   Vacuum-brazed mines.[11]

environments. The alloy has proven quite useful at cryogenic temperatures because of its very stable austenite. It was found that the brazing
of high-manganese stainless steel required braze filler metals and
procedures similar to the 300 series stainless steels. The following braze
filler metals appeared most desirable on the basis of maximum wettability and minimum erosion: 57Ag-33Cu-7Sn-3Mn and 65Ag-20Cu-
15Pd.[12]

From the previous study, not all of the braze filler metals used for
brazing stainless steels and other base metals found in high-
temperature applications are nickel-base. The noble-metal-base fillers
have been very successful; for example, the 85Au-15Ni alloy wets the
base metals well and has excellent oxidation resistance. Gold alloys are
expensive, however, so other filler metals are being developed and
evaluated constantly as potential substitutes for 85Au-15Ni and 82Au-
18Ni. The substitute filler metals used in one study are given in Table
9-3.[13]

The results of the study, based on property data and oxidation
resistance, showed that the silver-copper-palladium and the copper-
manganese-cobalt filler metals could be used for service to 800 and
1000°F (427 and 538°C), respectively. The shear strengths of some of
the joints produced are given in Table 9-4.

TABLE 9-3
Noble-Metal Braze Filler Metals for 410 Stainless Steel[13]

Alloy system	Nominal composition, wt%	Liquidus temperature		Braze temperature		Relative cost
		°F	°C	°F	°C	
1	82Au-18Ni	1740	949	1825	996	100%
2	18Au-45Cu-27Ni-10In	1800	982	1850	1010	30%
3	54Ag-25Pd-21Cu	1740	949	1800	982	40%
4	58.5Cu-31.5Mn-10Co	1730	943	1825	996	5%

TABLE 9-4
Elevated-Temperature Tensile Shear Strength of
Vacuum-Brazed 410 Stainless Steel[13]

Braze filler metal	Average tensile shear strength							
	RT* (20°C)		800°F (427°C)		1000°F (538°C)		1200°F (649°C)	
	ksi	MPa	ksi	MPa	ksi	MPa	ksi	MPa
1	63.9	441	40.1	277	31.5	217	21.7	150
2	42.0	290	31.0	214	11.5	79		
3	43.2	298	30.2	208	20.5	141	14.5	100
4	60.2	415	45.9	317	32.0	221	15.1	104

*RT: Room temperature.

Figure 9-7 depicts a Type 321 stainless steel vacuum-brazed flame and disperser manifold assembly which was joined with AMS 4777 braze filler metal at 1925°F (1051°C).[11] No tooling was required to hold the details during brazing and it was found that vacuum brazing of the manifold assemblies was an excellent method for fabricating a helium-leaktight part without evidence of warpage or distortion.

A 54Pd-36Ni-10Cr braze filler metal has produced ductile joints on Type 316 stainless steel after they were exposed to air for 500 h at 1800°F (982°C) plus an additional 90 h at 2000°F (1093°C). A 52.5-Cu-9.5Ni braze filler metal has been successfully used to braze Type 304 stainless steel, and test results are shown in Table 9-5.

There are two main types of heat exchangers currently being used for vehicular gas turbine applications. One is the fixed boundary recuperator, which is often referred to as a conventional direct-transfer heat exchanger. The austenitic stainless steel Type 304L has been used by several manufacturers for this exchanger. The second type is a periodic flow regenerator fabricated from the ferritic stainless steel

Fig. 9-7 Assembly tooling, detail parts, and vacuum-brazed manifold assembly.[11]

TABLE 9-5
Type 304 Stainless Steel Braze Results

Temperature	Nominal diameter of rod tested (butt)	Average (5 joints)		Maximum		Minimum	
		ksi	MPa	ksi	MPa	ksi	MPa
Room temperature	0.25 in (6.4 mm)	73.3	505	85.4	579	58.4	402
800°F (427°C)	0.25 in (6.4 mm)	55.6	383	58.6	403	47.2	325

Type 430. The brazing filler metal used to produce the full scale recuperator shown in Fig. 9-8 was BNi-7 (13Cr-10P-Rem Ni).[14]

Type 321 stainless steel heat-exchanger modules, the tubes and interconnecting fins of which are made by brazing together identical sections of corrugated strip in a stacked-honeycomb arrangement, are used in the oil systems of several large aircraft. This method has been successfully used to braze typical 12-in-cube (305-mm) modules at 2000°F (1093°C). Approximately 2000 joints are brazed on a single module.

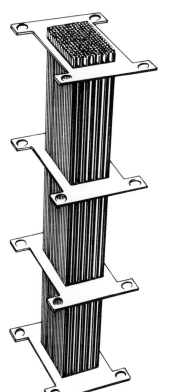

Fig. 9-8 Full-scale vacuum-brazed tubular recuperator.[14]

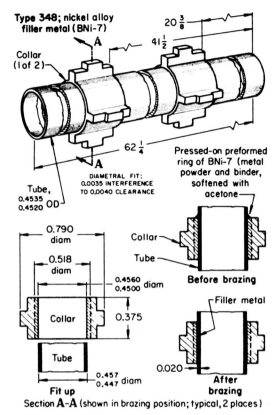

Fig. 9-9 Collar-and-tube assembly vacuum-induction-brazed.[15] (0.001 in = 0.03 mm)

A distinct advantage of induction brazing, as applied to stainless steel, is that it lends itself to simple applications that permit brazing in vacuum. Stainless steel collar-and-tube assemblies, such as that shown in Fig. 9-9,[15] were brazed in a setup that combined induction heating and the protection afforded by heating in vacuum. The twenty-two collar-and-tube components produced each day, with preformed BNi-7 filler-metal rings, were brazed at 1775°F (969°C).

Heat-Resistant Alloys

Heat-resistant alloys refer to those alloys suitable for use under moderate-to-high stresses in the temperature range 1000 to 2000°F (538 to 1093°C). These metals are complex austenitic alloys based on nickel and/or cobalt. They have often been termed superalloys. The term "superalloy" applies to a large family of alloys that show strengths and oxidation resistance at elevated temperatures and are superior to low-alloy steels. The distinct groups of these alloys based on their major or basic alloying ingredient are the following.

Nickel base

This group includes René 41, Hastelloy R-235, Nimonic family, Inconel 700 group, Waspaloy, and others; melting range 2300 to 2650°F (1260 to 1454°C). Two basic braze filler-metal systems will wet most of the alloys with only a few exceptions: precious-metal base and nickel base. A significant amount of new braze filler-metal development work has been conducted in the past ten years. Most of the reported successful results have required some processing gimmick to overcome the inherent characteristics of the available braze filler metals. A review of reported information has shown that the following filler metals are the best available: (1) Ni-Mn-Si-Cu, (2) Au-Ni-Cr, (3) Ni-Cr-Mn-Si, (4) Au-Pd-Ni, (5) Mn-Ni-Co-B, (6) Pd-Ni-Cr-Si, (7) Ni-Cr-Si, (8) Cu-Mn-Co-Ni,[16] (9) Pd-Ni-Cr, and (10) modified Ni-Mn-Si-Cu with Misch metal.

The brazing of age-hardenable nickel-base alloys (René 41, Waspaloy, Hastelloy R-235, Inconel 718) presents a different and a much more complex problem than the brazing of other nickel-base alloys (Monel, Inconel 625 and 600, Hastelloy C). In industry when these age-hardenable alloys must be brazed they are called "problem" alloys. The problem arises because they contain aluminum and/or titanium. In general, the magnitude of the problem varies directly with the sum of the amount of these elements present. The difference between lower and higher levels of aluminum and titanium, however, does not warrant concern because it is best to use the brazing procedure that assures good brazing under the worst possible conditions. The interactions between age-hardenable nickel-base alloys discussed above and braze filler metals listed above occur also with solid-solution-strengthening and nonaging nickel alloys if these aforementioned braze filler metals are used with them.

The age-hardening nickel-base alloys have titanium and aluminum oxides on their surfaces. These oxides cause difficulty because they are easily formed on exposure to air or other oxidizing conditions and cannot be reduced by even very dry pure hydrogen atmospheres. The results of great effort in developing brazing techniques for fabricating high-temperature, high-strength, nickel-base alloys into useful parts have shown that the problem alloys can be satisfactorily brazed by vacuum brazing at pressures of 0.002 torr (0.27 Pa) or lower.

The presence of titanium and/or aluminum in age-hardenable nickel-base alloys is not the only problem encountered when brazing these alloys. The interactions between the base metal and the braze filler metal at or near brazing temperature must also be recognized. The practical aspects of these interactions are manifest most when it becomes necessary to braze assemblies with relatively thin cross sections or when vibrational loading is anticipated. Penetration of elements such as carbon, boron, and sometimes silicon, which reduce the effective thickness of ductile base metal and replace it with nonductile metal compounds, is not tolerable.

Electroplating is one apparent solution, especially since it also aids in overcoming the effects of titanium and aluminum oxides. Recent development work utilizing the addition of rare earths in lieu of boron in filler metal (10) above, has produced the first real breakthrough in brazing nickel-base alloys in thick and thin sections (honeycomb) without any plating.

Another means for minimizing the interaction between the base metal and the braze filler metal involves strict control of the amount of braze filler metal used and of the brazing temperature cycle. The practice of very carefully controlling these two variables is probably the most widely used method for limiting the undesirable interactions.[17]

Most of the high-temperature braze filler metals are powders, which permit the use of another method to control braze filler-metal–base-metal reactions. Pure metal powders, such as nickel, or a powder with the base-metal composition added to the filler metal, inhibits reaction with the base metal. This technique is being utilized extensively today and will be common practice in the future as a means of combining brazing and diffusion welding.[18]

Many investigations have been undertaken to develop braze filler metals that fulfill all other requirements and do not react with the nickel-base alloy. A few of these have been successful,[19] but have not been widely accepted because they are high in expensive noble-metal (gold and palladium) content or do not always have the desired strength and oxidation resistance.

1. René 41 (20Cr-10Ni-15W-2Fe-Rem Co). A Ni-33Cr-24Pd-4Si braze filler metal, as well as the aforementioned rare-earth alloy addition (Ni-6Si-4.3Cu-22Mn-0.079 Misc. metal), has been found to exhibit excellent wetting and flow characteristics on René 41. This filler metal has provided the desired brazing temperature in combination with good wetting and flow on René 41 without excessive erosion or reaction with the base metal. The optimum brazing temperature for vacuum brazing René 41 with the Ni-Cr-Pd-Si is 2150°F (1177°C), while the second filler metal above (rare-earth additive) requires 1975°F (1080°C), and the two braze filler metals have the ability to braze René 41 thickness less than 0.015 in (0.38 mm) without erosion or embrittling effects.[20]

2. Inconel 700 group and other Inconels (Ni-Cr-Re-2Ti-Al). Inconel 718 can be brazed relatively more easily, Table 9-6, than can most nickel-base alloys hardened by the precipitation of aluminum and/or titanium compounds. Nickel-base and silver-base braze filler metals have been very successfully used on Inconel 718.[21] Inconel X has been very successfully brazed with an 82Au-18Ni braze filler metal[22] that has been proven the strongest braze filler metal between room temperature and 800°F (427°C), whereas above 800°F (427°C) a nickel-silicon-boron braze filler metal (AMS 4778) was equal to or better in tensile strength than the gold-nickel braze filler metal. The aforementioned Ni-Cr-Pd-Si braze filler metal has also been successful in joining René 41 and Inconel 718.

TABLE 9-6
Shear Strengths of Lap Joints in Inconel 718 vacuum-brazed
with Gold-Base Braze Filler Metals

Braze filler metal composition	Braze temperature		Test temperature		Failure* location	Failure stress	
	°F	°C	°F	°C		ksi	MPa
Au-22Ni-6Cr	2050	1121	RT†	20	BJ	50.9	351
	2050	1121	1000	538	BJ	31.3	216
Au-18Ni	1900	1038	RT	20	BJ	46.2	319
	1900	1038	1000	538	BJ	32.5	224

*BJ: Brazed joints.
†RT: Room temperature.

Cobalt base

This group includes L-605 and Haynes 188; melting range 2400 to 2570°F (1316 to 1410°C). The cobalt-base alloys are the easiest of the superalloys to braze as most of them do not contain titanium or aluminum. The following braze filler metals are the best available for cobalt-base alloys: (1) Au-Pd-Ni, (2) Ni-Cr-Si, (3) Co-Ni-Cr-Si-W-B, and (4) Pd-Ni-Cr.[23]

Iron base

This family consists of A-286 alloy; melting range 2500 to 2600°F (1371 to 1427°C). The Ni-Cr-Si braze filler metals are best suited for A-286.[23,24]

Other heat-resistant alloys

Dispersion-strengthened nickel and nickel alloys are new, useful materials for high-temperature applications. Submicron-sized thorium oxide or yttrium oxide particles provide inherent metallurgical stability up to 2400°F (1316°C). The desirable properties of nickel, such as high thermal and electrical conductivity and ease of fabrication are preserved while the remarkable strength is due to the dispersed phase. Because of their strength and oxidation resistance at elevated temperatures, these structural materials may be classed as superalloys also. However, the mechanism by which they are strengthened differs from those by which the conventional superalloys are strengthened and the difficulties experienced in brazing these base metals are different also. To obtain the advantages of using these materials, TD-nickel (TD-Ni), TD-nickel-chromium (TD-NiCr), and IN-853 must be joined to themselves and to other high-temperature materials. Because of the nature of the dispersion-hardening mechanism, joining processes that produce melting of the base metal disturb the thoria or yttria dispersion and nullify the strength advantage of these materials.[25,26,27]

TABLE 9-7
Braze Filler Metals Selected for Brazing TD-Ni and TD-NiCr[25,26]

Base metal	Braze filler metal	Braze temperature		Nominal composition
		°F	°C	
TD-Ni	TD-20	2375	1301	Ni-16Cr-25Mo-4Si-5W
	TD-6	2375	1301	Ni-22Cr-17Mo-4Si-5W
	J8600	2150	1177	Ni-33Cr-25Pd-4Si
	Ni-Pd	2275	1246	Ni-60Pd
TD-NiCr	TD-6	2375	1301	Ni-22Cr-17Mo-4Si-5W
	CM50	1950–2050	1066–1121	Ni-3.5Si-1.9B
	NX77	2150–2175	1177–1190	Ni-5Cr-7Si-1B-1W-4Co
	NSB	2350	1288	Ni-2Si-0.8B

New braze filler metals have been developed and evaluated for joining this new family of materials being used in propulsion systems and aerospace vehicle components.[20] Procedures were developed to braze TD-Ni and TD-NiCr foils for high-temperature service using the candidate filler metals shown in Table 9-7.[25,26]

Brazed joints with useful strengths have been made in IN-853 sheet with two commercial nickel-base braze filler metals, Cu-10Ni and 79Co-21Cb. The strongest joints were made with a Ni-Cr-Mo-W-Si and the 79Co-21Cb brazing filler metals. With $4t$ and $6t$ overlaps, tensile strengths at 1900°F (1038°C) corresponded to approximately 80% of the sheet strength. The oxidation resistance of the Ni-Cr-Mo-W-Si braze filler metal is similar to that of the IN-853 sheet.

This discussion of the brazing of heat-resistant alloys may seem unduly pessimistic. It is not intended to be. It must be noted that with due cognizance of the characteristics of all the materials involved, many complex structures have been built that have withstood very severe service conditions. This discussion has shown that the base metal, the braze filler metal, and the procedures for brazing must be selected very carefully. A thorough understanding of the physical metallurgy of the base-metal–braze-filler-metal interactions is necessary. In addition, the effect of brazing thermal cycles on the properties of the superalloy considered must be determined.

Refractory Metals and Their Alloys

The refractory metals family has attracted considerable interest because of their high melting points and excellent high-temperature strength. Alloys of the refractory metals are continually being evaluated with new braze-filler-metal combinations. In selecting new elevated-temperature braze filler metals in the range 2000 to 4000°F (1093 to 2210°C), consideration must not only be given to atmosphere purity and recrystallization behavior of the refractory metals, but also to the effects of the braze filler metal on the base metal. The braze filler metal must not cause severe degradation of the base metal through alloying, formation of brittle constituents, and erosion.

Columbium and Its Alloys

The most successful braze filler metal used to date on D-36 (10Ti-5Zr-Cb) alloy has been B-120VCA (Ti-13V-11Cr-3Al) alloy that flows at 2950°F (1621°C). Analysis of the microstructure of brazed joints shows metallurgical bonding along the braze-filler-metal–base-metal interface and complete alloying of the braze filler metal, especially with honeycomb foils. The joint is very ductile and can be bent double with fracture.[28,29]

As a result of high-remelt-temperature brazing techniques based on diffusion sink and reactive brazing concepts, two new braze filler metals have been developed for D-36 columbium. The diffusion sink technique involves either permitting the braze filler metal to react with the base metal under controlled conditions or adding base metal powder to the braze filler metal powder. One diffusion sink braze filler metal is Ti-33Cr, requiring a brazing temperature of 2650 to 2700°F (1454 to 1482°C).[30] The other alloy is a Ti-30V-4Be reactive braze filler metal that requires a brazing temperature of 2350 to 2400°F (1288 to 1316°C).[31]

Testing of the D-36 and Ti-33Cr braze filler metal was performed at temperatures above 2000°F (1093°C).

Joints that were mechanically tested varied from lap to tee to honeycomb. Test results indicate an increase in lap-shear strength of Ti-33Cr brazed joints from approximately 2.5 ksi (17 MPa) to greater than 4.5 ksi (31 MPa) at 2500°F (1371°C) and from 0 to 1 ksi (7 MPa) at 3000°F (1649°C). Thus a diffusion treatment 300°F (149°C) below the original brazing temperature actually increased the joint remelt temperature by 600°F (316°C), essentially doubled lap shear strength at 2500°F (1371°C), and produced excellent strength at 3000°F (1649°C).

The lap joints reactive brazed with Ti-30V-4Be exhibited substantially lower strength than similar joints diffusion sink brazed with Ti-33Cr, even though remelt temperatures were similar for both systems. Lap-shear strength of Ti-30V-4Be joints was approximately one-half and one-third the strength of Ti-33Cr braze-filler-metal joints at 2500°F (1371°C) and 3000°F (1649°C), respectively. Nevertheless the Ti-30V-4Be braze-filler-metal joints exhibited attractive potential for lower stress level applications.

Other columbium alloys, D-43 (10W-1Zr-0.1C-Cb), Cb-752 (10W-2.5Zr-Cb), and C-129Y (10W-11Hf-0.07Y-Cb), have been successfully brazed with two braze filler metals, B120VCA and Ti-8.5Si [braze temperature 2650°F (1454°C)]. A further demonstration of the variety of braze filler metals is the use of copper- or zirconium-base braze filler metals for brazing Cb-1Zr fins to Cb-1Zr tubes. On the basis of the test results, the Zr-28V-16Ti-0.1Be filler metal was used to braze full-scale heat receivers.[32]

Molybdenum and Its Alloys

There are three basic limits to brazing molybdenum and its alloys for use above 1800°F (982°C). The three metallurgical problems are the following:

1. Recrystallization of molybdenum.
2. Formation of intermetallics between refractory metal and braze filler metals.
3. Relative weakness of braze filler materials at elevated temperatures.

The formation of intermetallics between molybdenum and braze filler metals is harmful because of the brittleness of the intermetallics that may fracture at relatively low loads when the joint is stressed.

The relative weakness of braze filler materials at elevated temperature poses a basic limitation of using brazed molybdenum assemblies. Most of the nickel-base elevated-temperature-service braze filler materials melt in the range 1800 to 2100°F (982 to 1149°C), where the superior elevated-temperature strength of molybdenum begins to manifest itself. Special high-melting-point braze filler metals for molybdenum and its alloys are clearly indicated, provided of course that they do not cause recrystallization or form intermetallics with the metal.

Brazements of the diffusion-sink braze filler metal, Ti-8.5Si, which melts at approximately 2425°F (1330°C), exhibited excellent filleting and wetting with ductile joints and free from cracks.[23] Specimens with molybdenum powder added to the braze filler metal powder were brazed at 2550°F (1399°C).

Because of its excellent high-temperature properties and compatibility with certain environments, molybdenum is a prime candidate for use in isotopic power systems, certain nuclear reactor components, and chemical processing systems. As a result of these extremely stringent criteria (liquid alkali metals effects on braze filler metal) a series of iron-base brazing filler metals have been developed. The best filler metal based on overall performance is Fe-15Mo-5Ge-4C-1B.[33]

A molybdenum alloy, TZM (0.5Ti-0.08Zr-Mo), has also been successfully brazed at 2550°F (1399°C) with molybdenum powder added to the Ti-8.5Si braze filler metal.[23]

Other work in this same area has shown that other braze filler metals can be used. A Ti-25Cr-13Ni braze filler metal [braze temperature 2300°F (1260°C)] has produced the highest remelt temperatures on TZM. Tee and lap joint remelt temperatures were about 3100°F (1710°C).[31]

Other studies[34] were conducted to provide alloys and procedures for making refractory-metal joints possessing good load-carrying properties at 2000°F (1093°C) and with potential for operation at temperatures up to 3500°F (1925°C).

The results of shear tests at 2000°F (1093°C) are presented in Table 9-8. The strengths possessed by these joints are in the range of 20 to 30 ksi (138 to 207 MPa) and are considered excellent.

TABLE 9-8
Shear Strengths* of Ta-V-Cb and Ta-V-Ti
Brazed Joints in Vacuum at 2000°F (1093°C)[35]

Composition, wt%	Brazing temperature		Shear strength†	
	°F	°C	ksi	MPa
25Ta-50V-25Cb	3400	1870	24.4	168
30Ta-40V-30Cb	3500	1925	22.4	154
5Ta-65V-30Cb	3300	1815	24.6	170
30Ta-65V-5Cb	3400	1870	23.4	161
30Ta-65V-5Ti	3350	1845	25.6	177
25Ta-55V-20Ti	3350	1845	18.9	130
20Ta-50V-30Ti	3200	1760	30.2	208
10Ta-40V-50Ti	3200	1760	20.5	141

*Base metal used for all tests was TZM (Mo-0.5Ti-0.08Zr wt%).
†Each data point for shear strength is an average of two tests.

Tantalum and Its Alloys

Because most uses of tantalum and its alloys are for elevated-temperature applications [3000°F (1649°C) and above], investigations[20,36] have examined conventional brazing, reactive, and diffusion-sink brazing concepts. The reactive brazing concept uses a braze filler metal containing a strong melting-temperature depressant. The depressant is selected to react with the base material or powder additions to form a high-melting intermetallic compound during a post-braze diffusion treatment. By removing the depressant in this manner, the joint remelt temperature is increased. Successful application of this concept appears highly dependent on controlling the intermetallic compound reaction to form discrete particles.

Diffusion-sink brazing with titanium and Ti-30V filler metals, whose brazing temperatures are 3050 to 3200°F (1675 to 1760°C), has produced remelt temperatures exceeding 3800°F (2094°C) on tee and lap joints. Diffusion sink brazing with 33Zr-34Ti-33V [braze temperature 2600°F (1427°C)] has produced remelt temperatures exceeding 3200°F (1760°C). The remelt temperatures indicate that maximum service temperature for the titanium and Ti-30V filler metals could be 3500°F (1927°C) and for the 33Zr-34Ti-33V filler metal could be 3000°F (1649°C).

New braze filler metals are continually being developed to meet varying environments. Currently 90 to 95% of the available new braze filler metals are in powder form, which at times is difficult to work with at elevated temperatures. New powder braze filler metals such as Hf-7Mo, Hf-40Ta, and Hf-19Ta-2.5Mo are examples of these braze filler metals that are being developed for tantalum into foil-type braze filler metals, either by direct rolling of the braze filler metal or pack-diffusion heat treatment of hafnium foil.

Lap-shear testing at 3500°F (1927°C) temperature of the Ta-10W alloy using a Cb-1.3B braze filler metal has shown the following results:

Lap shear stress		Base metal tensile stress	
ksi	MPa	ksi	MPa
4.3	30	12.9	90
3.8	26	12.8	88
4.2	29	12.6	87

Tungsten

The brazing of tungsten structures has been done in vacuum very successfully. A wide variety of braze filler metals and pure metals having liquidus temperatures ranging from 1200 to 3500°F (649 to 1927°C) is potentially useful for brazing. Table 9-9 shows the variety of braze filler metals which have been used to braze not only tungsten, but also all the other refractory metals and their alloys.

TABLE 9-9
Braze Filler Metals for Refractory Metals[17]

Brazing filler metal	Liquidus temperature		Brazing filler metal	Liquidus temperature	
	°F	°C		°F	°C
Cb	4380	2416	Mn-Ni-Co	1870	1021
Ta	5425	2997			
Ag	1760	960	Co-Cr-Si-Ni	3450	1899
Cu	1980	1082	Co-Cr-W-Ni	2600	1427
Ni	2650	1454	Mo-Ru	3450	1899
Ti	3300	1816	Mo-B	3450	1899
Pd-Mo	2860	1571	Cu-Mn	1600	871
Pt-Mo	3225	1774	Cb-Ni	2175	1190
Pt-30W	4170	2299			
Pt-50Rh	3720	2049	Pd-Ag-Mo	2400	1306
			Pd-Al	2150	1177
Ag-Cu-Zn-Cd-Mo	1145–1295	619–701	Pd-Ni	2200	1205
Ag-Cu-Zn-Mo	1325–1450	718–788	Pd-Cu	2200	1205
Ag-Cu-Mo	1435	780	Pd-Ag	2400	1306
Ag-Mn	1780	971	Pd-Fe	2400	1306
			Au-Cu	1625	885
Ni-Cr-B	1950	1066	Au-Ni	1740	949
Ni-Cr-Fe-Si-C	1950	1066	Au-Ni-Cr	1900	1038
Ni-Cr-Mo-Mn-Si	2100	1149	Ta-Ti-Zr	3800	2094
Ni-Ti	2350	1288			
Ni-Cr-Mo-Fe-W	2380	1305	Ti-V-Cr-Al	3000	1649
Ni-Cu	2460	1349	Ti-Cr	2700	1481
Ni-Cr-Fe	2600	1427	Ti-Si	2600	1427
Ni-Cr-Si	2050	1121	Ti-Zr-Be†	1830	999
			Zr-Cb-Be†	1920	1049
			Ti-V-Be†	2280	1249
			Ta-V-Cb†	3300–3500	1816–1927
			Ta-V-Ti†	3200–3350	1760–1843

*Not all the filler metals listed are commercially available.
†Depends on the specific composition.

Reactive Metals and their Alloys (Titanium and Zirconium)

Titanium and its alloys have certain chemical and metallurgical characteristics that are important in brazing operations. One characteristic is
that titanium readily alloys with most molten braze filler metals. Because
of this characteristic, molten braze filler metals readily wet and flow on
titanium, but there is a strong tendency for excessive alloying to occur in
the brazed joint. Excessive alloying, which results in undercutting of the
titanium and the formation of brittle intermetallic compounds in the
joints, should be avoided because it lowers joint strength and ductility and
may embrittle the base metals when thin foils and fine wires are being
joined.

Several precautions have been taken to minimize alloying in brazed
joints. One is the development of braze filler metals that alloy only slightly
with titanium. Another is the use of brazing cycles in which the braze filler
metals, although they alloy with titanium, do not form brittle intermetallic
compounds.

Another characteristic is reactivity. Titanium and its alloys are
extremely sensitive to embrittlement by absorption of oxygen, nitrogen,
and hydrogen contamination. The presence of oxygen and nitrogen in
the brazing atmosphere should be avoided to prevent the formation of
brittle-contaminated surfaces on the titanium. The use of a vacuum for
brazing prevents this embrittlement of the titanium surface.

Early vacuum brazing of titanium was accomplished with silver-base
filler metals. Persistent problems were encountered with brittle intermetallic formation and crevice corrosion attack. Development of
aluminum-base fillers and improved joining methods has resulted in new
fabrication technology. Some of these braze filler metals for brazing
titanium alloys include 3003Al, 95Ag-5Al, 90Ag-10Sn, 94Ag-5Al-0.2Mn,
and 56Ag-24Cu-19Ge-1Ti. However, depending on the particular end
use, problems have been encountered with these braze filler metals:

- The formation of continuous TiAg[37] or TiAl intermetallic films
  along the joint interface.
- The tendency for galvanic and/or crevice corrosion in the joint
  interface.
- The tendency for prolonged braze cycles result in gradual
  deterioration of braze fillets because of sweating or flowaway of
  fillet braze materials.

The Ag-Cu-Ge braze filler metal had satisfactory flow at 1100°F (593°C)
temperature, but the mechanical properties of joints made with this
filler metal were poor in comparison with the mechanical properties of
similar joints made with 95Ag-5Al braze alloy that flowed at 1625°F
(885°C).[20,38,39]

The 3003 aluminum has been successfully used as a braze filler
metal to produce complex honeycomb sandwich structures exceeding
50 ft² (4.6 m²). Service temperature limitation for such aerospace hardware is about 500 to 600°F (260 to 316°C). Development and production scale-up programs proved the viability of the brazing system.[40] The

program produced 10,000 h creep-rupture strength of 0.8 and 0.4 ksi (5 and 3 MPa) at 450°F and 600°F (232 and 316°C). Corrosion resistance of the brazed titanium sandwich was shown to be essentially equivalent to 3003 aluminum sheet. No significant galvanic acceleration from the bimetal coupling with titanium was detected.[41] Finally, aircraft service experience up to about 5 years has shown no corrosion penetration of the honeycomb panels.[42] Not only has 3003 aluminum been used as a braze filler metal for honeycomb sandwich construction but also recently has been utilized in a weld-brazing process which combines resistance spot welding and brazing. The two approaches to the process that have been investigated, Figs. 9-10 and 9-11, have proven to be successful joining methods.[44] Typical cross sections of a weld-brazed joint taken from a compression panel are shown in Fig. 9-12. The upper portion of the figure depicts the joint and provides evidence that the faying surface gap is adequately filled by brazing. The braze filler metal which was placed adjacent to the flange of the stiffener is shown to have penetrated completely through the joint to form a generous fillet between the inner surface of the stiffener and the face sheet.

The photomicrograph on the lower portion of Fig. 9-12 provides further verification of adequate braze penetration, at least to the weld nugget. A good metallurgical bond is shown to exist between the braze and all adjoining titanium surfaces, although there is some evidence of

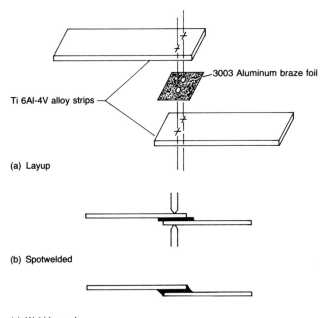

(a) Layup

Ti 6Al-4V alloy strips

3003 Aluminum braze foil

(b) Spotwelded

(c) Weld-brazed

Fig. 9-10 Weld brazing with prepunched foil.[43]

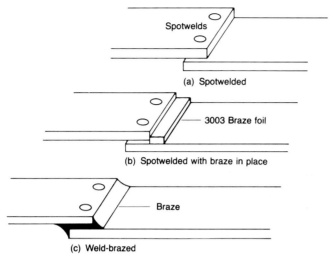

Fig. 9-11 Weld brazing with capillary flow.[43]

the formation of titanium aluminide. However, the formation of the intermetallic to the extent shown was not detrimental to the properties studied.

Other braze filler metals with high service capability and corrosion resistance include Ti-45Zr-8Ni-2Be, Ti-15Ni-15Cu, Ti-48Zr-4Be, and 82Ag-9Pd-9Ga.

A 6Al-4V titanium antiicing airfoil consisting of a wrap-around skin and corrugated core member (50,000 sheet-metal gas-turbine inlet guide vanes) has been successfully vacuum brazed with the Ti-15Cu-15Ni braze filler metal.

For future use in heat exchangers fabricated from titanium, which combines good corrosion resistance with light weight, brazing with the Ag-5Al, Ag-5Al-5Ti, Ti-15Ni-15Cu and Ti-48Zr-4Be braze filler metals has been considered.[45] Results showed that the Ti-48Zr-4Be filler metal had good flow characteristics and produced minimal base-metal erosion of the four filler metals evaluated.

The 82Ag-9Pd-9Ga filler metal was evaluated and tests showed improved metallurgical compatibility with titanium alloys and excellent burst, impulse fatigue, and corrosion resistance.[46]

Recently, investigations relating to brazing of damage-tolerant titanium structures and suitable braze filler metals for titanium operable at 800°F (427°C) were concluded. The first program[47] found that laminates made with a braze filler metal Al-7.5Si clad to a core of 6951 aluminum alloy exhibited the highest shear strength, S-N fatigue strength, and strain to failure in tension of eleven braze filler metals tested, and exhibited good damage-tolerance behavior. The second program[48] found that a newly developed braze filler metal, Ti-27.2Zr-15Ni-7Cu, proved to have excellent resistance to structural damage

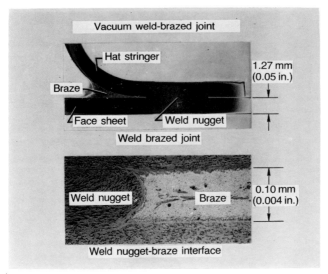

Fig. 9-12 Cross sections of a weld-brazed joint.[44]

from 800°F (427°C) oxidation and salt-corrosion reactions, and had stress-rupture properties similar to those of the parent titanium alloys, Ti-6Al-4V and Beta C (Ti-3Al-8V-6Cr-4Mo-4Zr).

Zirconium

The development of braze filler metals for zirconium has been directed toward those that would produce sound, corrosion-resistant joints in zirconium alloy tubing surrounded by pressurized water at elevated temperatures in nuclear reactors. Joints brazed in vacuum with a 4% beryllium addition to the zirconium alloy composition have shown excellent resistance to corrosion in 680°F (360°C) water. Other promising braze filler metals that have shown good corrosion resistance in 680°F (360°C) water are Ni-7P and Ni-20Pd-3In.

Additional studies to develop improved braze filler metals for brazing Zircaloy-base metals for use in water-cooled reactors were completed recently.[49] The following filler metals had acceptable corrosion resistance and mechanical strength:

1. Zr-50Ag: 2768°F (1520°C) brazing temperature
2. Zr-29Mn: 2516°F (1380°C) brazing temperature
3. Zr-24Sn: 3146°F (1730°C) brazing temperature

The Zr-5Be filler metal has been used extensively to braze zirconium-base metals to themselves and to other metals (e.g., stainless steel).[50] Because of its ability to wet ceramic-surfaces, Zr-5Be has been used to braze zirconium to uranium oxide and beryllium oxide.[51]

Ceramics

Ceramic materials are inherently difficult to wet with conventional braze filler metals. Most of these braze filler metals merely ball up at the joint with little or no wetting occurring. When bonding does occur, it can be mechanical or chemical. The strength of a mechanical bond can be attributed to interlocking particles or penetration into surface pores and voids, whereas the chemical bond derives strength from material transfer between the braze filler metal and the base material.

Another basic problem in brazing ceramics results from the differences in thermal expansion between the base material and the braze filler metal itself and, with ceramic-to-metal joints, between the two base materials to be joined. In addition, ceramics are poor conductors of heat, which means that it takes them longer to reach equilibrium temperature than it does metals. Both of these factors may result in a cracking problem in making such a joint. Since ceramics generally have low tensile and shear strength, crack propagation occurs at relatively low stresses as compared with metals. In addition, the low ductilities permit very little distribution of the stresses set up by stress raisers.

In some brazing processes a ceramic such as alumina, zirconia, beryllia, or forsterite (Mg_2SiO_4) is premetallized to facilitate wetting, and braze filler metals such as copper (BCu-1), silver-copper (BAg-8), gold-copper (BAu-8), and gold-nickel (BAu-4) have been used frequently.

Commercial braze filler metals, which have been used for brazing ceramics, are silver-copper-clad or nickel-clad titanium wires. A considerable amount of filler metal development has been under way and the several experimental braze filler metals shown in Table 9-9 for joining refractory materials are also suitable for brazing ceramics. An experimental assembly, with compartments cut into a ceramic plate of

Fig. 9-13 Demonstration compartmented aluminum oxide assembly, vacuum-brazed with 49Ti-49Cu-2Be braze filler metal at 1796°F (980°C) for 10 min.[51]

alumina, has been brazed with a 49Ti-49Cu-2Be filler metal, Fig. 9-13.[51]

Because of their inertness in many corrosive environments, ceramics are used as seals in fuel cells and other devices that convert chemical, nuclear, or thermionic energy to electricity. Ceramics are also used as friction materials for brakes, clutches, and other energy-absorbing devices; coatings for nuclear-fuel particles; constituents in high-temperature adhesives; and radomes to enclose antennas. One commercial use of a ceramic-to-metal joint is the insulation of electrical leads from another metal. A compilation of work on heat-resistant ceramic-metal joints has recently been completed in Europe.[52]

The usual industrial practice for brazing ceramic materials involves surface pretreatment of the components to be joined by either the molybdenum-manganese process or the titanium hydride process.[53] A recently completed program conducted at a government agency concerns the development of brazing filler metals for use in the 1830 to 3000°F (999 to 1649°C) temperature range by a direct brazing technique which requires that the brazing filler metal wet and flow on the nonmetal without need for base-material pretreatment. Such a treatment has been accomplished through the employment of active metals, e.g., titanium and zirconium, as components of the filler metals. Filler metals from the titanium-vanadium-chromium system have been used to make brazes between refractory metals and alumina and graphite. These brazes are strengthened by the flow of the filler metal into the pores (when present) of the nonmetallic materials. Filler metals from other ternary systems, such as titanium-zirconium-germanium, titanium-zirconium-tantalum, and titanium-zirconium-columbium, also have been developed and satisfactorily used. Dissimilar metal brazes, such as graphite to molybdenum, have been successfully employed at elevated temperatures and in various environments.

Glass-to-metal seals have been made for many years in the vacuum-tube industry, and the experience obtained gives a general insight into the problem of fabricating ceramic-to-metal joints. More recently, the fabrication of refractory-tipped tools has added to available knowledge and techniques. A variety of other applications make important use of ceramic-to-metal or ceramic-to-ceramic seals. The nuclear industry has several applications, including fuel elements, thermocouple attachments, and experimental devices.

Graphite

The joining problems associated with the brazing of graphite are similar to those encountered with the ceramic materials previously mentioned. For low- and intermediate-temperature applications, a titanium-cored silver-copper braze filler metal is suitable for brazing graphite. A new commercially available braze filler metal (48Ti-48Zr-4Be), shown in Fig. 9.14, has been particularly promising for the joining of graphite, for its major constituents are extremely strong

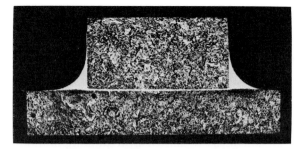

Fig. 9-14 Photomicrograph of graphite-to-graphite tee joint, vacuum-brazed with 48Zr-48Ti-4Be braze filler metal.[54]

carbide formers. Another braze filler metal, shown in Fig. 9-13 (49Ti-49Cu-2Be) also has brazed graphite very successfully.

Braze filler metals in the gold-nickel-molybdenum ternary system have been developed and found satisfactory to braze graphite-to-graphite joints. Filler metals in this system containing low percentages of molybdenum can be used for graphite-to-molybdenum joints, whereas filler metals with greater percentages of this carbide former can be used to braze graphite-to-graphite joints as well.

The 35Au-35Ni-30Mo composition is especially attractive as a general-purpose braze filler metal and can be used to braze both low- and high-porosity grades of graphite. The joints have strengths at least as great as that of the graphite.

Braze filler metals in the gold-nickel-tantalum system (60Au-10Ni-30Ta) have also been developed that have satisfactorily flowed on graphite. Compositions suitable for brazing graphite-to-graphite joints sometimes exhibited fillet cracking, but compositions containing lower percentages (less than approximately 30 wt%) of tantalum have been satisfactory for brazing graphite-to-metal joints.

Commercial braze filler metals which have been utilized to some extent by various investigators include silver-manganese, nickel-chromium-boron, gold-nickel-chromium and nickel-chromium-silicon. Graphite is also readily wet by molybdenum disilicide, titanium, zirconium, and titanium-chromium. The braze filler metals of 54Ti-21V-25Cr, 43Ti-42Zr-15Ge, and 47Ti-48Zr-5Cb have been developed to braze graphite for certain nuclear and aerospace applications.

Composites

Vacuum brazing boron/aluminum composite material, using aluminum-silicon braze filler metals, is more critical than soldering because of the high temperatures involved. Temperatures typically range from 1070 to 1140°F (577 to 616°C). At these temperatures, it is necessary to protect the boron filaments by coating them with a silicon carbide layer that prevents an aluminum/boron filament interaction and subsequent strength degradation.

A complete review of brazing metal-matrix fiber-reinforced composites is contained in numerous reports.[56]

Dissimilar Metal and/or Ceramic Combinations

The problems that arise from the desire to make dissimilar metal joints depends mainly on the difference in composition among the alloys. If they are similar or are metallurgically compatible over a wide composition range, problems will not be great, if good brazing practice is used.

The selection and use of dissimilar metals in structural applications is governed by the service requirements for the structure and the economics of material cost and fabrication. In general, dissimilar metals are used in a structure to provide high-temperature or low-temperature strength; resistance to oxidation, corrosion, or wear; resistance to radiation damage; or other required properties.

Titanium to stainless steel and to copper

A brazed transition section located between a titanium tank and stainless steel feed lines was evaluated during the course of the space program. Titanium alloy Ti-6Al-4V was vacuum-induction-brazed to Type 304L stainless steel with the Au-18Ni braze filler metal, Fig. 9-15. The presence of a brittle intermetallic compound and indication of cracking led to extended joint evaluations. It was concluded that the brazed joint could sustain loads in excess of the yield strength of the stainless steel. The successful performance of this joint has been attributed to the rigid control of all the brazing process variables. The formation of brittle intermetallic compounds was minimized because the joint was brazed rapidly and a minimum holding time at tempera-

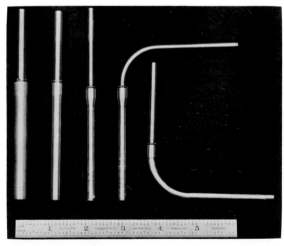

Fig. 9-15 Transition tubes of Ti-6Al-4V joined to Type 304L stainless steel.[57]

ture. The same procedures have been used to make joints between titanium and mild steel, Vascojet-1000, and other metals.

Alloy development studies have also been conducted to produce a braze filler metal for joining tubing that could be used to join titanium to stainless steel for other uses in the space program. The braze filler metal Pd-9.0Ag-4.2Si was developed and brazed the steel and titanium successfully in vacuum at 1360°F (738°C). Excellent flow properties were exhibited by this filler metal. In recent years titanium and its alloys have been successfully brazed to carbon and austenitic stainless steels with the 48Ti-48Zr-4Be filler metal.

Titanium alloy Ti-3Al-1.5Mn has been brazed to Cu-0.8Cr alloy using silver-base braze filler metals. Three braze filler metals were evaluated during this program: (1) Ag-28Cu, (2) Ag-40Cu-35Zn, and (3) Ag-27Cu-5Sn. The joints were brazed in a vacuum at a temperature of 1520°F (827°C) for 5 min. Using these conditions, shear strengths of 28.4 to 38.3 ksi (196 to 264 MPa) were obtained. The heating rate and brazing temperature were critical. For maximum joint strength, the brazing temperature had to be between 1518 and 1526°F (826 and 830°C).

A process for vacuum brazing copper-plated titanium has also been developed. Copper was electroplated on the surface of titanium alloy Ti-3Al-1.5Mn after the surface had been hydrided in a sulfuric acid solution. The hydriding of the titanium surface removed hydrogen or hydrogen compounds, thereby creating an effective surface for the copper plate. Joints were made between the titanium alloy and commercially pure copper as well as between Ti-3Al-1.5Mn and stainless steel or a nickel-base alloy using Ag-27Cu-5Sn braze filler metal. The joints were brazed at 1400 to 1500°F (760 to 816°C) for 15 to 20 min. Under ideal conditions, the average shear strength was 28 ksi (193 MPa).

Beryllium to stainless steel and to titanium

Type 303 stainless steel pressure fittings were joined to a 0.080-in-thick (2.2 mm) sheet of QMV beryllium using pure silver as the braze filler metal.[57] The joint was eutectic-diffusion-brazed at 1690°F (921°C) for 20 to 30 min in a vacuum; a pressure of 0.005 ksi (0.03 MPa) was applied to hold the joint members together. Other researchers found that brazing temperatures and times at temperature must be kept to a minimum to obtain highest joint strengths when only silver braze filler metal is used. Also other studies have reported that beryllium can be brazed to titanium or stainless steel at temperatures as low as 1652°F (900°C).

QMV beryllium was brazed to Type 304L stainless steel to demonstrate the feasibility of joining these metals for nuclear applications. The steel surface was coated with a thin film of the Ag-28Cu braze filler metal by vapor-deposition techniques, and brazing was conducted at 1510°F (821°C). Lap shear strengths ranged from 14.2 to 20.5 ksi (98 to 141 MPa).

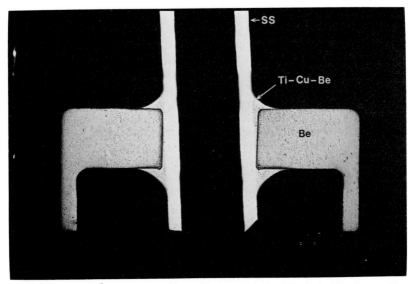

Fig. 9-16 Stainless-steel-to-beryllium joint brazed with 49Ti-49Cu-2Be braze filler metal.[57]

Stainless steel tubes have been successfully brazed to beryllium end caps with 49Ti-49Cu-2Be. Tests have indicated that the braze filler metal readily wets beryllium and that the joints exhibit adequate strength for the application, provided that the brazing time is kept sufficiently short to minimize the formation of intermetallic compounds. Induction brazing in vacuum provided a ready means for performing this operation. A photomicrograph of a typical sound stainless-steel-to-beryllium joint from one of these specimens is shown in Fig. 9-16.

The eutectic diffusion brazing of beryllium and B120VCA titanium alloy has been achieved with pure silver in a vacuum at 1650°F (899°C); these joints had shear strengths of about 20 ksi (138 MPa).

Refractory metals to steel, to copper, and to other refractory metals

A recent application of electron-beam brazing was for a Zircaloy-2 in-pile tube-burst specimen. A stainless steel capillary tube was brazed into a molybdenum adapter with copper, and the adapter was brazed into the Zircaloy-2 specimen with 48Ti-48Zr-4Be. Both brazes were made simultaneously by impinging the defocused beam from a conventional low-voltage electron gun on the molybdenum adapter. In the application described above, visual control of the brazing cycle was used.

Columbium and its alloys have been successfully joined to cobalt-base alloys with the 82Au-18Ni braze filler metal, Type 316 stainless steel to the Cb-1Zr alloy using 21Ni-21Cr-8Si-Rem Co braze filler metal at 2150°F (1177°C) and columbium brazed to alumina using zirconium-nickel as braze filler metal. Researchers[57] have vacuum brazed heat resistant alloys, Hastelloy X, L605, and René 41 and the following refractory metals: (1) B66 and D43 columbium alloys, (2) T111 tantalum alloy, and (3) TZM molybdenum alloy. The braze filler metals were NX-77 (Ni-7Si-5Fe-5Cr-4Co-3W-0.7B-0.1Mn), Hastelloy C (Ni-15.5Cr-16Mo-5Fe-4W-2.5Co-1Mn-1Si), Pd-40Ni, and 82Au-18Ni, Fig. 9-17.

Vacuum brazing was used to join tantalum sheet to OFHC copper plate with the following braze filler metals: (1) Cu-8Sn, (2) Au-18Ni, and (3) Ag-15Mn. Tantalum has also been brazed to molybdenum in vacuum at 3218°F (1770°C) with pure zirconium as the braze filler metal. The gold-nickel and pure copper braze filler metals have also produced excellent tensile test results in brazing Type 304 stainless steel to tantalum and Ta-10W alloy.

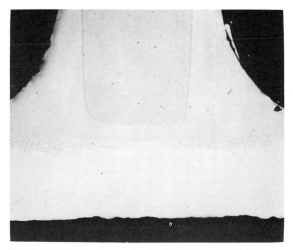

Fig. 9-17 Photomicrograph of columbium and cobalt-base alloy, vacuum-brazed with 82Au-18Ni braze filler metal.

Two binary braze filler metals, V-35Cb and Ti-30V, have been used to join Mo-0.5Ti to molybdenum base metal. Tee joints were brazed in a vacuum for 5 min at temperatures of 3000°F (1649°C) for the Ti-30V braze filler metal and 3400°F (1770°C) for the V-35Cb braze filler metal. The braze filler metals had excellent metallurgical compatibility with the molybdenum base metal, and minimum erosion of the base metal occurred during brazing.

Ceramics and Graphite to Metals

Extensive research has been conducted to join the refractory metals to graphite for aerospace and nuclear applications.[57] A variation of

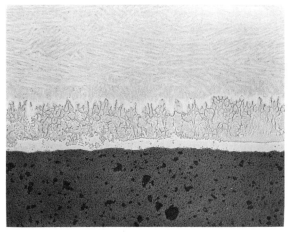

Fig. 9-18 Aluminum-oxide-to-Zircaloy-2 joint, vacuum-brazed with 48Ti-48Zv-4Be braze filler metal at 1922°F (1050°C) for 10 min.

diffusion welding, eutectic diffusion brazing, has been used to join molybdenum, columbium, and tantalum to graphite. A titanium-foil insert, electroplated with 0.0008- to 0.001-in-thick (0.002 to 0.003 mm) layer of copper, was placed between the graphite and the refractory metal. Joining was conducted under the following conditions: (1) temperature, 1634 to 1841°F (890 to 1004°C), (2) pressure, 0.04 to 0.1 ksi (0.3 to 0.7 MPa), and (3) time, 5 to 10 min. Under these conditions, a titanium-copper eutectic alloy was formed and wet the graphite and the refractory metal.

The alloy Cb-1Zr has been brazed to two types of graphite for a space radiation application using the following braze filler metals: (1) Ag-26Cu-8Ti, (2) 48Ti-48Zr-4Be, and (3) Au-10Ni-5Fe. Brazing was done in a vacuum of 10^{-5} torr (1.33 MPa).The braze filler metals were deposited on the metal substrates by plasma arc spraying procedures, and the braze filler metal compositions were adjusted to compensate for the losses of titanium and beryllium during spraying. The 48Ti-48Zr-4Be braze filler metal has also been successfully used to join alumina and Zircaloy 2, Fig. 9-18.

Braze filler metals have been developed to join molybdenum to graphite in association with a program for a nuclear molten-salt reactor. These braze filler metals had to wet graphite and molybdenum readily and be resistant to corrosion by molten fluoride salts. The braze filler metal Au-10Ni-30Ta was most effective in brazing molybdenum-to-graphite and graphite-to-graphite joints at 2370°F (1299°C); however, this braze filler metal had limited ductility and fillet cracking was observed.

Graphite joined to Hastelloy N for seals in a nuclear reactor has been successful using a transition section of tungsten-nickel-iron.[35]

Brazing graphite to AISI 430 steel has produced satisfactory results with nickel-base braze filler metals containing carbide formers.[58] The following filler metals, 70Ni-20Cr-10Si, 70Ni-18Cr-8Si-4Ti, and 65Ni-18Cr-8Si-9Ti, have been used to braze graphite to the ferritic stainless steel substrate at 2102°F (1150°C).

APPLICATIONS

Two areas where vacuum brazing is receiving the auto industry's attention are in the manufacturing of aluminum engine blocks and pistons. Virtually all engines use aluminum pistons. However, higher-strength aluminum alloys, such as the 7005 vacuum-brazed aluminum alloy discussed previously, will be required when engine designs incorporate higher cylinder pressures.

Vacuum-brazing programs that employed the 7005 aluminum alloy were the fabrication of heat exchangers for the environmental control system for the Apollo Lunar Excursion Module (LEM), the gas management assemblies for the Biosatellite, and Earth-orbiting spacecraft designed to study the effects of space flights on animal and plant life.

Several automotive firms are joining a variety of aluminum heat

Fig. 9-19   Vacuum-brazed aluminum air/Freon evaporator.[61]

Fig. 9-20 Beryllium brazed to Monel alloy 400 with 65Ag-20Cu-15Pd braze filler metal in the production of windows for x-ray tubes.[57]

exchangers, particularly the common automotive and aircraft types. Heat exchangers[59,60] and evaporators, Fig. 9-19, with components having base alloys of Types 1100, 3003, 5005, and 6951 have been successfully brazed. The clad brazing sheet has standard compositions shown in Table 9-10. Vacuum brazing of aluminum was utilized during fabrication of cold-plate cores for various manned spacecraft.[62] The cores were made of type 6061 aluminum alloy and the facing skins were made of No. 23 aluminum brazing sheet, which consists of a Type 6951 aluminum core material clad on one side with Type 4045 braze filler metal. The brazing temperature range was 1055 to 1095°F (568 to 590°C), held for 10 min. The brazed joints, which were designed to withstand internal pressures of 1 ksi (7 MPa), have withstood pressures exceeding 2.2 ksi (15 MPa) without failure.

X-ray-tube beryllium window assemblies, Fig. 9-20, have been vacuum-brazed into Monel retainers with silver braze filler metal. All assemblies are vacuum-tight and suitable for use in x-ray tubes.

Other vacuum brazing applications currently either being designed, developed, tested, or used include:

1. Titanium primary structure of honeycomb, seen in Fig. 9-21, and multiwalled sandwich for antennas (aluminum, magnesium, beryllium).
2. Space hulls and interstage adapters (aluminum, magnesium, beryllium).[64]
3. Heat exchangers where increased pressures demand high-strength material and stronger fittings, shown in Fig. 9-22; landing energy absorbers; honeycomb heat shields, Fig. 9-23; leading edges; and other structural brazed components, Fig. 9-24.

The role of vacuum brazing in the joining of heat-resistant super-alloys and stainless steels for jet engines has been very important. Components such as afterburner spray and fuel manifold assemblies, air ducts, air-cooled turbine blades, and stator assemblies with vanes have been joined successfully with the Au-18Ni filler metal.[67] See Figs. 9-25 and 9-26.

TABLE 9-10
Clad Aluminum Sheet for Brazing

Designation	Core	Cladding	Sides clad
X3	3003	X4003	Both
X5	6951	X4003	Both
X7	3003	X4004	Both
X8	3003	X4004	One
X9	3003	X4005	Both
X14	6951	X4004	Both

Others include engine flaps of Waspaloy with Inconel 718 honeycomb, Fig. 9-27, tailpipes of Inconel 718 honeycomb, Fig. 9-28, turbine blades of René 80 for marine engines,[68] and turbine rings with honeycomb seals, Fig. 9-29.[66]

Open-face honeycomb sandwiches can be brazed for high-temperature corrosion-resistant applications, and the development of these efficient air-seal structures has made major contributions to the evolution of large, lightweight turbojet and turbofan engines. Over $200 million in labyrinth and blade-tip types of brazed honeycomb seals have been manufactured. See Fig. 9-30. The unique attribute of such honeycomb shrouds is that the core structure provides an effective air seal and will tolerate actual interference or "rub" between rotating and stationary components without damaging the turbine/compressor rotors.

Vacuum-brazed nickel and cobalt-base alloys are currently used in commercial and military jet aircraft as deflector vanes and doors. The deflector vanes direct jet engine exhaust gases for thrust-reverser

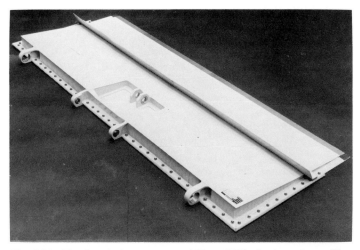

Fig. 9-21 Titanium facings, core, and Type 3003 aluminum braze filler metal in completed flight spoiler.[63]

Fig. 9-22 Six-thousand Type 430 stainless steel 0.004-in (0.1-mm) tubes simultaneously vacuum brazed into header of gas turbine recuperator.[65]

braking and perform the same function as reverser braking. The vanes perform the same function as reverse-pitch propellers on piston-engine planes; that is, they reduce landing speed and hence permit jet aircraft to land on shorter runways. See Fig. 9-31.

Vacuum-brazing techniques are being employed in the fabrication of a Type 304 stainless steel nozzle with 16 tubes for high-speed beverage can filling equipment. A 15Cr-3.5B-Rem Ni braze filler metal combined with a vacuum-brazing cycle of 2075°F (1135°C) has produced excellent results. Diaphragm assemblies, Fig. 9-32, for low-pressure, vacuum, and altitude-indicating instruments, of Ni-Span-C902 (nickel spring alloy) are vacuum-brazed in production at 1320°F (716°C) with BAg-7 (56Ag-22Cu-17Zn-5Sn) braze filler metal while vacuum brazing has

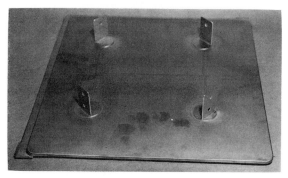

Fig. 9-23 TZM molybdenum heat shield.

Fig. 9-24 Completed titanium vacuum-brazed engine support beam test component.[66]

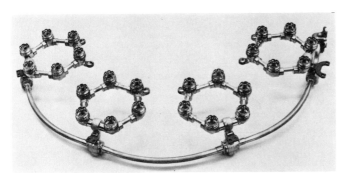

Fig. 9-25 Stainless-steel-to-Hastelloy fuel manifold assembly with vacuum-brazed fittings.[67]

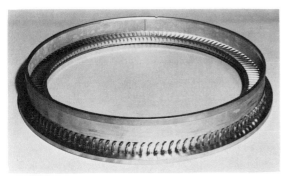

Fig. 9-26 Nickel-alloy compressor stator assembly with vacuum-brazed vanes and feltmetal air seal.[67]

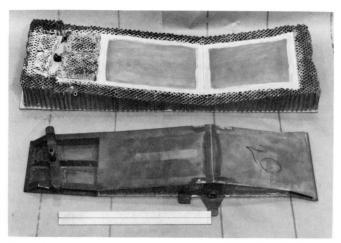

Fig. 9-27 Brazed Waspaloy honeycomb assembly with 71Ni-20Co-4.5Si-3.5B-.03C braze filler metal.

Fig. 9-28 Tailpipe of Inconel 718 for jet cargo aircraft.

Fig. 9-29 Nickel-alloy turbine ring with vacuum-brazed honeycomb air seal.[67]

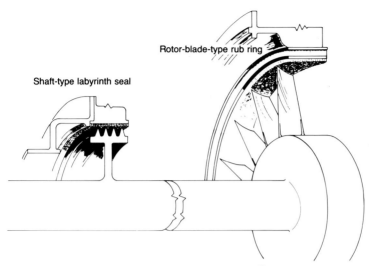

Fig. 9-30   Honeycomb seals for gas turbine engines.[17]

now been applied to the successful joining of two dissimilar cast irons for cylinders and blocks for automotive engines. The BNi-2 filler metal (6Cr-4Si-3.5B-3Fe-82Ni) is used at a braze temperature of 1868°F (1020°C).[70]

Among new applications are stainless steel bellows, gas actuators,[71] heater assemblies, cooler units, and preheaters for a new diesel engine (Stirling).[72] A production brazing plant has adapted vacuum furnace

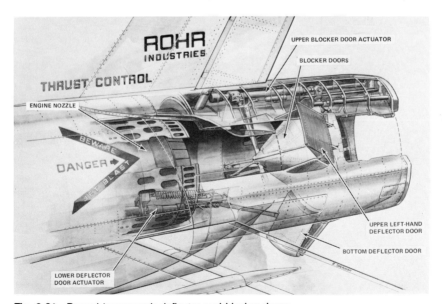

Fig. 9-31   Brazed honeycomb deflector and blocker doors.

Fig. 9-32 Arranging components of diaphragm assembly with brazing-filler-metal preforms prior to vacuum brazing.[69]

brazing to fabricate vacuum manifold components that are leaktight to the most exacting standards, while another plant has produced hydraulic manifolds, Fig. 9-33, for a missile system.

A unique application of vacuum brazing is for coatings. The environment in which the nozzle guide vanes of an aircraft gas turbine operate must surely be among the most hostile conditions imaginable. They operate at temperatures only marginally below their melting point, and are subject to a high-velocity gas stream containing sulfur-bearing combustion products and in some instances solid particles. The vanes must withstand thermal cycling and uneven heating, both combining to produce thermal fatigue cracking of the airfoil sections.

Fig. 9-33 Vacuum-brazed hydraulic manifold system and fixture.

In addition to the common oxidation mechanism, however, another phenomena called hot corrosion is recognized as being caused by the action of molten sodium sulfate on the vane surface. The use of a vacuum braze coating as an integral part of a crack repair scheme has proved to be a worthwhile technique. A 70Ni-20Cr-10Si filler metal has proved to be beneficial to nickel and cobalt-base alloys as a coating to protect vanes from surface erosion and oxidation.[73]

Molybdenum, tungsten, and tantalum are extensively used in construction of electron tubes and other vacuum devices, and are often brazed to each other or to other metals, Fig. 9-34.[19] Tungsten and molybdenum are readily brazed with pure platinum and palladium-gold-nickel braze filler metals. The choice between these available braze filler metals is generally determined by the operating temperature of parts to be brazed. Thus, tungsten electron-tube support rods can be brazed with either pure platinum or a Pt-4W braze filler metal. Molybdenum vacuum-tube "plate" structures are also commonly brazed with these braze filler metals. The tungsten contacts of vacuum switches have been brazed to copper conductors with the 82Au-18Ni braze filler metals, and tantalum is readily wet by copper-gold, gold-nickel, palladium-nickel, and palladium-gold-nickel braze filler metals.

Vacuum brazing has been most helpful in the extensive use of refractory metals. Since various gases (nitrogen, hydrogen, and oxygen) can create problems of brittleness and surface contamination, the use of vacuum has substantially aided in the use and manufacturing development of refractory metal alloy structures. These include:

- Honeycomb heat shields
- Thermionic converters composed of various refractory metals, and ion and magnetohydrodynamic propulsion devices

From these examples, it is evident that refractory metals and vacuum brazing have become inseparable. Future maneuverable reentry vehi-

Fig. 9-34 Thermionic valve for generating microwaves. The assembly involves a large number of sequential brazing operations, starting with pure platinum, gold-copper, gold-silver and gold-copper-silver braze filler metals. The last joint is made with a tin-lead solder.[19,74]

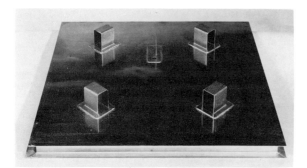

Fig. 9-35 Columbium alloy Cb752 vacuum-brazed with titanium-alloy braze filler metal at 3100°F (1710°C).

cles, Fig. 9-35, uncooled rocket engines, nose cones, and thrust deflectors will require the use of refractory metals and their subsequent joining by vacuum brazing.

The nuclear industry has employed vacuum brazing as a means of sealing graphite-clad fuel elements and for fabricating a variety of experimental assemblies.

An example of one of these assemblies was an electromagnetic pump that carries liquid sodium for a fast breeder reactor. This required vacuum brazing copper rods to Type 304 stainless steel tubes with BAu-3 (62Cu-35Au-3Ni) filler metal at 1925°F (1052°C). The choice of braze filler metal was to solidify the rod-to-tube assemblies. The gold imparted the reliability demanded in nuclear components.

The increasing use of ceramics in industrial and development applications results from their good insulating and ultra-high-temperature properties. In Fig. 9-36 is a ceramic-metal seal brazed at 3000°F (1649°C) that has operated for 1000 h at 2000°F (1093°C). The ceramic is Al_2O_3, the metal is columbium, and the braze filler metal is titanium.

Fig. 9-36 Ceramic-to-metal seal.

Almost nothing makes a good, all-around furnace atmosphere. Thus, understandably, vacuum brazing is no longer a novelty. The initial operating costs of furnaces have been substantially reduced and production rates have been increased, thereby contributing to the economical production joining of parts by vacuum brazing.

The future of fabrication by vacuum furnace or induction brazing is secure because of its many advantages. However, the brazing equipment and accessories must be improved and adapted to fully realize the potentials of the process. There is a need for larger furnaces, more sensitive temperature control, especially above 3000°F (1649°C), and more rapid heating capacities.

REFERENCES

1. Hawkins, W. D., "Physical Chemistry of Surface Films," Reinhold, New York, pp. 1–413, 1952.
2. Gilliland, R. G., "Wetting of Beryllium by Various Pure Metals and Alloys," *Weld. J.*, **43**(6), 248s–258s, June 1964.
3. Milner, D. R., "A Survey of the Scientific Principles Related to Wetting and Spreading," *Br. Weld. J.*, 5, 90–105, 1958.
4. Kohl, W. H., "Soldering and Brazing," *Vacuum*, 14, 175–198, 1964.
5. Singleton, O. R., "A Look at the Brazing of Aluminum—Particularly Fluxless Brazing," *Weld. J.*, **49**(11), 843–849, November 1970.
6. Terrill, J. R., Cochran, C. N., Stokes, J. J., and Haupin, W. E., "Understanding the Mechanisms of Aluminum Brazing," *Weld. J.*, **50**(12), 833–839, December 1971.
7. Gempler, E. B., "Parameters Evaluated in Long Cycle Aluminum Vacuum Brazing," *Weld. J.*, **55**(10), 293s–301s, October 1976.
8. Werner, W. J., Slaughter, G. M., and Gurtner, F. B., "Development of Filler Metals and Procedures for Vacuum Brazing of Aluminum," *Weld. J.*, **51**(2), 64s–70s, February 1972.
9. Brynes, Jr., E. R., "Vacuum Fluxless Brazing of Aluminum," *Weld. J.*, **50**(10), 712–716, October 1971.
10. Juntz, R. J., King, W. G., Tardiff, Jr., G., and Westlund, E. F., "Exploratory Study of a Fluxless Aluminum Brazing Process for Beryllium," *Weld. J.*, **52**(4), 187s–192s, April 1973.
11. Burrows, C. F., "Vacuum Brazing Gas-Quenching Process for the Manufacturing of Metal Materials, Components and Hardware," Dept. of the Army, Contr. DAAA15-68-C-0659, Final Report, February 1970.
12. Bennett, W. S., Hillyer, R. F., Keller, D. L., and Riefenberg, D. H., "Vacuum Brazing Studies on High Manganese Stainless Steel," *Weld. J.*, **53**(11), 510s–516s, November 1974.
13. Schaefer, R. P., et al., "Brazing Filler Metal Evaluation for an Aircraft Gas Turbine Engine Application," *Weld. J.*, **50**(9), 394s–400s, September 1971.
14. Amato, I., Cappelli, P. G., and Fenoglio, G., "Brazing of Stainless Steel Heat Exchangers for Gas Turbine Applications," *Weld. J.*, **54**(10), 338s–343s, October 1975.
15. "Metals Handbook," vol. 6, "Welding and Brazing," 8th ed., American Society of Metals, Metals Park, Ohio, pp. 602–682, 1971.
16. "Cu-Mn-Co Braze Alloy Beats Precious Metals," *Matls. Engr.*, p. 20, January 1976.
17. "Brazing Manual," 3rd ed., revised, American Welding Society, Miami, 1976.
18. Doherty, P. E., and Harraden, O. R., Materials Development Corp., private communication, May 1977.
19. Sloboda, M. H., "Industrial Gold Brazing Alloys," *Gold Bull.*, **4**(1), 2–8, January 1971.
20. Pattee, H. E., "High-Temperature Brazing," WRC Interpretive Bull. 187, September 1973.
21. Blair, W., "Procedure Development for Brazing Inconel 718 Honeycomb Sandwich Structures," *Weld. J.*, **52**(10), 433s–440s, October 1973.

22. Colbus, J., and Zimmermann, K. F., "Properties of Gold-Nickel Alloy Brazed Joints in High Temperature Materials," *Gold Bull.*, 7(2), 42–49, April 1974.
23. Schwartz, M. M., "Brazed Honeycomb Structures," WRC Interpretive Bull. 182, April 1973.
24. Schwartz, M. M., "Modern Metal Joining Techniques," Wiley, New York, 1969.
25. Brentnall, W. D., Stetson, A. R., and Metcalfe, A. G., "Joining of Superalloy Foils for Hypersonic Vehicles," Technical Rep. AFML TR-68-299, Contr. F33(615)-67-C-1211, October 1968.
26. Uhland, G. E., Rupert, E. J., and Maccalous, J. W., Martin-Marietta-Denver, private communication, May 1973.
27. Kenyon, N., and Hrubec, R. J., "Brazing of a Dispersion Strengthened Nickel Base Alloy Made by Mechanical Alloying," *Weld. J.*, 53(4), 145s–151s, April 1974.
28. McCown, J., Wilks, C., Schwartz, M. M., and Norton, A., "Final Report on Development of Manufacturing Methods and Processes for Fabricating Refractory Metal Components," ASD Proj. 7-937, AF33(657)–7276, September 1963.
29. Schwartz, M. M., "Brazing of Sandwich Structures of Columbium Alloys," *Weld. J.*, 40(4), 377–382, 1961.
30. Freedman, A. H., and Mikus, E. B., "Brazing of Columbium D-36 Honeycomb Structures," *Weld. J.*, 43(9), 385s–392s, November 1964.
31. Freedman, A. H., and Mikus, E. B., "High Remelt Temperature Brazing of Columbium Honeycomb Structures," *Weld. J.*, 45(6), 258s–265s, June 1966.
32. Smeltzer, C. E., and Compton, W. A., "A Brazing Process for Cb-1Zr Heat Receiver Tubes," Rep. NASA CR-95481, Solar Division, International Harvester Company, San Diego, CA, Contr. NAS 3-10603.
33. Cole, N. C., Gunkel, R. W., and Koger, J. W., "Development of Corrosion Resistant Filler Metals for Brazing Molybdenum," *Weld. J.*, 52(10), 466s–473s, October 1973.
34. Gilliland, R. G., and Slaughter, G. M., "The Development of Brazing Filler Metals for High Temperature Service," *Weld. J.*, 48(10), 463s–468s, October 1969.
35. Slaughter, G. M., Werner, W. J., Gilliland, R. G., and Hammond, J. P., "Recent Advances in Brazing," *5th Nat. SAMPE Technical Conf.*, vol. 5, pp. 115–123, Oct. 9–11, 1973, Kiamesha Lake, New York.
36. Stone, L. H., Freedman, A. H., and Mikus, E. B., "Brazing Alloys and Techniques for Tantalum Honeycomb Structures," *Weld. J.*, 46(8), 343s–350s, August 1967.
37. Tucker, M. S. and Wilson, K. R., "Attack of Ti-6Al-4V by Silver Base Brazing Alloys," *Weld. J.*, 48(12), 521s–527s, December 1969.
38. Key, R. E., Burnett, L. I., and Inouye, S., "Titanium Structural Brazing," *Weld. J.*, 53(10), 426s–431s, October 1974.
39. McHenry, H. I., and Key, R. E., "Brazed Titanium Fail-Safe Structures," *Weld. J.*, 53(10), 432s–439s, October 1974.
40. Kramer, B. E., "Brazed Titanium Honeycomb Core Sandwich," B. E. Kramer, *3d Air Force Metalworking Conf.*, WESTEC '72, March 14, 1972.
41. Elrod, S. D., Lovell, D. T., and Davis, R. A., "Aluminum Brazed Titanium Honeycomb Sandwich System," *Weld. J.*, 52(10), 425s–432s, October 1973.
42. Lovell, D. T., and Lindh, D. V., "Titanium Structures Technical Summary," DOT/SST Ph. I and Ph. II, Rep. FAA-SS-73-27, October 1974.
43. Bales, T., Royster, D. M., and Arnold, Jr., W. E., "Weld-Brazing—A New Joining Process," *NASA-LRC Symp.*, Williamsburg, Va., May 30–June 1, 1972.
44. Bales, T., et al., "Weld-Brazing of Titanium," *5th Nat. SAMPE Tech. Conf.*, vol. 5, pp. 481–500, Oct. 9–11, 1973, Kiamesha Lake, New York.
45. Howden, D. G., and Monroe, R. W., "Suitable Alloys for Brazing Titanium Heat Exchangers," *Weld. J.*, 51(1), 31–36, January 1972.
46. Gamer, N., and Richardson, J., "Investigation of Ductile Brazing Alloy Compositions for Use in Joining Titanium and Its Alloys," Wesgo Tech. Rep. 1492, pp. 1–32, April 1971.
47. Wells, R. R., "Low Temperature Large-Area Brazing of Damage Tolerant Titanium Structures," *Weld. J.*, 54(10), 348s–356s, October 1975, and Tech. Rep. AFML-TR-75-50, Contr. F-33615-73-C-5161, May 1975.
48. Smeltzer, C. E., and Hammer, A. N., "Titanium Braze System for High Temperature Applications," AFML-TR-76-145, Contr. F33615-74-C-5118, August 1976.

49. Beal, R. E., and Saperstein, Z. P., "Development of Brazing Filler Metals for Zircaloy," *Weld. J.*, **50**(7), 275s–291s, 1971.
50. Amato, I., and Ravizza, M., "Some Developments in Zircaloy Brazing Technology," *Energ. Nucl. (Milan)*, **16**(2), 35–39, 1969.
51. Fox, C. W., and Slaughter, G. M., "Brazing of Ceramics," *Weld. J.*, **43**(7), 591–597, 1964.
52. Grunling, H. W., "High-Temperature-Resistant Ceramic-Metal Joints," *Schweissen + Schneiden*, February 1973, and *Weld. Res. Abroad*, **20**(7), 45–57, August–September 1974.
53. Canonico, D. A., et al., "Direct Brazing of Ceramics, Graphite, and Refractory Metals," Rep. ORNL TM-5195, Oak Ridge National Laboratory, Oak Ridge, TN, Contr. W-7405-eng-26, March 1976.
54. Donnelly, R. G., and Slaughter, G. M., "The Brazing of Graphite," *Weld. J.*, **41**(5), 461–469, May 1962.
55. Robertson, A. R., Miller, M. F., and Maikish, C. R., "Soldering and Brazing of Advanced Metal-Matrix Structures," *Weld. J.*, **52**(10), 446s–453s, October 1973.
56. Metzger, G. E., "Joining of Metal-Matrix Fiber-Reinforced Composite," WRC Interpretive Bull. 207, July 1975.
57. Schwartz, M. M., "The Fabrication of Dissimilar Metal Joints Containing Reactive and Refractory Metals," WRC Interpretive Bull. 210, October 1975.
58. Amato, I., Cappelli, P., and Martinengo, P., "Brazing of Special Grade Graphite to Metallic Substrates," Fiat-DCR Laboratori Centrali, SMT-25, Orbassano, Italy, February 1974.
59. "Joining Processes for Aluminum Reduce Pollution, Cut Costs," *Mater. Eng.*, pp. 60–63, March 1973.
60. Patrick, E. P., "Successful Vacuum Brazing of Aluminum," *Weld. J.*, **54**(3), 159–163, March 1975.
61. Warner, J., Alcoa, private communication, April 1978.
62. Beuyukian, C. S., "Fluxless Brazing of Apollo Coldplate—Development and Production," *Weld. J.*, **47**(9), 710–719, September 1968.
63. Taylor, R. Q., Elrod, S. D., and Lovell, D. T., "Development and Evaluation of the Aluminum-Brazed Titanium System," vol. III, Rep. FAA-SS-73-5-3, D6-60277-3, May 1974.
64. Cremer, G. D., Grant, L. A., and Kamper, L. F., "Structural Beryllium Sheet for Spacecraft Use," *AIAA/ASME/SAE 13th Structures, Structural Dynamics, and Matls. Conf.*, San Antonio, TX, AIAA Paper 72-404, April 1972.
65. Troy, W., "Brazed Recuperator-Feasibility Study," Internal Reps. 2-071 and 6-037, Rohr Industries, February 1973.
66. Hurwitz, D., "Manufacturing Methods for Brazed Titanium Hybrid Structures," AFML-TR-76-119, Contr. F33615-74-C-5047, Final Report, June 1976.
67. Schwartz, M., "Applications for Gold-Base Brazing Alloys," *Gold Bull.*, **8**(4), October 1975.
68. "Nickel Alloy Foils Inflated Gold Prices," *Weld. J.*, **55**(4), 280–282, April 1976.
69. Englehard Industries, private communication, May 1978.
70. Bell, T., Green, A., and Constable, D., "Vacuum Brazing of Cast Iron Cylinders into Engine Blocks," *Weld. Met. Fabr.*, pp. 289–293, May 1976.
71. Barfield, C. J., "Vacuum Brazed Stainless Steel Hot Gas Actuators for Aerospace Components," *Weld. J.*, **49**(7), 559–564, July 1970.
72. Neelen, G. T. M., "Vacuum Brazing of Complex Heat Exchangers for the Stirling Engine," *Weld. J.*, **49**(5), 381–386, May 1970.
73. Malcolm, L. J., "Developments in Vacuum Braze Coating of Aero-Engine Nozzle Guide Vanes," *Weld. J.*, **51**(7), 483–488, July 1972.
74. English Electric Value Co. Ltd., private communication, April 1978.
75. Okamoto, I., Takemoto, T., and Den, K., "Vacuum Brazing of Aluminum Using Al-12% Si System Filler Alloy," *Transactions of JWRI*, **5**(2), 127–130, December 1976.
76. Christensen, J., and Rørbo, K., "Nickel Brazing Below 1025°C of Untreated Inconel 718," *Weld. J.*, **53**(10), 460s–464s, October 1974.

77. Steffens, H. D., and Lange, H., "Properties of High Temperature Brazed NiCr20Ti-Al PdNi40 Joints," *Weld. J.*, **53**(10), 476s–479s, October 1974.

78. "Solving an Al/Ti Brazing Problem," *Weld. J.*, **53**(10), 638, October 1974.

79. Baker, C. J., "The Application of Vacuum Brazing as a Repair Technique for Aero-Engine Components," *Weld. J.*, **50**(8), 559–566, August 1971.

80. Amato, I., Baudrocco, F., and Cappelli, P., "Wettability and Diffusion of Cermets Brazed to Stainless Steel for High-Temperature Resistant Coatings," Fiat Res. and Dev. Center, Turin, Italy, 1973.

81. "Fluxless Brazing goes High Production," *Iron Age*, pp. 56–57, Apr. 27, 1972.

82. Dumez, B., "Study of Vacuum Furnace Atmospheres for Brazing Titanium Honeycomb Panels," *Weld. J.*, **51**(7), 346s–348s, July 1972.

83. Barfield, C. J., "Vacuum Brazing in the Fabrication of Guided Missiles," *Lastechniek*, **35**(1), 6–10, January 1969.

84. "Gold Brazing in the Space Shuttle Engines," *Gold Bull.*, **8**(3), 79, July 1975.

85. Lovell, D. T., and Elrod, S. D., "Development and Evaluation of the Aluminum-Brazed Titanium System," vol. 1, Program Summary, Final Rep. FAA-SS-73-5-1, May 1974.

86. Ruza, V., "Vacuum Brazing of High Strength Steel," *Met. Constr. Br. Weld. J.*, January 1976, and *Welding Res. Abroad*, **23**(3), 57–59, March 1977.

87. "Precious Metals Boost Brazing Uses," *Weld. Eng.*, pp. 38–41, January 1970.

88. Schwartz, M., Gurtner, F. G., and Shutt, P. K., Jr., "Vacuum Brazing–Gas Quenching of 6061 Aluminum Alloy," Edgewood Arsenal Tech. Rep. EATR4085, March 1967.

89. Burrows, C. F., and O'Keefe, R., "Evaluation of Braze Alloys for Vacuum Treating–Gas Quenching," *Weld. J.*, **51**(2), 53s–63s, February 1972.

90. McCall, J. L., "Metallography of Vacuum Brazed and Vacuum Heat Treated and Gas Quenched Materials," *Weld. J.*, **51**(2), 71s–80s, February 1972.

91. Metzger, G. E., "Diffusion of Aluminum Alloys," Final Rep. AFML-TR-75-210, April 1976.

92. "High Temperature Brazing Demands Careful Selection of Filler Metals," *Mater. Eng.*, pp. 52–54, September 1975.

93. Gilliland, R. G., and Adams, C. M., Jr., "Improved Brazing Methods for Tungsten Carbide Tool Bits," *Weld. J.*, **50**(7), 267s–274s, July 1971.

94. Semeniuk, A., and Brady, G. R., "Properties of TZM and Nuclear Behavior of TZM Brazements," *Weld. J.*, **53**(10), October 1974.

95. "Furnace Brazing with Nickel Base Filler Metal Improves Beverage Can Filling Nozzles," *Weld. J.*, **55**(10), 860–861, October 1976.

96. "Brazing for Titanium Bicycle Frames," *Weld. J.*, **55**(10), 868, October 1976.

97. Fairbanks, N. P., "High Temperature Braze for Superalloys," AFML-TR-76, 155, Contr. F33615-75-C-5094, September 1976.

98. Canonico, D. A., Cole, N. C., and Slaughter, G., "Direct Brazing of Ceramics, Graphite and Refractory Metals," *Weld. J.*, **56**(8), 31–38, August 1977.

10

DIFFUSION WELDING

Diffusion welding (DFW) to date has found most of its application in the atomic energy and aerospace industries. To meet the stringent requirements of applications in these industries, it was not only necessary to develop new materials but, equally as important, it was also necessary to develop methods to fabricate them into useful engineering components. Diffusion welding is one such fabrication technique developed to keep pace with the requirements of the advancing technology. DFW is a process which carries many names because it can be applied in a large variety of ways. The essential details of the procedures and the metallurgical aspects are the same for all forms of the process.

DFW per se is not a completely new joining technique. Forge-welding processes have been used to join both wrought iron and low-carbon steels for many years. In fact, forge welding is one of the oldest joining methods known and was the only process in common use before the nineteenth century. It is interesting to note that the famous "Damascus blade" of medieval times was made by forge welding, and the technique has been even traced back in one form to at least 1500 B.C. in the Euphrates Valley.[1]

THEORY AND PRINCIPLES OF PROCESS

The formation of a diffusion weld can best be studied by separating it into three separate stages. The first stage involves the initial contact of the interfaces. This includes whatever deformation of surface asperities (microscopic roughness) and films is needed to establish some degree of initial mechanical contact. Second, there is a time-dependent deformation of the same interfaces which further establishes intimate interfacial contact. Finally, there is a diffusion-controlled elimination of the original interface. This final step may occur as the result of grain growth across this interface, the solution or dispersion of interfacial contaminant, or by simple diffusion of atoms along or across the original interface.

The initial interfacial accommodation occurs by the plastic flow of the surface asperities and by the simultaneous rupturing or displacement of surface films. Surface films, if present, may be oxides, organic deposits, or gaseous or aqueous films. This initial deformation is caused by the compressive load applied to the interfaces to be joined. It occurs essentially instantaneously at the welding temperature of the joint or at ambient temperature if the parts are assembled before heating.

In DFW, the first two stages serve to set up the third stage, the elimination of the original interface. This is essentially controlled by diffusional processes in its entirety. The influence of diffusional processes is felt in numerous ways which tend to overlap with the second stages of the welding process. The creep which dominates the second stage is largely a diffusion-activated process. All proposed mechanisms of eliminating the original interface are diffusion-controlled. Four possible mechanisms have been proposed to be involved in this final stage:

1. Atom transport occurs across the original interface and in doing so creates bonds between the parts.[2] This occurs by volume diffusion.
2. Recrystallization and/or grain growth occurs at the interface, resulting in the formation of a new grain structure which sweeps across the original boundary. It has also been suggested that during recrystallization, the yield strength of a metal is essentially zero. Thus total accommodation of the interface by deformation can occur with little or no applied pressure.[3] This brings surface atoms into sufficiently close proximity to permit metallic bonding at the interface.
3. Surface diffusion and sintering action cause the interfaces to grow together rapidly.[4]
4. Surface films and oxides are dissolved by the base metal and in doing so eliminate these barriers which resist the formation of normal metallic bonds. In the absence of interfering films, these bonds can form spontaneously.[5]

The concept of a bulk diffusion process simply transporting atoms across the interface to promote welding is rather inadequate. Ideally, atomic interchange in the bulk is not possible until interatomic distances across the interface are approximately equal to the lattice parameter. When the original interfaces reach this state of proximity, they become a grain boundary, and except for contaminant atoms, this state is essentially as strong as the metals to be joined, which contain numerous grain boundaries. Therefore, the entire interface is already in complete contact and the weld can be assumed complete.

It can be seen from the preceding discussion that to propose a simple universal model for all types of DFW is very difficult. The mechanism can involve one or any combination of a number of metallurgical and mechanical events. The specific conditions under which a diffusion weld is made, as well as the results desired from the weld, will determine which of the phenomenological events are dominant. However, the following elementary model has been proposed as a general description of the mechanism of DFW.

Initially two surfaces are brought together under load. If the pressure exerted on the joint is high or the temperature quite high, there will be considerable plastic flow of the surface asperities until the interfaces have achieved a high degree of conformity with each other. At this point, the joint has considerable strength because at certain regions of the interface, metallic bonds will form. If the initial pressure is lower, this same surface conformity may be achieved at longer times by creep and/or surface diffusion of atoms. During the deformation, any thin surface films are seriously disrupted and some plastic work may be put into the surfaces.

As the joint is held for some finite length of time at elevated temperature, there is a great degree of atom mobility in the joint. Recrystallization or grain-boundary motion may occur to extend and further strengthen atom-to-atom bonds and to cause further disruption of the surface films at the joint. Both dissolution and agglomeration of contaminants may occur, and both remove the barriers to the formation of additional metallic bonds. Again, these processes occur to varying degrees depending upon the temperature, time, interfacial deformation, metal characteristics, and other factors. In the last stages of joint formation, some additional exchange of atoms occurs across the initial interface with the effect of assisting in the process of structural and chemical homogenization of the joint area.

Another significant theory that has been proposed revolves around the essential role of diffusion.

The diffusion phenomenon is of prime importance from both the theoretical and practical aspects of metallurgy. This is due to the many phase changes which take place in metal alloys involving a redistribution of the atoms present. These changes occur at rates that are dependent upon the speed of the migrating atoms. Diffusion in metal systems is usually categorized into three different processes depending upon the path of the diffusing element. These are volume diffusion, grain-boundary diffusion, and surface diffusion, and each one has different diffusivity constants. The specific rates for grain-boundary and surface diffusion are higher than the rate for volume diffusion. However, because of the small number of atoms in these regions, their contribution to the total diffusion process is small. The basic equation for diffusion in metals is Fick's first law. Several mechanisms can account for the diffusion of atoms in metals. Two of these are the interstitial mechanism and the vacancy mechanism. The former is concerned with the movement of atoms having small atomic radii compared with the matrix atoms. These elements move from one location to another along the interstices of the crystal lattice, hence the name interstitial elements. These moves occur within the crystal without distorting or permanently displacing the matrix atoms. The matrix or substitutional atoms use the vacancy mechanism for their mode of transportation. Because of their size, it is literally impossible for these atoms to migrate along the interstices. The only path open to them is that of vacancy sites. Although the energy required to move a matrix atom is equal to that for an interstitial element, the rate is considerably slower. This is due to the fewer number of vacant locations available to the atoms.

Although not a part of the mechanism of DFW, the use of intermediate materials in DFW is of considerable importance. Intermediate materials can be used to:

1. Promote diffusion at much lower temperatures than for self-welding.
2. Promote plastic flow and surface conformance at lower pressures.
3. Prevent the formation of intermetallic compounds.
4. Obtain clean surfaces.

Intermediate or activating agent materials are commonly used in the form of either foil, electroplates or vapor deposits. Foreign-atom diffusion rates are generally much greater than self-diffusion rates. Thus, the intermediate layer can accelerate the diffusion stage in the bonding process. Intermediate materials with low yield strengths permit larger contact areas for a given applied pressure. In systems which form intermetallic compounds, an intermediate layer is used to restrict the interdiffusion of the components and thus prevent the formation of brittle compounds. For metals such as aluminum, which are difficult to clean for welding, an electroplate of some other more readily cleaned metal can be used to facilitate welding. Nickel is an example of such a material.

The purpose of the intermediate layer of material or activation agent is also to make welding possible in very short times.

KEY VARIABLES OF PROCESS

Since DFW is any joining process in which two or more solid phases are metallurgically joined without the creation of a liquid phase, the term "metallurgically joined" can be used to describe weld formation by the action of atomic forces rather than solely by mechanical interlocking or by a nonmetallic adhesive. DFW can be divided into two general categories: deformation welding and DFW. Deformation welding includes those techniques in which gross plastic flow that promotes intimate contact and breaks up surface oxides is the principal factor in the formation of a weld and diffusion is not essential. Processes in this category include friction welding (FRW), explosive welding (EXW, high-pressure and roll welding (HPW-ROW) (yield-stress controlled), and forge welding (FOW). In DFW, deformation occurs only on a microscale, and diffusion is the principal factor in the formation of a weld. Included in this group are

- Gas-pressure welding (isostatic)
- Vacuum-diffusion welding (creep controlled)
- Press or die pressure welding
- Transient and eutectic melt

In the numerous processes mentioned above there are basically two variations of the process, solid-state DFW and liquid-phase DFW. With the former, all reactions occur in the solid state, while with the latter, interdiffusion occurs between two dissimilar metal parts such that the change of composition at the interface results in the formation of a liquid phase at the welding temperature. Until the liquid is formed the liquid-phase process is identical with the solid-state process, but once the liquid has formed, the process becomes virtually an operation similar to brazing.[6,7]

It should be noted here that there has been much confusion when a joint produced with a brazing filler metal or in situ liquid phase has been miscellaneously incorporated under such terms as diffusion bonding, DFW, furnace brazing, or solid-state bonding.

The defining of "diffusion brazing" as a process is a departure from the past, since all brazing processes have previously been defined by their heating method, i.e., torch, induction, furnace, etc. Diffusion brazing (DFB) is a brazing process which produces coalescence of metals by heating them to suitable temperatures and by using a filler metal or an in situ liquid phase. The filler metal may be distributed by capillary attraction or may be placed or formed at the faying surfaces. The filler metal is diffused with the base metal to the extent that the joint properties have been changed to approach those of the base metal. While pressure is not specified in this definition, "pressure may or may not be applied."[8]

Whether the process is deformation welding or DFW or DFB, there are several key parameters which in theory must be controlled and in practice are effectively controlled.

Temperature

Temperature has received much attention as a process variable for a number of reasons:

- Temperature is the most readily controllable and measurable process variable.
- In any thermally activated process, incremental changes in temperature cause the greatest changes in process kinetics compared with other parameters.
- Virtually all the mechanisms involved in DFW are temperature sensitive.
- Physical and mechanical properties, critical temperatures, and phase transformations are important reference points in any effective use of DFW.

One of the most systematic published works on parametric evaluation of DFW was prepared by Kazakov.[9] In his work, abrupt change in strength with increased temperature is not evident at any stress or time. He shows a continuous temperature-time-pressure interdependence in which increased temperature results in increased strength. Increases in pressure and time also increase the joint strength.

An interesting comparison can be drawn between the 0.45% carbon steel in Kazakov's data and the 0.20% carbon steel in Parks' work.[10] Parks achieved welds at 820°F (438°C) in 1020 steel, whereas Kazakov's conditions for good welds were between 1460 and 2020°F (793 and 1104°C). This candidly illustrates how reported results can vary with small differences in composition, pressure, surface preparation, and by the effects of crystallographic changes made by allotropic transformation.

Temperatures encountered in the process range from 500°F (260°C) for joining some aluminum alloys to Ti-5Al-2.5Sn with silver as a diffusion aid, to as high as 2800°F (1538°C) for joining two pieces of tungsten.

In general, the temperature at which DFW takes place is greater than $0.5T_m$, where T_m is the melting point of the material, usually in kelvins. Many metals and alloys can be diffusion-welded at temperatures between $0.6T_m$ and $0.8T_m$.

Time

Time is closely related to temperature in that most diffusion-controlled reactions vary with time. Data presented by Kazakov illustrate the effect of time as a DFW variable. These data of Kazakov indicate that increasing time at temperature and pressure increases joint strength up to a point. Beyond this point no further gains are achieved. This illustrates that time is not a quantitively simple parameter. The simple relationship which describes the average distance traveled by an atom does not reflect the more complex changes in structure that result in the formation of a diffusion weld. Although atom motion continues indefinitely, structural changes tend to approach equilibrium. An example of similar behavior can be found in recrystallization.

A deformed sample, when heated, first undergoes recovery, then recrystallizes. At first the formation and growth of new grains are rapid, but as time progresses, the rate of grain-boundary motion and physical change diminishes. The decrease is caused by the relative stabilization of microstructure through reduction of internal energy. Thus the driving force for continued structural change is also reduced. The rate of atom motion does not decrease significantly throughout this entire sequence of events.

In a practical sense, time has been varied over an extremely broad range in DFW from seconds to hours. Realistic factors influence the time allowed for DFW, such as delay periods in the apparatus necessary to provide the heat and pressure. When systems have thermal and mechanical (or hydrostatic) inertia, DFW times are longer because of the impracticality of suddenly changing variables. When there are no inertial problems, welding times may vary from as little as 0.3 min for joining thoria-dispersed nickel to itself to as long as 4 h for joining columbium with zirconium as a diffusion aid. For economic reasons, it is desirable to reduce the time necessary for DFW to increase the potential production rates.

Pressure

Pressure is an important variable in DFW. It is less easy to deal with as a quantitative variable than either temperature or time. Pressure affects several aspects of the DFW process. The initial phase of bond formation is most certainly affected by the amount of deformation induced by the pressure applied. This is the most obvious single effect and probably is most frequently and thoroughly considered. Increased pressure invariably results in better joints for any given time-temperature value. The most apparent reason related to this effect is the greater interface deformation and asperity breakdown that comes from high pressures. There is also the effect of deformation on the recrystallization behavior. Increased pressure (and deformation) leads to lower recrystallization temperature. Conversely stated, the increased deformation accelerates the process of recrystallization at a given DFW temperature.

In practice, diffusion welds can be performed over a wide pressure range, e.g., 6 to 40 ksi (4 to 276 MPa). Practical limitations, in addition to metallurgical considerations, are the apparatus that is available to apply pressure and the geometry of the joint. Because the pressure needed to achieve success is related so closely to the other parameters of temperature and time, there is a great degree of latitude in the pressure needed to make good welds. Pressure has additional significance when dissimilar combinations are considered. From economic and manufacturing aspects, reductions in welding pressure are desirable. Increased pressures require costlier apparatus, greater need for control, and generally more complex part-handling procedures.

Surface Preparation

The surfaces of parts to be diffusion welded normally are carefully prepared before application of heat or pressure. A universal philosophy which is the bylaw for the preparation of parts is maximum attainable cleanliness. Surface preparation, however, involves more than just cleanliness. It also includes generation of an acceptable finish or smoothness, removal of chemically combined films (oxides, etc.), and cleansing of gaseous, aqueous, or organic surface films. The primary surface finish is obtained ordinarily by machining, abrading, grinding, or polishing.

One property of a correctly prepared surface is flatness. A certain degree of flatness and smoothness is required in order to assure that the interfaces can achieve the necessary compliance without excessive deformation. Machine finishes, grinding, or abrasive polishing are usually adequate to obtain the surface flatness and smoothness needed. A secondary effect of primary machining or abrading which is not always apparent is the plastic flow introduced into the surface during machining. Cold-worked surface layers have lower recrystallization temperatures than the bulk material. Chemical etching or pickling, commonly used as a form of preweld preparation, has two effects. The first is the removal of nonmetallic surface films, most frequently oxides. The second is the removal of part or all of the cold-worked layer that occurs during preliminary surface preparation. The benefits of oxide removal are apparent because it is difficult to cause two oxidized surfaces to adhere. Many chemical solvents are suitable for use with different metals systems.

Degreasing is a universal part of any procedure for prediffusion weld cleaning; alcohol, trichlorethylene, acetone, detergents, and many others have been used by numerous investigators. Choice seems to rely on individual preference. Frequently, the recommended techniques are very intricate and may include multiple rinse-wash-etch cycles in several solutions.

Vacuum bake-out has also been used occasionally to obtain clean surfaces. The usefulness of vacuum bake-out depends to a large extent on the material and the nature of its surface films. Organic, aqueous, or gaseous adsorbed layers can be easily removed by vacuum heat treatment at temperatures and pressures that cause boiling of these relatively volatile materials. Oxides are not easily dissociated by vacuum bake-out, particularly on such materials as titanium, aluminum, or alloys containing significant amounts of chromium. However, it is possible to dissolve adherent oxides in some base materials at elevated temperature. Zirconium, titanium, and others have reasonably high solubility for oxygen and will dissolve their own oxides at elevated temperature.[5] During vacuum bake-out, oxygen is not available for continued formation of additional oxide. As a result, surfaces may be cleaned and made ready for DFW. Baking in vacuum usually requires vacuum or controlled-atmosphere storage and careful handling before use to avoid the recurrence of surface adsorbed or chemisorbed layers. Many factors enter into selecting the total surface preparation treatment. In addition to those already mentioned, the specific welding conditions to be used may affect the selection. With higher welding temperatures and pressures, it becomes less important to obtain extremely clean surfaces because increased atomic mobility, surface-asperity deformation, and solubility for impurity elements all contribute to the self-removal of surface contaminants during welding. As a corollary, it can be stated that to lower the minimum DFW temperature or pressure, it is necessary to provide better-prepared, cleaner, and preserved surfaces.

Surface preservation is a necessary feature in a discussion on surface preparation. It is folly to exercise supreme caution in preparing surfaces before DFW if they are permitted to become recontaminated during subsequent handling. One solution to this potential dilemma lies in the effective use of protective environments during DFW. Vacuum protection during DFW provides continued freedom from contamination, as it does during surface preparation. Use of hydrogen as an atmosphere in DFW helps minimize the amount of oxide formed during welding and it may reduce existing oxides. However, it will form hydrides in alloys of titanium, zirconium, hafnium, columbium, and tantalum, which may be detrimental to weld properties. Argon, helium, and possibly nitrogen can be used to protect clean surfaces at elevated temperatures. When these inert gases are used, their purity must be very high. Inert gases offer none of the advantages of chemical or physical activity that hydrogen or vacuum does. Many of the precautions and principles applicable to brazing atmospheres can be applied directly to DFW.

Metallurgical Factors

In addition to those parameters already discussed, there are a number of metallurgically important factors which should be considered. Two factors of particular importance in conjunction with similar metal welds are allotropic transformations and microstructural factors that result in modification of diffusion rates. Allotropic transformations (or phase transformations) occur in a limited number of metals and alloys. Heat-treatable alloy steels are the most familiar of these, but other metals, such as titanium, zirconium, and cobalt, also undergo allotropic transformations. One reason for the importance of the transformation is that the metal is very plastic while undergoing a transformation. This tends to permit more rapid initial interface accommodation at lower pressures in much the same manner as does recrystallization.

Any other means of alteration of the diffusion rates affects DFW. We have already seen that direct or indirect alterations occur as a result of temperature changes and transformations. If the rate of atomic motion can be increased by other means, the process contributing to the formation of a weld may accelerate. Diffusion rates have been found to be higher in plastically deformed metals.

Another means of enhancing diffusion is alloying or, more specifically, introducing elements with high diffusivity in the system. The function of the high-diffusivity element is to accelerate the process of atomic motion at or across the interface. In addition to simple diffusion acceleration, the addition of these alloys may have secondary effects. The atoms that are selected as diffusion accelerating are usually those which have reasonable solubility in the metal to be joined, do not form stable compounds, and do depress the melting point locally. Melting point depression by alloying must be controlled because of the possibility of liquefaction at the joint interface.

When a diffusion-activated system is used, it is considered desirable, either during or after the welding process, to heat-treat sufficiently to disperse the high-diffusivity element away from the interface. If this is not done, the presence of the low-melting region may produce metallurgically unstable structures. This would be particularly important for joints that would be exposed to elevated-temperature service.

INTERMEDIATE MATERIALS

It has become rather common to use some form of interlayer or intermediate material in many applications which have been labeled DFW. In many instances the interlayer is a standard brazing filler metal that merely fills the gap and subsequently undergoes a diffusion reaction with the base metal.

Another purpose of the use of interlayers is to provide a significant difference in hardness between the base metals and the interfacial layer. A soft nickel interlayer placed between two very hard nickel alloys permits the use of lower pressures to achieve interface conformity. After the joint is achieved, the diffusion of alloy elements into the unalloyed layer results in minimal compositional and property gradients across the joint.

Intermediate diffusion aids may be necessary or advantageous in certain applications to:

- Reduce DFW temperature
- Reduce DFW pressure
- Reduce dwell time
- Increase diffusivity
- Scavenge undesirable elements

Diffusion aids can be applied in many forms. They can be electroplated, evaporated, or sputtered to the surface to be welded, or they can be used in the form of foil inserts or powders. Thickness of the interlayer should not exceed 0.010 in (0.25 mm).

Generally, the diffusion aid is a less-alloyed version of the base metals being joined. For example, unalloyed titanium often is used as an interlayer with titanium alloys. Nickel is used in DFW of chromium-containing nickel-base superalloys. However, silver can be used with aluminum. Interlayers with rapidly diffusing elements also can be used. Alloys containing beryllium can be used with nickel alloys to increase the rate of joint formation.

Diffusion aids form the basis of the transient-melt and liquid-phase methods of DFW. Here, the purpose of the aid is to form a liquid phase at the joint. Diffusion of the intermediate element or elements into the base metal and of the base-metal element or elements into the liquid phase causes the melt to resolidify at temperature, and a joint with high remelt capability results. It is of critical importance to select the intermediate diffusion aid with great care in any DFW application. An improperly chosen intermediate material can:

- Decrease the temperature capability of the joint
- Decrease the strength of the joint
- Cause microstructural degradation
- Cause thermodynamic incompatibility
- Result in corrosion problems at the joint

DEFORMATION WELDING

There are numerous DFW processes. One of these is isostatic DFW, also called Thermovac welding. The processing scheme of Thermovac is compared with the more conventional gas-pressure welding process in Figs. 10-1 and 10-2. The gas-pressure welding process is also known as hot isostatic pressure (HIP) welding. Both processes require an autoclave or other suitable source of gas pressure, and both extract pressure from the gas medium by isolating the joint interface from the gas through the use of a metal can or other method of sealing. In both processes, the internal volume within either the metal can or the welded structure is evacuated prior to the welding step. Hence the principal difference between Thermovac and HIP is the absence of internal support tooling in the thermovac method. Thus, unlike the situation during HIP welding, in which the stresses on the structure are ideally all compressive and balanced, the stress state is not in balance in the thermovac method.

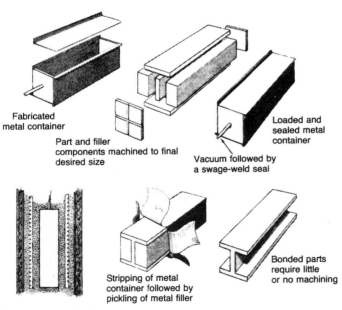

Fabricated metal container

Part and filler components machined to final desired size

Loaded and sealed metal container

Vacuum followed by a swage-weld seal

Stripping of metal container followed by pickling of metal filler

Bonded parts require little or no machining

Hot-gas-pressure bonding

Fig. 10-1   Schematic of gas-pressure welding.

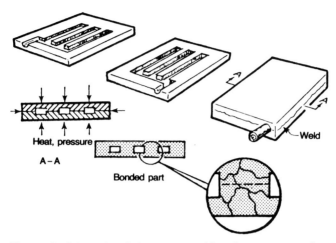

Fig. 10-2 Schematic of thermovac welding (no support tooling used).

Some of the advantages of the HIP welding process for joining complex shapes are as follows:

1. Adequate metallurgical bonds can be obtained.
2. Close dimensional control can be achieved.
3. Many similar or dissimilar materials can be welded together, usually in a one-step operation.
4. Components of brittle metals which cannot be joined by conventional techniques can be solid-state welded.
5. In some cases, fabricated costs can be lower than those for conventional processes.

Another DFW process is roll DFW. The diffusion-welded joint between structural details is accomplished by gross plastic flow during hot rolling.

The roll-weld process allows flexibility in selecting the structural arrangement and in the fabrication procedure. The process has been applied most frequently to titanium and its alloys.

The method consists of assembling the titanium parts to be joined in a protective jacket of mild steel that is quite similar to the pressure-cladding process.

The lower steel cover sheet and yoke are placed together on an assembly table after which the titanium sheets, core strips, and steel filler bars are fitted within the yoke cavity, as shown in Fig. 10-3. The steel top cover is then placed over the yoke and the entire pack is clamped together and welded. The steps in processing are shown in Fig. 10-4. The processing temperature will vary between 1400 and 1900°F (760 and 1038°C), depending on the titanium alloys being processed. The presently developed procedure is unidirection rolling (rolling parallel to the core elements) of the pack. See Fig. 10-5. Panels as large as 3 in high by 60 in wide by 120 in long (76 mm by 1524 mm by 3048 mm) have been rolled.[12]

The press-DFW process involves the assembly of premachined and cleaned titanium details in a tooling arrangement designed so that pressure can be applied to all interfaces being joined. This assembly is enclosed in a vacuumtight stainless steel retort, which is sandwiched between ceramic heating platens and encased on the lateral surfaces with ceramic insulation. This assembly is heated to the processing temperature of $1700 \pm 50°F$ ($927 \pm 10°C$), and pressure is applied by a modified hydraulic press designed to apply pressure in orthogonal horizontal directions in addition to the vertical press loading direction. The processing scheme is shown in Fig. 10-6.[13]

A relatively new process is continuous-seam diffusion bonding (CSDB).[14] This process joins material by "yield-controlled DFW." The parts, such as an end cap and webs held with tooling, are fed through a machine with four rollers. The top and bottom wheels are made of molybdenum and are hooked up to the machine much as a resistance weld wheel is hooked up to a resistance welder.

By electrical resistance, the wheel and part are heated to the desired temperature by a special control system. This temperature is usually around 1800 to 2000°F (983 to 1093°C) for titanium and in the 2000 to 2200°F (1093 to 1205°C) range for superalloys. The red-hot wheels apply pressure from 1 to 20 ksi (7 to 138 MPA) at the seam, depending on what materials are being joined. See Fig. 10-7.

Most DFW processes utilize low temperatures, long time periods,

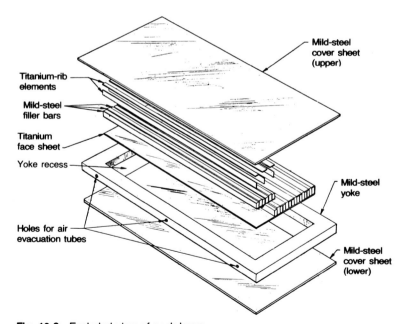

Titanium-rib elements

Mild-steel filler bars

Titanium face sheet

Yoke recess

Holes for air evacuation tubes

Mild-steel cover sheet (upper)

Mild-steel yoke

Mild-steel cover sheet (lower)

Fig. 10-3 Exploded view of pack layup.

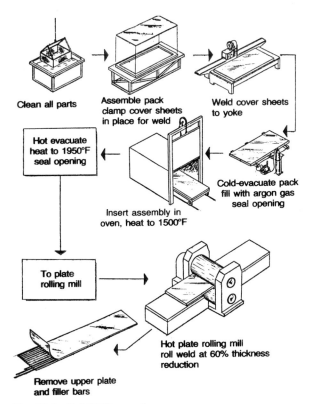

Clean all parts

Assemble pack clamp cover sheets in place for weld

Weld cover sheets to yoke

Hot evacuate heat to 1950°F seal opening

Cold-evacuate pack fill with argon gas seal opening

Insert assembly in oven, heat to 1500°F

To plate rolling mill

Hot plate rolling mill roll weld at 60% thickness reduction

Remove upper plate and filler bars

Fig. 10-4 Roll-DFW operations.

and high mechanical pressures. A new hydrodynamic welding process is a solid-state DFW process carried out below the melting temperatures of the materials being joined, and requires high temperatures and short times. Through the use of high-frequency induction currents, the joint interface is rapidly heated; then, at the optimum temperature, the mating surfaces are brought into intimate contact by

Fig. 10-5 Roll-DFW titanium part.[11]

pulsed, magnetic forces.[15] Unlike metallurgical bonding techniques, the pressures which create the bond are fast—less than $^1/_2$ ms.[16]

The joint is heated by induction heating to a temperature range somewhat below the parent-metal melting point. At this time, a large pulsed current is induced into the walls of the joint. This current produces pressures in excess of 10 ksi (69 MPa) at the interface simultaneously with temperatures far in excess of parent-metal melting points. While the metallic system is subjected to this temperature under high pressure, there is no evidence of melting of the base metals. However, at these elevated temperatures, the atoms have a strong tendency to migrate finite distances in short periods of time. It is these diffusion lengths that cause complete elimination of prior interfaces in the hydrodynamic or "thermomagnetic" welding process, and for most metals, with the exception of titanium, joints can be produced in ambient atmosphere.

The use of intermediate diffusion aids has produced several distinct DFW processes. One is "activated diffusion bonding," which is the name given a joining process for high-strength nickel-base superalloys. This process combines the manufacturing ease of brazing with the high joint strengths achievable by solid-state DFW. This new process basically involves vacuum furnace brazing with an ultra-high-strength bonding alloy (nearly identical in chemical composition to the base metal being joined), followed by diffusion and aging heat treatments to produce maximum joint strength.

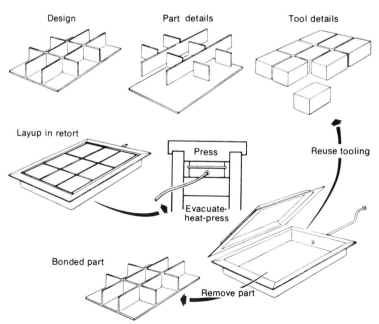

Fig. 10-6 Press-welding process.[13]

Fig. 10-7 Hot wheels are key feature of CSDB process.[14]

This process differs radically from solid state DFW in that only nominal pressures 0 to 0.01 ksi (0 to 0.07 MPa) are required to effect a sound joint. The process is similar to solid-state DFW in that high vacuums 10^{-3} torr (0.13 Pa) in leaktight furnaces are an absolute requirement for success and that a subsequent heat treatment is necessary to develop maximum joint mechanical properties. The low pressure used in this process allows it to be used for joining relatively fragile parts of complex configuration without risking deformation during joining.

The development of complex, high-strength brazing filler metals by the addition of small amounts of melting-point depressants to ultra-high-strength superalloy-base compositions has been successfully demonstrated. Melting point depressants such as silicon, boron, manganese, aluminum, titanium, and columbium have been added to base alloys, René 77, René 80, and René 100. The base alloy is simply "doped" with increasing amounts of depressants such that the resultant alloy is liquid at a temperature that does not impair the properties of the alloy to be joined. For example, the high-strength superalloy René 80 is normally solution-heat-treated at 2225°F (1219°C), and that is then the temperature for the brazing filler metal to be molten.[17]

Transient Liquid Phase (TLP) is another new DFW process used for producing diffusion bonds in nickel-base and cobalt-base heat-resistant alloys. Because pressure requirements during welding are extremely low [<0.01 ksi (<0.07 MPa)], complex-shaped parts can be joined economically without the need for elaborate tooling or bonding presses. Boron was found to be a key additive to the interlayer material because of its effectiveness as a melting-point depressant and because of its rapid diffusivity during postbond heat treatment. The boron content is controlled in the interlayers to obtain an optimum balance between melting point and ease of subsequent homogenization.

A typical example of one of the family of interlayer alloys is the Ni-15CR-15Co-5Mo-2.5B alloy used for joining Udimet 700. In this interlayer alloy, the chromium, cobalt, and molybdenum contents are matched to that of the nominal Udimet 700 composition. Aluminum and titanium are left out of the bonding interlayer and are diffused into the joint during the bonding cycle. This particular interlayer alloy has a melting range which allows it to be used at bonding temperatures ≥2050°F (1121°C).[18]

Several DFW processes have been developed for titanium and its alloys. One of these processes forms a metallurgical joint between the titanium surfaces with the aid of a thin film of a series of electroplated elements, Fig. 10-8. Upon the application of heat and a pressure sufficient to maintain contact between the surfaces, the intermediate film forms a transient molten phase with the titanium surfaces being joined. The intermediate alloy is then diluted in the base metal by thermal diffusion.[19]

During the controlled thermal cycle (in high vacuum) the eutectic liquid is formed in the faying surfaces at 1650°F (899°C) and fills the gap between mating joints. The eutectic liquid is quickly solidified as the hyper side of the eutectic composition is reached, because of rapid diffusion. This transient liquid establishes the atomic bridge through which diffusion takes place. If the part is left at temperature for 90 min, the materials are diluted into the substrate to result in a stable joint microstructure. Because the eutectic formers are beta stabilizers, the affected area is converted to a Widmanstatten structure. This type of joint is one of the few which can fully develop the strength properties of the parent metal.[20]

Another similar DFW process has been developed to produce a Ti-Cu eutectic composition at the joint interface at the relatively low temperature of 1635°F (890°C), thus forming a joint. The formation of Ti-Cu liquid phase in the joint allows a low bonding force to be used, which reduces distortion and eliminates any need for heavy equipment. The joint is then diffusion-treated to reduce the copper content below

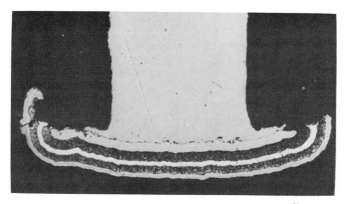

Fig. 10-8 Series of electroplated elements prior to heating.[20]

6%, giving good mechanical properties. A resistance seam-welding machine has been used to supply the heat required for welding. Instead of using an external heat source, an alternating current is passed through the joint, and the heating in the faying surface raises the joint temperature above 1625°F (885°C), where the electrolytically plated copper reacts with titanium to form a Ti-Cu eutectic. Solidification of the joint occurs upon cooling. Subsequent diffusion treating at 1700°F (927°C) for 4 h disperses the copper content from 70% to below 6% in the fillet and produces a strong, tough joint.[21,22]

Two new processes rely on the superplastic properties which enable certain metals or alloys to deform or flow at elevated temperatures to very high tensile elongations under very small applied loads, without necking or fracture. Titanium and its alloys exhibit this superplastic behavior over the temperature range of 1400 to 1700°F (760 to 927°C), where gas forming pressures ranging from 0.15 to several ksi (0.10 to several MPa) have been successfully used to form complex shapes. One of these processes is CRISP, which is an acronym for *creep isostatic pressing*.[23] CRISP is a two-step process combining creep or superplastic forming of titanium sheet structures with hot isostatic pressing to produce a diffusion-welded one-piece structure.

Inherent in the CRISP process is the mating of two external skins. This is accomplished through a combination of creep forming and isostatic welding to achieve a one-piece structure. First, one skin is creep-formed by gas pressure to the contour of a die. Then, shaped inserts are positioned in place and a second skin is creep formed by gas pressure over the first skin and inserts. DFW of the formed sheets and inserts is achieved by hot isostatic pressing in an autoclave, which eliminates the requirements both for expensive, precision-machined, matched die sets and for tight dimensional tolerances previously required in vacuum hot-press DFW.

The second process has been entitled SPF/DB. *Superplastic forming/diffusion bonding*[24] utilizes the same properties of titanium and its alloys described previously; however the DFW is performed under low-pressure conditions as compared with several high-pressure joining systems. SPF/DB is a two-stage process whereby titanium is joined without melting. The first stage is largely mechanical and involves plastic deformation of surface asperities through application of pressure, thereby achieving metal-to-metal contact. The second stage of the process is the strengthening of the bond by diffusion of atoms and grain growth across the joint interface. This is a function of the mobility of the exchange atoms and is accomplished by holding the material at an elevated temperature for the required period of time. Since superplastic forming and pressure DFW of selected titanium alloys can be accomplished with identical process temperatures, combining the two processes in a single fabrication cycle is possible. However, DFW in this manner must be accomplished under low-pressure conditions as opposed to the present high-pressure method generally in use.

Superplastic forming is a sheet metal fabrication process which uses the extensive tensile elongation and low deformation stresses of Ti-6Al-4V alloy. Forming is accomplished by application of low pressure argon gas [about 0.15 ksi (1.03 MPa)] on a titanium sheet diaphragm at 1700°F (927°C) in a sealed die.

The pressures to be used for the concurrent low-pressure DFW process are less than 0.3 ksi (2 MPa), which is considerably less than that normally used for press DFW [2 ksi (14 MPa)] of heavy-section titanium hardware.

EQUIPMENT AND TOOLING

A wide variety of equipment and tooling is employed in DFW activities. The only basic requirements are that pressure and temperature must be applied and maintained in a controlled environment. Various classes of DFW equipment, each with its own special advantages and disadvantages, have been developed. Within a given class of equipment or approach there are numerous variations employed depending upon the specific situation. A general description of four classes of DFW equipment is given below.

High-Pressure Isostatic Equipment

Gas-pressure welding is a specific technique utilizing high-pressure isostatic equipment to achieve DFW. This technique is basically a hot-pressing operation performed in a high-pressure autoclave. The working fluid is an inert gas providing true isostatic pressure application to any part within the chamber.

The primary component of gas-pressure welding is a cold-wall autoclave which permits pressures up to 150 ksi (1034 MPa) to be employed even though specimen temperatures in excess of 3000°F (1649°C) might be employed. Internal cooling is usually provided to aid in maintaining a low wall temperature. Closures in each end provide access to the vessel cavity. Utilities and instrumentation are brought into the vessel through high-pressure fittings located in the end closures. The high temperatures are possible because the heater is located inside the autoclave. Resistance-wound furnaces of varying designs are employed. Alumina or silica insulation is used to reduce heat losses to the wall. Temperature is monitored and controlled by thermocouples located throughout the furnace and vessel. Pressurization is achieved by pumping the inert gas from its storage area through a multistage piston-type compressor. Control of temperature and pressure are independent and any combination of heating and pressurizing rates can be programmed.

The tooling required is minimal. The most important consideration is the gastight envelope, or can, in which the specimen must be contained. If a leak develops in the can, no pressure differential can be maintained and no useful work can be accomplished. Internal tooling may also be required if cavities exist in the geometry to be diffusion-welded. Usually sufficient pressure is applied so that plastic flow will occur until all void space is filled. If proper tooling is not provided, the structure might collapse. With proper conditions, essentially no deformation occurs and no change in dimensions will occur during the operation.

Presses

A very common approach to DFW employs a mechanical or hydraulic press of some sort. The basic requirements for the press are: (1) sufficient load and size capacity, (2) an available means for heating, and (3) the maintenance of uniform pressure for the required time. It is also desirable and often necessary that some provision for protective atmosphere around the weldment be made.

Because of the wide latitude available in using presses, and the far-reaching ingenuity of users, there really is no standard equipment established for press DFW. However, some units have been produced for sale commercially. Some units provide for a vacuum or an inert atmosphere to surround the part. One such unit uses radiant heating from tungsten-mesh heating elements. Equally effective, however, are induction heating and self-resistance heating. The advantage of such a setup is the ease of operation and the excellent parametric control available. The disadvantage is the practical limitation of size in view of the larger components to be diffusion-welded. Also, this approach does not lend itself to high production rates; it is not suited to rapid turn-around or batch operation.

Some of the limitations on size can be overcome by eliminating the protective chamber and operating in large forming or forging presses.

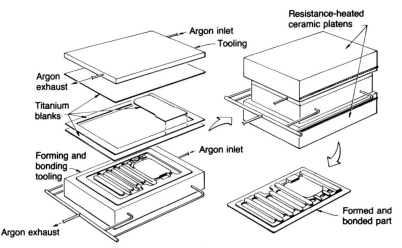

Fig. 10-9 Concurrent SPF/DB of titanium.[24]

Fig. 10-10   Inside a retort which holds titanium beam parts
and 22-4-9 stainless steel tooling.

Heated platens are used to apply both temperature and pressure to the
components to be diffusion-welded. The platens may be metallic or
ceramic depending upon the temperature and pressure employed; see
Fig. 10-9. Castable ceramics are particularly useful because contours
can easily be accommodated without extensive machining. Heating
elements can be cast into the ceramic die to provide the required
uniform heat during bonding. Care must be taken to ensure close
tolerances between the die and the part so that uniform pressure will
be applied. This is a major problem with DFW on press-type equipment. It is extremely difficult to maintain uniform pressure across the
section, and variations in weld quality can result.

Tooling requirements vary with application. If no lateral restraint is
provided, upsetting may occur during processing. In such cases, lower
pressures are usually required. The process is quite similar to closed-
die press forging except that lower pressures and longer times are
employed. Because of the time factor, heated dies are required and die
materials become a problem. The die must be able to withstand both
the temperature and pressure as well as be compatible with the
material to be diffusion-welded. Interaction between the part and the
die can be controlled by stop-off agents or by oxidizing the surface in

Fig. 10-11 When retort is positioned in press, side and end hydraulic jacks together with vertical cylinders exert 2 ksi (14 MPa) in all directions.

many instances. Atmosphere protection is often achieved by sealing parts in evacuated metal cans which are flexible and conform to die shapes.

Equipment that can be adapted to DFW applications is frequently available. Nearly every sizable manufacturing or development organization has a press of some type that can be modified to perform DFW.

In Fig. 10-10 is a retort which holds titanium parts for a beam in position. Tooling blocks and spacers of 22-4-9 stainless steel fill the voids between the titanium pieces to hold the structure to dimensions. Figure 10-11 shows a press with side and end hydraulic jacks which, with pressure from the vertical, exert 2 ksi (14 MPa) on the retort in all directions. In actual production, the technicians heat the completed assembly packs (retort, heating pads, insulation, and evacuation equipment) before moving them into the press. Large structures may require a preheat and soak of possibly 40 h. Several packs may be in assembly and preheat at one time. The actual time in the press will vary from 2 to 12 h, depending on the shape of the structure and the mass of titanium. Four days of cooling follow before the assembly is dismantled and the retort cut open. This approach is also quite slow and may not be scaled readily to high production rates.

Resistance DFW Equipment

Excellent application of resistance welding equipment has been made to DFW. In general, no modification of standard equipment is necessary to achieve successful resistance diffusion welds. Both spot and seam DFW have been accomplished, although seam DFW is not so well developed. Closed-loop control systems are being developed that provide fast and reproducible results.

As in standard resistance welding, selection of electrode materials is important. The electrodes must be electrical conductors, possess high strength at welding temperatures, resist thermal shock, and resist sticking to the materials to be welded. There is no universal electrode material, because of potential interaction with the workpiece. Each system must be carefully evaluated from a metallurgical compatibility standpoint to ensure success.

One modification often employed is the addition of an atmospheric control device. This usually takes the form of a small chamber surrounding the electrodes to provide an inert atmosphere or vacuum during the DFW process. The seam welder is less sensitive to potential weld contamination by the atmosphere because of the nature of the applied force. This tends to force the contamination by the atmosphere out of the joint as the rollers move forward.

The biggest advantage in using this type of equipment for DFW is the speed at which joints can be made. Cycle times are measured in seconds rather than hours (as with other DFW approaches). However, it must be recognized that only a small area is welded at a time and the preparation of large weld areas becomes time-consuming and requires numerous overlaps to achieve welding over an area larger than the electrodes.

Specialized Equipment Approaches

In addition to the major equipment discussed above, engineers have devised numerous other approaches to DFW. An incomplete listing of

Fig. 10-12 Type 321 stainless steel mandrel used to produce titanium sandwich structures.[20]

Fig. 10-13 Largest vacuum furnace used for DFW.[20]

apparatus would include retorts, fixtures, dead weights and differential thermal expansion fixtures. In all cases, the apparatus used provides the pressure required and is used in conjunction with a separate heating source, which normally is a furnace with vacuum or inert atmosphere.

In Fig. 10-12 is an example of a Type 321 stainless steel tool used as a thermal differential fixture in producing cylindrical parts in the furnace seen in Fig. 10-13.[20]

Other specialized pieces of equipment include automated rolling mills used in the roll DFW process,[12] described earlier and seen in Figs. 10-3 and 10-4.

Tooling

A number of important considerations must be observed when selecting fixturing materials. The main criteria for selection of tooling are:

1. Ease of operation
2. Reproducibility of welding cycle
3. Operational maintenance required
4. Weld cycle time required
5. Initial cost of tooling

Furthermore, the fixture materials must be capable of maintaining their proper position throughout the heating cycle.

Second, suitable fixture materials may be limited when DFW temperatures above 2500°F (1371°C) are encountered. Only the refractory metals themselves and certain nonmetallics have sufficient creep strength for fixturing. Tantalum and graphite have been used for fixturing tungsten. Ceramics make suitable fixturing materials provided that they are completely outgassed.

Third, since pressure is required for DFW, the fixtures should be designed to take advantage of the difference in thermal expansion between the materials being joined and the fixture material itself. For example, by appropriate selection of fixture material and gap clearances, it is possible for the fixtured parts to generate at least part, if not all, of the external pressure required for welding. These principles were also used to join 2219 aluminum alloy tubing to 321 stainless steel.[25] A precise method was devised to apply the correct bonding force to the tubular assembly. This method ensured application of sufficient uniform force to the mating surfaces to provide complete welding, yet not apply so much force that excessive compressive yielding of the aluminum component would result in deformation of the welded joint. By taking advantage of the difference between the thermal-expansion coefficients of low-alloy steel and stainless steel, tooling was developed that provided a uniform and reproducible welding pressure.

JOINT DESIGN

It has been a difficult problem to devise tests for determining mechanical properties, and to determine the most suitable joint designs for the various types of DFW processes. For example, the configuration of the weld interface in clad plate makes it difficult to determine the joint strength experimentally. For this reason, joints are usually evaluated by indirect or qualitative methods such as bending, twisting, or pulling the clad sheet in tension to determine whether the weld will separate.

By utilizing a simple and unique application of differential thermal expansion, stainless steel and aluminum have been diffusion-welded. Literature shows that 2219 aluminum alloy has a thermal contraction that is approximately 30% greater than that of stainless steel. Therefore, since the aluminum alloy has a greater contraction in the temperature range 77 to −423°F (25.1 to −253°C), the aluminum alloy should be on the outer surface to give the most reliable joint. The joint configuration that was selected for DFW is similar to a lap shear joint used in brazing, and is designed to have an overlap of approximately 1.0 in (25.4 mm). This type of joint prevents the entrapment of corrosive cleaning solutions and foreign particles in the joint faying surface and allows for variation of joint interface area, depending on the shear strength required. Room temperature single- and double-lap shear strengths greater than approximately 15 ksi (103 MPa) have

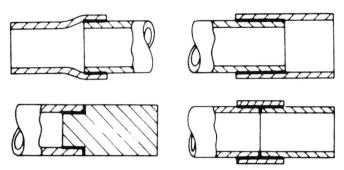

Fig. 10-14 Typical welded joints.

consistently been obtained for diffusion-welded joints. At test temperatures of −320 and −423°F (−196 and −253°C), the joint strengths increased approximately 20 and 30%, respectively.[25]

The utilization of roll DFW which was discussed earlier has been mainly applied to titanium alloys to date. With this technique, however, certain structural geometries can be designed. The minimum weight of this geometry depends on the type of loading involved for the specific structural component, illustrating that a variety of structural shapes are usually required for a minimum-weight design. For example, a corrugation design and a strip-and-key design[12] are two different construction methods for roll DFW of a truss-core sandwich. Edge members can be incorporated easily into the design. Diffusion welds of 100% efficiency have been obtained with properties equal to the basic material when roll DFW is used.

At the present state of development of the HDW process, joint geometrics must provide closed surfaces, such as tube to tube, plug to tube, and rod to rod. Socket or lap welds and butt welds also have been made successfully, as seen in Fig. 10-14.

In press DFW, no special precautions are required for the joints. Machining titanium details for welding is a low-cost operation because all cuts are straight—and planned to be. Welding of straight-cut ends to opposing flat surfaces is all that is required because welding pressure produces corner fillets which require no machining. Reverse fillets machined on 22-4-9 alloy tooling blocks, where they meet titanium intersections, accurately mold fillets during bonding. The pressure crushes out any irregularities at an intersection. This is seen in Fig. 10-15.

Three basic joint types made by the CSDB process are the lap, tee, and butt. The lap joint is made by passing the workpiece between two wheels or by supporting the workpiece on a suitable weld fixture and using a single wheel to produce the weld. The single-wheel method, used most frequently as a reference surface, is thereby provided for controlling flatness or curvature in the part being welded. See Fig. 10-16.

The decrease in thickness of the lap joint caused by the welding pass

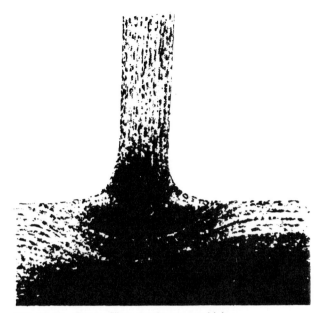

Fig. 10-15 Corner fillets require no machining.

is typically less than 1.5% of the original sheet thickness. Other forms of DFW, such as press-roll welding, typically require a reduction of thickness from 10% to more than 50%. This feature of CSDB makes possible the joining of hollow structures without need for internal tooling to support the hollow cavities. Applications include simple joining of sheets, edge closure of vanes, bimetal heat exchangers, and hollow compressor blades.

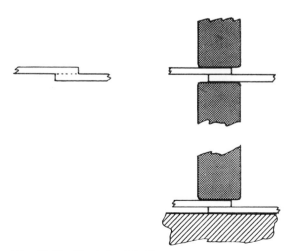

Fig. 10-16 Simple lap joint.[14]

Tee joints are made by the methods depicted schematically in Fig. 10-17. Figure 10-17a shows the method used most frequently to join a stiffening rib to another sheet-metal component, such as in tee beam or panel applications.

To make a two-piece joint, the vertical member is clamped between electrically conductive tooling, with an edge extending a controlled distance above the top surface of the tool. With the horizontal member positioned over the vertical member, the extended edge of the vertical member is heated and upset to form fillets and produce a diffusion weld. As the fillets are formed, the upset edge penetrates slightly in the horizontal member, producing a nonplanar weld interface with both members contributing metal to formation of the fillet.

A three-piece tee joint can also be made, as shown in Fig. 10-17b. In this case the edge of the vertical member extends through and above two horizontal members. Fillets are formed against the tooling, and diffusion welds are made between vertical members and the abutting edge of each horizontal member. This joint is used in rib-stiffened struts or similar parts where displacement of curved surfaces must be avoided.

To produce a butt joint, the members are clamped in an abutting position on an electrically conductive tooling rail. The butt joint has

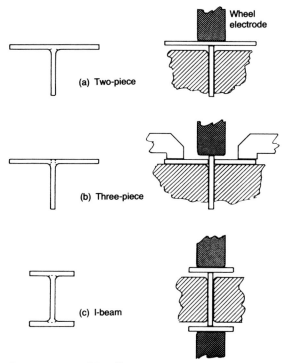

(a) Two-piece

(b) Three-piece

(c) I-beam

Wheel electrode

Fig. 10-17 Tee joints.[14]

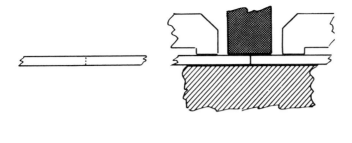

Fig. 10-18 Butt joints.[14]

found an important application to fabrication of hollow rotor spars for helicopters from titanium-alloy sheet. See Fig. 10-18.

Joint designs for producing parts which utilize intermediate diffusion aids to produce a diffusion weld are similar to those used for conventional brazing. The fundamental butt and lap joints with modifications such as scarf joints are used universally.

ECONOMICS, ADVANTAGES, AND DISADVANTAGES

DFW is not a universal substitute for other joining techniques, by any means. Pure metals and alloys of every class have been joined. Some of the advantages of DFW metals include the following:

- Numerous materials are severely embrittled, when joined by conventional methods, from exposure to contaminating atmosphere.
- Fusion-welding recrystallization damages mechanical properties.
- DFW makes weight reduction possible by (1) avoiding large overlaps and rivets, (2) reducing the number of gages by welding closely spaced stiffeners.

An example is seen in Fig. 10-19, which illustrates a currently forged Ti-6Al-6V-6Sn fitting for a military aircraft; the fitting is completely

Fig. 10-19 Ti-6Al-6V-2Sn forging and machined fitting.

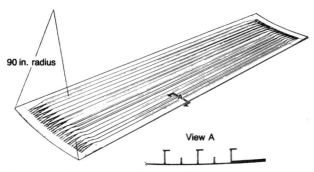

90 in. radius

View A

Fig. 10-20 Fuselage and wing panel.[26] (0.001 in = 0.03 mm)

machined. A weight comparison of the conventional forged and machined fitting with one made by DFW indicates about a 17% savings in weight, or about 500 lb (226.8 kg) per ship. Cost comparisons show it to be competitive pricewise.

DFW provides economical methods of adding doublers or stiffening members, for example, at attachment holes. This is depicted in Fig. 10-20, which shows a trial fuselage and wing panel. Several of these were built for evaluation for a supersonic transport airplane. The fuselage skin panel was 6Al-4V titanium and was 36 in (914 mm) wide by 240 in (6096 mm) long. The panel skin was 0.036 in (0.91 mm) thick and built up to 0.060 in (1.5 mm) around the edge to form a doubler. Stiffeners consisted of L sections, between which were shortened-height ribs.

Along with advantages there are limitations. Several general limitations include lack of equipment, an indefinite dimensional (size) capability, and inability to join surfaces that are inaccessible or have a peculiar configuration.

One of the chief advantages of press welding is the relatively inexpensive equipment required. Conventional hydraulic presses can supply the required welding pressures. Welding temperatures can be provided by a wide range of methods including resistance, induction, and radiant heaters, or simply by heating with an oxyacetylene torch. And, since many pressure-welding operations can be carried out in air, additional equipment to provide protective atmospheres is not required in many applications.

Depending on the equipment available and the characteristics of the materials to be joined, welding time can be very short, sometimes on the order of seconds. Another advantage of the process is that the finish of joint surfaces is not very critical. However, deformation is common with pressure welding, and, if subsequent machining to remove this deformation is required, joint surface preparation may reduce cost savings.

Transient-melt DFW has a very significant advantage in that low welding pressures are always used. However, there are two important limitations: prolonged diffusion treatment is required to eliminate joint remelt temperatures, and the high diffusivity of the liquid phase accelerates tendencies for void formation that can result from interdiffusion of dissimilar metals in the weld area.

The chief limitations of gas-pressure welding stem from the high cost of the equipment it requires and the limited size of workpiece that current equipment can handle. Because of high equipment costs, conventional joints by gas-pressure welding are more expensive than those of other DFW processes. In addition, because of the slow heat-up characteristics of autoclaves, welding cycle times usually range 3 h and more.

The roll DFW process can be performed on conventional rolling mills, and the only restriction on the size of the structure that can be produced is the capacity of the rolling mill. The range of materials that can be joined by roll welding is broad. However, the limitation exists that high-temperature, high-strength materials may require roll pressures not possible with conventional equipment, and expensive modification of conventional rolling facilities may be required.

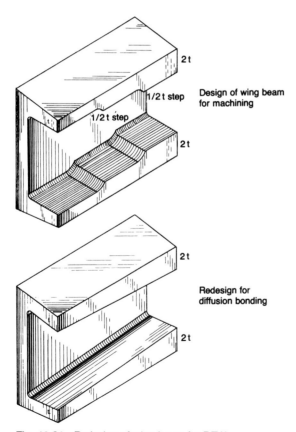

Fig. 10-21 Redesign of wing beam for DFW.

Redesign may be necessary to achieve maximum cost-effectiveness. The wing beam shown in Fig. 10-21 was designed to be manufactured by machining from plate or from a forging. Stepwise thickness changes in web and caps were used to facilitate machining. Redesign was possible with uniform thickness throughout most of the web and a continuous taper in the caps. It will be noted that in the design for machining, provision for access for the cutter leads to a nonoptimum cap configuration that tapers to its extremity. A more efficient design with uniform-thickness caps was possible by diffusion welding from constant-thickness or simple tapered sheets. In this example, cost-effectiveness results from:

- Metal recovery increase from less than 10% to greater than 90% of the raw material.
- Less than 5% of the final part surface is generated by machining, in contrast to 100% in the original design.
- More effective cap shape is possible with DFW.

In conclusion, DFW can be an extremely effective means to reduce costs and increase part effectiveness. The process will require appreciation by the designer of the requirements for effective fabrication by DFW, generation of design data for use by the structural analyst, demonstration of producibility and reproducibility by the manufacturing engineer, and development of acceptance criteria and inspection methods by quality control engineers.

MATERIALS

A wide variety of materials have been joined by DFW. Pioneer work in this area was conducted primarily in the nuclear field; in recent years, however, work has been extended to cover many structural materials. A summary of materials which have been joined follows.

Aluminum and Its Alloys

Aluminum is quite difficult to diffusion weld because of its tightly adhering oxide film. Once the oxide is removed, DFW, without a diffusion aid, is performed by holding parts at temperatures between 850 and 1000°F (454 and 538°C) for up to 4 h. With a diffusion aid such as silver, copper, Ag-28Cu, Alclad, or aluminum foil, the time-temperature requirements are reduced considerably. For example, a typical weld cycle for Type 6061 or 2219 alloy without diffusion aids is 4 h at 870°F (466°C); with an Alclad surface, 7075 can be welded in 1 h at 325°F (163°C) and 24 ksi (165 MPa) pressure. The strength of diffusion welds varies, depending on whether a diffusion aid is used. Lap shear strengths of 9 to 11 ksi (62 to 76 MPa) are possible with Alclad 7075, and of 5.6 ksi (39 MPa) with alloys 6061 and 2219 welded without a diffusion aid.

Beryllium and Its Alloys

Beryllium's high strength-to-weight ratio and low neutron-absorption cross section make it especially interesting for aircraft and nuclear applications. Its usage, however, has been limited because of the difficulty of joining or fabricating this characteristically brittle metal into desired shapes without extensive machining. Cold-worked beryllium can be diffusion-welded by holding it at temperatures of 1500 to 1650°F (816 to 899°C) and pressures of about 10 ksi (69 MPa) for 4 h. In general, mechanical cleaning followed by wiping with acetone or ether constitutes good surface preparation for beryllium. It also can be prepared by grinding with wet silicon carbide paper and polishing with alumina in dilute oxalic acid. On the other hand, Be-38Al alloy can be diffusion-welded without special surface preparation.

Beryllium-copper (Cu-1.7Be) is readily diffusion-welded. Joint tensile strengths average 108 ksi (745 MPa), or well over twice that of brazed beryllium-copper joints. Good welds are obtained with a minimum pressure—about 0.006 ksi (0.04 MPa)—by using a silver-indium-copper diffusion aid. Using either a hydrogen atmosphere or vacuum, the weld cycle is approximately 30 min at 1475 to 1550°F (801 to 843°C).

A study has demonstrated that the weldability of beryllium is influenced by the BeO content and thickness. Welding conditions of 3 h at 1.5 ksi (10 MPa) pressure at 1400 to 1500°F (760 to 815°C) produced welds with shear strengths exceeding 90% of the base-metal shear strength at both room temperature and 800°F (427°C). It was apparent, however, that the beryllium oxide content effected weldability and that high efficiency and strength was obtained only in materials with about 1.0% BeO. All the work was performed in a vacuum hot press.[27,28]

Spot DFW is a new means of joining beryllium. It looks promising for double lap or butt shear joints in beryllium sheet. Ultimate strength of a double lap shear joint with multiple spot welds is about 59 ksi (407 MPa), lower than the ultimate strength of the sheet [70 ksi (483 MPa)], but higher than its minimum yield strength [50 ksi (345 MPa)].

Copper and Its Alloys

A limited amount of work has been done utilizing copper in DFW except in basic studies and as an intermediate diffusion aid material. Copper-copper and copper-nickel welds have been made by HIP welding. The high joint strength reported for copper to copper that was heat-treated at low temperatures is a reflection of the initial joint strength.[29] DFW has taken place in 15 min at 1000°F (538°C) and 5 ksi (34 MPa). The strength of copper-nickel joints improves with postweld heat treatment up to 1112°F (600°C).

Heat-Resistant Alloys

Nickel and cobalt alloys can be diffusion-welded with or without diffusion aids. Using various alloys containing from 9 to 16% beryllium as diffusion aids, Inconel X-750 can be diffusion welded in about 10 min at approximately 2000°F (1093°C). Resulting welds have shear strengths of about 70 ksi (483 MPa) at room temperature and 38 ksi (262 MPa) at 1500°F (816°C).

Butt joints made by the activated diffusion-bonding process of nickel-base superalloys which are difficult to weld (such as René 80, René 100, or René 77) have been exhaustively tested in elevated-temperature tensile, stress-rupture, and high-cycle fatigue. These tests have demonstrated that butt-joint efficiencies of 70 to 90% can be developed in both cast and wrought nickel-base superalloys; see Fig. 10-22. This represents an eightfold increase in strength over the strongest joints producible by conventional brazing.[17]

In addition to Udimet 700, DFW with the TLP process has successfully joined Inconel 713C, In-100, B-1900, MAR-M-200, MAR-M-302, Stellite 31, and Hastelloy X. Welds have been demonstrated in both similar and dissimilar metal combinations, including nickel-to-cobalt alloys. Bond strengths can be achieved which are effectively equivalent to that of the base metal even in high-temperature stress-rupture testing. Process flexibility has also resulted in welding of some coated turbine parts without degradation of their oxidation-resistant coating.

Production reliability and reproducibility has been demonstrated for this process by the high yield (>99.8%) of successfully welded parts in

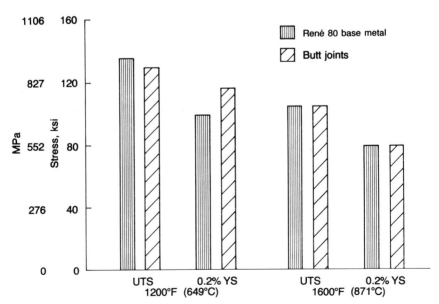

Fig. 10-22 Tensile properties of activated diffusion-welded butt joints in René 80 vs. those of the base metal.[17]

the initial production run of more than 18,000 turbine vane clusters; see Fig. 10-23. Other applications include welding of wear-resistant materials on turbine-blade shrouds and joining of tips onto turbine blades. Longer-range applications under study involve fabrication of

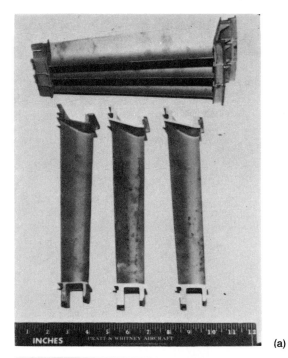

(a)

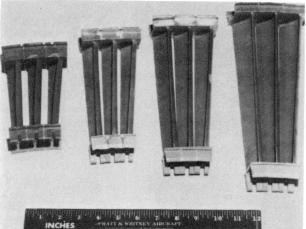

(b)

Fig. 10-23 TLP diffusion-welded low-pressure turbine vane clusters (In-713C). (a) Vanes read for DFW; (b) diffusion-welded vane cluster.[18]

(c)

Fig. 10-23 (cont.) (c) Diffusion-welded vane clusters.[18]

multipiece turbine vanes and other construction and repair concepts aimed at reducing manufacturing costs and increasing component performance.[18,30]

DFW systems were evaluated for their applicability to the fabrication of advanced-design air-cooled gas turbine blades from split halves. The joining systems evaluated were based upon the use of intermediate diffusion aids to promote and enhance DFW of a directionally solidified superalloy (modification of MAR-M-200). Particular emphasis was placed on increasing the ability of the joining systems to accommodate lack of fit, which is a major concern in DFW of complex-shaped hollow parts. The three systems, an electroplated nickel-cobalt alloy, a nickel-cobalt-tungsten-chromium dispersion-electroplated intermediate aid, and thin foil intermediaries, all produced excellent shear test results.[31]

Steels

Aircraft gas turbine engine rotor bearings run at fairly high speeds, but in the next decade, engine design will call for bearings to operate at twice the present-day pace. At these future speeds, the strong centrifugal forces between the rolling elements and outer race are beyond the capabilities of current bearings. A possible solution to this fatigue-life problem is spherically hollow balls that are fabricated by welding two hemispherical shells together. The AISI-M-2 shells are diffusion-butt-welded in an atmosphere of 2×10^{-5} torr (2.67 MPa) at 2130°F (1165°C) for 4 h with a pressure of 0.004 ksi (0.03 MPa) holding the hemispheres together.

The faying surfaces of the two hemispheres are put together in a welding jig made of aluminum oxide. A dead weight in the form of a tungsten rod placed on the upper hemisphere presses the two members together while they are vacuum-diffusion-welded. The process has produced a complete weld with no discernible weld lines and, because of the low pressure used, no macrodeformation.

DFW of 1.5- to 2-in-thick (38.4 to 50.8 mm) AISI 1020 steel plate in air was accomplished using the autogenous (self-generated) faying-surface cleaning principle, designated autovac cleaning. Butt joints with ground and degreased surfaces were prepared. Evaluation of weld quality was based on metallographic examination and room-temperature tensile and bend tests. Results were as follows:[32]

1. Excellent diffusion welds were produced in air with no macrodeformation of the AISI 1020 steel base metal. Diffusion promoted grain growth across the weld line and eliminated the original interface. The welds were as strong as the base metal as judged by transverse tensile and bend tests.
2. The best diffusion welds in AISI 1020 steel were obtained by using either set of the following welding parameters:
   a. No autovac cleaning; DFW at 2195°F (1200°C) for 2 h at 0.005 ksi (0.04 MPa).
   b. Autovac cleaning at 2195°F (1200°C) for $2^{1}/_{2}$ h; DFW at 1991°F (1090°C) for 2 h at 0.005 ksi (0.04 MPa).

Autovac cleaning of Type 304 stainless steel, Fig. 10-24, makes it possible to subsequently produce high-quality welds. Type 304 stainless

Effect of auto-vac cleaning
Hot press welds in type 304 bar at 980° C

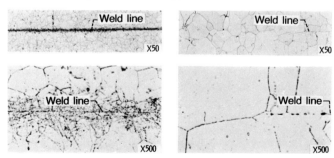

No auto-vac cleaning   Auto-vac cleaned at 1200° C for 1 hr

Fig. 10-24 Diffusion welds in Type 304 stainless steel, illustrating the effect of preweld autovac cleaning. Left, no autovac cleaning prior to DFW at 1796°F (980°C); right, autovac-cleaned at 2192°F (1200°C) for 1 h prior to DFW at 1796°F (980°C).[32]

steel was autovac-cleaned in 1 h at 2195°F (1200°C) and diffusion-welded at 1796°F (980°C) for 5 min at 2.7 ksi (18 MPa).

DFW has been used to join martensitic steel to tool steel with nickel foils 0.001 to 0.003 in thick (0.03 to 0.08 mm) for blanking and drawing dies.[33]

Dispersion-Strengthened Alloys

HIP welds made in 0.5-in-diameter (12.7 mm) TD-nickel bar in both butt joints (with and without intermediate aids) and lap joints were accomplished in a 2-h cycle. The DFW temperature was 2000°F (1093°C), pressure was 20 ksi (138 MPa), and all work was performed in helium atmosphere. The criteria for selection of the diffusion aids is shown in Table 10-1.[34] The following results were obtained:

1. For the joints with intermediate diffusion aids, stress-rupture tests at 2000°F (1093°C) were a much more severe criterion of joint strength than 2000°F (1093°C) tensile tests. The strongest joints in stress-rupture [with the 0.004-in. (0.10-mm) cobalt-alloy diffusion aid] for 100 h life had 15% joint efficiency.
2. Short-time shear tests of lap joints indicate that the HIP welds are about as strong as the base metal at room temperature and at 2000°F (1093°C).
3. In 2000°F (1093°C) tensile tests, butt joints with cobalt-alloy and Hastelloy X diffusion aids had up to 100% and 87% joint efficiency, respectively. This represented the best results of the various aid materials evaluated. Without aids, maximum joint efficiency was about 55%.[34]

TABLE 10-1
Criteria for Selection of Materials[34]

Interlayer material	Primary basis for selection
W, Mo, Cb, Ta	Good strength at 2000°F (1093°C) for the interlayer.
Ti, Cr, V, Pd, Fe	Increase in diffusion across the weld interfaces to promote grain growth and eliminate the original weld interface. Also selected to avoid ordered phase formation.
ThO_2	Extra thoria to compensate for possible losses.
TD-Ni sheet	Relatively good strength at 2000°F (1093°C) for the interlayer.
Hastelloy X	Relatively good strength at 2000°F (1093°C) for the interlayer. Strong Ni-base alloy in sheet form. Good tensile strength to 2000°F (1093°C). Good stress-rupture strength to 1800°F (982°C).
Cobalt-base alloy (2.8Cr-25W-2Re-0.9Ti-0.4Zr-0.15C-Rem Co)	Strongest cobalt-base alloy available in sheet form at 2000°F* (1093°C); ultimate tensile strength—15 ksi (172 MPa). At 2000°F (1093°C) stress for rupture in 100 h—10 ksi (69 Mpa).

*Strength given here is for tests of as-cast material.[34]

A vacuum-hot-press DFW method was used in recent work[35,36] to produce tensile-shear and creep-rupture shear strengths equal to parent material at 2000°F (1090°C) with specially processed (unrecrystallized) TD-NiCr. The lap joints were made with 0.015- and 0.060-in-thick (0.38 and 1.5 mm) TD-NiCr. Specifically, the following conclusions resulted from these studies:

1. The DFW process was applicable in joining both commercial-grade and specially processed TD-NiCr sheets to themselves or to each other. Use of the specially processed material was preferred because of better reliability of joint quality.
2. The conditions recommended for the one-step weld cycles developed in this study were as follows:
   a. The specially processed TD-NiCr: 1400°F (760°C) with 20 ksi (138 MPa) for 1 h.
   b. For commercial TD-NiCr: 1400°F (760°C) with 40 ksi (276 MPa) for 1 h.
   c. For specially processed TD-NiCr to commercial TD-NiCr: 1400°F (760°C) with 30 ksi (207 MPa) for 1 h.
   Postheating at 2150°F (1180°C) for 2 h in a nonoxiding atmosphere was recommended for all of these cycles to produce recrystallization and/or grain growth across the weld line.
3. The recommended preweld joint preparation method involved surface sanding with 320-grit paper followed by chemical polishing.

More recently resistance spot welding[37] was used to produce diffusion welds in TD-NiCr using lap-joint specimens, specially processed material, and postheating at 2192°F (1200°C) for 2 h in hydrogen. The excellent results showed that the weld was indistinguishable from the base metal. In 2012°F (1100°C) stress-rupture shear tests, the welds were as strong as the base metal. Base-metal failure, rather than weld failure, took place in the stress-rupture tests and the other mechanical tests that included room-temperature and 2012°F (1100°C) tensile shear, and room-temperature fatigue tests.

The CSDB process has been successfully applied to joining TD-Ni and TD-NiCr.[38] Combustion cans fabricated by this method have withstood 2000°F (1093°C) temperature tests without any mechanical failures.

Columbium and Its Alloys

HIP welds in Cb and Cb-V alloys have been successfully made at 2400°F (1316°C), 10 ksi (70 MPa), for 3 h in vacuum. Columbium alloy Cb-752 (10W-2.5Zr-Rem Cb) has been successfully diffusion-welded by blanket and resistance heating method. A diffusion aid of titanium foil, 0.002 in (0.05 mm) and a DFW cycle of 2200°F (1204°C), 1×10^{-6} torr (0.133 MPa), for 6 h were used to produce the components

TABLE 10-2
DFW Results for Molybdenum and Its Alloys

Material	DFW process	Parameters			Comments
		Temperature	Pressure	Time	
Pure molybdenum	Hot isostatic press (HIP)	2600°F (1427°C)	10 ksi (69 MPa)	3 h	HIP welds produced were of high quality with complete grain growth across the original weld interface. HIP produced loss of ductility, but 25% cold rolling restored ductility.
	Vacuum hot press	1840°F (1004°C)	30 ksi (207 MPa)	1 h	Columbium foil, 0.001 in (0.03 mm), has been successfully used as a diffusion aid to produce excellent welded joints below the recrystallization temperature of molybdenum.
	Induction heating with and without intermediate diffusion aids[39]	2012°F (1150°C)	5 ksi (35 MPa)	15 min	Diffusion welds without an intermediate aid were produced at higher temperatures than the recrystallization temperature of pure molybdenum with 5 to 10% deformation, but the joints made at higher temperatures than 2192°F (1200°C) were brittle because of recrystallization.[39] Grain growth across the interface was observed to occur at 2282°F (1250°C) for 5 min and migration of grain boundaries took place easily at relatively low temperatures. See Fig. 25. It was also found that the formation of the molybdenum joint without recrystallization and large deformation was accomplished with an intermediate aid such as iron, nickel, copper, or silver prepared by electroplating. The remelting temperature of the joint was much higher than the melting one of the intermediate aid. Although nickel formed an intermetallic compound with molybdenum, the nickel intermediate aid made a stronger joint at low temperatures than the others. Copper was also found to be applicable as an intermediate aid, but it did not alloy with molybdenum.[39]

TABLE 10-2
(Continued)

Material	DFW process	Parameters			Comments
		Temperature	Pressure	Time	
Molybdenum-0.5Ti	HIP	2600°F (1427°C)	10 ksi (69 MPa)	3 h	
	Resistance heating	2100°F (1149°C)	0.5 ksi (3 MPa)	15 min	Titanium and nickel 0.001-in (0.03-mm) foils as diffusion aids. The shear strength of the joint with titanium was 20.7 ksi (143 MPa) while the nickel joint produced 33.8 ksi (233 MPa).
	Vacuum hot press	For titanium 1680°F (916°C)	30 ksi (207 MPa)	20 min	
		For nickel 1700°F (927°C)	30 ksi (207 MPa)	20 min	
TZM (0.5Ti-0.1 Zr-Rem Mo)	Induction heating	2200°F (1204°C)	10 ksi (69 MPa)	1 min	Columbium, tantalum, and vanadium 0.001-in (0.03-mm) foils as diffusion aids. The tantalum yielded the highest room temperature shear strength 0.7 ksi (4 MPa).

(honeycomb sandwich) with the electric-blanket method. Utilizing resistance heat, the cycle entailed 2100°F (1149°C), 1 ksi (7 MPa), and 15 min. The atmosphere protecting the parts for both methods was argon.

Columbium alloy D-36 (10Ti-5Zr-Rem Cb) has been diffusion-welded by resistance and induction heating methods. Diffusion aids of vanadium, tantalum and columbium foil have been used successfully to join the alloy, and self-welding has been used as well. All systems produced welds, but the self-weld condition gave the highest joint strengths and the vanadium foil provided a good alternative system. Although surface preparation was found to be not critical when an intermediate material was used, an abraded and degreased surface was optimum in the self-welding of this alloy.

Columbium alloy B-66 (5Mo-5V-1Zr-Rem Cb) has been successfully diffusion-welded by induction heat both in the self-weld condition and with a 0.003-in (0.01-mm) tantalum intermediate foil. Columbium, Tantalum, and vanadium foils have also been used as intermediates in the resistance DFW of B-66 alloy. The optimum surface preparation for DFW B-66 alloy with an intermediate foil was degreasing in a salt solution. This preparation produced the highest-strength lap joints. One last Cb alloy, D-43 (10W-1Zr-0.1C-Rem Cb), has been diffusion-welded by induction heating, and high peel strengths have been obtained in the self-welded condition and with vanadium and tantalum intermediates.

Molybdenum and Its Alloys

Several DFW techniques have been applied to join molybdenum and its alloys with a fair amount of success. See Table 10-2.

Tantalum and Its Alloys

Pure tantalum has been diffusion-welded successfully by HIP with the following parameters: 2350°F (1288°C) at 10 ksi (69 MPa) in 2.5 h. An intermediate diffusion aid, zirconium, has produced excellent joints at temperatures as low as 1600°F (871°C), well below the normal recrystallization temperatures.

Resistance heating of the 90Ta-10W alloy has produced diffusion welds in 15 min at 2500°F (1371°C) and 0.5 ksi (3 MPa) in an argon atmosphere. The tantalum alloy T-111 (8W-2Hf-Rem Ta) has been resistance and induction diffusion-welded with and without any aids. The most successful system has used a 0.003-in (0.01-mm) tantalum foil at 2600°F (1427°C) at 24 ksi (165 MPa) for 20 s.

Tungsten and Its Alloys

HIP welding of tungsten has been accomplished at 2800°F (1538°C) and 10 ksi (69 MPa) for 3 h. Vacuum-hot-press DFW has been successful on tungsten, and for sustained high-temperature application, either a tungsten-titanium or a tungsten-columbium intermediate system has produced minimum diffusion activity.

Titanium and Its Alloys

Electroplating has become a popular method for applying an intermediate diffusion aid material on titanium and alloys (6Al-4V, 6Al-6V-2Sn, 6Al-2Sn-4Zr-2Mo, 3Al-2.5V, 5Al-2.5Sn, 8Al-1Mo-1V, 3Al-13V-11Cr, and Beta III) and subsequently creating a diffusion weld.[40] A typical joint is shown in Fig. 10-25. Applications have been found in honeycomb sandwich construction for aircraft and engine components.[19,20] These components include engine cases, aircraft wing and fuselage assemblies, flaps and nozzle vanes for engines, firewalls for helicopters, and components for space vehicles. All the DFW is performed in vacuum furnaces at 10^{-5} torr (1.33 MPa).

The credibility of this diffusion-aided joining system was recently shown in a government-sponsored program.[41] It involved ground testing and Mach 3 flight verification testing of full-scale, primary structural panels on the upper wing surface of a research airplane, and laboratory testing of representative structural element specimens.

Test data showed that exposure temperatures of 600°F (316°C) and 800°F (427°C) do not significantly affect the flatwise tensile strength of diffusion-welded sandwich structures. This type of exposure was for periods up to 5000 h. Additional testing has shown no deterioration of the structure as seen in Table 10-3.[20,41] Other thin-film DFW systems have been applied to 6Al-4V titanium sheet metal and plate materials, successfully producing high-integrity joints that resulted in excellent mechanical and metallurgical properties.[21,42]

As aircraft engines become more complex, they also must be lighter, diffusion-welded hollow titanium compressor blades are 50% lighter

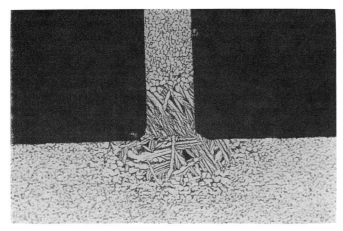

Fig. 10-25 Photomicrograph of Ti-6Al-4V sheet diffusion-welded to Ti-3Al-2.5V foil.

TABLE 10-3
Static Test Results of Panels[20,41]

Test panel number	Test temperature		Exposure	% ultimate load*
	°F	°C		
1	RT†	20	None	111
2	RT	20	100 h at 600°F (316°C)	121
3	600	316	None	127‡
4	600	316	100 h at 600°F (316°C)	134
5	RT	20	1000 cycles—65°F (−54°C) to 600°F (316°C)	121
6	RT	20	10,000 h at 600°F (316°C)	119

*Corrected for temperature as required.
†RT: Room temperature.
‡Fixture bottomed out—no failure.

than conventional solid titanium blades.[43] Development work using vacuum-hot-press DFW techniques in conjunction with forging and chemical milling is being conducted. Two parts are first formed by forging, then hollowed out by chemical milling. The parts are ground to prepare concave and convex mating surfaces for DFW. After cleaning, the parts are brought into intimate contact by external pressure. The assembly is heated in a vacuum and held at elevated temperature, and a diffusion weld is achieved. These blades, which when finished are about 5 in (127 mm) wide and 16.5 in (419 mm) long and are made from Ti-6Al-4V alloy, have been produced at a cost savings of at least 50% over the cost of fabricating by other methods.

One of the vital elements in making diffusion-welded joints (aside from temperature and time) is pressure. A novel approach where this can be applied with reasonable economy is a forging press. The system seems to work well on titanium parts. The parts are chemically cleaned at their mating surfaces, electron-beam-welded together, heated in a furnace, and them pressed together for only 1 to 2 min.

The idea works well on prototype parts. No special dies are required and parts are blocked in the press to equalize ram forces. The edges that were electron-beam-welded together are machined away after DFW. The surfaces of the part that have been exposed to high temperature may also have to be etched. A good example is a titanium jet-engine compressor wheel composed of a flat-type wheel with a welded ring to produce a high-coupling wheel. See Fig. 10-26. Experiments have demonstrated the feasibility of joining different titanium alloys. Composites of as many as three different alloys have been made. A notable example is the compressor wheel, where a high-creep-resistance alloy is desirable at the rim section and a high-tensile-strength alloy is desirable at the hub where temperatures are generally lower.

Property tests across welded joints, including room- and elevated-temperature tensile, stress-rupture, creep, fracture toughness, and fatigue properties, show that welded areas have properties equivalent to the parent metal.[44]

Press DFW has found practical applications in a new airplane. There are now sixty-six diffusion-welded parts in critical fracture areas which have been designed and fabricated by DFW.[13,45] One of the advantages is that DFW saves metal. An initial 1000-lb (454-kg) forging, for example, has to be machined into a 440-lb (199-kg) part. With DFW, no metal is lost to machining the unit, and lighter, less expensive machines are employed than with forging.

The titanium is primarily annealed 6Al-4V and is used in many of the aircraft's bulkheads, parts of engine nacelles, and other hot sections. Bulkheads are diffusion-welded and assembled with mechanical fasteners. The extremely large wing carry-through structure also uses some diffusion-welded titanium parts.

Aircraft designers are finding that DFW might be suitably applied in the wing pivot section, the vertical tail, and fuselage skin panels of aircraft.

The joints produced by roll DFW are metallurgically indistinguishable from the base material. Consequently, structures which have been properly welded show that base-metal properties can essentially be retained across the joined section.

Tensile tests of Ti-8Al-1Mo-1V showed no significant differences in strength between welded and base-line specimens, nor between materials reduced 40 and 60%. Ductility (reduction in area) was less for welded specimens than for base-line specimens, however. Tensile data are summarized in Table 10-4.

Other recent successes utilizing roll DFW include a titanium chamber for a synchrotron. The chamber basically is a long, shallow

Fig. 10-26 Jet-engine compressor wheel with diffusion-welded coupling ring.[44]

TABLE 10-4
Tensile Data on Ti-8Al-1Mo-1V[12]

Class	Fabrication reduction level, %	Yield strength		Ultimate strength		Reduction in area, %
		ksi	MPa	ksi	MPa	
Base	40	145	1000	152	1048	29.5
Bonded	40	148	1020	153	1055	22
Base	60	145	1000	152	1048	32
Bonded	60	145	1000	152	1048	10

box with the upper and lower skins stiffened by exterior tee members. Full-size shrouded centrifugal impellers 12 in (305 mm) in diameter for liquid hydrogen pumps were diffusion-welded from 16 pieces of forged and machined Ti-5Al-2.5Sn alloy.[46]

The autovac cleaning and subsequent DFW process applied to steels, etc., previously discussed, provides oxide-free welding surfaces and greatly speeds DFW of titanium and its alloys by hot-press and roll techniques.

For hot-press DFW, surfaces to be welded are ground flat, cleaned with acetone, and butted together, and the joints are seam-welded on all sides to form a seal. The assembly is then heated in an inert-gas atmosphere for 2 h at 1800°F (983°C). This dissolves oxides and gases trapped between the welding surfaces into the parent material and creates a vacuum. The welded seal prevents reforming of surface oxides. Subsequently only 5 min of pressing time is required at 1800°F (983°C) with a pressure of 0.2 ksi (1 MPa) to make the diffusion weld. The resultant weld strength and ductility of test specimens equal parent metal properties.[47]

For roll welding, accomplished with only 10% deformation, the surfaces to be welded are ground flat, pickled, washed and cleaned with acetone. The surfaces are clamped together, sealed by welding on all sides, and canned in 0.015-in (0.38-mm) stainless steel to prevent oxidation during rolling. The canned sheet assemblies are then auto-vacuum-cleaned by heating in air for 2 h at 1800°F (983°C).

Alternatively, auto-vacuum cleaning can be done during heat-up to the rolling temperature, heat soak, rolling, and cool-down. Heating the sealed assemblies high enough to decompose and dissolve oxides and gases trapped between welding surfaces eliminates the high degree of deformation normally required to break up these films and dissolve the gases. This method has been used to roll-diffusion-weld 0.06-in-thick (1.5 mm) sheets of Ti-6Al-4V at 1750°F (954°C).

Investigators recently evaluated titanium alloys Ti-6Al-4V, Ti-5Al-2.5Sn, Ti-8Al-1Mo-1V, and Ti-3Al-2.5Sn and found that at temperatures of 1500 to 1900°F (816 to 1038°C), at pressures of 5 to 10 ksi (34 to 69 MPa), and for time periods of 30 min to 6 h, excellent DFW can be accomplished, while some investigators found that only 2 ksi (14 MPa) was required to produce diffusion welds with thick-section Ti-6Al-4V.

Zirconium and Its Alloys

Diffusion aids such as silver, copper, and iron have produced excellent diffusion welds in zirconium alloys (Zircaloy). The technique has been very effective for DFW plate-type nuclear fuel elements. The best welded properties have been obtained with a 0.003-in (0.08-mm) copper coating diffusion-welded at 1900°F (1038°C) and 0.03 ksi (0.2 MPa) in 30 min to 2 h. HIP welds have also been satisfactorily made in Zircaloy parts in 3 h at 1550°F (843°C) and 10 ksi (69 MPa).

Composites

One of the most promising fields in which DFW seems destined to play a significant role is that of composite materials. Composites are materials which contain high-strength or high-modulus filamentary materials to reinforce common matrices in a manner which resembles the principles used in reinforced concrete. By this technique, higher-strength, higher-modulus materials can be made. Reinforcing materials commonly used are carbon, boron, alumina, silicon carbide, tungsten, columbium, beryllium, boron nitride, and others.

In metal-matrix composites, i.e., where the material which is reinforced is a metal, DFW is one of the most common means for producing the shapes which contain fiber and matrix. Many of the composite-material combinations have been made by press and roll DFW as well as HIP. Among the metals studied as matrix materials are aluminum, titanium, copper, nickel, and magnesium. A nickel-tungsten composite was produced by HIP, a beryllium-titanium composite was produced by roll DFW, and an aluminum-nickel plated graphite composite and titanium-tungsten and titanium-graphite composites[48] have been hot-press-welded.

DFW is being used not only to produce composites but also to join them to each other. A development program has shown that layups of B/Al tape having a plasma-sprayed layer of brazing material (713 Al) can be diffusion-welded at pressures below 0.2 ksi (1 MPa), compared with 10 ksi (69 MPa) for welding Type 6061 aluminum matrix composites.

Boron/aluminum composites and titanium alloys can be joined by resistance DFW without melting of the aluminum matrix. This is accomplished with standard electrodes. A molten nugget, centered in the titanium, conducts heat into the aluminum matrix of the composite. Temperature of the aluminum is maintained near, but below, its melting point.

Mechanical properties of joints are excellent over a wide temperature range from room temperature to 600°F (21 to 315°C). Average lap shear of 0.32-in-diameter (8 mm) spots between 0.030-in (0.76-mm) B/Al and 0.036-in (0.92-mm) titanium is 105 ksi (724 MPa) at 70°F (21°C), 120 ksi (827 MPa) at 250°F (121°C), and 85 ksi (586 MPa) at 600°F (316°C). Joints have useful creep strength up to 600°F (316°C). At 70°F (21°C), diffusion spots sustain over 40% of static strength for more than 2 million cycles without failure. At 600°F (316°C), fatigue strength decreases with life because of creep. At 10 million cycles, more than 25% of the static strength remains.

Resistance DFW is used primarily for joining B/Al "hat" sections to titanium web panels. The new process is expected to find further application in fabrication of lightweight aerospace components.[49]

Dissimilar Metal and Ceramic Combinations

Joining nonferrous metals to ferrous metals

Joints between ferrous and nonferrous metals are of interest to industry because they combine the strength and toughness of steel with the special properties, such as oxidation resistance, corrosion resistance, etc. provided by the nonferrous metal. The joining of ferrous to nonferrous metals is far more complicated than the joining of dissimilar ferrous metals, because of the wider variation in the physical, mechanical, and metallurgical properties of the metals being joined. The extent of these property differences is an excellent indication of the difficulty to be anticipated in joining such metals.

Titanium to Steel. The DFW of Ti-8Al-1Mo-1V titanium alloy to Type 321 stainless steel, utilizing the differences in coefficients of expansion of the two materials, was investigated in the course of a program to develop procedures to fabricate transition sections for cryogenic tubing applications.[50,51] Joints were diffusion-welded in air and in a vacuum; both bare and electroplated base metals were used. On the basis of metallurgical studies, corrosion tests, and mechanical tests, the following conditions were selected for DFW: (1) bare base metals, 1425°F (774°C) for 10 min in a vacuum; and (2) silver-plated base metals, 700°F (371°C) for 30 min in air. The silver-plated specimens were prediffused at 1350°F (732°C) for 10 min prior to welding. Helium-leak tests before and after thermal cycling from room temperature to −320°F (−196°C) indicated the soundness of these joints; the shear load to failure was 12,800 lb (5805 kg). Failure occurred in the titanium-alloy tubing. In an extension of this program, joints between Ti-8Al-1Mo-1V titanium alloy and Type 321 stainless steel were diffusion-welded to produce transition sections with diameters of 0.5, 2.0, 4.0 and 8.0 in[51] (12.7, 51, 102, and 203 mm). The joint properties evaluated were thermal-shock tests, helium-leak checks, vibration tests, cyclic pressure tests, and burst tests.

The silver-plated surfaces were diffusion-welded at temperatures ranging from 500 to 1600°F (260 to 871°C) and contact pressures from 5.5 to 30 ksi (38 to 207 MPa) in a vacuum or an argon atmosphere for periods ranging from 10 min to 8 h. Satisfactory welds were obtained over a wide range of experimental conditions, but a minimum temperature of 1100 to 1300°F (593 to 704°C) was required to ensure proper adherence of the silver plate to the titanium alloy.

By this method, reliable DFW of the dissimilar metals was effected at relatively low temperatures, with better control to minimize the formation of detrimental intermetallic phases and to provide a greater tolerance of processing parameters such as cleanliness, time, pressure, and temperature.[50,51]

Titanium and its alloys have been joined to iron-, nickel-, or cobalt-base alloys by DFW techniques using a copper/nickel to titanium eutectic. The basic concept behind this approach was that if a eutectic can be formed between two pieces of titanium and a thin film of an intermediate material, then another material could be substituted for one of the pieces of titanium, and the eutectic would still be formed through the agency of the remaining titanium member.

The film of joining material was commercially pure copper or nickel, or an alloy containing up to 3% foreign elements such as Cr, Mn, Al, Sn, Si, etc. It could also be a Cu/Ni alloy such as Monel, constantan, or an alloy containing up to 8% foreign elements as in R-, K-, H-, or S-Monel. Film thickness could vary from 0.00004 to 0.003 in (0.001 to 0.08 mm). Its placement involved the use of various techniques such as chemical plating, electroplating, vapor deposition, and metallizing; also shims or foils were preplaced.

Titanium to Nickel-Base Alloy. The DFW of titanium alloy Ti-8Al-1Mc-1V to nickel alloy Inconel 600 was also investigated during a program to fabricate transition sections for cryogenic tubing applications.[50] The joints were diffusion-welded in air or in a vacuum, using bare, silver-plated, or nickel-plated base metals. The following conditions were used for welding: (1) bare base metals, 1625°F (885°C) for 15 min in a vacuum; (2) silver-plated base metals, 600°F (316°C) for 30 min in air; and (3) nickel-plated base metals, 1325°F (719°C) for 30 min in a vacuum.

Either the silver or nickel plating functions as an effective diffusion aid, resulting in lower permissible welding temperatures; however, the joint strength was not improved by plating.

During the same program, Ti-8Al-1Mo-1V was roll-welded to Inconel 600 at a temperature of 1050°F (566°C); no diffusion aid was used.

Beryllium to Steel. Cast beryllium has been diffusion-welded to Type 316 stainless steel impact targets.[52] Joining was performed in vacuum at 1450°F (788°C) for 2 h, and silver was used as a diffusion aid. A 0.5-in-diameter (12.7 mm) stainless steel tube was positioned inside a drilled section of beryllium rod 1.25 in (32 mm) in diameter. Pressure was supplied by differential thermal expansion. Other Type 316 stainless-to-beryllium impact targets have been HIP diffusion-welded under the same parameters as above with 10 ksi (69 MPa) pressure.[53,54]

Refractory Metals to Steel. The DFW of molybdenum and columbium alloys to stainless steel was investigated.[55] Small disks of columbium alloy F-48, molybdenum alloy Mo-0.5Ti, and Type 316 stainless steel were assembled in a molybdenum capsule for joining; pressure was applied by means of a threaded screw in the capsule. Joints made between F-48 and 316 and between Mo-0.5Ti and 316 were diffusion-welded at temperatures of 1800 and 2000°F (982 and 1093°C) for 4 h.

The Cb-1Zr alloy has been diffusion-welded to Type 316 stainless steel using a Cb-1Zr diffusion aid. DFW was accomplished at 1800°F (982°C) in 4 h. Shear tests showed 10.7 ksi (74 MPa) at room temperature (20°C), 11.4 ksi (79 MPa) at 600°F (316°C), 11.9 ksi (82 MPa) at 1200°F (649°C), and 4.2 ksi (29 MPa) at 1800°F (982°C).

The HDW process has produced excellent joints between AISI 4140 steel rod and molybdenum.[56]

For some parts, such as a filter in which the filter material was porous tungsten, it was necessary to ensure tight connection with a bushing made from stainless steel. Evaluation of the diffusion welds was done by rupture tests. Satisfactory conditions were those which ensured rupture in the filter bed without exfoliation of it on its border with the steel. The DFW conditions were pressure 0.2 to 0.3 ksi (1 to 2 MPa), temperature 2192°F (1200°C), and time 30 min.[9]

Zircaloy has been successfully diffusion-welded to stainless steel with resultant tensile strength of 68 ksi (400 MPa).[57] With diffusion aids as joining media, nuclear applications have utilized the properties of Zircaloy and stainless steel. Joining has been done in a vacuum furnace at temperatures of 1870°F (1021°C) in 5 to 30 min and by induction heating in 30 s to 1 min at a temperature of 1900°F (1038°C). Vacuums of 3 to 5×10^{-5} torr (0.004 to 0.008 MPa) have been used with either of these heating methods to prevent oxidation and contamination of the joint materials.

Aluminum to Steel. Successful DFW of 2219 aluminum alloy and Type 321 stainless steel has been accomplished: (1) temperature of 500 to 600°F (260 to 316°C), (2) pressures of 20 to 25 ksi (138 to 172 MPa), and (3) times of 2 to 4 h. With these combinations of metals, the joint faying surfaces were electroplated with silver before joining. The silver prevented the formation of oxide-film barriers and embrittling phases.

For these processing parameters, techniques for DFW of large diameter assemblies have been successfully developed and demonstrated with the fabrication and testing of 20-in-diameter (508 mm) joints. Hoop stresses developed during burst testing exceeded the yield strength of the Type 2219-T62 aluminum alloy. The unique DFW method developed utilized simple differential thermal expansion tooling that could be economically adapted for production requirements.[50,51,57]

Bronze to Steel. DFW is reported to provide faster, more effective joining of Type 4130 steel and a TFE-bronze composite. The TFE-bronze composite is used as a dry lubricant for steel gears operating in the hostile environment of space. Previously, the materials were joined by adhesive bonding, but this method often presented such problems as adhesive out-gassing and radiation damage.

With the use of a diffusion aid at the TFE-steel interface, procedures are basically standard. Parts to be joined are first cleaned with methyl alcohol. The metal interfaces are copper-flashed, and a coat of flux is treated with fine-mesh, oxygen-free copper granules. The parts are then placed in a press, subjected to heat at 580°F (305°C) and 25 ksi

(17 MPa) for 15 to 20 min, and allowed to cool to room temperature. The process requires $1^1/_2$ h and produces excellent joints.

Joining nonferrous metals to nonferrous metals

The inherent problems in joining dissimilar nonferrous metals are similar to those encountered when ferrous and nonferrous metals are joined, because of the differences in the physical and metallurgical properties of the base metals. Some dissimilar nonferrous metals have been joined routinely for many years; others, such as aluminum to titanium, titanium to nickel, aluminum to uranium, etc., are new combinations.

Aluminum to Titanium. The DFW of Type 2219 aluminum alloy to Ti-5Al-2.5Sn alloy was investigated during a program to fabricate transition sections for cryogenic tubing applications.[50,51] The joints were diffusion-welded in air or in a vacuum and bare or silver-plated base metals were used. On the basis of metallurgical studies, corrosion tests, and mechanical tests, the following conditions were selected for welding: (1) bare base metals, 940°F (504°C) for 30 min in a vacuum; and (2) silver-plated base metals, 500°F (260°C) for 2 h in air. Acceptable shear strengths at all test temperatures were obtained with bare base metals. Joints made with silver-plated base metals had acceptable strengths at room temperature and −320°F (20 and −196°C). Tubular transition sections were made according to the joint design shown in Fig. 10-27. The same tooling and joint designs were applicable to aluminum and titanium as well as stainless steel. In an extension to this program, joints between Type 2219 aluminum alloy and Ti-5Al-2.5Sn alloy 0.060 in (1.5 mm) thick were diffusion-welded to produce transition sections of 0.5, 2.0, 4.0, and 8.0 in (12.7, 51, 102, and 203 mm) diameter.[51] The joint properties were evaluated by thermal-shock tests, helium-leak tests, vibration tests, cyclic pressure tests, and burst tests.

Aluminum to Uranium and Zirconium. Joining of aluminum alloys and alloys of uranium and zirconium is encountered in the fabrication of fuel elements for nuclear reactors, and an extensive technology for

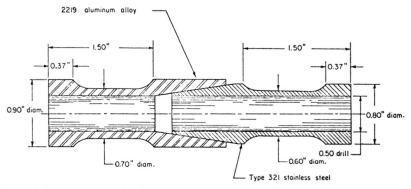

Fig. 10-27   Joint design for DFW dissimilar metal tubing.[50] (0.001 in = 0.03 mm).

joining these metals has been developed. DFW methods have included HIP and roll techniques and use of diffusion aids. Aluminum and Al-4.5U alloy have been successfully joined with diffusion aids. Aids have included zinc, tin, and nickel.[58,59,60,61] The use of silver was also investigated.[62] Roll DFW was successful with Type 6061 aluminum alloy and uranium.[63,64,65] HIP welds of Zircaloy-2 and aluminum for tubing have been successfully produced.[66,67]

Titanium to Beryllium. DFW using 0.003-in-thick (0.08 mm) silver as a diffusion aid has been successful in joining beryllium to Ti-6Al-4V at 1570°F (854°C) and a pressure of 0.64 ksi (4 MPa) in vacuum. Joint strength was approximately 5 ksi (34 MPa).

Titanium to Copper. DFW of alloys Ti-3Al-1.5Mn, Ti-4Al-3Mo-1V, and Ti-3Al-8Mo-11Cr to Cu-0.8Cr with a columbium foil diffusion aid 0.004 in (0.10 mm) thick has been investigated.[68] The optimum joining conditions were (1) temperature, 1760 to 1796°F (960 to 980°C); (2) pressure, 0.28 to 0.5 ksi (2 to 3 MPa); and (3) time, 5 h. The tensile strength of these joints ranged from 28 to 41 ksi (191 to 283 MPa).

Recently techniques required to diffusion weld commercial bronze (Cu-10Zn) to a titanium alloy (Ti-6Al-6V-2Sn) at 900°F (482°C) were developed. Since this titanium alloy will age-harden at 900°F (482°C), a process was developed such that welding was carried out during the titanium alloy aging treatment. The results of this investigation were then directly applied to DFW obturator bands on experimental 6.1-in (155-mm) artillery projectiles.[69]

All welding was done in a vacuum of 10^{-4} torr (13.3 MPa). Under optimal welding conditions, failure occurred in the gilding metal matrix adjacent to the weld, and joint shear strengths of up to 29 ksi (200 MPa) were achieved. Since the assembly was two concentric cylinders which were welded on a circumferential joint, the differential thermal constraint technique was used to apply a uniform stress in the axial and radial directions. This was accomplished by placing a TZM molybdenum ring around the gilding metal, which in turn surrounded the titanium alloy. Since the coefficient of thermal expansion for molybdenum is lower than that of the other materials, it provided constraint as the assembly was heated and subsequently diffusion-welded.

Molybdenum to Tungsten, Columbium, and Others. Numerous examples of HIP dissimilar-metal diffusion welds have been documented.[70] Columbium and Ta-10W alloy have been welded to 0.5Ti-Mo alloy, and molybdenum has been welded to tungsten. The welds were produced below 2500°F (1371°C).

Recently extensive work was conducted on the DFW of composite cathodes for electrovacuum devices for molybdenum and tungsten. Parts have been successfully produced under industrial conditions. The mechanical and electrical characteristics of welded cathodes completely satisfy technical specifications.[9]

Another example of current experimental work[9] is DFW of cathode assemblies for welding ignitrons. This work involved welding molybdenum to Kovar. A new area of investigation is DFW of carbides of zirconium and columbium to refractory metals. Titanium carbide was joined to molybdenum at temperatures of 2912 to 3452°F (1600 to 1900°C), and zirconium carbide to columbium at 2552 to 2912°F (1400 to 1600°C).[9]

Graphite to Metals. Extensive research has been conducted to join the refractory metals to graphite. DFW with the use of diffusion aids was used[71] to join molybdenum, columbium, and tantalum to graphite. A titanium-foil insert, electroplated with a 0.0008- to 0.001-in-thick (0.02 to 0.03 mm) layer of copper, was placed between the graphite and the refractory metal. Joining was conducted under the following conditions: (1) temperature, 1634 to 1841°F (890 to 1005°C); (2) pressure, 0.04 to 0.1 ksi (0.3 to 0.7 MPa); and (3) time, 5 to 10 min. Under these conditions, the titanium-copper eutectic alloy formed and wet the graphite and the refractory metal.

Ceramics to Metals. HIP welding has been used to fabricate joints between columbium and high-purity ceramic materials.[72] Of the two metal-ceramic systems examined, the columbium-chromium-alumina system is a three-component system in which the intermediate material provides the necessary diffusion characteristics with columbium; its oxide is completely soluble in alumina. The columbium-zirconia system represents a two-component system in which the metal oxide has limited solubility in the ceramic. Two types of specimens were used for columbium-chromium-alumina systems, as shown in Fig. 10-28; the stainless steel sections were incorporated in each specimen for attachment to the grips in a tensile testing machine. The cermet section was composed of 50 vol% chromium and 50 vol% alumina. The welds were made in 3 h with the temperature 2200 to 2300°F (1205 to 1260°C) and pressure 10 ksi (69 MPa).

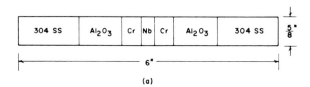

(a)

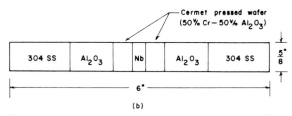

(b)

Fig. 10-28 Alumina-chromium-columbium assemblies.[72] (*a*) Metal wafer composite; (*b*) cermet composite. (0.001 in = 0.03 mm)

Columbium-zirconia specimens were prepared in the same manner and under the same joining conditions, but no intermediate material was present in these joints.

Mechanically strong seals have been produced between molybdenum sheet and the metallized surface of a high-purity alumina body. An alumina cylinder was first metallized with a layer of composition 85% molybdenum, 10% manganese and 5% titanium hydride. After this layer was sintered to the alumina cylinder, a second metallizing layer was slurry-coated to the ceramic surface and fired; the composition of this layer was 80% molybdenum and 20% chromium. The faying surfaces of the molybdenum sheet and metallized alumina ceramic were then lapped and the joint members assembled. Joining proceeded in a dry argon atmosphere at 3272°F (1800°C). While joints made in this manner had acceptable strength properties, it was necessary to infiltrate the metallized ceramic with a manganese oxide–alumina eutectic mixture before welding to obtain hermetic sealing.[73,74]

Additional joints have been made between a 99.5% alumina body and the following metals: stainless steel, Kovar, nickel, palladium, titanium, nichrome, low-alloy steel, and iron.[74] The welding conditions were pressure, 0.01 ksi (0.06 MPa); temperature, 2282 to 2372°F (1250 to 1300°C); and time, 10 min. Satisfactory joints were obtained between all of these ceramic-to-metal combinations. When joints between alumina and several refractory metals were attempted, welding did not occur either in a vacuum or in hydrogen; however, satisfactory joints were obtained when a ductile metal such as copper, nickel, or stainless steel was used as a diffusion aid material between the metal and ceramic surfaces.

APPLICATIONS

It can be seen from the previous pages that many industries have taken advantage of the benefits of the DFW process. The aircraft industry has taken the lead, especially with the increased potential usage of titanium alloys. Two new vehicles,[20] one for space travel and the other a long range bomber aircraft, are utilizing DFW extensively. The engine mount of each Space Shuttle will have 28 diffusion-welded titanium parts. They will range from large frames to interconnecting box tubes. This structure is capable of withstanding 3,000,000 lb (1,359,000 kg) of thrust. Basic tubes with 0.75-in-thick (19 mm) walls and approximately 8 in (203 mm) square were diffusion welded in lengths up to 180 in (4600 mm), and weigh 3500 lb (1586 kg). The advanced airplane has sixty-six Ti-6Al-4V alloy diffusion-welded parts which are being utilized in each of the first three aircraft. These parts range in weight from about 40 lb (18 kg) to over 400 lb (181 kg). The wing carry-through structure is without doubt the largest diffusion-welded composite structure in existence. It is the most critical structure in the air vehicle (see Fig. 10-29), and fully 75% of the assembly, by weight, is diffusion-welded.

Fig. 10-29 B-1 bomber wing carry-through structure.[11]

Dimensionally, press-diffusion-welded parts probably are limited only by the length and breadth of press beds. Future DFW consideration is being given to main landing gear beams for commercial airliners which now are fabricated from extrusions and sheet metal parts with mechanical fasteners. Future consideration will also be given to a new process, diffusion-weld riveting, and an example is shown in Fig. 10-30.

The press DFW process has been successful in producing a helicopter rotor hub, Fig. 10-31, and CSDB was evaluated in producing main rotor blade spars of Ti-6Al-4V alloy, Fig. 10-32. The laminated hub required a 4500-ton (4.1-Mg) press and only 64 lb (29 kg) of metal had

Fig. 10-30 Hat section of Ti-6Al-4V diffusion-weld riveted.[75]

Fig. 10-31 Helicopter rotor hub.[76]

to be removed after DFW. This new approach could remove one of the main limits in fabricating rotor hubs for heavy-lift helicopters.

The three most recently developed DFW processes are being utilized by design engineers who are continually finding aircraft uses. Shown in Fig. 10-33 is an 81-in-long (2057 mm) sandwich honeycomb structure of Ti-6-2-4-2 which weighs 6 lb (2.7 kg) and is used to carry hot gases. The structure was diffusion-welded with plated diffusion aid materials. The same process produced the Ti-6Al-4V alloy engine cases seen in Fig. 10-34 for the newest high powered engines.

The second process of note is CSDB. Shown in Fig. 10-35 is an example of a tee-stiffened skin fabricated as an integral one-piece structure, which is typical of aircraft designs.

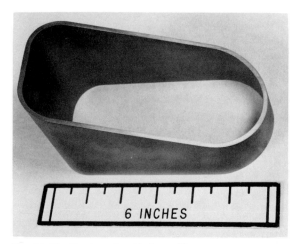

6 INCHES

Fig. 10-32 Section of welded spar.[77]

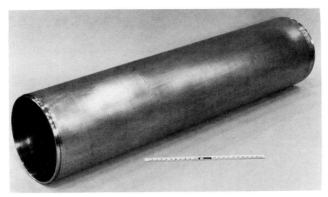

Fig. 10-33 Diffusion-welded honeycomb sandwich tubing of Ti-6Al-2Sn-4Zr-2Mo.

The third process is SPF/DB. The use of this process is gaining momentum not only from industry but also from government-sponsored programs. Figures 10-36 and 10-37 show some typical parts.[78] Other more complex components are currently being redesigned for SPF/DB. One of the largest parts to be diffusion-welded will

Fig. 10-34 Diffusion-welded Ti-6Al-4V honeycomb engine case.

Fig. 10-35 Ti-6Al-4V tee-stiffened panel welded by CSDB.

be the engine nozzle fairing shown in Fig. 10-38. Future unique structures emerging from design conceptual studies are seen in Fig. 10-39.

The joining specialist and engine designer have found that several DFW processes are quite amenable to weight and cost reductions in current and future high-thrust engines. These include CSDB, HIP, and intermediate diffusion aids. An aircraft turbine-engine fan blade of Ti-6Al-4V alloy, seen in Fig. 10-40, was locally stiffened by DFW of an inlay of Ti-6Al-4V/50B composite in recesses in the blade surface. Various dynamic tests, including engine tests, of blades resulted in no failures at the composite inlay. The advantage of the composite inlay, in this case, was a significant improvement in blade vibration stability because of the high elastic modulus of the composite.

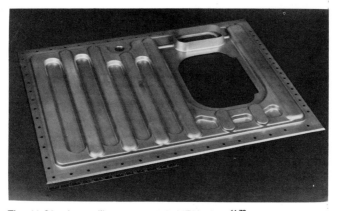

Fig. 10-36 An auxiliary power unit (APU) door.[11,78]

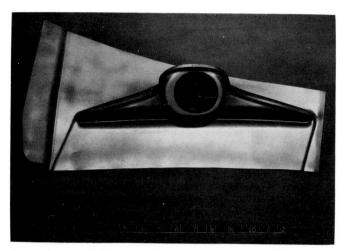

Fig. 10-37 An SPF/DB windshield hot-air blast nozzle.[11,78]

With HIP, diffusion welds have been achieved in the fabrication of rotors from AISI 4340 and Inconel 718.[81]

Blades, vanes, and disks are important components of engines, and with the use of diffusion aid materials, considerable advances have been and will be achieved in joining Udimet 700, Ti-6Al-4V and Ti-6Al-2Sn-4Zr-6Mo, René 80, TD-NiCr, and Bl900.[82,83,84] Figure 10-41 shows the fan disk design, while Table 10-5 illustrates several blade configurations.[84]

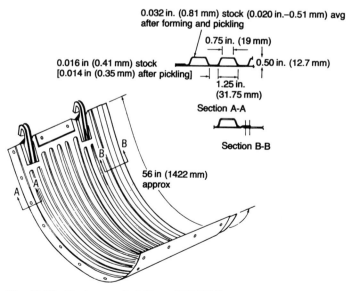

Fig. 10-38 Engine nozzle fairing—SPF/DB.[79]

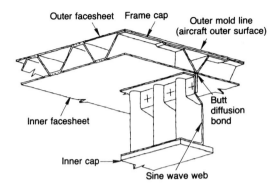

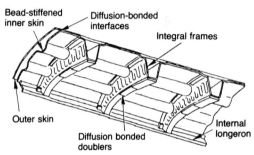

Fig. 10-39 Potential SPF/DB applications include wing/fuselage (top) and skin/frame/stringer (bottom) structures.[78]

Future development programs such as CRISP,[23] described earlier, will attempt to form and diffusion-weld cases such as that shown in Fig. 10-42.

One of the first applications for the CSDB process was for curved Ti-6Al-4V I beams used as structural members supporting boron-aluminum composite on a fighter airplane. These beams were made

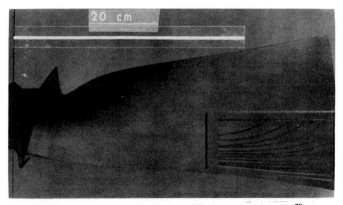

Fig. 10-40 Jet engine fan blade with diffusion-welded insert.[80]

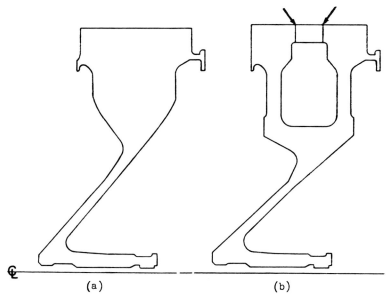

Fig. 10-41 Diagrams of fan-disk cross sections.[80] (a) Conventional solid-rim disk; (b) one concept of lightweight hollow-rim disk. Arrows show locations of diffusion welds.

from 0.025-in (0.6-mm) Ti-6Al-4V sheet. The alternate method of fabrication was machining from 1-in (25.4-mm) plate stock; material savings with CSDB exceeded 90%.

Other I beams have been produced from 0.070-in (1.7-mm) Ti-6Al-4V sheet and tested in a reverse-bending mode. The results demonstrated a fatigue life exceeding 10^7 cycles at flange stresses of 83 ksi (572 MPa), and all failures originated at the edges of the flanges well away from the diffusion welds. Sections are currently produced by machining extrusions that are 0.25 to 0.35 in (6.4 to 9 mm) thick and more than 70% of the metal is machined away.

Another aircraft prototype part fabricated was a rear wing beam. This part was made from Ti-6Al-6V-2Sn sheet. See Fig. 10-43.

Two companies have recently described their production of hollow titanium rotor-blade spars. A 4000-lb (1814-kg) titanium-alloy billet is forged and extruded into a 3400-lb (1542-kg), 33-ft (100.5-m) hollow tube, then machined and creep-formed. The companies have been able to apply the CSDB process to such spars; 120-in (3048-mm) lengths were made from 0.125-in (3.2-mm) Ti-6Al-4V sheet with a diffusion-welded butt joint. Preliminary fatigue results on this spar were encouraging and show that DFW offers an approach that will markedly improve metal recovery, will offer a high-performance product, and will reduce cost.

Closed structures are also possible with CSDB. A typical engine strut was fabricated from 0.063-in (1.6-mm) Ti-6Al-4V. The part was made

TABLE 10-5
Application of Joining Processes to Composite Blade Configurations[84]

Composite configuration	Configuration cross-section	Process applicability	
		Activated diffusion brazing	Gas pressure welding
Finned shell to strut (A) Fins at midchord region (B) Fins at leading edge	Chordwise fins Midchord region Leading edge region	(A) Very good (B) Not applicable unless gas pressure is used	(A) or (B) good but shell needs support in nonfinned region (A) and (B) combined very good
Nonfinned shell to strut webs (A) Solid shell (B) Porous shell		(A) Very good (B) Not applicable because braze clogs pores	(A) or (B) good but shell needs internal support
Shell segments with spanwise joints	Material B Material A	Good	Not applicable

by welding two vee gutters to the median stiffening rib. Removable, reusable internal tooling supported all three members and provided surfaces against which fillet radii were formed.

A more complex hollow strut is the inlet guide vane for a new engine being developed in Europe. Through prototype production of this vane by CSDB and structural evaluation, it has been demonstrated that significant cost reduction and improved performance can be achieved over vanes made by fusion welding. Six vanes have been fabricated from 0.070-in (1.7-mm) Ti-2.5Cu alloy sheet by CSDB. Each vane was made by joining six sheet-metal components. First, tee-joint welds were made to join the ribs to the two outer skins. Then lap-type

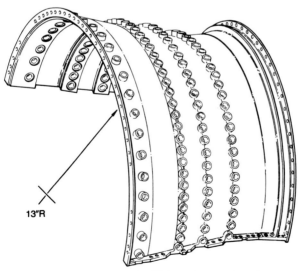

13"R

Fig. 10-42 Compressor casing.[23] (0.001 in = 0.03 mm)

joints were made to weld a filler strip into the leading and trailing edges. Removable internal tooling was used to produce controlled radii at all joints.

Another example of a hollow sheet-metal part made by CSDB is the vanes for an advanced new engine. These vanes were made by joining two preformed skins of 0.035-in (0.89-mm) Ti-6Al-4V along the leading and trailing edges. The vane performance was excellent in engine tests. Multiple tee joints can be combined in a single part to make rib-stiffened panels. The panels can be flat or curved, and the tooling is reusable. A Ti-6Al-4V panel 36 in (914 mm) in length, stiffened by five ribs, has been fabricated. The uniformity of the fillet radius and the absence of a weld line in all ten sections has been demonstrated. The process has been applied to structures in a variety of metals including mild, stainless, and precipitation-hardening steels, superalloys, zirconium, and refractory metals. In general, the process is not ideally suited to aluminum, although very satisfactory aluminum-to-steel joints have been made.

A T joint in Hastelloy X that forms the support members for the open-face honeycomb-core turbine seals on a commercial aircraft engine has been made. These seals are segmented. The T beams are made in straight 120-in (3048-mm) lengths by DFW of a 0.095-in

Fig. 10-43 Rear wing beam in Ti-6Al-6V-2Sn.[14]

(2.4-mm) stem to a 0.045-in-thick (1.2 mm) cap. For turbine seals, CSDB has replaced machined ring forgings, reducing cost while increasing metal recovery by a very significant amount. Approximately 40,000 ft (122 km) of tee section has been made for this application, seen in Fig. 10-44. Other applications include gas-cooled walls in jet engine combustors and cooled walls for pressure vessels.

Other industries are starting to utilize DFW. Columbium wires in a copper-tin alloy matrix is a prime example of new-generation composite superconductors developed through the use of diffusion welds to form the superconductive phase in situ. A flat-cable connecting system that terminates wires by DFW is now being marketed. The machine puts terminals on 800 wires per hour, or 100 contacts at a time. Furthermore, users of the system no longer have to strip insulation or crimp the connection. The machine will handle closely spaced terminals, as close as 0.050 in (1.3 mm). A short pulse of heat from the machine vaporizes and gets rid of the wire insulation, and also joins the wire to the terminal connector. Diffusion and grain growth form a weld of greater tensile strength and electrical continuity than crimping, soldering, and fusion welding.

Another application has been in the refrigeration industry, where the thermomagnetic process was used, substituting aluminum tubing for copper in refrigerant line sets and subsequently joining the aluminum tubing to brass end fittings. The metallurgical weld is created without melting either the brass or aluminum. The joint is characterized by complete disappearance of the prior interface, and material cost savings are considerable.

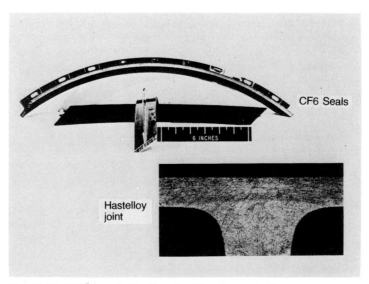

Fig. 10-44 CSDB applied to Hastelloy X engine seals.[14]

The general areas of current and future application are:

- Large-area overlap joints
- High strength/weight ratio structures
- Heat exchangers
- Composite structures
  Filled composites
  Laminar composites
  Cellular composites
  Metal/ceramic composites
- Hybrid structures
- Complex forgings

Finally, as little as 6 years ago the application of DFW to large-scale structures and components, except in very special cases, was a mere possibility on a far horizon. Developments in the intervening period have revealed the true potential of these techniques, and general large-scale application is an exciting prospect for the forthcoming decade.

The transformation has been from a process for unusual materials to a process for ordinary materials, and from a process for the small component to one for major structural assemblies.

The ability of DFW to produce high-quality joints in all types of material has been long known, but now its competitive potential in relation to conventional fusion-welding processes has been revealed.

The difficulties associated with future development center upon joint assessment and the mechanical aspects of equipment construction, but both can be readily overcome.

REFERENCES

1. Tylecote, R. F., "Diffusion Bonding," *Weld. Met. Fabr.*, **35**(12), 483–489, December 1967.
2. Feduska, W., and Horigan, W. L., *Weld. J.*, **41**(1), 28–35, January 1962.
3. Vaidyanath, L. R., Nicholas, M. G., and Milner, D. R., *Br. Weld. J.*, **6**(1), January 13, 1959.
4. Tylecote R. G., and Wynne, E. J., *Br. Weld. J.*, **10**(8), 385–394, August 1963.
5. Wilford, C. F., and Tylecote, R. F., *Br. Weld. J.*, **7**(12), 708–712, December 1960.
6. Bartle, P. M., "Introduction to Diffusion Bonding," *Met. Constr. Br. Weld. J.*, **1**(5), May 1969, and *Weld. Res. Abroad*, **15**(9), 33–36, November 1969.
7. Bartle, P. M., "Diffusion Bonding: A Look at the Future," *Weld. J.*, **54**(11), 799–804, November 1975.
8. Peaslee, R. L., "Diffusion Brazing," *Weld. J.*, **55**(8), 695–696, August 1976.
9. Kazakov, N. F., "Diffusion Welding in a Vacuum," Moska, Izdvo, Mashionostroyniye, pp. 1–332, 1968.
10. Parks, J. M., *Weld. J.*, **32**(5), 209–222, May 1953.
11. Weisert, D., Rockwell International, private communication, May 1978.
12. Houck, J. A., and Bartlett, E. S., "The Roll-Diffusion Bonding of Structural Shapes & Panels," DMIC Rep. S-17, pp. 1–37, October 1967.
13. Bangs, J., "Diffusion Bonding: No Longer a Mysterious Process," *Weld. Des. Fabr.*, pp. 43–46, January 1976.
14. Thorsrud, E. C., Rose, F. K., and Metcalfe, A. G., "Improved Metal Recovery by the CSDB Process," SAE 740835, pp. 1–10, Oct. 1–3, 1974.

15. Morin, T. J., "Speedy Solid-State Joining," *Weld. Eng.*, pp. 15–16, December 1974.
16. Morin, T. J., Whitehead, R. J., and Zotos, J., "Hydrodynamic Welding of Steel Tubes to Ferrous and Nonferrous Alloys," *ASF Trans.*, 76, 515–520, 1968.
17. Hoppin, G. S., III, and Berry, T. F., "Activated Diffusion Bonding," *Weld. J.*, **49**(11), 505s–509s, November 1970.
18. Duvall, D. S., Owczarski, W. A., and Panlonis, D. F., "TLP* Bonding: A New Method for Joining Heat Resistant Alloys," *Weld. J.*, **53**(4), 203–214, April 1974.
19. Schwartz, M., "LID Bonding," *Golden Gate Weld. Conf.*, San Francisco, 1972.
20. Schwartz, M., "Rohrbond," SME, AD76-280, Cleveland, April 1976.
21. Freedman, A. H., "Basic Properties of Thin-Film Diffusion Brazed Joints in Ti-6Al-4V," *Weld. J.*, **50**(8), 343s–356s, August 1971.
22. Freedman, A. H., "Nor-Ti-Bond," AWS, San Francisco, 1971; Mikus, E., *Westec Conf.*, Los Angeles, 1972.
23. Rajala, R., "Manufacturing Methods for Low Cost Non-Rotating Titanium Engine Components," IR-875-5 (IV) (v), October 1975 to March, 1976, AFML Contr. F33615-75-C-5079.
24. Hamilton, C. H., Stacher, G. W., and Li, H. W., "Manufacturing Methods for SPF/DB Process," IR-798-5 (I through VIII), January 1975 to January 1977, AFML Contr. F33615-75-C-5058.
25. Crane, C., Lovell, D., and Baginski, W., "Research Study for Development of Techniques for Joining of Dissimilar Metals," NAS 8-11307, DCNI-4-50-01068-01 (1F).
26. "Diffusion Bonding on Verge of Wider Market," *Steel*, pp. 66–67, Dec. 2, 1968.
27. Bosworth, T. J., "Diffusion Welding of Beryllium: Part I—Basic Studies," *Weld. J.*, **51**(12), 579s–590s, December 1972.
28. Bosworth, T. J., "Diffusion Welding of Beryllium: Part II—The Role of the Microalloying Elements," *Weld. J.*, **52**(1), 38s–48s, January 1973.
29. Gerken, J. W., and Owczarski, W., TRW Rep. ER 6563, June 23, 1965.
30. Duvall, D. S., Owczarski, W. A., Paulonis, D. F., and King, W. H., "Methods for Diffusion Welding the Superalloy Udimet 700," *Weld. J.*, **51**(2), 41s–49s, February 1972.
31. Nessler, C. G., "Joining Techniques for Fabrication of High-Temperature Superalloy Blades," AFML-TR-71-237, Contr. F33615-70-C-1784, December 1971.
32. Moore, T. J., and Holko, K. H., "Practical Method for Diffusion Welding of Steel Plate in Air," *Weld. J.*, **51**(3), 106s–116s, March 1972.
33. Kazakov, N. F., Samoilov, V. S., and Polyakova, M. L., "Vacuum Diffusion Bonding of VK20 Hard Alloy to Steel," *Svar. Proizvod.*, 2, pp. 18–19, 1972, and IIW Doc. IV-127-73.
34. Moore, T. J., and Holko, K. H., "Solid-State Welding of TD-Nickel Bar," *Weld. J.*, **49**(9), 395s–409s, September 1970.
35. Holko, K. H., and Moore, T. J., "Enhanced Diffusion Welding of TD-NiCr Sheet," *Weld. J.*, **51**(2), 81s–89s, February 1972.
36. Holko, K. H., "An Improved Diffusion Welding Technique for TD-NiCr Sheet," *Weld. J.*, **52**(11), 515s–523s, November 1973.
37. Moore, T. J., "Solid State and Fusion Resistance Spot Welding of TD-NiCr Sheet," *Weld. J.*, **53**(1), 37s–48s, January 1974.
38. Metcalfe, A. G., and Rose, F. K., "Production Tool for Diffusion Bonding," Rep. AFML-TR-68-213, vol. 1, Contr. AF 33(615)-2304, August 1968.
39. Hashimoto, T., and Tanuma, K., "Diffusion Welding of Molybdenum," *Trans. Nat. Res. Inst. Met.*, **11**(5), 1969; *Welding Res. Abd*; **26**(7), 2–10, August–September 1970.
40. Woodward, J., "Titanium Honeycomb Sandwich Fabrication Process," *5th Nat. SAMPE Tech. Conf.*, vol. 5, pp. 432–437, Oct. 9–11, 1973, Kiamesha Lake, NY.
41. "Supersonic Cruise Aircraft Research Structural Panel Program," 8th Semiannual rep., Nov. 1, 1976, NASA, SP-4557.
42. Wu, K. C., "Resistance Nor-Ti-Bond Joining of Titanium Shapes," *Weld. J.*, **50**(9), 386s–393s, September 1971.
43. Cogan, R. M., and Shamblem, C. E., "Development of a Manufacturing Process for Fabricated Diffusion Bonded Hollow Blades," Rep. AFML-TR-69-219, General Electric Com., Cincinnati, Contr. F33615-68-C-1215, August 1969.

44. "Joining Diffusion Bonding with Forging Lowers Cost," *Materials Engr.*, pp. 12–13, July 1971.
45. Hamilton, C. H., "Diffusion Bonding on the B1 Aircraft", *ASM Conf.—Joining Titanium for Aerospace Applications*, Feb. 5–6, 1975.
46. Wolf, J. E., "Fabrication Techniques for Shrouded Titanium Impeller," Final Rep. NASA CR-102589, Rocketdyne Division, North American Rockwell Corp., Canoga Park, CA, Contr. NAS 8-20761, Dec. 10, 1969 (N70-23376).
47. Holko, K. H., "Hot Press and Roll Welding of Titanium–6% Aluminum–4% Vanadium Bar and Sheet with Auto-Vacuum Cleaning," NASATND-6958, September 1972.
48. Kennedy, J. R., "Fusion Welding of Titanium-Tungsten and Titanium-Graphite Composites," *Weld. J.*, 51(5), 250s–259s, May 1972.
49. Hersh, M. S., "Resistance Diffusion Bonding Boron/Aluminum Composite to Titanium," *Weld. J.*, 52(8), 370s–376s, August 1973.
50. Crane, C. H., Torgerson, R. T., Lovell, D. T., and Baginski, W. A., "Study of Dissimilar Metal Joining by Solid State Bonding," NASA Contr. NAS 8-20156, October 1966.
51. Crane, C. H., Lovell, D. T., and Johnson, H. A., "Study of Dissimilar Metal Joining by Solid State Welding," NASA Contr. NAS 8-20156 (Amendment No. 2), July 15, 1967.
52. Patenaude, C. J., and Santschi, W. H., "Casting of Beryllium-Stainless Steel and Beryllium-Columbium Impact Target Composites," Summary Rep., Beryllium Corp., Reading, PA, NASA Contr. NAS 3-3729, June 9, 1964.
53. Diersing, R. J., Hanes, H. D., and Hodge, E. S., "Fabrication of Beryllium-Clad Tubular Hypervelocity Impact Targets by Gas-Pressure Bonding," Summary Rep. NASA Cr-54058, Battelle Memorial Institute, Columbus, OH, Contr. NAS 3-3651, Nov. 6, 1963.
54. Diersing, R. J., Carmichael, D. C., Hanes, H. D., and Hodge, E. S., "Gas-Pressure Bonding of Stainless Steel-Reinforced Beryllium Hypervelocity Impact Targets," Rep. NASA CR-54173, Battelle Memorial Institute, Columbus, OH, Contr. NAS 3-5139, July 1965.
55. Young, W. R., and Jones, E. S., "Joining of Refractory Metals by Brazing and Diffusion Bonding," Tech. Documentary Rep. ASD-TDR-63-88, Contr. AF33(616)-7484, January 1963.
56. Morin, T. J., Whitehead, R. J., and Zotos, J., "Hydrodynamic Welding of Steel Tubes to Ferrous and Nonferrous Alloys," *ASF Trans.*, 76, 515–520, 1968.
57. Bartle, P. M., and Ellis, C. R. G., "Diffusion Bonding & Friction Welding, Two Newer Processes for the Dissimilar Metal Joint," *Met. Constr. Brit. Weld. J.*, 1(12s), 88–95, December 1969.
58. Schneider, G., "Metallic Bonding Between Uranium and Aluminum for Reactor Fuel Elements," *Metallurgy*, 15(7), 675–679, July 1961.
59. Schneider, G., "Leak-Tight Joints in the Fabrication of Nuclear Fuel Elements," Deutsche Luft und Raum-Fahrt Rep. 64-07, Deutscher Verlag für Schweiss-Technik (DVS) GMGH, Dusseldorf, West Germany, December 1964.
60. Angerman, C. L., "Metallographic Studies of Al-Ni-U Bonds in Nuclear Fuel Elements," *ASME Trans. Quart.*, 54(3), 260–275, September 1961.
61. Auleta, J. J., Finch, D. B., Goodman, L., Lew, D. E., Mandel, H., and Rubenstein, H. J., "Piqua Nuclear Power Facility Operations Analysis Program," Prog. Rep. 2, Fiscal Year 1963, USAEC Rep. NAA-SR-8722, Atomics International, Nov. 30, 1963.
62. Kendall, E. G., et al., "Fabrication Development of APM Alloys for Fuel Elements," USAEC Rep. NAA-SR-6213, Atomics International, Dec. 15, 1961.
63. Francis, W. C., and Craig, S. E., "Progress Report on Fuel-Element Development and Associated Projects," USAEC Rep. IDO-16574, Philips Petroleum Co., Aug. 16, 1970.
64. Baskey, R. H., "Fuel-Bearing Fiberglas in Aluminum-Base Fuel Elements," USAEC Reps. ORO-303 (June 13, 1960), ORO-304 (July 7, 1960), ORO-316 (Sept. 2, 1960), and ORO-322 (Sept. 12, 1960), Clevite Corp.
65. Lloyd, H., and Davies, J. M., "Roll Bonding of Nuclear Fuel Plates," British Rep. AERE-R-4634, June 1964.
66. Watson, R. D., "Diffusionless Bonding of Aluminum to Zircaloy-2," Rep. AECL-2243, Atomic Energy of Canada, Ltd., Chalk River, Canada, 1965.
67. Watson, R. D., "Techniques for Hot-Press Bonding Dissimilar Metal Combinations," Rep. AECL-2853, Atomic Energy of Canada, Ltd., Chalk River, Canada, 1966.

68. Shmakov, V. M., and Izmirlieva, A. N., "Diffusion Welding of Titanium to Bronze," *Weld. Prod. (USSR)*, **13**(1), 14–17, January 1966.
69. Zanner, F. J., and Fisher, R. W., "Diffusion Welding of Commercial Bronze to a Titanium Alloy," *Weld. J.*, **54**(4), 105s–112s, April 1975.
70. Albom, M. J., "Solid State Bonding," *Weld. J.*, **43**(6), 491, June 1964.
71. Bondarev, V. V., "On the Problem of Brazing Graphite and Some Other Materials," *Weld. Prod. (USSR)*, **14**(6), 17–19, June 1967.
72. Porembka, S. W., "Nonglassy Phase Ceramic-Metal Bonding," Final Rep., Battelle Memorial Institute, Columbus, OH, Nov. 29, 1963.
73. Dring, M. L., "Ceramic-to-Metal Seals for High-Temperature Thermionic Converters," Red Bank Division, Bendix Corp., Eatontown, NJ, Tech. Doc. Rep. TDR-63-4109, Contr. AF33(657)-10038, October 1963.
74. Metelkin, J. J., Makarkin, A. Y., and Pavlova, M. A., "Welding Ceramic Materials to Metals," *Weld. Prod. (USSR)*, **14**(6), 10–12, 1967.
75. Hersh, M., General Dynamics, Convair Division, private communication, May 1978.
76. Kearns, W., Editor, "Welding Handbook," private communication, April 1978.
77. Lucas, J. J., and Doyle, P. J., "Diffusion Bonded Ti-6Al-4V Heliocopter Rotor Hub & Blade Spar Development," *ASM Conf.—Joining Titanium for Aerospace Applications*, Feb. 5–6, 1975, Contracts DAAG46-72-C-0175 and DAAG-46-73-C-0126.
78. Weisert, E. D., and Stacher, G. W., "Fabricating Titanium Parts with SPF/DB Process," *Met. Prog.*, pp. 32–37, March 1977.
79. Miska, K. H., "Diffusion Welding Joins Similar to Dissimilar Metals," *Mat. Eng.*, pp. 18–20, December 1976.
80. Metzger, G. E., "Joining of Metal-Matrix Fiber-Reinforced Composite Materials," Weldg. Res. Council Interpretive Rep. 207, July 1975.
81. Lessman, G. G., and Bryant, W. A., "Complex Rotor Fabrication by Hot Isostatic Pressure Welding," *Weld. J.*, **51**(12), 606s–614s, December 1972.
82. Duvall, D. S., and Owczarski, W. A., "Fabrication and Repair of Titanium Engine Components by Welding," *5th Nat. SAMPE Tech. Conf.*, vol. 5, pp. 472–485, Oct. 9–11, 1973, Kiamesha Lake, NY.
83. Meiners, K. E., "Diffusion Bonding of Specialty Structures," *5th Nat. SAMPE Tech. Conf.*, vol. 5, pp. 703–712, Oct. 9–11, 1973, Kiamesha Lake, NY.
84. Kaufman, A., Berry, T. F., and Meiners, K. E., "Joining Techniques for Fabrication of Composite Air-Cooled Turbine Blades and Vanes," ASME 71-GT-32, pp. 1–9, Gas and Turbine Conf., Houston, March 28–Apr. 1, 1971.
85. Brick, R. M., "Hot Roll Bonding of Steel," *Weld. J.*, **49**(9), 440s–444s, September 1970.
86. Bryant, W. A., "A Method for Specifying Hot Isostatic Pressure Welding Parameters," *Weld. J.*, **54**(12), 433s–435s, December 1975.
87. O'Brien, M., Rice, C. R., and Olson, D. L., "High Strength Diffusion Welding of Silver Coated Base Metals," *Weld. J.*, **55**(1), 25–27, January 1976.
88. Signes, E. G., "Diffusion Welding of Steel in Air," *Weld. J.*, **47**(12), 571s–574s, December 1968.
89. Ozelton, M. W., et al., "Reactive Bonding of Solution Treated Titanium Alloys," Air Force Contr. F33615-69C-1908, AFML-TR-70-23, April 1970.
90. Makara, A. M., and Nazarchuk, A., "The Mechanism of Diffusion Welding and the Improvement of the Quality of Diffusion Welds," *Avtom. Svarka*, **22**(4), 193, April 1969.
91. Kharchenko, G. K., "Problems in Diffusion Welding of Dissimilar Metals," *Avtom. Svarka*, **22**(4), 193, April 1969.
92. Wiesner, P., "Diffusion Welding in the G.D.R.," Doc. IV-174-75, Zentralinstitut für Schweisstechnik der DDR, Halle (Saale).
93. Carlson, C. E., Delgrasso, E. J., and Varholak, E. M., "Mechanical Properties of Braze Bonded Borsic™-Aluminum Composites," *15th SAMPE Nat. Meeting*, Los Angeles, April 1969.
94. Stocker, B. P. W., "Full-Scale Fatigue Test of a Diffusion Bonded Heliocopter Main Rotor Hub," Contr. F33615-70-C-1327, AFML-TR-72-63, April 1972.
95. Brunken, R. D., et al., "Manufacturing Methods for Roll Diffusion Bonded Stiffened Skin Structure," Contr. F33615-69-C-1877, AFML-TR-72-169, January 1973.

96. Mohamed, H. A., and Washburn, J., "Mechanism of Solid State Pressure Welding," *Weld. J.*, **54**(9), 302s–310s, September 1975.
97. Wells, R. R., "Microstructural Control of Thin-Film Diffusion-Brazed Titanium," *Weld. J.*, **55**(1), 20s–28s, January 1976.
98. Perun, K. R., "Diffusion Welding and Brazing of Titanium 6Al-4V Process Development," *Weld. J.*, **46**(9), 385s–390s, September 1967.
99. King, W. H., and Owczarski, W. A., "Additional Studies on the Diffusion Welding of Titanium," *Weld. J.*, **47**(10), 444s–450s, October 1968.
100. Castle, C. H., Melnyk, P., and West, W. G., "Process Development for Boron-Aluminum Fan Blades," Tech. Memo TM-4663, TRW, Cleveland, 1972.
101. Kazakov, N. F., et al., "Vacuum Diffusion Bonding of L62 Brass for Type AMts Alloy Via a Nickel Interlayer," *Svar. Proizvod.*, 10, 15–16, and IIW Doc. IV-128-73.
102. Arata, Y., Shima, K., Terai, K., and Nagai, Y., "The Forecasting of Welding Processes in the Future by the Delphi Method," *Trans. Jpn Weld. Soc.*, **3**(1), April 1972, and *Weld. Res. Abroad*, **19**(7), 14–40, August–September 1973.
103. Martin, D. C., and Miller, F. R., "Using Solid-State Joining in Gas Turbine Engines," ASME 72-GT-74, pp. 1–16, *Gas Turbine and Fluids Engrg. Conf.*, San Francisco, March 26, 1972.

INDEX

1